2
edition

College Accounting

Chapters 1–14

John J. Wild
University of Wisconsin at Madison

Vernon J. Richardson
University of Arkansas

Ken W. Shaw
University of Missouri at Columbia

COLLEGE ACCOUNTING

Published by McGraw-Hill/Irwin, a business unit of The McGraw-Hill Companies, Inc., 1221
Avenue of the Americas, New York, NY, 10020. Copyright © 2011, 2008 by The McGraw-Hill
Companies, Inc. All rights reserved. No part of this publication may be reproduced or distributed
in any form or by any means, or stored in a database or retrieval system, without the prior written
consent of The McGraw-Hill Companies, Inc., including, but not limited to, in any network or other
electronic storage or transmission, or broadcast for distance learning.

Some ancillaries, including electronic and print components, may not be available to customers
outside the United States.

This book is printed on acid-free paper.

4 5 6 7 8 9 0 DOW/DOW 1 0 9 8 7 6 5 4 3

ISBN   978-0-07-813667-2 (chapters 1–29)
MHID   0-07-813667-9 (chapters 1–29)
ISBN   978-0-07-726873-2 (chapters 1–14)
MHID   0-07-726873-3 (chapters 1–14)

Vice president and editor-in-chief: *Brent Gordon*
Editorial director: *Stewart Mattson*
Publisher: *Tim Vertovec*
Executive editor: *Steve Schuetz*
Director of development: *Ann Torbert*
Senior development editor: *Christina A. Sanders*
Vice president and director of marketing: *Robin J. Zwettler*
Marketing manager: *Michelle Heaster*
Vice president of editing, design and production: *Sesha Bolisetty*
Managing editor: *Lori Koetters*
Lead production supervisor: *Carol A. Bielski*
Lead designer: *Matthew Baldwin*
Senior photo research coordinator: *Lori Kramer*
Photo researcher: *Sarah Evertson*
Lead media project manager: *Brian Nacik*
Cover design: *Matthew Baldwin*
Interior design: *Matthew Baldwin*
Cover image: *© Getty Images*
Typeface: *10.5/12 Times Roman*
Compositor: *Aptara®, Inc.*
Printer: *R. R. Donnelley*

Library of Congress Cataloging-in-Publication Data

Wild, John J.
    College accounting : chapters 1–29 / John J. Wild, Vernon J. Richardson,
Ken W. Shaw.—2nd ed.
        p. cm.
    Includes index.
    ISBN-13: 978-0-07-813667-2 (chapters 1–29 : alk. paper)
    ISBN-10: 0-07-813667-9 (chapters 1–29 : alk. paper)
    ISBN-13: 978-0-07-726873-2 (chapters 1–14 : alk. paper)
    ISBN-10: 0-07-726873-3 (chapters 1–14 : alk. paper)
    1. Accounting. I. Richardson, Vernon J. II. Shaw, Ken W. III. Title.
HF5635.W693 2011
657—dc22
                                                            2009041924

To my wife **Gail** and children, **Kimberly**, **Jonathan**, **Stephanie**, and **Trevor**.

To my parents, **Jay** and **Lavona Richardson**.

To my wife **Linda** and children, **Erin**, **Emily**, and **Jacob**.

College Accounting

Dear Friends and Colleagues,

We all struggle with many of the same teaching challenges: motivating students to learn, making accounting relevant to them, integrating technology, and covering crucial material. We wrote this book intending to give our students and us the means to confront each of those challenges.

One problem with many college accounting books is that their dated examples and boring companies fail to engage students. As instructors, we are responsible for bringing accounting to life through interesting and contemporary examples of exciting companies and industries. This book's chapter-opening vignettes and its many examples showcase successful, dynamic entrepreneurs that excite and engage students. Discussions of ethics, fraud, and the Sarbanes-Oxley Act further engage students. We also illustrate many key accounting concepts using the financial statements of Best Buy, RadioShack, and other well-recognized companies.

We all believe that our students must be able to prepare and interpret accounting information to successfully enter the business world. We use short learning sessions, with clear examples and objectives, to ensure student success. To help students transition, we show students where and how business decisions draw on accounting knowledge.

Students today learn in ways beyond reading chapters and attending classes. Important developments in technology are creating new avenues for learning accounting. Working together, this book's publisher and we developed new tools to reach and sustain students throughout the course. An exciting example of those tools is Connect Accounting™ or Connect Accounting Plus™ (which includes an interactive eBook). Connect Accounting is our application of the accounting adage that "perfect practice makes perfect." Other highly successful tools include the book's Online Learning Center and Carol Yacht's Quickbooks Guide.

This is an exciting time to be an accounting instructor. We welcome your thoughts on how we can continue to engage today's accounting students and prepare them for tomorrow's business world.

John   Vern   Ken

John J. Wild is a professor of accounting and the Robert and Monica Beyer Distinguished Professor at the University of Wisconsin at Madison. He previously held appointments at Michigan State University and the University of Manchester in England. He received his BBA, MS, and PhD from the University of Wisconsin.

Professor Wild teaches accounting courses at both the undergraduate and graduate levels. He has received the Mabel W. Chipman Excellence-in-Teaching Award, the departmental Excellence-in-Teaching Award, and the Teaching Excellence Award from the 2003 and 2005 business graduates at the University of Wisconsin. He also received the Beta Alpha Psi and Roland F. Salmonson Excellence-in-Teaching Award from Michigan State University. Professor Wild is a past KPMG Peat Marwick National Fellow and is a recipient of fellowships from the American Accounting Association and the Ernst and Young Foundation.

Professor Wild is an active member of the American Accounting Association and its sections. He has served on several committees of these organizations, including the Outstanding Accounting Educator Award, Wildman Award, National Program Advisory, Publications, and Research Committees. Professor Wild is author of *Fundamental Accounting Principles, Financial Accounting,* and *Financial Statement Analysis*, published by McGraw-Hill/Irwin. His research appears in The Accounting Review, Journal of Accounting Research, Journal of Accounting and Economics, Contemporary Accounting Research, Journal of Accounting, Auditing and Finance, Journal of Accounting and Public Policy, and other journals. He is past associate editor of Contemporary Accounting Research and has served on several editorial boards including The Accounting Review.

Professor Wild, his wife, and four children enjoy travel, music, sports, and community activities.

Vernon J. Richardson is Professor of Accounting and the S. Robson Walton Distinguished Chair in the Sam M. Walton College of Business at the University of Arkansas. He currently serves as Accounting department chair. He received his B.S., Masters of Accountancy, and MBA from Brigham Young University and a Ph.D. in accounting from the University of Illinois at Urbana-Champaign. He has taught students at the University of Arkansas, University of Illinois, Brigham Young University, University of Kansas, and the China Europe International Business School (Shanghai).

Professor Richardson is a member of the American Accounting Association. He currently serves as the president of the American Accounting Association Information Systems section. Professor Richardson has published articles in the Accounting Review, the Journal of Accounting and Economics, Journal of Accounting and Public Policy, Journal of Business, Finance, and Accounting, Financial Analysts Journal, MIS Quarterly, Journal of Operations Management, Journal of Marketing, and the American Business Law Journal.

Professor Richardson, his wife, and their twelve children all enjoy music, traveling, sports, and watching movies.

Ken W. Shaw is an associate professor of accounting and the Deloitte Professor at the University of Missouri at Columbia. He previously was on the faculty at the University of Maryland at College Park. He received an accounting degree from Bradley University and an MBA and PhD from the University of Wisconsin. He is a Certified Public Accountant with work experience in public accounting.

Professor Shaw teaches financial accounting at the undergraduate and graduate levels. He was voted the "Most Influential Professor" by the 2005 and 2006 School of Accountancy graduating classes, won the Williams-Keepers Teaching Excellence Award in 2007, and won O'Brien Excellence in Teaching Awards in 2003 and 2008. He is also the advisor to his school's chapter of the Association of Certified Fraud Examiners.

Professor Shaw is an active member of the American Accounting Association and its sections. He has served on committees of these organizations and presented his research papers at national and regional meetings. Professor Shaw is co-author of *Fundamental Accounting Principles*, *Financial and Managerial Accounting*, and *Managerial Accounting* published by McGraw-Hill/ Irwin. Professor Shaw's research appears in the Accounting Review; the Journal of Accounting Research; Contemporary Accounting Research; Journal of Financial and Quantitative Analysis; Strategic Management Journal; Journal of the American Taxation Association; Journal of Accounting, Auditing, and Finance; Journal of Business, Finance, and Accounting; Journal of Financial Research; Research in Accounting Regulation; and other journals. He currently serves on the editorial boards of Issues in Accounting Education and the Journal of Business Research.

In his leisure time, Professor Shaw enjoys tennis, cycling, music, and coaching his children's sports teams.

College Accounting

Help get your students on the path to success. *College Accounting (CA)* will help your students succeed by leading them through engaging accounting content and providing state-of-the-art technology.

One of the greatest challenges students confront in a college accounting course is seeing the relevance of materials. *CA* tackles this issue head-on with **engaging content** and a **motivating style**. Students are motivated when reading materials that are **clear and relevant**. *CA* chapter-opening vignettes showcase dynamic, successful, entrepreneurial individuals and companies guaranteed to **interest and excite readers**. This text's featured companies—Best Buy and RadioShack—engage students with their annual reports, which are great vehicles for **learning** financial statements. Further, this book's coverage of the accounting cycle fundamentals is widely praised for its **clarity and effectiveness**.

CA also delivers **state-of-the-art technology** to help students succeed. **Connect Accounting** provides students with instant grading and feedback for assignments that are completed online. **Connect Accounting Plus** integrates an online version of the textbook with our popular Connect Accounting system. *CA* also offers accounting students portable **iPod-ready content**.

We're confident you'll agree that *CA* **will lead your students on the path to succeed**.

Engaging Content

College Accounting 2e by Wild, Richardson, and Shaw brings excitement to your College Accounting course in its extensive use of small business examples, integration of computerized learning tools, superior end-of-chapter material, and a highly engaging pedagogical design. *College Accounting* motivates students with real-world applications and examples including motivating chapter openers featuring real entrepreneurs. The text also includes the financial statements of Best Buy and RadioShack to further engage students by applying knowledge learned in the course directly to a familiar company.

Cutting-Edge Technology

College Accounting offers the most advanced and comprehensive technology on the market in a seamless, easy-to-use platform. As students learn in different ways, *CA* provides a technology smorgasbord that helps students learn more effectively and efficiently. Connect Accounting, eBook options, and iPod content are some of the options available. Connect Accounting Plus takes learning to another level by integrating an online version of the textbook with all the power of Connect Accounting. Technology offerings include the following:

- Connect Accounting
- Connect Accounting Plus
- iPod content
- Quickbooks Templates

- Online Learning Center
- ALEKS for the Accounting Cycle
- ALEKS for Financial Accounting

McGraw-Hill Connect Accounting

Less Managing. More Teaching. Greater Learning.

McGraw-Hill Connect Accounting is an online assignment and assessment solution that connects students with the tools and resources they'll need to achieve success. McGraw-Hill Connect Accounting helps prepare students for their future by enabling faster learning, more efficient studying, and higher retention of knowledge.

McGraw-Hill Connect Accounting features

Connect Accounting offers a number of powerful tools and features to make managing assignments easier, so faculty can spend more time teaching. With Connect Accounting, students can engage with their coursework anytime and anywhere, making the learning process more accessible and efficient. Connect Accounting offers you the features described below.

Simple assignment management

With Connect Accounting, creating assignments is easier than ever, so you can spend more time teaching and less time managing. The assignment management function enables you to:

- Create and deliver assignments easily with selectable end-of-chapter questions and test bank items.
- Streamline lesson planning, student progress reporting, and assignment grading to make classroom management more efficient than ever.
- Go paperless with the eBook and online submission and grading of student assignments.

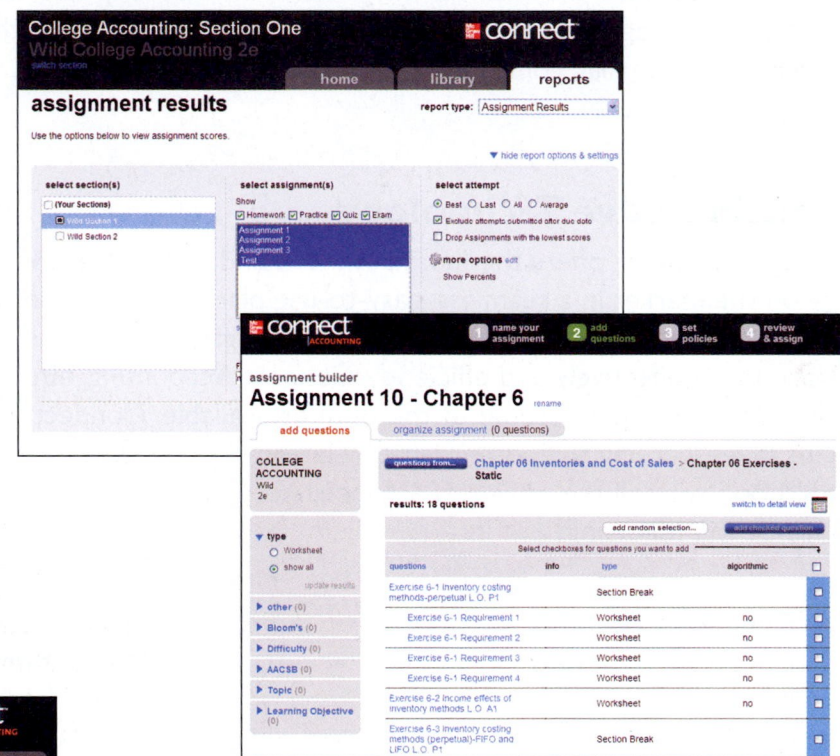

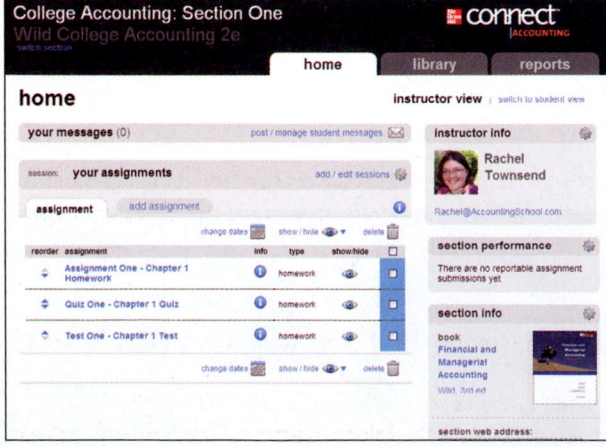

Smart grading

When it comes to studying, time is precious. Connect Accounting helps students learn more efficiently by providing feedback and practice material when they need it, where they need it. When it comes to teaching, your time also is precious. The grading function enables you to:

- Have assignments scored automatically, giving students immediate feedback on their work and side-by-side comparisons with correct answers.
- Access and review each response; manually change grades or leave comments for students to review.
- Reinforce classroom concepts with practice tests and instant quizzes.

Student study center

The Connect Accounting Student Study Center is the place for students to access additional resources. The Student Study Center:

- Offers students quick access to lectures, practice materials, eBooks, and more.
- Provides instant practice material and study questions, easily accessible on the go.

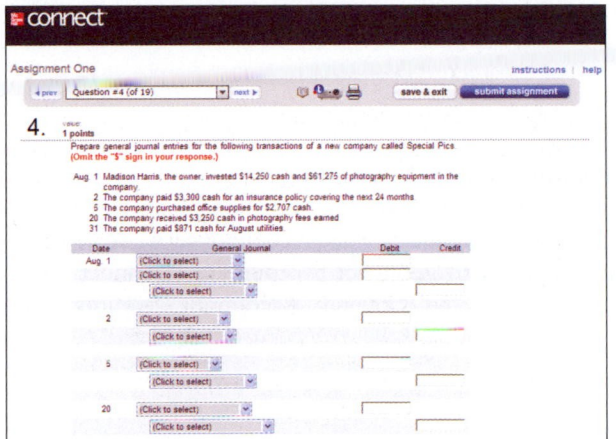

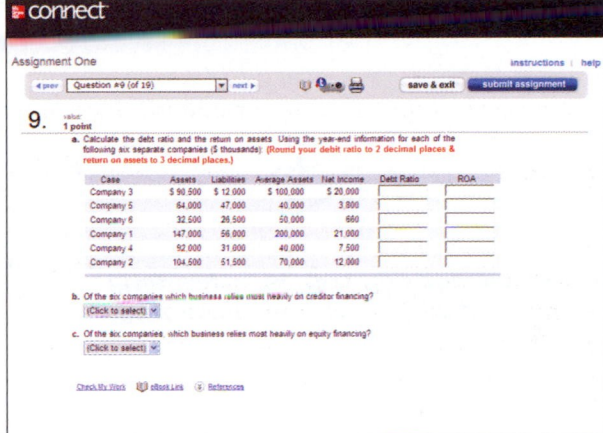

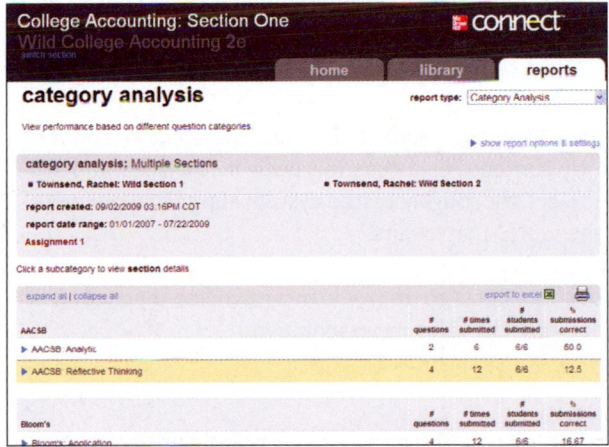

Student progress tracking

Connect Accounting keeps instructors informed about how each student, section, and class is performing, allowing for more productive use of lecture and office hours. The progress-tracking function enables you to:

- View scored work immediately and track individual or group performance with assignment and grade reports.
- Access an instant view of student or class performance relative to learning objectives.
- Collect data and generate reports required by many accreditation organizations, such as AACSB and AICPA.

Lecture capture

Increase the attention paid to lecture discussion by decreasing the attention paid to note taking. For an additional charge Lecture Capture offers new ways for students to focus on the in-class discussion, knowing they can revisit important topics later. Lecture Capture enables you to:

- Record and distribute your lecture with a click of the button.
- Record and index PowerPoint presentations and anything shown on your computer so it is easily searchable, frame by frame.
- Offer access to lectures anytime and anywhere by computer, iPod, or mobile device.
- Increase intent listening and class participation by easing students' concerns about note-taking. Lecture Capture will make it more likely you will see students' faces, not the tops of their heads.

How does Technology guide your

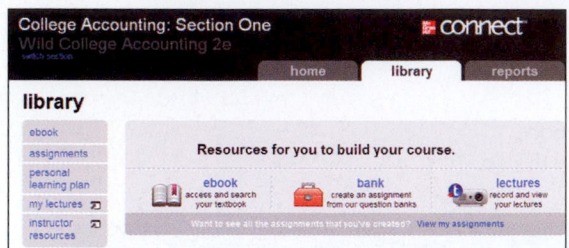

Instructor library

The Connect Accounting Instructor Library is your repository for additional resources to improve student engagement in and out of class. You can select and use any asset that enhances your lecture. The Connect Accounting Instructor Library includes the Solutions Manual, Instructor's Resource Manual, Test Bank, and PowerPoint lecture slides.

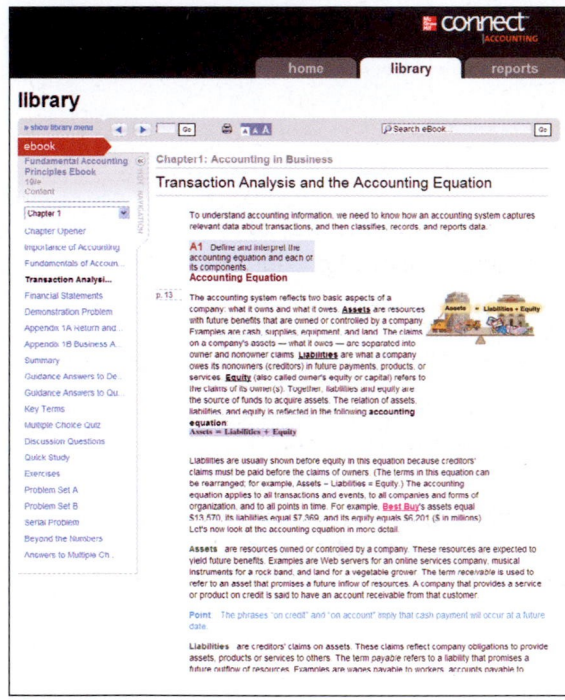

McGraw-Hill Connect Plus Accounting

McGraw-Hill reinvents the textbook learning experience for the modern student with Connect Plus Accounting. A seamless integration of an eBook and Connect Accounting, Connect Plus Accounting provides all of the Connect Accounting features plus the following:

- An integrated eBook, allowing for anytime, anywhere access to the textbook.
- Dynamic links between the problems or questions you assign to your students and the location in the eBook where that problem or question is covered.
- A powerful search function to pinpoint and connect key concepts in a snap.

In short, Connect Accounting offers you and your students powerful tools and features that optimize your time and energies, enabling you to focus on course content, teaching, and student learning. Connect Accounting also offers a wealth of content resources for both instructors and students. This state-of-the-art, thoroughly tested system supports you in preparing students for the world that awaits.

For information about Connect, go to www.mcgrawhillconnect.com, or contact your local McGraw-Hill sales representative.

Tegrity Campus: Lectures 24/7

Tegrity Campus is a service that makes class time available 24/7 by automatically capturing every lecture. With a simple one-click start-and-stop process, you capture all computer screens and corresponding audio in a format that is easily searchable, frame by frame. Students can replay any part of any class with easy-to-use browser-based viewing on a PC or Mac, an iPod, or other mobile device. Educators know that the more students can see, hear, and experience class resources, the better they learn. In fact, studies prove it. Tegrity Campus's unique search feature helps students efficiently find what they need, when they need it, across an entire semester of class recordings. Help turn your students' study time into learning moments immediately supported by your lecture. With Tegrity Campus, you also increase intent listening and class participation by easing students' concerns about note-taking. Lecture Capture will make it more likely you will see students' faces, not the tops of their heads.

To learn more about Tegrity, watch a 2-minute Flash demo at http://tegritycampus.mhhe.com.

Assurance of Learning Ready

Many educational institutions today are focused on the notion of assurance of learning, an important element of some accreditation standards. College Accounting is designed specifically to support your assurance of learning initiatives with a simple, yet powerful solution. Each test bank question for College Accounting maps to a specific chapter learning outcome/objective listed in the text. You can use our test bank software, EZ Test and EZ Test Online, or in Connect Accounting to easily query for learning outcomes/objectives that directly relate to the learning objectives for your course. You can then use the reporting features of EZ Test to aggregate student results in similar fashion, making the collection and presentation of assurance of learning data simple and easy.

AACSB Statement

The McGraw-Hill Companies is a proud corporate member of AACSB International. Understanding the importance and value of AACSB accreditation, College Accounting, 2nd edition recognizes the curricula guidelines detailed in the AACSB standards for business accreditation by connecting selected questions in the test bank to the six general knowledge and skill guidelines in the AACSB standards. The statements contained in College Accounting, 2nd edition are provided only as a guide for the users of this textbook. The AACSB leaves content coverage and assessment within the purview of individual schools, the mission of the school, and the faculty. While College Accounting, 2nd edition and the teaching package make no claim of any specific AACSB qualification or evaluation, we have within College Accounting, 2nd edition labeled selected questions according to the six general knowledge and skills areas.

McGraw-Hill Customer Care Contact Information

At McGraw-Hill, we understand that getting the most from new technology can be challenging. That's why our services don't stop after you purchase our products. You can e-mail our Product Specialists 24 hours a day to get product training online. Or you can search our knowledge bank of Frequently Asked Questions on our support Website. For Customer Support, call 800-331-5094 or visit www.mhhe.com/support. One of our Technical Support Analysts will be able to assist you in a timely fashion.

ALEKS®

ALEKS® for the Accounting Cycle and ALEKS® for Financial Accounting

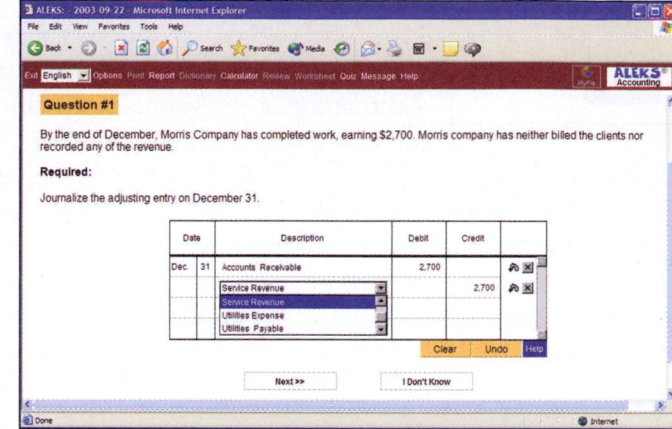

Available from McGraw-Hill over the World Wide Web, ALEKS (Assessment and LEarning in Knowledge Spaces) provides precise assessment and individualized instruction in the fundamental skills your students need to succeed in accounting.

ALEKS motivates your students because ALEKS can tell what a student knows, doesn't know, and is most ready to learn next. ALEKS does this using the ALEKS Assessment and Knowledge Space Theory as an artificial intelligence engine to exactly identify a student's knowledge of accounting. When students focus on precisely what they are ready to learn, they build the confidence and learning momentum that fuel success.

To learn more about adding ALEKS to your principles course, visit www.business.aleks.com.

How Can Students Study on the Go Using Their iPod?

iPod Content

Harness the power of one of the most popular technology tools students use today—the Apple iPod. Our innovative approach allows students to download audio and video presentations right into their iPod and take learning materials with them wherever they go. Students just need to visit the Online Learning Center at **www.mhhe.com/wildCA2e** to download our iPod content. For each chapter of the book they will be able to download audio-narrated lecture presentations designed for use on various versions of iPods.

It makes review and study time as easy as putting in headphones.

How Can Text-Related Web Resources Enhance My Course?

Online Learning Center (OLC)

We offer an Online Learning Center (OLC) that follows *College Accounting* chapter by chapter. It doesn't require any building or maintenance on your part. It's ready to go the moment you and your students type in the URL: www.mhhe.com/wildCA2e. As students study and learn from *College Accounting*, they can visit the Student Edition of the OLC Website to work with a multitude of helpful tools:

- Generic Template Working Papers
- Chapter Learning Objectives
- Interactive Chapter Quizzes
- PowerPoint® Presentations
- Narrated PowerPoint® Presentations
- iPod Content
- Excel Template Assignments

A secured Instructor Edition stores essential course materials to save you prep time before class. Everything you need to run a lively classroom and an efficient course is included. All resources available to students, plus . . .

- Sample Syllabi
- Test Bank
- Instructor's Manual
- Solutions Manual
- Solutions to Excel Template Assignments

The OLC Website also serves as a doorway to other technology solutions, like course management systems.

Learning Objectives

Each chapter opens with Learning Objectives that are highlighted throughout the chapter body and end-of-chapter materials. These Learning Objectives give students direction on the concepts that they are building on and focus their learning. The chapter opener also provides "A Look Back," "A Look at This Chapter," and "A Look Ahead" to inform students where they are, where they were, and where they will be going to help better direct them on their journey through *College Accounting*.

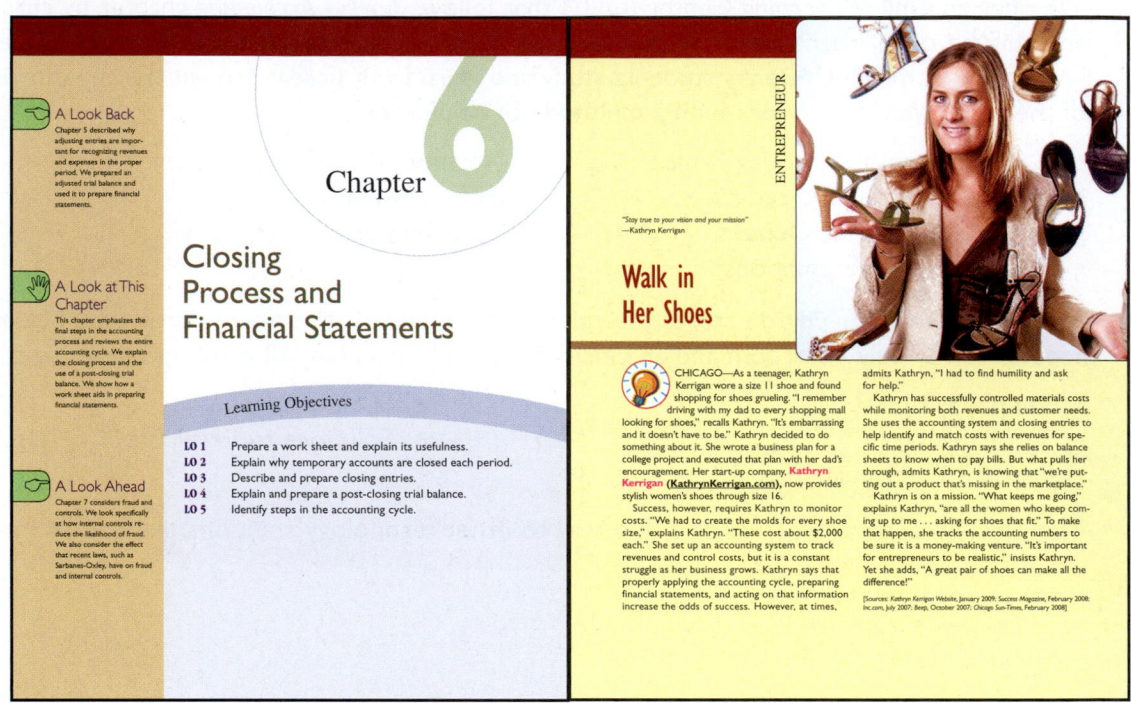

Whether we prepare, analyze, or apply accounting information, one skill remains essential: decision making. To help develop good decision-making habits and to illustrate the relevance of accounting, *College Accounting* uses a unique pedagogical framework comprised of a variety of approaches, giving students insight into every aspect of business decision making. Many later chapters also include a tool, such as ratio analysis, that uses accounting data to better understand company operations. An "In the News" feature offers information relevant to students entering the business world.

IN THE NEWS

Perpetual Accounting **Wal-Mart** uses a network of information links with its point-of-sale cash registers to coordinate sales, purchases, and distribution. Its supercenters, for instance, ring up to 15,000 separate sales on heavy days. By using cash register information, the company can fix pricing mistakes quickly and capitalize on sales trends.

TOTAL ASSET TURNOVER

A company's assets are important in determining its ability to generate sales and earn income. Managers devote much attention to deciding what assets a company acquires, how much it invests in assets, and how to use assets most efficiently and effectively. One important measure of a company's ability to use its assets is **total asset turnover,** defined in Exhibit 18.19.

LO9 Compute total asset turnover and apply it for analysis.

$$\text{Total asset turnover} = \frac{\text{Net sales}}{\text{Average total assets}}$$

Exhibit 18.19
Total Asset Turnover

Chapter Preview with Flow Chart

This feature provides a handy textual/visual guide at the start of each chapter. Students can begin their reading with a clear understanding of what they will learn and when, which allows them to stay more focused and organized along the way.

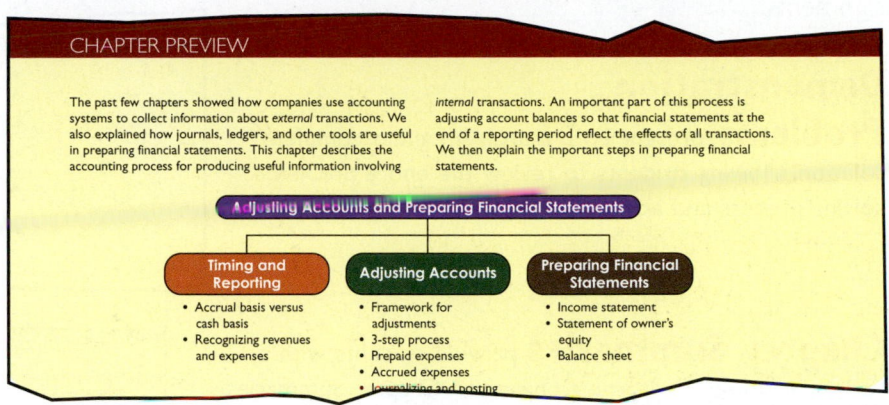

CHAPTER PREVIEW

The past few chapters showed how companies use accounting systems to collect information about *external* transactions. We also explained how journals, ledgers, and other tools are useful in preparing financial statements. This chapter describes the accounting process for producing useful information involving *internal* transactions. An important part of this process is adjusting account balances so that financial statements at the end of a reporting period reflect the effects of all transactions. We then explain the important steps in preparing financial statements.

Adjusting Accounts and Preparing Financial Statements

Timing and Reporting
- Accrual basis versus cash basis
- Recognizing revenues and expenses

Adjusting Accounts
- Framework for adjustments
- 3-step process
- Prepaid expenses
- Accrued expenses
- Journalizing and posting

Preparing Financial Statements
- Income statement
- Statement of owner's equity
- Balance sheet

How You Doin'?

These short question/answer features reinforce the material immediately preceding them. They allow the reader to pause and reflect on the topics described, then receive immediate feedback before going on to new topics. Answers are provided at the end of each chapter.

HOW YOU DOIN'? Answers—p. 61

1. Identify each of the following as either an asset, a liability, or equity: (a) Prepaid Rent, (b) Unearned Fees, (c) Building, (d) Wages Payable, and (e) Office Supplies.
2. What is a T-account?
3. Does *debit* always mean increase and *credit* always mean decrease?

Marginal Student Annotations

These annotations provide students with additional hints, tips, and examples to help them more fully understand the concepts and retain what they have learned. The annotations also include notes on global implications of accounting and further examples.

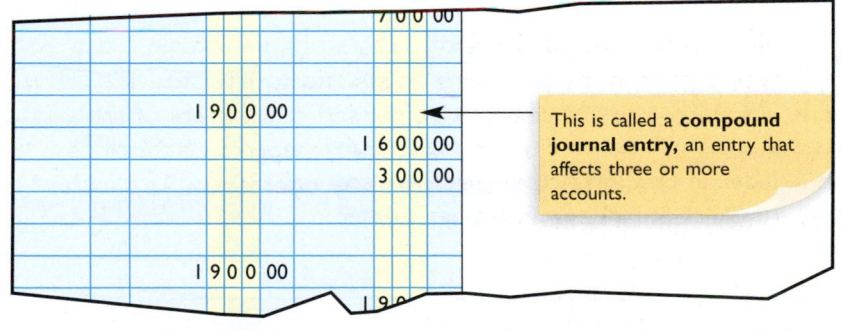

This is called a **compound journal entry,** an entry that affects three or more accounts.

FastForward

FastForward is a case that takes students through the Accounting Cycle, Chapters 2–6. The FastForward icon is placed in the margin whenever this case is discussed.

1. Investment by Owner

Transaction: Chuck Taylor invests $30,000 cash in Fa

Analysis:

Assets	=	Liabilities
Cash		
+30,000	=	0

Total debits equal total credits for each transaction.

Cash and C. Taylor, Capital increase by $3
is debited and C. Taylor, Capital is credited

Once a student has finished reading the chapter, how well he or she retains the material can depend greatly on the questions, exercises, and problems that reinforce it. This book leads the way in comprehensive, accurate end-of-chapter assignments.

Demonstration Problems
present both a problem and a complete solution, allowing students to review the entire problem-solving process and achieve success.

Chapter Summaries
provide students with a review organized by learning objectives. Chapter Summaries recap each learning objective.

Key Terms
are bolded in the text and repeated at the end of the chapter with definitions and page numbers indicating their location. The book also includes a complete Glossary of Key Terms.

Multiple Choice Quizzes
In response to review and focus group feedback, the authors have created Multiple Choice Quizzes that quickly test chapter knowledge before a student moves on to complete Quick Studies, Exercises, and Problems.

Quick Study
assignments are short exercises that often focus on one learning objective. All are included in Connect Accounting. There are usually 8–10 Quick Study assignments per chapter.

Exercises
are one of this book's many strengths and a competitive advantage. There are about 10–15 per chapter and all are included in Connect Accounting.

Problem Sets A & B
are proven problems that can be assigned as homework or for in-class projects. All problems are coded according to one or more learning objectives, and items from Problem Set A are included in Connect Accounting.

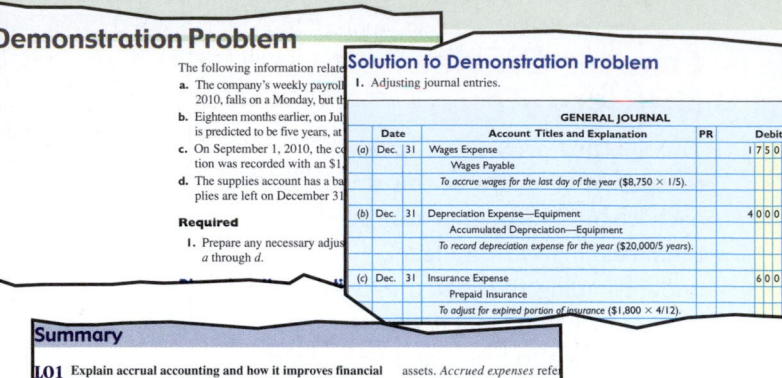

Demonstration Problem
The following information relate...
a. The company's weekly payroll... 2010, falls on a Monday, but th...
b. Eighteen months earlier, on Jul... is predicted to be five years, at...
c. On September 1, 2010, the co... tion was recorded with an $1,...
d. The supplies account has a ba... plies are left on December 31...

Required

1. Prepare any necessary adjus... *a* through *d*.

Solution to Demonstration Problem
1. Adjusting journal entries.

GENERAL JOURNAL

Date		Account Titles and Explanation	PR	Debit
(a) Dec.	31	Wages Expense		1 7 5 0 0
		Wages Payable		
		To accrue wages for the last day of the year ($8,750 × 1/5).		
(b) Dec.	31	Depreciation Expense—Equipment		4 0 0 0 0
		Accumulated Depreciation—Equipment		
		To record depreciation expense for the year ($20,000/5 years).		
(c) Dec.	31	Insurance Expense		6 0 0 0
		Prepaid Insurance		
		To adjust for expired portion of insurance ($1,800 × 4/12).		

Summary

LO1 Explain accrual accounting and how it improves financial statements. Accrual accounting recognizes revenues when earned and expenses as they occur—not necessarily when cash inflows and outflows occur. This better reflects a company's financial position and performance.

LO2 Identify the types of accounting adjustments and their purpose. Adjustments can be grouped according to the timing of cash receipts or payments relative to the timing of the related work performed. Adjusting entries are made for prepaid expenses,

assets. *Accrued expenses* refer... are both unpaid and unrecorde... accrued expenses involve incr... creasing (crediting) liabilities.

LO4 Explain and prepare a... adjusted trial balance is... pared after recording and post... statements are often prepared

LO5

Key Terms

Accrual basis accounting (p. 104) Accounting system that recognizes revenues when earned and expenses as they occur; the basis for GAAP.

Accrued expenses (p. 109) Costs incurred in a period that are both unpaid and unrecorded; adjusting entries for recording accrued expenses involve increasing expenses and increasing liabilities.

Adjusted trial balance (p. 110) List of accounts and balances prepared after period-end adjustments are recorded and posted.

Adjusting entry (p. 106) Journal entry at the end of an accounting period to bring an asset or liability account to its proper amount and

Contra account (p. 108... having an opposite norm... other account's balance.

Depreciation (p. 108) ... and equipment to period... expense of using the asse...

Fiscal year (p. 105) Co... chosen as the organizatio...

Interim financial state...

Multiple Choice Quiz   Answers on p. 125

Additional Multiple Choice Quizzes are available at the book's Website.

1. A company forgot to record accrued and unpaid employee wages of $350,000 at period-end. This oversight would
a. Understate net income by $350,000.
b. Overstate net income by $350,000.
c. Have no effect on net income.
d. Overstate assets by $350,000.
e. Understate assets by $350,000.

2. Prior to recording adjusting entries, the Office Supplies account has a $450 debit balance. A physical count of supplies shows $125 of unused supplies still available. The required adjusting entry is:

a. $4,000
b. $8,000
c. $12,000
d. $20,000
e. $24,000

4. A company purchases a del... 2010. The truck is estimated... zero salvage value. The com... of depreciation. How much... on th...

QUICK STUDY   *connect*

QS 5-1
Computing accrual income and cash income **LO1**

In its first year of operations, Case Co. earned $60,000 in revenues and received $52,000 cash from these customers. The company recorded expenses of $37,500 but had not paid $6,000 of them by the end of the year. The company also prepaid $3,250 cash for next year's insurance premium. Calculate Case Co.'s first year net income under (a) the cash basis and (b) the accrual basis of accounting.

EXERCISES   *connect*

Exercise 5-1
Determining assets and expenses for accrual and cash accounting **LO1**

On November 1, 2009, a company paid a $15,300 premium on a 36-month insurance policy for coverage beginning on that date. Refer to that policy and fill in the blanks in the following table.

Balance Sheet Prepaid Insurance Asset Using			Insurance Expense Using		
	Accrual Basis	Cash Basis		Accrual Basis	Cash Basis
Dec. 31, 2009	$_____	$_____	2009	$_____	$_____
Dec. 31, 2010	_____	_____	2010	_____	_____
Dec. 31, 2011	_____	_____	2011	_____	_____
Dec. 31, 2012	_____	_____	2012	_____	_____
			Total	$_____	$_____

Check 2011 insurance expense: Accrual, $5,100; Cash, $0. Dec. 31, 2011, asset: Accrual, $4,250; Cash, $0.

PROBLEM SET A

Problem 5-1A
Preparing adjusting entries, adjusted trial balance, and financial statements
LO3 LO4 LO5

eXcel
mhhe.com/wildCA2e

Wells Technical Institute (WTI), a sc... pay tuition directly to the school. W... trial balance as of December 31, 2010... tries on December 31, 2010, follow.

Additional Information

a. An analysis of the school's insura...
b. A count shows that teaching supp...
c. Annual depreciation on the equip...
d. Annual depreciation on the profes...
e. The school's two employees are p... at the rate of $100 per day for eac...
f. The balance in the Prepaid Rent a...

...as of December 31, 2010. The Institute... rectly to the business and offers exten... al balance are items *a* through *f* that re-...

PROBLEM SET B

Problem 5-1B
Preparing adjusting entries, adjusted trial balance, and financial statements **LO3 LO4 LO5**

Beyond the Numbers exercises ask students to use accounting figures and understand their meaning. Students also learn how accounting applies to a variety of business situations. These creative and fun exercises are divided into sections:

- Reporting in Action
- Comparative Analysis
- Ethics Challenge
- Workplace Communication
- Taking It To The Net

- Teamwork in Action
- Entrepreneurs in Business
- Your Ethics Call
- You Call It

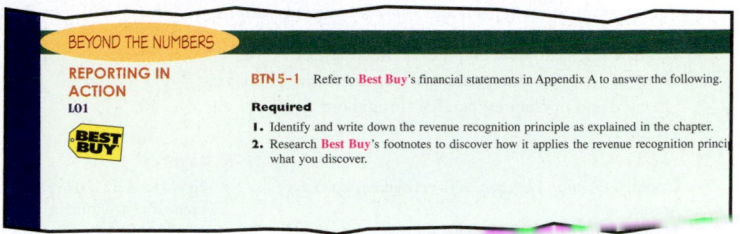

Serial Problems use a continuous running case study to illustrate chapter concepts in a familiar context. Serial Problems can be followed continuously from the first chapter or picked up at any later point in the book; enough information is provided to ensure students can get right to work.

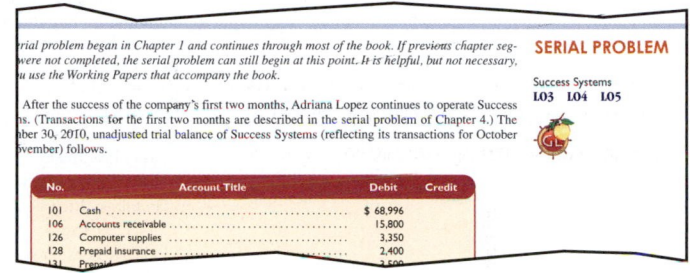

Appendix on Accounting Principles discusses a rules-based versus a principles-based accounting system. It also describes the objectives, characteristics, and assumptions of accounting principles.

The End of the Chapter Is Only the Beginning

Our valuable and proven assignments aren't just confined to the book. From problems that require technological solutions to materials found exclusively online, this book's end-of-chapter material is fully integrated with its technology package.

connect
- Quick Studies, Exercises, and Problems available on Connect Accounting (see page ix) are marked with an icon.

- Problems supported by the Quickbooks Software are marked with an icon.

- The Online Learning Center (OLC) includes Personal Interactive Quizzes and Excel template assignments.

mhhe.com/wildCA2e
- Problems supported with Microsoft Excel template assignments are marked with an icon.

Put Away Your Red Pen

We pride ourselves on the accuracy of this book's assignment materials. Independent research reports that instructors and reviewers point to the accuracy of this book's assignment materials as one of its key competitive advantages.

The authors extend a special thanks to accuracy checker Anna Boulware, St. Charles Community College.

Enhancements for College Accounting 2e

This edition's revisions are driven by feedback from instructors and students. Many of the revisions are summarized here. Feedback suggests that this is the book instructors want to teach from and students want to learn from. General revisions include:

- Updated design-visual graphics and text layout
- New and revised entrepreneurial elements throughout text
- Revised end of chapter material throughout text
- New feature company, Best Buy, with Annual Report, and comparison to RadioShack

Chapter 1

- Updated Opener, **LoveSac,** with revised entrepreneurial assignment
- Improved discussion and graphic on users of accounting information
- Updated graphic on accounting salaries
- New discussion on experience and education requirements for entry-level accounting jobs
- Expanded discussion on sources of ethical guidance
- New discussion of organization structures
- New discussion of types of businesses
- New graphic on recent publicized accounting scandals
- New reference to the Public Company Accounting Oversight Board
- New information on real-world companies' use of accounting principles
- Revised end-of-chapter material, including 7 new questions

Chapter 2

- New Opener, **SPANX,** with new entrepreneurial assignment
- Simplified discussion of 3-step process for analyzing transactions
- New exhibit on links between financial statements
- New discussion of financial statement headings and alternative names
- Clarified discussion of items that impact owner's equity
- Revised end-of-chapter material, including 15 new questions

Chapter 3

- Updated Opener, **Cake Love,** with revised entrepreneurial assignment
- Clarified discussion of T-accounts
- New simplified 3-step process for determining postings to T-accounts
- Enhanced discussion of normal balances
- Enhanced discussion on prepayments
- Increased clarity of exhibit illustrating expanded accounting equation
- Increased clarity of exhibit illustrating the rules of debit and credit
- Revised end-of-chapter material, including 10 new questions

Chapter 4

- Updated Opener, **Vosges Haut Chocolate,** with revised entrepreneurial assignment
- Enhanced exhibit on the recording process
- Clarified discussion and added exhibit comparing the T-account with the general ledger account
- Simplified discussion of the journalizing and posting process
- New exhibits on the journalizing and posting process
- Enhanced discussion of correcting errors
- Revised end-of-chapter material, including 14 new questions

Chapter 5

- New Opener, **PopCap Games,** with revised entrepreneurial assignment
- New discussion of accrual basis versus cash basis accounting
- New exhibit comparing effects of accrual basis versus cash basis accounting
- New discussion of why certain accounts are adjusted
- New exhibit on framework for adjustments
- Simplified 3-step adjusting process and examples
- New exhibits on journalizing and posting adjusting entries
- Revised end-of-chapter material, including 11 new questions

Chapter 6

- New Opener, **Kathryn Kerrigan,** with revised entrepreneurial assignment
- New discussion on the benefits and uses of a work sheet
- New discussion of preparing pro-forma financial statements
- Simplified discussion on preparing the work sheet
- New graphic on sorting accounts to financial statement columns on the work sheet
- New graphic on how to determine income or loss from work sheet totals
- Clarified discussion on how to balance the work sheet for either income or loss
- New discussion and exhibit on treatment of additional owner investment
- New discussion of handling errors on the work sheet
- Simplified discussion of the closing process
- Enhanced graphic on closing process
- Enhanced exhibit showing the use of the work sheet in the closing process
- Revised end-of-chapter material, including 6 new questions
- Two new practice sets covering the full accounting cycle

Chapter 7

- New Opener, **Dylan's Candy Bar,** with revised entrepreneurial assignment
- New graphic, ways to detect fraud
- New discussion on fraud detection
- New exhibit, fraud red flags
- Added examples of real fraud cases

Chapter 8

- Updated Opener, **Wildflower Linen,** with revised entrepreneurial assignment
- New exhibit illustrating signature card document
- New section and exhibit on blank and restrictive endorsements
- New graphic and explanation of non-sufficient funds and overdraft fees
- Revised end-of-chapter material, including 8 new questions

Chapter 9

- New Opener, **Feed Granola Company,** with revised entrepreneurial assignment
- New discussion of independent contractors
- Enhanced discussion of self-employment taxes
- New illustration of Social Security taxes that exceed the maximum earnings limit
- New illustration of the Medicare tax
- Updated with new minimum wage (as of July 24, 2009)
- Updated with 2009 tax withholding tables

Chapter 10

- Updated Opener, **1-800-GOT-JUNK,** with revised entrepreneurial assignment
- Added new How You Doin'? questions
- Simplified discussion of federal unemployment taxes and credit for state unemployment taxes
- Simplified journal entries for federal and state unemployment taxes

Chapter 11

- Updated Opener, **Life is Good,** with revised entrepreneurial assignment
- Enhanced examples of wholesalers and retailers
- Enhanced discussion of cash receipts journal with associated end of chapter assignments

Chapter 12

- Updated Opener, **CoCaLo,** with revised entrepreneurial assignment
- Chapter now begins with section on Accounting for Merchandise Purchases
- Enhanced discussion of cash disbursements journal with associated end of chapter assignments
- Revised end-of-chapter material, including 10 new questions
- Two new practice sets covering special journals and subsidiary ledgers

Chapter 13

- New Opener, **BigBadToyStore,** with new entrepreneurial assignment
- Continues Z-Mart example from previous merchandising chapters for continuity and clarity
- New discussion and computation examples of net sales, net purchases, cost of goods sold, and gross profit
- Simplified presentation of the work sheet for merchandisers
- New discussion of adjustment for merchandise inventory
- New exhibits on journalizing and posting adjustments for merchandise inventory
- Simplified chart and discussion of framework for adjustments
- Simplified discussion of adjusting journal entries for a merchandiser
- Simplified discussion of unearned revenues and their adjustment
- New second Demonstration Problem added
- Revised end-of-chapter material, including 15 new questions

Chapter 14

- New Opener, **RockBottomGolf,** with revised entrepreneurial assignment
- Continued Z-Mart example from previous merchandising chapters for continuity and clarity
- Simplified work sheet presentation and exhibit
- New section on statement of owner's equity
- New table showing items that impact owner's equity and their information sources
- Simplified closing entries section
- New section on post-closing trial balance
- New exhibit, postings to Income Summary account
- New exhibit on use of work sheet in preparing closing entries
- Revised end-of-chapter material, including 14 new questions

Acknowledgments

xix

The authors and McGraw-Hill/Irwin would like to recognize the following instructors for their valuable feedback and involvement in the development of *College Accounting 2e*. We are thankful for their suggestions, counsel, and encouragement.

Cornelia Alsheimer-Barthel, Santa Barbara City College

Jack Aschkenazi, American Intercontinental University Online

Marjorie Ashton, Truckee Meadows Community College

Jeanne Bedell, Keiser University

Sean Bell, Advanced Career Training

Jason Bess, Stautzenberger College

Juanita Garza Blankenship, Del Mar College

Sara Bottomley, Indiana Business College

Anna Boulware, St. Charles Community College

Judith Brierley, Seminole Community College

Peggy Brock, Central New Mexico Community College

Rebecca F. Brown, Des Moines Area Community College

Joan Cook, Milwaukee Area Technical College

Dean Danielson, San Joaquin Delta College

Lorie Darche, Southwest Florida College

Susan Snow Davis, Green River Community College

Vincent DeBiase II, San Joaquin Valley College

Carol Easley, National College

Steven Ernest, Baton Rouge Community College

Vanessa Escalante, LA College International

Richard Firth, Colorado Technical University

Mark Fronke, Cerritos College

Marina Grau, Houston Community College

Betty Habershon, Prince George's Community College

Toni Hartley, Laurel Business Institute

Christina Hata, MiraCosta College

Keith Hendrick, DeKalb Technical College

YuanRong Jia-Reid, Huntington Junior College

Dennis Jirkovsky, Indiana Business College and Longview Community College

Vern Jorgensen, Southwestern College

Dmitriy Kalyagin, Chabot College

Rosemary Keasey, Butler County Community College

Donna Kimmerling, Indiana Business College

Barbara Krause, South Hills School of Business

Kimberly Lamb, Stautzenberger College

Greg Lauer, North Iowa Area Community College-Mason

David Laurel, South Texas College

Harold Lea, Fashion Institute of Design

Mary E. Leslie, Grossmont College

Lolita Lockett, Jones College

Delores Loedel, MiraCosta College

Thomas Lynch, Hocking College

James B. Meir, Cleveland State Community College

Julie Miller-Millmann, Chippewa Valley Tech College

Anita Morgan, Colorado Technical University Online

Cathy Nash, Dekalb Technical College

Joe Nicassio, Westmoreland County Community College

Sharon Owens, Westwood College

Gary Reynolds, Ozarks Technical Community College

Brenda Richter, Santa Barbara City College

Alberta E. Robinson, Indiana Business College

Amanda J. Salinas, Palo Alto College

Jan Sedely, Ohio Business College

Elizabeth Serapin, Columbia Southern University

Gabrielle Serrano, Elgin Community College

Daniel P. Small, J. Sargeant Reynolds Community College

Lauren Smith, Front Range Community College

Joan Thomas, National College

Bill Thompson, Full Sail Real World Education

Patricia Walczk, Lansing Community College

Roger Waller, San Joaquin Delta Community College

Elry Wallman, Institute of Business and Medical Careers

We would like to thank the entire McGraw-Hill/Irwin *College Accounting* team, including Stewart Mattson, Tim Vertovec, Steve Schuetz, Christina Sanders, Lori Koetters, Matthew Baldwin, Carol Bielski, Lori Kramer, and Brian Nacik as well as Aaron Downey from Matrix Productions. We also thank the great marketing and sales support staff, including Kathleen Klehr, Michelle Heaster, Sankha Basu, and Abbey Woodward. Many talented educators and professionals worked hard to create the supplements for this book, and for their efforts we're grateful. Finally, many more people we either did not meet or whose efforts we did not personally witness nevertheless helped to make this book everything that it is, and we thank them all.

John Wild   Vernon Richardson   Ken Shaw

Supplements

Instructor

Instructor's Resource CD-ROM

ISBN: 9780077268817
MHID: 0077268814

This is your all-in-one resource. It allows you to create custom presentations from your own materials or from the following text-specific materials provided in the CD's asset library:

- Instructor's Resource Manual
- Solutions Manual. *Prepared by John J. Wild, Vernon J. Richardson, and Ken W. Shaw.*
- Test Bank, Computerized Test Bank. *Prepared by Linda Muren and Veronica Czekaj, Cuyahoga Community College.*
- PowerPoint® Presentations allow for revision of lecture slides, and include a viewer, allowing screens to be shown with or without the software. *Prepared by Jason Bess, Stautzenberger College.*
- Excel Template Assignments
- Link to PageOut

Student

Study Guide and Working Papers

Vol. 1, Chapters 1–14
ISBN: 9780077268855
MHID: 0077268857

Written by John J. Wild, Vernon J. Richardson and Ken W. Shaw.

Electronic Study Guide and Excel Working Papers CD

Chapters 1–29
ISBN: 9780077268787
MHID: 0077268784

Written by John J. Wild, Vernon J. Richardson, and Ken W. Shaw.

Study Guide and Working Papers delivered in Excel spreadsheets. Excel Working Papers are available on CD-ROM and can be bundled with the printed Working Papers; see your representative for information. The Study Guide covers each chapter and appendix with reviews of the learning objectives, outlines of the chapters, summaries of chapter materials, and additional problems with solutions.

QuickBooks Pro2010 Student Guide and Templates

ISBN: 9780077399443
MHID: 0077399447

Prepared by Carol Yacht.

To better prepare students for accounting in the real world, select end-of-chapter material in the text is tied to Quickbooks software. The accompanying student guide provides a step-by-step walkthrough for students on how to complete the problem in the software.

The authors extend special thanks to the supplement authors and accuracy checkers:

Test Bank: Linda Muren and Veronica Czekaj, Cuyahoga Community College

PowerPoint Presentations: Jason Bess, Stautzenberger College

Online Quizzes: Anna Boulware, St. Charles Community College

Supplement accuracy and quality assurance: Helen Roybark, Radford University; Beth Woods, Accuracy Counts; Lorie Darche, Southwest Florida College

Brief Contents

1   Introduction to Accounting 2

2   Accounting for Business Transactions 20

3   Applying Double-Entry Accounting 44

4   Preparing the General Journal and General Ledger 72

5   Adjusting Accounts and Preparing Financial Statements 102

6   Closing Process and Financial Statements 126

7   Fraud, Ethics, and Controls 156

8   Cash and Cash Controls 176

9   Employee Earnings, Deductions, and Payroll 204

10 Employer Payroll Tax Reporting 230

11 Merchandise Sales and Accounts Receivable 260

12 Merchandise Purchases and Accounts Payable 284

13 Merchandiser's Adjustments and Trial Balance 314

14 Merchandiser's Financial Statements and the Closing Process 344

A   Financial Statement Information A-1

B   Accounting Principles B-1

C* Capital Budgeting Decisions

D* Time Value of Money

*Appendixes C and D are not printed in the text; they are available on the book's Website, mhhe.com/wildCA2e.

Contents

1 Introduction to Accounting 2

Importance of Accounting 4
   Accounting Information Uses 4
   Accounting Information Users 5
Opportunities in Accounting 7
   Entry-Level Jobs 7
   Career Paths 7
   Certifications 8
Fundamentals of Accounting 9
   Ethics—A Key Concept 9
   Generally Accepted Accounting Principles 10
   Ownership Structures 11

2 Accounting for Business Transactions 20

Transaction Analysis and the Accounting Equation 22
   Accounting Equation 22
   Transactions and the Accounting Equation 23
   Summary of Transactions 28
Financial Statements 29
   Income Statement 30
   Statement of Owner's Equity 30
   Balance Sheet 31

3 Applying Double-Entry Accounting 44

Analyzing and Recording Transactions 46
   The T-Account 46
   Double-Entry Accounting 47
   Recording Transactions—An Illustration 48
   Summary of T-Account Illustration 54
Trial Balance 55
   Preparing a Trial Balance 55
   Using a Trial Balance to Prepare Financial Statements 56

4 Preparing the General Journal and General Ledger 72

Analyzing and Recording Process 74
   Source Documents 75
   Chart of Accounts 76
Journalizing and Posting 77
   The General Journal 77
   The General Ledger 80
   Journalizing and Posting—An Illustration 82
   Trial Balance 83
   Correcting Errors in the Journal and the Ledger 85

5 Adjusting Accounts and Preparing Financial Statements 102

Timing and Reporting 104
   Accrual Basis versus Cash Basis 104
   Recognizing Revenues and Expenses 105
Adjusting Accounts 105
   Framework for Adjustments 105
   3-Step Adjusting Process 106
   Prepaid (Deferred) Expenses 106
   Accrued Expenses 109
   Journalizing and Posting Adjusting Entries 110
   Adjusted Trial Balance 110
Preparing Financial Statements 112

6 Closing Process and Financial Statements 126

Work Sheet as a Tool 128
   Benefits of a Work Sheet 128
   Use of a Work Sheet 128
   Work Sheet Applications and Analysis 132

Closing Process 133
  Temporary and Permanent Accounts 133
  Recording Closing Entries 134
  Post-Closing Trial Balance 137
Accounting Cycle 137

7 Fraud, Ethics, and Controls 156

Workplace Fraud 158
  Elements of Workplace Fraud Schemes 158
  Major Types of Workplace Fraud 158
Internal Control 160
  Purpose of Internal Control 160
  Principles of Internal Control 160
  Technology and Internal Control 162
  Limitations of Internal Control 163
  Voucher System of Control 164
The Sarbanes-Oxley Act 165
  Requirements of the Sarbanes-Oxley Act 165
Appendix 7A Documentation and Verification 166

8 Cash and Cash Controls 176

Control of Cash 178
  Cash and Liquidity 178
  Control of Cash Receipts 178
  Control of Cash Disbursements 180
Banking Activities as Controls 183
  Basic Bank Services 183
  Bank Statement 185
  Bank Reconciliation 186

9 Employee Earnings, Deductions, and Payroll 204

Legal Aspects of Employee Payroll 206
  Fair Labor Standards Act 206
  Federal and State Income Tax Withholding 206
  Federal Insurance Contributions Act (FICA) 207

Employee Earnings and Witholdings 208
  Compute Employee Gross Pay 208
  Compute Withholdings from Employee Gross Pay 209
  Compute Net Pay 213
Payroll Accounting 213
  Payroll Register 213
  Recording and Settling Payroll 214
  Employee Earnings Records 216
Control over Payroll 216
  Payroll Fraud 217
  Payroll Control 217

10 Employer Payroll Tax Reporting 230

Laws Impacting Employer's Payroll Tax 232
  Employer Identification Number 232
  Employer FICA Tax 232
  Federal and State Unemployment Tax Acts 232
  Workers' Compensation Insurance 233
Employer's Payroll Taxes 233
  Computing Employer's FICA Tax 233
  General Journal Entry to Record Employer FICA Tax 233
  Payroll Tax Deposits 234
Employer's Payroll Tax Reporting 236
  Employer's Quarterly Federal Tax Return 236
  Employer's Annual Withholding Reporting 238
Federal (FUTA) and State (SUTA) Unemployment Taxes 240
  Computing Employer's Unemployment Taxes 240
  Reporting Employer's Unemployment Taxes 241
Workers' Compensation Insurance 244
  Computing Estimated Workers' Compensation Insurance Premium 244
  Computing Actual Workers' Compensation Insurance Premium 244

11 Merchandise Sales and Accounts Receivable 260

Merchandising Sales 262
   Sales of Merchandise 262
   Sales Discounts 262
   Sales Returns and Allowances 264
   Recording and Posting Merchandise Sales 265
Special Journals and Subsidiary Ledgers 266
   Sales Journal 266
   Accounts Receivable Subsidiary Ledger 267
   Cash Receipts Journal 270

12 Merchandise Purchases and Accounts Payable 284

Accounting for Merchandise Purchases 286
   Purchasing Procedures 286
   Accounting for Purchases and Freight Charges 287
   Trade Discounts 287
   Purchase Discounts 288
   Purchase Returns and Allowances 289
   Transportation Costs and Ownership Transfer 290
Purchases Journal and Accounts Payable Subsidiary Ledger 291
   Purchases Journal 292
   Posting to the Accounts Payable Subsidiary Ledger 294
   Cash Disbursements Journal 294

13 Merchandiser's Adjustments and Trial Balance 314

Merchandiser's Trial Balance 316
   Using a Trial Balance 317
   Adjusting Entries for Merchandise Inventory 317
Expense Adjustments 318
   Adjusting Process 318
   Adjusting Prepaid Expenses (Including Depreciation) 319
   Adjusting Accrued Expenses 320

Partial Work Sheet 320
   Adjusted Trial Balance 320
   Computing Net Sales and Net Purchases for a Merchandiser 322
   Computing Cost of Goods Sold 322
   Computing Gross Profit 323
Revenue Adjustments 323
   Accrued Revenues 324
   Unearned (Deferred) Revenues 324
Links to Financial Statements 326
Appendix 13A Alternative Accounting for Prepayments 329

14 Merchandiser's Financial Statements and the Closing Process 344

The Work Sheet 346
   Preparing the Work Sheet 346
Financial Statement Formats 347
   Multiple-Step Income Statement 347
   Single-Step Income Statement 349
   Statement of Owner's Equity 349
   Classified Balance Sheet 349
Completing the Accounting Cycle 352
   Closing Entries 352
   Post-Closing Trial Balance 353
Appendix 14A Reversing Entries 356

A   Financial Statement Information A-1
     Best Buy A-2
     RadioShack A-21
B   Accounting Principles B-1
C* Capital Budgeting Decisions
D* Time Value of Money
     Glossary G-1
     Index IND-1

College Accounting

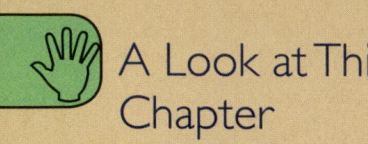

Chapter

Introduction to Accounting

Learning Objectives

LO 1	Explain the purpose and importance of accounting in the information age.
LO 2	Identify users and uses of accounting.
LO 3	Identify career opportunities in accounting and related fields.
LO 4	Explain why ethics are crucial to accounting.
LO 5	Explain the meaning of generally accepted accounting principles.
LO 6	Identify the groups that establish generally accepted accounting principles.
LO 7	Identify the three types of ownership structures.

A **short article** launches each chapter showing the relevance of accounting for a real entrepreneur. An **Entrepreneurs In Business** problem at the end of the assignments returns to this article with a mini-case.

"Ask everyone to give you money…
remember, you hold the opportunity for them"
—Shawn Nelson

Love, Peace, and Profits

SALT LAKE CITY—Trying to get comfortable while watching TV, Shawn Nelson thought "a huge beanbag thing" would be far more relaxing than his old couch. So he made one—a big one! Seven feet across and shaped like a baseball, Shawn's creation was the talk of friends and neighbors. Shortly after making and selling a few "huge beanbag things," Shawn knew it needed a better name. Drawing on the 1960s retro spirit of "love and peace," Shawn named his invention the **LoveSac** and his company (**LoveSac.com**) was born.

Yet LoveSac's launch was anything but smooth. Shawn began by working out of his mother's basement. He then set up shop at trade shows and even the local drive-in cinema. He got his first big break when **Limited Too** called after seeing his display at a trade show. "I answered the phone," says Shawn, "Twelve thousand Sacs? Sure, no problem." Who was he kidding?

Shawn's debt swelled to over $50,000 as he worked 19-hour days and slept in the aged building in which he manufactured the Sacs. "It nearly broke me emotionally, physically, mentally," Shawn recalls.

"We finished the order but ate up all our profits." Without profits his business, too, would soon be retro. So Shawn approached furniture retailers to ask if they would carry Sacs. "Shawn can still hear the laughter," states LoveSac's Website.

Just when things seemed bleakest, Shawn's cousin suggested he open a retail location. Desperate, Shawn took a three-month lease in a shopping mall. His goal: sell one SuperSac per day. This would cover rent and pay him and his cousin a $5 hourly wage. Shawn then developed a transaction-based accounting system to get a handle on orders and sales.

Incredibly, customers crowded into his store within days of opening. Four weeks later and just before Christmas, customers were lined up outside the door waiting for Sacs to arrive from the factory. By Christmas Eve, Shawn's store was nearly sold out. Today, Shawn has more than 20 stores projected to generate over $30 million in sales. With results like that we'd all love Sacs!

[Sources: *LoveSac Website*, January 2009; *CNBC Business Nation interview*, February 2008; *Entrepreneur*, November 2004; *LA Confidential*, Fall 2004; *Life & Style Weekly*, June 2005.]

*A **Preview** opens each chapter with a summary of topics covered.*

Today's world is one of information—its preparation, communication, analysis, and use. Accounting is at the heart of this information age. Knowledge of accounting provides career opportunities and the insight to take advantage of them. This book introduces concepts, procedures, and analyses that help us make better decisions. In this chapter we describe accounting, the users and uses of accounting information, and career opportunities in accounting. We also emphasize the importance of ethics for accounting.

Introduction to Accounting

Importance of Accounting	Opportunities in Accounting	Fundamentals of Accounting
• Accounting information uses • Accounting information users	• Entry-level jobs • Careers in accounting • Accounting certifications	• Ethics is key • Generally accepted accounting principles • Ownership structures

Importance of Accounting

LO1 Explain the purpose and importance of accounting in the information age.

We live in an information age—a time of communication and immediate access to data, news, facts, and commentary. Information affects how we live, whom we associate with, and our opportunities. To fully benefit from the available information, we need knowledge of how the information system collects, processes, and reports information to decision makers.

Accounting Information Uses

Providing information about what businesses own, what they owe, and how they perform is an important aim of accounting. **Accounting** is an information and measurement system that identifies, records, and communicates information about an organization's business activities. *Identifying* business activities requires selecting transactions relevant to an organization. Examples are the sale of iPods by **Apple** and the receipt of ticket fees by **TicketMaster**. *Recording* business activities requires keeping a chronological log of transactions measured in dollars and classified and summarized in a useful format. *Communicating* business activities requires preparing accounting reports such as financial statements. It also requires analyzing and interpreting such reports. (The financial statements and notes of **Best Buy** and **RadioShack** are shown in Appendix A of this book.) Exhibit 1.1 summarizes accounting activities.

Real company names are printed in bold magenta.

All aspects of business involve accounting. The most common contact with accounting is through credit approvals, checking accounts, tax forms, and payroll. These experiences tend to focus on the recordkeeping role of accounting. **Recordkeeping,** or **bookkeeping,** is the recording of transactions and events, either manually or electronically. This is just one part of accounting.

Exhibit 1.1

Accounting Activities

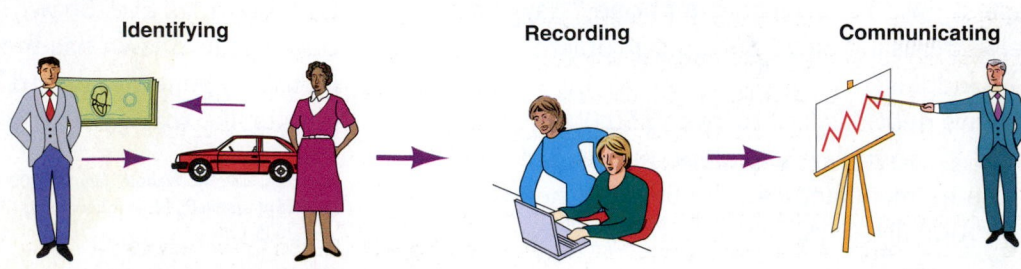

Identifying	Recording	Communicating
Select transactions and events	Input, measure, and classify	Prepare, analyze, and interpret

Accounting also identifies and communicates information on transactions and events, and it includes the crucial processes of analysis and interpretation.

Technology is a key part of modern business and plays a major role in accounting. Accounting software packages like *QuickBooks* and *Simply Accounting* reduce the time, effort, and cost of recordkeeping while improving clerical accuracy.

Accounting Information Users

Accounting is often called the *language of business* because all organizations set up an accounting information system to communicate information to help people make better decisions. Exhibit 1.2 shows that accounting users can be divided into two groups: internal users and external users.

Internal users

- Owners
- Managers
- Internal auditors
- Sales staff
- Budget officers
- Controllers

External users

- Lenders
- Shareholders
- Governments
- Consumer groups
- External auditors
- Customers

Exhibit 1.2

Users of Accounting Information

Infographics reinforce key concepts through visual learning.

Internal Information Users   **Internal users** of accounting information are those directly involved in managing and operating an organization. They use the information to help improve the efficiency and effectiveness of an organization. **Managerial accounting** is the area of accounting that serves the decision-making needs of internal users. Internal reports are not subject to the same rules as external reports and instead are designed with the special needs of internal users in mind.

Several types of internal users rely on accounting reports, including:

Owners   As the owner of **LoveSac**, Shawn Nelson needs accounting data to answer questions like:

- Are we keeping our production costs low enough?
- Should we expand into clothing and other accessories?
- Should we open more retail outlets?
- Do we need to borrow money?

Managers   As a business grows, its owner often must assign managers to certain duties.

- *Purchasing managers* need to know what, when, and how much to purchase.
- *Marketing managers* use reports about sales and costs to target customers; set prices; and monitor customer needs, tastes, and price concerns.
- *Human resource managers* need information about employees' payroll, benefits, performance, and compensation.
- *Production managers* depend on information to monitor costs and ensure quality.
- *Distribution managers* need reports for timely, accurate, and efficient delivery of products.
- *Service managers* need to know the costs and benefits of looking after products and services.
- *Research and development managers* need information about projected costs and revenues of any proposed changes in products and services.

Internal auditors   Internal auditors design and test their employer's internal controls. *Internal controls* are procedures designed to protect company property, ensure reliable reports, promote efficiency, and ensure employees follow company policies. Examples are good records, physical controls (locks, passwords, guards), and independent reviews.

LO2 Identify users and uses of accounting.

External Information Users   **External users** of accounting information are *not* directly involved in running the organization. They include shareholders (investors), lenders, directors, customers, suppliers, regulators, lawyers, brokers, and the press. External users have limited access to an organization's information. Yet their business decisions depend on information that is reliable, relevant, and comparable.

Financial accounting is the area of accounting aimed at serving external users by providing them with financial statements. These statements are known as *general-purpose financial statements*. The term *general-purpose* refers to the broad range of purposes for which external users rely on these statements.

Each external user has special information needs depending on the types of decisions to be made, including the following:

Capital providers

- *Lenders* (creditors) loan money or other resources to a business. Banks often are lenders. Lenders look for information to help them assess whether a business is likely to repay its loans with interest.
- *Shareholders* (investors) are the owners of a corporation. They use accounting reports in deciding whether to buy, hold, or sell stock. Shareholders typically elect a *board of directors* to oversee their interests in an organization. Since directors are responsible to shareholders, their information needs are similar.

External auditors

- *External* (independent) *auditors* examine financial statements to verify that they are prepared according to generally accepted accounting principles. Their work is overseen by the Public Company Accounting Oversight Board (PCAOB).

Labor unions

- *Labor unions* use financial statements to judge the fairness of wages, assess job prospects, and bargain for better wages.

Regulators

- The Internal Revenue Service (IRS) requires organizations to file accounting reports in computing taxes.
- Utility boards use accounting information to set utility rates.
- The Securities and Exchange Commission (SEC) requires reports for companies that sell their stock to the public.

Business associates

- *Suppliers* use accounting information to judge the soundness of a customer before making sales on credit.
- *Customers* use financial reports to assess the staying power of potential suppliers.

IN THE NEWS

In The News highlight relevant items from practice.

They Fought the Law   Our economic and social welfare depends on reliable accounting information. A few managers in recent years forgot that and are now paying their dues. They include L. Dennis Kozlowski of **Tyco**, convicted of falsifying accounting records; Bernard Ebbers of **WorldCom**, convicted of an $11 billion accounting scandal, and Andrew Fastow of **Enron**, guilty of hiding debt and inflating income.

Entrepreneurs, particularly in small companies, perform many of the tasks demanded of both external and internal users, and thus rely heavily on accounting information.

Answers—p. 13

HOW YOU DOIN'?

1. What is the purpose of accounting?
2. What is the relation between accounting and recordkeeping?
3. Who are the internal and external users of accounting information?
4. Identify at least five types of managers who are internal users of accounting information.
5. What are internal controls and why are they important?

How You Doin'? is a chance to stop and reflect on key points.

Opportunities in Accounting

Entry-Level Jobs

L03 Identify career opportunities in accounting and related fields.

Accounting offers many types of jobs. Typical education and experience requirements for common entry-level jobs are described in Exhibit 1.3 below.

Job Title	Education	Experience
Accounting clerk	1–2 accounting courses	Little or none
Bookkeeper	1–2 years of accounting courses	Some as an accounting clerk
Accountant	Two-year or four-year college degree	Little or none

Exhibit 1.3

Common Entry-Level Jobs

Career Paths

Accounting has four broad areas of opportunities: financial, managerial, taxation, and accounting-related. Exhibit 1.4 lists selected opportunities in each area.

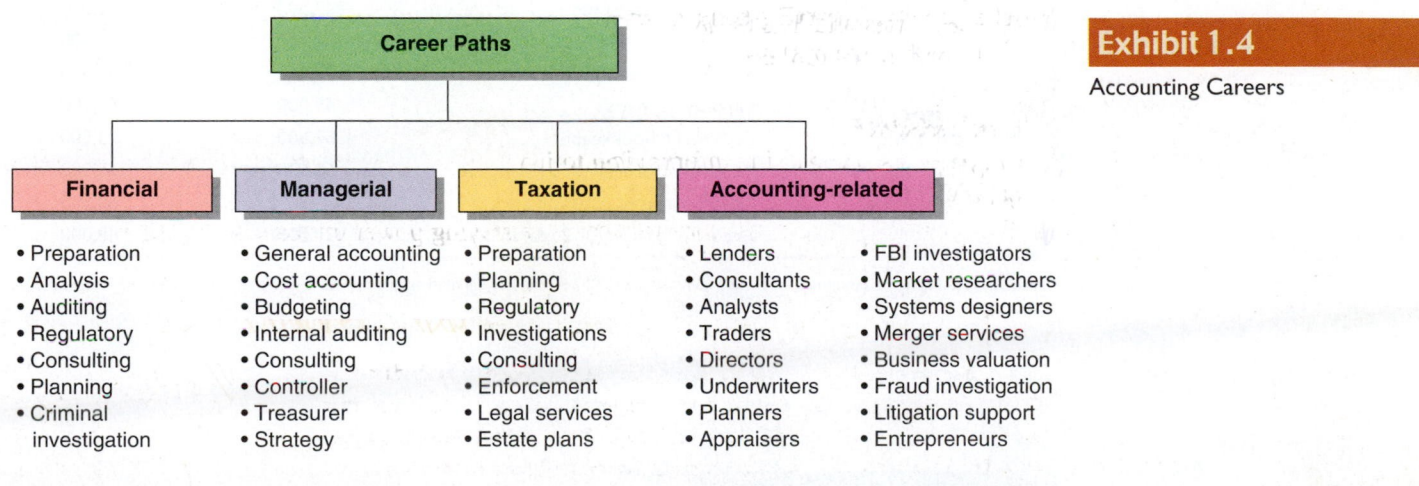

Exhibit 1.4

Accounting Careers

The majority of accounting opportunities are in *private accounting,* as shown in Exhibit 1.5. *Public accounting* offers the next largest number of opportunities. Private accountants are employed by a single company. Public accountants provide auditing, tax, and consulting work for

Exhibit 1.5

Accounting Jobs by Area

Graphical displays are often used to illustrate key points.

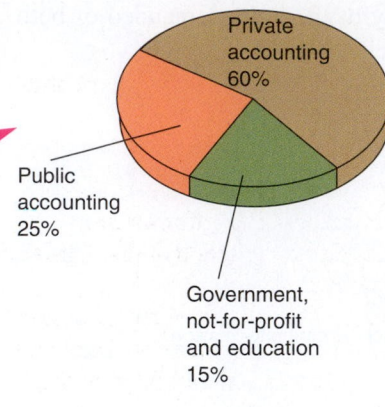

Private accounting 60%

Public accounting 25%

Government, not-for-profit and education 15%

other companies for service fees. Still other opportunities exist in government (and not-for-profit) agencies, including business regulation and investigation of law violations.

Certifications

Accounting specialists are highly regarded. Their professional standing often is denoted by a certificate. Employers look for specialists with designations such as certified bookkeeper (CB), certified payroll professional (CPP), personal financial specialist (PFS), certified fraud examiner (CFE), and certified forensic accountant (CrFA). Certified public accountants (CPAs) must meet education and experience requirements, pass an examination, and exhibit ethical character. Many accounting specialists hold certificates in addition to or instead of the CPA. Two of the most common are the certificate in management accounting (CMA) and the certified internal auditor (CIA).

Individuals with accounting knowledge are always in demand. Benefit packages can include flexible work schedules, telecommuting options, career path alternatives, casual work environments, extended vacation time, and child and elder care.

Demand for accounting specialists is booming. Exhibit 1.6 reports average annual salaries for several accounting positions. Salary variation depends on location, company size, professional designation, experience, and other factors. For example, salaries for full-charge bookkeepers average $57,500 per year. Likewise, annual salaries for accounting clerks averages $37,500.

Exhibit 1.6

Accounting Salaries for Selected Fields

Field	Title (experience)	2007 Salary	2012 Estimate*
Public Accounting	Partner	$190,000	$242,500
	Manager (6–8 years)	94,500	120,500
	Senior (3–5 years)	72,000	92,000
	Junior (0–2 years)	51,500	65,500
Private Accounting	CFO	232,000	296,000
	Controller/Treasurer	147,500	188,000
	Manager (6–8 years)	87,500	111,500
	Senior (3–5 years)	72,500	92,500
	Junior (0–2 years)	49,000	62,500
Recordkeeping	Full-charge bookkeeper	57,500	73,500
	Accounts manager	51,000	65,000
	Payroll manager	54,500	69,500
	Accounting clerk (0–2 years)	37,500	48,000

*Estimates assume a 5% compounded annual increase over 2007 levels. For updated salary data go to www.aicpa.org, Abbott-Langer.com, or Kforce.com.

HOW YOU DOIN'?   Answers—p. 13

6. What career opportunities exist in the taxation area?

7. What types of certificates are available in accounting?

Fundamentals of Accounting

Accounting is guided by concepts and principles. This section describes two key fundamentals of accounting.

LO4 Explain why ethics are crucial to accounting.

Ethics—A Key Concept

The goal of accounting is to provide useful information for decisions. For information to be useful, it must be trusted. This demands ethics in accounting. **Ethics** are beliefs that distinguish right from wrong. They are accepted standards of good and bad behavior.

Identifying the ethical path is sometimes difficult. The preferred path is a course of action that avoids casting doubt on one's decisions. For example, accounting users are less likely to trust an auditor's report if the auditor's pay depends on the success of the client being audited. To avoid such concerns, ethical rules are often set. For example, external auditors are banned from direct investment in their client and cannot accept pay that depends on figures in the client's reports. Exhibit 1.7 gives guidelines for making ethical decisions.

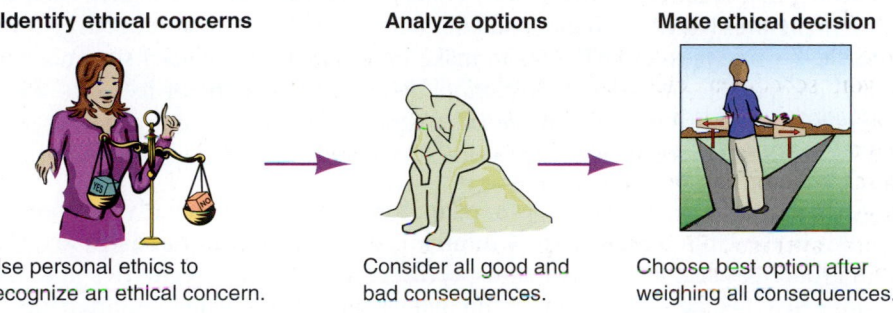

| Identify ethical concerns | Analyze options | Make ethical decision |
| Use personal ethics to recognize an ethical concern. | Consider all good and bad consequences. | Choose best option after weighing all consequences. |

Exhibit 1.7

Guidelines for Ethical Decision Making

Providers of accounting information often face ethical choices as they prepare financial reports. These choices can affect the price a buyer pays and the wages paid to workers. They can even affect the success of products and services. Misleading information can lead to a wrongful closing of a division that harms workers, customers, and suppliers. There is an old saying worth remembering: *Good ethics are good business.*

Accountants have many sources of ethical guidance. For example, the American Institute of Certified Public Accountants' *Code of Professional Ethics* is available at **www.aicpa.org**. The Institute of Management Accountants' *Statement of Ethical Professional Practice* (at **www.imanet.org**) provides guidance on ethical principles and how to resolve ethical conflicts. The **Sarbanes-Oxley Act** requires each issuer of securities to disclose whether it has adopted a code of ethics for its senior officers and the contents of that code. This act also requires that financial statements filed with the SEC be certified by the CEO and CFO as fairly representing the company's financial performance and position. Violators can receive a $5 million fine and/or up to 20 years in prison. Nevertheless, accounting abuses occur, as the listing below of some recent accounting scandals shows.

Company	Alleged Accounting Abuses
Enron	Inflated income, hid debt, and bribed officials
WorldCom	Understated expenses to inflate income and hid debt
Fannie Mae	Inflated income
Adelphia Communications	Understated expenses to inflate income and hid debt
AOL Time Warner	Inflated revenues and income
Xerox	Inflated income
Bristol-Myers Squibb	Inflated revenues and income
Nortel Networks	Understated expenses to inflate income
Global Crossing	Inflated revenues and income
Tyco	Hid debt, and CEO evaded taxes
Halliburton	Inflated revenues and income
Qwest Communications	Inflated revenues and income

IN THE NEWS

Virtuous Returns   Virtue is not always its own reward. Compare the S&P 500 with the Domini Social Index (DSI), which covers 400 companies that have especially good records of social responsibility. We see that returns for companies with socially responsible behavior are at least as high as those of the S&P 500.

Copyright © 2007 by KLD Research & Analytics, Inc. The "Domini 400 Social Index" is a service mark of KLD Research & Analytics.

Graphical displays are often used to illustrate key points.

Generally Accepted Accounting Principles

LO5 Explain the meaning of generally accepted accounting principles.

Financial accounting practice is governed by concepts and rules known as **generally accepted accounting principles (GAAP).** To use and interpret financial statements effectively, we need to understand these principles. GAAP aims to make information in financial statements relevant, reliable, and comparable. *Relevant information* affects the decisions of its users. *Reliable information* is trusted by users. *Comparable information* is helpful in contrasting organizations. Appendix B provides a more detailed discussion of generally accepted accounting principles.

LO6 Identify the groups that establish generally accepted accounting principles.

Setting Accounting Principles   Two main groups establish generally accepted accounting principles in the United States. The **Financial Accounting Standards Board (FASB)** is the private group that sets both broad and specific principles. The **Securities and Exchange Commission (SEC)** is the government group that establishes reporting requirements for companies that issue stock to the public.

In today's global economy, there is increased demand by external users for comparability in accounting reports. This often arises when companies wish to raise money from lenders and investors in different countries. To that end, the **International Accounting Standards Board (IASB)** issues *International Financial Reporting Standards (IFRS)* that identify preferred accounting practices. The IASB hopes to create more harmony among accounting practices of different countries. If standards are harmonized, one company can potentially use a single set of financial statements in all financial markets. Many countries' standard setters support the IASB, and differences between U.S. GAAP and IASB's practices are fading. Yet, the IASB does not have authority to impose its standards on companies.

Rules–Based versus Principles–Based   U.S. accounting practices are often viewed as *rules-based*. This means that companies apply technical, specific, and detailed rules in preparing financial statements. A *principles-based* approach is sometimes argued as preferable. A principles-based system would develop and apply broad, fundamental concepts for reporting. Companies would have more flexibility in preparing principles-based reports. For example, a broad principle might be that a company must report all debt it might have to repay. Certain executives of **Enron** were able to mislead investors by not reporting some of its debt. While many of Enron's reports technically followed rules-based standards, the reports failed to adequately disclose its debts.

IN THE NEWS

Principles and Scruples   Auditors, directors, and lawyers are using principles to improve accounting reports. Examples include accounting restatements at **Navistar**, financial restatements at **Nortel**, accounting reviews at **Echostar**, and expense adjustments at **Electronic Data Systems**. Principles-based accounting has led accounting firms to drop clients deemed too risky. Examples include **Grant Thornton**'s resignation as auditor of **Fremont General** due to alleged failures in providing information when promised, and **Ernst and Young**'s resignation as auditor of **Catalina Marketing** due to alleged accounting errors.

8. What three-step guidelines can help people make ethical decisions?
9. Why are ethics and social responsibility valuable to organizations?
10. Why are ethics crucial in accounting?
11. Who sets U.S. accounting rules?
12. How are U.S. companies affected by international accounting standards?

Ownership Structures

The **business entity assumption** means that a business is accounted for separately from other business and from its owners. This is necessary for making good business decisions. Businesses generally are of one of three major legal forms: *proprietorships, partnerships,* and *corporations.* In this book you will learn the accounting for each of these different business types.

LO7 Identify the three types of ownership structures.

1. A **sole proprietorship,** or simply **proprietorship,** is a business owned by one person. No special legal requirements must be met to start a proprietorship. It is a separate entity for accounting purposes, but it is *not* a separate legal entity from its owner. This means, for example, that a court can order an owner to sell personal belongings to pay a proprietorship's debt. This *unlimited liability* of a proprietorship is a disadvantage. However, an advantage is that a proprietorship's income is not subject to a business income tax but is instead reported and taxed on the owner's personal income tax return. Business characteristics are summarized in Exhibit 1.8.

Characteristic	Proprietorship	Partnership	Corporation
Business entity	yes	yes	yes
Legal entity	no	no	yes
Limited liability	no*	no*	yes
Unlimited life	no	no	yes
Business taxed	no	no	yes
One owner allowed	yes	no	yes

Exhibit 1.8

Characteristics of Businesses

* Proprietorships and partnerships that are set up as LLCs provide limited liability.

2. A **partnership** is a business owned by two or more people called *partners.* Like a proprietorship, no special legal requirements must be met in starting a partnership. The only requirement is an agreement between partners to run a business together. The agreement can be either oral or written and usually indicates how income and losses are to be shared. A partnership, like a proprietorship, is *not* legally separate from its owners. This means that each partner's share of profits is reported and taxed on that partner's tax return. It also means *unlimited liability* for its partners. However, several types of partnerships limit liability. The most common of these, a *limited liability company (LLC),* offers the limited liability of a corporation and the tax treatment of a partnership (and proprietorship).

3. A **corporation** is a business legally separate from its owners, meaning it is responsible for its own acts and its own debts. Separate legal status means that a corporation can conduct business with the rights, duties, and responsibilities of a person. A corporation acts through its managers, who are its legal agents. Separate legal status also means that its owners, who are called **shareholders** (or **stockholders**), are not personally liable for corporate acts and debts. This limited liability is its main advantage. A main disadvantage is what's called *double taxation*—meaning that (1) the corporation's income is taxed and (2) any distribution of income to the corporation's owners through dividends is taxed as part of the owners' personal income.

Types of Businesses   Businesses can also be classified by the type of product or service they provide. A **service business** provides services to customers. These could include computer repair, catering, tax preparation, and many others. A **merchandising business** buys products from other companies and then resells them to consumers. **Best Buy**, **RadioShack**, and **Target** are well-known merchandisers. **Manufacturing businesses,** like **LoveSac**, make products to sell to either merchandisers and/or consumers. We will study the accounting for each of these business types in this book.

HOW YOU DOIN'?   Answers—p. 13

13. Why is the business entity assumption important?

14. What are the three basic forms of business organization?

15. What is the name given the owners of a corporation? What is the name given to the ownership units of a corporation?

*The **Demonstration Problem** is a review of key chapter content. Planning the Solution offers strategies in solving the problem.*

Demonstration Problem

After months of planning, Polly Guthrie opens SuperSub, a sandwich shop. Because this is her first time running a business, Polly is wondering who will use her financial statements.

Required

List four potential external or internal users of SuperSub's financial statements. Explain how they might use these statements.

Planning the Solution

• Look back at the list of possible external and internal users on pages 5 and 6 and think about how each might use SuperSub's financial statements.

• Consider any user that might use and need SuperSub's financial statements.

Solution to Demonstration Problem

Interested users would include:

1. Polly Guthrie, owner and internal user. Polly will use the financial statements to see where she is earning and spending her money. She can also use her financial statements to predict and budget for future sales and costs.

2. Internal Revenue Service, external user. This regulator will need to see SuperSub's accounting reports to compute and monitor the accurate payment of income tax.

3. Lenders (or a bank), external user. Owners periodically need loans to operate or expand their businesses. The bank often requests financial statements, which it can use to assess whether SuperSub will be able to repay its loans.

4. Suppliers (creditors), external user. Suppliers of the foodstuffs like assurance that they will get paid promptly. They will often ask for financial statements or additional financial information to get the information they need.

*A **Summary** organized by learning objectives concludes each chapter.*

Summary

LO1 Explain the purpose and importance of accounting in the information age. Accounting is an information and measurement system that aims to identify, record, and communicate relevant, reliable, and comparable information about business activities. It helps assess opportunities, products, investments, and social and community responsibilities.

LO2 Identify users and uses of accounting. Users of accounting are both internal and external. Some users and uses of accounting include (a) managers in controlling, monitoring, and planning; (b) lenders for measuring the risk and repayment of loans; (c) shareholders for assessing the return and risk of stock; (d) directors for overseeing management; and (e) employees for judging employment opportunities.

LO3 Identify career opportunities in accounting and related fields. Opportunities in accounting include financial, managerial, and tax accounting. They also include accounting-related fields such as lending, consulting, managing, and planning.

LO4 Explain why ethics are crucial to accounting. The goal of accounting is to provide useful information for decision making. For information to be useful, it must be trusted. This demands ethical behavior in accounting.

LO5 Explain the meaning of generally accepted accounting principles. Generally accepted accounting principles are a common set of standards applied by accountants. Accounting principles aid in producing relevant, reliable, and comparable information.

LO6 Identify the groups that establish generally accepted accounting principles. Generally accepted accounting principles (GAAP) are established by two main groups in the United States: the Financial Accounting Standards Board (FASB) and the Securities and Exchange Commission (SEC). The FASB is a private entity that sets financial accounting principles. The SEC is the governmental entity that establishes financial reporting requirements for companies that issue stock to the public.

LO7 Identify the three types of ownership structures. Proprietorships, partnerships, and corporations are the three main types of ownership structures. A proprietorship is a business owned by one person, while a partnership is owned by two or more partners. Proprietorships and partnerships are not separate legal entities from their owners. Corporations are separate legal entities from their owners, who are called shareholders.

Guidance Answers to   HOW YOU DOIN'?

1. Accounting is an information and measurement system that identifies, records, and communicates relevant information to help people make better decisions.

2. Recordkeeping, also called *bookkeeping,* is the recording of financial transactions and events, either manually or electronically. Recordkeeping is essential to data reliability; but accounting is this and much more. Accounting includes identifying, measuring, recording, reporting, and analyzing business events and transactions.

3. External users of accounting include lenders, shareholders, directors, customers, suppliers, regulators, lawyers, brokers, and the press. Internal users of accounting include managers, officers, and other internal decision makers involved with strategic and operating decisions.

4. Internal users (managers) include those from research and development, purchasing, human resources, production, distribution, marketing, and servicing.

5. Internal controls are procedures designed to protect assets, ensure reliable accounting reports, promote efficiency, and encourage adherence to company policies. Internal controls are crucial for relevant and reliable information.

6. Tax preparation, tax planning, and tax enforcement are among the various career opportunities in the taxation area.

7. Some of the certificates that exist in accounting include: certified public accountant (CPA), certified management accountant (CMA), certified internal auditor (CIA), certified fraud examiner (CFE), certified bookkeeper (CB), certified payroll professional (CPP), and personal financial specialist (PFS).

8. Ethical guidelines are threefold: (1) identify ethical concerns using personal ethics, (2) analyze options considering all good and bad consequences, and (3) make ethical decisions after weighing all consequences.

9. Ethics and social responsibility yield good behavior, and they often result in higher income and a better working environment.

10. For accounting to provide useful information for decisions, it must be trusted. Trust requires ethics in accounting.

11. Two major participants in setting rules include the SEC and the FASB.

12. Most U.S. companies are not directly affected by international accounting standards. International standards are put forth as preferred accounting practices. However, stock exchanges and other parties are increasing the pressure to narrow differences in worldwide accounting practices. International accounting standards are playing an important role in that process.

13. Users desire information about the performance of a specific entity. If information is mixed between two or more entities, its usefulness decreases.

14. The three basic forms of business organization are sole proprietorships, partnerships, and corporations.

15. Owners of corporations are called *shareholders* (or *stockholders*). Corporate ownership is divided into units called *shares* (or *stock*). The most basic of corporate shares is common stock (or capital stock).

← *A list of key terms with page references concludes each chapter (a complete glossary is at the end of the book).*

Key Terms

Accounting (p. 4) Information and measurement system that identifies, records, and communicates relevant information about a company's business activities.

Business entity assumption (p. 11) Concept that assumes a business will be accounted for separately from its owner(s) and any other entity.

Corporation (p. 11) Business that is a separate legal entity under state or federal laws with owners called *shareholder* or *stockholders*.

Ethics (p. 9) Codes of conduct by which actions are judged as right or wrong, fair or unfair, honest or dishonest.

External users (p. 6) Persons using accounting information who are not directly involved in running the organization.

Financial accounting (p. 6) Area of accounting mainly aimed at serving external users.

Financial Accounting Standards Board (FASB) (p. 10) Independent group of full-time members responsible for setting accounting rules.

Generally accepted accounting principles (GAAP) (p. 10) Rules that specify acceptable accounting principles.

Internal users (p. 5) Persons using accounting information who are directly involved in managing the organization.

International Accounting Standards Board (IASB) (p. 10) Group that identifies preferred accounting practices and encourages global acceptance; issues International Financial Reporting Standards (IFRS).

Managerial accounting (p. 5) Area of accounting mainly aimed at serving the decision-making needs of internal users; also called *management accounting*.

Manufacturing business (p. 12) A business that makes products for sale.

Merchandising business (p. 12) A business that buys goods from manufacturers and then sells them to consumers.

Partnership (p. 11) Unincorporated association of two or more persons to pursue a business for profit as co-owners.

Proprietorship (p. 10) Business owned by one person that is not organized as a corporation.

Recordkeeping (p. 4) Part of accounting that involves recording transactions and events, either manually or electronically; also called *bookkeeping*.

Sarbanes-Oxley Act (p. 9) Created the *Public Company Accounting Oversight Board,* regulates analyst conflicts, imposes corporate governance requirements, enhances accounting and control disclosures, impacts insider transactions and executive loans, establishes new types of criminal conduct, and expands penalties for violations of federal securities laws.

Securities and Exchange Commission (SEC) (p. 10) Federal agency Congress has charged to set reporting rules for organizations that sell ownership shares to the public.

Service business (p. 11) A business that provides services to customers.

Shareholders (p. 11) Owners of a corporation; also called *stockholders*.

Multiple Choice Quiz   Answers on p. 19   mhhe.com/wildCA2e

Additional Multiple Choice Quizzes are available at the book's Website.

1. Accounting is an information and measurement system that _____ information about an organization's business activities.
   a. Translates
   b. Records
   c. Chooses
   d. Prints out

2. External users of financial information include:
   a. Purchasing managers
   b. Service managers
   c. The chief executive officer
   d. Lenders

3. Typical accounting specialists with designations include all of the following except:
   a. Certified Financial Analyst (CFA)
   b. Certified Public Accountant (CPA)
   c. Certified Bookkeeper (CB)
   d. Certified Payroll Professional (CPP)

4. Generally accepted accounting principles do not aim to make information in financial statements:
   a. Reasonable
   b. Relevant
   c. Reliable
   d. Comparable

5. The Financial Accounting Standards Board is the:
   a. Governmental group that sets financial accounting principles.
   b. International group that identifies preferred international accounting principles.
   c. Private group that sets both broad and specific accounting principles.
   d. Governmental group that sets standards for state and local governmental financial statements.

Discussion Questions

1. What is the purpose of accounting in society?

2. Technology is increasingly used to process accounting data. Why then must we study and understand accounting?

3. Identify at least four kinds of external users and describe how they use accounting information.

4. What are at least three questions business owners and managers might be able to answer by looking at accounting information?

5. Identify three actual businesses that offer services and three actual businesses that offer products.

6. Describe the internal role of accounting for organizations.

7. Identify three types of services typically offered by accounting professionals.

8. What type of accounting information might be useful to the marketing managers of a business?

9. Why is accounting described as a service activity?

10. What are some accounting-related professions?

11. How do ethics rules affect auditors' choice of clients?

12. What work do tax accounting professionals perform in addition to preparing tax returns?

13. Refer to the financial statements of **Best Buy** in Appendix A near the end of the book. Look at the consolidated statements of earnings (income statement). How many years are included and what are their dates?

Connect Accounting repeats assignments via the Web, which allows instructors to monitor, promote, and assess student learning. It can be used in practice, homework, or exam mode.

Quick Study exercises give readers a brief test of key elements.

connect

(*a*) Define these accounting-related acronyms: GAAP, SEC, FASB and IASB. (*b*) Briefly explain the importance of the knowledge base or organization that is referred to for each of the accounting-related acronyms.

QUICK STUDY

QS 1–1
Identifying accounting terms
LO5   LO6

Identify the following users as either external users (E) or internal users (I).

a. Customers **d.** Business press **g.** Shareholders **j.** FBI and IRS
b. Suppliers **e.** Managers **h.** Lenders **k.** Consumer group
c. Brokers **f.** District attorney **i.** Controllers **l.** Sales staff

QS 1–2
Identifying accounting users   **LO2**

An important responsibility of many accounting professionals is to design and implement internal control procedures for organizations. Explain the purpose of internal control procedures. Provide two examples of internal controls applied by companies.

QS 1–3
Explaining internal control   **LO2**

Identify at least three main areas of opportunities for accounting professionals. For each area, identify at least three job possibilities linked to accounting.

QS 1–4
Accounting opportunities   **LO3**

Accounting professionals must sometimes choose between two or more acceptable methods of accounting for business transactions and events. Explain why these situations can involve difficult matters of ethical concern.

QS 1–5
Identifying ethical concerns   **LO4**

Using the information provided in the chapter, determine what the 2012 estimate of salaries is for the following selected accounting fields:

QS 1–6
Identifying career opportunities
LO3

Accounting Position	Expected 2012 Salary
Controller/treasurer	$?
Private accounting (senior)	$?
Payroll manager	$?
Public accounting (manager)	$?

QS 1-7
Generally accepted accounting principles   **LO5**

Generally accepted accounting principles aim to make information relevant, reliable, and comparable. Choose the correct definition on the right for each of these terms:

1. Relevant	**a.** Information is both broad and specific
2. Reliable	**b.** Information is helpful in contrasting organizations
3. Comparable	**c.** The information affects the decisions of its users.
	d. Information is trusted by users

QS 1-8
Ownership structures   **LO7**

Businesses generally are of three major legal forms. List and briefly describe these three alternative legal forms of business ownership structure.

connect™

EXERCISES

Exercise 1-1
Describing accounting responsibilities   **LO2   LO3**

Many accounting professionals work in one of the following three areas.

A. Financial accounting   **B.** Managerial accounting   **C.** Tax accounting

Identify the area of accounting that is most involved in each of the following responsibilities.

_____ **1.** Internal auditing.		_____ **5.** Investigating violations of tax laws.
_____ **2.** External auditing.		_____ **6.** Planning transactions to minimize taxes.
_____ **3.** Cost accounting.		_____ **7.** Preparing external financial statements.
_____ **4.** Budgeting.		_____ **8.** Reviewing reports for SEC compliance.

Exercise 1-2
Identifying accounting users and uses   **LO2**

Much of accounting is directed at serving the information needs of those users that are external to an organization. Identify at least three external users of accounting information and indicate two questions they might seek to answer through their use of accounting information.

Exercise 1-3
Identifying ethical concerns   **LO4**

Assume the following roles and describe a situation in which ethical considerations play an important part in guiding your decisions and actions.

a. You are a student in an introductory accounting course.
b. You are a manager with responsibility for several employees.
c. You are an accounting professional preparing tax returns for clients.
d. You are an accounting professional with audit clients that are competitors in business.

Exercise 1-4
Learning the language of business
LO3   LO4   LO5   LO6

Match each of the numbered descriptions 1 through 7 with the term or phrase it best reflects. Indicate your answer by writing the letter for the term or phrase in the blank provided.

A. Audit	**C.** Ethics	**E.** SEC	**G.** IASB
B. GAAP	**D.** Tax accounting	**F.** Public accountants	

_____ **1.** Principles that determine whether an action is right or wrong.
_____ **2.** Accounting professionals who provide services to many clients.
_____ **3.** An accounting area that includes planning future transactions to minimize taxes paid.
_____ **4.** An examination of an organization's accounting system and records that adds credibility to financial statements.
_____ **5.** Government group that establishes reporting requirements for companies that issue stock to the public.
_____ **6.** Concepts and rules that govern financial accounting practice.
_____ **7.** Group that issues preferred international accounting practices.

Exercise 1-5
Ownership structures   **LO7**

Following are descriptions of several different business organizations. Determine whether the description refers to a sole proprietorship, partnership, or corporation.

a. Ownership of Zander Company is divided into 1,000 shares of stock.
b. Wallingford is owned by Trent Malone, who is personally liable for the company's debts.

c. Elijah Fong and Ava Logan own Financial Services, a financial services provider. Neither Fong nor Logan has personal responsibility for the debts of Financial Services.

d. Dylan Bailey and Emma Kayley own Speedy Packages, a courier service. Both are personally liable for the debts of the business.

e. IBC Services does not have separate legal existence apart from the one person who owns it.

f. Physio Products does not pay income taxes and has one owner.

g. Aaliyah Services pays its own income taxes and has two owners.

Accounting specialists are often denoted by certifications. Several of these are mentioned in the chapter. Write the full name of each of the certifications below:

a. CMA   d. CB   g. CPP

b. CPA   e. PFS

c. CFE   f. CIA

Exercise 1-6
Professional certifications **L03**

---

connect

The following is a list of selected users of accounting information. Match the appropriate user A through E to the following information needs 1 through 5.

A. Suppliers   **C.** Shareholders   **E.** Employees

B. Lenders   **D.** Production managers

_____ **1.** Monitor costs and ensure quality.

_____ **2.** Judge the soundness of a customer before making sales on credit.

_____ **3.** Assessing employment opportunities.

_____ **4.** Assessing whether a loan is likely to be repaid.

_____ **5.** Deciding whether to buy, hold, or sell stock.

PROBLEM SET A

Problem 1-1A
Identifying accounting users **L02**

The following is a list of broad opportunities in accounting. Match the appropriate broad opportunity A through D to the specific accounting opportunity 1 through 8.

A. Financial   **C.** Taxation

B. Managerial   **D.** Accounting-related

_____ **1.** Appraiser   _____ **5.** Litigation support

_____ **2.** Estate planning   _____ **6.** Internal audit

_____ **3.** External audit   _____ **7.** Financial statement preparation

_____ **4.** Budgeting   _____ **8.** Tax planning

Problem 1-2A
Identify opportunities in accounting **L03**

The following is a list of selected internal users of accounting information. Match the appropriate user A through E to the following information needs 1 through 5.

A. Research and development managers   **C.** Distribution managers   **E.** Service managers

B. Human resource managers   **D.** Purchasing managers

_____ **1.** Assessing when and how much to purchase.

_____ **2.** Judge the costs and benefits of looking after products and services.

_____ **3.** Monitor timely, accurate, and efficient delivery of products and services.

_____ **4.** Assessing employees' payroll, benefits, performance, and compensation.

_____ **5.** Measuring projected costs and revenues of any proposed changes in products and services.

PROBLEM SET B

Problem 1-1 B
Identifying accounting users **L02**

The following is a list of accounting terms. Match the appropriate accounting term A through D to its definition 1 through 4.

A. Accounting   **C.** Managerial accounting

B. Bookkeeping   **D.** Financial accounting

Problem 1-2B
Definition of accounting terms
L01 L02

_____ **1.** Area of accounting aimed at serving external users by providing them with financial statements.

_____ **2.** Information and measurement system that identifies, records, and communicates information about an organization's business activities.

_____ **3.** The recording of transactions and events, either manually or electronically.

_____ **4.** Area of accounting that serves the decision-making needs of internal users.

The serial problem starts in this chapter and continues throughout most chapters of the book. It is most readily solved if you use the Working Papers that accompany this book.

SERIAL PROBLEM

Success Systems

SP 1   On October 1, 2010, Adriana Lopez launched a computer services company, **Success Systems,** that is organized as a proprietorship and provides consulting services, computer system installations, and custom program development. Lopez will prepare the company's first set of financial statements on December 31, 2010.

Required

List at least five potential internal and external users of Success Systems' financial statements. Explain why each user would be interested in the financial statements.

Beyond the Numbers (BTN) is a special problem section aimed to refine communication, conceptual, analysis, and research skills. It includes many activities helpful in developing an active learning environment.

BEYOND THE NUMBERS

REPORTING IN ACTION
L01

BTN 1–1   Find **Best Buy**'s annual report included in Appendix A near the end of the book.

Required

List at least three likely users of Best Buy's financial statements and how they would use financial statements.

ETHICS CHALLENGE
L04

BTN 1–2   Managerial accounting professionals follow a code of ethics. As a member of the Institute of Management Accountants, the managerial accountant must comply with Standards of Ethical Conduct.

Required

1. Identify, print, and read the *Statement of Ethical Professional Practice* posted at **www.IMAnet.org**. (Search using "ethical professional practice.")

2. What four overarching ethical principles underlie the IMA's statement?

3. Describe the courses of action the IMA recommends in resolving ethical conflicts.

WORKPLACE COMMUNICATION
L06

BTN 1–3   The Financial Accounting Standards Board (FASB) sets accounting standards. The FASB's mission is described at its Website (**FASB.org**) under the tab "About FASB."

Required

Prepare a half-page report outlining the mission of the FASB. Identify the ways it has set out to accomplish that mission.

TAKING IT TO THE NET
L02

BTN 1–4   Find **Best Buy**'s most current financial statements by going to their Website (**BestBuy.com**) and click on the link "For Our Investors" at the bottom of the page. Click on "Annual Reports" in the right column. Click on the most recent "Form 10-K" tab.

Required

1. What is the date of this annual report?
2. What are the titles of the financial statements included in this report?

BTN 1–5   Teamwork is important in today's business world. Successful teams schedule convenient meetings, maintain regular communications, and cooperate with and support their members. This assignment aims to establish support/learning teams, initiate discussions, and set meeting times.

TEAMWORK IN ACTION
L01

Required

1. Form teams and open a team discussion to determine a regular time and place for your team to meet between each scheduled class meeting. Notify your instructor via a memorandum or e-mail message as to when and where your team will hold regularly scheduled meetings.
2. Develop a list of telephone numbers and/or e-mail addresses of your teammates.

BTN 1–6   Refer to this chapter's opening feature about **LoveSac**. Assume that Shawn Nelson decides to open a new manufacturing facility to meet customer demand. To open the new facility, Shawn would have to get a loan from a bank.

ENTREPRENEURS IN BUSINESS
L02

Required

1. Which external users would be interested in reviewing LoveSac's financial statements? Why?
2. What specific information would a loan officer want to review before extending a loan to LoveSac?

BTN 1–7   You and a friend develop a new design for in-line skates that improves speed and performance by 25 to 40 percent. You plan to form a business to manufacture and market these skates. You and your friend want to minimize taxes, but your prime concern is potential lawsuits from individuals who might be injured on these skates. What form of organization do you set up?

YOU CALL IT — ENTREPRENEUR

---

1. b	4. a
2. d	5. c
3. a	

ANSWERS TO MULTIPLE CHOICE QUIZ

A Look Back

Chapter 1 explained the importance of accounting to different types of organizations. We also described the use and users of accounting information.

A Look at This Chapter

This chapter explains the accounting equation and how it helps to describe business transactions. We also show how accounting information is reflected in financial statements.

A Look Ahead

Chapter 3 further describes the analysis of business transactions. We also introduce and explore the basics of double-entry accounting.

Chapter 2

Accounting for Business Transactions

Learning Objectives

LO 1	Define the accounting equation and each of its components.
LO 2	Analyze business transactions using the accounting equation.
LO 3	Identify and prepare basic financial statements and explain how they interrelate.

"It has been a dream come true"
—Sara Blakely

The Bottom Line

ATLANTA—"Working as a sales trainer by day and performing stand-up comedy at night, I didn't know the first thing about the pantyhose industry," admits Sara Blakely. "Except, I dreaded wearing most pantyhose." One night Sara cut the feet out of her pantyhose to wear with white pants and open-toed shoes, and at that moment, Sara knew she had a unique idea. Sara took $5,000 in savings and launched **SPANX** (**Spanx.com**), a manufacturer of footless pantyhose, slimming intimates, hosiery, and other women's apparel.

To pursue her business ambitions, Sara studied business activities and learned the value of accounting information. She established recordkeeping processes, transaction analysis, inventory accounting, and financial statement reporting. I had to get a handle on my financial situation, says Sara, as I wanted to remain self-funded. To this day, Sara remains self-funded and has a reliable accounting system to help her make good business decisions.

I had to account for product costs, office expenses, supplier payments, patent fees, and other expenses, says Sara. At the same time, Sara expanded sales and struggled to stay profitable. "I had no money to advertise, so I hit the road," laughs Sara. "For the entire first year, I did in-store rallies . . . staying all day introducing customers to Spanx."

In her first three months, Sara sold over 50,000 pairs of footless pantyhose. Today, just seven short years from her launch, Sara reports over $150 million in retail sales. "We are still a small company of women," claims Sara, "obsessed with inventing and improving comfortable undergarments." Sara continues to track and account for all revenues and expenses. She maintains that success requires proper accounting for and analysis of the financial side.

The bigger message of SPANX, says Sara, is promoting comfort and confidence for women. Insists Sara, "We believe all women deserve the opportunity to make the most of their assets!"

[Sources: *SPANX Website*, January 2009; *Entrepreneur*, May 2007; *Smart Money*, September 2002; *TV Guide*, July 2007; *Financial Times*, 2006; *ABC Television*, 2007]

Accounting identifies, records, and communicates information about an organization's business activities. In this chapter, we introduce the accounting equation as a means of identifying and recording business transactions. We also introduce basic financial statements that communicate accounting information about the company's performance and financial position.

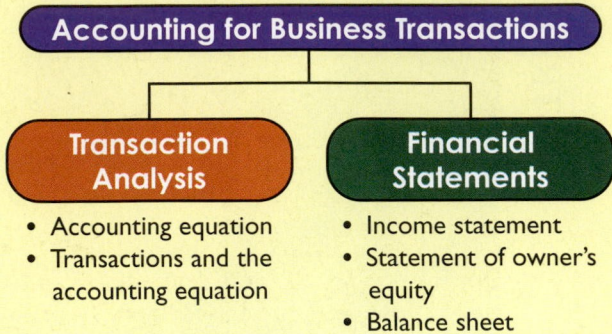

Accounting for Business Transactions

Transaction Analysis
- Accounting equation
- Transactions and the accounting equation

Financial Statements
- Income statement
- Statement of owner's equity
- Balance sheet

Transaction Analysis and the Accounting Equation

LO1 Define the accounting equation and each of its components.

To understand accounting information, we need to know how an accounting system captures relevant data about transactions, and then classifies, records, and reports data. In this section, we introduce the accounting equation and then show how the accounting equation represents each business transaction.

Accounting Equation

The accounting system reflects two basic aspects of a company: what it owns and what it owes. **Assets** are resources with future benefits that are owned or controlled by a company. The claims on a company's assets—what it owes—are separated into owner and nonowner claims. **Liabilities** are what a company owes its nonowners (creditors) in future payments, products, or services. **Equity** (also called owner's equity or capital) refers to the claims of its owner(s). Together, liabilities and equity are the source of funds to acquire assets. The relation of assets, liabilities, and equity is reflected in the following **accounting equation:**

$$\text{Assets} = \text{Liabilities} + \text{Equity}$$

Liabilities are usually shown before equity in this equation because creditors' claims must be paid before the claims of owners. (The terms in this equation can be rearranged; for example, Assets − Liabilities = Equity.) The accounting equation applies to all transactions and events, to all companies and forms of organization, and to all points in time. Let's now look at the accounting equation in more detail.

Assets Assets are resources owned or controlled by a company that are expected to yield future benefits. Examples of assets include Web servers for an online services company, musical instruments for a rock band, land for a vegetable grower, and cash in the company's bank account. The term *receivable* refers to an asset that promises a future inflow of resources. A company that provides a service or product on credit is said to have an account receivable from that customer. The phrases *on credit* and *on account* imply that cash payment will occur at a future date. Other typical assets include supplies, equipment, land, and buildings.

Liabilities Liabilities are creditors' claims on assets. **Creditors** are individuals and organizations that own the right to receive payment from a company. These claims reflect obligations

IN THE NEWS

Web Info   Most organizations maintain Websites that include accounting data—see **Best Buy** (**BestBuy.com**) as an example. The SEC keeps an online database called **EDGAR** (**www.SEC.gov/edgar.shtml**), which has accounting information for thousands of companies that issue stock to the public. Information services such as **Finance.Google.com** and **Finance.Yahoo.com** offer additional online data and analysis.

to provide assets, products, or services to others. The term *payable* refers to a liability that promises a future outflow of resources. Examples are wages payable to workers, accounts payable to suppliers, loans (or notes) payable to banks, and taxes payable to the government.

Equity   **Equity** is the owner's claim on assets. Equity is equal to assets minus liabilities. This is the reason equity is also called *net assets* or *residual equity*.

Equity for a proprietorship (or partnership)—commonly called owner's equity—increases and decreases as follows: owner investments and revenues *increase* equity, whereas owner withdrawals and expenses *decrease* equity. **Owner investments** are assets an owner puts into the company and are included under the generic account **Owner, Capital. Owner withdrawals** are assets an owner takes from the company for personal use.

Revenues increase equity and are the assets earned from a company's earnings activities. Examples are consulting services provided, sales of products, facilities rented to others, and commissions from services. **Expenses** decrease equity and are the cost of assets or services used to earn revenues. Examples are costs of employee time, use of supplies, and advertising, utilities, and insurance services from others. At any point in time, equity is the accumulated revenues and owner investments minus the accumulated expenses and owner withdrawals since the company began. This breakdown of equity yields the following **expanded accounting equation.**

$$\text{Assets} = \text{Liabilities} + \underbrace{\text{Owner, Capital} - \text{Owner, Withdrawals} + \text{Revenues} - \text{Expenses}}_{\text{Equity}}$$

Net income occurs when revenues exceed expenses. Net income increases equity. A **net loss** occurs when expenses exceed revenues, which decreases equity. Owner investments and withdrawals are not included in net income.

Transactions and the Accounting Equation

A transaction is defined as a business activity that affects the accounting equation. **External transactions** are exchanges of value between two entities, which yield changes in the accounting equation. An example is a company's payment of its electric bill. **Internal transactions** are exchanges within an entity; they can also affect the accounting equation. An example is a company's use of its supplies, which are reported as expenses when used. **Events** refer to those happenings that affect an entity's accounting equation *and* can be reliably measured. They include natural events such as floods and fires that destroy assets and create losses. They do not include, for example, the signing of service or product contracts, which by themselves do not impact the accounting equation.

An **account** is a record within an accounting system in which increases and decreases are entered and stored. Specific asset, liability, equity, revenue, and expense items are recorded in separate accounts. This section uses the accounting equation and accounts to analyze 11 selected transactions and events of FastForward, a start-up consulting (service) business, in its first month

LO2   Analyze business transactions using the accounting equation.

of operations. We focus on two questions when analyzing the effects of a transaction on the accounting equation.

1. Which accounts are affected by the transaction?
2. How is the accounting equation affected?

Remember that each transaction and event leaves the accounting equation in balance and that assets *always* equal the sum of liabilities and equity.

Starting the Business   On December 1, Chuck Taylor forms a consulting business, focused on assessing the performance of athletic footwear and accessories, which he names FastForward. He sets it up as a proprietorship; he owns and manages the business. The marketing plan for the business is to focus primarily on consulting with sports clubs, amateur athletes, and others who place orders for athletic footwear and accessories with manufacturers.

Transaction 1: Investment by Owner

Chuck Taylor invests $30,000 cash in FastForward.

Taylor personally invests $30,000 cash in the new company and deposits the cash in a bank account opened under the name of FastForward. The accounts in this transaction are Cash (an asset) and C. Taylor, Capital (owner's equity). (Owner investments are always included under the title "Owner name," Capital). Both accounts increase by $30,000 as a result of this transaction. After this transaction, Fastforward's assets equal its equity, and the accounting equation is in balance. The effect of this transaction on FastForward is reflected in the accounting equation as follows.

	Assets	=	Liabilities	+	Equity
	Cash	**=**			**C. Taylor, Capital**
(1)	**+$30,000**	**=**			**+$30,000**

Transaction 2: Purchase Supplies for Cash

FastForward pays $2,500 cash for supplies.

FastForward uses $2,500 of its cash to buy supplies of brand name athletic footwear for performance testing over the next few months. This transaction is an exchange of cash, an asset, for another kind of asset, supplies. It merely changes the form of assets from cash to supplies. The decrease in cash exactly equals the increase in supplies. Fastforward's total assets and owner's equity each remain at $30,000 after this transaction. The supplies of athletic footwear are assets because of the expected future benefits from the test results of their performance. This transaction is reflected in the accounting equation as follows:

	Assets			=	Liabilities	+	Equity
	Cash	**+**	**Supplies**	**=**			**C. Taylor, Capital**
Old Bal.	$30,000			=			$30,000
(2)	**−2,500**	**+**	**$2,500**				
New Bal.	$27,500	+	$ 2,500	=			$30,000
		$30,000				$30,000	

Transaction 3: Purchase Equipment for Cash

FastForward pays $26,000 cash for equipment.

FastForward spends $26,000 to acquire equipment for testing athletic footwear. Like transaction 2, transaction 3 is an exchange of one asset, cash, for another asset, equipment. The equipment is an asset because of its expected future benefits from testing athletic footwear. This purchase changes the makeup of assets but does not change the asset total. The accounting equation remains in balance. Transactions 2 and 3 illustrate a fundamental idea in accounting: *Payments of cash are not always expenses.*

	Assets					=	Liabilities	+	Equity
	Cash	+	Supplies	+	Equipment	=			C. Taylor, Capital
Old Bal.	$27,500	+	$2,500			=			$30,000
(3)	−26,000			+	$26,000				
New Bal.	$ 1,500		$2,500	+	$ 26,000	=			$30,000
			$30,000						$30,000

Transaction 4: Purchase Supplies on Credit

FastForward purchases $7,100 of supplies on credit.

Taylor decides he needs more supplies of athletic footwear and accessories. These additional supplies total $7,100, but as we see from the accounting equation in transaction 3, FastForward has only $1,500 in cash. Taylor arranges to purchase the supplies on credit from CalTech Supply Company. Thus, FastForward acquires supplies in exchange for a promise to pay for them later. This purchase increases assets by $7,100 in supplies, and liabilities (called *accounts payable*) increase by the same amount. The effects of this purchase follow:

	Assets					=	Liabilities	+	Equity
	Cash	+	Supplies	+	Equipment	=	Accounts Payable	+	C. Taylor, Capital
Old Bal.	$1,500	+	$2,500	+	$26,000	=			$30,000
(4)		+	7,100				+$7,100		
New Bal.	$1,500	+	$9,600	+	$26,000	=	$ 7,100	+	$30,000
			$37,100					$37,100	

Transaction 5: Provide Services for Cash

FastForward provides consulting services and immediately collects $4,200 cash.

FastForward earns revenues by consulting with clients about test results on athletic footwear and accessories. In one of its first jobs, FastForward provides consulting services to an athletic club and immediately collects $4,200 cash. The accounting equation reflects this increase in cash of $4,200 and in equity of $4,200. This increase in equity is shown in the far right column under Revenues because the cash received is earned by providing consulting services. Using separate accounts to record revenues and owner investments (transaction 1) helps in preparing accurate financial statements.

	Assets					=	Liabilities	+	Equity		
	Cash	+	Supplies	+	Equipment	=	Accounts Payable	+	C. Taylor, Capital	+	Revenues
Old Bal.	$1,500	+	$9,600	+	$26,000	=	$7,100	+	$30,000		
(5)	+4,200									+	$4,200
New Bal.	$5,700	+	$9,600	+	$26,000	=	$7,100	+	$30,000	+	$ 4,200
			$41,300						$41,300		

Transactions 6 and 7: Payment of Expenses in Cash

FastForward pays $1,000 in cash for December rent.
FastForward pays $700 cash for employee salaries.

In transaction 6, FastForward pays $1,000 rent to the landlord of the building where its facilities are located. Paying this amount allows FastForward to occupy the space for the month of December. In transaction 7, FastForward pays the biweekly $700 salary of the company's only employee. Both transactions 6 and 7 are December expenses for FastForward. The costs of both rent and salary are expenses, as opposed to assets, because their benefits are used in December (they have no future benefits after December). The accounting equation shows that both transactions reduce cash and equity. The far right column identifies these decreases as Expenses.

By definition, increases in expenses yield decreases in equity.

	Assets					=	Liabilities	+			Equity		
	Cash	+	Supplies	+	Equipment	=	Accounts Payable	+	C. Taylor, Capital	+	Revenues	−	Expenses
Old Bal.	$5,700	+	$9,600	+	$26,000	=	$7,100	+	$30,000	+	$4,200		
(6)	−1,000											−	$1,000
Bal.	4,700	+	9,600	+	26,000	=	7,100	+	30,000	+	4,200	−	1,000
(7)	− 700											−	700
New Bal.	$4,000	+	$9,600	+	$26,000	=	$7,100	+	$30,000	+	$4,200	−	$ 1,700

$39,600 = $39,600

Transaction 8: Provide Services and Facilities for Credit

FastForward provides consulting services of $1,600 and rents its test facilities for $300. The customer is billed $1,900 for these services.

FastForward provides consulting services of $1,600 and rents its test facilities for $300 to an amateur sports club. The rental involves allowing club members to try recommended footwear and accessories at FastForward's testing grounds. The sports club is billed for the $1,900 total. This transaction results in a new asset, called *accounts receivable*, which means the client has not yet paid the $1,900 bill. Since FastForward has already provided the consulting services and the rental, FastForward considers the full $1,900 as Revenues. These two revenue items increase equity as shown in the Revenues column of the accounting equation below. Transaction 8 reveals another important concept: *Revenues do not require immediate receipt of cash.*

	Assets								=	Liabilities	+			Equity		
	Cash	+	Accounts Receivable	+	Supplies	+	Equipment	=	Accounts Payable	+	C. Taylor, Capital	+	Revenues	−	Expenses
Old Bal.	$4,000	+		+	$9,600	+	$26,000	=	$7,100	+	$30,000	+	$4,200	−	$1,700
(8)		+	$1,900									+	1,600		
												+	300		
New Bal.	$4,000	+	$ 1,900	+	$9,600	+	$26,000	=	$7,100	+	$30,000	+	$6,100	−	$1,700

$41,500 = $41,500

Transaction 9: Receipt of Cash from Accounts Receivable

FastForward receives $1,900 cash from the customer billed in transaction 8.

The client in transaction 8 (the amateur sports club) pays $1,900 to FastForward 10 days after it is billed for consulting services. This transaction 9 does not change the total amount of assets and does not affect liabilities or equity. It converts the receivable (an asset) to cash (another asset). It does not create new revenue. Revenue was recognized when FastForward rendered the services in transaction 8, not when the cash is now collected. Transaction 9 shows that *receipt of cash is not always a revenue*. The new balances follow:

	Assets						=	Liabilities	+		Equity			
	Cash	+	Accounts Receivable	+	Supplies	+	Equipment	=	Accounts Payable	+	C. Taylor, Capital	+	Revenues	−	Expenses
Old Bal.	$4,000	+	$1,900	+	$9,600	+	$26,000	=	$7,100	+	$30,000	+	$6,100	−	$1,700
(9)	+1,900	−	1,900												
New Bal.	$5,900	+	$ 0	+	$9,600	+	$26,000	=	$7,100	+	$30,000	+	$6,100	−	$1,700

$41,500 $41,500

Transaction 10: Payment of Accounts Payable

FastForward pays its supplier $900 cash toward the account payable from transaction 4.

FastForward pays CalTech Supply $900 cash as partial payment for its earlier $7,100 purchase of supplies (transaction 4), leaving $6,200 unpaid. The accounting equation shows that this transaction decreases FastForward's cash by $900 and decreases its liability to CalTech Supply by $900. Equity does not change. This event does not create an expense even though cash flows out of FastForward. Instead, the expense is recorded when FastForward uses the supplies. (We show this and other adjustments in later chapters).

	Assets						=	Liabilities	+		Equity			
	Cash	+	Accounts Receivable	+	Supplies	+	Equipment	=	Accounts Payable	+	C. Taylor, Capital	+	Revenues	−	Expenses
Old Bal.	$5,900	+	$ 0	+	$9,600	+	$26,000	=	$7,100	+	$30,000	+	$6,100	−	$1,700
(10)	− 900								− 900						
New Bal.	$5,000	+	$ 0	+	$9,600	+	$26,000	=	$6,200	+	$30,000	+	$6,100	−	$1,700

$40,600 $40,600

Transaction 11: Withdrawal of Cash by Owner

Chuck Taylor withdraws $200 cash from FastForward for personal use.

The owner of FastForward withdraws $200 cash for personal use. Withdrawals are accounted for as a decrease in equity. Withdrawals are not expenses because they are not part of the company's earning process. Since withdrawals are not company expenses, they are not used in computing net income.

By definition, increases in withdrawals yield decreases in equity.

	Assets						=	Liabilities	+		Equity					
	Cash	+	Accounts Receivable	+	Supplies	+	Equipment	=	Accounts Payable	+	C. Taylor, Capital	−	C. Taylor, Withdrawals	+	Revenues	−	Expenses
Old Bal.	$5,000	+	$ 0	+	$9,600	+	$26,000	=	$6,200	+	$30,000			+	$6,100	−	$1,700
(11)	− 200											− $200				
New Bal.	$4,800	+	$ 0	+	$9,600	+	$26,000	=	$6,200	+	$30,000	−	$200	+	$6,100	−	$1,700

$40,400 $40,400

Summary of Transactions

We summarize in Exhibit 2.1 the effects of these 11 transactions of FastForward using the accounting equation. Two points should be noted. First, the accounting equation remains in balance after each transaction. Second, transactions can be analyzed by their effects on components of the accounting equation. For example, in transactions 2, 3, and 9, one asset increased while another asset decreased by equal amounts.

Exhibit 2.1

Summary of Transactions Using the Accounting Equation

	Cash	+	Accounts Receivable	+	Supplies	+	Equipment	=	Accounts Payable	+	C. Taylor, Capital	−	C. Taylor, Withdrawals	+	Revenues	−	Expenses
(1)	$30,000							=			$30,000						
(2)	− 2,500			+	$2,500												
Bal.	27,500			+	2,500			=			30,000						
(3)	−26,000					+	$26,000										
Bal.	1,500			+	2,500	+	26,000	=			30,000						
(4)				+	7,100				+$7,100								
Bal.	1,500			+	9,600	+	26,000	=	7,100	+	30,000						
(5)	+ 4,200													+	$4,200		
Bal.	5,700			+	9,600	+	26,000	=	7,100	+	30,000			+	4,200		
(6)	− 1,000															−	$1,000
Bal.	4,700			+	9,600	+	26,000	=	7,100	+	30,000			+	4,200	−	1,000
(7)	− 700															−	700
Bal.	4,000			+	9,600	+	26,000	=	7,100	+	30,000			+	4,200	−	1,700
(8)		+	$1,900											+	1,600		
														+	300		
Bal.	4,000	+	1,900	+	9,600	+	26,000	=	7,100	+	30,000			+	6,100	−	1,700
(9)	+ 1,900	−	1,900														
Bal.	5,900	+	0	+	9,600	+	26,000	=	7,100	+	30,000			+	6,100	−	1,700
(10)	− 900								− 900								
Bal.	5,000	+	0	+	9,600	+	26,000	=	6,200	+	30,000			+	6,100	−	1,700
(11)	− 200											−	$200				
Bal.	$ 4,800	+	$ 0	+	$9,600	+	$ 26,000	=	$ 6,200	+	$ 30,000	−	$ 200	+	$6,100	−	$1,700

IN THE NEWS

Women Entrepreneurs   The Center for Women's Business Research reports that
women-owned businesses, such as **SPANX**, are growing and that they

- Total approximately 11 million and employ nearly 20 million workers.
- Generate $2.5 trillion in annual sales and tend to embrace technology.
- Are philanthropic—70% of owners volunteer at least once per month.
- Are more likely funded by individual investors (73%) than venture firms (15%).

Financial Statements

This section shows how three basic financial statements are prepared from the analysis of business transactions. The financial statements and their purposes are:

1. **Income statement**—describes a company's revenues and expenses along with the resulting net income or loss over a period of time due to earnings activities. This statement is sometimes called a *profit and loss statement,* or *P&L.*
2. **Statement of owner's equity**—explains changes in owner's equity from net income (or loss) and from any owner investments and withdrawals over a period of time. This statement is also called the *statement of changes in owner's equity.*
3. **Balance sheet**—describes a company's financial position (types and amounts of assets, liabilities, and equity) at a point in time.

LO3 Identify and prepare basic financial statements and explain how they interrelate.

Exhibit 2.2 shows the links between financial statements across time. A balance sheet reflects financial position at a *point in time*. The income statement and the statement of owner's equity reflect activity over a *period of time*. Information from these two financial statements updates the balance sheet at the next *point in time*.

We prepare these financial statements using the 11 selected transactions of FastForward from Exhibit 2.1. Note, a financial statement's heading lists the 3 W's: **W**ho—name of organization; **W**hat—name of statement; and **W**hen—statement's point in time or period of time.

Exhibit 2.2

Links between Financial Statements across Time

Income Statement

The income statement shows the profitability of business operations over a period of time. FastForward's income statement for December is shown at the top of Exhibit 2.3. Information about revenues and expenses is from the Equity columns of Exhibit 2.1. Revenues are reported first on the income statement. They include consulting revenues of $5,800 from transactions 5 and 8 and rental revenue of $300 from transaction 8. Expenses are reported after revenues. (Here we list larger amounts first, but we can sort expenses in different ways.) Rent and salary expenses are from transactions 6 and 7. Expenses reflect the costs to generate the revenues reported. Net income (or loss) is reported at the bottom of the income statement. During the month of December, FastForward had net income, or profit, of $4,400. Notice that owner's investments and withdrawals are *not* part of income.

Exhibit 2.3

Financial Statements and Their Links

> A single ruled line denotes an addition or subtraction. Final totals are double underlined.

> Arrow lines show how the statements interrelate. ① Net income is used to update equity (capital) ② Ending capital is used to prepare the balance sheet.

FASTFORWARD
Income Statement
For Month Ended December 31, 2010

Revenues		
Consulting revenue	$ 5,800	
Rental revenue	300	
Total revenues		$ 6,100
Expenses		
Rent expense	1,000	
Salaries expense	700	
Total expenses		1,700
Net income		$ 4,400

FASTFORWARD
Statement of Owner's Equity
For Month Ended December 31, 2010

C. Taylor, Capital, December 1, 2010		$ 0
Plus: Investments by owner	$30,000	
Net income	4,400	34,400
		34,400
Less: Withdrawals by owner		200
C. Taylor, Capital, December 31, 2010		$34,200

FASTFORWARD
Balance Sheet
December 31, 2010

Assets		Liabilities	
Cash	$ 4,800	Accounts payable	$ 6,200
Supplies	9,600		
Equipment	26,000	**Equity**	
		C. Taylor, Capital	34,200
Total assets	$40,400	Total liabilities and equity	$ 40,400

Statement of Owner's Equity

The statement of owner's equity reports information about how equity changes over the reporting period. This statement shows beginning capital, events that increase it (owner investments and net income), and events that decrease it (owner withdrawals and net loss). FastForward's statement of owner's equity is the second report in Exhibit 2.3. The beginning capital balance is measured as of the start of business on December 1. It is zero because FastForward did not exist before then. An existing business reports the beginning balance as of the end of the prior reporting period (such as from November 30). FastForward's statement shows that Taylor's initial investment created $30,000 of equity. It also shows the $4,400 of net income earned during the period. This links the income statement to the statement of owner's equity (see line ①). The statement also reports Taylor's $200 cash withdrawal and FastForward's end-of-period capital balance of $34,200. This ending capital is carried over and reported on the balance sheet. This links the statement of owner's equity to the balance sheet (see line ②).

Balance Sheet

The balance sheet reports the type and amounts of assets, liabilities, and owner's equity at a point in time. FastForward's balance sheet is the third report in Exhibit 2.3. This statement refers to FastForward's financial condition at the close of business on December 31. The left side of the balance sheet lists FastForward's assets: cash, supplies, and equipment. The upper right side of the balance sheet shows that FastForward owes $6,200 to creditors. Any other liabilities (such as a bank loan) would be listed here. The equity (capital) balance is $34,200. Note again the link between the ending balance of the statement of owner's equity and the equity balance here—see line ②.

HOW YOU DOIN'?   Answers—p. 33

5. Explain the link between the income statement and the statement of owner's equity.

6. Describe the link between the balance sheet and the statement of owner's equity.

Demonstration Problem

After several months of planning, Jasmine Worthy started a haircutting business called Expressions. The following events occurred during its first month of business.

a. On August 1, Worthy invested $3,000 cash and $15,000 of equipment in Expressions.

b. On August 2, Expressions paid $600 cash for furniture for the shop.

c. On August 3, Expressions paid $500 cash to rent space in a strip mall for August.

d. On August 4, it purchased $1,200 of equipment on credit for the shop (using an account payable).

e. On August 5, Expressions opened for business. Cash received from services provided in the first week and a half of business (ended August 15) is $825.

f. On August 15, it provided $100 of haircutting services on account.

g. On August 17, it received a $100 check for services previously rendered on account on August 15.

h. On August 17, it paid $125 cash to an assistant for working during the grand opening.

i. Cash received from services provided during the second half of August is $930.

j. On August 31, it paid $400 toward the account payable entered into on August 4.

k. On August 31, Worthy made a $900 cash withdrawal for personal use.

Required

1. Arrange the following asset, liability, and equity titles in a table similar to the one in Exhibit 2.1: Cash; Accounts Receivable; Furniture; Store Equipment; Accounts Payable; J. Worthy, Capital; J. Worthy, Withdrawals; Revenues; and Expenses. Show the effects of each transaction using the accounting equation.

2. Prepare an income statement for August.

3. Prepare a statement of owner's equity for August.

4. Prepare a balance sheet as of August 31.

Planning the Solution

- Set up a table like Exhibit 2.1 with the appropriate columns for accounts.
- Analyze each transaction and show its effects as increases or decreases in the appropriate columns. Be sure the accounting equation remains in balance after each transaction.
- Prepare the income statement, and identify revenues and expenses. List those items on the statement, compute the difference, and label the result as *net income* or *net loss*.
- Use information in the Equity columns to prepare the statement of owner's equity.
- Use information in the last row of the transactions table to prepare the balance sheet.

Solution to Demonstration Problem

1.

	Assets						=	Liabilities	+		Equity				
	Cash	+	Accounts Receivable	+	Furniture	+	Store Equipment	=	Accounts Payable	+	J. Worthy, Capital	− J. Worthy, Withdrawals	+ Revenues	− Expenses
a.	$3,000						$15,000				$18,000			
b.	− 600			+	$600									
Bal.	2,400	+		+	600	+	15,000	=			18,000			
c.	− 500													− $500
Bal.	1,900	+		+	600	+	15,000	=			18,000			− 500
d.						+	1,200		+$1,200					
Bal.	1,900	+		+	600	+	16,200	=	1,200	+	18,000			− 500
e.	+ 825												+ $ 825	
Bal.	2,725	+		+	600	+	16,200	=	1,200	+	18,000		+ 825	− 500
f.		+	$100										+ 100	
Bal.	2,725	+	100	+	600	+	16,200	=	1,200	+	18,000		+ 925	− 500
g.	+ 100	−	100											
Bal.	2,825	+	0	+	600	+	16,200	=	1,200	+	18,000		+ 925	− 500
h.	− 125													− 125
Bal.	2,700	+	0	+	600	+	16,200	=	1,200	+	18,000		+ 925	− 625
i.	+ 930												+ 930	
Bal.	3,630	+	0	+	600	+	16,200	=	1,200	+	18,000		+ 1,855	− 625
j.	− 400								− 400					
Bal.	3,230	+	0	+	600	+	16,200	=	800	+	18,000		+ 1,855	− 625
k.	− 900											− $900		
Bal.	$ 2,330	+	$ 0	+	$600	+	$ 16,200	=	$ 800	+	$ 18,000	− $900	+ $1,855	− $625

2.

EXPRESSIONS Income Statement For Month Ended August 31		
Revenues		
Haircutting services revenue		$1,855
Expenses		
Rent expense	$500	
Wages expense	125	
Total expenses		625
Net income		$1,230

3.

EXPRESSIONS Statement of Owner's Equity For Month Ended August 31		
J. Worthy, Capital, August 1*		$ 0
Plus: Investments by owner	$18,000	
Net income	1,230	19,230
		19,230
Less: Withdrawals by owner		900
J. Worthy, Capital, August 31		$18,330

* If Expressions had been an existing business from a prior period, the beginning capital balance would equal the Capital account balance from the end of the prior period.

4.

EXPRESSIONS Balance Sheet August 31			
Assets		**Liabilities**	
Cash	$ 2,330	Accounts payable	$ 800
Furniture	600	**Equity**	
Store equipment	16,200	J. Worthy, Capital	18,330
Total assets	$19,130	Total liabilities and equity	$19,130

Summary

LO1 Define the accounting equation and each of its components. The accounting equation is: Assets = Liabilities + Equity. Assets are resources owned by a company. Liabilities are creditors' claims on assets. Equity is the owner's claim on assets (*the residual*). The expanded accounting equation is: Assets = Liabilities + [Owner Capital − Owner Withdrawals + Revenues − Expenses].

LO2 Analyze business transactions using the accounting equation. A *transaction* is an exchange of value between two parties. Examples include exchanges of products, services, money, and

rights to collect money. Transactions always have at least two effects on one or more components of the accounting equation. This equation is always in balance.

LO3 Identify and prepare basic financial statements and explain how they interrelate. Three basic financial statements report on an organization's activities: balance sheet, income statement, and statement of owner's equity. Net income from the income statement updates equity on the statement of owner's equity. Ending owner's equity is reported on the ending balance sheet.

Guidance Answers to   HOW YOU DOIN'?

1. The accounting equation is: Assets = Liabilities + Equity. This equation is always in balance, both before and after each transaction. This means that a company's assets are equal to the claims on those assets.

2. A transaction that changes the makeup of assets would not affect liability and equity accounts. FastForward's transactions 2, 3, and 9 are examples. Each exchanges one asset for another.

3. Earning revenue by performing services, as in FastForward's transaction 5, increases equity (and assets). Incurring expenses while servicing clients, such as in transactions 6 and 7, decreases equity (and assets). Other examples include owner investments that increase equity and owner withdrawals that decrease equity.

4. Paying a liability with an asset reduces both asset and liability totals. One example is FastForward's transaction 10 that reduces a payable by paying cash.

5. An income statement reports a company's revenues and expenses along with the resulting net income or loss. A statement of owner's equity shows changes in equity, including that from net income or loss. Both statements report transactions occurring over a period of time.

6. The balance sheet describes a company's financial position (assets, liabilities, and equity) at a point in time. The equity amount in the balance sheet is obtained from the statement of owner's equity.

Key Terms

Account (p. 23) Record within an accounting system in which increases and decreases are entered and stored in a specific asset, liability, equity, revenue, or expense.

Accounting equation (p. 22) Equality involving a company's assets, liabilities, and equity; Assets = Liabilities + Equity; also called *balance sheet equation*.

Assets (p. 22) Resources a business owns or controls that are expected to provide current and future benefits to the business.

Balance sheet (p. 29) Financial statement that lists types and dollar amounts of assets, liabilities, and equity at a specific date.

Creditors (p. 22) Individuals and organizations that are entitled to receive payment from a company.

Equity (p. 23) Owner's claim on the assets of a business; equals the residual interest in an entity's assets after deducting liabilities; also called *net assets*.

Events (p. 23) Those happenings that affect an entity's accounting equation *and* can be reliably measured.

Expanded accounting equation (p. 23) Assets = Liabilities + Equity; Equity equals [Owner capital − Owner withdrawals + Revenues − Expenses].

Expenses (p. 23) Outflows or using up of assets as part of operations of a business to generate sales.

External transactions (p. 23) Exchanges of value between one entity and another entity.

Income statement (p. 29) Financial statement that subtracts expenses from revenues to yield a net income or loss over a specified period of time; also includes any gains or losses.

Internal transactions (p. 23) Activities within an organization that can affect the accounting equation.

Liabilities (p. 22) Creditors' claims on an organization's assets; involves a probable future payment of assets, products, or services that a company is obliged to make due to past transactions or events.

Net income (p. 23) Amount earned after subtracting all expenses necessary for and matched with sales for a period; also called *income, profit,* or *earnings.*

Net loss (p. 23) Excess of expenses over revenues for a period.

Owner, Capital (p. 23) Account showing the owner's claim on company assets; equals owner investments plus net income (or less net losses) minus owner withdrawals since the company's inception; also referred to as *equity.*

Owner investment (p. 23) Assets put into the business by the owner.

Owner withdrawals (p. 23) Payment of cash or other assets from a proprietorship or partnership to its owner or owners.

Revenues (p. 23) Gross increase in equity from a company's business activities that earn income; also called *sales.*

Statement of owner's equity (p. 29) Report of changes in equity over a period; adjusted for increases (owner investment and net income) and for decreases (withdrawals and net losses).

Multiple Choice Quiz

Answers on p. 43   mhhe.com/wildCA2e

Additional Multiple Choice Quizzes are available at the book's Website.

1. When supplies are paid for with cash, which accounts increase or decrease?
   a. Supplies increase; cash increases.
   b. Supplies increase; accounts payable increases.
   c. Supplies increase; cash neither increases nor decreases.
   d. Supplies increase; cash decreases.

2. When supplies are purchased on account, which accounts increase or decrease?
   a. Supplies increase; accounts payable increases.
   b. Supplies increase; accounts receivable increases.
   c. Supplies increase; accounts payable decreases.
   d. Supplies increase; equity decreases.

3. If the assets of a company increase by $100,000 during the year and its liabilities increase by $35,000 during the same year, then the change in equity of the company during the year must have been:
   a. An increase of $135,000.
   b. A decrease of $135,000.
   c. A decrease of $65,000.
   d. An increase of $65,000.
   e. An increase of $100,000.

4. A company borrows $50,000 cash from Third National Bank. How does this transaction affect the accounting equation for this company?

   a. Assets increase by $50,000; liabilities increase by $50,000; no effect on equity.
   b. Assets increase by $50,000; no effect on liabilities; equity increases by $50,000.
   c. Assets increase by $50,000; liabilities decrease by $50,000; no effect on equity.
   d. No effect on assets; liabilities increase by $50,000; equity increases by $50,000.
   e. No effect on assets; liabilities increase by $50,000; equity decreases by $50,000.

5. Geek Squad performs services for a customer and bills the customer for $500. How would Geek Squad record this transaction?
   a. Accounts receivable increase by $500; revenues increase by $500.
   b. Cash increases by $500; revenues increase by $500.
   c. Accounts receivable increase by $500; revenues decrease by $500.
   d. Accounts receivable increase by $500; accounts payable increase by $500.
   e. Accounts payable increase by $500; revenues increase by $500.

Discussion Questions

1. Define (*a*) *assets,* (*b*) *liabilities,* (*c*) *equity,* and (*d*) *net assets.*
2. What events or transactions change equity?
3. What do accountants mean by the term *revenue*?
4. Define *net income* and explain its computation.
5. Identify the three basic financial statements of a business.
6. What information is reported in an income statement?
7. Give two examples of expenses a business might incur.
8. What is the purpose of the statement of owner's equity?

9. What information is reported in a balance sheet?
10. Refer to the financial statements of **Best Buy** in Appendix A near the end of the book. To what level are dollar amounts rounded? What time period does its income statement cover?
11. Refer to the financial statements for **RadioShack** in Appendix A near the  end of the book. What time period does its balance sheet cover? To what level are dollar amounts rounded?

connect

a. Total assets of Charter Company equal $700,000 and its equity is $420,000. What is the amount of its liabilities?

b. Total assets of Martin Marine equal $500,000 and its liabilities and equity amounts are equal to each other. What is the amount of its liabilities? What is the amount of its equity?

QUICK STUDY

QS 2-1
Applying the accounting equation
L01

Use the accounting equation to compute the missing financial statement amounts (*a*), (*b*), and (*c*).

Company	Assets	=	Liabilities	+	Equity
1	$75,000		$ (a)		$40,000
2	$ (b)		$25,000		$70,000
3	$85,000		$20,000		$ (c)

QS 2-2
Applying the accounting equation
L01

Indicate in which financial statement each item would most likely appear: income statement (I), balance sheet (B), or statement of owner's equity (E).

a. Assets   **c.** Equipment   **e.** Liabilities   **g.** Total liabilities and equity

b. Withdrawals   **d.** Expenses   **f.** Revenues

QS 2-3
Identifying items with financial statements   **L03**

Use RadioShack's December 31, 2007, financial statements, in Appendix A near the end of the book, to answer the following:

a. Identify the dollar amounts of RadioShack's 2007 (1) total assets, (2) total liabilities, and (3) total equity.

b. Using RadioShack's amounts from part *a,* verify that Assets = Liabilities + Equity.

QS 2-4
Identifying and computing assets, liabilities, and equity   **L01**

Explain how the transactions below impact the accounting equation.

a. Collect $4,000 cash from a customer for consulting services provided.

b. Bill a customer $2,800 for consulting services provided.

QS 2-5
Using the accounting equation
L02

Explain how the transactions below impact the accounting equation.

a. Pay $1,800 cash for employee wages.

b. Pay $10,000 cash for office equipment.

QS 2-6
Using the accounting equation
L02

Explain how the transactions below impact the accounting equation.

a. Owner invests $50,000 cash in her new business.

b. Owner withdraws $4,000 cash from the business for personal use.

QS 2-7
Using the accounting equation
L02

Explain how the transactions below impact the accounting equation.

a. Pay $1,200 in cash for supplies.

b. Purchase $2,000 of office supplies on credit.

QS 2-8
Using the accounting equation
L02

EXERCISES

Exercise 2-1
Using the accounting equation
L01

Determine the missing amount from each of the separate situations a, b, and c below.

	Assets	=	Liabilities	+	Equity
a.	?	=	$20,000	+	$45,000
b.	$100,000	=	$34,000	+	?
c.	$154,000	=	?	+	$40,000

Exercise 2-2
Classifying accounts
L01   L02

Classify each of the following accounts as an asset (A), liability (L), or equity (E) account.

_____ **1.** Accounts Payable   _____ **5.** Supplies

_____ **2.** Loan (or Notes) Payable   _____ **6.** Equipment

_____ **3.** Accounts Receivable   _____ **7.** Rod Smith, Capital

_____ **4.** Cash

Exercise 2-3
Identifying effects of transactions
on the accounting equation
L01   L02

Provide an example of a transaction that creates the described effects for the separate cases *a* through *g*.

a. Decreases an asset and decreases equity.   **e.** Increases an asset and decreases an asset.

b. Increases an asset and increases a liability.   **f.** Increases a liability and decreases equity.

c. Decreases a liability and increases a liability.   **g.** Increases an asset and increases equity.

d. Decreases an asset and decreases a liability.

Exercise 2-4
Using the accounting equation
L01   L02

Answer the following questions. (*Hint:* Use the accounting equation.)

a. Cadence Office Supplies has assets equal to $123,000 and liabilities equal to $47,000 at year-end. What is the total equity for Cadence at year-end?

b. At the beginning of the year, Addison Company's assets are $300,000 and its equity is $100,000. During the year, assets increase $80,000 and liabilities increase $50,000. What is the equity at the end of the year?

Check (c) Beg. equity, $60,000

c. At the beginning of the year, Quasar Company's liabilities equal $70,000. During the year, assets increase by $60,000, and at year-end assets equal $190,000. Liabilities decrease $5,000 during the year. What are the beginning and ending amounts of equity?

Exercise 2-5
Identifying effects of transactions
using the accounting equation
L01   L02

Leora Holden began a professional practice on June 1 and plans to prepare financial statements at the end of each month. During June, Holden (the owner) completed these transactions.

a. Owner invested $60,000 cash along with equipment that had a $15,000 market value.

b. Paid $1,500 cash for rent of office space for the month.

c. Purchased $10,000 of additional equipment on credit (payment due within 30 days).

d. Completed work for a client and immediately collected the $2,500 cash earned.

e. Completed work for a client and sent a bill for $8,000 to be received within 30 days.

f. Purchased additional equipment for $6,000 cash.

g. Paid an assistant $3,000 cash as wages for the month.

h. Collected $5,000 cash on the amount owed by the client described in transaction *e*.

i. Paid $10,000 cash to settle the liability created in transaction *c*.

j. Owner withdrew $1,000 cash for personal use.

Required

Check   Net income, $6,000

Create a table like the one in Exhibit 2.1, using the following headings for columns: Cash; Accounts Receivable; Equipment; Accounts Payable; Holden, Capital; Holden, Withdrawals; Revenues; and Expenses. Then use additions and subtractions to show the effects of the transactions on individual items of the accounting equation. Show new balances after each transaction.

The following table shows the effects of five transactions (*a* through *e*) on the assets, liabilities, and equity of Trista's Boutique. Write short descriptions of what likely happened in each transaction.

	Assets				=	Liabilities	+	Equity		
	Cash	+ Accounts Receivable	+ Office Supplies	+ Land	=	Accounts Payable	+ Trista, Capital	+ Revenues		
	$ 21,000	+ $ 0	+ $3,000	+ $ 19,000	=	$ 0	+ $43,000	+ $ 0		
a.	− 4,000			+ 4,000						
b.			+ 1,000			+1,000				
c.		+ 1,900						+ 1,900		
d.	− 1,000					−1,000				
e	+ 1,900	− 1,900								
	$ 17,900	+ $ 0	+ $4,000	+ $ 23,000	=	$ 0	+ $43,000	+ $1,900		

On October 1, Keisha King organized Real Answers, a new consulting firm. On October 31, the company's records show the following items and amounts. Use this information to prepare an October income statement for the business.

Cash	$11,500	Cash withdrawals by owner	$ 2,000
Accounts receivable	12,000	Consulting fees earned	14,000
Office supplies	24,437	Rent expense	2,520
Land	46,000	Salaries expense	5,600
Office equipment	18,000	Telephone expense	760
Accounts payable	25,037	Miscellaneous expenses	580
Owner investments	84,360		

Use the information in Exercise 2-7 to prepare an October statement of owner's equity for Real Answers.

Use the information in Exercise 2-7 (if completed, you can also use your solution to Exercise 2-8) to prepare an October 31 balance sheet for Real Answers.

The following is selected financial information for Elko Energy Company for the year ended December 31, 2010: revenues, $55,000; expenses, $40,000; net income, $15,000.

Required

Prepare the 2010 income statement for Elko Energy Company.

The following is selected financial information for Amity Company as of December 31, 2010: liabilities, $44,000; equity, $46,000; assets, $90,000.

Required

Prepare the balance sheet for Amity Company as of December 31, 2010.

Following is selected financial information for Kasio Co. for the year ended December 31, 2010.

K. Kasio, Capital, Dec. 31, 2010	$14,000	K. Kasio, Withdrawals	$1,000
Net income	8,000	K. Kasio, Capital, Dec. 31, 2009	7,000

Required

Prepare the 2010 statement of owner's equity for Kasio.

Exercise 2-13
Preparing a statement of
owner's equity   **LO3**

Following is selected financial information of First Act for the year ended December 31, 2010.

| I. Firstact, Capital, Dec. 31, 2010 . . . . | $47,000 | I. Firstact, Withdrawals . . . . | $ 7,000 |
| Net income . . . . | 5,000 | I. Firstact, Capital, Dec. 31, 2009 . . . . | 49,000 |

Required

Prepare the 2010 calendar-year statement of owner's equity for First Act.

Exercise 2-14
Analyzing effects of transactions
LO1   LO2

Isabel Lopez started Biz Consulting, a new business, and completed the following transactions during its first year of operations.

a. I. Lopez invests $70,000 cash and office equipment valued at $10,000 in the business.

b. Purchased a $20,000 building to use as an office. Biz paid $20,000 in cash.

c. Purchased office equipment for $15,000 cash.

d. Purchased $1,200 of office supplies credit.

Required

1. Create a table like the one in Exhibit 2.1, using the following headings for the columns: Cash; Office Supplies; Office Equipment; Building; Accounts Payable; I. Lopez, Capital.

2. Use additions and subtractions to show the effects of these transactions on individual items of the accounting equation. Show new balances after each transaction.

Exercise 2-15
Preparing financial statements **LO3**

Isabel Lopez's consulting business, Biz Consulting, reports the following accounting equation balances on December 31, 2010, the end of its first year of operations.

Assets					=	Liabilities	+	Equity				
Cash	+ Accounts Receivable	+ Office Supplies	+ Office Equipment	+ Building	= Accounts Payable		+ I. Lopez, Capital	− I. Lopez, Withdrawals	+ Revenues	− Expenses
Bal. $34,525	+ $1,000	+ $1,200	+ $26,700	+ $150,000	= $132,200		+ $80,000	− $3,275	+ $6,800	− $2,300

Required

Check   (2) I. Lopez Capital,
December 31, $81,225

1. Compute net income for 2010.

2. Prepare a statement of owner's equity for 2010 and a balance sheet as of December 31, 2010.

Problem Set B located at the end of Problem Set A is provided for each problem to reinforce the learning process.

PROBLEM SET A

Problem 2-1A
Computing missing information
using accounting knowledge and
the accounting equation
LO1   LO2

The following financial statement information is from five separate companies.

	Company A	Company B	Company C	Company D	Company E
December 31, 2009					
Assets	$55,000	$34,000	$24,000	$60,000	$119,000
Liabilities	24,500	21,500	9,000	40,000	?
December 31, 2010					
Assets	58,000	40,000	?	85,000	113,000
Liabilities	?	26,500	29,000	24,000	70,000
During year 2010					
Owner investments	6,000	1,400	9,750	?	6,500
Net income	8,500	?	8,000	14,000	20,000
Owner cash withdrawals	3,500	2,000	5,875	0	11,000

Required

1. Answer the following questions about Company A.

  a. What is the amount of equity on December 31, 2009?

  b. What is the amount of equity on December 31, 2010?

  c. What is the amount of liabilities on December 31, 2010?

Check   (1b) $41,500

2. Answer the following questions about Company B.

   a. What is the amount of equity on December 31, 2009?

   b. What is the amount of equity on December 31, 2010?

   c. What is net income for year 2010?

3. Calculate the amount of assets for Company C on December 31, 2010.

4. Calculate the amount of owner investments for Company D during year 2010.

5. Calculate the amount of liabilities for Company E on December 31, 2009.

Check   (2c) $1,600

(3) $55,875

Identify how each of the following separate transactions affects financial statements. For the balance sheet, identify how each transaction affects total assets, total liabilities, and total equity. For the income statement, identify how each transaction affects net income. For increases, place a "+" in the column or columns. For decreases, place a "−" in the column or columns. If both an increase and a decrease occur, place a "+/−" in the column or columns. The first transaction is completed as an example.

Problem 2-2A

Identifying effects of transactions on financial statements

LO1   LO2

	Transaction	Balance Sheet			Income Statement
		Total Assets	**Total Liab.**	**Total Equity**	**Net Income**
I	Owner invests cash in business	+		+	
2	Receives cash for services provided				
3	Pays cash for employee wages				
4	Owner withdraws cash				
5	Provides services on credit				
6	Buys office equipment for cash				
7	Collects cash on receivable from (6)				

Holden Graham started The Graham Co., a new business that began operations on May 1. Graham Co. completed the following transactions during that first month.

May	1	H. Graham invested $40,000 cash in the business.
	1	Rented a furnished office and paid $2,200 cash for May's rent.
	3	Purchased $1,890 of office equipment on credit.
	5	Paid $750 cash for this month's cleaning services.
	8	Provided consulting services for a client and immediately collected $5,400 cash.
	12	Provided $2,500 of consulting services for a client on credit.
	15	Paid $750 cash for an assistant's salary for the first half of this month.
	20	Received $2,500 cash payment for the services provided on May 12.
	22	Provided $3,200 of consulting services on credit.
	25	Received $3,200 cash payment for the services provided on May 22.
	26	Paid $1,890 cash for the office equipment purchased on May 3.
	27	Purchased $80 of advertising in this month's (May) local paper on credit.
	28	Paid $750 cash for an assistant's salary for the second half of this month.
	30	Paid $300 cash for this month's telephone bill.
	30	Paid $280 cash for this month's utilities.
	31	Graham withdrew $1,400 cash for personal use.

Problem 2-3A

Analyzing transactions and preparing financial statements

LO2   LO3

mhhe.com/wildCA2e

Required

1. Arrange the following asset, liability, and equity titles in a table like Exhibit 2.1: Cash; Accounts Receivable; Office Equipment; Accounts Payable; H. Graham, Capital; H. Graham, Withdrawals; Revenues; and Expenses.

2. Show effects of the transactions on the accounts of the accounting equation by recording increases and decreases in the appropriate columns. Do not determine new account balances after each transaction. Determine the final total for each account and verify that the equation is in balance.

3. Prepare an income statement for May, a statement of owner's equity for May, and a May 31 balance sheet.

Check   (2) Ending balances: Cash, $42,780; Expenses, $5,110

(3) Net income, $5,990; Total assets, $44,670

Problem 2-4A

Analyzing transactions and
preparing financial statements
LO2   LO3

mhhe.com/wildCA2e

Helga Ander started a new business and completed these transactions during December.

Dec. 1   Helga Ander transferred $65,000 cash from a personal savings account to a checking account
          in the name of Ander Electric.
      2   Rented office space and paid $1,000 cash for the December rent.
      3   Purchased $13,000 of electrical equipment by paying $4,800 cash and agreeing to pay the
          $8,200 balance in 30 days.
      5   Purchased office supplies by paying $800 cash.
      6   Completed electrical work and immediately collected $1,200 cash for the work.
      8   Purchased $2,530 of office equipment on credit.
      15 Completed electrical work on credit in the amount of $5,000.
      18 Purchased $350 of office supplies on credit.
      20 Paid $2,530 cash for the office equipment purchased on December 8.
      24 Billed a client $900 for electrical work completed.
      28 Received $5,000 cash for the work completed on December 15.
      29 Paid the assistant's salary of $1,400 cash for this month.
      30 Paid $540 cash for this month's utility bill.
      31 Ander withdrew $950 cash for personal use.

Required

1. Arrange the following asset, liability, and equity titles in a table like Exhibit 2.1: Cash; Accounts
Receivable; Office Supplies; Office Equipment; Electrical Equipment; Accounts Payable; H. Ander,
Capital; H. Ander, Withdrawals; Revenues; and Expenses.

Check   (2) Ending balances: Cash,
$59,180, Accounts Payable, $8,550

2. Use additions and subtractions to show the effects of each transaction on the accounts in the accounting equation. Show new balances after each transaction.

   (3) Net income, $4,160;
Total assets, $76,760

3. Use the increases and decreases in the columns of the table from part 2 to prepare an income statement
and a statement of owner's equity for the month. Also prepare a balance sheet as of the end of the month.

PROBLEM SET B

Problem 2-1B

Computing missing information
using accounting knowledge
LO1   LO2

The following financial statement information is from five separate companies.

	Company V	Company W	Company X	Company Y	Company Z
December 31, 2009					
Assets	$54,000	$ 80,000	$141,500	$92,500	$144,000
Liabilities	25,000	60,000	68,500	51,500	?
December 31, 2010					
Assets	59,000	100,000	186,500	?	170,000
Liabilities	36,000	?	65,800	42,000	42,000
During year 2010					
Owner investments	5,000	20,000	?	48,100	60,000
Net income	?	40,000	18,500	24,000	32,000
Owner cash withdrawals	5,500	2,000	0	20,000	8,000

Required

1. Answer the following questions about Company V.

   a. What is the amount of equity on December 31, 2009?

Check   (1b) $23,000

   b. What is the amount of equity on December 31, 2010?

   c. What is the net income or loss for the year 2010?

2. Answer the following questions about Company W.

   a. What is the amount of equity on December 31, 2009?

   b. What is the amount of equity on December 31, 2010?

   (2c) $22,000

   c. What is the amount of liabilities on December 31, 2010?

3. Calculate the amount of owner investments for Company X during 2010.

   (4) $135,100

4. Calculate the amount of assets for Company Y on December 31, 2010.

5. Calculate the amount of liabilities for Company Z on December 31, 2009.

Identify how each of the following separate transactions affects financial statements. For the balance sheet, identify how each transaction affects total assets, total liabilities, and total equity. For the income statement, identify how each transaction affects net income. For increases, place a "+" in the column or columns. For decreases, place a "−" in the column or columns. If both an increase and a decrease occur, place "+/−" in the column or columns. The first transaction is completed as an example.

Problem 2–2B
Identifying effects of transactions on financial statements
L01   L02

		Balance Sheet			Income Statement
	Transaction	Total Assets	Total Liab.	Total Equity	Net Income
1	Owner invests cash in business	+		+	
2	Pays cash for salaries				
3	Provides services for cash				
4	Pays cash for rent				
5	Buys store equipment for cash				
6	Owner withdraws cash				
7	Provides services on credit				
8	Collects cash on receivable from (7)				

Holly Nikolas launched a new business, Holly's Maintenance Co., that began operations on June 1. The following transactions were completed by the company during that first month.

Problem 2–3B
Analyzing transactions and preparing financial statements
L02   L03

June 1   H. Nikolas invested $130,000 cash in the business.
     2   Rented a furnished office and paid $6,000 cash for June's rent.
     4   Purchased $2,400 of equipment on credit.
     6   Paid $1,150 cash for the next week's advertising of the opening of the business.
     8   Completed maintenance services for a customer and immediately collected $850 cash.
    14   Completed $7,500 of maintenance services for City Center on credit.
    16   Paid $800 cash for an assistant's salary for the first half of the month.
    20   Received $7,500 cash payment for services completed for City Center on June 14.
    21   Completed $7,900 of maintenance services for Paula's Beauty Shop on credit.
    24   Completed $675 of maintenance services for Build-It Coop on credit.
    25   Received $7,900 cash payment from Paula's Beauty Shop for the work completed on June 21.
    26   Made payment of $2,400 cash for the equipment purchased on June 4.
    28   Paid $800 cash for an assistant's salary for the second half of this month.
    29   Nikolas withdrew $4,000 cash for personal use.
    30   Paid $150 cash for this month's telephone bill.
    30   Paid $890 cash for this month's utilities.

Required

1. Arrange the following asset, liability, and equity titles in a table like Exhibit 2.1: Cash; Accounts Receivable; Equipment; Accounts Payable; H. Nikolas, Capital; H. Nikolas, Withdrawals; Revenues; and Expenses.

2. Show the effects of the transactions on the accounts of the accounting equation by recording increases and decreases in the appropriate columns. Do not determine new account balances after each transaction. Determine the final total for each account and verify that the equation is in balance.

3. Prepare a June income statement, a June statement of owner's equity, and a June 30 balance sheet.

Check   (2) Ending balances: Cash, $130,060; Expenses, $9,790

(3) Net income, $7,135; Total assets, $133,135

Truro Excavating Co., owned by Raul Truro, began operations in July and completed the following transactions during that first month.

Problem 2–4B
Analyzing transactions and preparing financial statements
L02   L03

July 1   R. Truro invested $80,000 cash in the business.
     2   Rented office space and paid $700 cash for the July rent.
     3   Purchased excavating equipment for $5,000 by paying $1,000 cash and agreeing to pay the $4,000 balance in 30 days.
     6   Purchased office supplies for $600 cash.
     8   Completed work for a customer and immediately collected $7,600 cash for the work.

10 Purchased $2,300 of office equipment on credit.
15 Completed work for a customer on credit in the amount of $8,200.
17 Purchased $3,100 of office supplies on credit.
23 Paid $2,300 cash for the office equipment purchased on July 10.
25 Billed a customer $5,000 for work completed.
28 Received $8,200 cash for the work completed on July 15.
30 Paid an assistant's salary of $1,560 cash for this month.
31 Paid $295 cash for this month's utility bill.
31 Truro withdrew $1,800 cash for personal use.

Required

Check (2) Ending balances: Cash, $87,545; Accounts Payable, $7,100

(3) Net income, $18,245; Total assets, $103,545

1. Arrange the following asset, liability, and equity titles in a table like Exhibit 2.1: Cash; Accounts Receivable; Office Supplies; Office Equipment; Excavating Equipment; Accounts Payable; R. Truro, Capital; R. Truro, Withdrawals; Revenues; and Expenses.

2. Use additions and subtractions to show the effects of each transaction on the accounts in the accounting equation. Show new balances after each transaction.

3. Use the increases and decreases in the columns of the table from part 2 to prepare an income statement, and a statement of owner's equity. Also prepare a balance sheet as of the end of the month.

SERIAL PROBLEM

Success Systems

(This serial problem started in Chapter 1 and continues through most of the chapters. If the Chapter 1 segment was not completed, the problem can begin at this point. It is helpful, but not necessary, to use the Working Papers that accompany this book.)

SP 2 On October 1, 2010, Adriana Lopez started a computer services company, **Success Systems,** that provides consulting services, computer system installations, and custom program development. Lopez expects to prepare the company's first set of financial statements on December 31, 2010.

Required

Create a table like the one in Exhibit 2.1 using the following headings for columns: Cash; Accounts Receivable; Computer Supplies; Computer System; Office Equipment; Accounts Payable; A. Lopez, Capital; A. Lopez, Withdrawals; Revenues; and Expenses. Then use additions and subtractions to show the effects of the October transactions for Success Systems on the individual items of the accounting equation. Show new balances after each transaction.

Oct. 1 Adriana Lopez invested $75,000 cash, a $25,000 computer system, and $10,000 of office equipment in the business.
3 Purchased $1,600 of computer supplies on credit from Corvina Office Products.
6 Billed Easy Leasing $6,200 for services performed in installing a new Web server.
8 Paid $1,600 cash for the computer supplies purchased from Corvina Office Products on October 3.
12 Billed Easy Leasing another $1,950 for services performed.
15 Received $6,200 cash from Easy Leasing toward its account.
17 Paid $900 cash to repair computer equipment damaged when moving it.
20 Paid $1,790 cash for an advertisement in the local newspaper.
22 Received $1,950 cash from Easy Leasing toward its account.
28 Billed Clark Company $7,300 for services performed.
31 Paid $1,050 cash for Michelle Jones's wages for seven days of work this month.
31 Lopez withdrew $4,000 cash for personal use.

Check Ending balances: Cash, $73,810; Revenues, $15,450; Expenses, $3,740

BEYOND THE NUMBERS

REPORTING IN ACTION

LO1

BEST BUY

BTN 2–1 Key financial figures for **Best Buy**'s fiscal year ended March 1, 2008, follow.

Key Figure	In Millions
Liabilities + Equity	$12,758
Net income	1,407
Revenues	40,023

Required

1. What is the total amount of assets invested in **Best Buy**?

2. How much are total expenses for Best Buy for the year ended March 1, 2008?

BTN 2-2   **WorldCom** committed fraud by accounting for some expenses as if they were assets.

Required

1. Using the accounting equation, show the accounting for an expense and the accounting for an asset (assume $1,000 cash is paid in each instance). Does the accounting equation balance in both instances?

2. What ethical concerns would you have if your business accounted for an expense as if it were an asset?

ETHICS CHALLENGE

L01   L02

BTN 2-3   Refer to this chapter's opening feature about **SPANX**. Assume that the founder, Sara Blakely, is having difficulty assessing how well her business has performed over the past year. Write Sara Blakely a half-page memo to explain which financial statement will provide her the best information on her company's performance and which particular number she should focus on.

WORKPLACE COMMUNICATION

L03

BTN 2-4   Visit the EDGAR database at (www.SEC.gov). Under "Filings and Forms" click on "Search for Company Filings." Access the Form 10-K report of **Rocky Mountain Chocolate Factory** (ticker RMCF) filed on May 14, 2007, covering its 2007 fiscal year.

Required

1. Item 6 of its 10-K report provides comparative financial highlights of RMCF for the years 2004–2007. How would you describe the revenue trend for RMCF over this five-year period?

2. Has RMCF been profitable (see net income) over this four-year period? Support your answer.

TAKING IT TO THE NET

L03

BTN 2-5   Divide the class into teams and play **Monopoly**™. Each team takes 10 turns. Each team starts with $1,500 of owners' capital, in cash.

Required

1. Each team accounts for its first 10 transactions using the accounting equation. Use a table like Exhibit 2.1.

2. Each team presents its accounting equation entries to one other team.

TEAMWORK IN ACTION

L01   L02

BTN 2-6   Assume that Sara Blakely of SPANX wants to expand her business. She is considering financing her expansion in one of two ways: (1) contributing more of her own cash to the business or (2) borrowing cash from a bank.

Required

Identify the issues that Blakely should consider when trying to decide on the method for financing the expansion.

ENTREPRENEURS IN BUSINESS

L02   L03

BTN 2-7   You open a wholesale business selling entertainment equipment to retail outlets. You find that most of your customers demand to buy on credit. How can you use the balance sheets of these customers to help you decide which ones to extend credit to?

YOU CALL IT— ENTREPRENEUR

---

1. d

2. a

3. d;

4. a

5. a

ANSWERS TO MULTIPLE CHOICE QUIZ

Assets	=	Liabilities	+	Equity
+$100,000	=	+35,000	+	?

Change in equity = $100,000 − $35,000 = $65,000

A Look Back

Chapter 2 introduced the accounting equation and accounts for various transactions. We also introduced the basic financial statements.

A Look at This Chapter

This chapter introduces double-entry accounting. We explain the analysis and recording of transactions using debits and credits and T-accounts. We show how a trial balance is used to check the accuracy of debits and credits.

A Look Ahead

Chapter 4 introduces the general journal and general ledger. We show how transactions are journalized (recorded) in a general journal and then posted in a general ledger.

Chapter

Applying Double-Entry Accounting

Learning Objectives

LO 1	Describe a T-account and its use in recording transactions.
LO 2	Define debits and credits and explain their role in double-entry accounting.
LO 3	Post transactions in T-accounts.
LO 4	Prepare and explain the use of a trial balance.
LO 5	Prepare financial statements from a trial balance.

"Each individual problem you face is totally surmountable"—Warren Brown

Making Dough

WASHINGTON, DC—Warren Brown started baking cakes to reduce stress, but his friends' appetites demanded more. "Friends were jumping on the bed" saying how much they loved the cakes and insisting that I set up shop, says Warren.

Starting small, Warren baked cakes from scratch using all-natural ingredients in his apartment for hours after work each evening. He sold his sweet concoctions mostly to co-workers and friends, and even held a cake open house at the local art gallery. But Warren was determined to grow his business. He took a course in entrepreneurship at his local community college, and there he discovered the importance of accounting.

Launching his fledgling cake business presented Warren with many challenges. He borrowed $125,000 from the Small Business Administration to buy the equipment to get his business started. He established inventory accounting, transaction analysis, and accounting entries. Rapidly changing prices for his cake ingredients require Warren to closely monitor his selling prices and costs to enable a profit. "Everything feels like a disaster when it's right in your face," says Warren. "You just have to be calm, look at what you're doing, and fix the problem." Warren fixed the

problems and unveiled his shop called **Cake Love (CakeLove.com)**. "I opened up this tiny retail, walk-up bakery . . . [to sell] goodies that are baked from scratch," Warren recalls.

Today, Cake Love entices customers with the scents of fresh bakery at each of its six locations. Warren's Love Café offers customers an inviting place to lounge for hours with free wireless Internet and comfy chairs. "I want it to be relaxed and comfortable," says Warren. "People can bring their work, their kids, their friends, and just relax."

Warren continues to experiment with new treats. "I'm always getting better, improving my skills," he said. Warren also shows a keen appetite for using accounting information to make good business decisions. "But," says Warren, "I love eating what I make more."

"The bigger message of Cake Love is finding your passion and working to reach your goals," says Warren. That's a slice of advice worth more than any amount of dough.

[Sources: *Cake Love Website,* January 2009; *Black Enterprise,* September 2004; *Georgetown Voice,* March 2005; *National Public Radio (NPR) Website,* May 2005; *Inc.com,* April 2005; *Modern Baking,* November 1, 2004; Diamondback online, February 21, 2007.]

Financial statements report on the financial performance and condition of an organization. A main goal of this chapter is to illustrate how transactions are recorded and how they are reflected in financial statements. Debits and credits are introduced and identified as a tool in helping analyze and process transactions.

Applying Double-Entry Accounting

Analyzing and Recording Transactions
- The T-account
- Double-entry
- An illustration

Preparing and Using a Trial Balance
- Trial balance preparation
- Trial balance use

Analyzing and Recording Transactions

In Chapter 2, we introduced the accounting equation, Assets = Liabilities + Equity, as a way to understand what resources the organization owns and who has rights to those resources. However, organizations do not record their transactions in accounting equation form. Instead, they record increases and decreases in individual accounts.

The T-Account

LO1 Describe a T-account and its use in recording transactions.

An account is a record of increases and decreases in a specific asset, liability, equity, revenue, or expense item due to an organization's transactions. A **T-account** is a tool used to understand the effects of these transactions. Its name comes from its shape like the letter T. The layout of a T-account (shown in Exhibit 3.1) is (1) the account title on top, (2) a left, or **debit,** side, and (3) a right, or **credit,** side. We can think of the terms *debit* and *credit* as accounting terms for left and right. In addition, to debit an account means to post a dollar amount on the left side of the T-account. To credit an account means to post a dollar amount on the right side of the T-account. This is true for all types of accounts.

In Chapter 2, we accounted for the December transactions of FastForward using the accounting equation. As an illustration of the use of the T-account, we show how increases and decreases in cash are accounted for. The T-account for FastForward's Cash account, reflecting its first 11 transactions (from Exhibit 2.1), is shown in Exhibit 3.2. (Only nine of FastForward's first 11 transactions impact its Cash account). We include descriptions of each transaction for illustration purposes. T-accounts usually include only numbers.

Exhibit 3.1

The T-Account

Account Title	
(Left side)	(Right side)
Debit	*Credit*

LO2 Define debits and credits and explain their role in double-entry accounting.

Exhibit 3.2

Computing the Balance for a T-Account

Cash			
Investment by owner	30,000	Purchase of supplies	2,500
Consulting services revenue earned	4,200	Purchase of equipment	26,000
Collection of account receivable	1,900	Payment of rent	1,000
Footing	**36,100**	Payment of salary	700
		Payment of account payable	900
		Withdrawal by owner	200
		Footing	**31,300**
Balance	**4,800**		

Note that the numbers in a T-account are not identified with either plus or minus signs. In the next section we explain how the accountant knows how debits and credits impact individual accounts. At this point, simply understand that increases in cash are shown on the left (or debit) side and decreases in cash are shown on the right (or credit) side. The increases in FastForward's Cash account total $36,100, and the decreases total $31,300. These totals are called **footings.** To foot a column of numbers means to compute the total of that column. The difference between total debits and total credits for an account, including any beginning balance, is the **account balance.** When the sum of debits exceeds the sum of credits, the account has a *debit balance*. It has a *credit balance* when the sum of the credits exceeds the sum of debits. When the sum of debits equals the sum of credits, the account has a zero balance. Since the total increases (debits) exceed the total decreases (credits) for FastForward's Cash account, its ending balance in cash is a debit balance of $4,800, (computed as $36,100 minus $31,300).

Double-Entry Accounting

Double-entry accounting requires that each transaction be recorded in at least two accounts. It also means the *total amount debited must equal the total amount credited* for each transaction. Thus, the sum of the debits for all entries must equal the sum of the credits for all entries, and the sum of debit account balances must equal the sum of credit account balances. This means the accounting equation is in balance.

The system for recording debits and credits follows from the usual accounting equation—see Exhibit 3.3. Two points are important here. First, accounts on the left side of the accounting equation (assets) increase with entries in the left side of the T-account (debits). Accounts on the

"Total debits equal total credits for each entry."

Assets		=	Liabilities		+	Equity	
Debit for increases	Credit for decreases		Debit for decreases	Credit for increases		Debit for decreases	Credit for increases
+	–		–	+		–	+

Exhibit 3.3

Debits and Credits in the Accounting Equation

right side of the accounting equation (liabilities and equity) increase with entries on the right side of the T-account (credits). Second, an account's **normal balance** is the side of the account on which increases are recorded. Thus, the left side is the *normal balance* side for assets, and the right side of the T-account is the *normal balance* side for liabilities and equity. This matches their layout in the accounting equation where assets are on the left side of this equation, and liabilities and equity are on the right.

Recall that equity increases from revenues and owner investments and it decreases from expenses and owner withdrawals. These important equity relations are conveyed by expanding the accounting equation to include debits and credits in double-entry form as shown in Exhibit 3.4. The abbreviation "Dr." is for debit, and the abbreviation "Cr." is for credit.

Exhibit 3.4

Debit and Credit Effects for Expanded Accounting Equation

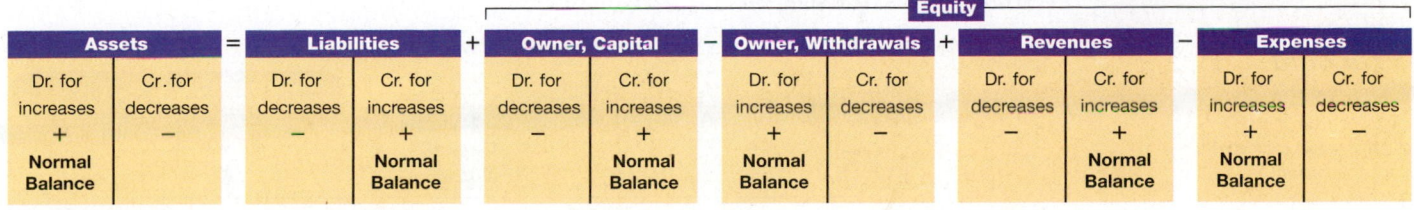

Assets		=	Liabilities		+	Owner, Capital		–	Owner, Withdrawals		+	Revenues		–	Expenses	
Dr. for increases	Cr. for decreases		Dr. for decreases	Cr. for increases		Dr. for decreases	Cr. for increases		Dr. for increases	Cr. for decreases		Dr. for decreases	Cr. for increases		Dr. for increases	Cr. for decreases
+	–		–	+		–	+		+	–		–	+		+	–
Normal Balance				**Normal Balance**			**Normal Balance**		**Normal Balance**				**Normal Balance**		**Normal Balance**	

Increases (credits) to capital and revenues *increase* equity; increases (debits) to withdrawals and expenses *decrease* equity. The normal balance of each account (asset, liability, capital, withdrawals, revenue, or expense) refers to the left or right (debit or credit) side where *increases* are recorded.

Recording Transactions—An Illustration

LO3 Post transactions in T-accounts.

We return to the activities of FastForward to show how to record transactions in T-account form. Study each transaction thoroughly before proceeding to the next. The first 11 transactions are from Chapter 2, and we analyze five additional December transactions of FastForward (numbered 12 through 16) that were omitted earlier.

Here is a simple three-step process to follow to record a transaction in T-account form. We use the letters *TAP* to stand for the steps: Transaction, Analysis, and Post.

1. *Transaction:* Determine which accounts are affected by the transaction.
2. *Analysis:* Analyze the transaction using the accounting equation.
   a. Label the affected accounts as either assets, liabilities, or equity (including revenues and expenses).
   b. Determine whether the transaction increases or decreases the affected accounts.
   c. Verify the accounting equation remains in balance.
3. *Post:* Using the rules of debit and credit, post the transactions to T-accounts. To **post** means to make an entry in an account. We summarize the rules of debit and credit in Exhibit 3.5.

Exhibit 3.5

Debit and Credit Rules

	Debit and Credit Rules		
Accounts		**Increase (normal bal.)**	**Decrease**
Asset		Debit	Credit
Liability		Credit	Debit
Capital		Credit	Debit
Withdrawals		Debit	Credit
Revenue		Credit	Debit
Expense		Debit	Credit

1. Investment by Owner

FASTForward

Total debits equal total credits for each transaction.

Transaction: Chuck Taylor invests $30,000 cash in FastForward.

Analysis:

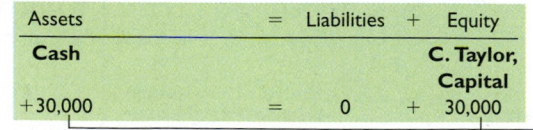

Assets	=	Liabilities	+	Equity
Cash				**C. Taylor, Capital**
+30,000	=	0	+	30,000

Cash and C. Taylor, Capital increase by $30,000. Cash is debited and C. Taylor, Capital is credited.

Post in T-accounts:

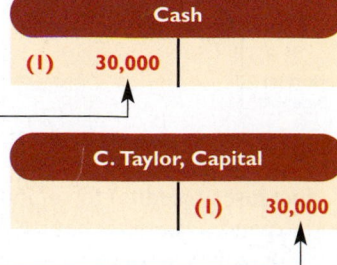

Cash	
(1) 30,000	

C. Taylor, Capital	
	(1) 30,000

2. Purchase Supplies for Cash

Transaction: FastForward pays $2,500 cash for supplies.

Analysis:

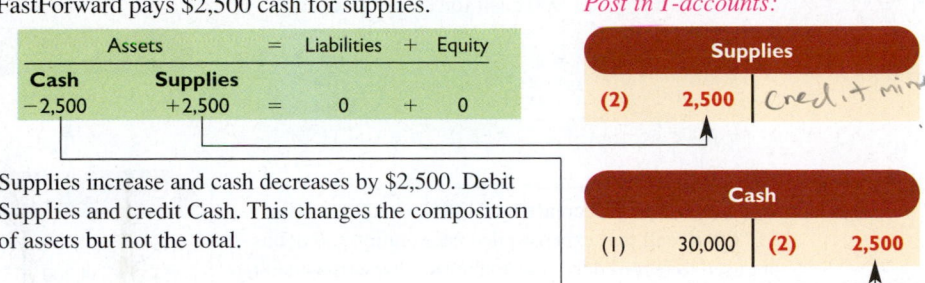

Supplies increase and cash decreases by $2,500. Debit Supplies and credit Cash. This changes the composition of assets but not the total.

3. Purchase Equipment for Cash

Transaction: FastForward pays $26,000 cash for equipment.

Analysis:

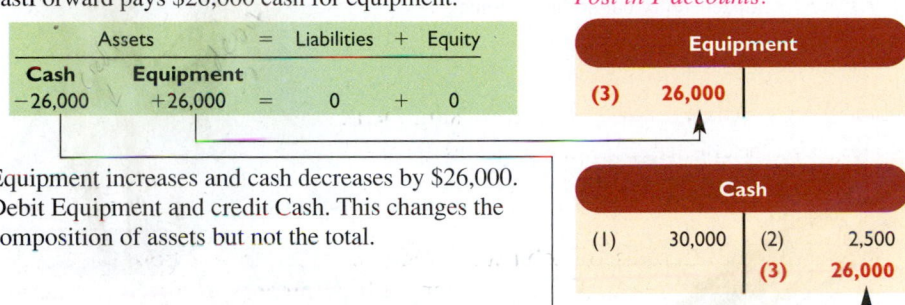

Equipment increases and cash decreases by $26,000. Debit Equipment and credit Cash. This changes the composition of assets but not the total.

4. Purchase Supplies on Credit

Transaction: FastForward purchases $7,100 of supplies on credit from a supplier.

Analysis:

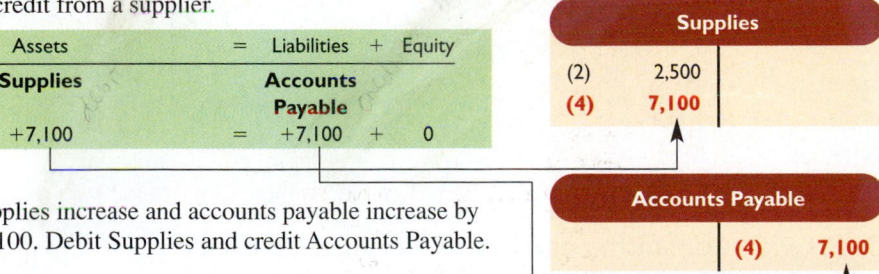

Supplies increase and accounts payable increase by $7,100. Debit Supplies and credit Accounts Payable.

5. Provide Services for Cash

Transaction: FastForward provides consulting services and immediately collects $4,200 cash.

Analysis:

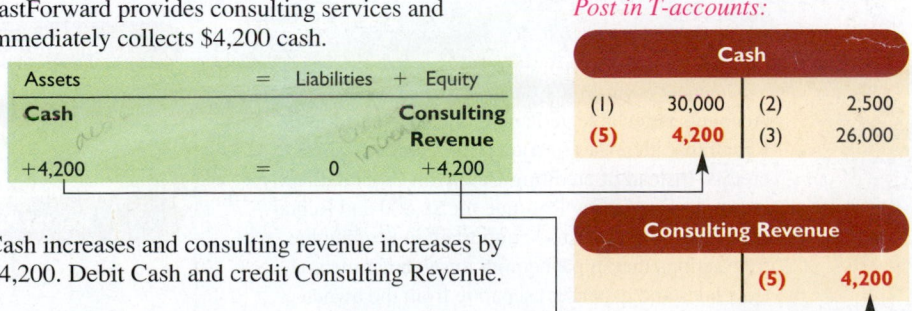

Cash increases and consulting revenue increases by $4,200. Debit Cash and credit Consulting Revenue.

6. Payment of Expense in Cash

Transaction: FastForward pays $1,000 cash for December rent.

Analysis:

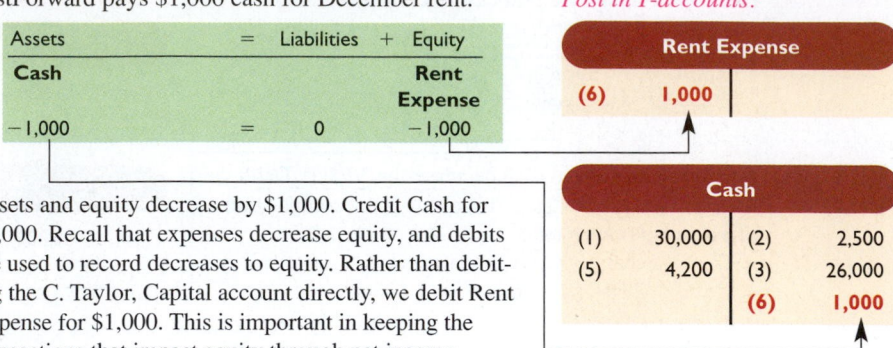

Assets and equity decrease by $1,000. Credit Cash for $1,000. Recall that expenses decrease equity, and debits are used to record decreases to equity. Rather than debiting the C. Taylor, Capital account directly, we debit Rent Expense for $1,000. This is important in keeping the transactions that impact equity through net income (revenues and expenses) separate from the owner transactions (withdrawals and contributions) that impact equity but not net income.

7. Payment of Expense in Cash

Transaction: FastForward pays $700 cash for employee salaries.

Analysis:

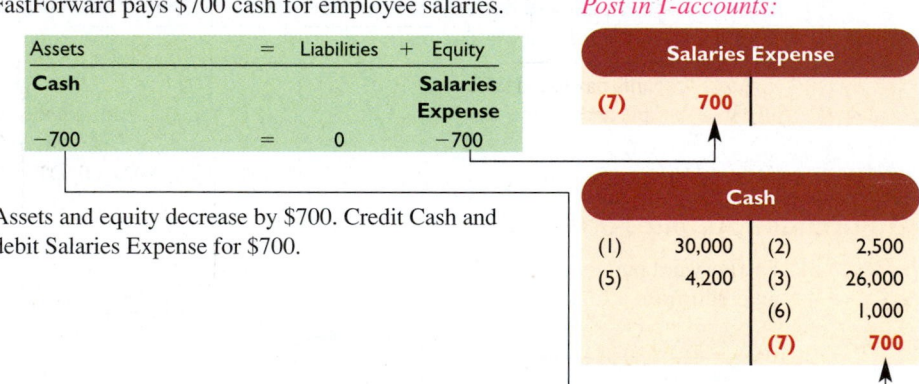

Assets and equity decrease by $700. Credit Cash and debit Salaries Expense for $700.

8. Provide Consulting and Rental Services on Credit

Transaction: FastForward provides consulting services of $1,600 and rents its test facilities for $300. The customer is billed $1,900 for these services.

Analysis:

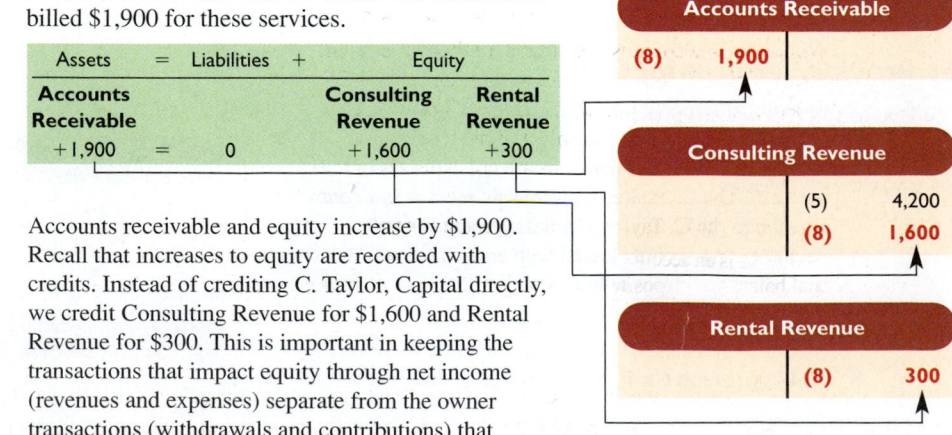

Accounts receivable and equity increase by $1,900. Recall that increases to equity are recorded with credits. Instead of crediting C. Taylor, Capital directly, we credit Consulting Revenue for $1,600 and Rental Revenue for $300. This is important in keeping the transactions that impact equity through net income (revenues and expenses) separate from the owner transactions (withdrawals and contributions) that impact equity but not net income.

9. Receipt of Cash on Account

Transaction: FastForward receives $1,900 cash from the client billed in transaction 8.

Analysis:

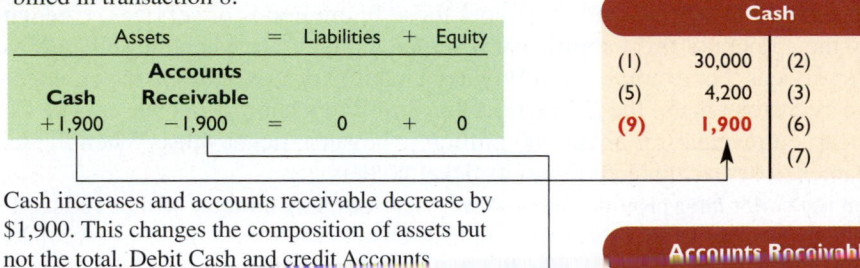

Cash increases and accounts receivable decrease by $1,900. This changes the composition of assets but not the total. Debit Cash and credit Accounts Receivable.

10. Partial Payment of Accounts Payable

Transaction: FastForward pays the supplier $900 cash toward the account payable from transaction 4.

Analysis:

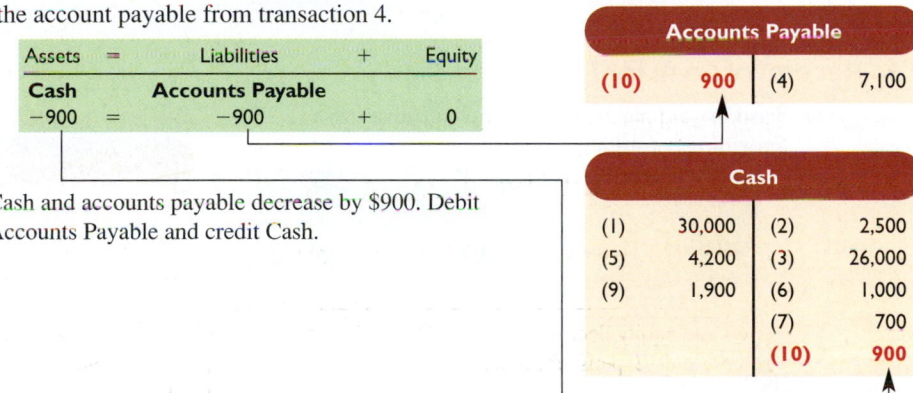

Cash and accounts payable decrease by $900. Debit Accounts Payable and credit Cash.

11. Withdrawal of Cash by Owner

Transaction: Chuck Taylor withdraws $200 cash from FastForward for personal use.

Analysis:

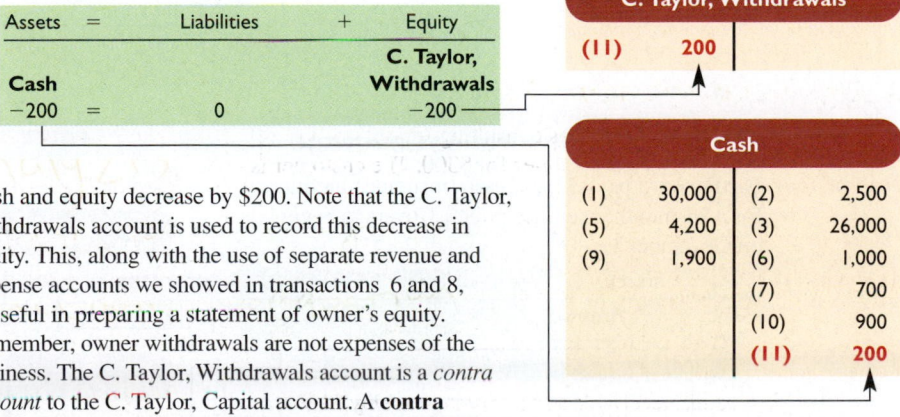

Cash and equity decrease by $200. Note that the C. Taylor, Withdrawals account is used to record this decrease in equity. This, along with the use of separate revenue and expense accounts we showed in transactions 6 and 8, is useful in preparing a statement of owner's equity. Remember, owner withdrawals are not expenses of the business. The C. Taylor, Withdrawals account is a *contra account* to the C. Taylor, Capital account. A **contra account** is an account linked with another account. Its normal balance is opposite that of the linked account's balance.

Prepayments So far we have used the transactions from Chapter 2 to show how to post transactions to T-accounts. We now introduce five additional transactions of FastForward for December. The first two of these transactions illustrate how to account for *prepayments* of cash.

Cash collected before services are provided   Sometimes customers pay in advance for products or services to be provided later. Examples include magazine subscriptions collected in advance by a publisher, gift certificates by stores, and season ticket sales by sports teams. When this happens, the seller owes the customer those future goods or services. **Unearned revenue** refers to the amount of this liability that is settled in the future when the seller delivers goods or provides services. For example, Best Buy has a liability of $332 million for unredeemed gift certificates; as customers use the gift certificates, Best Buy's liability decreases. The Chicago Bears have unearned revenues of about $60 million in advance ticket sales. When the team plays its home games, it settles this liability to its ticket holders.

When the seller later provides the goods or services, this liability will be reduced and revenue will be recorded. We show this process in later chapters.

Cash paid before services are received   Sometimes a business pays in advance for goods or services to be provided later. Common examples of these prepaid amounts include prepaid rent and prepaid insurance. **Prepaid assets** (also called *prepaid expenses*) refers to amounts a business has paid in advance for future goods or services. These prepayments are assets, since the business expects future benefits from the prepayments. These prepaid assets become expenses as the goods or services are provided, a process we show in later chapters.

12. Receipt of Cash for Future Services

Transaction: FastForward receives $3,000 cash in advance of providing consulting services to a customer.

Post in T-accounts:

Analysis:

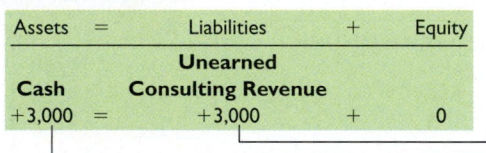

Assets	=	Liabilities	+	Equity
Cash		**Unearned Consulting Revenue**		
+3,000	=	+3,000	+	0

Accepting $3,000 cash obligates FastForward to perform future services. Unearned revenue is a liability created when customers pay in advance for services (or products). Cash increases and liabilities increase by $3,000. Debit Cash and credit Unearned Consulting Revenue.

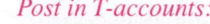

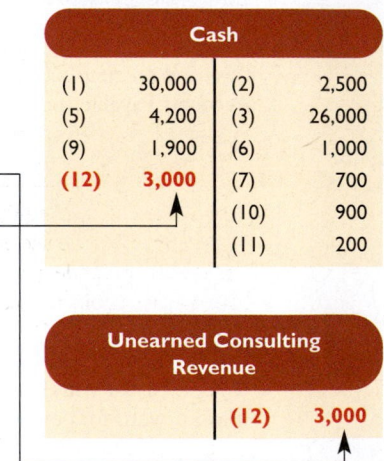

Cash			
(1)	30,000	(2)	2,500
(5)	4,200	(3)	26,000
(9)	1,900	(6)	1,000
(12)	3,000	(7)	700
		(10)	900
		(11)	200

Unearned Consulting Revenue			
		(12)	3,000

13. Pay Cash for Future Insurance Coverage

Transaction: FastForward pays $2,400 cash (insurance premium) for a 24-month insurance policy. Coverage begins on December 1.

Post in T-accounts:

Analysis:

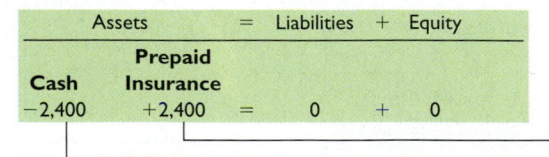

Assets		=	Liabilities	+	Equity
Cash	**Prepaid Insurance**				
−2,400	+2,400	=	0	+	0

This prepayment provides FastForward with insurance coverage over the next 24 months. This insurance coverage is an asset. The asset prepaid insurance increases by $2,400, and cash decreases by $2,400. This changes the composition of assets but not the total. Debit Prepaid Insurance and credit Cash.

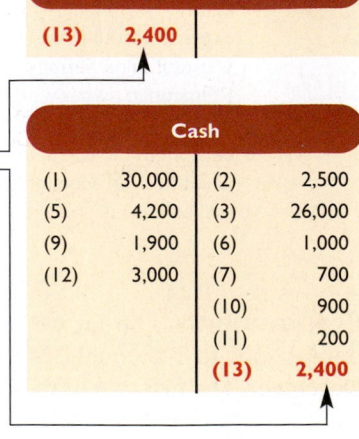

Prepaid Insurance			
(13)	2,400		

Cash			
(1)	30,000	(2)	2,500
(5)	4,200	(3)	26,000
(9)	1,900	(6)	1,000
(12)	3,000	(7)	700
		(10)	900
		(11)	200
		(13)	2,400

14. Purchase Supplies for Cash

Transaction: FastForward pays $120 cash for supplies.

Analysis:

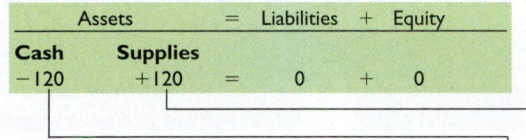

Assets		=	Liabilities	+	Equity
Cash	**Supplies**				
−120	+120	=	0	+	0

Supplies increase and cash decreases by $120. This changes the composition of assets but not the total. Debit Supplies and credit Cash.

Post in T-accounts:

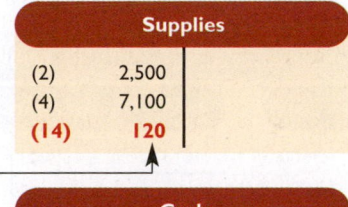

Supplies

(2)	2,500
(4)	7,100
(14)	**120**

Cash

(1)	30,000	(2)	2,500
(5)	4,200	(3)	26,000
(9)	1,900	(6)	1,000
(12)	3,000	(7)	700
		(10)	900
		(11)	200
		(13)	2,400
		(14)	**120**

15. Payment of Expense in Cash

Transaction: FastForward pays $230 cash for December utilities expense.

Analysis:

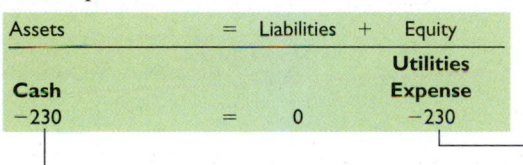

Assets	=	Liabilities	+	Equity
				Utilities Expense
Cash				
−230	=	0		−230

Cash decreases and equity decreases by $230. Remember that we use expense accounts to record transactions that decrease equity through net income. As debits reduce equity, debit Utilities Expense and credit Cash.

Post in T-accounts:

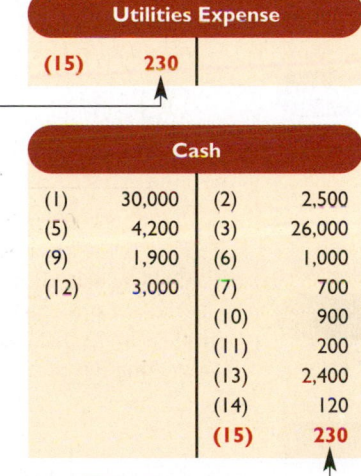

Utilities Expense

(15)	**230**

Cash

(1)	30,000	(2)	2,500
(5)	4,200	(3)	26,000
(9)	1,900	(6)	1,000
(12)	3,000	(7)	700
		(10)	900
		(11)	200
		(13)	2,400
		(14)	120
		(15)	**230**

16. Payment of Expense in Cash

Transaction: FastForward pays $700 cash in employee salaries for work performed in the latter part of December.

Analysis:

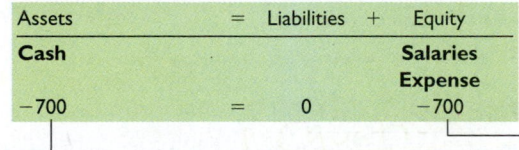

Assets	=	Liabilities	+	Equity
Cash				**Salaries Expense**
−700	=	0		−700

Cash decreases and equity decreases (through expenses) by $700. Debit Salaries Expense and credit Cash.

Post in T-accounts:

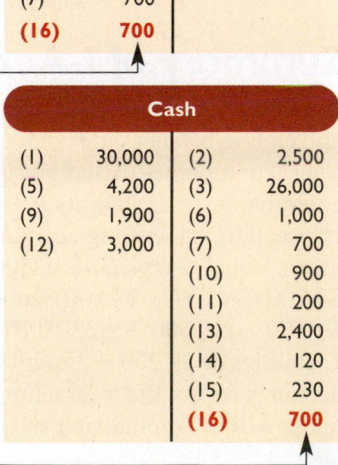

Salaries Expense

(7)	700
(16)	**700**

Cash

(1)	30,000	(2)	2,500
(5)	4,200	(3)	26,000
(9)	1,900	(6)	1,000
(12)	3,000	(7)	700
		(10)	900
		(11)	200
		(13)	2,400
		(14)	120
		(15)	230
		(16)	**700**

Exhibit 3.6

T-Accounts for FastForward

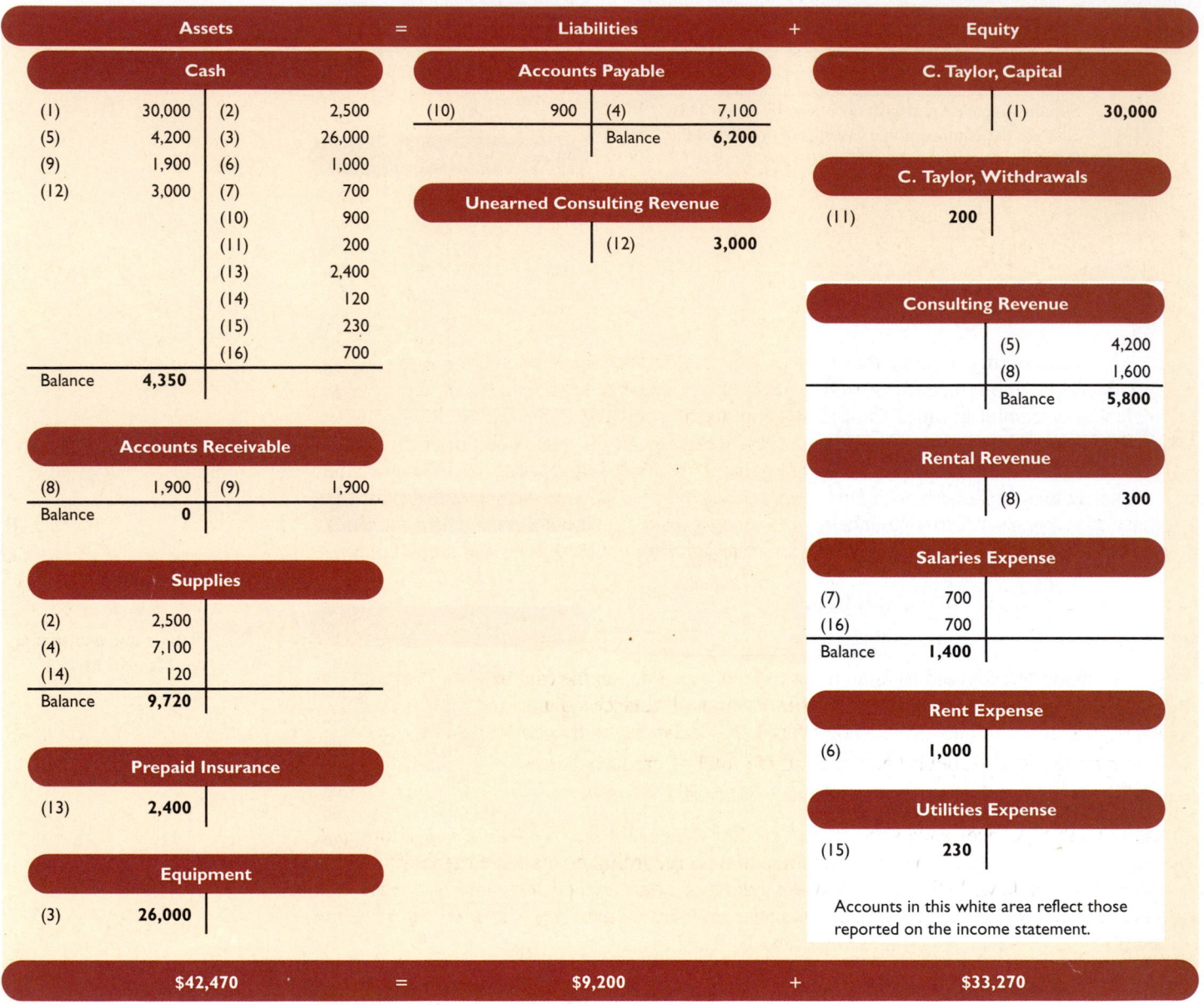

Assets			=	Liabilities		+	Equity	

Cash

(1)	30,000	(2)	2,500
(5)	4,200	(3)	26,000
(9)	1,900	(6)	1,000
(12)	3,000	(7)	700
		(10)	900
		(11)	200
		(13)	2,400
		(14)	120
		(15)	230
		(16)	700
Balance	4,350		

Accounts Receivable

(8)	1,900	(9)	1,900
Balance	0		

Supplies

(2)	2,500		
(4)	7,100		
(14)	120		
Balance	9,720		

Prepaid Insurance

(13)	2,400	

Equipment

(3)	26,000	

Accounts Payable

(10)	900	(4)	7,100
		Balance	6,200

Unearned Consulting Revenue

	(12)	3,000

C. Taylor, Capital

	(1)	30,000

C. Taylor, Withdrawals

(11)	200	

Consulting Revenue

	(5)	4,200
	(8)	1,600
	Balance	5,800

Rental Revenue

	(8)	300

Salaries Expense

(7)	700	
(16)	700	
Balance	1,400	

Rent Expense

(6)	1,000	

Utilities Expense

(15)	230	

Accounts in this white area reflect those reported on the income statement.

$42,470	=	$9,200	+	$33,270

Summary of T-Account Illustration

Exhibit 3.6 shows the T-accounts of FastForward after all 16 transactions are posted to T-accounts and ending balances are computed. The numbers in brackets in each of the T-accounts refer to the transaction number from our illustration. The accounts are grouped according to the accounting equation: assets, liabilities, and equity. Note several important points. First, as with each transaction, the ending account balances must obey the accounting equation. Specifically, total assets equal $42,470 ($4,350 + $0 + $9,720 + $2,400 + $26,000); total liabilities equal $9,200 ($6,200 + $3,000); and total equity equals $33,270 ($30,000 − $200 + $5,800 + $300 − $1,400 − $1,000 − $230). These numbers prove the accounting equation: Assets of $42,470 = Liabilities of $9,200 + Equity of $33,270. Second, the capital, withdrawals, revenue, and expense accounts reflect the transactions that change equity. Third, the revenue and expense account balances will be summarized and reported in the income statement.

HOW YOU DOIN'?   Answers—p. 61

4. What types of transactions increase equity? What types decrease equity?

5. Why are accounting systems called *double entry*?

6. For each transaction, double-entry accounting requires which of the following: (*a*) Debits to asset accounts must create credits to liability or equity accounts, (*b*) a debit to a liability account must create a credit to an asset account, or (*c*) total debits must equal total credits.

7. An owner invests $15,000 cash along with equipment having a market value of $23,000 in a company. Describe how T-accounts will be used to record this transaction.

8. Matt Waller receives $3,000 cash for his consulting services provided. Describe how T-accounts will be used to record this transaction.

Trial Balance

Double-entry accounting requires the sum of debit account balances to equal the sum of credit account balances. A trial balance is used to verify this. A **trial balance** is a list of accounts and their balances at a point in time. The accounts are usually ordered according to the accounting equation in Exhibit 3.4. Account balances are reported in the appropriate debit or credit column of a trial balance. Exhibit 3.7 shows the trial balance for FastForward after its 16 transactions have been recorded in T-accounts. (This is an *unadjusted* trial balance—Chapter 5 explains the necessary adjustments.) A trial balance is *not* a financial statement but a mechanism for checking the equality of debits and credits. Financial statements do not have debit and credit columns.

Preparing a Trial Balance

Preparing a trial balance involves three steps:

LO4 Prepare and explain the use of a trial balance.

1. List each account title and its amount (from the T-accounts) in the trial balance. If an account has a zero balance, list it with a zero in its normal balance column (or omit it entirely). Investigate any accounts that do not have normal balances, as this could indicate errors.
2. Compute the total of debit balances and the total of credit balances.
3. Verify (*prove*) total debit balances equal total credit balances.

The total of debit balances equals the total of credit balances for the trial balance in Exhibit 3.7. Equality of these two totals does not guarantee that no recording errors were made. For example, the column totals will still be equal when a debit or credit of a correct amount is made to a wrong account. Another error that does not cause unequal column totals is when equal debits and credits of an incorrect amount are recorded.

Searching for and Correcting Errors   If the trial balance does not balance (its column totals are not equal), the error (or errors) must be found. Follow these steps to search for an error:

1. Verify that the trial balance columns are correctly added.
2. Verify that account balances are accurately entered from the T-account to the trial balance.
3. Check to see whether a debit (or credit) balance is mistakenly listed in the trial balance as a credit (or debit).
4. Recompute each account balance in the T-accounts.
5. Verify that the debits equal the credits for each transaction.

At this point the error should be uncovered.[1]

---

[1] *Transposition* occurs when two digits are switched, or transposed, within a number. If transposition is the only error, it yields a difference between the two trial balance totals that is evenly divisible by 9. For example, assume that a $691 debit in an entry is incorrectly posted to the ledger as $619. Total credits are then larger than total debits by $72 ($691 − $619). The $72 error is evenly divisible by 9 (72/9 = 8). The first digit of the quotient (in our example it is 8) equals the difference between the digits of the two transposed numbers (the 9 and the 1).

Exhibit 3.7

Trial Balance (unadjusted)

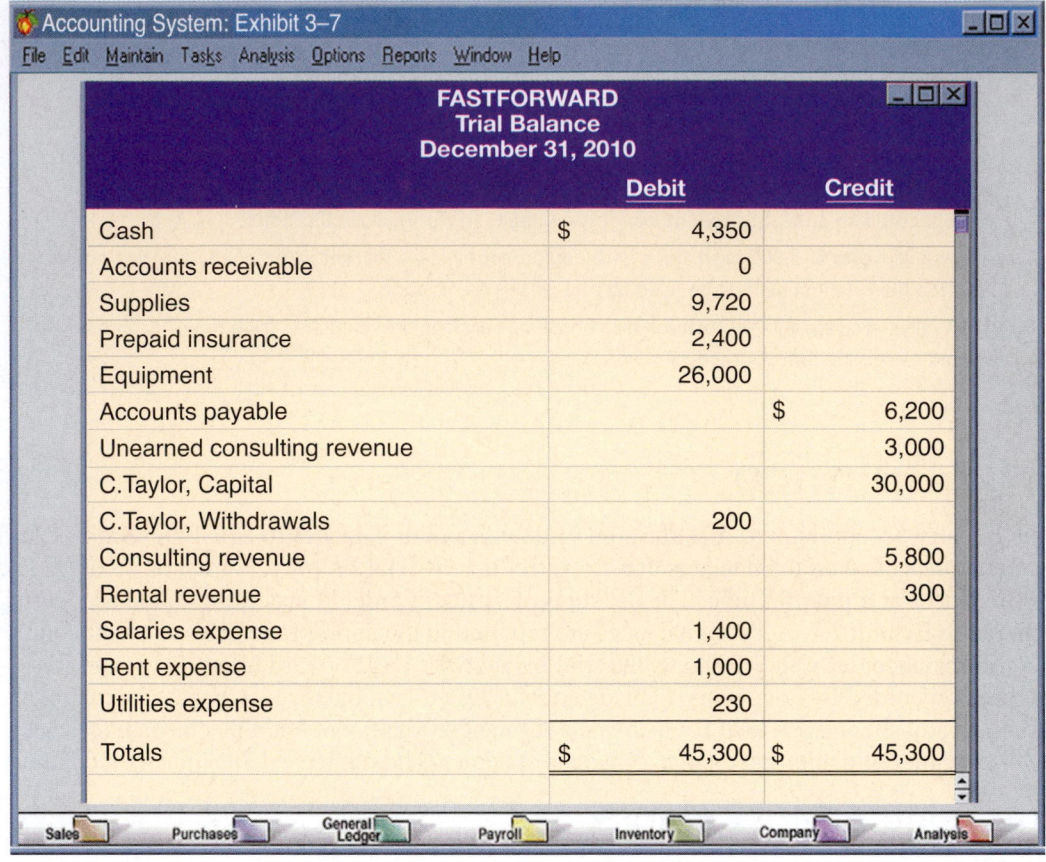

Accounting System: Exhibit 3–7

File Edit Maintain Tasks Analysis Options Reports Window Help

FASTFORWARD
Trial Balance
December 31, 2010

	Debit	Credit
Cash	$ 4,350	
Accounts receivable	0	
Supplies	9,720	
Prepaid insurance	2,400	
Equipment	26,000	
Accounts payable		$ 6,200
Unearned consulting revenue		3,000
C.Taylor, Capital		30,000
C.Taylor, Withdrawals	200	
Consulting revenue		5,800
Rental revenue		300
Salaries expense	1,400	
Rent expense	1,000	
Utilities expense	230	
Totals	$ 45,300	$ 45,300

Sales   Purchases   General Ledger   Payroll   Inventory   Company   Analysis

Using a Trial Balance to Prepare Financial Statements

L05 Prepare financial statements from a trial balance.

This section shows how to prepare *financial statements* from the trial balance in Exhibit 3.7 and information on the December transactions of FastForward. The statements differ from those in Chapter 2 because of several additional transactions. These statements are also more precisely called *unadjusted statements* because we need to make some further accounting adjustments (described in Chapter 5).

Income Statement   An income statement reports a company's revenues earned minus its expenses over a period of time. FastForward's income statement for December is shown at the top of Exhibit 3.8. Information about revenues and expenses is taken from the trial balance in Exhibit 3.7. The income statement reports total revenues ($6,100) and total expenses ($2,630). Net income (revenues minus expenses) of $3,470 is reported at the bottom of the statement. Owner investments and withdrawals are *not* part of income.

Statement of Owner's Equity   The statement of owner's equity reports information about how equity changes over the reporting period. FastForward's statement of owner's equity is the second report in Exhibit 3.8. It shows the $30,000 owner investment, the $3,470 of net income, the $200 withdrawal, and the $33,270 end-of-period (capital) balance. (The beginning balance in the statement of owner's equity is rarely zero; an exception is for the first period of operations. The beginning capital balance in January 2011 is $33,270, which is December 2010's ending balance.)

Balance Sheet   The balance sheet reports the financial position of a company at a point in time, usually at the end of a month, quarter, or year. FastForward's balance sheet is the third

Exhibit 3.8

Financial Statements and
Their Links

FASTFORWARD
Income Statement
For Month Ended December 31, 2010

Revenues

Consulting revenue	$ 5,800	
Rental revenue	300	
Total revenues		$ 6,100

Expenses

Rent expense	1,000	
Salaries expense	1,400	
Utilities expense	230	
Total expenses		2,630
Net income		**$ 3,470**

FASTFORWARD
Statement of Owner's Equity
For Month Ended December 31, 2010

C. Taylor, Capital, December 1, 2010		$ 0
Plus: Investments by owner	$30,000	
Net income	**3,470**	33,470
		33,470
Less: Withdrawals by owner		200
C. Taylor, Capital, December 31, 2010		**$33,270**

Arrow lines show how the statements are linked. Net income for the period updates the owner's equity at the end of the period. The ending owner's equity appears on the balance sheet at the end of the period.

FASTFORWARD
Balance Sheet
December 31, 2010

Assets		Liabilities	
Cash	$ 4,350	Accounts payable	$ 6,200
Supplies	9,720	Unearned revenue	3,000
Prepaid insurance	2,400	Total liabilities	9,200
Equipment	26,000	**Equity**	
		C. Taylor, Capital	**33,270**
Total assets	$42,470	Total liabilities and equity	$ 42,470

report in Exhibit 3.8. This statement refers to financial condition at the close of business on December 31, 2010. The left side of the balance sheet lists FastForward's assets: cash, supplies, prepaid insurance, and equipment. The upper right side of the balance sheet shows that it owes $6,200 to creditors and $3,000 in services to customers who paid in advance. The equity section shows an ending capital balance of $33,270. Note the link between the ending balance of C. Taylor, on the statement of owner's equity and its disclosure on the balance sheet. This means that FastForward's financial performance for December updates its financial position at the end of December. This updating is a key feature of accounting.

Presentation Issues   Dollar signs are not used in T-accounts, but they do appear in financial statements. The usual practice is to put dollar signs beside only the first and last numbers in a column. **Best Buy**'s financial statements in Appendix A show this. Companies also commonly round amounts in reports to the nearest dollar, or even to a higher level. Best Buy is typical of many large companies in that it rounds dollar amounts in its financial statements to the nearest million. This decision is based on the perceived impact of rounding for users' business decisions.

HOW YOU DOIN'?   Answers—p. 61

9. Where are dollar signs typically entered in financial statements?

10. Describe the link between the income statement and the statement of owner's equity.

11. Explain the link between the balance sheet and the statement of owner's equity.

12. Define and describe revenues and expenses.

13. Define and describe assets, liabilities, and equity.

Demonstration Problem

(This problem extends the demonstration problem of Chapter 2.) After several months of planning, Jasmine Worthy started a haircutting business called Expressions. The following events occurred during its first month.

a. On August 1, Worthy invested $3,000 cash and $15,000 of equipment in Expressions.

b. On August 2, Expressions paid $600 cash for furniture for the shop.

c. On August 3, Expressions paid $500 cash to rent space in a strip mall for August.

d. On August 4, it purchased $1,200 of equipment on credit for the shop (using an account payable).

e. On August 5, Expressions opened for business. Cash received from services provided in the first week and a half of business (ended August 15) is $825.

f. On August 15, it provided $100 of haircutting services on account.

g. On August 17, it received a $100 check for services previously rendered on account.

h. On August 17, it paid $125 to an assistant for working during the grand opening.

i. Cash received from services provided during the second half of August is $930.

j. On August 31, it paid $400 toward the account payable entered into on August 4.

k. On August 31, Worthy withdrew $900 cash for personal use.

Required

1. Post each transaction in the appropriate T-account. Open T-accounts for the following accounts: Cash; Accounts Receivable; Furniture; Store Equipment; Accounts Payable; J. Worthy, Capital; J. Worthy, Withdrawals; Haircutting Services Revenue; Wages Expense; Rent Expense.

2. Prepare a trial balance from the T-accounts as of August 31.

3. Prepare an income statement for August.

4. Prepare a statement of owner's equity for August.

5. Prepare a balance sheet as of August 31.

Planning the Solution

- Analyze each transaction.
- Post each transaction in the appropriate T-accounts.
- Calculate each ending account balance and list the accounts with their balances on a trial balance.
- Verify that the total debits in the trial balance equal the total credits.
- To prepare the income statement, identify revenues and expenses. List those items on the statement, compute the difference between total revenues and total expenses, and label the result as net income or net loss.
- Use information in the trial balance to prepare the statement of stockholder's equity.
- Use information in the trial balance to prepare the balance sheet.

Solution to Demonstration Problem

1. Post each transaction to the appropriate T-account.

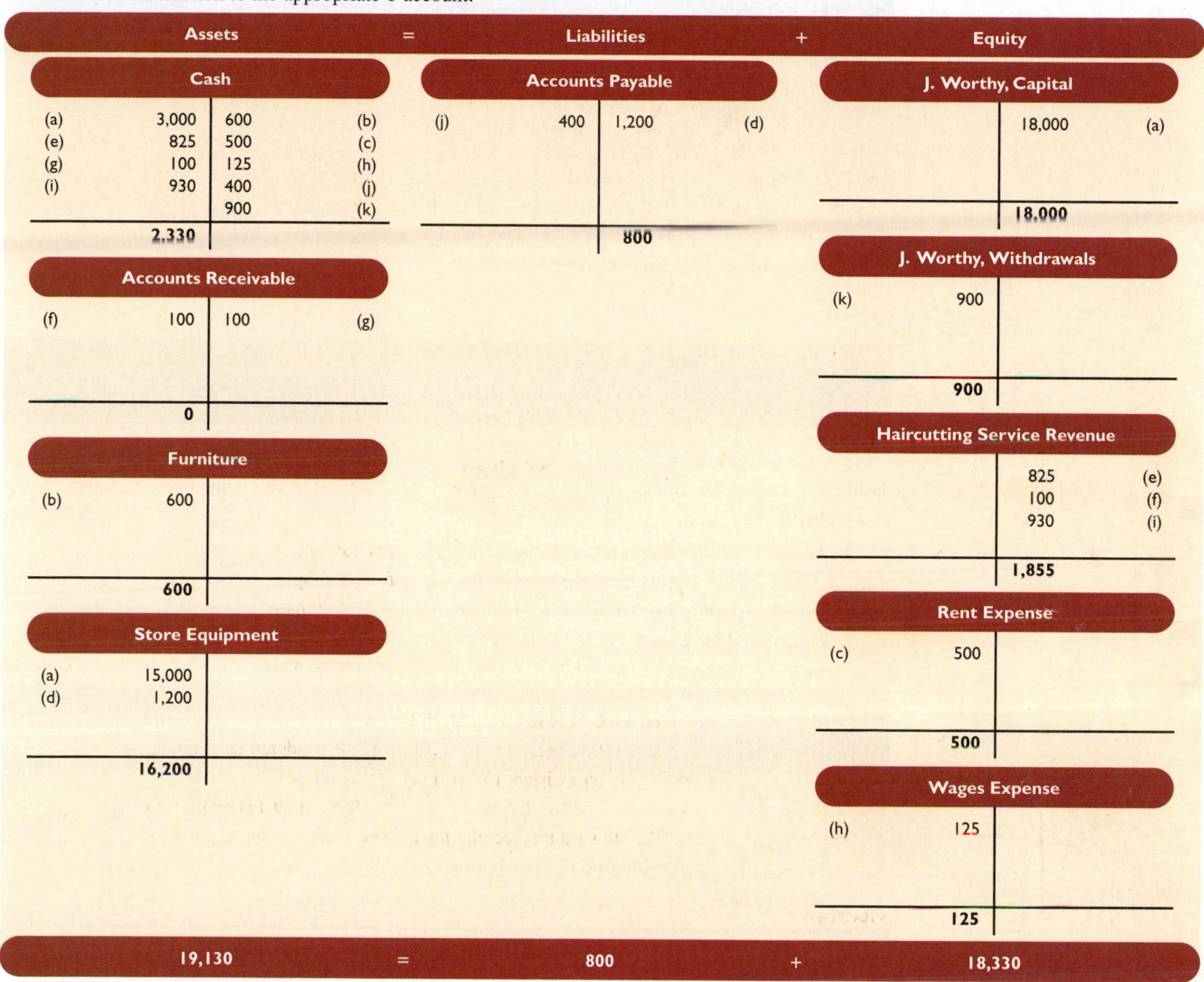

| Assets | = | Liabilities | + | Equity |

Cash

(a)	3,000	600	(b)
(e)	825	500	(c)
(g)	100	125	(h)
(i)	930	400	(j)
		900	(k)
	2,330		

Accounts Receivable

| (f) | 100 | 100 | (g) |
| | **0** | | |

Furniture

| (b) | 600 | |
| | **600** | |

Store Equipment

(a)	15,000	
(d)	1,200	
	16,200	

Accounts Payable

| (j) | 400 | 1,200 | (d) |
| | | **800** | |

J. Worthy, Capital

| | 18,000 | (a) |
| | **18,000** | |

J. Worthy, Withdrawals

| (k) | 900 | |
| | **900** | |

Haircutting Service Revenue

	825	(e)
	100	(f)
	930	(i)
	1,855	

Rent Expense

| (c) | 500 | |
| | **500** | |

Wages Expense

| (h) | 125 | |
| | **125** | |

| **19,130** | = | **800** | + | **18,330** |

2. Prepare a trial balance from the T-accounts.

EXPRESSIONS
Trial Balance
August 31, 2010

	Debit	Credit
Cash	$ 2,330	
Accounts receivable	0	
Furniture	600	
Store equipment	16,200	
Accounts payable		$ 800
J. Worthy, Capital, August 1		18,000
J. Worthy, Withdrawals	900	
Haircutting service revenue		1,855
Wages expense	125	
Rent expense	500	
Totals	$20,655	$20,655

3.

EXPRESSIONS
Income Statement
For Month Ended August 31, 2010

Revenues		
Haircutting service revenue		$1,855
Operating expenses		
Rent expense	$500	
Wages expense	125	
Total operating expenses		625
Net income		$1,230

4.

EXPRESSIONS
Statement of Owner's Equity
For Month Ended August 31, 2010

J. Worthy, Capital, August 1			$ 0
Plus: Investments by owner	$18,000		
Net income	1,230	19,230	
		19,230	
Less: Withdrawals by owner		900	
J. Worthy, Capital, August 31		$18,330	

5.

EXPRESSIONS
Balance Sheet
August 31, 2010

Assets		Liabilities	
Cash	$ 2,330	Accounts payable	$ 800
Furniture	600	**Equity**	
Store equipment	16,200	J. Worthy, Capital, August 31	18,330
Total assets	$19,130	Total liabilities and equity	$19,130

Summary

LO1 **Describe a T-account and its use in recording transactions.** A T-account is a tool to show the effects of transactions and events on accounts. A T-account has both a left (debit) and right (credit) side.

LO2 **Define debits and credits and explain their role in double-entry accounting.** *Debit* refers to left, and *credit* refers to right. Debits increase assets, expenses, and withdrawals while credits decrease them. Credits increase liabilities, owner capital, and revenues; debits decrease them. Double-entry accounting means each transaction affects at least two accounts and has at least one debit and one credit. The system for recording debits and credits follows from the accounting equation. The left side of an account is the normal balance for assets, withdrawals, and expenses, and the right side is the normal balance for liabilities, capital, and revenues.

LO3 **Post transactions in T-accounts.** We analyze transactions using concepts of double-entry accounting. This analysis is performed by determining a transaction's effects on accounts. Posting is the process of entering dollar amounts for transactions in the appropriate debit or credit side of the affected T-accounts.

LO4 **Prepare and explain the use of a trial balance.** A trial balance is a list of accounts, showing their debit or credit balances in separate columns. The trial balance is useful in preparing financial statements and in revealing recordkeeping errors.

LO5 **Prepare financial statements from a trial balance.** The balance sheet, the statement of owner's equity and the income statement use the trial balance for their preparation.

1.

Assets	Liabilities	Equity
a,c,e	b,d	—

2. A T-account is a tool to record increases and decreases in a specific asset, liability, equity, revenue, or expense.

3. No. Debit and credit both can mean increase or decrease. The particular meaning in a circumstance depends on the *type of account*. For example, a debit increases the balance of asset, withdrawals, and expense accounts, but it decreases the balance of liability, capital, and revenue accounts.

4. Equity is increased by revenues and by owner investments. Equity is decreased by expenses and owner withdrawals.

5. The name *double entry* is used because all transactions affect at least two accounts. There must be at least one debit in one account and at least one credit in another account.

6. Answer is (*c*).

7. Debit Cash for $15,000, debit Store Equipment for $23,000, and credit Owner, Capital for $38,000.

8. Debit Cash for $3,000 and credit Consulting Services Revenue for $3,000.

9. At a minimum, dollar signs are placed beside the first and last numbers in a column. It is also common to place dollar signs beside any amount that appears after a ruled line to indicate that an addition or subtraction has occurred.

10. An income statement reports a company's revenues and expenses along with the resulting net income or loss. A statement of owner's equity reports changes in equity, including that from net income or loss. Both statements report transactions occurring over a period of time.

11. The balance sheet describes a company's financial position (assets, liabilities, and equity) at a point in time. The capital amount in the balance sheet is obtained from the statement of owner's equity.

12. Revenues are inflows of assets in exchange for products or services provided to customers as part of the main operations of a business. Expenses are outflows or the using up of assets that result from providing products or services to customers.

13. Assets are the resources a business owns or controls that carry expected future benefits. Liabilities are the obligations of a business, representing the claims of others against the assets of a business. Equity reflects the owner's claims on the assets of the business after deducting liabilities.

Key Terms

Account balance (p. 47) Difference between total debits and total credits (including the beginning balance for an account.

Contra account (p. 51) An account linked with another account. Its normal balance is opposite that of the other account's balance.

Credit (p. 46) Recorded on the right side; an entry that decreases asset and expense accounts, and increases liability, revenue and most equity accounts; abbreviated Cr.

Debit (p. 46) Recorded on the left side; an entry that increases asset and expense accounts, and decreases liability, revenue, and most equity accounts; abbreviated Dr.

Double-entry accounting (p. 47) Accounting system in which each transaction affects at least two accounts and has at least one debit and one credit.

Footing (p. 47) The total of a column of numbers.

Normal balance (p. 47) The side of a T-account on which increases are recorded. Asset accounts have normal debit balances. Liability and equity accounts have normal credit balances.

Post (p. 47) Make an entry in an account.

Prepaid assets (p. 52) Asset created when a company pays in advance for products or services to be received later. Also called prepaid expenses.

T-account (p. 46) Tool used to show the effects of transactions and events on individual accounts.

Trial balance (p. 55) List of accounts and their balances at a point in time; total debit balances equal total credit balances.

Unearned revenue (p. 52) Liability created when customers pay in advance of products or services to be provided later; earned when the products or services are later delivered.

Multiple Choice Quiz

Answers on p. 71   mhhe.com/wildCA2e

Additional Multiple Choice Quizzes are available at the book's Website.

1. Asset and expense accounts normally have
 a. Zero balances
 b. Credit balances
 c. Debit balances
 d. Negative balances

2. The accounting equation requires that if assets have a balance of $1 million and equity has a balance of $600,000, then liabilities must equal
   a. $600,000
   b. $1,600,000
   c. $0
   d. $400,000

3. Kirk Hinrich starts a new business by making an investment of $600,000 cash. Using the double-entry method, this increase in cash should be accounted for by
   a. Debiting Cash
   b. Crediting Cash
   c. Debiting Accounts Receivable
   d. Crediting Inventory

4. To record the payment of wages to its employees, Roy Beach Co. would
   a. Debit Wage Expense, debit Cash
   b. Debit Wage Expense, credit Cash
   c. Debit Cash, credit Wage Expense
   d. Credit Cash, credit Wage Expense

5. On May 1, Mattingly Lawn Service collected $2,500 cash from a customer in advance of five months of lawn service. Mattingly records this increase in liability as a
   a. Credit to Unearned Lawn Service Fees for $2,500.
   b. Debit to Lawn Service Fees Earned for $2,500.
   c. Credit to Cash for $2,500.
   d. Debit to Unearned Lawn Service Fees for $2,500.
   e. Credit to Capital for $2,500.

Discussion Questions

1. Provide the names of two (*a*) asset accounts, (*b*) liability accounts, and (*c*) equity accounts.

2. What is the normal balance for an asset account? What is the normal balance for a liability account?

3. What is an unearned revenue account? Why would customers pay in advance for services (or products) not yet received?

4. If assets are valuable resources and asset accounts have debit balances, why do expense accounts also have debit balances?

5. Why does the recordkeeper prepare a trial balance?

6. Identify the three basic financial statements of a business.

7. What information is reported in an income statement?

8. Why does the user of an income statement need to know the time period that it covers?

9. What information is reported in a balance sheet?

10. Define (*a*) *assets,* (*b*) *liabilities,* (*c*) *equity,* and (*d*) *net assets.*

11. Which financial statement is sometimes called the *statement of financial position*?

12. Review the **Best Buy** balance sheet in Appendix A. Identify three accounts on its balance sheet that carry debit balances and three accounts on its balance sheet that carry credit balances.

QUICK STUDY

QS 3–1
Identifying financial statement items
LO5

Identify the financial statement(s) where each of the following items appears. Use I for income statement, E for statement of owner's equity, and B for balance sheet.
   a. Cash withdrawal by owner
   b. Office equipment
   c. Accounts payable
   d. Cash
   e. Utilities expenses
   f. Office supplies
   g. Prepaid rent
   h. Unearned fees
   i. Service fees earned

QS 3–2
Linking debit or credit with
normal balance   **LO2**

Using Exhibit 3.4 as a guide, indicate whether a debit or credit *decreases* the normal balance of each of the following accounts.
   a. Repair Services Revenue
   b. Interest Payable
   c. Accounts Receivable
   d. Salaries Expense
   e. Owner Capital
   f. Prepaid Insurance
   g. Buildings
   h. Interest Revenue
   i. Owner Withdrawals
   j. Unearned Revenue
   k. Accounts Payable
   l. Office Supplies

QS 3–3
Analyzing debit or credit
by account   **LO2**

Using Exhibit 3.4 as a guide, identify whether a debit or credit yields the indicated change for each of the following accounts.
   a. To increase Land
   b. To decrease Cash
   c. To increase Utilities Expense
   d. To increase Fees Earned
   e. To decrease Unearned Revenue
   f. To decrease Prepaid Insurance
   g. To increase Accounts Payable
   h. To decrease Accounts Receivable
   i. To increase Owner Capital
   j. To increase Store Equipment

Identify the normal balance (debit or credit) for each of the following accounts.

a. Office Supplies   **d.** Wages Expense   **g.** Wages Payable
b. Owner Withdrawals   **e.** Cash   **h.** Building
c. Fees Earned   **f.** Prepaid Insurance **i.** Owner Capital

QS 3–4
Identifying normal balance   **LO2**

Post the following transactions to the appropriate T-accounts and compute the ending balance in each account.

a. On January 13, DeShawn Tyler opens a landscaping business called Elegant Lawns by investing $70,000 cash along with equipment having a $30,000 value.
b. On January 21, Elegant Lawns purchases office supplies on credit for $280.
c. On January 29, Elegant Lawns receives $7,800 cash for performing landscaping services.
d. On January 30, Elegant Lawns receives $1,000 cash in advance of providing landscaping services to a customer.

QS 3–5
Posting to T-accounts   **LO3**

Indicate the financial statement on which each of the following items appears. Use I for income statement, E for statement of owner's equity, and B for balance sheet.

a. Services Revenue   **e.** Equipment   **h.** Depreciation Expense
b. Wages Payable   **f.** Prepaid Insurance   **i.** Owner Withdrawals
c. Accounts Receivable **g.** Buildings   **j.** Office Supplies
d. Salaries Expense

QS 3–6
Classifying accounts in financial statements   **LO1**   **LO5**

Post the following transactions to the appropriate T-accounts.
a. Owner invests $10,000 cash to start an auto repair shop.
b. Received $3,500 cash for providing repair services.
c. Paid $1,700 cash for this month's rent.
d. Owner withdraws $500 cash for personal use.

QS 3–7
Posting to T-accounts   **LO3**

Foot the cash T-account below and compute its ending balance.

Cash	
40,000	15,000
7,800	6,200
1,000	

QS 3–8
Footing T-accounts   **LO3**

connect

For each of the following (1) identify the type of account as an asset, liability, equity, revenue, or expense, (2) enter *debit* (Dr.) or *credit* (Cr.) to identify the kind of entry that would increase the account balance, and (3) identify the normal balance of the account.

a. Accounts Payable   **e.** Owner Capital   **i.** Equipment
b. Postage Expense   **f.** Accounts Receivable   **j.** Fees Earned
c. Prepaid Insurance   **g.** Owner Withdrawals   **k.** Wages Expense
d. Land   **h.** Cash   **l.** Unearned Revenue

EXERCISES

Exercise 3–1
Identifying type and normal balances of accounts   **LO1**   **LO2**

Record the transactions below for Amena Company by recording debit and credit amounts directly in the following T-accounts: Cash; Accounts Receivable; Office Supplies; Office Equipment; Accounts Payable; A. Amena, Capital; A. Amena, Withdrawals; Fees Earned; and Rent Expense. Use the letters *a* through *i* to identify transactions in the T-accounts. Determine the ending balance of each T-account.

a. Ahmad Amena, owner, invested $13,325 cash in the business.
b. Purchased office supplies for $475 cash.

Exercise 3–2
Recording effects of transactions in T-accounts   **LO1**   **LO2**   **LO3**

c. Purchased $6,235 of office equipment on credit.

d. Received $2,000 cash as fees for services provided to a customer.

e. Paid $6,235 cash to settle the payable for the office equipment purchased in transaction *c*.

f. Billed a customer $3,300 as fees for services provided.

g. Paid $775 cash for the monthly rent.

h. Collected $2,300 cash toward the account receivable created in transaction *f*.

Check   Cash ending balance, $9,340

i. Ahmad Amena withdrew $800 cash for personal use.

Exercise 3-3

Preparing a trial balance

LO3   LO4

After recording the transactions of Exercise 3-2 in T-accounts and calculating the ending balance of each account, prepare a trial balance. Use May 31, 2010, as its report date.

Exercise 3-4

Analyzing revenue transactions

LO1   LO2   LO3

Examine the following transactions and identify those that create revenues for Valdez Services, a company owned by Brina Valdez. Use T-accounts to record the transactions that create revenues. Explain why the other transactions did not create revenues.

a. Brina Valdez invests $39,350 cash in the business.

b. Provided $2,300 of services on credit.

c. Provided services to a client and immediately received $875 cash.

d. Received $10,200 cash from a client in payment for services to be provided next year.

e. Received $3,500 cash from a client in partial payment of an account receivable.

f. Borrowed $120,000 cash from the bank by signing a promissory note.

Exercise 3-5

Analyzing expense transactions

LO1   LO2   LO3

Examine the following transactions and identify those that create expenses for Valdez Services. Use T-accounts to record the transactions that create expenses. Explain why the other transactions did not create expenses.

a. Paid $12,200 cash for office supplies that were purchased on account more than 1 year ago.

b. Paid $1,233 cash for the receptionist's salary for the two weeks just completed.

c. Paid $39,200 cash for equipment.

d. Paid $870 cash for this month's utilities.

e. Owner (B. Valdez) withdrew $4,500 cash for personal use.

Exercise 3-6

Analyzing changes in equity   **LO3**

Compute the missing amount in each of the following separate companies *a* through *d*.

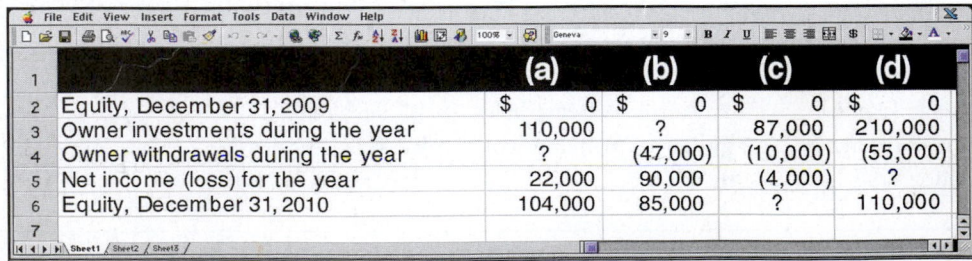

	(a)	(b)	(c)	(d)
Equity, December 31, 2009	$ 0	$ 0	$ 0	$ 0
Owner investments during the year	110,000	?	87,000	210,000
Owner withdrawals during the year	?	(47,000)	(10,000)	(55,000)
Net income (loss) for the year	22,000	90,000	(4,000)	?
Equity, December 31, 2010	104,000	85,000	?	110,000

Exercise 3-7

Interpreting and describing transactions from T-accounts   **LO3**

Assume the following T-accounts reflect Belle Co.'s accounts and that seven transactions are posted to them. Provide a short description of each of the seven transactions *a* through *g* of Belle Co. Include dollar amounts in your descriptions.

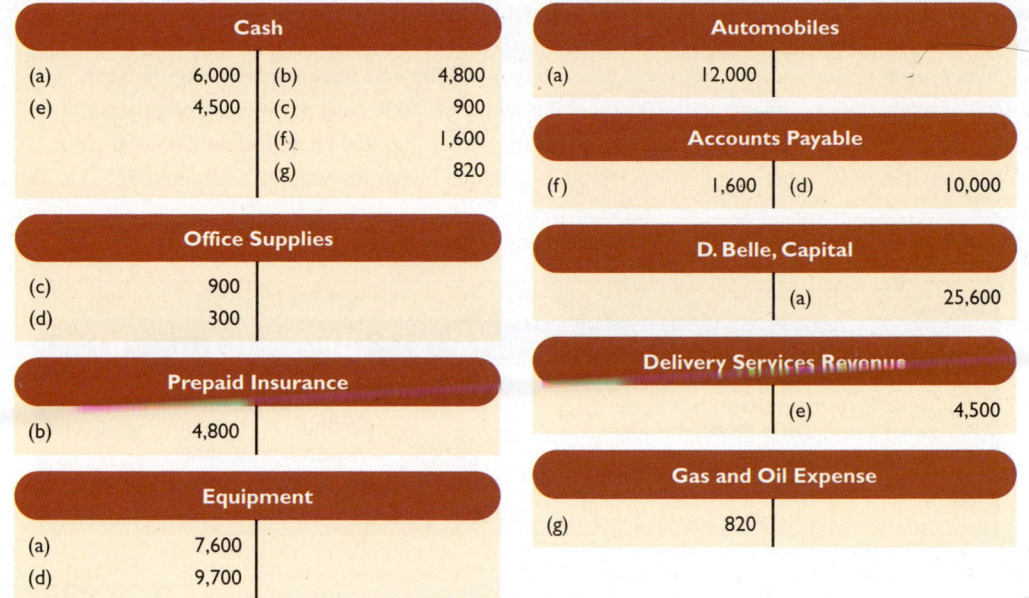

Cash

(a)	6,000	(b)	4,800
(e)	4,500	(c)	900
		(f)	1,600
		(g)	820

Office Supplies

(c)	900
(d)	300

Prepaid Insurance

(b)	4,800

Equipment

(a)	7,600
(d)	9,700

Automobiles

(a)	12,000

Accounts Payable

(f)	1,600	(d)	10,000

D. Belle, Capital

		(a)	25,600

Delivery Services Revenue

		(e)	4,500

Gas and Oil Expense

(g)	820

Refer to the T-accounts in Exercise 3-7. Compute ending balances and prepare Belle Company's income statement and statement of owner's equity for the month ended December 31, 2010.

Exercise 3-8
Preparing an income statement and statement of owner's equity **LO5**

Refer to the T-accounts in Exercise 3-7. Compute ending balances and prepare Belle Company's balance sheet. Assume the balance sheet is dated December 31, 2010. (*Hint:* The December 31, 2010, D. Belle, Capital account balance is $29,280.)

Exercise 3-9
Preparing a balance sheet   **LO5**

On October 1, Diondre Shabazz organized a new consulting firm called Tech Talk. On October 31, the company's records show the following accounts and amounts. Use this information to prepare an October income statement for the business.

Exercise 3-10
Preparing an income statement   **LO5**

Cash	$ 12,614	D. Shabazz, Withdrawals	$ 2,000
Accounts receivable	25,648	Consulting fees earned	25,620
Office supplies	4,903	Rent expense	6,859
Land	69,388	Salaries expense	12,405
Office equipment	27,147	Telephone expense	560
Accounts payable	12,070	Miscellaneous expenses	280
D. Shabazz, Capital	124,114		

Check   Net income, $5,516

Use the information in Exercise 3-10 to prepare an October statement of owner's equity for Tech Talk. (The owner invested $124,114 to launch the company.)

Exercise 3-11
Preparing a statement of owner's equity   **LO5**

Use the information in Exercise 3-10 (if completed, you can also use your solution to Exercise 3-11) to prepare an October 31 balance sheet for Tech Talk.

Exercise 3-12
Preparing a balance sheet   **LO5**

A company had the following assets and liabilities at the beginning and end of a recent year.

Exercise 3-13
Computing net income   **LO5**

	Assets	Liabilities
Beginning of the year	$131,000	$56,159
End of the year	180,000	72,900

Determine the net income earned or net loss incurred by the business during the year for each of the following *separate* cases:

a. Owner made no investments in the business and no withdrawals were made during the year.

b. Owner made no investments in the business but withdrew $650 cash per month for personal use.

c. No withdrawals were made during the year but the owner invested an additional $45,000 cash.

d. Withdrew $650 cash per month for personal use and the owner invested an additional $25,000 cash.

Exercise 3–14

Analyzing changes in a company's equity   **LO3**

Compute the missing amount in each of the following separate companies *a* through *d*.

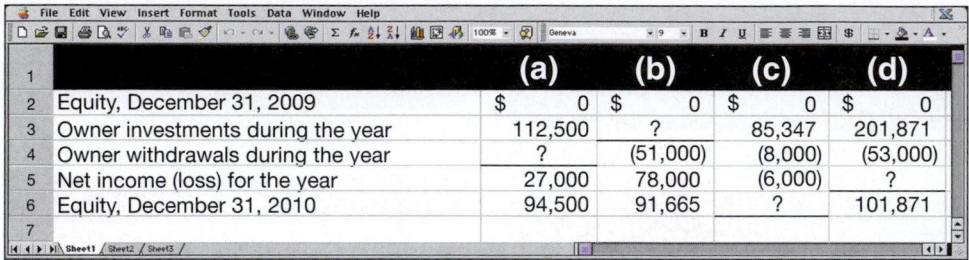

	(a)	(b)	(c)	(d)
Equity, December 31, 2009	$ 0	$ 0	$ 0	$ 0
Owner investments during the year	112,500	?	85,347	201,871
Owner withdrawals during the year	?	(51,000)	(8,000)	(53,000)
Net income (loss) for the year	27,000	78,000	(6,000)	?
Equity, December 31, 2010	94,500	91,665	?	101,871

PROBLEM SET A

Denzel Brooks opens a Web consulting business called Venture Consultants and completes the following transactions in March.

Problem 3–1A

Posting transactions to T-accounts; preparing a trial balance

LO2   LO3   LO4

mhhe.com/wildCA2e

March   1   Brooks invested $150,000 cash along with $22,000 of office equipment in the business.
        2   Prepaid $6,000 cash for six months' rent for an office. (*Hint:* Debit Prepaid Rent (an asset) for $6,000.)
        3   Made credit purchases of office equipment for $3,000 and office supplies for $1,200.
        6   Completed services for a client and immediately received $4,000 cash.
        9   Completed a $7,500 project for a client, who must pay within 30 days.
       12   Paid $4,200 cash to settle the account payable created on March 3.
       19   Paid $5,000 cash for the premium on a 12-month insurance policy.
       22   Received $3,500 cash as partial payment for the work completed on March 9.
       25   Completed work for another client for $3,820 on credit.
       29   Brooks withdrew $5,100 cash for personal use.
       30   Purchased $600 of additional office supplies on credit.
       31   Paid $500 cash for this month's utility bill.

Required

1. Open the following T-accounts—Cash; Accounts Receivable; Office Supplies; Prepaid Insurance; Prepaid Rent; Office Equipment; Accounts Payable; D. Brooks, Capital; D. Brooks, Withdrawals; Services Revenue; and Utilities Expense. Post the transactions in the T-accounts.

2. Prepare a trial balance as of the end of March.

Problem 3–2A

Posting transactions to T-accounts; preparing a trial balance; preparing financial statements

LO1   LO2   LO3   LO4   LO5

Kendis Lanelle opened a computer consulting business called Viva Consultants and completed the following transactions in the first month of operations.

April   1   Lanelle invested $80,000 cash along with office equipment valued at $26,000 in the business.
       2   Prepaid $9,000 cash for 12 months' rent for office space. (*Hint:* Debit Prepaid Rent (an asset) for $9,000.)
       3   Made credit purchases for $8,000 in office equipment and $3,600 in office supplies.
       6   Completed services for a client and immediately received $4,000 cash.
       9   Completed a $6,000 project for a client, who must pay within 30 days.
      13   Paid $11,600 cash to settle the account payable created on April 3.
      19   Paid $2,400 cash for the premium on a 12-month insurance policy. (*Hint:* Debit Prepaid Insurance (an asset) for $2,400.)
      22   Received $4,400 cash as partial payment for the work completed on April 9.
      25   Completed work for another client for $2,890 on credit.
      28   Lanelle withdrew $5,500 cash for personal use.
      29   Purchased $600 of additional office supplies on credit.
      30   Paid $435 cash for this month's utility bill.

Required

1. Open the following T-accounts—Cash; Accounts Receivable; Office Supplies; Prepaid Insurance; Prepaid Rent; Office Equipment; Accounts Payable; K. Lanelle, Capital; K. Lanelle, Withdrawals; Services Revenue; and Utilities Expense. Post the transactions in the T-accounts.

2. Prepare a trial balance as of April 30.

3. Prepare an income statement for the month of April.

4. Prepare a statement of owner's equity for the month of April.

5. Prepare a balance sheet as of April 30.

Check (1) Ending balances: Cash, $59,465; Accounts Receivable, $4,490; Accounts Payable, $600

(2) Total debits, $119,490

AE Consulting reports the following trial balance as of December 31, 2010, the end of its first month of operations.

Problem 3-3A
Preparing financial statements
LO4 LO5

AE CONSULTING Trial Balance December 31		
	Debit	Credit
Cash	$ 39,670	
Accounts receivable	2,750	
Office supplies	1,700	
Office equipment	48,100	
Building	165,000	
Land	40,000	
Accounts payable		$169,100
A. Emitt, Capital		120,800
A. Emitt, Withdrawals	2,900	
Fees earned		14,350
Salaries expense	3,500	
Utilities expense	630	
Total	$304,250	$304,250

Required

1. Prepare an income statement for the month.

2. Prepare a statement of owner's equity for the month.

3. Prepare a balance sheet as of the end of the month.

Diella Management Services opens for business and completes these transactions in November.

PROBLEM SET B

Problem 3-1B
Posting transactions to T-accounts, preparing a trial balance
LO2 LO3 LO4

Nov. 1 Cicely Diella, the owner, invested $30,000 cash along with $15,000 of office equipment in the business.

2 Prepaid $4,500 cash for six months' rent for an office. (*Hint:* Debit Prepaid Rent (an asset) for $4,500.)

4 Made credit purchases of office equipment for $2,500 and of office supplies for $600.

8 Completed work for a client and immediately received $3,400 cash.

12 Completed a $10,200 project for a client, who must pay within 30 days.

13 Paid $3,100 cash to settle the payable created on November 4.

19 Paid $1,800 cash for the premium on a 24-month insurance policy.

22 Received $5,200 cash as partial payment for the work completed on November 12.

24 Completed work for another client for $1,750 on credit.

28 Cicely Diella withdrew $5,300 cash for personal use.

29 Purchased $249 of additional office supplies on credit.

30 Paid $831 cash for this month's utility bill.

Required

1. Open the following T-accounts—Cash; Accounts Receivable; Office Supplies; Prepaid Insurance; Prepaid Rent; Office Equipment; Accounts Payable; C. Diella, Capital; C. Diella, Withdrawals; Services Revenue; and Utilities Expense. Post the transactions in the T-accounts.

2. Prepare a trial balance as of the end of November.

Problem 3-2B
Posting transactions to T-accounts preparing a trial balance; preparing financial statements
LO1 LO2 LO3 LO4 LO5

Johnson Management Services opens for business and completes these transactions in September.

Sept.	1	John Johnson, the owner, invests $38,000 cash along with office equipment valued at $15,000 in the business.
	2	Prepaid $9,000 cash for 12 months' rent for office space. (*Hint:* Debit Prepaid Rent (an asset) for $9,000.)
	4	Made credit purchases for $8,000 in office equipment and $2,400 in office supplies.
	8	Completed work for a client and immediately received $3,280 cash.
	12	Completed a $15,400 project for a client, who must pay within 30 days.
	13	Paid $10,400 cash to settle the payable created on September 4.
	19	Paid $1,900 cash for the premium on an 18-month insurance policy. (*Hint:* Debit Prepaid Insurance (an asset) for $1,900.)
	22	Received $7,700 cash as partial payment for the work completed on September 12.
	24	Completed work for another client for $2,100 on credit.
	28	John Johnson withdrew $5,300 cash for personal use.
	29	Purchased $550 of additional office supplies on credit.
	30	Paid $860 cash for this month's utility bill.

Required

1. Open the following T-accounts—Cash; Accounts Receivable; Office Supplies; Prepaid Insurance; Prepaid Rent; Office Equipment; Accounts Payable; J. Johnson, Capital; J. Johnson, Withdrawals; Service Fees Earned; and Utilities Expense. Post the transactions in the T-accounts.

2. Prepare a trial balance as of the end of September.

3. Prepare an income statement for the month of September.

4. Prepare a statement of owner's equity for the month of September.

5. Prepare a balance sheet as of September 30.

Problem 3-3B
Preparing financial statements
LO5

Witter Consulting provides the following trial balance as of June 30, 2010, the end of its first month of operations.

WITTER CONSULTING Trial Balance June 30		
	Debit	**Credit**
Cash	$ 34,570	
Accounts receivable	2,500	
Office supplies	2,200	
Office equipment	48,500	
Building	165,000	
Land	50,000	
Accounts payable		$173,300
D. Witter, Capital		121,800
D. Witter, Withdrawals	2,700	
Fees earned		14,500
Salaries expense	3,500	
Utilities expense	630	
Total	$309,600	$309,600

Required

1. Prepare an income statement for the month.

2. Prepare a statement of owner's equity for the month.

3. Prepare a balance sheet as of the end of the month.

(This serial problem started in Chapter 1 and continues through most of the chapters. If the Chapter 1 segment was not completed, the problem can begin at this point. It is helpful, but not necessary, to use the Working Papers that accompany this book.)

SERIAL PROBLEM

Success Systems
LO2   LO3

SP 3   On October 1, 2010, Adriana Lopez launched a computer services company called **Success Systems,** which provides consulting services, computer system installations, and custom program development. Lopez adopts the calendar year for reporting purposes and expects to prepare the company's first set of financial statements on December 31, 2010. The company uses the following accounts:

Account	Account
Cash	A. Lopez, Capital
Accounts Receivable	A. Lopez, Withdrawals
Computer Supplies	Computer Services Revenue
Prepaid Insurance	Wages Expense
Prepaid Rent	Advertising Expense
Office Equipment	Mileage Expense
Computer Equipment	Miscellaneous Expenses
Accounts Payable	Repairs Expense—Computer

Required

1. Post each of the following transactions to the appropriate T-accounts.

Oct. 1   Lopez invested $75,000 cash, a $25,000 computer system, and $10,000 of office equipment in the business.
  2   Paid $3,500 cash for four months' rent. (*Hint:* Debit Prepaid Rent for $3,500.)
  3   Purchased $1,600 of computer supplies on credit from Corvina Office Products.
  5   Paid $2,400 cash for one year's premium on a property and liability insurance policy. (*Hint:* Debit Prepaid Insurance for $2,400.)
  6   Billed Easy Leasing $6,200 for services performed in installing a new Web server.
  8   Paid $1,600 cash for the computer supplies purchased from Corvina Office Products on October 3.
  12   Billed Easy Leasing another $1,950 for services performed.
  15   Received $6,200 cash from Easy Leasing on its account.
  17   Paid $900 cash to repair computer equipment that was damaged when moving it.
  20   Paid $1,790 cash for an advertisement in the local newspaper.
  22   Received $1,950 cash from Easy Leasing on its account.
  28   Billed Clark Company $7,300 for services performed.
  31   Paid $1,050 cash for Michelle Jones's wages for seven days' work.
  31   Lopez withdrew $4,000 cash for personal use.
Nov. 1   Reimbursed Lopez in cash for business automobile mileage allowance (Lopez logged 1,200 miles at $0.32 per mile).
  2   Received $3,600 cash from Edge Corporation for computer services performed.
  5   Purchased computer supplies for $1,750 cash from Corvina Office Products.
  8   Billed Gomez Co. $6,500 for services performed.
  18   Received $5,000 cash from Clark Company as partial payment of the October 28 bill.
  22   Donated $300 cash to the United Way in the company's name.
  24   Completed work for Alex's Engineering Co. and sent it a bill for $7,000.
  28   Reimbursed Lopez in cash for business automobile mileage (1,500 miles at $0.32 per mile).
  30   Paid $2,100 cash for Michelle Jones's wages for 14 days' work.
  30   Lopez withdrew $2,500 cash for personal use.

2. Prepare a trial balance (dated November 30, 2010) from the ending balances of the T-accounts from part 1.

BEYOND THE NUMBERS

REPORTING IN ACTION
LO5

BTN 3-1   Refer to **Best Buy**'s financial statements in Appendix A for the following questions.

Required

1. What amount of cash does Best Buy report for each of the years ended March 1, 2008, and March 3, 2007?
2. Did Best Buy's cash balance increase or decrease during the year ended March 1, 2008?

ETHICS CHALLENGE
LO5

BTN 3-2   Craig Thorne works in a public accounting firm and hopes to eventually be a partner. The management of Allnet Company invites Thorne to prepare a bid to audit Allnet's financial statements. In discussing the audit fee, Allnet's management suggests a fee range in which the amount depends on the reported profit of Allnet. The higher its profit, the higher will be the audit fee paid to Thorne's firm.

Required

1. Identify the parties potentially affected by this audit and the fee plan proposed.
2. What are the ethical factors in this situation? Explain.
3. Would you recommend that Thorne accept this audit fee arrangement? Why or why not?
4. Describe some ethical considerations guiding your recommendation.

WORKPLACE COMMUNICATION
LO5

BTN 3-3   Lila Corentine is an aspiring entrepreneur and your friend. She is having difficulty understanding the purposes of financial statements and how they fit together across time.

Required

Write a one-page memorandum to Corentine explaining the purposes of the three basic financial statements and how they are linked across time.

TAKING IT TO THE NET

BTN 3-4   Search the Web for answers to the following questions on accounting careers. One suitable Website is CareerOneStop (**www.CareerOneStop.org**). For documentation print copies of the Website information accessed.

1. Identify the number of listings for accounting positions and the various accounting job titles.
2. Identify the number of listings for other job titles, with examples, that require or prefer accounting knowledge/experience but are not specifically accounting positions.
3. Specify the salary range for the accounting and accounting-related positions if provided.
4. Identify a job that appeals to you, the reason for its appeal, and its requirements.

TEAMWORK IN ACTION
LO2   LO3

BTN 3-5   The expanded accounting equation consists of assets, liabilities, capital, withdrawals, revenues, and expenses. It can be used to reveal insights into changes in a company's financial position.

Required

1. Form *learning teams* of six (or more) members. Each team member must select one of the six components and each team must have at least one expert on each component: (*a*) assets, (*b*) liabilities, (*c*) capital, (*d*) withdrawals, (*e*) revenues, and (*f*) expenses.
2. Form *expert teams* of individuals who selected the same component in part 1. Expert teams are to draft a report that each expert will present to his or her learning team addressing the following:
   a. Identify for its component the (i) increase and decrease side of the account and (ii) normal balance side of the account.
   b. Describe a transaction, with amounts, that increases its component.

c. Using the transaction and amounts in (*b*), verify the equality of the accounting equation.

d. Describe a transaction, with amounts, that decreases its component.

e. Using the transaction and amounts in (*d*), verify the equality of the accounting equation.

3. Each expert should return to his/her learning team. In rotation, each member presents his/her expert team's report to the learning team. Team discussion is encouraged.

BTN 3-6 Assume Warren Brown of **Cake Love** wishes to expand but needs a $30,000 loan. The bank requests Warren to prepare a balance sheet. Warren has not kept formal records but is able to provide the following accounts and their amounts as of December 31, 2010:

ENTREPRENEURS IN BUSINESS

LO5

Cash	$ 3,600	Accounts Receivable	$9,600	Prepaid Insurance	$ 1,500
Prepaid Rent	9,400	Store Supplies	6,600	Equipment	50,000
Accounts Payable	17,800			Total Equity*	62,900
Annual net income	40,000				

* The total equity amount reflects all owner investments, withdrawals, revenues, and expenses as of December 31, 2010.

Required

1. Prepare a balance sheet as of December 31, 2010, for Cake Love.

2. Do you think the prospects of Cake Love repaying a $30,000 bank loan are good? Why or why not?

---

1. c; Assets and expenses normally have debit balances.

2. d; Assets = Liabilities + Equity.

3. a; The cash investment should be accounted for as a debit to cash (and a credit to K. Hinrich, Capital).

4. b; The accountant would debit Wage Expense and credit Cash.

5. a; Debit Cash for $2,500 and credit Unearned Lawn Service Fees for $2,500.

ANSWERS TO MULTIPLE CHOICE QUIZ

A Look Back

Chapter 3 explained the analysis and recording of transactions. We showed how to apply and interpret T-accounts, double-entry accounting, and trial balances.

A Look at This Chapter

This chapter continues our focus on the accounting process. We introduce source documents as inputs for analysis and describe a company's chart of accounts. We also explain how transactions are journalized and posted to the general ledger.

A Look Ahead

Chapter 5 explains the need to adjust accounts. We describe the various types of adjustments and the adjusted trial balance. We show how the adjusted trial balance is used to prepare financial statements.

Chapter **4**

Preparing the General Journal and General Ledger

Learning Objectives

LO 1	Explain the steps in processing transactions.
LO 2	Describe source documents and their purpose.
LO 3	Describe a chart of accounts.
LO 4	Record transactions in a general journal.
LO 5	Post entries to a general ledger.
LO 6	Prepare financial statements from a trial balance.
LO 7	Explain how to correct errors in the general journal and general ledger.

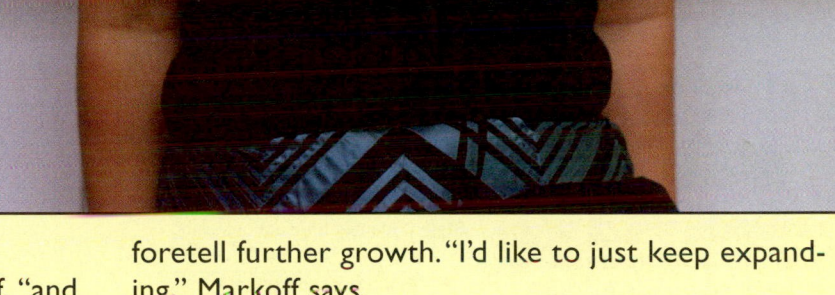

"You just have to do it. There are no limitations."
—Katrina Markoff

Culinary Adventures

CHICAGO—"My heritage is Macedonian," says Katrina Markoff, "and my love of cooking has been with me from childhood. I began to think, why not combine international spices and chocolate?" Markoff ultimately created a chocolate confectionary company, **Vosges Haut Chocolat [VosgesChocolate.com],** with an "East-meets-West" feel. "I noticed a lack of creativity in chocolate," says Markoff. "They were all gold boxes with chocolate that tasted lousy and had raspberry and strawberry filling."

With ingredients such as wasabi, balsamic vinegar, jasmine flower, curry, and anise, you won't confuse her chocolate with any others. "When I tell people stories about the ingredients," says Markoff, "they tend to slow down and pay attention to what they're putting in their mouths."

Markoff is also a businessperson. "I couldn't help it," says Markoff, "my mother is an entrepreneur." That business sense mixed with her culinary skills gives her unique insights. Last year's sales were almost $12 million. The company's current best seller is "Mo's Bacon Bar," which contains pieces of applewood smoked bacon, she explains. Such results

foretell further growth. "I'd like to just keep expanding," Markoff says.

Markoff insists that a timely and reliable accounting system is crucial for Vosges Haut Chocolat's success. This system gives Markoff the financial statement information that has enabled her company to obtain the necessary financing to feed its growth. This chapter focuses on the accounting system underlying financial statements.

The accounting system also gives her information on key expenses. She personally inspects and purchases each spice, flower, and chocolate used. "Right now, I'm trying out a Jamaican-style truffle, flavored with rum and allspice." Once new products meet her culinary standards, they are appropriately priced.

"We want people to experience chocolate through the use of their senses—all six!" exclaims Markoff. One of her newer products is the Aztec collection that combines chocolate with spices of the vanilla bean, ancho chili pepper, Ceylon cinnamon, and cashews. Adds Markoff, both chocolate and spices have a long history as aphrodisiacs. Now we're cooking!

[Sources: *Vosges Haut Chocolat Website,* January 2009; *Inc.* magazine, April 2005; *Entrepreneur,* 2002; Chocomap, January 2007; *Entrepreneur,* May 2008; *The Wall Street Journal,* D1, February 14, 2008.

Knowledge of how the accounting system processes transactions into financial statements is important. The goal of this chapter is to illustrate how transactions are recorded in a general journal and then posted to a general ledger. The chapter also shows how general ledger account balances are used to prepare financial statements.

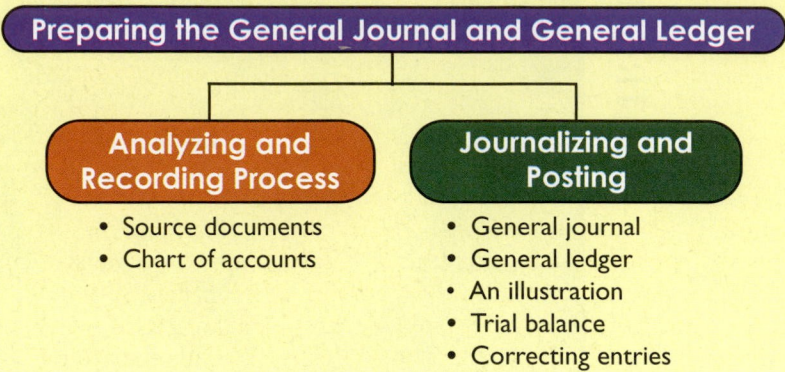

Preparing the General Journal and General Ledger

Analyzing and Recording Process
- Source documents
- Chart of accounts

Journalizing and Posting
- General journal
- General ledger
- An illustration
- Trial balance
- Correcting entries

Analyzing and Recording Process

LO1 Explain the steps in processing transactions.

In Chapter 3 we used T-accounts and the accounting equation as tools to understand transactions. Businesses don't use T-accounts to maintain their books; instead, the accounting process for analyzing and recording transactions and events follows the steps shown in Exhibit 4.1.

Exhibit 4.1

Steps in Processing Transactions

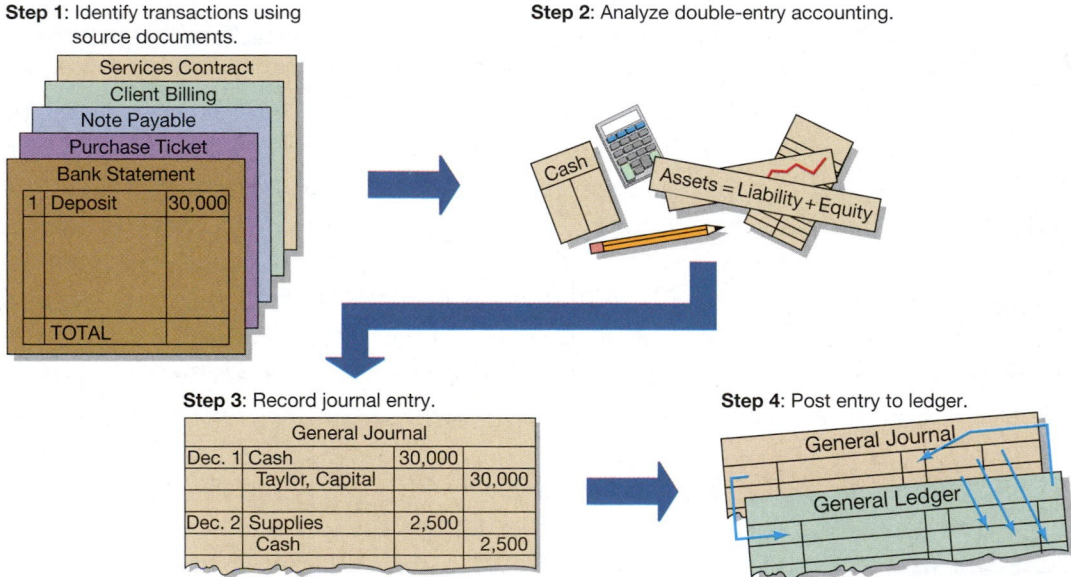

Steps 1 and 2—involving transaction analysis and double-entry accounting—were introduced in Chapters 2 and 3. This chapter extends that discussion and focuses on steps 3 and 4 of the accounting process. Step 3 is to record each transaction in a journal. A **journal** gives a complete record of each transaction in one place. It also shows debits and credits for each transaction. The process of recording transactions in a journal is called **journalizing.** Step 4 is to transfer (or *post*) entries from the journal to the ledger. The process of transferring journal entry information to the ledger is called **posting.** We can summarize this process with the letters *TARP,* which stand for: Transaction, Analysis, Record, and Post. The complete collection of all accounts in an accounting information system is called a **ledger** (or **general ledger**).

A journal is often referred to as the *book of original entry.* The ledger is referred to as the *book of final entry* because financial statements are prepared from it.

Business transactions and events are the starting points. Relying on source documents, transactions and events are analyzed using the accounting equation to understand how they affect accounts. These effects are recorded in accounting records, informally referred to as the *accounting books,* or simply the *books.* Additional steps such as posting and then preparing a trial balance help summarize and classify the effects of transactions and events. Ultimately, the accounting process provides information in useful reports or financial statements to decision makers.

Source Documents

Source documents identify and describe transactions entering the accounting process. They are the sources of accounting information and can be in either hard copy or electronic form. Examples are sales invoices, checks, purchase orders, bills from suppliers, employee earnings records, and bank statements (as shown in Exhibit 4.2). To illustrate, when an item is purchased on credit, the seller usually prepares at least two copies of a sales invoice. One copy is given to the buyer. Another copy, often sent electronically, is used by the seller to record the sale. Sellers use invoices for recording sales and for control; buyers use them for recording purchases and for monitoring purchasing activity. Many cash registers record information for each sale on a tape or electronic file locked inside the register. This record can be used as a source document for recording sales in the accounting records. Source documents, especially if obtained from outside the organization, provide objective and reliable evidence about transactions and their amounts.

LO2 Describe source documents and their purpose.

Exhibit 4.2

Sampling of Source Documents

A. Sales invoice (for goods or services provided)

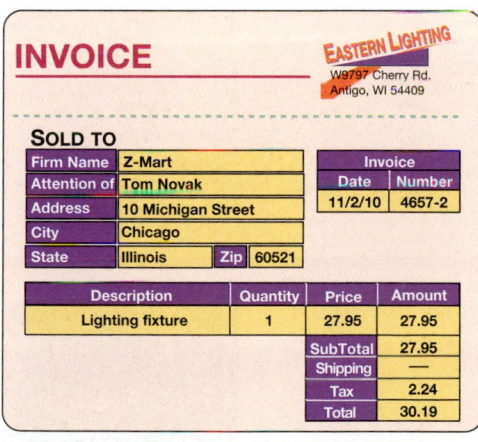

B. Cash register summary (detail of cash receipts)

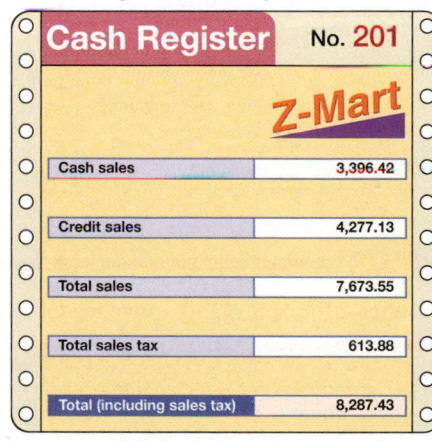

C. Processed check images (detail of cash payments)

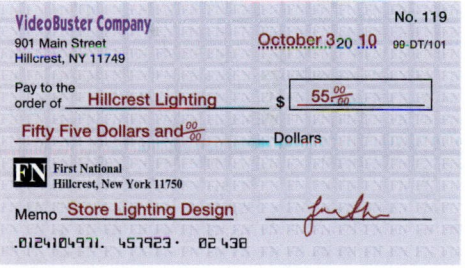

E. Deposit ticket (record of bank deposits)

D. Bill from supplier (for goods or services received)

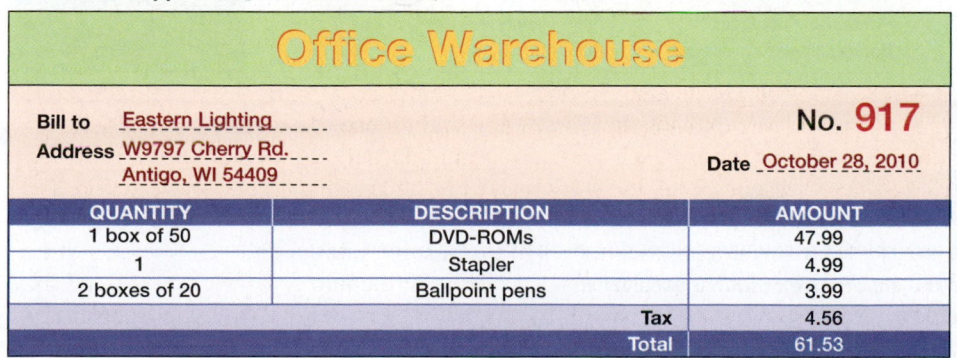

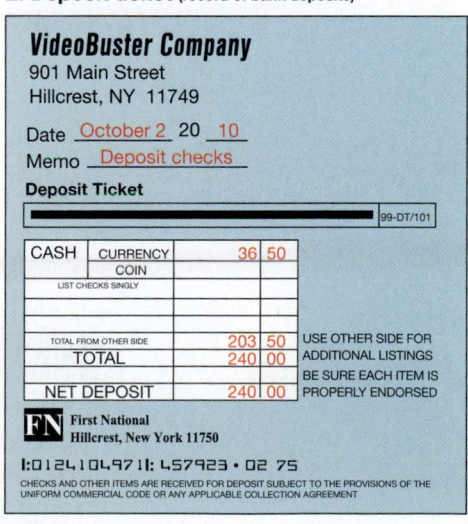

Chart of Accounts

LO3 Describe a chart of accounts.

To know which account is affected in a transaction, we must know which accounts a particular company uses. A company's size and diversity of operations affect the number of accounts needed. A small company can get by with as few as 20 or 30 accounts; a large company can require several thousand. The **chart of accounts** is a list of all accounts a company uses and includes an identification number assigned to each account. A small business might use the following numbering system for its accounts:

101–199	Asset accounts
201–299	Liability accounts
301–399	Equity accounts
401–499	Revenue accounts
501–699	Expense accounts

These numbers provide a three-digit code that is useful in recordkeeping. In this case, the first digit assigned to asset accounts is a 1, the first digit assigned to liability accounts is a 2, and so on. The second and third digits relate to the accounts' subcategories. Exhibit 4.3 shows a *partial* chart of accounts for FastForward, the focus company of Chapters 2 and 3. Different companies use different account titles. An example of the variety of accounts and their titles can be seen by looking at the chart of accounts located before the index at the back of the book.

Exhibit 4.3

Partial Chart of Accounts for FastForward

Account Number	Account Name	Account Number	Account Name
101	Cash	301	C. Taylor, Capital
106	Accounts receivable	302	C. Taylor, Withdrawals
126	Supplies	403	Consulting revenue
128	Prepaid insurance	406	Rental revenue
167	Equipment	622	Salaries expense
201	Accounts payable	637	Insurance expense
236	Unearned consulting revenue	640	Rent expense
		652	Supplies expense
		690	Utilities expense

IN THE NEWS

Sporting Accounts   The **Miami Heat** have the following major revenue and expense accounts:

Revenues	Expenses
Basketball ticket sales	Team salaries
TV & radio broadcast fees	Game costs
Advertising revenues	NBA franchise costs
Basketball playoff receipts	Promotional costs

HOW YOU DOIN'?   Answers—p. 89

1. Identify examples of accounting source documents.

2. Explain the importance of source documents.

3. What determines the number and types of accounts a company uses?

4. Describe a chart of accounts.

Journalizing and Posting

The General Journal

The process of journalizing transactions requires an understanding of a journal. While companies can use various journals, every company uses a **general journal.** It can be used to record any transaction. Exhibit 4.4 provides an example. The general journal contains columns to record:

1. Date of transaction.
2. Titles of affected accounts.
3. Dollar amount of each debit.
4. Dollar amount of each credit.
5. Posting reference.

Computerized journals are often designed to look like a manual journal page and also include error-checking routines that ensure debits equal credits for each entry. Shortcuts allow record-keepers to select account names and numbers from pull-down menus.

LO4 Record transactions in a general journal.

GENERAL JOURNAL				Page 1
Date	Account Titles and Explanation	PR	Debit	Credit

Exhibit 4.4

Sample General Journal

Journalizing Transactions   To record entries in a general journal, use this four-step process.

1. Date the transaction: Enter the year at the top of the first column and the month and day on the first line of each journal entry.
2. Enter titles of accounts **debited** and then enter amounts in the Debit column on the same line. Account titles are taken from the chart of accounts and are aligned with the left margin of the Account Titles and Explanation column.
3. Enter titles of accounts **credited** and then enter amounts in the Credit column on the same line. Account titles are from the chart of accounts and are indented from the left margin of the Account Titles and Explanation column to distinguish them from debited accounts.
4. Enter a brief explanation of the transaction on the line below the entry (it often references a source document). This explanation is indented about half as far as the credited account titles to avoid confusing it with accounts.

There are no exact rules for writing journal entry explanations. An explanation should be short yet describe why an entry is made.

We use the 16 transactions of FastForward from Chapter 3 to show how to journalize transactions. These transactions are summarized in Exhibit 4.5. A detailed journalizing example using FastForward's first transaction in December follows:

Transaction 1

Chuck Taylor invests $30,000 cash in FastForward on December 1.

Step 1: Enter the date in the date column. Enter the year at the top of the first column and then enter the month and the day.

Date	Account Titles and Explanation	PR	Debit	Credit
2010 Dec. 1				

Step 2: Enter the titles of the accounts debited and enter the debit amount in the Debit column on the same line. Note that dollar signs are not used in journals.

Date		Account Titles and Explanation	PR	Debit	Credit
2010 Dec.	1	Cash		30 000 00	

Step 3: Enter the titles of the accounts credited and enter the credit amount in the credit column on the same line. Indent the credit account title from the left margin of the Account Titles and Explanation column.

Date		Account Titles and Explanation	PR	Debit	Credit
2010 Dec.	1	Cash		30 000 00	
		C. Taylor, Capital			30 000 00

Step 4: Enter an explanation, indented about half as far the credited account title.

Date		Account Titles and Explanation	PR	Debit	Credit
2010 Dec.	1	Cash		30 000 00	
		C. Taylor, Capital			30 000 00
		Investment by owner.			

Exhibit 4.5

FastForward's December Transactions

Date	Transaction
(1) Dec. 1	Chuck Taylor invests $30,000 cash in FastForward.
(2) Dec. 2	FastForward pays $2,500 cash for supplies.
(3) Dec. 3	FastForward pays $26,000 cash for equipment.
(4) Dec. 4	FastForward purchases $7,100 of supplies on credit.
(5) Dec. 5	FastForward provides consulting services and immediately collects $4,200 in cash.
(6) Dec. 6	FastForward pays $1,000 cash for December rent.
(7) Dec. 12	FastForward pays $700 cash for employee salaries.
(8) Dec. 13	FastForward provides consulting services of $1,600 and rents its test facilities for $300. The customer is billed $1,900 for these services.
(9) Dec. 19	FastForward receives $1,900 cash from the client billed in transaction 8.
(10) Dec. 20	FastForward pays the supplier $900 cash toward the account payable from transaction 4.
(11) Dec. 21	Chuck Taylor withdraws $200 cash from FastForward for personal use.
(12) Dec. 22	FastForward receives $3,000 cash in advance of providing consulting services to a customer.
(13) Dec. 23	FastForward pays $2,400 cash (insurance premium) for a 24-month insurance policy. Coverage begins on December 1.
(14) Dec. 23	FastForward pays $120 cash for supplies.
(15) Dec. 23	FastForward pays $230 cash for December utilities expense.
(16) Dec. 26	FastForward pays $700 cash in employee salaries for work performed in the latter part of December.

FastForward's transactions are journalized in Exhibit 4.6. Review this carefully. We identify each transaction with its number (1–16) in our example; this information is not usually seen in journals.

A blank line is left between each journal entry for clarity. When a transaction is first recorded, the **posting reference (PR) column** is left blank (in a manual system). Later, when posting entries to the general ledger, the identification numbers of the individual ledger accounts are entered in the PR column. We show how to post journal entries to the general ledger next.

Exhibit 4.6

Journal Entries for FastForward Transactions

	Date		GENERAL JOURNAL Account Titles and Explanation	PR	Debit	Credit
						Page 1
(1)	2010 Dec.	1	Cash		30 000 00	
			C. Taylor, Capital			30 000 00
			Investment by owner.			
(2)	Dec.	2	Supplies		2 500 00	
			Cash			2 500 00
			Purchased supplies for cash.			
(3)	Dec.	3	Equipment		26 000 00	
			Cash			26 000 00
			Purchased equipment for cash.			
(4)	Dec.	4	Supplies		7 100 00	
			Accounts Payable			7 100 00
			Purchased supplies on credit.			
(5)	Dec.	5	Cash		4 200 00	
			Consulting Revenue			4 200 00
			Provide services for cash.			
(6)	Dec.	6	Rent Expense		1 000 00	
			Cash			1 000 00
			Payment of rent expense in cash.			
(7)	Dec.	12	Salaries Expense		700 00	
			Cash			700 00
			Payment of salaries expense in cash.			
(8)	Dec.	13	Accounts Receivable		1 900 00	
			Consulting Revenue			1 600 00
			Rental Revenue			300 00
			Provide rental and consulting services on credit.			
(9)	Dec.	19	Cash		1 900 00	
			Accounts Receivable			1 900 00
			Receipt of cash on account.			
(10)	Dec.	20	Accounts Payable		900 00	
			Cash			900 00
			Payment of accounts payable (partial).			
(11)	Dec.	21	C. Taylor, Withdrawals		200 00	
			Cash			200 00
			Withdrawal of cash by owner.			
(12)	Dec.	22	Cash		3 000 00	
			Unearned Consulting Revenue			3 000 00
			Receipt of cash for future services			
(13)	Dec.	23	Prepaid Insurance		2 400 00	
			Cash			2 400 00
			Cash payment for insurance coverage.			

This is called a **compound journal entry,** an entry that affects three or more accounts.

[continued on next page]

[continued from previous page]

(14)	Dec.	23	Supplies		1 2 0 00	
			Cash			1 2 0 00
			Purchased supplies for cash.			
(15)	Dec.	23	Utilities Expense		2 3 0 00	
			Cash			2 3 0 00
			Payment of utilities expense in cash.			
(16)	Dec.	26	Salaries Expense		7 0 0 00	
			Cash			7 0 0 00
			Payment of salaries expense in cash.			

The General Ledger

The general journal gives a complete record of each transaction in one place. To determine the current balance of each specific account, however, information in the journal must be transferred (or posted) to each account.

Balance Column Account   The T-accounts that were introduced in Chapter 3 are a simple way to show how the accounting process works. However, actual accounting systems need more structure, and therefore use **balance column accounts** in ledgers. We compare T-accounts to the balance column accounts found in ledgers in Exhibit 4.7, using the first few transactions for FastForward. The T-account is a useful classroom tool which represents the more formal balance column account.

Exhibit 4.7

Comparing T-account with Balance Column account

Cash	
30,000	2,500
4,200	26,000
Balance 5,700	

		Cash			Account No. 101
Date	Explanation	PR	Debit	Credit	Balance
2010					
Dec. 1		G1	30,000		30,000
Dec. 2		G1		2,500	27,500
Dec. 3		G1		26,000	1,500
Dec. 10		G1	4,200		**5,700**

The balance column account format is similar to a T-account in having columns for debits and credits. It differs from a T-account by including the account number (101) from FastForward's chart of accounts, transaction date, posting reference (PR), and explanation columns. It also has a column with the running balance of the account after each entry is recorded. To illustrate, FastForward's Cash account in Exhibit 4.7 is debited on December 1 for the $30,000 owner investment, yielding a $30,000 debit balance. The account is credited on December 2 for $2,500, yielding a $27,500 debit balance. On December 3, it is credited again, this time for $26,000, and its debit balance is reduced to $1,500. The Cash account is debited for $4,200 on December 10, and its debit balance increases to $5,700.

The heading of the Balance column does not show whether it is a debit or credit balance. Instead, an account is assumed to have a *normal balance*. Unusual events can sometimes temporarily give an account an abnormal balance. An *abnormal balance* refers to a balance on the side where decreases are recorded. For example, a customer might mistakenly overpay a bill. This gives that customer's account receivable an abnormal (credit) balance. An abnormal balance is often identified by circling it or by entering it in red or some other unusual color in manual systems. An abnormal balance might be shown in brackets in a computerized system. A zero balance for an account is usually shown by writing zeros or a dash in the Balance column to avoid confusion between a zero balance and one omitted in error. Explanations are typically included in ledger accounts only for unusual transactions or events.

Posting Journal Entries   Step 4 of processing transactions is to post journal entries to ledger accounts (see Exhibit 4.1). To ensure that the ledger is up-to-date, entries are posted as soon as possible. This might be daily, weekly, or when time permits. All entries must be posted to the ledger before financial statements are prepared to ensure that account balances are up-to-date. When entries are posted to the ledger, the debits in journal entries are transferred into ledger accounts as debits, and credits are transferred into ledger accounts as credits. The steps to post a journal entry to a general ledger account are:

LO5   Post entries to a general ledger.

1. Identify the ledger account that is debited in the journal entry and enter the date of the transaction in the date column.
2. Enter the debit amount in the debit column.
3. Update the balance of the ledger account.

`In the ledger`

4. Enter the journal and page in the PR column of the ledger. For example, the letter *G* shows the journal entry came for the General Journal; the number 1 indicates the journal entry came from page 1 of that journal.
5. Enter the general ledger account number in the PR column of the journal. This creates a link between the general ledger and the journal entry in the general journal. This link is a useful cross-reference for tracing an amount from one record to another. Also, if an accountant is interrupted during the posting process, PR numbers enable the accountant or others to determine where to resume.

`In the journal`

   Next, to complete the posting of that entry, repeat the above process for the credit part of the journal entry.

   In Exhibit 4.8 we provide a detailed example of the posting process using FastForward's first journal entry from December 1.

Posting a Debit

1. Enter the year, 2010, and the date (December 1) of FastForward's first transaction in the Cash account in the ledger.
2. Enter the $30,000 debit to cash in the debit column of the Cash account.

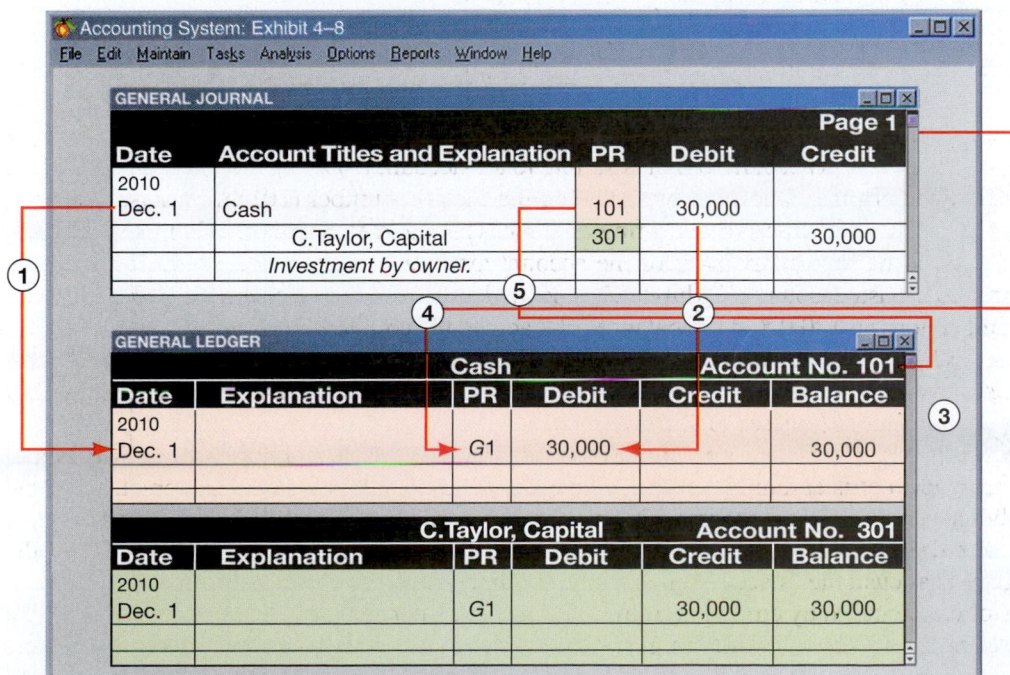

Exhibit 4.8

Posting an Entry to the Ledger

Arrow lines show the posting steps for the *debit* of this journal entry. The steps are similar for the *credit* of this journal entry. Step ③ occurs only in the ledger.

3. Update the balance of the Cash account to $30,000.

[In the ledger]

4. Enter *G1* in the PR column, indicating the journal entry is from page 1 of the general journal.

[In the journal]

5. Put 101, the account number for the Cash general ledger account, in the PR column of the journal.

Posting a Credit

1. Enter the year, 2010, and the date (December 1) of FastForward's first transaction in the C. Taylor, Capital, account in the ledger.

2. Enter the $30,000 credit in the credit column of the C. Taylor, Capital, account.

3. Update the balance of the C. Taylor, Capital, account to $30,000.

[In the ledger]

4. Enter *G1* in the PR column, indicating the journal entry is from page 1 of the general journal.

[In the journal]

5. Put 301, the account number for the C. Taylor, Capital, general ledger account, in the PR column of the journal.

Journalizing and Posting—An Illustration

We return to the activities of FastForward to show how to journalize and post their first 16 transactions. We first show the 16 transactions as journal entries in the general journal (Exhibit 4.9). Note that account numbers are included in the "PR" column, indicating the entries have been

---

Exhibit 4.9

Journal Entries for FastForward Transactions, after Posting to General Ledger

GENERAL JOURNAL   Page 1

	Date		Account Titles and Explanation	PR	Debit	Credit
(1)	2010 Dec.	1	Cash	101	30 000 00	
			C. Taylor, Capital	301		30 000 00
			Investment by owner.			
(2)	Dec.	2	Supplies	126	2 500 00	
			Cash	101		2 500 00
			Purchased supplies for cash.			
(3)	Dec.	3	Equipment	167	26 000 00	
			Cash	101		26 000 00
			Purchased equipment for cash.			
(4)	Dec.	4	Supplies	126	7 100 00	
			Accounts Payable	201		7 100 00
			Purchased supplies on credit.			
(5)	Dec.	5	Cash	101	4 200 00	
			Consulting Revenue	403		4 200 00
			Provide services for cash.			
(6)	Dec.	6	Rent Expense	640	1 000 00	
			Cash	101		1 000 00
			Payment of rent expense in cash.			
(7)	Dec.	12	Salaries Expense	622	700 00	
			Cash	101		700 00
			Payment of salaries expense in cash.			

[continued on next page]

[continued from previous page]

				Ref.	Debit	Credit
(8)	Dec.	13	Accounts Receivable	106	1 9 0 0 00	
			Consulting Revenue	403		1 6 0 0 00
			Rental Revenue	406		3 0 0 00
			Provide rental and consulting services on credit.			
(9)	Dec.	19	Cash	101	1 9 0 0 00	
			Accounts Receivable	106		1 9 0 0 00
			Receipt of cash on account.			
(10)	Dec.	20	Accounts Payable	201	9 0 0 00	
			Cash	101		9 0 0 00
			Payment of accounts payable (partial).			
(11)	Dec.	21	C. Taylor, Withdrawals	302	2 0 0 00	
			Cash	101		2 0 0 00
			Withdrawal of cash by owner.			
(12)	Dec.	22	Cash	101	3 0 0 0 00	
			Unearned Consulting Revenue	236		3 0 0 0 00
			Receipt of cash for future services.			
(13)	Dec.	23	Prepaid Insurance	128	2 4 0 0 00	
			Cash	101		2 4 0 0 00
			Cash payment for insurance coverage.			
(14)	Dec.	23	Supplies	126	1 2 0 00	
			Cash	101		1 2 0 00
			Purchased supplies for cash.			
(15)	Dec.	23	Utilities Expense	690	2 3 0 00	
			Cash	101		2 3 0 00
			Payment of utilities expense in cash.			
(16)	Dec.	26	Salaries Expense	622	7 0 0 00	
			Cash	101		7 0 0 00
			Payment of salaries expense in cash.			

posted to the general ledger. We then show the results of posting these transactions to ledger accounts (Exhibit 4.10).

The general ledger accounts in Exhibit 4.10 do not include a column for explanations. Explanations are typically included in ledger accounts only for unusual transactions or events. If an explanation is needed, it can be added in the date column, directly below the date of the unusual transaction or event.

The fundamental concepts of the manual (pencil-and-paper) system we illustrate are identical to those of a computerized accounting system. However, posting is automatic and immediate in a computerized system. Accounting software also typically includes features that reduce the chance for errors, for example computing updated account balances and ensuring all journal entries have equal debits and credits.

Trial Balance

After all entries have been posted, a trial balance is prepared to ensure the equality of debits and credits in the general ledger. All of the accounts in the ledger are entered into the trial balance, typically in account number order. The balance for each account is obtained from the last row of

Exhibit 4.10

General Ledger for FastForward

Cash — Account No. 101

Date	PR	Debit	Credit	Balance
Dec. 1	G1	30,000		30,000
2	G1		2,500	27,500
3	G1		26,000	1,500
5	G1	4,200		5,700
6	G1		1,000	4,700
12	G1		700	4,000
19	G1	1,900		5,900
20	G1		900	5,000
21	G1		200	4,800
22	G1	3,000		7,800
23	G1		2,400	5,400
23	G1		120	5,280
23	G1		230	5,050
26	G1		700	4,350

Accounts Receivable — Account No. 106

Date	PR	Debit	Credit	Balance
Dec. 13	G1	1,900		1,900
19	G1		1,900	0

Supplies — Account No. 126

Date	PR	Debit	Credit	Balance
Dec. 2	G1	2,500		2,500
4	G1	7,100		9,600
23	G1	120		9,720

Prepaid Insurance — Account No. 128

Date	PR	Debit	Credit	Balance
Dec. 23	G1	2,400		2,400

Equipment — Account No. 167

Date	PR	Debit	Credit	Balance
Dec. 3	G1	26,000		26,000

Accounts Payable — Account No. 201

Date	PR	Debit	Credit	Balance
Dec. 4	G1		7,100	7,100
20	G1	900		6,200

Unearned Consulting Revenue — Account No. 236

Date	PR	Debit	Credit	Balance
Dec. 22	G1		3,000	3,000

C. Taylor, Capital — Account No. 301

Date	PR	Debit	Credit	Balance
Dec. 1	G1		30,000	30,000

C. Taylor, Withdrawals — Account No. 302

Date	PR	Debit	Credit	Balance
Dec. 21	G1	200		200

Consulting Revenue — Account No. 403

Date	PR	Debit	Credit	Balance
Dec. 5	G1		4,200	4,200
13	G1		1,600	5,800

Rental Revenue — Account No. 406

Date	PR	Debit	Credit	Balance
Dec. 13	G1		300	300

Salaries Expense — Account No. 622

Date	PR	Debit	Credit	Balance
Dec. 12	G1	700		700
26	G1	700		1,400

Rent Expense — Account No. 640

Date	PR	Debit	Credit	Balance
Dec. 6	G1	1,000		1,000

Utilities Expense — Account No. 690

Date	PR	Debit	Credit	Balance
Dec. 23	G1	230		230

L06 Prepare financial statements from a trial balance.

information for that account in the ledger and entered in the trial balance. As in Chapter 3, if the total debits do not equal the total credits in the trial balance, the accountant must determine why. In Exhibit 4.11 we provide FastForward's trial balance, prepared from the general ledger accounts in Exhibit 4.10 as of the end of December. You will notice it is the same as the trial balance we prepared from T-accounts in Chapter 3. The income statement, statement of owner's equity, and balance sheet shown in Exhibit 4.11 can then be prepared from this trial balance. We showed in detail how to prepare these three financial statements in Chapter 3.

Exhibit 4.11

Preparing Financial Statements from Trial Balance

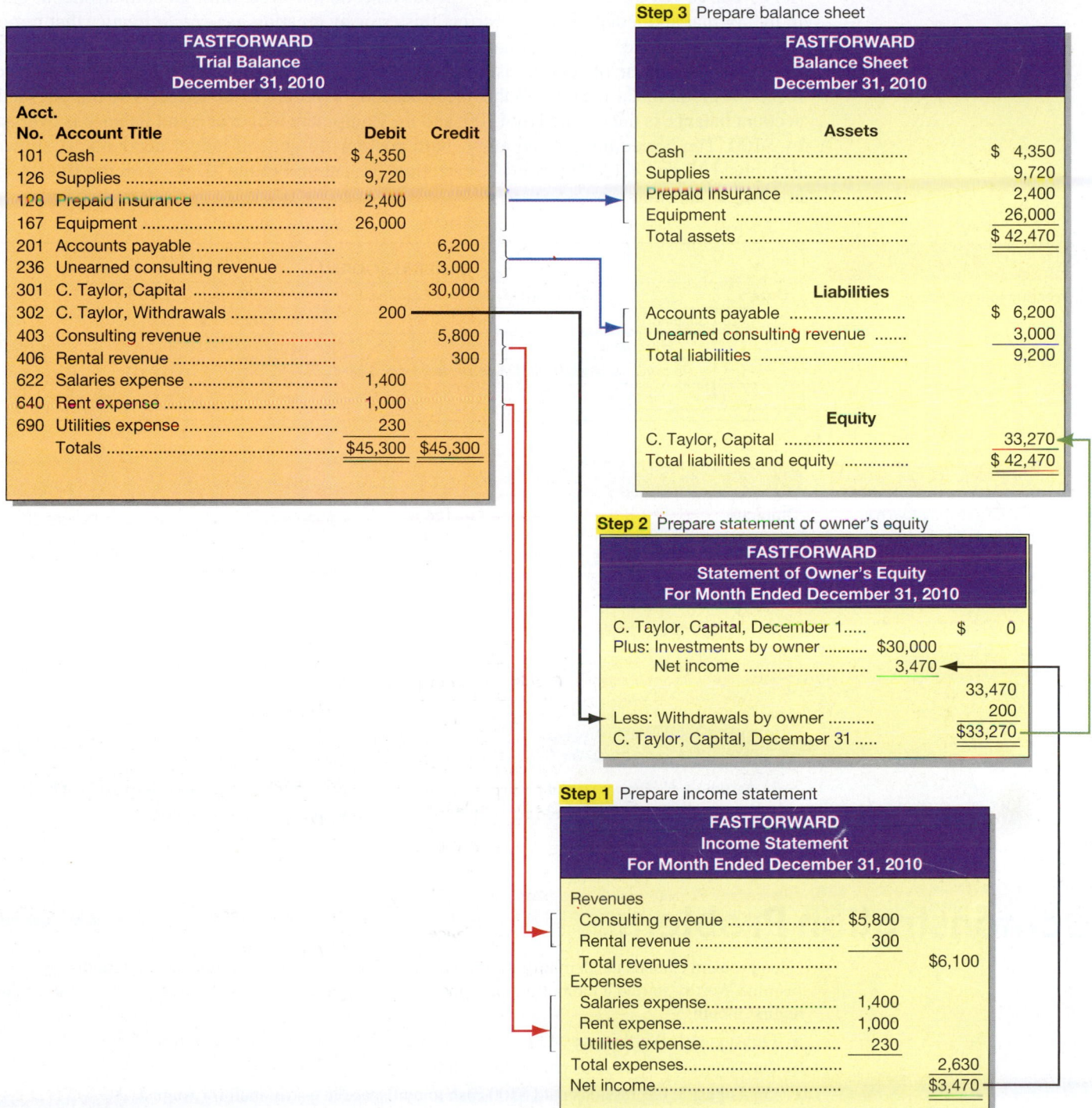

Correcting Errors in the Journal and the Ledger

Errors sometimes occur in journal entries. When they occur, we must correct them. How we correct the error depends on whether it is discovered before or after the journal entry is posted.

LO7 Explain how to correct errors in the general journal and general ledger.

Error Discovered before Posting   In this case, the error can be corrected in a manual system by drawing a line through the incorrect information. The correct information is written above it to create a record of change for the auditor. Many computerized systems allow the operator to replace the incorrect information directly.

Error Discovered after Posting   In this case, do not strike through both erroneous entries in the journal and ledger. Instead, correct this error by creating a *correcting entry* that removes the amount from the wrong account and records it in the correct account. As an example, suppose a $100 purchase of supplies is journalized with an incorrect debit to Equipment and a correct $100 credit to Cash, and then this incorrect entry is posted to the ledger. The Supplies ledger account balance is understated by $100, and the Equipment ledger account balance is overstated by $100. The correcting journal entry, with postings to general ledger accounts, is shown in Exhibits 4.12 and 4.13. The word "Correcting" is entered in the "Date" column in each general ledger account.

Exhibit 4.12

Correcting Journal Entry

	GENERAL JOURNAL			
Date	Account Titles and Explanation	PR	Debit	Credit
2010 July 28	Supplies	126	1 0 0 00	
	Equipment	167		1 0 0 00
	To correct error where equipment was incorrectly debited.			

Exhibit 4.13

Effects of a Correcting Journal Entry on Ledger Accounts

	General Ledger								
Supplies			Account No. 126		**Equipment**			Account No. 167	
Date	PR	Debit	Credit	Balance	Date	PR	Debit	Credit	Balance
2010 July 28					2010 July 15	G1	800		800
Correcting	G1	100		100	22	G1	100		900
					28				
					Correcting	G1		100	800

> **HOW YOU DOIN'?**   Answer—p. 89
>
> **5.** Assume a $500 purchase of prepaid insurance is journalized with an incorrect debit to Supplies, and this incorrect entry is posted to the ledger. Prepare the correcting journal entry.

Demonstration Problem

(This problem extends the demonstration problem of Chapters 2 and 3.) After several months of planning, Jasmine Worthy started a haircutting business called Expressions. The following events occurred during its first month.

a. On August 1, Worthy invested $3,000 cash and $15,000 of equipment in Expressions.

b. On August 2, Expressions paid $600 cash for furniture for the shop.

c. On August 3, Expressions paid $500 cash to rent space in a strip mall for August.

d. On August 4, it purchased $1,200 of equipment on credit for the shop (using an account payable).

e. On August 5, Expressions opened for business. Cash received from services provided in the first week and a half of business (ended August 15) is $825.

f. On August 15, it provided $100 of haircutting services on account.

g. On August 17, it received a $100 check for services previously rendered on account.

h. On August 17, it paid $125 to an assistant for working during the grand opening.

i. Cash received from services provided during the second half of August is $930.

j. On August 31, it paid $400 on the account payable entered into on August 4.

k. On August 31, Worthy withdrew $900 cash for personal use.

Required

1. Open the following ledger accounts in balance column format (account numbers are in parentheses): Cash (101); Accounts Receivable (102); Furniture (161); Store Equipment (165); Accounts Payable (201); J. Worthy, Capital (301); J. Worthy, Withdrawals (302); Haircutting Services Revenue (403); Wages Expense (623); and Rent Expense (640). Prepare general journal entries for the transactions.

2. Post the journal entries from (1) to the ledger accounts.

3. Prepare a trial balance as of August 31.

Extended Analysis

4. In the coming months, Expressions will experience a greater variety of business transactions. Identify which accounts are debited and which are credited for the following transactions. (*Hint:* We must use some accounts not opened in part 1.)

   a. Purchase supplies with cash.

   b. Pay cash for future insurance coverage.

   c. Receive cash for services to be provided in the future.

   d. Purchase supplies on account.

Planning the Solution

- Analyze each transaction and use the debit and credit rules to prepare a journal entry for each.
- Post each debit and each credit from journal entries to their ledger accounts and cross-reference each amount in the PR columns of the journal and ledger.
- Calculate each account balance and list the accounts with their balances on a trial balance.
- Verify that total debits in the trial balance equal total credits.
- Analyze the future transactions to identify the accounts affected and apply debit and credit rules.

Solution to Demonstration Problem

1. General journal entries:

		GENERAL JOURNAL			
Date		**Account Titles and Explanation**	**PR**	**Debit**	**Credit**
Aug. 2010	1	Cash	101	3 000 00	
		Store Equipment	165	15 000 00	
		J. Worthy, Capital	301		18 000 00
		Owner's investment.			
	2	Furniture	161	6 00 00	
		Cash	101		6 00 00
		Purchased furniture for cash.			
	3	Rent Expense	640	5 00 00	
		Cash	101		5 00 00
		Paid rent for August.			
	4	Store Equipment	165	1 200 00	
		Accounts Payable	201		1 200 00
		Purchased additional equipment on credit.			
	15	Cash	101	8 25 00	
		Haircutting Services Revenue	403		8 25 00
		Cash receipts from first half of August.			
	15	Accounts Receivable	102	1 00 00	
		Haircutting Services Revenue	403		1 00 00
		To record revenue for services provided on account.			

[continued on next page]

[continued from previous page]

	Date	Account	PR	Debit	Credit
	17	Cash	101	100 00	
		Accounts Receivable	102		100 00
		To record cash received as payment on account.			
	17	Wages Expense	623	125 00	
		Cash	101		125 00
		Paid wages to assistant.			
	31	Cash	101	930 00	
		Haircutting Services Revenue	403		930 00
		Cash receipts from second half of August.			
	31	Accounts Payable	201	400 00	
		Cash	101		400 00
		Paid an installment on the account payable.			
	31	J. Worthy, Withdrawals	302	900 00	
		Cash	101		900 00
		Cash withdrawal by owner.			

2. Post journal entries from part 1 to the ledger accounts:

General Ledger

Cash   Account No. 101

Date	PR	Debit	Credit	Balance
Aug. 1	G1	3,000		3,000
2	G1		600	2,400
3	G1		500	1,900
15	G1	825		2,725
17	G1	100		2,825
17	G1		125	2,700
31	G1	930		3,630
31	G1		400	3,230
31	G1		900	2,330

Accounts Receivable   Account No. 102

Date	PR	Debit	Credit	Balance
Aug. 15	G1	100		100
17	G1		100	0

Furniture   Account No. 161

Date	PR	Debit	Credit	Balance
Aug. 2	G1	600		600

Store Equipment   Account No. 165

Date	PR	Debit	Credit	Balance
Aug. 1	G1	15,000		15,000
4	G1	1,200		16,200

Accounts Payable   Account No. 201

Date	PR	Debit	Credit	Balance
Aug. 4	G1		1,200	1,200
31	G1	400		800

J. Worthy, Capital   Account No. 301

Date	PR	Debit	Credit	Balance
Aug. 1	G1		18,000	18,000

J. Worthy, Withdrawals   Account No. 302

Date	PR	Debit	Credit	Balance
Aug. 31	G1	900		900

Haircutting Services Revenue   Account No. 403

Date	PR	Debit	Credit	Balance
Aug. 15	G1		825	825
15	G1		100	925
31	G1		930	1,855

Wages Expense   Account No. 623

Date	PR	Debit	Credit	Balance
Aug. 17	G1	125		125

Rent Expense   Account No. 640

Date	PR	Debit	Credit	Balance
Aug. 3	G1	500		500

3. Prepare a trial balance from the ledger:

EXPRESSIONS Trial Balance August 31	Debit	Credit
Cash	$ 2,330	
Accounts receivable	0	
Furniture	600	
Store equipment	16,200	
Accounts payable		$ 800
J. Worthy, Capital		18,000
J. Worthy, Withdrawals	900	
Haircutting services revenue		1,855
Wages expense	125	
Rent expense	500	
Totals	$20,655	$20,655

4a. Supplies *debited*
    Cash *credited*
4b. Prepaid Insurance *debited*
    Cash *credited*

4c. Cash *debited*
    Unearned Services Revenue *credited*
4d. Supplies *debited*
    Accounts Payable *credited*

Summary

LO1 **Explain the steps in processing transactions.** The accounting process identifies business transactions and events, analyzes and records their effects, and summarizes and prepares information useful in making decisions. Transactions and events are the starting points in the accounting process. Source documents help in their analysis. The effects of transactions and events are recorded in journals. Posting along with a trial balance helps summarize and classify these effects.

LO2 **Describe source documents and their purpose.** Source documents identify and describe transactions and events. Examples are sales tickets, checks, purchase orders, bills, and bank statements. Source documents provide objective and reliable evidence, making information more useful.

LO3 **Describe a chart of accounts.** The chart of accounts is a list of all accounts and usually includes an identification number assigned to each account.

LO4 **Record transactions in a general journal.** Transactions are recorded in a journal. The journal includes columns for dates, account titles and explanations, debit amounts, credit amounts, and a posting reference column.

LO5 **Post entries to a general ledger.** Each entry in a journal is posted to a ledger. The ledger provides information that is used to produce financial statements. Balance column accounts are widely used and include columns for debits, credits, and the account balance. A posting reference column provides a link between the ledger and the entry in the journal.

LO6 **Prepare financial statements from a trial balance.** A trial balance is prepared from the general ledger, and then used to prepare the income statement, statement of owner's equity, and the balance sheet.

LO7 **Explain how to correct errors in the general journal and general ledger.** If an error in a journal entry is discovered before the error is posted, it can be corrected by drawing a line through the incorrect information. If an error in a journal entry is not discovered until after it is posted, correct this error with a *correcting entry* that removes the amount from the erroneous accounts and records it to the correct accounts.

1. Examples of source documents are sales tickets, checks, purchase orders, charges to customers, bills from suppliers, employee earnings records, and bank statements.

2. Source documents serve many purposes, including recordkeeping and internal control. Source documents, especially if obtained from outside the organization, provide objective and reliable evidence about transactions and their amounts.

3. A company's size and diversity affect the number of accounts in its accounting system. The types of accounts depend on information the company needs to both effectively operate and report its activities in financial statements.

4. A chart of accounts is a list of all of a company's accounts and their identification numbers.

5. The Supplies ledger account balance is overstated by $500 and the Prepaid Insurance ledger account balance is understated by $500. The correcting journal entry is: debit Prepaid Insurance and credit Supplies (both for $500).

Key Terms

Balance column account (p. 80) Account with debit and credit columns for recording entries and another column for showing the balance of the account after each entry.

Chart of accounts (p. 76) List of accounts used by a company; includes an identification number for each account.

Compound journal entry (p. 79) An entry that affects three or more accounts.

General journal (p. 77) All-purpose journal for recording the debits and credits of transactions and events.

Journal (p. 74) Record in which transactions are entered before they are posted to ledger accounts; also *book of original entry*.

Journalizing (p. 74) Process of recording transactions in a journal.

Ledger (p. 74) Record containing all accounts (with amounts) for a business; also called *general ledger*.

Posting (p. 74) Process of transferring journal entry information to a ledger; computerized systems automate this process.

Posting reference (PR) column (p. 78) A column in journals and ledgers in which individual ledger account numbers are entered when entries are posted to those ledger accounts.

Source documents (p. 75) Source of information for accounting entries that can be in either paper or electronic form; also called *business papers*.

Multiple Choice Quiz

Answers on p. 101   mhhe.com/wildCA2e

Additional Multiple Choice Quizzes A and B are available at the book's Website.

1. The process of transferring debits and credits from the journal to the ledger is called
   a. Transferring
   b. Posting
   c. Journalizing
   d. Referencing

2. Unearned revenue exists when customers pay in advance for products or services and is accounted for as a(n)
   a. Asset
   b. Revenue
   c. Expense
   d. Liability

3. Amalia Company received its utility bill for the current period of $700 and immediately paid it. Its journal entry to record this transaction includes a
   a. Credit to Utility Expense for $700.
   b. Debit to Utility Expense for $700.
   c. Debit to Accounts Payable for $700.
   d. Debit to Cash for $700.
   e. Credit to Capital for $700.

4. Liang Shue contributed $250,000 cash and land worth $500,000 to open his new business, Shue Consulting. Which of the following journal entries does Shue Consulting make to record this transaction?

		Debit	Credit
a.	Cash Assets	750,000	
	L. Shue, Capital		750,000
b.	L. Shue, Capital	750,000	
	Assets		750,000
c.	Cash	250,000	
	Land	500,000	
	L. Shue, Capital		750,000
d.	L. Shue, Capital	750,000	
	Cash		250,000
	Land		500,000

5. A trial balance prepared at year-end shows total credits exceed total debits by $765. This discrepancy could have been caused by
   a. An error in the general journal where a $765 increase in Accounts Payable was recorded as a $765 decrease in Accounts Payable.
   b. The ledger balance for Accounts Payable of $7,650 being entered in the trial balance as $765.
   c. A general journal error where a $765 increase in Accounts Receivable was recorded as a $765 increase in Cash.
   d. The ledger balance of $850 in Accounts Receivable was entered in the trial balance as $85.
   e. An error in recording a $765 increase in Cash as a credit.

Discussion Questions

1. Discuss the steps in processing business transactions.
2. What kinds of transactions can be recorded in a general journal?
3. Are debits or credits typically listed first in general journal entries? Are the debits or the credits indented?
4. Should a transaction be recorded first in a journal or the ledger? Why?
5. If an incorrect amount is journalized and posted to the accounts, how should the error be corrected?
6. If assets are valuable resources and asset accounts have debit balances, why do expense accounts also have debit balances?
7. What is the difference between a T-account and a general ledger account?

connect

Identify the items from the following list that are likely to serve as source documents.

a. Sales ticket	**d.** Telephone bill	**g.** Balance sheet
b. Income statement	**e.** Invoice from supplier	**h.** Prepaid insurance
c. Trial balance	**f.** Company revenue account	**i.** Bank statement

QUICK STUDY

QS 4–1

Identifying source documents

LO2

Prepare journal entries for each of the following selected transactions.

a. On January 13, DeShawn Tyler opens a landscaping business called Elegant Lawns by investing $70,000 cash along with equipment having a $30,000 value.

b. On January 21, Elegant Lawns purchases office supplies on credit for $280.

c. On January 29, Elegant Lawns receives $7,800 cash for performing landscaping services.

d. On January 30, Elegant Lawns receives $1,000 cash in advance of providing landscaping services to a customer.

QS 4–2

Preparing journal entries   **LO4**

Refer to QS 4-2. Post each of the journal entries to the correct T-accounts.

QS 4–3

Posting to T-accounts   **LO5**

Goro Co. bills a client $62,000 for services provided and agrees to accept the following two items in full payment: (1) $10,000 cash, and (2) computer equipment worth $52,000. What journal entry should Goro make to record this transaction?

QS 4–4

Compound journal entry   **LO4**

A trial balance has total debits of $20,000 and total credits of $24,500. Which one of the following errors would create this imbalance? Explain.

a. A $2,250 debit to Rent Expense in a journal entry is incorrectly posted to the ledger as a $2,250 credit.

b. A $4,500 debit to Salaries Expense in a journal entry is incorrectly posted to the ledger as a $4,500 credit.

c. A $2,250 credit to Consulting Fees Earned in a journal entry is incorrectly posted to the ledger as a $2,250 debit.

QS 4–5

Identifying a posting error   **LO7**

On August 4, 2010, a company incorrectly debits Rent Expense instead of Salaries Expense when recording payroll for the month. On August 30, the error is discovered while preparing the trial balance. Propose a correcting journal entry to correct the books. If the error had not been discovered, how would the company's income statement have been affected?

QS 4–6

Preparing a correcting journal entry   **LO7**

Prepare journal entries for the following selected transactions and post them to the appropriate general ledger accounts. In posting the entries, use account numbers from the chart of accounts at the back of the book, and assume the journal entries are made on page 4 of the general journal.

a. Harley Vance invests $60,000 of cash along with fitness equipment valued at $25,000 in her startup business named HV Fitness.

b. Vance withdraws $2,800 cash for personal use.

QS 4–7

Journalizing and posting owner transactions   **LO4   LO5**

QS 4–8
Journalizing and posting
transactions   **LO4**   **LO5**

Prepare journal entries for the following selected transactions of JK Design and post them to the appropriate general ledger accounts. In posting the entries, use account numbers from the chart of accounts at the back of the book, and assume the journal entries are made on page 4 of the general journal.

a. Completed $6,250 of design work for a client, who agrees to pay within 30 days.

b. Received $4,000 cash as partial payment from the customer in transaction *a*.

c. Paid $1,800 cash salary to an assistant.

QS 4–9
Journalizing transactions   **LO4**

Prepare journal entries for the following selected transactions of Custom Cabinets.

a. Purchased $2,000 of office supplies on credit.

b. Provided services to a client and collected $8,000 cash.

c. Paid $635 in cash for this month's utilities.

d. Paid $2,000 in cash to settle the payable created in transaction *a*.

EXERCISES

Exercise 4–1
Preparing general journal entries
LO4

Prepare general journal entries for the following transactions of a new business called Pose-for-Pics.

Aug.	1	Madison Harris, the owner, invested $6,500 cash and $33,500 of photography equipment in the business.
	2	Paid $2,100 cash for an insurance policy covering the next 24 months.
	5	Purchased office supplies for $880 cash.
	20	Received $3,000 cash in photography fees earned.
	29	Paid $675 cash for August utilities.

Exercise 4–2
Preparing T-accounts (ledger)
and a trial balance   **LO5**

Use the information in Exercise 4-1 to prepare an August 31 trial balance for Pose-for-Pics. Open these T-accounts: Cash; Office Supplies; Prepaid Insurance; Photography Equipment; M. Harris, Capital; Photography Fees Earned; and Utilities Expense. Post the general journal entries to these T-accounts (which will serve as the ledger), and prepare a trial balance.

Exercise 4–3
Preparing an income statement
LO6

On October 1, Diondre Shabazz organized a new consulting firm called OnTech. On October 31, the company's general ledger shows the following items and amounts. Use this information to prepare an October income statement for the business.

Cash	$11,360		D. Shabazz, Withdrawals	$ 2,000
Accounts receivable	14,000		Consulting fees earned	14,000
Office supplies	3,250		Rent expense	3,550
Patents	46,000		Salaries expense	7,000
Office equipment	18,000		Telephone expense	760
Accounts payable	8,500		Miscellaneous expenses	580
D. Shabazz, Capital	84,000			

Check   Net income, $2,110

Exercise 4–4
Preparing a statement of
owner's equity   **LO6**

Use the information in Exercise 4-3 to prepare an October statement of owner's equity for OnTech.

Use the information in Exercise 4-3 (if completed, you can also use your solution to Exercise 4-4) to pre-pare an October 31 balance sheet for OnTech.

Exercise 4-5
Preparing a balance sheet   **LO6**

Assume the following T-accounts reflect Belle Co.'s general ledger and that seven transactions *a* through *g* are posted to them. Use information from the T-accounts to prepare general journal entries for each of the seven transactions (a) through (g). Provide a short description of each transaction.

Exercise 4-6
Preparing general journal entries
LO4

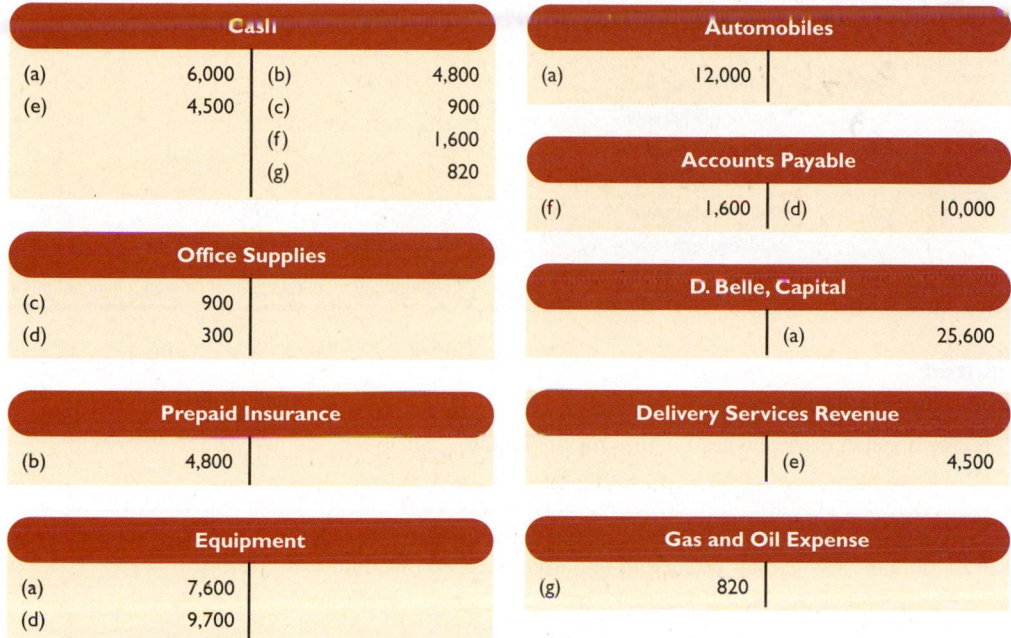

Cash			
(a)	6,000	(b)	4,800
(e)	4,500	(c)	900
		(f)	1,600
		(g)	820

Office Supplies	
(c)	900
(d)	300

Prepaid Insurance	
(b)	4,800

Equipment	
(a)	7,600
(d)	9,700

Automobiles	
(a)	12,000

Accounts Payable			
(f)	1,600	(d)	10,000

D. Belle, Capital			
		(a)	25,600

Delivery Services Revenue			
		(e)	4,500

Gas and Oil Expense	
(g)	820

Bonnie Stradling opened a computer consulting business called Stradling Consultants and completed the following transactions in the first month of operations.

Exercise 4-7
Preparing journal entries   **LO4**

April 1   Bonnie invested $80,000 cash along with office equipment valued at $26,000 in the business.
2   Prepaid $9,000 cash for 12 months' rent for office space. (*Hint:* Debit Prepaid Rent for $9,000.)
3   Made credit purchases for $8,000 in office equipment and $3,600 in office supplies. Payment is due within 10 days.
6   Completed services for a client and immediately received $4,000 cash.
9   Completed a $6,000 project for a client, who must pay within 30 days.
13   Paid $11,600 cash to settle the account payable created on April 3.
19   Paid $2,400 cash for the premium on a 12-month insurance policy. (*Hint:* Debit Prepaid Insurance for $2,400.)
22   Received $4,400 cash as partial payment for the work completed on April 9.
25   Completed work for another client for $2,890 on credit.
28   Bonnie withdrew $5,500 cash for personal use.
29   Purchased $600 of additional office supplies on credit.
30   Paid $435 cash for this month's utility bill.

Required

Prepare general journal entries to record these transactions (use the account titles listed below). Cash (101); Accounts Receivable (106); Office Supplies (124); Prepaid Insurance (128); Prepaid Rent (131); Office Equipment (163); Accounts Payable (201); B. Stradling, Capital (301); B. Stradling, Withdrawals (302); Services Revenue (403); and Utilities Expense (690).

Exercise 4–8
Preparing financial statements from the trial balance   **LO6**

After posting the journal entries from Exercise 4-7 to general ledger accounts, Stradling Consultants reports the following trial balance.

STRADLING CONSULTANTS Trial Balance April 30		
	Debit	**Credit**
Cash	$ 59,465	
Accounts receivable	4,490	
Office supplies	4,200	
Prepaid insurance	2,400	
Prepaid rent	9,000	
Office equipment	34,000	
Accounts payable		$ 600
B. Stradling, Capital		106,000
B. Stradling, Withdrawals	5,500	
Services revenue		12,890
Utilities expense	435	
Total	$119,490	$119,490

Required

1. Prepare an income statement for the month.

2. Prepare a statement of owner's equity for the month.

Check   Ending owner's equity, $112,955

Exercise 4–9
Preparing a balance sheet from the trial balance   **LO6**

Refer to the trial balance in Exercise 4-8 and prepare a balance sheet for Stradling Consultants as of the end of the month. The ending balance in the owner's capital account is $112,955.

Exercise 4–10
Chart of accounts   **LO3**

Using the chart of accounts provided at the back of this book, determine the account names and their account numbers that would be used to record the following transactions.

a. Owner invests cash and office equipment in a new business.

b. Purchase office supplies on credit.

c. Provide services to a client and collect cash.

d. Pay cash for utilities expenses.

e. Provide services to a client, who agrees to pay within 30 days.

f. Owner withdraws cash for personal use.

Exercise 4–11
Preparing journal entries   **LO4**

Kamilos Management Services opens for business and completes these transactions in September.

Sept. 1   Tom Kamilos, the owner, invests $38,000 cash along with office equipment valued at $15,000 in the business.

2   Prepaid $9,000 cash for 12 months' rent for office space. (*Hint:* Debit Prepaid Rent for $9,000.)

4   Made credit purchases for $8,000 in office equipment and $2,400 in office supplies. Payment is due within 10 days.

8   Completed work for a client and immediately received $3,280 cash.

12   Completed a $15,400 project for a client, who must pay within 30 days.

13   Paid $10,400 cash to settle the payable created on September 4.

19   Paid $1,900 cash for the premium on an 18-month insurance policy. (*Hint:* Debit Prepaid Insurance for $1,900.)

22   Received $7,700 cash as partial payment for the work completed on September 12.

24   Completed work for another client for $2,100 on credit.

28   Tom Kamilos withdrew $5,300 cash for personal use.

29   Purchased $550 of additional office supplies on credit.

30   Paid $860 cash for this month's utility bill.

Required

Prepare general journal entries to record these transactions (use account titles listed below). Cash (101); Accounts Receivable (106); Office Supplies (124); Prepaid Insurance (128); Prepaid Rent (131); Office Equipment (163); Accounts Payable (201); T. Kamilos, Capital (301); T. Kamilos, Withdrawals (302); Service Fees Earned (401); and Utilities Expense (690).

After posting the journal entries from Exercise 4-11, Kamilos Management Services reports the following trial balance.

Exercise 4-12
Preparing financial statements from the trial balance   **LO6**

KAMILOS MANAGEMENT SERVICES
Trial Balance
September 30

	Debit	Credit
Cash	$21,520	
Accounts receivable	9,800	
Office supplies	2,950	
Prepaid insurance	1,900	
Prepaid rent	9,000	
Office equipment	23,000	
Accounts payable		$ 550
T. Kamilos, Capital		53,000
T. Kamilos, Withdrawals	5,300	
Service fees earned		20,780
Utilities expense	860	
Totals	$74,330	$74,330

Required

1. Prepare an income statement for the month.
2. Prepare a statement of owner's equity for the month.

Check Ending T. Kamilos, Capital $67,620

Refer to the trial balance provided in Exercise 4-12 and prepare a balance sheet as of the end of the month. The ending balance in the owner's capital account is $67,620.

Exercise 4-13
Preparing a balance sheet from the trial balance   **LO6**

connect

Aracel Engineering completed the following transactions in the month of June.

a. Jenna Aracel, the owner, invested $100,000 cash, office equipment with a value of $5,000, and $60,000 of drafting equipment to launch the business.
b. Purchased land worth $6,300 for an office by paying $6,300 cash.
c. Purchased a portable building with $55,000 cash and moved it onto the land acquired in b.
d. Paid $3,000 cash for the premium on a 12-month insurance policy.
e. Completed and delivered a set of plans for a client and collected $6,200 cash.
f. Purchased $9,500 of additional drafting equipment by paying $9,500 cash.
g. Completed $14,000 of engineering services for a client. This amount is to be received in 30 days.
h. Purchased $1,150 of additional office equipment on credit.
i. Completed engineering services for $22,000 on credit.
j. Received a bill for rent of equipment that was used on a recently completed job. The $1,000 rent cost must be paid within 30 days.
k. Collected $7,000 cash in partial payment from the client described in transaction g.
l. Paid $1,200 cash for wages to a drafting assistant.
m. Paid $1,150 cash to settle the account payable created in transaction h.
n. Paid $925 cash for minor repairs to its drafting equipment.
o. Jenna Aracel withdrew $9,480 cash for personal use.
p. Paid $1,200 cash for wages to a drafting assistant.
q. Paid $2,500 cash for advertisements in the local newspaper during June.

PROBLEM SET A

Problem 4-1A
Preparing and posting journal entries; preparing a trial balance
LO3   LO4   LO5

Required

1. Prepare general journal entries to record these transactions (use the account titles listed in part 2).
2. Open the following ledger accounts—their account numbers are in parentheses (use the balance column format): Cash (101); Accounts Receivable (106); Prepaid Insurance (108); Office Equipment (163); Drafting Equipment (164); Building (170); Land (172); Accounts Payable (201); J. Aracel, Capital (301); J. Aracel, Withdrawals (302); Engineering Fees Earned (402); Wages Expense (601); Equipment Rental Expense (602); Advertising Expense (603); and Repairs Expense (604). Post the journal entries from part 1 to the accounts and enter the balance after each posting.
3. Prepare a trial balance as of the end of June.

Check   (2) Ending balances: Cash, $22,945; Accounts Receivable, $29,000; Accounts Payable, $1,000

(3) Trial balance totals, $208,200

Problem 4-2A

Preparing and posting journal entries; preparing a trial balance

LO3 LO4 LO5

mhhe.com/wildCA2e

Kasey Reese opens a consulting business called Cougar Consulting and completes the following transactions in March.

March	1	Reese invested $150,000 cash along with $22,000 of office equipment in the business.
	2	Prepaid $6,000 cash for six months' rent for an office. (*Hint:* Debit Prepaid Rent for $6,000.)
	3	Made credit purchases of office equipment for $3,000 and office supplies for $1,200. Payment is due within 10 days.
	6	Completed services for a client and immediately received $4,000 cash.
	9	Completed a $7,500 project for a client, who must pay within 30 days.
	12	Paid $4,200 cash to settle the account payable created on March 3.
	19	Paid $5,000 cash for the premium on a 12-month insurance policy.
	22	Received $3,500 cash as partial payment for the work completed on March 9.
	25	Completed work for another client for $3,820 on credit.
	29	Reese withdrew $5,100 cash for personal use.
	30	Purchased $600 of additional office supplies on credit.
	31	Paid $500 cash for this month's utility bill.

Required

1. Prepare general journal entries to record these transactions (use the account titles listed in part 2).
2. Open the following ledger accounts—their account numbers are in parentheses (use the balance column format): Cash (101); Accounts Receivable (106); Office Supplies (124); Prepaid Insurance (128); Prepaid Rent (131); Office Equipment (163); Accounts Payable (201); K. Reese, Capital (301); K. Reese, Withdrawals (302); Services Revenue (403); and Utilities Expense (690). Post the journal entries from part 1 to the ledger accounts and enter the balance after each posting.
3. Prepare a trial balance as of the end of March.

Check   (2) Ending balances: Cash, $136,700; Accounts Receivable, $7,820; Accounts Payable, $600

(3) Total debits, $187,920

Problem 4-3A

Preparing financial statements from the trial balance **LO6**

Below is the trial balance for HV Consulting for the month ended September 30.

HV CONSULTING Trial Balance September 30		
	Debit	**Credit**
Cash	$ 12,665	
Accounts receivable	2,250	
Office supplies	2,000	
Office equipment	50,900	
Automobiles	16,500	
Building	160,000	
Land	40,000	
Accounts payable		$ 5,600
H. Venedict, Capital		271,500
H. Venedict, Withdrawals	2,800	
Fees earned		14,250
Salaries expense	3,600	
Utilities expense	635	
Total	$291,350	$291,350

Required

1. Prepare an income statement for the month.

2. Prepare a statement of owner's equity for the month.

3. Prepare a balance sheet as of the end of the month.

After all journal entries have been posted, Levi Hancock finds that errors have been made in recording some company transactions. Help Levi prepare correcting journal entries for each of the following errors.

1. The following journal entry was made to record the purchase of supplies for $700 cash.

Equipment	700	
Cash		700

2. The following journal entry was made to record the cash payment of $1,850 for prepaid rent.

Prepaid Insurance	1,850	
Cash		1,850

3. The following journal entry was made to record the cash receipt of $2,000 for consulting services.

Accounts Receivable	2,000	
Consulting Services Revenue		2,000

4. The following journal entry was made to record the cash payment of $1,375 for utilities expense.

Utilities Expense	1,375	
Accounts Payable		1,375

Problem 4–4A

Correcting errors with journal entries   **LO7**

At the beginning of April, Bernadette Grechus launched a custom computer solutions company called Softworks. The company had the following transactions during April.

a. Bernadette Grechus invested $75,000 cash, office equipment with a value of $5,750, and $30,000 of computer equipment in the company.

b. Purchased land worth $22,000 for an office by paying $22,000 cash.

c. Purchased a portable building with $34,500 cash and moved it onto the land acquired in *b*.

d. Paid $5,000 cash for the premium on a two-year insurance policy.

e. Provided services to a client and immediately collected $4,600 cash.

f. Purchased $4,500 of additional computer equipment by paying $4,500 cash.

g. Completed $4,250 of services for a client. This amount is to be received within 30 days.

h. Purchased $950 of additional office equipment on credit.

i. Completed client services for $10,200 on credit.

j. Received a bill for rent of a computer testing device that was used on a recently completed job. The $580 rent cost must be paid within 30 days.

k. Collected $8,800 cash from the client described in transaction *i*.

l. Paid $1,800 cash for wages to an assistant.

m. Paid $950 cash to settle the payable created in transaction *h*.

n. Paid $608 cash for minor repairs to the company's computer equipment.

o. Grechus withdrew $6,230 cash for personal use.

p. Paid $1,800 cash for wages to an assistant.

q. Paid $750 cash for advertisements in the local newspaper during April.

PROBLEM SET B

Problem 4–1B

Preparing and posting journal entries; preparing a trial balance

LO3   LO4   LO5

Required

1. Prepare general journal entries to record these transactions (use account titles listed in part 2).

2. Open the following ledger accounts—their account numbers are in parentheses (use the balance column format): Cash (101); Accounts Receivable (106); Prepaid Insurance (108); Office Equipment

Check   (2) Ending balances: Cash, $10,262; Accounts Receivable, $5,650; Accounts Payable, $580

(163); Computer Equipment (164); Building (170); Land (172); Accounts Payable (201); B. Grechus, Capital (301); B. Grechus, Withdrawals (302); Fees Earned (402); Wages Expense (601); Computer Rental Expense (602); Advertising Expense (603); and Repairs Expense (604). Post the journal entries from part 1 to the accounts and enter the balance after each posting.

(3) Trial balance totals, $130,380

3. Prepare a trial balance as of the end of April.

Problem 4–2B

Preparing and posting journal entries; preparing a trial balance

LO3   LO4   LO5

Barry Wells Management Group opens for business and completes these transactions in November.

Nov.   1   Barry Wells, the owner, invested $30,000 cash along with $15,000 of office equipment in the business.
     2   Prepaid $4,500 cash for six months' rent for an office. (*Hint:* Debit Prepaid Rent for $4,500.)
     4   Made credit purchases of office equipment for $2,500 and of office supplies for $600. Payment is due within 10 days.
     8   Completed work for a client and immediately received $3,400 cash.
    12   Completed a $10,200 project for a client, who must pay within 30 days.
    13   Paid $3,100 cash to settle the payable created on November 4.
    19   Paid $1,800 cash for the premium on a 24-month insurance policy.
    22   Received $5,200 cash as partial payment for the work completed on November 12.
    24   Completed work for another client for $1,750 on credit.
    28   Barry Wells withdrew $5,300 cash for personal use.
    29   Purchased $249 of additional office supplies on credit.
    30   Paid $831 cash for this month's utility bill.

Required

1. Prepare general journal entries to record these transactions (use account titles listed in part 2).

Check   (2) Ending balances: Cash, $23,069; Accounts Receivable, $6,750; Accounts Payable, $249

2. Open the following ledger accounts—their account numbers are in parentheses (use the balance column format): Cash (101); Accounts Receivable (106); Office Supplies (124); Prepaid Insurance (128); Prepaid Rent (131); Office Equipment (163); Accounts Payable (201); B. Wells, Capital (301); B. Wells, Withdrawals (302); Services Revenue (403); and Utilities Expense (690). Post the journal entries from part 1 to the ledger accounts and enter the balance after each posting.

(3) Total debits, $60,599

3. Prepare a trial balance as of the end of November.

Problem 4–3B

Preparing financial statements from the trial balance   **LO6**

Below is the trial balance for Nuncio Consulting for the month ended June 30.

NUNCIO CONSULTING Trial Balance June 30		
	Debit	**Credit**
Cash	$17,860	
Accounts receivable	2,000	
Office supplies	500	
Office equipment	15,600	
Automobiles	8,000	
Building	40,000	
Land	7,500	
Accounts payable		$ 1,200
A. Nuncio, Capital		86,500
A. Nuncio, Withdrawals	1,100	
Fees earned		7,400
Salaries expense	2,000	
Utilities expense	540	
Total	$95,100	$95,100

Required

1. Prepare an income statement for the month.

2. Prepare a statement of owner's equity for the month.

3. Prepare a balance sheet as of the end of the month.

After all journal entries have been posted, Kasey Beck finds that errors have been made in recording some company transactions. Help Kasey prepare correcting journal entries for each of the following errors.

Problem 4-4B
Correcting errors with journal entries **LO7**

1. The following journal entry was made to record the purchase of equipment for $1,450 cash.

Supplies	1,450	
Cash		1,450

2. The following journal entry was made to record the cash purchase of $870 for prepaid rent.

Rent Expense	870	
Cash		870

3. The following journal entry was made to record the cash payment of $1,780 for utilities expense.

Salaries Expense	1,780	
Cash		1,780

4. The following journal entry was made to record $2,000 for consulting services on account.

Cash	2,000	
Consulting Services Revenue		2,000

(This serial problem started in Chapter 1 and continues through most of the chapters. If previous chapter segments were not completed, the problem can begin at this point. It is helpful, but not necessary, to use the Working Papers that accompany this book.)

SERIAL PROBLEM

Success Systems
LO3 LO4 LO5

SP 4 On October 1, 2010, Adriana Lopez launched a computer services company called Success Systems, which provides consulting services, computer system installations, and custom program development. Lopez adopts the calendar year for reporting purposes and expects to prepare the company's first set of financial statements on December 31, 2010. The company's initial chart of accounts follows.

Account	No.	Account	No.
Cash	101	A. Lopez, Capital	301
Accounts Receivable	106	A. Lopez, Withdrawals	302
Computer Supplies	126	Computer Services Revenue	403
Prepaid Insurance	128	Wages Expense	623
Prepaid Rent	131	Advertising Expense	655
Office Equipment	163	Mileage Expense	676
Computer Equipment	167	Miscellaneous Expenses	677
Accounts Payable	201	Repairs Expense—Computer	684

Required

1. Prepare journal entries to record each of the following transactions for Success Systems.

Oct. 1 Lopez invested $75,000 cash, a $25,000 computer system, and $10,000 of office equipment in the business.

      2 Paid $3,500 cash for four months' rent. (*Hint:* Debit Prepaid Rent for $3,500.)

      3 Purchased $1,600 of computer supplies on credit from Corvina Office Products.

      5 Paid $2,400 cash for one year's premium on a property and liability insurance policy. (*Hint:* Debit Prepaid Insurance for $2,400.)

      6 Billed Easy Leasing $6,200 for services performed in installing a new Web server.

	8	Paid $1,600 cash for the computer supplies purchased from Corvina Office Products on October 3.
	12	Billed Easy Leasing another $1,950 for services performed.
	15	Received $6,200 cash from Easy Leasing on its account.
	17	Paid $900 cash to repair computer equipment that was damaged when moving it.
	20	Paid $1,790 cash for an advertisement in the local newspaper.
	22	Received $1,950 cash from Easy Leasing on its account.
	28	Billed Clark Company $7,300 for services performed.
	31	Paid $1,050 cash for Michelle Jones's wages for seven days' work.
	31	Lopez withdrew $4,000 cash for personal use.
Nov.	1	Reimbursed Lopez in cash for business automobile mileage allowance (Lopez logged 1,200 miles at $0.32 per mile).
	2	Received $3,600 cash from Edge Corporation for computer services performed.
	5	Purchased computer supplies for $1,750 cash from Corvina Office Products.
	8	Billed Gomez Co. $6,500 for services performed.
	18	Received $5,000 cash from Clark Company as partial payment of the October 28 bill.
	22	Donated $300 cash to the United Way in the company's name.
	24	Completed work for Alex's Engineering Co. and sent it a bill for $7,000.
	28	Reimbursed Lopez in cash for business automobile mileage (1,500 miles at $0.32 per mile).
	30	Paid $2,100 cash for Michelle Jones's wages for 14 days' work.
	30	Lopez withdrew $2,500 cash for personal use.

Check (2) Cash, Nov. 30 bal., $68,996

(3) Trial bal. totals, $142,550

2. Open ledger accounts (in balance column format) and post the journal entries from part 1 to them.

3. Prepare a trial balance (dated November 30, 2010) from the ending balances in the ledger accounts from part 1.

BEYOND THE NUMBERS

REPORTING IN ACTION
LO2

BTN 4-1   **Best Buy** sells consumer electronics in its retail outlets and from its online stores.

Required

Based on your understanding of Best Buy, identify at least four types of source documents that Best Buy would likely use in its operations.

ETHICS CHALLENGE
LO2

BTN 4-2   Your manager requires that you, as cashier, immediately enter each sale. Recently, lunch hour traffic has increased and the assistant manager asks you to avoid delays by taking customers' cash and making change without entering sales. The assistant manager says she will add up cash and enter sales after lunch. She says that, in this way, the register will always match the cash amount when the manager arrives at three o'clock. What do you do?

Required

Discuss the advantages to the process proposed by the assistant manager and the concerns you have with the proposal. Decide what you would do.

WORKPLACE COMMUNICATION
LO4   LO5

BTN 4-3   Mark Ellingson is an aspiring entrepreneur and your friend. He is having difficulty understanding the link between the general journal and the general ledger.

Required

Write a half-page memorandum to Ellingson explaining how the general journal and the general ledger are linked to each other.

TAKING IT TO THE NET
LO4   LO5   LO7

BTN 4-4   **Quickbooks** is an accounting software program with both a general journal and general ledger. Access Quickbooks' Website (**QuickBooks.com**) and review the various Quickbooks' software programs to answer the following requirements.

Required

1. Which Quickbooks' program would be most appropriate for a small business? Which would be most appropriate for a large business?
2. Many of the examples given in this chapter assumed manual journal entries, where journal entries are recorded and then later posted. How would a computerized program be different? How would the correction of errors differ?

BTN 4–5   Refer to the chapter's opening feature about Katrina Markoff and her **Vosges Haut Chocolat** company.

ENTREPRENEURS IN BUSINESS
LO3

Required

What are some examples of accounts you would expect to see in the Vosges Haut Chocolat company chart of accounts?

---

1. b
2. d
3. b; debit Utility Expense for $700, and credit Cash for $700.

4. c; debit Cash for $250,000, debit Land for $500,000, and credit L. Shue, Capital for $750,000.
5. d

ANSWERS TO MULTIPLE CHOICE QUIZ

A Look Back

Chapters 3 and 4 explained the analysis and recording of transactions. We showed how to apply and interpret T-accounts, double-entry accounting, ledgers, postings, and trial balances.

A Look at This Chapter

This chapter introduces the need to adjust accounts. Adjusting accounts is important for recognizing revenues and expenses in the proper period. We describe the adjusted trial balance and how it is used to prepare financial statements.

A Look Ahead

Chapter 6 highlights the completion of the accounting cycle. We explain the important final steps in the accounting process. These include closing procedures and the post-closing trial balance. We show how a work sheet can aid in this process.

Chapter 5

Adjusting Accounts and Preparing Financial Statements

Learning Objectives

LO 1 Explain accrual accounting and how it improves financial statements.

LO 2 Identify the types of accounting adjustments and their purpose.

LO 3 Prepare and explain adjusting entries.

LO 4 Explain and prepare an adjusted trial balance.

LO 5 Prepare financial statements from an adjusted trial balance.

"Get a good accountant"
—Jason Kapalka (from left: John Vechey, Brian Feite, Jason Kapalka)

High Score

SEATTLE—Jason Kapalka met John Vechey and Brian Feite, both 19 at the time, after the two had created an online game. "We hit it off really well," explains Jason. "We were all a little unhappy with our jobs. We thought, 'Hey, we could start our own company.'" Their startup company, **PopCap Games** (**PopCap.com**), is a creator and provider of downloadable games. Jason recalls that their friends considered them crazy.

Undaunted, the three scraped together the little cash they had. Jason explains that each worked out of their respective apartments to save money. "We survived," admits Jason, "because we didn't have many expenses." The young trio quickly developed a system to account for everything, including cash, revenues, receivables, and payables. They also adjusted to the deferral and accrual of revenues and expenses. Setting up a good accounting system is an important part of success, explains Jason. "Don't wait until . . . everything is a big mess."

Most of PopCap's sales are paid for in advance of game delivery. This means few uncollectible accounts.

The team also defers payment of their expenses to the time permitted—which is good management. "We're trying to keep a very simple business model," insists Jason. The team continues to fine-tune their accounting system as they remain focused on revenues, income, assets, and liabilities. "No matter what you do," argues Jason, "there's always something that you haven't done."

Financial statements preparation and analysis are a process that the three continue to work on. Although they insist on timely and accurate accounting reports, Jason says "it really helped us to keep things simple." To help make it simple, they took time to understand accounting adjustments and their effects. It is part of the larger picture. "You're not going to get breaks unless you're working hard."

Today, PopCap is a success story. "Now we can afford Mac and Cheese, and the occasional bottle of water," laughs Jason. "Life is good!"

[Sources: *PopCap Website,* January 2009; *Entrepreneur,* February 2008; *Wired,* March 2008; *2o2p Magazine,* September 2006; *Washington Post,* March 2008]

The past few chapters showed how companies use accounting systems to collect information about *external* transactions. We also explained how journals, ledgers, and other tools are useful in preparing financial statements. This chapter describes the accounting process for producing useful information involving *internal* transactions. An important part of this process is adjusting account balances so that financial statements at the end of a reporting period reflect the effects of all transactions. We then explain the important steps in preparing financial statements.

Adjusting Accounts and Preparing Financial Statements

Timing and Reporting
- Accrual basis versus cash basis
- Recognizing revenues and expenses

Adjusting Accounts
- Framework for adjustments
- 3-step process
- Prepaid expenses
- Accrued expenses
- Journalizing and posting adjusting entries
- Adjusted trial balance

Preparing Financial Statements
- Income statement
- Statement of owner's equity
- Balance sheet

Timing and Reporting

This section describes how the use of accrual basis accounting impacts the recording of revenues and expenses.

Accrual Basis versus Cash Basis

LO1 Explain accrual accounting and how it improves financial statements.

After external transactions and events are recorded, several accounts still need adjustment before their balances appear in financial statements. This need arises because internal transactions and events remain unrecorded. **Accrual basis accounting** uses the adjusting process to recognize revenues when earned and expenses when incurred (matched with revenues). Sometimes cash is received before (or after) the revenue is earned. Likewise, sometimes cash is paid before an expense is incurred. **Cash basis accounting** recognizes revenue when cash is received and records expenses when cash is paid. This means that cash basis net income is the difference between cash receipts and cash payments. It is commonly held that accrual accounting better reflects business performance than does cash basis accounting.

As an example, FastForward's insurance costs $100 per month, but FastForward paid $2,400 in advance for 24 months of insurance coverage beginning on December 1, 2010. Accrual accounting requires FastForward to record $100 of insurance expense per month. Exhibit 5.1 illustrates this allocation of insurance cost across these three years. The accrual basis balance sheet reports any unexpired insurance as a Prepaid Insurance asset. For example, FastForward would report an asset of $2,300 at the end of 2010.

Exhibit 5.1

Accrual Basis Accounting for Allocating Prepaid Insurance to Expense

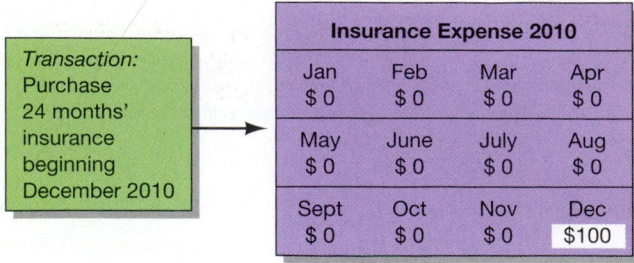

Transaction: Purchase 24 months' insurance beginning December 2010

Insurance Expense 2010			
Jan $0	Feb $0	Mar $0	Apr $0
May $0	June $0	July $0	Aug $0
Sept $0	Oct $0	Nov $0	Dec $100

Insurance Expense 2011			
Jan $100	Feb $100	Mar $100	Apr $100
May $100	June $100	July $100	Aug $100
Sept $100	Oct $100	Nov $100	Dec $100

Insurance Expense 2012			
Jan $100	Feb $100	Mar $100	Apr $100
May $100	June $100	July $100	Aug $100
Sept $100	Oct $100	Nov $100	Dec $0

Alternatively, a cash basis income statement for December 2010 reports insurance expense of $2,400, as shown in Exhibit 5.2. The cash basis income statements for years 2011 and 2012 show no insurance expense. Also, the cash basis balance sheet never reports an insurance asset.

Exhibit 5.2

Cash Accounting for Allocating Prepaid Insurance to Expense

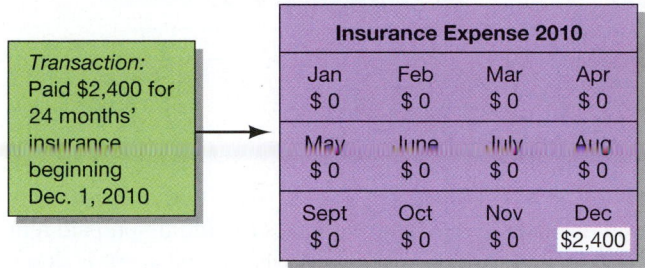

Transaction: Paid $2,400 for 24 months' insurance beginning Dec. 1, 2010

Insurance Expense 2010			
Jan $0	Feb $0	Mar $0	Apr $0
May $0	June $0	July $0	Aug $0
Sept $0	Oct $0	Nov $0	Dec $2,400

Insurance Expense 2011			
Jan $0	Feb $0	Mar $0	Apr $0
May $0	June $0	July $0	Aug $0
Sept $0	Oct $0	Nov $0	Dec $0

Insurance Expense 2012			
Jan $0	Feb $0	Mar $0	Apr $0
May $0	June $0	July $0	Aug $0
Sept $0	Oct $0	Nov $0	Dec $0

Recognizing Revenues and Expenses

To provide timely information, accountants prepare reports at regular intervals. The **time period assumption** assumes a business's activities can be divided into specific periods, such as a month or year. Reports covering a one-year period are called **annual financial statements.** Annual financial statements can be for a **fiscal year** made up of any 12 consecutive months, and are not always for a calendar year ending on December 31. **Interim financial statements** cover one, three, or six months of activity.

We use the time period assumption to divide a company's activities into specific time periods, but not all activities are complete when financial statements are prepared. Thus, adjustments often are required to get correct account balances.

We rely on two principles in the adjusting process: revenue recognition and matching. The **revenue recognition principle** requires that revenue be recorded when earned. Most companies earn revenue when they provide services and products to customers. A major goal of the adjusting process is to have revenue recognized (reported) in the time period when it is earned.

The **matching principle** aims to record expenses in the same accounting period as the revenues that are earned as a result of these expenses. This matching of expenses with the revenue benefits is a major part of the adjusting process.

Matching expenses with revenues often requires us to predict certain events. When we use financial statements, we must understand that they require estimates and therefore include measures that are not always precise. **Walt Disney**'s annual report explains that its production costs from movies, such as *Pirates of the Caribbean,* are matched to revenues based on a ratio of current revenues from the movie divided by its predicted total revenues.

Answers—p. 115

HOW YOU DOIN'?

1. What two accounting principles most directly drive the adjusting process?

2. If your company pays a $4,800 premium on April 1, 2010, for two years' insurance coverage, how much insurance expense is reported in 2011 using cash basis accounting? Using accrual basis accounting?

Adjusting Accounts

In this section we suggest a framework for considering the types of adjustments that must be made at the end of the reporting period.

LO2 Identify the types of accounting adjustments and their purpose.

Framework for Adjustments

Adjustments are necessary for transactions that extend over more than one accounting period. It is helpful to group adjustments by the timing of cash receipt or cash payment in relation to when the work is performed. Exhibit 5.3 identifies types of adjustments.

Exhibit 5.3

Types of Adjustments

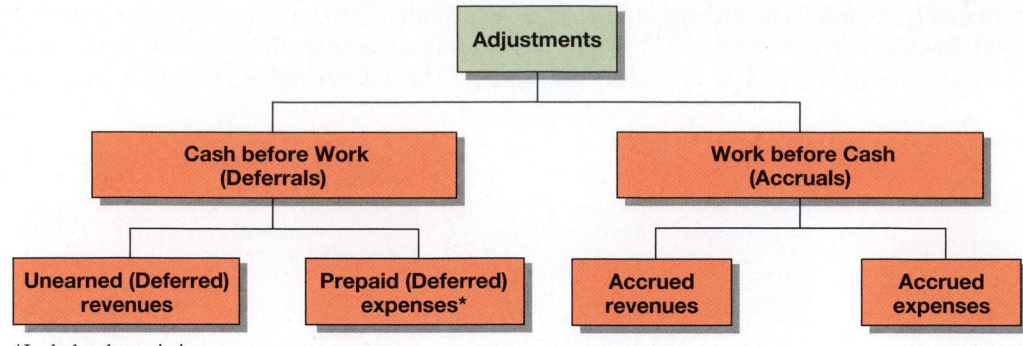

*Includes depreciation.

The left side of this exhibit shows unearned revenues and prepaid expenses (including prepaid rent and depreciation), which reflect transactions when cash is paid or received *before* work is done. They are also called *deferrals* because the recognition of an expense (or revenue) is *deferred* until after the related work is done. The right side of this exhibit shows accrued revenues and accrued expenses, which reflect transactions when work is done before cash is paid or received.

   Adjusting entries are necessary for each of these so that revenues, expenses, assets, and liabilities are correctly reported. It is helpful to remember that each adjusting entry affects one or more income statement accounts *and* one or more balance sheet accounts (but never the Cash account). Adjusting entries are posted to general ledger accounts just like other general journal entries. In this chapter we show the adjustments for prepaid expenses and accrued expenses. In Chapter 13 we show the adjustments for unearned revenues and accrued revenues.

LO3 Prepare and explain adjusting entries.

FASTForward

3-Step Adjusting Process

Adjusting accounts is a three-step process:

Step 1: **Determine the current account balance.**

Step 2: **Determine what the current account balance should be.**

Step 3: **Record the adjusting journal entry to get from step 1 to step 2.**

Prepaid (Deferred) Expenses

Prepaid expenses refer to items *paid for* before receiving their benefits. Prepaid expenses are assets. When these assets are used, their costs become expenses. Adjusting entries for prepaid assets increase expenses and decrease assets as shown in the T-accounts of Exhibit 5.4. Such adjustments reflect transactions and events that use up prepaid expenses (including passage of time). To illustrate the accounting for prepaid expenses, this section focuses on prepaid insurance, supplies, and depreciation.

Exhibit 5.4

Adjusting for Prepaid Expenses

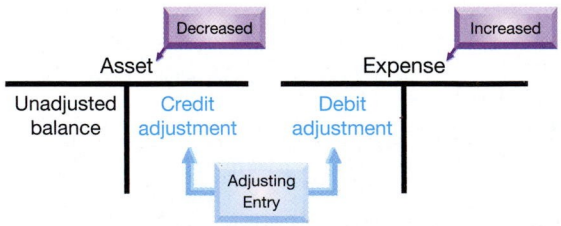

Prepaid Insurance   We use our three-step process for this and all accounting adjustments.

Step 1:   We determine the current balance of FastForward's prepaid insurance to be its payment of $2,400 for 24 months of insurance benefits beginning on December 1, 2010. The balance in insurance expense is $0.

Step 2:   As time passes, the benefits of the insurance gradually expire and some of the Prepaid Insurance asset becomes expense. For instance, one month's insurance coverage expires by December 31, 2010. This expense is $100, or $2,400/24.

Step 3:   The adjusting entry to record this expense and reduce the asset, along with postings to T-accounts, follows:

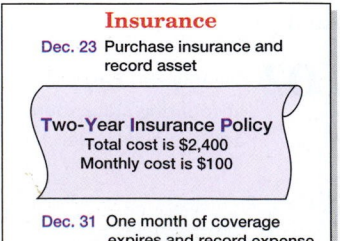

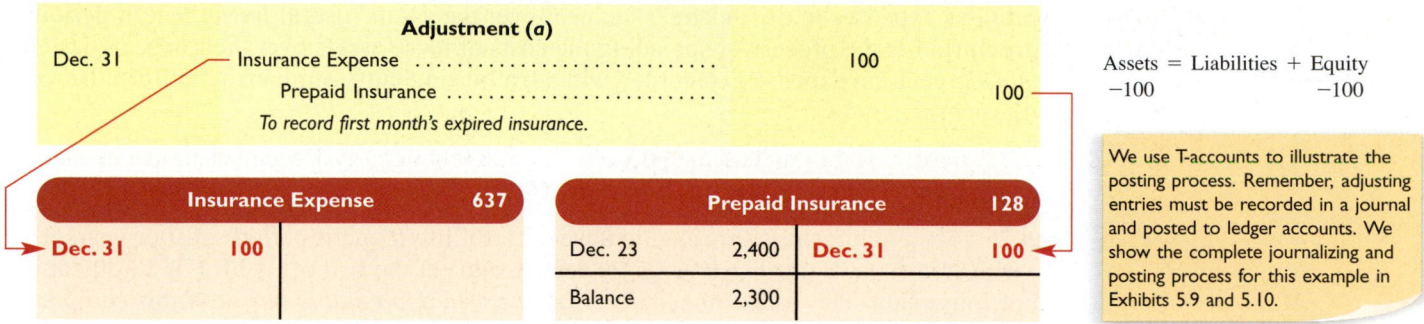

Adjustment (a)

Dec. 31   Insurance Expense   100
           Prepaid Insurance   100
           To record first month's expired insurance.

Assets = Liabilities + Equity
−100   −100

Insurance Expense	637
Dec. 31 100	

Prepaid Insurance		128
Dec. 23 2,400	Dec. 31	100
Balance 2,300		

We use T-accounts to illustrate the posting process. Remember, adjusting entries must be recorded in a journal and posted to ledger accounts. We show the complete journalizing and posting process for this example in Exhibits 5.9 and 5.10.

After adjusting and posting, the $100 balance in Insurance Expense and the $2,300 balance in Prepaid Insurance are ready for reporting in financial statements.

Supplies   Supplies are a prepaid expense requiring adjustment.

Step 1:   Recall that FastForward purchased $9,720 of supplies in December and used some of them during the month. When financial statements are prepared at December 31, the cost of supplies used during December must be included in computing net income.

Step 2:   On December 31 FastForward counts its *unused* supplies and finds $8,670 remaining of the $9,720 supplies. The $1,050 difference between these two amounts ($9,720 − $8,670) is December's supplies expense.

Step 3:   The adjusting entry to record this expense and reduce the Supplies asset account, along with T-account postings, follows:

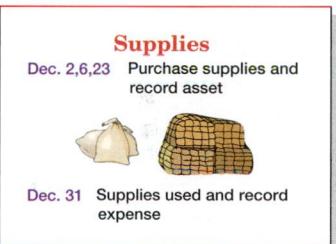

Supplies

Dec. 2,6,23   Purchase supplies and record asset

Dec. 31   Supplies used and record expense

Adjustment (b)

Dec. 31   Supplies Expense   1,050
           Supplies   1,050
           To record supplies used.

Assets = Liabilities + Equity
−1,050   −1,050

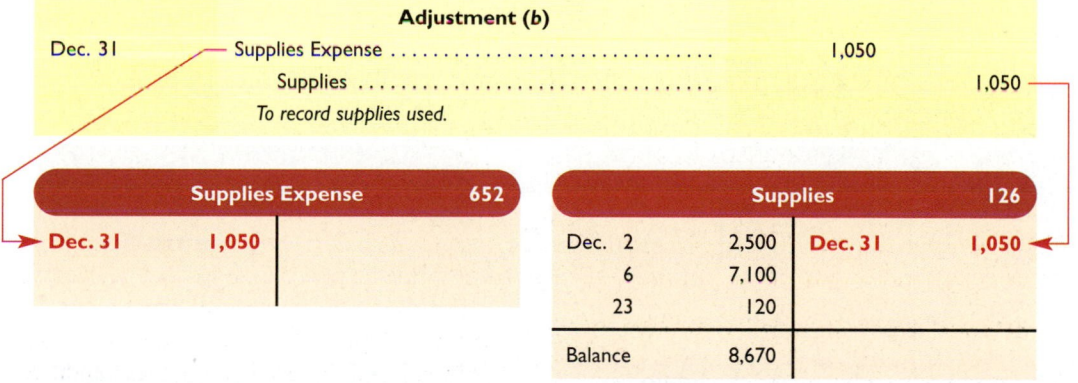

Supplies Expense	652
Dec. 31 1,050	

Supplies		126
Dec. 2 2,500	Dec. 31	1,050
6 7,100		
23 120		
Balance 8,670		

The balance of the Supplies account is $8,670 after posting—equaling the cost of the remaining supplies.

Other Prepaid Expenses   Other prepaid expenses, like Prepaid Rent, are accounted for exactly like Insurance and Supplies. Also, note that some prepaid expenses are both paid for and fully used up within a single accounting period. One example is when a company pays monthly rent on one of the first few days each month. This payment creates a prepaid asset early in each month that fully expires by the end of that month. In these special cases we can record the cash paid with a debit to an expense account instead of an asset account.

Depreciation   A special category of prepaid expenses is **plant assets,** which refers to long-term tangible assets used to produce and sell products and services. Plant assets are expected to provide benefits for more than one period. Examples of plant assets are buildings, machines, vehicles, and fixtures. All plant assets, with the exception of land, eventually wear out or decline in usefulness. The costs of using these assets are deferred and are gradually reported as expenses in the income statement over the assets' useful lives (benefit periods). **Depreciation** is the process of spreading the costs of these assets over their expected useful lives. Depreciation expense is recorded with an adjusting entry similar to that for other prepaid expenses.

Step 1:   FastForward purchased equipment for $26,000 in early December to use in earning revenue. This equipment's cost must be depreciated.

Step 2:   The equipment is expected to have a useful life (benefit period) of four years. It is also expected to have a *salvage value* (expected value at the end of its life) of $8,000 at the end of four years. This means the *net* cost (also called *depreciable basis*) of this equipment over its useful life is $18,000 (equal to $26,000 − $8,000). There are many methods to allocate this $18,000 net cost to expense over the equipment's four-year useful life. FastForward uses a method called **straight-line depreciation,** which allocates equal amounts of the asset's net cost to depreciation during its useful life. The monthly depreciation expense is computed as:

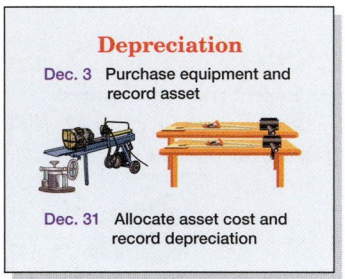

Depreciation

Dec. 3 Purchase equipment and record asset

Dec. 31 Allocate asset cost and record depreciation

$$\text{Monthly depreciation expense} = \frac{\text{Cost} - \text{Salvage value}}{\text{Useful life}}$$

$$= \frac{(\$26,000 - 8,000)}{48 \text{ months}} = \$375 \text{ per month}$$

Step 3:   The adjusting entry to record monthly depreciation expense, along with T-account postings follows:

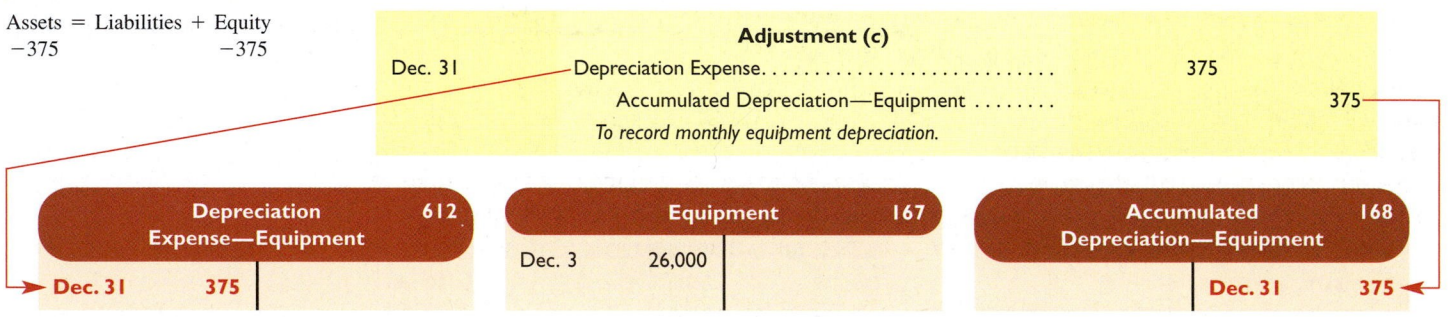

Assets = Liabilities + Equity
−375   −375

Adjustment (c)

Dec. 31 ┌─ Depreciation Expense............................   375
        │   Accumulated Depreciation—Equipment   375
        │   *To record monthly equipment depreciation.*

Depreciation Expense—Equipment	612		Equipment	167		Accumulated Depreciation—Equipment	168
Dec. 31 375			Dec. 3 26,000				Dec. 31 375

After posting the adjustment, the Equipment account ($26,000) less its Accumulated Depreciation ($375) account equals $25,625. The $375 balance in the Depreciation Expense account is reported in the December income statement.

Accumulated depreciation is kept in a separate contra account, not in the Equipment account. A **contra account** is an account linked with another account. Its normal balance is opposite of, and is reported as a subtraction from, that other account's balance.

A contra account allows balance sheet readers to know both the full costs of assets and the total amount of accumulated depreciation. By knowing both these amounts, decision makers can better assess a company's capacity and its need to replace assets. For example, FastForward's December 31 balance sheet shows both the $26,000 original cost of equipment and the $375 balance in the accumulated depreciation contra account. This information reveals that the equipment is close to new. If FastForward reports equipment only at its net amount of $25,625, users cannot assess the equipment's age or its need for replacement. The title of the contra account, *Accumulated Depreciation,* indicates that this account includes total depreciation expense for all prior periods for which the asset was used. To illustrate how Accumulated Depreciation increases as the asset's useful life expires, the Equipment and the Accumulated Depreciation accounts appear as in Exhibit 5.5 on February 29, 2011, after three months of adjusting entries.

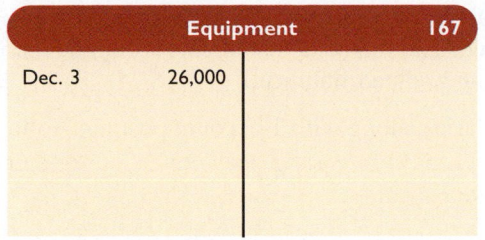

Exhibit 5.5

Accounts after Three Months of Depreciation Adjustments

The $1,125 balance in the accumulated depreciation account is subtracted from its related $26,000 asset cost. The difference ($24,875) between these two balances is the cost of the asset that has not yet been depreciated. This difference is called the **book value,** or *net amount,* which equals the asset's cost less its accumulated depreciation. These account balances are reported in the assets section of FastForward's February 29, 2011, balance sheet in Exhibit 5.6.

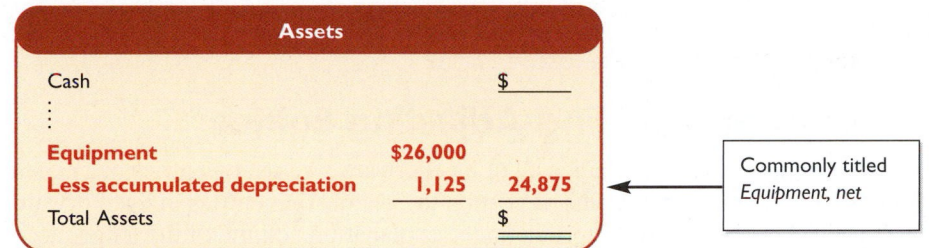

Accrued Expenses

Accrued expenses refer to costs that occur in a period but are both unpaid and unrecorded at the end of the period. Accrued expenses must be reported on the income statement in the period they occur. Adjusting entries for recording accrued expenses involves increasing expenses and increasing liabilities as shown in Exhibit 5.7. Common examples of accrued expenses are salaries, interest, rent, and taxes. We use salaries to show how to adjust accounts for accrued expenses.

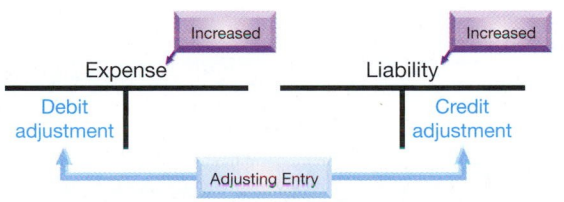

Exhibit 5.7

Adjusting for Accrued Expenses

Accrued Salaries Expense FastForward's employee earns $70 per day, or $350 for a five-day workweek beginning on Monday and ending on Friday.

Step 1: Its employee is paid every two weeks on Friday. On December 12 and 26, the salary is paid, recorded in the journal, and posted to the ledger. The balance in Salaries Payable is $0.

Step 2: The calendar in Exhibit 5.8 shows three working days after the December 26 payday (29, 30, and 31). This means the employee has earned three days' salary by the close of

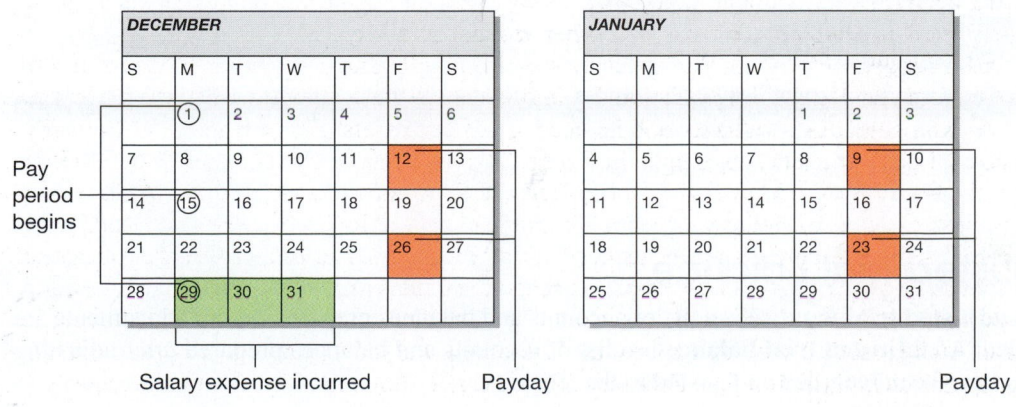

Exhibit 5.8

Salary Accrual and Paydays

business on Wednesday, December 31. This equals $210, computed as 3 days × $70 per day. Yet, this salary cost has not been paid nor recorded. The financial statements would be incomplete if FastForward fails to record this expense and related liability.

Step 3:   The adjusting entry to record accrued salaries, along with T-account postings, follows:

Assets = Liabilities + Equity
 +210   −210

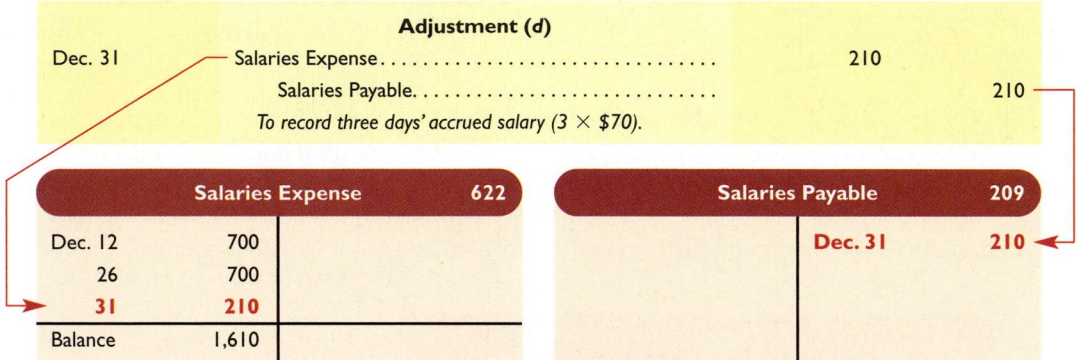

Journalizing and Posting Adjusting Entries

In Exhibit 5.9 we show how to journalize all of FastForward's adjusting entries in a general journal. Exhibit 5.10 then shows the results of posting these adjusting entries in FastForward's general ledger. The abbreviation "Adj." appears in the explanation column of the ledger accounts to note the amount is from an adjusting journal entry.

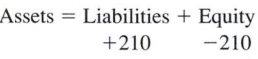

Exhibit 5.9

Recording Adjusting Entries in the General Journal

The title "Adjusting Entries" can be written at the beginning of a series of adjusting entries, rather than writing detailed explanations below each journal entry.

	Date		Account Titles and Explanation	PR	Debit	Credit
			GENERAL JOURNAL			Page 1
			Adjusting Entries			
(a)	Dec. 2010	31	Insurance Expense	637	1 0 0 00	
			Prepaid Insurance	128		1 0 0 00
(b)	Dec.	31	Supplies Expense	652	1 0 5 0 00	
			Supplies	126		1 0 5 0 00
(c)	Dec.	31	Depreciation Expense	612	3 7 5 00	
			Accumulated Depreciation-Equipment	168		3 7 5 00
(d)	Dec.	31	Salaries Expense	622	2 1 0 00	
			Salaries Payable	209		2 1 0 00

HOW YOU DOIN'?   Answers—p. 115

3. What is a contra account? Explain its purpose.
4. What is an accrued expense? Give an example.
5. Describe how a prepaid expense arises. Give an example.

Adjusted Trial Balance

LO4 Explain and prepare an adjusted trial balance.

An **unadjusted trial balance** is a list of accounts and balances prepared *before* adjustments are recorded. An **adjusted trial balance** is a list of accounts and balances prepared *after* adjusting entries have been recorded and posted to the ledger.

Exhibit 5.10
General Ledger after Posting Adjusting Entries

Asset Accounts

Cash   Acct. No. 101

Date	Explan.	PR	Debit	Credit	Balance
2010					
Dec. 1		G1	30,000		30,000
2		G1		2,500	27,500
3		G1	26,000		1,300
5		G1	4,200		5,700
6		G1		1,000	4,700
12		G1		700	4,000
19		G1	1,900		5,900
20		G1		900	5,000
21		G1		200	4,800
22		G1	3,000		7,800
23		G1		2,400	5,400
23		G1		120	5,280
23		G1		230	5,050
26		G1		700	**4,350**

Accounts Receivable   Acct. No. 106

Date	Explan.	PR	Debit	Credit	Balance
2010					
Dec. 13		G1	1,900		1,900
19		G1		1,900	**0**

Supplies   Acct. No. 126

Date	Explan.	PR	Debit	Credit	Balance
2010					
Dec. 2		G1	2,500		2,500
4		G1	7,100		9,600
23		G1	120		9,720
31	Adj.	G1		1,050	**8,670**

Prepaid Insurance   Acct. No. 128

Date	Explan.	PR	Debit	Credit	Balance
2010					
Dec. 23		G1	2,400		2,400
31	Adj.	G1		100	**2,300**

Equipment   Acct. No. 167

Date	Explan.	PR	Debit	Credit	Balance
2010					
Dec. 3		G1	26,000		**26,000**

Accumulated Depreciation—Equipment   Acct. No. 168

Date	Explan.	PR	Debit	Credit	Balance
2010					
Dec. 31	Adj.	G1		375	375

Liability and Equity Accounts

Accounts Payable   Acct. No. 201

Date	Explan.	PR	Debit	Credit	Balance
2010					
Dec. 4		G1		7,100	7,100
20		G1	900		**6,200**

Salaries Payable   Acct. No. 209

Date	Explan.	PR	Debit	Credit	Balance
2010					
Dec. 31	Adj	G1		210	210

Unearned Consulting Revenue   Acct. No. 236

Date	Explan.	PR	Debit	Credit	Balance
2010					
Dec. 22		G1		3,000	**3,000**

C. Taylor, Capital   Acct. No. 301

Date	Explan.	PR	Debit	Credit	Balance
2010					
Dec. 1		G1		30,000	**30,000**

C. Taylor, Withdrawals   Acct. No. 302

Date	Explan.	PR	Debit	Credit	Balance
2010					
Dec. 21		G1	200		**200**

Revenue and Expense Accounts

Consulting Revenue   Acct. No. 403

Date	Explan.	PR	Debit	Credit	Balance
2010					
Dec. 5		G1		4,200	4,200
13		G1		1,600	**5,800**

Rental Revenue   Acct. No. 406

Date	Explan.	PR	Debit	Credit	Balance
2010					
Dec. 13		G1		300	**300**

Depreciation Expense—Equipment   Acct. No. 612

Date	Explan.	PR	Debit	Credit	Balance
2010					
Dec. 31	Adj.	G1	375		375

Salaries Expense   Acct. No. 622

Date	Explan.	PR	Debit	Credit	Balance
2010					
Dec. 12		G1	700		700
26		G1	700		1,400
31	Adj.	G1	210		**1,610**

Insurance Expense   Acct. No. 637

Date	Explan.	PR	Debit	Credit	Balance
2010					
Dec. 31	Adj.	G1	100		100

Rent Expense   Acct. No. 640

Date	Explan.	PR	Debit	Credit	Balance
2010					
Dec. 6		G1	1,000		**1,000**

Supplies Expense   Acct. No. 652

Date	Explan.	PR	Debit	Credit	Balance
2010					
Dec. 31	Adj.	G1	1,050		**1,050**

Utilities Expense   Acct. No. 690

Date	Explan.	PR	Debit	Credit	Balance
2010					
Dec. 23		G1	230		**230**

Exhibit 5.11

Unadjusted and Adjusted
Trial Balances

C. Taylor, Capital balance is
not updated in the adjusted
trial balance.

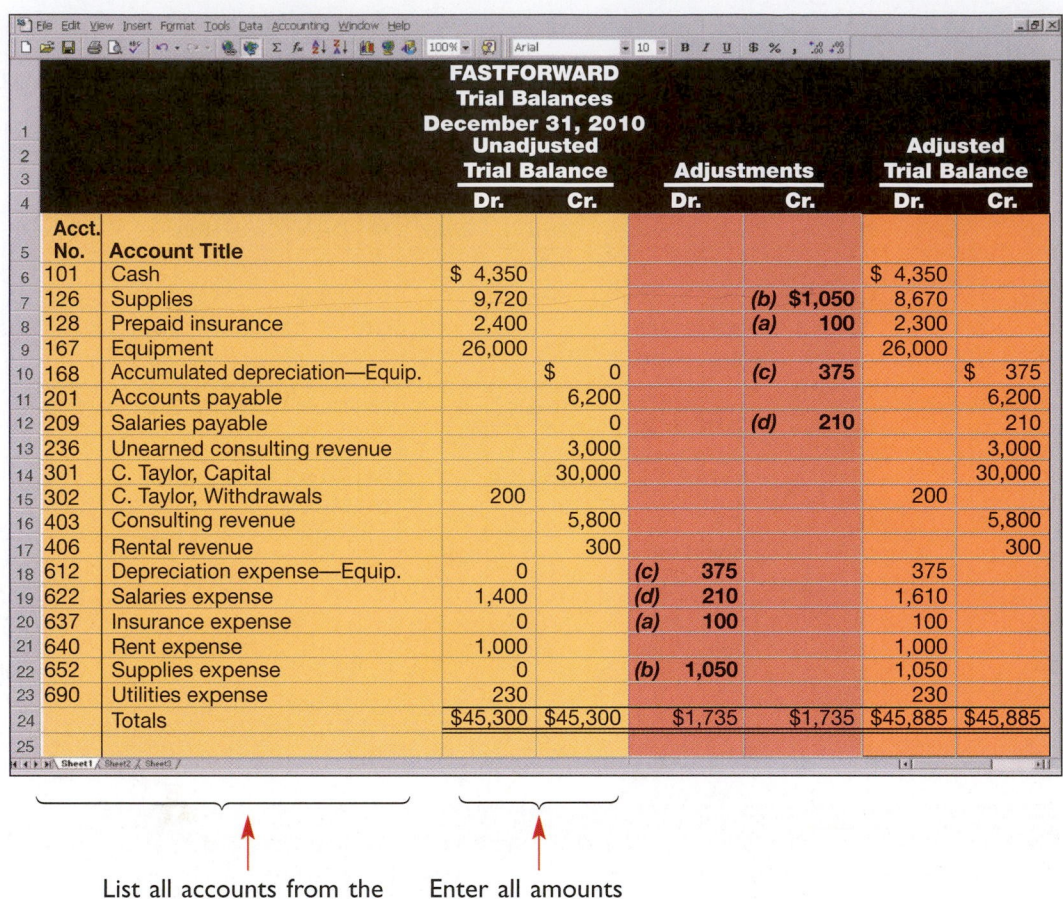

Acct. No.	Account Title	Unadjusted Trial Balance Dr.	Unadjusted Trial Balance Cr.	Adjustments Dr.	Adjustments Cr.	Adjusted Trial Balance Dr.	Adjusted Trial Balance Cr.
101	Cash	$ 4,350				$ 4,350	
126	Supplies	9,720			(b) $1,050	8,670	
128	Prepaid insurance	2,400			(a) 100	2,300	
167	Equipment	26,000				26,000	
168	Accumulated depreciation—Equip.		$ 0		(c) 375		$ 375
201	Accounts payable		6,200				6,200
209	Salaries payable		0		(d) 210		210
236	Unearned consulting revenue		3,000				3,000
301	C. Taylor, Capital		30,000				30,000
302	C. Taylor, Withdrawals	200				200	
403	Consulting revenue		5,800				5,800
406	Rental revenue		300				300
612	Depreciation expense—Equip.	0		(c) 375		375	
622	Salaries expense	1,400		(d) 210		1,610	
637	Insurance expense	0		(a) 100		100	
640	Rent expense	1,000				1,000	
652	Supplies expense	0		(b) 1,050		1,050	
690	Utilities expense	230				230	
	Totals	$45,300	$45,300	$1,735	$1,735	$45,885	$45,885

List all accounts from the ledger and those expected to arise from adjusting entries.

Enter all amounts available from ledger accounts. Column totals must be equal.

Exhibit 5.11 shows both the unadjusted and the adjusted trial balances for FastForward at December 31, 2010. The order of accounts in the trial balance usually matches the order in the chart of accounts. Several new accounts arise from the adjusting entries. Each adjustment (see middle columns) is identified by a letter in parentheses that links it to an adjusting entry explained earlier. Each amount in the Adjusted Trial Balance columns is computed by taking that account's amount from the Unadjusted Trial Balance columns and adding or subtracting any adjustment(s). To illustrate, Supplies has a $9,720 Dr. balance in the unadjusted columns. Subtracting the $1,050 Cr. amount shown in the adjustments columns yields an adjusted $8,670 Dr. balance for Supplies. Notice that the amounts in the Adjusted Trial Balance column agree with their ending balances in the general ledger, shown in Exhibit 5.10. Not all accounts require adjustment each period, so some accounts have blanks in the adjustments columns.

Preparing Financial Statements

LO5 Prepare financial statements from an adjusted trial balance.

We can prepare financial statements directly from information in the *adjusted* trial balance. Exhibit 5.12 shows how revenue and expense balances are transferred from the adjusted trial balance to the income statement (red lines). The net income and the withdrawals amount are then used to prepare the statement of owner's equity (black lines). Asset and liability balances on the adjusted trial balance are then transferred to the balance sheet (blue lines). The ending capital is determined on the statement of owner's equity and transferred to the balance sheet (green line). The ending capital balance is computed; it *does not* come from the adjusted trial balance.

Even though balance sheet accounts are listed first in a trial balance, we usually prepare financial statements in the following order: income statement, statement of owner's equity, and balance sheet. This order makes sense since the balance sheet uses information from the statement of owner's equity, which in turn uses information from the income statement.

Exhibit 5.12

Preparing Financial Statements (Adjusted Trial Balance from Exhibit 5.11)

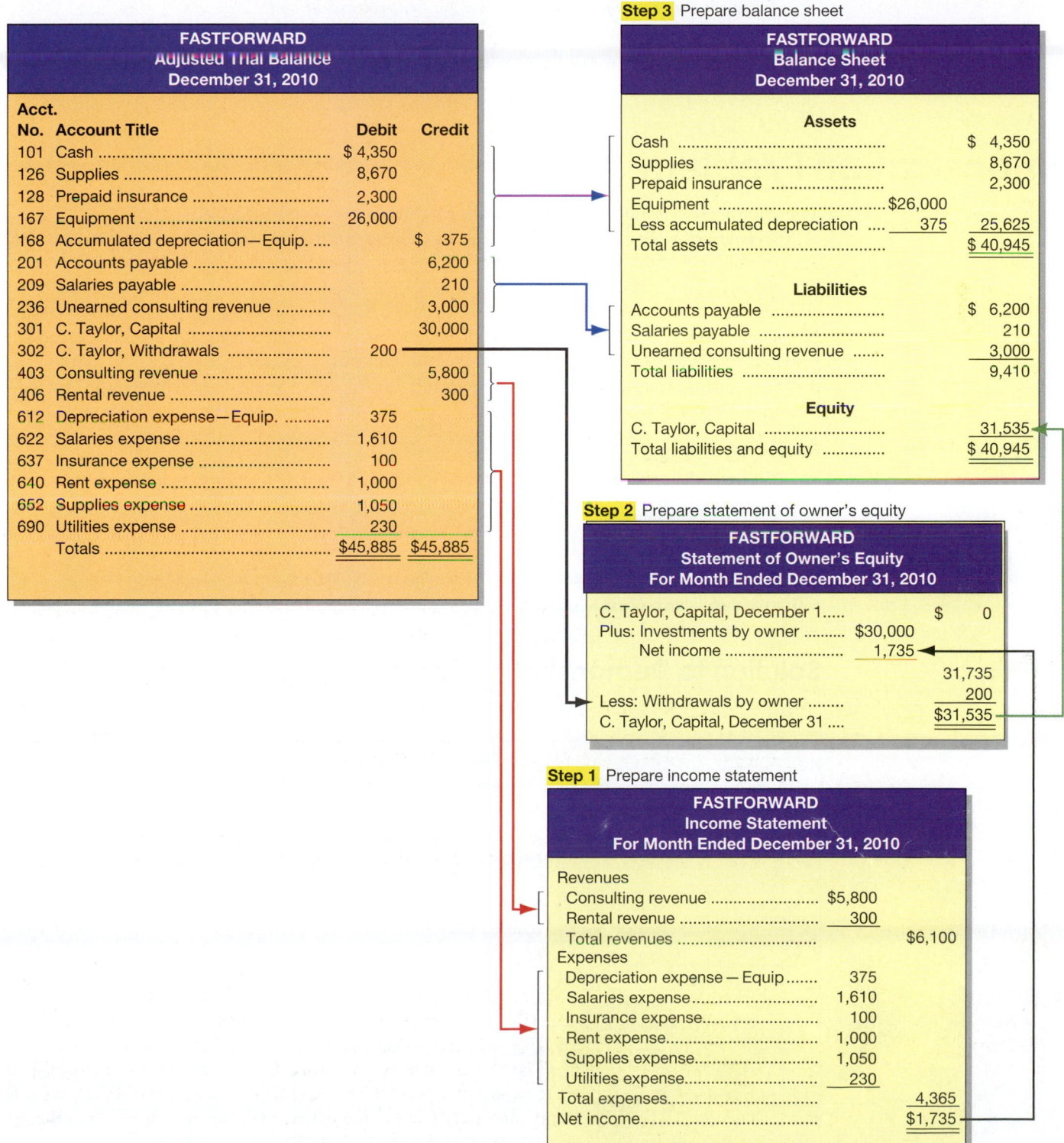

Step 3 Prepare balance sheet

FASTFORWARD
Adjusted Trial Balance
December 31, 2010

Acct. No.	Account Title	Debit	Credit
101	Cash	$ 4,350	
126	Supplies	8,670	
128	Prepaid insurance	2,300	
167	Equipment	26,000	
168	Accumulated depreciation—Equip.		$ 375
201	Accounts payable		6,200
209	Salaries payable		210
236	Unearned consulting revenue		3,000
301	C. Taylor, Capital		30,000
302	C. Taylor, Withdrawals	200	
403	Consulting revenue		5,800
406	Rental revenue		300
612	Depreciation expense—Equip.	375	
622	Salaries expense	1,610	
637	Insurance expense	100	
640	Rent expense	1,000	
652	Supplies expense	1,050	
690	Utilities expense	230	
	Totals	$45,885	$45,885

FASTFORWARD
Balance Sheet
December 31, 2010

Assets
Cash		$ 4,350
Supplies		8,670
Prepaid insurance		2,300
Equipment	$26,000	
Less accumulated depreciation	375	25,625
Total assets		$ 40,945

Liabilities
Accounts payable	$ 6,200
Salaries payable	210
Unearned consulting revenue	3,000
Total liabilities	9,410

Equity
C. Taylor, Capital	31,535
Total liabilities and equity	$ 40,945

Step 2 Prepare statement of owner's equity

FASTFORWARD
Statement of Owner's Equity
For Month Ended December 31, 2010

C. Taylor, Capital, December 1		$ 0
Plus: Investments by owner	$30,000	
Net income	1,735	
		31,735
Less: Withdrawals by owner		200
C. Taylor, Capital, December 31		$31,535

Step 1 Prepare income statement

FASTFORWARD
Income Statement
For Month Ended December 31, 2010

Revenues		
Consulting revenue	$5,800	
Rental revenue	300	
Total revenues		$6,100
Expenses		
Depreciation expense — Equip.	375	
Salaries expense	1,610	
Insurance expense	100	
Rent expense	1,000	
Supplies expense	1,050	
Utilities expense	230	
Total expenses		4,365
Net income		$1,735

6. Jordan Air has the following information in its unadjusted and adjusted trial balances.

	Unadjusted		Adjusted	
	Debit	Credit	Debit	Credit
Prepaid insurance	$6,200		$5,900	
Salaries payable		$ 0		$1,400

What are the adjusting entries that Jordan Air likely recorded?

7. What accounts are taken from the adjusted trial balance to prepare an income statement?

8. In preparing financial statements from an adjusted trial balance, what statement is usually prepared second?

Demonstration Problem

The following information relates to Fanning's Electronics on December 31, 2010.

a. The company's weekly payroll is $8,750, paid each Friday for a five-day workweek. Assume December 31, 2010, falls on a Monday, but the employees will not be paid their wages until Friday, January 4, 2011.

b. Eighteen months earlier, on July 1, 2009, the company purchased equipment that cost $20,000. Its useful life is predicted to be five years, at which time the equipment is expected to be worthless (zero salvage value).

c. On September 1, 2010, the company purchased a 12-month insurance policy for $1,800. The transaction was recorded with an $1,800 debit to Prepaid Insurance.

d. The supplies account has a balance of $2,500 before adjustment. A count reveals that only $675 of supplies are left on December 31.

Required

1. Prepare any necessary adjusting entries on December 31, 2010, in relation to transactions and events *a* through *d*.

Planning the Solution

- Analyze each situation to determine which accounts need to be updated with an adjustment.
- Use the three-step process to compute the amount of each adjustment and prepare the necessary adjusting journal entries.

Solution to Demonstration Problem

1. Adjusting journal entries.

This solution provides explanations for each adjusting entry. The accountant can instead write "Adjusting Entries" at the beginning of a series of adjusting entries.

			GENERAL JOURNAL			Page 9
	Date		**Account Titles and Explanation**	**PR**	**Debit**	**Credit**
(a)	Dec.	31	Wages Expense		1 7 5 0 00	
			Wages Payable			1 7 5 0 00
			To accrue wages for the last day of the year ($8,750 × 1/5).			
(b)	Dec.	31	Depreciation Expense—Equipment		4 0 0 0 00	
			Accumulated Depreciation—Equipment			4 0 0 0 00
			To record depreciation expense for the year ($20,000/5 years).			
(c)	Dec.	31	Insurance Expense		6 0 0 00	
			Prepaid Insurance			6 0 0 00
			To adjust for expired portion of insurance ($1,800 × 4/12).			
(d)	Dec.	31	Supplies Expense		1 8 2 5 00	
			Supplies			1 8 2 5 00
			To record supplies used ($2,500 − $675).			

Summary

LO1 Explain accrual accounting and how it improves financial statements. Accrual accounting recognizes revenues when earned and expenses as they occur—not necessarily when cash inflows and outflows occur. This better reflects a company's financial position and performance.

LO2 Identify the types of accounting adjustments and their purpose. Adjustments can be grouped according to the timing of cash receipts or payments relative to the timing of the related work performed. Adjusting entries are made for prepaid expenses, unearned revenues, accrued expenses, and accrued revenues.

LO3 Prepare and explain adjusting entries. *Prepaid expenses* refer to items paid for in advance of receiving their benefits. Prepaid expenses are assets. Adjusting entries for prepaids involve increasing (debiting) expenses and decreasing (crediting)

assets. *Accrued expenses* refer to costs incurred in a period that are both unpaid and unrecorded. Adjusting entries for recording accrued expenses involve increasing (debiting) expenses and increasing (crediting) liabilities.

LO4 Explain and prepare an adjusted trial balance. An adjusted trial balance is a list of accounts and balances prepared after recording and posting adjusting entries. Financial statements are often prepared from the adjusted trial balance.

LO5 Prepare financial statements from an adjusted trial balance. Revenue and expense balances are reported on the income statement. Asset, liability, and equity balances are reported on the balance sheet. We usually prepare statements in the following order: income statement, statement of owner's equity, and balance sheet.

Guidance Answers to HOW YOU DOIN'?

1. The revenue recognition and the matching principle lead most directly to the adjusting process.

2. No expense is reported in 2011 under cash basis accounting. Under cash basis accounting, all $4,800 is reported as expense in April 2010 when paid. Under accrual basis accounting $2,400 (computed as $4,800/24 \times 12$) is reported as expense in 2011.

3. A contra account is an account that is subtracted from the balance of a related account. Use of a contra account provides more information than simply reporting a net amount.

4. An accrued expense is a cost incurred in a period that is both unpaid and unrecorded prior to adjusting entries. One example is salaries earned but not yet paid at period-end.

5. A prepaid expense arises when items have been paid for in advance of receiving their benefits. Examples are prepaid insurance, prepaid rent, and supplies.

6. The probable adjusting entries of Jordan Air are:

Insurance Expense	300	
Prepaid Insurance		300
To record insurance expired.		
Salaries Expense	1,400	
Salaries Payable		1,400
To record accrued salaries.		

7. Revenue accounts and expense accounts.

8. Statement of owner's equity.

Key Terms

Accrual basis accounting (p. 104) Accounting system that recognizes revenues when earned and expenses as they occur; the basis for GAAP.

Accrued expenses (p. 109) Costs incurred in a period that are both unpaid and unrecorded; adjusting entries for recording accrued expenses involve increasing expenses and increasing liabilities.

Adjusted trial balance (p. 110) List of accounts and balances prepared after period-end adjustments are recorded and posted.

Adjusting entry (p. 106) Journal entry at the end of an accounting period to bring an asset or liability account to its proper amount and update the related expense or revenue account.

Annual financial statements (p. 105) Financial statements covering a one-year period; often based on a calendar year, but any consecutive 12-month (or 52-week) period is acceptable.

Book value (p. 109) Asset's acquisition cost less its accumulated depreciation; also sometimes used synonymously as the *carrying value* of an account.

Cash basis accounting (p. 104) Accounting system that recognizes revenues when cash is received and recognizes expenses as cash is paid; not consistent with GAAP.

Contra account (p. 108) Account linked with another account and having an opposite normal balance; reported as a subtraction from the other account's balance.

Depreciation (p. 108) Expense created by allocating the cost of plant and equipment to periods in which the asset is used; represents the expense of using the asset.

Fiscal year (p. 105) Consecutive 12-month (or 52-week) period chosen as the organization's annual accounting period.

Interim financial statements (p. 105) Financial statements covering periods of less than one year; usually based on one-, three-, or six-month periods.

Matching principle (p. 105) Prescribes expenses to be reported in the same period as the revenues earned as a result of those expenses.

Plant assets (p. 107) Tangible long-lived assets used to produce or sell products and services; also called *property, plant and equipment (PP&E)* or *fixed assets*.

Prepaid expenses (p. 106) Items paid for in advance of receiving their benefits; classified as assets.

Revenue recognition principle (p. 105) Prescribes that revenue is recognized on the income statement in the period it is earned.

Straight-line depreciation method (p. 108) Method that allocates an equal portion of the depreciable cost of plant asset (cost minus salvage value) to each accounting period in its useful life.

Time period assumption (p. 105) Assumption that an organization's activities can be divided into specific time periods such as months or years.

Unadjusted trial balance (p. 110) List of accounts and balances prepared before accounting adjustments are recorded and posted.

Multiple Choice Quiz   Answers on p. 125   mhhe.com/wildCA2e

Additional Multiple Choice Quizzes are available at the book's Website.

1. A company forgot to record accrued and unpaid employee wages of $350,000 at period-end. This oversight would
   a. Understate net income by $350,000.
   b. Overstate net income by $350,000.
   c. Have no effect on net income.
   d. Overstate assets by $350,000.
   e. Understate assets by $350,000.

2. Prior to recording adjusting entries, the Office Supplies account has a $450 debit balance. A physical count of supplies shows $125 of unused supplies still available. The required adjusting entry is:
   a. Debit Office Supplies $125; Credit Office Supplies Expense $125.
   b. Debit Office Supplies $325; Credit Office Supplies Expense $325.
   c. Debit Office Supplies Expense $325; Credit Office Supplies $325.
   d. Debit Office Supplies Expense $325; Credit Office Supplies $125.
   e. Debit Office Supplies Expense $125; Credit Office Supplies $125.

3. On May 1, 2010, a two-year insurance policy was purchased for $24,000 with coverage to begin immediately. What is the amount of insurance expense that appears on the company's income statement for the year ended December 31, 2010?
   a. $4,000
   b. $8,000
   c. $12,000
   d. $20,000
   e. $24,000

4. A company purchases a delivery truck for $39,000 on July 1, 2010. The truck is estimated to have a useful life of 6 years and zero salvage value. The company uses the straight-line method of depreciation. How much depreciation expense is recorded on the truck for the year ended December 31, 2010?
   a. $3,500
   b. $3,250
   c. $4,000
   d. $6,500
   e. $7,000

5. A company purchased a machine for $80,000 on January 1, 2008. Straight-line depreciation expense on the machine is $8,000 per year. The machine's book value on December 31, 2010, is
   a. $0.
   b. $24,000.
   c. $56,000.
   d. $72,000.
   e. $80,000.

Discussion Questions

1. What is the difference between the cash basis and the accrual basis of accounting?

2. Why is the accrual basis of accounting generally preferred over the cash basis?

3. What is a prepaid expense and where is it reported in the financial statements?

4. What type of assets require adjusting entries to record depreciation?

5. What contra account is used when recording and reporting the effects of depreciation? Why is it used?

6. Review the balance sheet of **Best Buy** in Appendix A. Identify the asset accounts that require adjustment before annual financial statements can be prepared. What would be the effect on the income statement if these asset accounts were not adjusted?

QUICK STUDY

QS 5-1
Computing accrual income and cash income   **LO1**

In its first year of operations, Case Co. earned $60,000 in revenues and received $52,000 cash from these customers. The company recorded expenses of $37,500 but had not paid $6,000 of them by the end of the year. The company also prepaid $3,250 cash for next year's insurance premium. Calculate Case Co.'s first year net income under (a) the cash basis and (b) the accrual basis of accounting.

Classify the following adjusting entries as involving prepaid expenses (PE) or accrued expenses (AE).

a. _____ To record employee wages earned but not yet paid (nor recorded).

b. _____ To record annual depreciation expense.

c. _____ To record the cost of supplies used.

QS 5–2
Types of adjusting entries   **LO2**

Adjusting entries affect at least one balance sheet account and at least one income statement account. For the following entries, identify the account to be debited and the account to be credited. Indicate which of the accounts is the income statement account and which is the balance sheet account.

a. Entry to record wage expenses incurred but not yet paid (nor recorded).

b. Entry to record expiration of prepaid insurance.

c. Entry to record annual depreciation expense.

QS 5–3
Recording and analyzing adjusting entries   **LO3**

---

a. On July 1, 2010, Lamis Company paid $1,200 for six months of insurance coverage. No adjustments have been made to the Prepaid Insurance account, and it is now December 31, 2010. Prepare the journal entry to reflect expiration of the insurance as of December 31, 2010.

b. Shandi Company has a Supplies account balance of $500 on January 1, 2010. During 2010, it purchased $2,000 of supplies. As of December 31, 2010, $800 of supplies are available. Prepare the adjusting journal entry to correctly report the balance of the Supplies account and the Supplies Expense account as of December 31, 2010.

QS 5–4
Adjusting prepaid expenses   **LO3**

---

a. Chika Company purchases $20,000 of equipment on January 1, 2010. The equipment is expected to last five years and be worth $2,000 at the end of that time. Prepare the journal entry to record one year's depreciation expense for the equipment as of December 31, 2010. Use the straight-line method.

b. What is the book value of the equipment on December 31, 2010?

QS 5–5
Adjusting for depreciation   **LO3**

An employee gets paid $500 for a five-day workweek. At the end of July, she has worked one day for which she has not been paid. What adjusting journal entry must her employer make to correctly record salaries expense for July?

QS 5–6
Accruing salaries   **LO3**

The following information is taken from Brooke Company's unadjusted and adjusted trial balances.

QS 5–7
Interpreting adjusting entries
LO3

	Unadjusted		Adjusted	
	Debit	**Credit**	**Debit**	**Credit**
Prepaid insurance	$4,100		$3,700	
Salaries payable		$ 0		$800

Given this information, what were the adjusting journal entries?

In the blank space beside each adjusting entry, enter the letter of the explanation A through C that most closely describes the entry.

A. To record this period's depreciation expense.

B. To record amounts earned but not yet paid.

C. To record this period's use of a prepaid expense.

QS 5–8
Classifying adjusting entries   **LO3**

____	1.	Insurance Expense	3,180
		Prepaid Insurance	3,180
____	2.	Depreciation Expense	38,217
		Accumulated Depreciation	38,217
____	3.	Salaries Expense	13,280
		Salaries Payable	13,280

connect™

EXERCISES

Exercise 5-1
Determining assets and expenses for accrual and cash accounting
LO1

On November 1, 2009, a company paid a $15,300 premium on a 36-month insurance policy for coverage beginning on that date. Refer to that policy and fill in the blanks in the following table.

Balance Sheet Prepaid Insurance Asset Using			Insurance Expense Using		
	Accrual Basis	Cash Basis		Accrual Basis	Cash Basis
Dec. 31, 2009	$_____	$_____	2009	$_____	$_____
Dec. 31, 2010	_____	_____	2010	_____	_____
Dec. 31, 2011	_____	_____	2011	_____	_____
Dec. 31, 2012	_____	_____	2012	_____	_____
			Total	$_____	$_____

Check 2011 insurance expense: Accrual, $5,100; Cash, $0. Dec. 31, 2011, asset: Accrual, $4,250; Cash, $0.

Exercise 5-2
Preparing adjusting entries   LO3

Prepare adjusting journal entries for the year ended (date of) December 31, 2010, for each of these separate situations.

a. Depreciation on the company's equipment for 2010 is computed to be $18,000.

b. The Prepaid Insurance account had a $6,000 debit balance at December 31, 2010, before adjusting for the costs of any expired coverage. An analysis of the company's insurance policies showed that $1,100 of unexpired insurance coverage remains.

Check (c) Dr. Office Supplies Expense, $3,882;

c. The Office Supplies account had a $700 debit balance on December 31, 2009, and $3,480 of office supplies was purchased during the year. The December 31, 2010, count showed $298 of supplies available.

(d) Dr. Insurance Expense, $5,800

d. The Prepaid Insurance account had a $6,800 debit balance at December 31, 2010, before adjusting for the costs of any expired coverage. An analysis of insurance policies showed that $5,800 of coverage had expired.

e. Wage expenses of $3,200 have been incurred but are not paid as of December 31, 2010.

Exercise 5-3
Preparing adjusting entries   LO3

For each of the following separate cases, prepare adjusting entries required of financial statements for the year ended (date of) December 31, 2010.

a. Wages of $8,000 are earned by workers but not paid as of December 31, 2010.

b. Depreciation on the company's equipment for 2010 is $18,531.

c. The Office Supplies account had a $240 debit balance on December 31, 2009. During 2010, $5,239 of office supplies is purchased. A count of supplies at December 31, 2010, shows $487 of supplies available.

Check (d) Dr. Insurance Expense, $2,800

d. The Prepaid Insurance account had a $4,000 balance on December 31, 2009. An analysis of insurance policies shows that $1,200 of unexpired insurance benefits remain at December 31, 2010.

Exercise 5-4
Adjusting and paying accrued wages   LO3

Lopez Management has five part-time employees, each of whom earns $250 per day. They are normally paid on Fridays for work completed Monday through Friday of the same week. They were paid in full on Friday, December 28, 2010. The next week, the five employees worked only four days because New Year's Day was an unpaid holiday. Show (a) the adjusting entry that would be recorded on Monday, December 31, 2010, and (b) the journal entry that would be made to record payment of the employees' wages on Friday, January 4, 2011.

Exercise 5-5
Determining cost flows through accounts   LO3

Determine the missing amounts in each of these four separate situations a through d.

	a	b	c	d
Supplies available—prior year-end	$ 400	$1,200	$1,260	?
Supplies purchased during the current year	2,800	6,500	?	$3,000
Supplies available—current year-end	650	?	1,350	700
Supplies expense for the current year	?	1,200	8,400	4,588

Total weekly salaries expense for all employees is $10,000. This amount is paid at the end of the day on Friday of each five-day workweek. April 30 falls on Tuesday of this year, which means that the employees had worked two days since the last payday. The next payday is May 3.

What is the required adjusting journal entry as of April 30? What is the journal entry needed to record payment of the salaries on May 3?

Exercise 5-6
Adjusting and paying accrued expenses   **LO3**

Arnez Co.'s annual accounting period ends on December 31, 2010. The following information concerns the adjusting entries to be recorded as of that date.

a. The Office Supplies account started the year with a $4,000 balance. During 2010, the company purchased supplies for $13,400, which was added to the Office Supplies account. The amount of supplies available at December 31, 2010, totaled $2,554.

b. An analysis of the company's insurance policies provided the following facts.

Policy	Date of Purchase	Months of Coverage	Total Cost
A	April 1, 2009	24	$14,400
B	April 1, 2010	36	12,960
C	August 1, 2010	12	2,400

The total cost for each policy was paid in full (for all months) at the purchase date, and the Prepaid Insurance account was debited for the full cost. (Year-end adjusting entries for Prepaid Insurance were properly recorded in all prior years.)

c. The company has 15 employees, who earn a total of $1,960 in salaries each working day. They are paid each Monday for their work in the five-day workweek ending on the previous Friday. Assume that December 31, 2010, is a Tuesday, and all 15 employees worked the first two days of that week. Because New Year's Day is a paid holiday, they will be paid salaries for five full days on Monday, January 6, 2011.

d. The company purchased a building on January 1, 2010. It cost $960,000 and is expected to have a $45,000 salvage value at the end of its predicted 30-year life. Annual depreciation is $30,500.

Required

Use the information to prepare adjusting entries as of December 31, 2010.

Exercise 5-7
Preparing adjusting journal entries   **LO3**

Check   (b) Dr. Insurance Expense, $11,440 (d) Dr. Depreciation Expense, $30,500

Natsu Co.'s annual accounting period ends on October 31, 2010. The following information concerns the adjusting entries that need to be recorded as of that date.

a. The Office Supplies account started the fiscal year with a $600 balance. During the fiscal year, the company purchased supplies for $4,570, which was added to the Office Supplies account. The supplies available at October 31, 2010, totaled $800.

b. An analysis of the company's insurance policies provided the following facts.

Policy	Date of Purchase	Months of Coverage	Total Cost
A	April 1, 2009	24	$6,000
B	April 1, 2010	36	7,200
C	August 1, 2010	12	1,320

The total cost for each policy was paid in full (for all months) at the purchase date, and the Prepaid Insurance account was debited for the full cost. (Year-end adjusting entries for Prepaid Insurance were properly recorded in all prior fiscal years.)

c. The company has four employees, who earn a total of $1,000 for each workday. They are paid each Monday for their work in the five-day workweek ending on the previous Friday. Assume that

Exercise 5-8
Recording adjusting journal entries   **LO3**

October 31, 2010, is a Monday, and all five employees worked the first day of that week. They will be paid salaries for five full days on Monday, November 7, 2010.

d. The company purchased a building on November 1, 2009, that cost $175,000 and is expected to have a $40,000 salvage value at the end of its predicted 25-year life. Annual depreciation is $5,400.

Check (b) Dr. Insurance Expense, $5,350; (d) Dr. Depreciation Expense, $5,400.

Required

Use the information to prepare adjusting entries as of October 31, 2010.

 connect™

PROBLEM SET A

Problem 5-1A

Preparing adjusting entries, adjusted trial balance, and financial statements

LO3   LO4   LO5

eXcel

mhhe.com/wildCA2e

Wells Technical Institute (WTI), a school owned by Tristana Wells, provides training to individuals who pay tuition directly to the school. WTI also offers training to groups in off-site locations. Its unadjusted trial balance as of December 31, 2010, follows. Descriptions of items *a* through *f* that require adjusting entries on December 31, 2010, follow.

Additional Information

a. An analysis of the school's insurance policies shows that $2,400 of coverage has expired.

b. A count shows that teaching supplies costing $2,800 are available at year-end 2010.

c. Annual depreciation on the equipment is $13,200.

d. Annual depreciation on the professional library is $7,200.

e. The school's two employees are paid weekly. As of the end of the year, two days' salaries have accrued at the rate of $100 per day for each employee.

f. The balance in the Prepaid Rent account represents rent for December.

WELLS TECHNICAL INSTITUTE
Unadjusted Trial Balance
December 31, 2010

	Debit	Credit
Cash	$ 34,000	
Accounts receivable	0	
Teaching supplies	8,000	
Prepaid insurance	12,000	
Prepaid rent	3,000	
Professional library	35,000	
Accumulated depreciation—Professional library		$ 10,000
Equipment	80,000	
Accumulated depreciation—Equipment		15,000
Accounts payable		38,500
Salaries payable		0
T. Wells, Capital		90,000
T. Wells, Withdrawals	50,000	
Tuition fees earned		123,900
Training fees earned		40,000
Depreciation expense—Professional library	0	
Depreciation expense—Equipment	0	
Salaries expense	50,000	
Insurance expense	0	
Rent expense	33,000	
Teaching supplies expense	0	
Advertising expense	6,000	
Utilities expense	6,400	
Totals	$ 317,400	$ 317,400

Required

1. Using Exhibit 5.11 as a guide, create a seven-column sheet with the following headings:

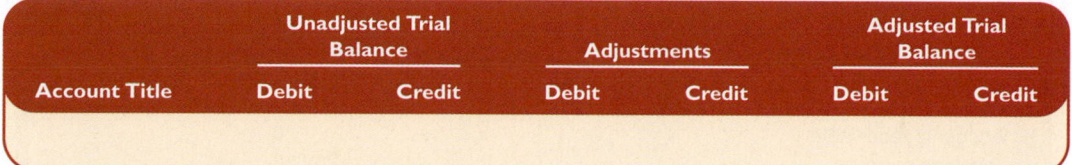

Account Title	Unadjusted Trial Balance		Adjustments		Adjusted Trial Balance	
	Debit	Credit	Debit	Credit	Debit	Credit

2. Enter the account titles and balances in the unadjusted trial balance columns onto your sheet.
3. Prepare the necessary adjusting journal entries for items *a* through *f* and record them in the adjustments column. Assume that adjusting entries are made only at year end.
4. Compute adjusted account balances and enter the balances in the adjusted trial balance columns.
5. Prepare Wells Technical Institute's income statement and statement of owner's equity for the year 2010 and prepare its balance sheet as of December 31, 2010. The owner made no additional investments during the year.

Check   (4) Adj. Trial balance totals $338,200; (5) Net income, $37,100; Ending T. Wells, Capital $77,100

The adjusted trial balance for Chiara Company as of December 31, 2010, follows.

Problem 5–2A
Preparing financial statements from the adjusted trial balance
LO5

	Debit	Credit
Cash	$ 30,000	
Accounts receivable	52,000	
Office supplies	16,000	
Automobiles	168,000	
Accumulated depreciation—Automobiles		$ 50,000
Equipment	138,000	
Accumulated depreciation—Equipment		18,000
Land	78,000	
Accounts payable		90,000
Salaries payable		19,000
R. Chiara, Capital		255,800
R. Chiara, Withdrawals	46,000	
Fees earned		484,000
Depreciation expense—Automobiles	26,000	
Depreciation expense—Equipment	18,000	
Salaries expense	188,000	
Wages expense	40,000	
Office supplies expense	34,000	
Advertising expense	58,000	
Repairs expense—Automobiles	24,800	
Totals	$916,800	$916,800

Required

Use the information in the adjusted trial balance to prepare (*a*) the income statement for the year ended December 31, 2010; (*b*) the statement of owner's equity for the year ended December 31, 2010; and (*c*) the balance sheet as of December 31, 2010. The owner made no additional investments during the year.

Check   (c) Total assets, $414,000

Following is the unadjusted trial balance for Augustus Institute as of December 31, 2010. The Institute provides one-on-one training to individuals who pay tuition directly to the business and offers extension training to groups in off-site locations. Shown after the trial balance are items *a* through *f* that require adjusting entries as of December 31, 2010.

PROBLEM SET B

Problem 5–1B
Preparing adjusting entries, adjusted trial balance, and financial statements **LO3 LO4 LO5**

		Debit	Credit
	AUGUSTUS INSTITUTE		
	Unadjusted Trial Balance		
	December 31, 2010		
3	Cash	$ 60,000	
4	Accounts receivable	0	
5	Teaching supplies	70,000	
6	Prepaid insurance	19,000	
7	Prepaid rent	3,800	
8	Professional library	12,000	
9	Accumulated depreciation—Professional library		$ 2,500
10	Equipment	40,000	
11	Accumulated depreciation—Equipment		20,000
12	Accounts payable		39,800
13	Salaries payable		0
14	C. Augustus, Capital		71,500
15	C. Augustus, Withdrawals	20,000	
16	Tuition fees earned		129,200
17	Training fees earned		68,000
18	Depreciation expense—Professional library	0	
19	Depreciation expense—Equipment	0	
20	Salaries expense	44,200	
21	Insurance expense	0	
22	Rent expense	29,600	
23	Teaching supplies expense	0	
24	Advertising expense	19,000	
25	Utilities expense	13,400	
26	Totals	$ 331,000	$ 331,000

Additional Information

a. An analysis of the Institute's insurance policies shows that $9,500 of coverage has expired.

b. An inventory count shows that teaching supplies costing $20,000 are available at year-end 2010.

c. Annual depreciation on the equipment is $5,000.

d. Annual depreciation on the professional library is $2,400.

e. The Institute's only employee is paid weekly. As of the end of the year, three days' salaries have accrued at the rate of $150 per day.

f. The balance in the Prepaid Rent account represents rent for December.

Required

1. Using Exhibit 5.11 as a guide, create a seven-column sheet with the following headings:

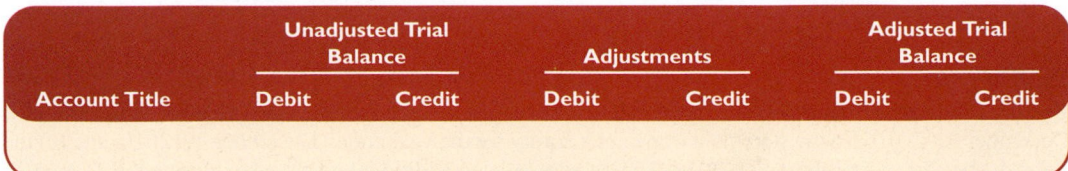

	Unadjusted Trial Balance		Adjustments		Adjusted Trial Balance	
Account Title	Debit	Credit	Debit	Credit	Debit	Credit

2. Enter the account titles and balances in the unadjusted trial balance columns onto your sheet.

3. Prepare the necessary adjusting journal entries for items *a* through *f* and record them in the adjustments column. Assume that adjusting entries are made only at year end.

4. Compute adjusted account balances and enter the balances in the adjusted trial balance columns.

5. Prepare Augustus Institute's income statement and statement of owner's equity for the year 2010, and prepare its balance sheet as of December 31, 2010. The owner made no additional investments during the year.

Check (4) Adj. trial balance totals, $338,850; (5) Net income, $19,850; Ending C. Augustus, Capital, $71,350

The adjusted trial balance for Speedy Courier as of December 31, 2010, follows.

Problem 5-2B
Preparing financial statements
from the adjusted trial balance
LO5

	Debit	Credit
Cash	$ 58,000	
Accounts receivable	120,000	
Office supplies	22,000	
Trucks	134,000	
Accumulated depreciation—Trucks		$ 58,000
Equipment	270,000	
Accumulated depreciation—Equipment		200,000
Land	100,000	
Accounts payable		276,000
Salaries payable		28,000
L. Horace, Capital		125,000
L. Horace, Withdrawals	50,000	
Delivery fees earned		611,800
Depreciation expense—Trucks	29,000	
Depreciation expense—Equipment	48,000	
Salaries expense	74,000	
Wages expense	300,000	
Office supplies expense	31,000	
Advertising expense	27,200	
Repairs expense—Trucks	35,600	
Totals	$1,298,800	$1,298,800

Required

Use the information in the adjusted trial balance to prepare (*a*) the income statement for the year ended December 31, 2010, (*b*) the statement of owner's equity for the year ended December 31, 2010, and (*c*) the balance sheet as of December 31, 2010. The owner made no additional investments during the year.

Check (c) Total assets $446,000

This serial problem began in Chapter 1 and continues through most of the book. If previous chapter segments were not completed, the serial problem can still begin at this point. It is helpful, but not necessary, that you use the Working Papers that accompany the book.

SERIAL PROBLEM

Success Systems
LO3 LO4 LO5

QB

SP 5 After the success of the company's first two months, Adriana Lopez continues to operate Success Systems. (Transactions for the first two months are described in the serial problem of Chapter 4.) The November 30, 2010, unadjusted trial balance of Success Systems (reflecting its transactions for October and November) follows.

No.	Account Title	Debit	Credit
101	Cash	$ 68,996	
106	Accounts receivable	15,800	
126	Computer supplies	3,350	
128	Prepaid insurance	2,400	
131	Prepaid rent	3,500	
163	Office equipment	10,000	
164	Accumulated depreciation—Office equipment		$ 0
167	Computer equipment	25,000	
168	Accumulated depreciation—Computer equipment		0
201	Accounts payable		0
210	Wages payable		0
236	Unearned computer services revenue		0
301	A. Lopez, Capital		110,000
302	A. Lopez, Withdrawals	6,500	
403	Computer services revenue		32,550

[continued on next page]

[continued from previous page]

612	Depreciation expense—Office equipment	0
613	Depreciation expense—Computer equipment	0
623	Wages expense	3,150
637	Insurance expense	0
640	Rent expense	0
652	Computer supplies expense	0
655	Advertising expense	1,790
676	Mileage expense	864
677	Miscellaneous expenses	300
684	Repairs expense—Computer	900
	Totals	$142,550 $142,550

Success Systems had the following transactions and events in December 2010.

Dec.   2   Paid $1,200 cash to Hilldale Mall for Success Systems' share of mall advertising costs.
       3   Paid $500 cash for minor repairs to the company's computer.
       4   Received $7,000 cash from Alex's Engineering Co. for the receivable from November.
      10   Paid cash to Michelle Jones for six days of work at the rate of $150 per day.
      14   Notified by Alex's Engineering Co. that Success's bid of $9,000 on a proposed project has been accepted. Alex's paid a $2,500 cash advance to Success Systems.
      15   Purchased $2,100 of computer supplies on credit from Cain Office Products.
      16   Sent a reminder to Gomez Co. to pay the fee for services recorded on November 8.
      20   Completed a project for Chang Corporation and received $3,620 cash.
   22–26   Took the week off for the holidays.
      26   Received $3,000 cash from Gomez Co. on its receivable.
      26   Reimbursed Lopez's business automobile mileage (800 miles at $0.32 per mile).
      27   Lopez withdrew $2,000 cash for personal use.

The following additional facts are collected for use in making adjusting entries prior to preparing financial statements for the company's first three months:

a. The December 31 count of computer supplies shows $775 still available.

b. Three months have expired since the 12-month insurance premium was paid in advance.

c. As of December 31, Michelle Jones has not been paid for four days of work at $150 per day.

d. The company's computer is expected to have a five-year life with no salvage value.

e. The office equipment is expected to have a four-year life with no salvage value.

f. Three of the four months' prepaid rent has expired.

Required

1. Prepare journal entries to record each of the December transactions and events for Success Systems. Post those entries to the accounts in the ledger.

2. Prepare adjusting entries to reflect *a* through *f*. Post those entries to the accounts in the ledger.

Check   (3) Adjusted trial balance totals, $153,245

3. Prepare an adjusted trial balance as of December 31, 2010.

4. Prepare an income statement for the three months ended December 31, 2010.

5. Prepare a statement of owner's equity for the three months ended December 31, 2010.

(6) Total assets, $122,635

6. Prepare a balance sheet as of December 31, 2010.

BEYOND THE NUMBERS

REPORTING IN ACTION
L01

BTN 5-1   Refer to **Best Buy**'s financial statements in Appendix A to answer the following.

Required

1. Identify and write down the revenue recognition principle as explained in the chapter.

2. Research **Best Buy**'s footnotes to discover how it applies the revenue recognition principle. Report what you discover.

BTN 5-2 At year-end the president of your company asks you, the accountant, not to record accrued expenses until next year because they will not be paid until then. The president also directs you to record in current year revenue a prepayment from a customer for services that won't be provided until next year. Your company would report a net income instead of a net loss if you carry out the president's instructions. What do you do?

BTN 5-3 Access the **Gap**'s Website (**gap.com**) to answer the following requirements.

Required

1. What are Gap's main brands?
2. Access Gap's 2008 annual report either at the company's Website (or at **www.SEC.gov**). What is Gap's fiscal year-end?
3. What is Gap's net sales for the period ended February 2, 2008?
4. What is Gap's net income for the period ended February 2, 2008?

BTN 5-4 Two types of adjustments are described in the chapter: (1) prepaid expenses and (2) accrued expenses.

Required

1. Form *learning teams* of two (or more) members. Each team member must select one of the two adjustments as an area of expertise (each team must have at least one expert in each area).
2. Form *expert teams* from the individuals who have selected the same area of expertise. Expert teams are to discuss and write a report that each expert will present to his or her learning team addressing the following:
   a. Description of the adjustment and why it's necessary.
   b. Example of a transaction or event, with dates and amounts, that requires adjustment.
   c. Adjusting entry(ies) for the example in requirement *b*.
   d. Status of the affected account(s) before and after the adjustment in requirement *c*.
   e. Effects on financial statements of not making the adjustment.
3. Each expert should return to his or her learning team. In rotation, each member should present his or her expert team's report to the learning team. Team discussion is encouraged.

BTN 5-5 Review the opening feature of this chapter dealing with **PopCap Games**.

Required

1. Assume that PopCap sells a $300 gift certificate to a customer, collecting the $300 cash in advance. Prepare the journal entry for the collection of $300 cash under (*a*) cash basis accounting and (*b*) accrual basis accounting.
2. PopCap understands that many companies carry inventories, and the owners are thinking of carrying an inventory of games on CDs. The owners desire your advice on the pros and cons of carrying such inventory. Provide at least one reason for and one reason against carrying inventories.

BTN 5-6 A small publishing company signs a well-known athlete to write a book. The company pays the athlete $500,000 to sign plus future book royalties. A note to the company's financial statements says that "prepaid expenses include $500,000 in author signing fees to be matched against future expected sales." Is this accounting for the signing bonus acceptable? How does it affect your analysis?

1. b; the forgotten adjusting entry is: *dr.* Wages Expense, *cr.* Wages Payable.
2. c; Supplies used = $450 − $125 = $325
3. b; Insurance expense = $24,000 × (8/24) = $8,000; adjusting entry is: *dr.* Insurance Expense for $8,000, *cr.* Prepaid Insurance for $8,000.
4. b; $3,250 = [($39,000 − $0)/6 years] × ½ year
5. c; Book value = $80,000 − (3 × $8,000) = $56,000

A Look Back

Chapter 5 described why adjusting entries are important for recognizing revenues and expenses in the proper period. We prepared an adjusted trial balance and used it to prepare financial statements.

A Look at This Chapter

This chapter emphasizes the final steps in the accounting process and reviews the entire accounting cycle. We explain the closing process and the use of a post-closing trial balance. We show how a work sheet aids in preparing financial statements.

A Look Ahead

Chapter 7 considers fraud and controls. We look specifically at how internal controls reduce the likelihood of fraud. We also consider the effect that recent laws, such as Sarbanes-Oxley, have on fraud and internal controls.

Chapter 6

Closing Process and Financial Statements

Learning Objectives

LO 1	Prepare a work sheet and explain its usefulness.
LO 2	Explain why temporary accounts are closed each period.
LO 3	Describe and prepare closing entries.
LO 4	Explain and prepare a post-closing trial balance.
LO 5	Identify steps in the accounting cycle.

"Stay true to your vision and your mission"
—Kathryn Kerrigan

Walk in Her Shoes

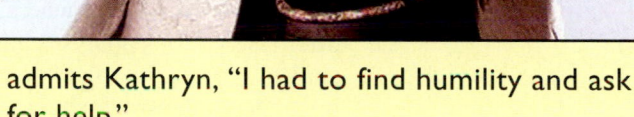

CHICAGO—As a teenager, Kathryn Kerrigan wore a size 11 shoe and found shopping for shoes grueling. "I remember driving with my dad to every shopping mall looking for shoes," recalls Kathryn. "It's embarrassing and it doesn't have to be." Kathryn decided to do something about it. She wrote a business plan for a college project and executed that plan with her dad's encouragement. Her start-up company, **Kathryn Kerrigan (KathrynKerrigan.com),** now provides stylish women's shoes through size 16.

Success, however, requires Kathryn to monitor costs. "We had to create the molds for every shoe size," explains Kathryn. "These cost about $2,000 each." She set up an accounting system to track revenues and control costs, but it is a constant struggle as her business grows. Kathryn says that properly applying the accounting cycle, preparing financial statements, and acting on that information increase the odds of success. However, at times,

admits Kathryn, "I had to find humility and ask for help."

Kathryn has successfully controlled materials costs while monitoring both revenues and customer needs. She uses the accounting system and closing entries to help identify and match costs with revenues for specific time periods. Kathryn says she relies on balance sheets to know when to pay bills. But what pulls her through, admits Kathryn, is knowing that "we're putting out a product that's missing in the marketplace."

Kathryn is on a mission. "What keeps me going," explains Kathryn, "are all the women who keep coming up to me . . . asking for shoes that fit." To make that happen, she tracks the accounting numbers to be sure it is a money-making venture. "It's important for entrepreneurs to be realistic," insists Kathryn. Yet she adds, "A great pair of shoes can make all the difference!"

[Sources: *Kathryn Kerrigan Website*, January 2009; *Success Magazine*, February 2008; *Inc.com*, July 2007; *Beep*, October 2007; *Chicago Sun-Times*, February 2008]

Earlier chapters described how transactions and events are analyzed, journalized, and posted. We also described important adjustments that are necessary in preparing financial statements. This chapter explains the closing process that readies revenue, expense, and withdrawal accounts for the next reporting period and updates the capital account. A work sheet is shown to be a useful tool for that process and in preparing financial statements.

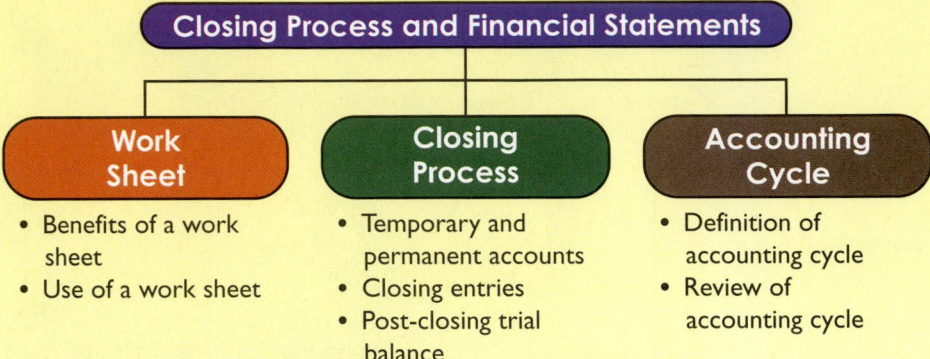

Work Sheet as a Tool

In Chapter 5 we showed how to prepare financial statements from an adjusted trial balance. This approach is good when the number of accounts and/or adjustments is low. Accountants often use various analyses and internal documents when preparing formal reports and financial statements. Internal documents are often called **working papers.** One widely used working paper is the **work sheet,** which helps accountants prepare financial statements and aids in the closing process.

Benefits of a Work Sheet

LO1 Prepare a work sheet and explain its usefulness.

A work sheet is *not* a required report, yet using a manual or electronic work sheet has several potential benefits. Specifically, a work sheet

- Aids the preparation of financial statements.
- Reduces the possibility of errors when working with many accounts and adjustments.
- Links accounts and adjustments to their impacts in financial statements.
- Assists in planning and organizing an audit of financial statements—as it can be used to reflect any adjustments necessary.
- Helps in preparing interim (monthly and quarterly) financial statements when the journalizing and posting of adjusting entries are postponed until year-end.
- Shows the effects of proposed or "what-if" transactions.
- Aids in closing temporary accounts.

Since a work sheet is *not* a required report or an accounting record, its format is flexible and can be modified by its user to fit his/her preferences. In this chapter we show a common format for the work sheet.

Use of a Work Sheet

When a work sheet is used to prepare financial statements, it is constructed at the end of a period before the adjusting process. The complete work sheet includes a list of the accounts, their balances and adjustments, and their sorting into financial statement columns. It provides two columns each for the unadjusted trial balance, the adjustments, the adjusted trial balance, the income statement, and the balance sheet (including the statement of owner's equity).

To describe and interpret the work sheet, we use the information from FastForward. Preparing the work sheet has five important steps. Each step, 1 through 5, is color-coded and explained with reference to Exhibit 6.1.

❶ Step 1. Enter Unadjusted Trial Balance

Refer to Exhibit 6.1. The first step in preparing a work sheet is to list the title of every account and its account number that is expected to appear on its financial statements. This includes all accounts in the ledger plus any new ones expected from adjusting entries. Most adjusting entries—including expenses from salaries, supplies, depreciation, and insurance—are predictable and recurring. The unadjusted balance for each account is then entered in the appropriate Debit or Credit column of the unadjusted trial balance columns. The totals of these two columns must be equal. Exhibit 6.1 shows FastForward's work sheet after completing this first step.

❷ Step 2. Enter Adjustments

Refer to Exhibit 6.1a (turn over first transparency). The second step in preparing a work sheet is to enter adjustments in the Adjustments columns. The adjustments shown are the same ones shown in Chapter 5. An identifying letter links the debit and credit of each adjusting entry. This is called *keying* the adjustments. **After preparing a work sheet, adjusting entries must still be entered in the journal and posted to the ledger.** The Adjustments columns provide the information for those entries.

❸ Step 3. Prepare Adjusted Trial Balance

Refer to Exhibit 6.1b (turn over second transparency). The adjusted trial balance is prepared by combining the adjustments with the unadjusted balances for each account. To avoid omitting the transfer of an account balance, start with the first line (cash) and continue in account order. As an example, the Prepaid Insurance account has a $2,400 debit balance in the Unadjusted Trial Balance columns. This $2,400 debit is combined with the $100 credit in the Adjustments columns to give Prepaid Insurance a $2,300 debit in the Adjusted Trial Balance columns. The totals of the Adjusted Trial Balance columns confirm the equality of debits and credits.

❹ Step 4. Sort Adjusted Trial Balance Amounts to Financial Statements

Refer to Exhibit 6.1c (turn over third transparency). This step involves sorting account balances from the adjusted trial balance to their proper financial statement columns as follows:

Accounts	Sorted to Column
Expenses	Income Statement Debit
Revenues	Income Statement Credit
Assets	Balance Sheet and Statement of Owner's Equity Debit
Withdrawals	Balance Sheet and Statement of Owner's Equity Debit
Liabilities	Balance Sheet and Statement of Owner's Equity Credit

❺ Step 5. Total Statement Columns, Compute Income or Loss, and Balance Columns

Refer to Exhibit 6.1d (turn over fourth transparency). Compute totals for each financial statement column. At this point, debit and credit totals will probably not equal. Use the difference in the totals of the Income Statement columns to determine whether the business has a net income or a net loss:

Credits > Debits	Net income
Credits < Debits	Net loss

For example, for Fastforward the Income Statement Credit column total of $6,100 is greater than the Income Statement Debit column total of $4,365. The difference of $1,735 is

[text continued on p. 131]

Exhibit 6.1

Work Sheet with Unadjusted Trial Balance

File Edit View Insert Format Tools Data Window Help												

FastForward
Work Sheet
For Month Ended December 31, 2010

		Unadjusted Trial Balance		Adjustments		Adjusted Trial Balance		Income Statement		Balance Sheet & Statement of Owner's Equity	
No.	**Account**	**Dr.**	**Cr.**	**Dr.**	**Cr.**	**Dr.**	**Cr.**	**Dr.**	**Cr.**	**Dr.**	**Cr.**
101	Cash	4,350									
126	Supplies	9,720									
128	Prepaid insurance	2,400									
167	Equipment	26,000									
168	Accumulated depreciation—Equip.		0								
201	Accounts payable		6,200								
209	Salaries payable		0								
236	Unearned consulting revenue		3,000								
301	C. Taylor, Capital		30,000								
302	C. Taylor, Withdrawals	200									
403	Consulting revenue		5,800								
406	Rental revenue		300								
612	Depreciation expense—Equip.	0									
622	Salaries expense	1,400									
637	Insurance expense	0									
640	Rent expense	1,000									
652	Supplies expense	0									
690	Utilities expense	230									
	Totals	45,300	45,300								

Sheet1 / Sheet2 / Sheet3

List all accounts from the ledger and those expected to arise from adjusting entries.

Enter all amounts available from ledger accounts. Column totals must be equal.

A work sheet collects and summarizes information used to prepare adjusting entries, financial statements, and closing entries.

FastForward's net income for the month. In the case of *net income* do the following on the work sheet:

■ Enter the net income in the Income Statement Debit column, in the Net income row.

■ Enter the net income in the Net income row in the Balance Sheet and Statement of Owner's Equity Credit column. Adding net income to the Credit column implies this amount will increase owner's equity.

■ Compute new column totals for the Income Statement Debit and Balance Sheet and Statement of Owner's Equity Credit columns. Total debits should now equal total credits.

For example, after entering net income of $1,735 in the work sheet, FastForward's Income Statement columns each total $6,100, and its Balance Sheet and Statement of Owner's Equity columns each total $41,520.

In the case of *net loss* do the following on the work sheet:

■ Enter the net loss in the Income Statement Credit column, in the Net income row.

■ Enter the net loss in the Net income row in the Balance Sheet and Statement of Owner's Equity Debit column. Carrying the net loss to the Debit column implies this amount will reduce owner's equity.

■ Compute new column totals for the Income Statement Credit and Balance Sheet and Statement of Owner's Equity Debit columns. Total debits should now equal total credits.

Updating owner's equity   Note that owner's equity is not updated on the work sheet. Instead, ending owner's capital is computed using amounts from the work sheet—beginning owner's capital plus net income minus withdrawals. This is done in the Statement of Owner's Equity (see Exhibit 6.3).

Additional owner investments   Care must be taken in reporting owner's equity when the owner makes additional investments during the year. In this case, the ending balance of owner's equity in the ledger would equal last year's ending owner's equity *plus* the additional owner investments during the year. The accountant reviews the activity in the owner's equity general ledger account to find these separate amounts. Exhibit 6.2 provides an example.

	Owner, Capital			Acct. No. 301	
Date	Explanation	PR	Debit	Credit	Balance
2010					
Nov. 30	Balance				40,000
Dec. 28	Additional owner investment	GI		5,000	45,000

Exhibit 6.2

Owner's Equity Ledger Account with Additional Owner Investment

In this case, the Statement of Owner's Equity for December would begin with the $40,000 beginning balance, and the next row of the statement would show the $5,000 additional investment.

If the Balance Sheet columns don't balance   The totals of the last two work sheet columns *must* balance after adding the net income or loss. If they do not, errors have been made. Perform the following steps to find the errors:

1. Add the column totals again.
2. Make sure the net income or loss has been sorted to the correct column.
3. Add the Income Statement columns again and make sure they equal and you have computed the correct net income.

IN THE NEWS

Accoun-tech   An electronic work sheet using spreadsheet software such as Excel allows us to easily change numbers, assess the impact of alternative strategies, and quickly prepare financial statements at less cost. It can also increase the available time for analysis and interpretation.

Work Sheet Applications and Analysis

A work sheet does not replace financial statements. It is a tool we can use at the end of an accounting period to help organize data and prepare financial statements. FastForward's financial statements are shown in Exhibit 6.3. Its income statement amounts are taken from the Income

Exhibit 6.3

Financial Statements Prepared from the Work Sheet

FASTFORWARD
Income Statement
For Month Ended December 31, 2010

Revenues		
Consulting revenue	$ 5,800	
Rental revenue	300	
Total revenues		$ 6,100
Expenses		
Depreciation expense—Equipment	375	
Salaries expense	1,610	
Insurance expense	100	
Rent expense	1,000	
Supplies expense	1,050	
Utilities expense	230	
Total expenses		4,365
Net income		$ 1,735

FASTFORWARD
Statement of Owner's Equity
For Month Ended December 31, 2010

C. Taylor, Capital, December 1		$ 0
Add: Investment by owner	$30,000	
Net income	1,735	31,735
		31,735
Less: Withdrawals by owner		200
C. Taylor, Capital, December 31		$31,535

Net income increases ending owner's capital.

FASTFORWARD
Balance Sheet
December 31, 2010

Assets		
Cash		$ 4,350
Supplies		8,670
Prepaid insurance		2,300
Equipment	$26,000	
Less: Accumulated depreciation—Equipment	375	25,625
Total assets		$40,945
Liabilities		
Accounts payable		$ 6,200
Salaries payable		210
Unearned consulting revenue		3,000
Total liabilities		9,410
Equity		
C. Taylor, Capital		31,535
Total liabilities and equity		$40,945

Ending owner's capital appears on the balance sheet.

Statement columns of the work sheet. Similarly, amounts for its balance sheet and its statement of owner's equity are taken from the Balance Sheet & Statement of Owner's Equity columns of the work sheet.

A work sheet is also useful to journalize adjusting entries as the information is in the Adjustments columns. It is important to remember that a work sheet is not a journal. This means that even when a work sheet is prepared, it is necessary to both journalize adjustments and post them to the ledger.

Work sheets can also help in analyzing proposed, or what-if, transactions. This is done by entering financial statement amounts in the Unadjusted columns. Proposed transactions are then entered into the Adjustments columns. We then compute adjusted amounts from the proposed transactions. The extended amounts in the last four columns of the work sheet then show the financial statement effects of these proposed transactions. These financial statement columns yield **pro forma financial statements** because they show the statements *as if* the proposed transactions happened.

HOW YOU DOIN'?   Answers—p. 141

1. Where do we get the amounts to enter in the Unadjusted Trial Balance columns of a work sheet?

2. What are the advantages of using a work sheet to help prepare adjusting entries?

Closing Process

The **closing process** is an important step at the end of an accounting period *after* financial statements are completed. The purpose of the closing process is to:

LO2 Explain why temporary accounts are closed each period.

- Set revenue, expense, and owner withdrawal accounts to zero. This is done so these accounts can properly measure income and withdrawals in the *next* period.
- Update the owner capital account balance to its proper ending balance.

The closing process involves three tasks:

Task 1: Identify accounts used in the closing process.

Task 2: Journalize and post closing entries.

Task 3: Prepare a post-closing trial balance.

We discuss these tasks next.

Temporary and Permanent Accounts

Temporary (or *nominal*) **accounts** accumulate data for one accounting period. They include all revenue and expense accounts, the owner withdrawal account, and the Income Summary account (discussed below). They are temporary because they start with balances of zero at the beginning of a period, they record transactions and events for that period, and then are closed to have zero balances at the end of the period. For example, FastForward's net income of $1,735 for this period cannot also be included in its net income for the next period; starting each period with zero balances in revenue and expense accounts ensures proper income measurement. **Permanent** (or *real*) **accounts** carry their balances into the next period and generally consist of all balance sheet accounts. For example, FastForward's ending cash balance of $4,350 on December 31 will be its beginning cash balance on January 1 of the next year. A simple rule applies to the closing process: *Only temporary accounts are closed.*

Temporary Accounts

Temporary Accounts
Revenues
Expenses
Owner Withdrawals
Income Summary

Permanent Accounts

Permanent Accounts
Assets
Liabilities
Owner Capital

Income Summary **Income Summary** is a temporary account used only in the closing process. Note, Income Summary does not appear in our work sheet in Exhibit 6.1, and it is not used for recording transactions during the year. The Income Summary account has these features:

- It starts the closing process with a zero balance.
- It is credited for the sum of all the revenue accounts for the period.
- It is debited for the sum of all the expense accounts for the period.
- It is closed to the owner capital account.
- It ends the closing process with a zero balance. Just before it is closed, its balance is equal to the net income or loss for that period.

Owner, Capital   The Owner, Capital account is the only permanent account that appears in the closing process. This is so this account can be updated to reflect that period's performance. Recall that the balance for Owner, Capital on the work sheet *is not* its ending balance; closing journal entries are necessary to obtain the correct ending balance of Owner, Capital in the ledger.

Recording Closing Entries

To record and post **closing entries** is to transfer the ending balances in the temporary accounts to the Owner, Capital account. To close a temporary account means to make an entry to reduce its account balance to zero. If all accounts have normal balances, revenue accounts are closed with debit entries and expense and withdrawal accounts are closed with credit entries. The four-step closing process is shown in Exhibit 6.4.

Exhibit 6.4

The Four-Step Closing Process

Accounts Being Closed	Closing Entry Made to
1. Revenue accounts	Cr. Income Summary
2. Expense accounts	Dr. Income Summary
3. Income Summary account	To Owner, Capital*
4. Withdrawals account	Dr. Owner, Capital

* Cr. for net income. Dr. for net loss.

After completing steps 1 and 2, the income statement accounts are now ready for the next period. After completing steps 3 and 4, the balance in the Owner, Capital account in the general ledger equals the ending amount shown on the Statement of Owner's Equity. Exhibits 6.5 and 6.6 illustrate the four-step closing process for FastForward, using ending balances in the Income Statement and Balance Sheet and Statement of Owner's Equity columns from the work sheet in Exhibit 6.1d. We next use this work sheet information to explain the four-step closing process.

LO3 Describe and prepare closing entries.

Step 1: Close Credit Balances in Revenue Accounts to Income Summary   The first closing entry transfers credit balances in revenue accounts to the Income Summary account. We bring accounts with credit balances to zero by debiting them. For FastForward, this journal entry is step 1 in Exhibit 6.6. This entry closes revenue accounts and leaves them with zero balances. The accounts are now ready to record revenues when they occur in the next period. The $6,100 credit entry to Income Summary equals total revenues for the period.

Step 2: Close Debit Balances in Expense Accounts to Income Summary   The second closing entry transfers debit balances in expense accounts to the Income Summary account. We bring expense accounts' debit balances to zero by crediting them. With a balance of zero, these accounts are ready to record expenses for the next period. This second closing entry for FastForward is step 2 in Exhibit 6.6. Exhibit 6.5 shows that posting this entry gives each expense account a zero balance. The sum of these expense account debit balances before closing is $4,365 ($375 + 1,610 + 100 + 1,000 + 1,050 + 230). This amount is debited to Income Summary and represents total expenses for the period.

It is possible to close revenue and expense accounts directly to owner's capital. Computerized accounting systems do this.

Step 3: Close Income Summary to Owner's Capital   After steps 1 and 2, the balance (credit) of Income Summary is equal to December's net income of $1,735. The third closing entry transfers the balance of the Income Summary account to the capital account. This entry closes the Income Summary account and is step 3 in Exhibit 6.6. The Income Summary account has a zero balance after posting this entry. It continues to have a zero

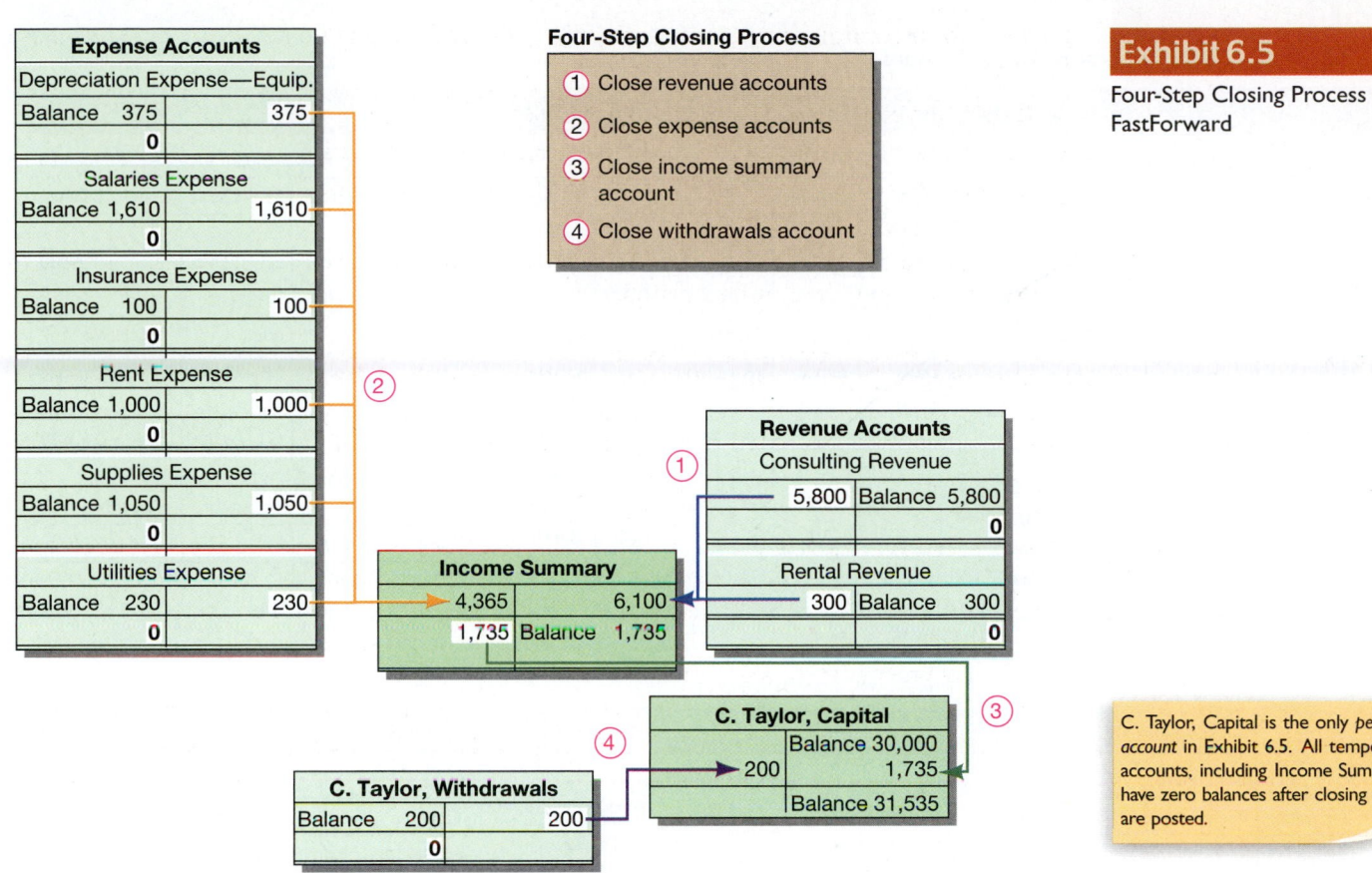

Exhibit 6.5

Four-Step Closing Process for FastForward

C. Taylor, Capital is the only *permanent account* in Exhibit 6.5. All temporary accounts, including Income Summary, have zero balances after closing entries are posted.

Exhibit 6.6

Preparing Closing Entries

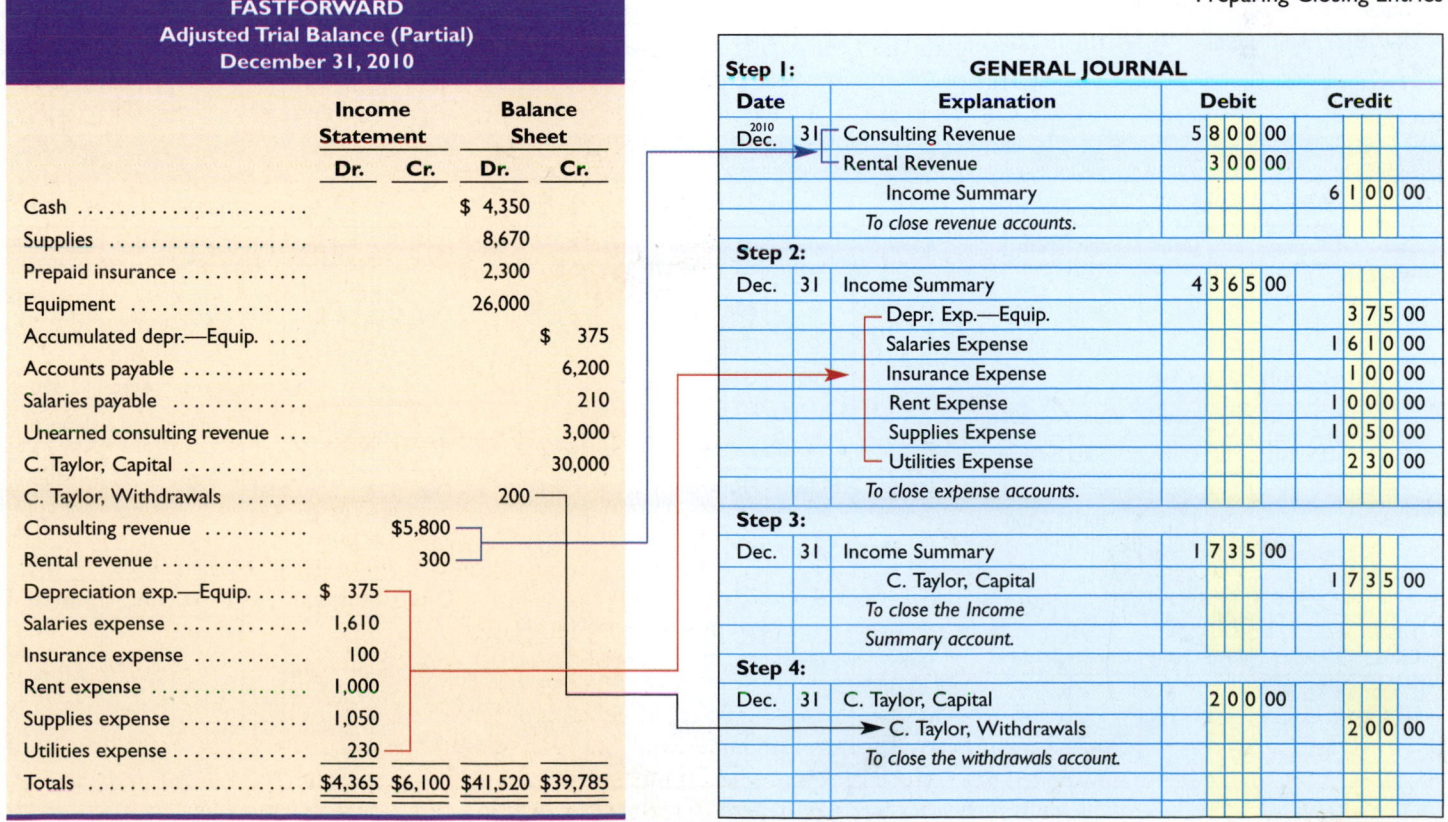

Exhibit 6.7

General Ledger after the Closing Process for FastForward

Asset Accounts

Cash   Acct. No. 101

Date	Explan.	PR	Debit	Credit	Balance
2010					
Dec. 1		G1	30,000		30,000
2		G1		2,500	27,500
3		G1		26,000	1,500
5		G1	4,200		5,700
6		G1		1,000	4,700
12		G1		700	4,000
19		G1	1,900		5,900
20		G1		900	5,000
21		G1		200	4,800
22		G1	3,000		7,800
23		G1		2,400	5,400
23		G1		120	5,280
23		G1		230	5,050
26		G1		700	**4,350**

Accounts Receivable   Acct. No. 106

Date	Explan.	PR	Debit	Credit	Balance
2010					
Dec. 13		G1	1,900		1,900
19		G1		1,900	**0**

Supplies   Acct. No. 126

Date	Explan.	PR	Debit	Credit	Balance
2010					
Dec. 2		G1	2,500		2,500
4		G1	7,100		9,600
23		G1	120		9,720
31	Adj.	G1		1,050	**8,670**

Prepaid Insurance   Acct. No. 128

Date	Explan.	PR	Debit	Credit	Balance
2010					
Dec. 23		G1	2,400		2,400
31	Adj.	G1		100	**2,300**

Equipment   Acct. No. 167

Date	Explan.	PR	Debit	Credit	Balance
2010					
Dec. 3		G1	26,000		**26,000**

Accumulated Depreciation— Equipment   Acct. No. 168

Date	Explan.	PR	Debit	Credit	Balance
2010					
Dec. 31	Adj.	G1		375	**375**

Liability and Equity Accounts

Accounts Payable   Acct. No. 201

Date	Explan.	PR	Debit	Credit	Balance
2010					
Dec. 4		G1		7,100	7,100
20		G1	900		**6,200**

Salaries Payable   Acct. No. 209

Date	Explan.	PR	Debit	Credit	Balance
2010					
Dec. 31	Adj	G1		210	**210**

Unearned Consulting Revenue   Acct. No. 236

Date	Explan.	PR	Debit	Credit	Balance
2010					
Dec. 22		G1		3,000	**3,000**

C. Taylor, Capital   Acct. No. 301

Date	Explan.	PR	Debit	Credit	Balance
2010					
Dec. 1		G1		30,000	30,000
31	Closing	G1		1,735	31,735
31	Closing	G1	200		31,735

C. Taylor, Withdrawals   Acct. No. 302

Date	Explan.	PR	Debit	Credit	Balance
2010					
Dec. 21		G1	200		200
31	Closing	G1		200	0

Revenue and Expense Accounts (including Income Summary)

Consulting Revenue   Acct. No. 403

Date	Explan.	PR	Debit	Credit	Balance
2010					
Dec. 5		G1		4,200	4,200
13		G1		1,600	5,800
31	Closing	G1	5,800		0

Rental Revenue   Acct. No. 406

Date	Explan.	PR	Debit	Credit	Balance
2010					
Dec. 13		G1		300	300
31	Closing	G1	300		0

Depreciation Expense— Equipment   Acct. No. 612

Date	Explan.	PR	Debit	Credit	Balance
2010					
Dec. 31	Adj.	G1	375		375
31	Closing	G1		375	0

Salaries Expense   Acct. No. 622

Date	Explan.	PR	Debit	Credit	Balance
2010					
Dec. 12		G1	700		700
26		G1	700		1,400
31	Adj.	G1	210		1,610
31	Closing	G1		1,610	0

Insurance Expense   Acct. No. 637

Date	Explan.	PR	Debit	Credit	Balance
2010					
Dec. 31	Adj.	G1	100		100
31	Closing	G1		100	0

Rent Expense   Acct. No. 640

Date	Explan.	PR	Debit	Credit	Balance
2010					
Dec. 6		G1	1,000		1,000
31	Closing	G1		1,000	0

Supplies Expense   Acct. No. 652

Date	Explan.	PR	Debit	Credit	Balance
2010					
Dec. 31	Adj.	G1	1,050		1,050
31	Closing	G1		1,050	0

Utilities Expense   Acct. No. 690

Date	Explan.	PR	Debit	Credit	Balance
2010					
Dec. 23		G1	230		230
31	Closing	G1		230	0

Income Summary   Acct. No. 901

Date	Explan.	PR	Debit	Credit	Balance
2010					
Dec. 31	Closing	G1		6,100	6,100
31	Closing	G1	4,365		1,735
31	Closing	G1	1,735		0

balance until the closing process again occurs at the end of the next period. (If a net loss occurred because expenses exceeded revenues, the third entry is reversed: debit Owner, Capital and credit Income Summary.)

Step 4: Close Withdrawals Account to Owner's Capital   The fourth closing entry transfers any debit balance in the withdrawals account to the owner's capital account—see step 4 in Exhibit 6.6. This entry gives the withdrawals account a zero balance, and the account is now ready to accumulate next period's withdrawals. This entry also reduces the capital account balance to the $31,535 amount reported on the balance sheet.

Post-Closing Trial Balance

Exhibit 6.7 shows the entire ledger of FastForward as of December 31 after adjusting and closing entries are posted. (The transaction and adjusting entries are in Chapters 3, 4, and 5.) The temporary accounts (revenues, expenses, and withdrawals) have ending balances equal to zero. The final task in the closing process is to ensure that debit and credit balances equal for the *permanent* accounts in the general ledger.

A **post-closing trial balance** is a list of permanent accounts and their balances from the ledger after all closing entries have been journalized and posted. It lists the balances for all accounts not closed. These accounts comprise a company's assets, liabilities, and equity, which are those in the balance sheet. The aim of a post-closing trial balance is to verify that (1) total debits equal total credits for permanent accounts and (2) all temporary accounts have zero balances. FastForward's post-closing trial balance is shown in Exhibit 6.8. The post-closing trial balance usually is the last step in the accounting process.

LO4 Explain and prepare a post-closing trial balance.

FASTFORWARD Post-Closing Trial Balance December 31, 2010	Debit	Credit
Cash	$ 4,350	
Supplies	8,670	
Prepaid insurance	2,300	
Equipment	26,000	
Accumulated depreciation—Equipment		$ 375
Accounts payable		6,200
Salaries payable		210
Unearned consulting revenue		3,000
C. Taylor, Capital		31,535
Totals	$41,320	$41,320

Exhibit 6.8

Post-Closing Trial Balance

The post-closing trial balance does not include revenues, expenses, or owner withdrawals. All of those accounts have zero balances after closing.

Accounting Cycle

Chapters 2 through 6 can be usefully summarized by examining the accounting cycle. The term **accounting cycle** refers to the steps from processing transactions through preparing financial statements. It is called a *cycle* because the steps are repeated each reporting period. Exhibit 6.9 shows the nine steps in the cycle, beginning with analyzing transactions and ending with a post-closing trial balance. Steps 1 through 3 usually occur regularly as a company enters into transactions. Steps 4 through 9 are done at the end of a period.

LO5 Identify steps in the accounting cycle.

HOW YOU DOIN'?
Answers—p. 141

3. What are the major steps in preparing closing entries?
4. Why are revenue and expense accounts called *temporary*? Can you identify and list any other temporary accounts?
5. What accounts are listed on the post-closing trial balance?

Exhibit 6.9

Steps in the Accounting Cycle*

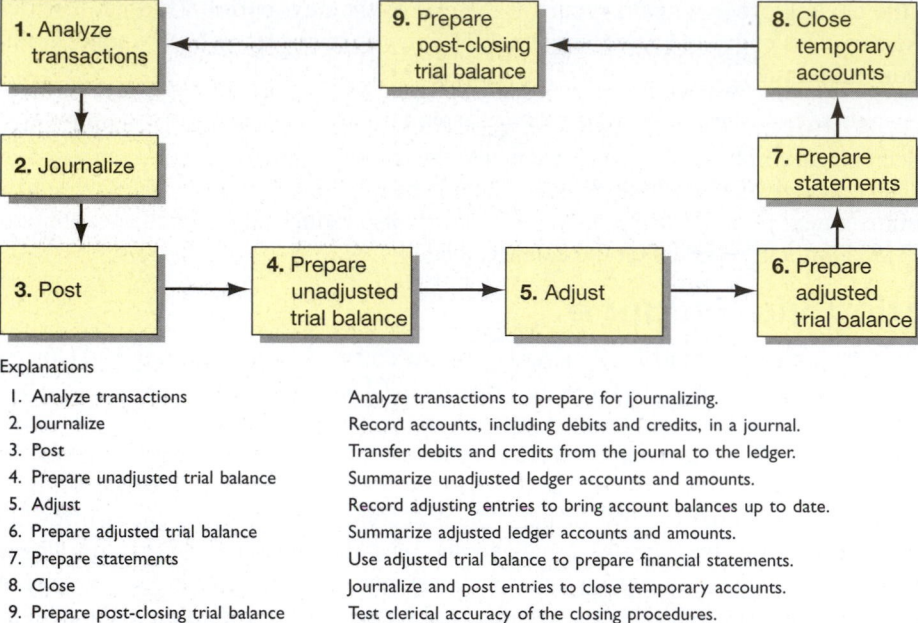

Explanations

1. Analyze transactions	Analyze transactions to prepare for journalizing.
2. Journalize	Record accounts, including debits and credits, in a journal.
3. Post	Transfer debits and credits from the journal to the ledger.
4. Prepare unadjusted trial balance	Summarize unadjusted ledger accounts and amounts.
5. Adjust	Record adjusting entries to bring account balances up to date.
6. Prepare adjusted trial balance	Summarize adjusted ledger accounts and amounts.
7. Prepare statements	Use adjusted trial balance to prepare financial statements.
8. Close	Journalize and post entries to close temporary accounts.
9. Prepare post-closing trial balance	Test clerical accuracy of the closing procedures.

*Steps 4, 6, and 9 can be done on a work sheet. A work sheet is useful in *planning* adjustments, but adjustments (step 5) must always be journalized and posted. Steps 3, 4, 6, and 9 are automatic with a computerized system.

Demonstration Problem

The partial work sheet of Midtown Repair Company at December 31, 2010, follows.

	Adjusted Trial Balance		Income Statement		Balance Sheet and Statement of Owner's Equity	
	Debit	Credit	Debit	Credit	Debit	Credit
Cash	95,600					
Prepaid insurance	16,000					
Prepaid rent	4,000					
Equipment	170,000					
Accumulated depreciation—Equipment		57,000				
Accounts payable		52,000				
C. Trout, Capital		178,500				
C. Trout, Withdrawals	30,000					
Repair services revenue		180,800				
Consulting revenue		14,800				
Depreciation expense—Equipment	28,500					
Wages expense	85,000					
Rent expense	48,000					
Insurance expense	6,000					
Totals	483,100	483,100				

Required

1. Complete the work sheet by extending the adjusted trial balance totals to the appropriate financial statement columns.
2. Prepare closing entries for Midtown Repair Company. Assume you are using page 7 of the General Journal.
3. Set up the Income Summary and the C. Trout, Capital account in the general ledger (in balance column format) and post the closing entries to these accounts.
4. Determine the balance of the C. Trout, Capital account to be reported on the December 31, 2010, balance sheet.
5. Prepare an income statement, statement of owner's equity, and balance sheet as of December 31, 2010.

Planning the Solution

- Extend the adjusted trial balance account balances to the appropriate financial statement columns.
- Prepare entries to close the revenue accounts to Income Summary, to close the expense accounts to Income Summary, to close Income Summary to the capital account, and to close the withdrawals account to the capital account.
- Post the first and second closing entries to the Income Summary account. Examine the balance of income summary and verify that it agrees with the net income shown on the work sheet.
- Post the third and fourth closing entries to the capital account.
- Use the work sheet's two right-most columns and your answer in part 4 to prepare the balance sheet.

Solution to Demonstration Problem

1. Completing the work sheet.

	Adjusted Trial Balance		Income Statement		Balance Sheet and Statement of Owner's Equity	
	Debit	Credit	Debit	Credit	Debit	Credit
Cash	95,600				95,600	
Prepaid insurance	16,000				16,000	
Prepaid rent	4,000				4,000	
Equipment	170,000				170,000	
Accumulated depreciation—Equipment		57,000				57,000
Accounts payable		52,000				52,000
C. Trout, Capital		178,500				178,500
C. Trout, Withdrawals	30,000				30,000	
Repair services revenue		180,800		180,800		
Consulting revenue		14,800		14,800		
Depreciation expense—Equipment	28,500		28,500			
Wages expense	85,000		85,000			
Rent expense	48,000		48,000			
Insurance expense	6,000		6,000			
Totals	483,100	483,100	167,500	195,600	315,600	287,500
Net income			28,100			28,100
Totals			195,600	195,600	315,600	315,600

2. Closing entries.

	GENERAL JOURNAL			Page 7
Date	Explanation		Debit	Credit
2010 Dec. 31	Repair Services Revenue		180 800 00	
	Consulting Revenue		14 800 00	
	Income Summary			195 600 00
	To close revenue accounts.			
Dec. 31	Income Summary		167 500 00	
	Depreciation Expense—Equipment			28 500 00
	Wages Expense			85 000 00
	Rent Expense			48 000 00
	Insurance Expense			6 000 00
	To close expense accounts.			
Dec. 31	Income Summary		28 100 00	
	C. Trout, Capital			28 100 00
	To close the Income Summary account.			
Dec. 31	C. Trout, Capital		30 000 00	
	C. Trout, Withdrawals			30 000 00
	To close the withdrawals account.			

*We exclude posting reference details in the general journal above.

3. Set up the Income Summary and the capital ledger accounts and post the closing entries.

		INCOME SUMMARY								Account No. 901	
Date		**Explanation**	**PR**	**Debit**		**Credit**		**Balance**			
2010 Jan.	1	Beginning balance								0	00
Dec.	31	Close revenue accounts	G7			195 600 00		195 600 00			
	31	Close expense accounts	G7	167 500 00				28 100 00			
	31	Close income summary	G7	28 100 00						0	00

		C. TROUT, CAPITAL								Account No. 301	
Date		**Explanation**	**PR**	**Debit**		**Credit**		**Balance**			
2010 Jan.	1	Beginning balance						178 500 00			
Dec.	31	Close Income Summary	G7			28 100 00		206 600 00			
	31	Close C. Trout, Withdrawals	G7	30 000 00				176 600 00			

4. The final capital balance of $176,600 (from part 3) will be reported on the December 31, 2010, balance sheet. The final capital balance reflects the increase due to the net income earned during the year and the decrease for the owner's withdrawals during the year.

5. Prepare financial statements.

MIDTOWN REPAIR COMPANY
Income Statement
For Year Ended December 31, 2010

Revenues		
Repair services revenue	$180,800	
Consulting revenue	14,800	
Total revenues		$195,600
Expenses		
Depreciation expense—Equipment	28,500	
Wages expense	85,000	
Rent expense	48,000	
Insurance expense	6,000	
Total expenses		167,500
Net income		$ 28,100

MIDTOWN REPAIR COMPANY
Statement of Owner's Equity
For Year Ended December 31, 2010

C. Trout, Capital, December 31, 2009		$178,500
Add: Investment by owner	$ 0	
Net income	28,100	28,100
		206,600
Less: Withdrawals by owner		30,000
C. Trout, Capital, December 31, 2010		$176,600

MIDTOWN REPAIR COMPANY
Balance Sheet
December 31, 2010

Assets

Cash		$ 95,600
Prepaid insurance		16,000
Prepaid rent		4,000
Equipment	$170,000	
Less: Accumulated depreciation—Equipment	57,000	113,000
Total assets		$228,600

Liabilities

Accounts payable	$ 52,000

Equity

C. Trout, Capital	176,600
Total liabilities and equity	$228,600

Summary

LO1 **Prepare a worksheet and explain its usefulness.** A work sheet can be a useful tool in preparing and analyzing financial statements. It is helpful at the end of a period in preparing adjusting entries, an adjusted trial balance, and financial statements. A work sheet usually contains five pairs of columns: Unadjusted Trial Balance, Adjustments, Adjusted Trial Balance, Income Statement, and Balance Sheet & Statement of Owner's Equity.

LO2 **Explain why temporary accounts are closed each period.** Temporary accounts are closed at the end of each accounting period for two main reasons. First, the closing process updates the capital account to include the effects of all transactions and events recorded for the period. Second, it prepares revenue, expense, and withdrawals accounts for the next reporting period by giving them zero balances.

LO3 **Describe and prepare closing entries.** Closing entries involve four steps: (1) close credit balances in revenue accounts to Income Summary, (2) close debit balances in expense accounts to Income Summary, (3) close Income Summary to the capital account, and (4) close the withdrawals account to owner's capital.

LO4 **Explain and prepare a post-closing trial balance.** A post-closing trial balance is a list of permanent accounts and their balances after all closing entries have been journalized and posted. Its purpose is to verify that (1) total debits equal total credits for permanent accounts and (2) all temporary accounts have zero balances.

LO5 **Identify steps in the accounting cycle.** The accounting cycle consists of 9 steps: (1) analyze transactions, (2) journalize, (3) post, (4) prepare an unadjusted trial balance, (5) adjust accounts, (6) prepare an adjusted trial balance, (7) prepare statements, (8) close temporary accounts, and (9) prepare a post-closing trial balance.

Guidance Answers to HOW YOU DOIN'?

1. Amounts in the Unadjusted Trial Balance columns are taken from current account balances in the ledger. The balances for new accounts expected to arise from adjusting entries can be left blank or set at zero.

2. A work sheet offers the advantage of listing on one page all necessary information to make adjusting entries.

3. The major steps in preparing closing entries are to close (1) credit balances in revenue accounts to Income Summary, (2) debit balances in expense accounts to Income Summary, (3) Income Summary to owner's capital, and (4) any withdrawals account to owner's capital.

4. Revenue and expense accounts are called *temporary* because they are opened and closed each period. The Income Summary and owner's withdrawals accounts are also temporary.

5. Permanent accounts make up the post-closing trial balance, which consist of asset, liability, and equity accounts.

Key Terms

Accounting cycle (p. 137) Recurring steps performed each accounting period, starting with analyzing transactions and continuing through the post-closing trial balance.

Closing entries (p. 134) Entries recorded at the end of each accounting period to transfer end-of-period balances in revenue, expense, and withdrawal accounts to the capital account.

Closing process (p. 133) Necessary end-of-period steps to prepare the accounts for recording the transactions of the next period.

Income Summary (p. 133) Temporary account used only in the closing process to which the balances of revenue and expense accounts are transferred; its balance is transferred to the capital account.

Permanent accounts (p. 133) Accounts that reflect activities related to one or more future periods; balance sheet accounts whose balances are not closed; also called *real accounts*.

Post-closing trial balance (p. 137) List of permanent accounts and their balances from the ledger after all closing entries are journalized and posted.

Pro forma financial statements (p. 133) Statements that show the effects of proposed transactions and events as if they had occurred.

Temporary accounts (p. 133) Accounts used to record revenues, expenses, and withdrawals; they are closed at the end of each period; also called *nominal accounts*.

Work sheet (p. 128) Spreadsheet used to draft an unadjusted trial balance, adjusting entries, adjusted trial balance, and financial statements.

Working papers (p. 128) Analyses and other internal documents prepared by accountants when organizing information for formal reports and financial statements.

Multiple Choice Quiz   Answers on p. 155   mhhe.com/wildCA2e

Additional Multiple Choice Quizzes are available at the book's Website.

1. G. Venda, owner of Venda Services, withdrew $25,000 from the business during the current year. The entry to close the withdrawals account at the end of the year is:

a.	G. Venda, Withdrawals	25,000	
	G. Venda, Capital		25,000
b.	Income Summary	25,000	
	G. Venda, Capital		25,000
c.	G. Venda, Withdrawals	25,000	
	Cash		25,000
d.	G. Venda, Capital	25,000	
	Salary Expense		25,000
e.	G. Venda, Capital	25,000	
	G. Venda, Withdrawals		25,000

2. The following information is available for the R. Kandamil Company before closing the accounts. After all of the closing entries are made, what will be the balance in the R. Kandamil, Capital account?

Total revenues	$300,000
Total expenses	195,000
R. Kandamil, Capital	100,000
R. Kandamil, Withdrawals	45,000

   a. $360,000
   b. $250,000

   c. $160,000
   d. $150,000
   e. $60,000

3. Which of the following is a permanent account?
   a. Income Summary
   b. Sales Revenue
   c. Utilities Expense
   d. Rent Expense
   e. Cash

4. A work sheet's Income Statement debit column totals $92,000 and its Income Statement credit column totals $86,700 at the end of the year. Based on this, the company made
   a. Net loss of $5,300 for the year
   b. Net income of $5,300 for the year
   c. Total revenues of $92,000 for the year
   d. Total expenses of $86,700 for the year

5. The temporary account used only in the closing process to hold the amounts of revenues and expenses before the net difference is added or subtracted from the owner's capital account is called the
   a. Closing account.
   b. Nominal account.
   c. Income Summary account.
   d. Balance Column account.
   e. Contra account.

Discussion Questions

1. What accounts are affected by closing entries? What accounts are not affected?

2. What two purposes are accomplished by recording closing entries?

3. What are the steps in recording closing entries?

4. What is the purpose of the Income Summary account?

5. Explain whether an error has occurred if a post-closing trial balance includes a Depreciation Expense account.

6. What tasks are aided by a work sheet?

7. Why are the debit and credit entries in the Adjustments columns of the work sheet identified with letters?

8. What are the overall benefits of a work sheet?

connect

Gloriosa Company began the current period with a $28,000 credit balance in the M. Gloriosa, Capital account. At the end of the period, the company's adjusted account balances include the following temporary accounts with normal balances.

Service fees earned	$45,000	Interest revenue	$6,000
Salaries expense	29,000	M. Gloriosa, Withdrawals	7,200
Depreciation expense	9,000	Utilities expense	3,000

After closing the revenue and expense accounts, what will be the balance of the Income Summary account? After all closing entries are journalized and posted, what will be the balance of the M. Gloriosa, Capital account?

QUICK STUDY

QS 6-1
Determining effects of
closing entries   **LO2   LO3**

List the following steps of the accounting cycle in their proper order.

a. Posting the journal entries.

b. Journalizing and posting adjusting entries.

c. Preparing the adjusted trial balance.

d. Journalizing and posting closing entries.

e. Analyzing transactions and events.

f. Preparing the financial statements.

g. Preparing the unadjusted trial balance.

h. Journalizing transactions and events.

i. Preparing the post-closing trial balance.

QS 6-2
Identifying the accounting cycle
LO5

The following information is taken from the work sheet for Warton Company as of December 31, 2010. Using this information, determine the amount for B. Warton, Capital that should be reported on its December 31, 2010, balance sheet.

QS 6-3
Interpreting a work sheet   **LO1**

	Income Statement		Balance Sheet and Statement of Owner's Equity	
	Dr.	Cr.	Dr.	Cr.
B. Warton, Capital				72,000
B. Warton, Withdrawals			39,000	
Totals	122,000	181,000		

In preparing a work sheet, indicate the financial statement Debit column to which a normal balance in the following accounts should be extended. Use I for the Income Statement Debit column and B for the Balance Sheet and Statement of Owner's Equity Debit column.

_____ **a.** Equipment

_____ **b.** Owner, Withdrawals

_____ **c.** Prepaid rent

_____ **d.** Depreciation expense—Equipment

_____ **e.** Accounts receivable

_____ **f.** Insurance expense

QS 6-4
Applying a work sheet   **LO1**

List the following steps in preparing a work sheet in their proper order by writing numbers 1–5 in the blank spaces provided.

a. _____ Total the statement columns, compute net income (loss), and complete work sheet.

b. _____ Extend adjusted balances to appropriate financial statement columns.

c. _____ Prepare an unadjusted trial balance on the work sheet.

d. _____ Prepare an adjusted trial balance on the work sheet.

e. _____ Enter adjustments data on the work sheet.

QS 6-5
Ordering work sheet steps   **LO1**

The ledger of Claudell Company includes the following unadjusted normal balances: Prepaid Rent $1,000 and Wages Expense $25,000. Adjusting entries are required for (a) rent expense of $200 and (b) accrued wages expense of $700. Enter the unadjusted balances of Prepaid Rent and Wages Expense and the necessary adjustments on a partial work sheet and complete the work sheet for these accounts. Use Exhibit 6.1 as a guide.

QS 6-6
Preparing a partial work sheet
LO1

The ledger of Mai Company includes the following accounts with normal balances: D. Mai, Capital $9,000; D. Mai, Withdrawals $800; Services Revenue $13,000; Wages Expense $8,400; and Rent Expense $1,600. Prepare the necessary closing entries from the available information at December 31.

QS 6-7
Prepare closing entries from
the ledger   **LO3**

QS 6-8
Identify post-closing accounts
LO4

Identify the accounts listed in QS 6-7 that would be included in a post-closing trial balance.

connect™

EXERCISES

Exercise 6-1
Preparing and posting
closing entries   **LO3**

Use the year-end information from the following ledger accounts (assume that all accounts have normal balances) to prepare closing journal entries and then post those entries to the appropriate ledger accounts. Assume the closing entries are made on page 2 of a general journal.

Check   M. Muncel, Capital (ending balance), $46,200

General Ledger				

M. Muncel, Capital   **Acct. No. 301**

Date	PR	Debit	Credit	Balance
Dec. 31				40,000

M. Muncel, Withdrawals   **Acct. No. 302**

Date	PR	Debit	Credit	Balance
Dec. 31				22,000

Services Revenue   **Acct. No. 401**

Date	PR	Debit	Credit	Balance
Dec. 31				76,000

Depreciation Expense   **Acct. No. 603**

Date	PR	Debit	Credit	Balance
Dec. 31				15,000

Salaries Expense   **Acct. No. 622**

Date	PR	Debit	Credit	Balance
Dec. 31				20,000

Insurance Expense   **Acct. No. 637**

Date	PR	Debit	Credit	Balance
Dec. 31				4,400

Rent Expense   **Acct. No. 640**

Date	PR	Debit	Credit	Balance
Dec. 31				8,400

Income Summary   **Acct. No. 901**

Date	PR	Debit	Credit	Balance

Exercise 6-2
Preparing closing entries and a
post-closing trial balance
LO3   LO4

The adjusted trial balance for Salonika Marketing Co. follows. Complete the four right-most columns of the table by first entering information for the four closing entries (keyed *1* through *4*) and second by completing the post-closing trial balance.

No.	Account Title	Adjusted Trial Balance		Closing Entry Information		Post-Closing Trial Balance	
		Dr.	Cr.	Dr.	Cr.	Dr.	Cr.
101	Cash	$ 9,200					
106	Accounts receivable	25,000					
153	Equipment	42,000					
154	Accumulated depreciation—Equipment		$ 17,500				
193	Franchise	31,000					
201	Accounts payable		15,000				
209	Salaries payable		4,200				
233	Unearned fees		3,600				
301	E. Salonika, Capital		68,500				
302	E. Salonika, Withdrawals	15,400					
401	Marketing fees earned		80,000				
611	Depreciation expense—Equipment	12,000					
622	Salaries expense	32,500					
640	Rent expense	13,000					
677	Miscellaneous expenses	8,700					
901	Income summary						
	Totals	$188,800	$188,800				

The following adjusted trial balance contains the accounts and balances of Cruz Company as of December 31, 2010, the end of its fiscal year. (1) Prepare the December 31, 2010, closing entries for Cruz Company. (2) Prepare the December 31, 2010, post-closing trial balance for Cruz Company.

Exercise 6-3
Preparing closing entries and a post-closing trial balance
LO2   LO3   LO4

No.	Account Title	Debit	Credit
101	Cash	$19,000	
126	Supplies	13,000	
128	Prepaid insurance	3,000	
167	Equipment	24,000	
168	Accumulated depreciation—Equipment		$ 7,500
301	T. Cruz, Capital		47,600
302	T. Cruz, Withdrawals	7,000	
404	Services revenue		44,000
612	Depreciation expense—Equipment	3,000	
622	Salaries expense	22,000	
637	Insurance expense	2,500	
640	Rent expense	3,400	
652	Supplies expense	2,200	
	Totals	$99,100	$99,100

Check   (2) T. Cruz, Capital (ending), $51,500; Total debits, $59,000

Use the following December 31, 2010, adjusted trial balance of Wilson Trucking Company to prepare the (1) income statement, (2) statement of owner's equity, and (3) balance sheet for the year ended December 31, 2010. The K. Wilson, Capital account balance is $175,000 at December 31, 2009.

Exercise 6-4
Preparing financial statements
LO1

Account Title	Debit	Credit
Cash	$ 8,000	
Accounts receivable	17,500	
Office supplies	3,000	
Trucks	172,000	
Accumulated depreciation—Trucks		$ 36,000
Land	85,000	
Accounts payable		65,000
Wages payable		4,000
K. Wilson, Capital		175,000
K. Wilson, Withdrawals	20,000	
Trucking fees earned		130,000
Depreciation expense—Trucks	23,500	
Salaries expense	61,000	
Office supplies expense	8,000	
Repairs expense—Trucks	12,000	
Totals	$410,000	$410,000

These 14 accounts are from the Adjusted Trial Balance columns of a company's 10-column work sheet. In the blank space beside each account, write the letter of the appropriate financial statement column (A, B, C, or D) to which a normal account balance is extended on the work sheet.

A. Debit column for the Income Statement columns.

B. Credit column for the Income Statement columns.

C. Debit column for the Balance Sheet and Statement of Owner's Equity columns.

D. Credit column for the Balance Sheet and Statement of Owner's Equity columns.

Exercise 6-5
Extending adjusted account balances on a work sheet
LO1

_____	**1.** Unearned Revenue	_____	**8.** Accounts Receivable
_____	**2.** Machinery	_____	**9.** Accumulated Depreciation
_____	**3.** Owner, Withdrawals	_____	**10.** Office Supplies
_____	**4.** Depreciation Expense	_____	**11.** Insurance Expense
_____	**5.** Accounts Payable	_____	**12.** Cash
_____	**6.** Service Fees Revenue	_____	**13.** Rent Expense
_____	**7.** Owner, Capital	_____	**14.** Wages Payable

Exercise 6-6

Extending accounts in a work sheet **LO1**

The Adjusted Trial Balance columns of a 10-column work sheet for Planta Company follow. Complete the work sheet by extending the account balances into the appropriate financial statement columns and by entering the amount of net income for the reporting period.

No.	Account Title	Debit	Credit
101	Cash	$ 7,000	
106	Accounts receivable	27,200	
153	Trucks	42,000	
154	Accumulated depreciation—Trucks		$ 17,500
183	Land	32,000	
201	Accounts payable		15,000
209	Salaries payable		4,200
233	Unearned fees		3,600
301	F. Planta, Capital		65,500
302	F. Planta, Withdrawals	15,400	
401	Plumbing fees earned		84,000
611	Depreciation expense—Trucks	6,500	
622	Salaries expense	38,000	
640	Rent expense	13,000	
677	Miscellaneous expenses	8,700	
	Totals	$189,800	$189,800

Check   Net income, $17,800

Exercise 6-7

Completing the income statement columns and preparing closing entries **LO1 LO3**

These partially completed Income Statement columns from a 10-column work sheet are for Brown's Bike Rental Company. (1) Use the information to determine the amount that should be entered on the net income line of the work sheet. (2) Prepare the company's closing entries. The owner, H. Brown, did not make any withdrawals this period.

Account Title	Debit	Credit
Rent earned		120,000
Salaries expense	46,300	
Insurance expense	7,400	
Office supplies expense	16,000	
Bike repair expense	4,200	
Depreciation expense—Bikes	20,500	
Totals		
Net income		
Totals		

Check   Net income, $25,600

Exercise 6-8

Preparing a work sheet and recording closing entries

LO1 LO3

The following unadjusted trial balance contains the accounts and balances of Dylan Delivery Company as of December 31, 2010, its first year of operations.

(1) Use the following information about the company's adjustments to complete a 10-column work sheet for Dylan Delivery Company.

a. Unrecorded depreciation on the trucks at the end of the year is $40,000.

b. An additional $1,000 of salaries must be accrued at year-end.

c. The cost of unused office supplies still available at year-end is $2,000.

(2) Prepare the year-end closing entries for Dylan Delivery Company, and determine the capital amount to be reported on its year-end balance sheet.

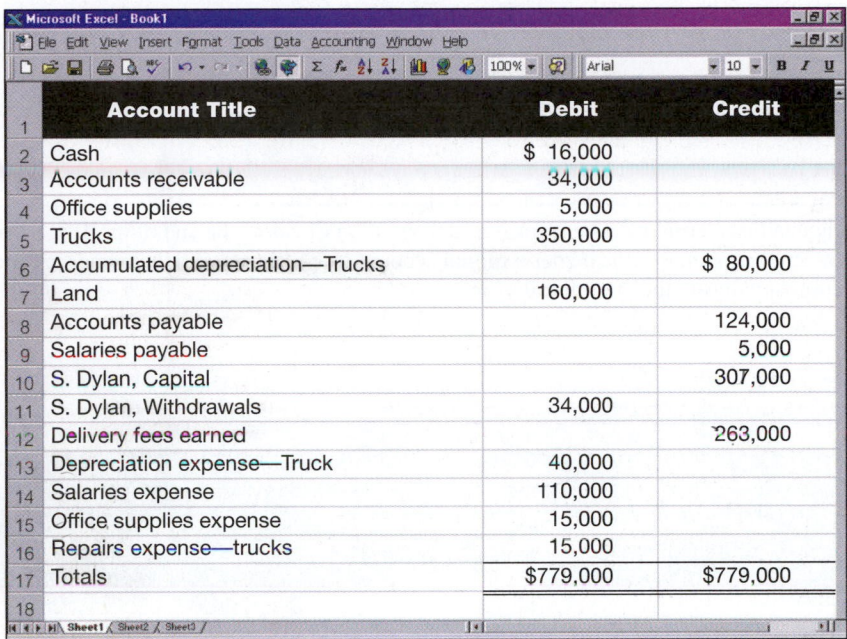

Account Title	Debit	Credit
Cash	$ 16,000	
Accounts receivable	34,000	
Office supplies	5,000	
Trucks	350,000	
Accumulated depreciation—Trucks		$ 80,000
Land	160,000	
Accounts payable		124,000
Salaries payable		5,000
S. Dylan, Capital		307,000
S. Dylan, Withdrawals	34,000	
Delivery fees earned		263,000
Depreciation expense—Truck	40,000	
Salaries expense	110,000	
Office supplies expense	15,000	
Repairs expense—trucks	15,000	
Totals	$779,000	$779,000

Check Adj. trial balance totals, $820,000; Net income, $39,000

---

connect

The adjusted trial balance of Karise Repairs on December 31, 2010, follows.

KARISE REPAIRS
Adjusted Trial Balance
December 31, 2010

No.	Account Title	Debit	Credit
101	Cash	$ 14,000	
124	Office supplies	1,300	
128	Prepaid insurance	2,050	
167	Equipment	50,000	
168	Accumulated depreciation—Equipment		$ 5,000
201	Accounts payable		14,000
210	Wages payable		600
301	C. Karise, Capital		33,000
302	C. Karise, Withdrawal	16,000	
401	Repair fees earned		90,950
612	Depreciation expense—Equipment	5,000	
623	Wages expense	37,500	
637	Insurance expense	800	
640	Rent expense	10,600	
650	Office supplies expense	3,600	
690	Utilities expense	2,700	
	Totals	$143,550	$143,550

PROBLEM SET A

Problem 6-1A
Preparing trial balances, closing entries, and financial statements
L01 L03 L04 L05

QB

mhhe.com/wildCA2e

Required

1. Prepare an income statement and a statement of owner's equity for the year 2010, and a balance sheet at December 31, 2010. There are no owner investments in 2010.
2. Prepare closing journal entries.
3. Prepare a post-closing trial balance.

Problem 6-2A

Preparing a work sheet, adjusting and closing entries, and financial statements **LO1 LO3**

The following unadjusted trial balance is for Ace Construction Co. as of the end of its 2010 fiscal year. The June 30, 2009, credit balance of the owner's capital account was $53,660, and the owner invested $35,000 cash in the company during the 2010 fiscal year.

File Edit View Insert Format Tools Data Window Help			
ACE CONSTRUCTION CO.			
Unadjusted Trial Balance			
June 30, 2010			
No.	Account Title	Debit	Credit
101	Cash	$ 18,500	
126	Supplies	9,900	
128	Prepaid insurance	7,200	
167	Equipment	132,000	
168	Accumulated depreciation—Equipment		$ 26,250
201	Accounts payable		31,800
208	Rent payable		0
210	Wages payable		0
301	V. Ace, Capital		88,660
302	V. Ace, Withdrawals	33,000	
401	Construction fees earned		132,100
612	Depreciation expense—Equipment	0	
623	Wages expense	49,610	
637	Insurance expense	0	
640	Rent expense	12,000	
652	Supplies expense	0	
684	Repairs expense	10,710	
690	Utilities expense	5,890	
	Totals	$ 278,810	$ 278,810

Required

1. Using Exhibit 6.1 as a guide, prepare a 10-column work sheet for fiscal year 2010, starting with the unadjusted trial balance and including adjustments based on these additional facts.
   a. The supplies available at the end of fiscal year 2010 had a cost of $3,300.
   b. The cost of expired insurance for the fiscal year is $3,800.
   c. Annual depreciation on equipment is $8,400.
   d. The June utilities expense of $650 is not included in the unadjusted trial balance because the bill arrived after the trial balance was prepared. The $650 amount owed needs to be recorded.
   e. The company's employees have earned $1,800 of accrued wages at fiscal year-end.
   f. The rent expense incurred and not yet paid or recorded at fiscal year-end is $500.

2. Use the work sheet to enter the adjusting entries, then journalize the adjusting entries.
3. Prepare an adjusted trial balance.
4. Extend the adjusted trial balance amounts to the proper financial statement column of the work sheet.
5. Prepare closing entries.
6. Prepare the income statement and the statement of owner's equity for the year ended June 30 and the balance sheet at June 30, 2010.

Check (3) Total assets, $122,550; Total liabilities, $34,750; Net income, $32,140

Holt Company's adjusted trial balance on December 31, 2010, follows.

PROBLEM SET B

Problem 6-1B
Preparing trial balances, closing entries, and financial statements
L01   L03   L04   L05

	HOLT COMPANY		
	Adjusted Trial Balance		
	December 31, 2010		
No.	**Account Title**	**Debit**	**Credit**
101	Cash	$ 14,450	
125	Store supplies	5,140	
128	Prepaid insurance	1,200	
167	Equipment	31,000	
168	Accumulated depreciation—Equipment		$8,000
201	Accounts payable		1,500
210	Wages payable		2,700
301	P. Holt, Capital		35,650
302	P. Holt, Withdrawals	15,000	
401	Repair fees earned		54,700
612	Depreciation expense—Equipment	2,000	
623	Wages expense	26,400	
637	Insurance expense	600	
640	Rent expense	3,600	
651	Store supplies expense	1,200	
690	Utilities expense	1,960	
	Totals	$102,550	$102,550

Required

1. Prepare an income statement and a statement of owner's equity for the year 2010, and a balance sheet at December 31, 2010. There are no owner investments in 2010.
2. Prepare closing journal entries.
3. Prepare a post-closing trial balance.

Check (1) Ending capital balance, $39,590

(3) P-C trial balance totals, $51,790

The following unadjusted trial balance is for Power Demolition Company as of the end of its April 30, 2010, fiscal year. The April 30, 2009, credit balance of the owner's capital account was $46,900, and the owner invested $40,000 cash in the company during the 2010 fiscal year.

Problem 6-2B
Preparing a work sheet, adjusting and closing entries, and financial statements   **L01   L03**

File   Edit   View   Insert   Format   Tools   Data   Window   Help

POWER DEMOLITION COMPANY
Unadjusted Trial Balance
April 30, 2010

No.	Account Title	Debit	Credit
101	Cash	$ 7,000	
126	Supplies	16,000	
128	Prepaid insurance	12,600	
167	Equipment	200,000	
168	Accumulated depreciation—Equipment		$ 14,000
201	Accounts payable		36,800
208	Rent payable		0
210	Wages payable		0
301	J. Bonair, Capital		86,900
302	J. Bonair, Withdrawals	12,000	
401	Demolition fees earned		187,000
612	Depreciation expense—Equipment	0	
623	Wages expense	44,700	
637	Insurance expense	0	
640	Rent expense	13,200	
652	Supplies expense	0	
684	Repairs expense	14,400	
690	Utilities expense	4,800	
	Totals	$ 324,700	$ 324,700

Sheet1 Sheet2 Sheet3

Required

1. Using Exhibit 6.1 as a guide, prepare a 10-column work sheet for fiscal year 2010, starting with the unadjusted trial balance and including adjustments based on these additional facts.

   a. The supplies available at the end of fiscal year 2010 had a cost of $7,900.

   b. The cost of expired insurance for the fiscal year is $10,600.

   c. Annual depreciation on equipment is $7,000.

   d. The April utilities expense of $800 is not included in the unadjusted trial balance because the bill arrived after the trial balance was prepared. The $800 amount owed needs to be recorded.

   e. The company's employees have earned $2,000 of accrued wages at fiscal year-end.

   f. The rent expense incurred and not yet paid or recorded at fiscal year-end is $3,000.

2. Enter the adjusting entry information in the work sheet; then journalize adjusting entries.

3. Prepare an adjusted trial balance.

4. Extend the adjusted trial balance amounts to the proper financial statement column of the work sheet.

5. Prepare closing entries.

6. Prepare the income statement and the statement of owner's equity for the year ended April 30, and the balance sheet at April 30, 2010.

Check (3) Total assets, $195,900; Total liabilities, $42,600; Net income, $78,400

---

connect

PRACTICE SET 1

Adventure Travel

Applying the accounting cycle

LO3 LO4 LO5

eXcel

mhhe.com/wildCA2e

QB

On April 1, 2010, Jiro Nozomi created a new travel agency, Adventure Travel. The following transactions occurred during the company's first month.

April	1	Nozomi invested $30,000 cash and computer equipment worth $20,000 in the business.
	2	Rented furnished office space by paying $1,800 cash for the first month's (April) rent. (Hint: Adventure Travel debited Rent Expense for this payment.)
	3	Purchased $1,000 of office supplies for cash.
	10	Paid $2,400 cash for the premium on a 12-month insurance policy. Coverage begins on April 11.
	14	Paid $1,600 cash for two weeks' salaries earned by employees.
	24	Collected $8,000 cash on commissions from airlines on tickets obtained for customers.
	26	Paid another $1,600 cash for two weeks' salaries earned by employees.

27   Paid $350 cash for minor repairs to the company's computer.
27   Paid $750 cash for this month's telephone bill.
28   Nozomi withdrew $1,500 cash for personal use.

The company's chart of accounts follows:

101	Cash	405	Commissions Earned
106	Accounts Receivable	612	Depreciation Expense—Computer Equip.
124	Office Supplies	622	Salaries Expense
128	Prepaid Insurance	637	Insurance Expense
167	Computer Equipment	640	Rent Expense
168	Accumulated Depreciation—Computer Equip.	650	Office Supplies Expense
209	Salaries Payable	684	Repairs Expense
301	J. Nozomi, Capital	688	Telephone Expense
302	J. Nozomi, Withdrawals	901	Income Summary

Required

1. Use the balance column format to set up each ledger account listed in the chart of accounts.

2. Prepare journal entries to record the transactions for April and post them to the ledger accounts.

3. Prepare an unadjusted trial balance as of April 30.

4. Use the following information to journalize and post adjusting entries for the month:

  a. Two-thirds of one month's insurance coverage has expired. (Round your answer to the nearest dollar).

  b. At the end of the month, $600 of office supplies are still available.

  c. This month's depreciation on the computer equipment is $500.

  d. Employees earned $420 of unpaid and unrecorded salaries as of month-end.

5. Prepare the income statement and the statement of owner's equity for the month of April and the balance sheet at April 30, 2010.

6. Prepare journal entries to close the temporary accounts and post these entries to the ledger.

7. Prepare a post-closing trial balance.

Check   (3) Unadj. trial balance totals, $58,000

(4*a*) Dr. Insurance Expense, $133

(5) Net income, $447; J. Nozomi, Capital (4/30/2010), $48,947; Total assets, $49,367

(7) P-C trial balance totals, $49,867

On July 1, 2010, Lula Plume created a new self-storage business, Safe Storage Co. The following transactions occurred during the company's first month.

July 1   Plume invested $30,000 cash and buildings worth $150,000 in the business.
  2   Rented equipment by paying $2,000 cash for the first month's (July) rent. (Hint: Safe Storage debited Rent Expense for this payment.)
  5   Purchased $2,400 of office supplies for cash.
  10 Paid $7,200 cash for the premium on a 12-month insurance policy. Coverage begins on July 11.
  14 Paid an employee $1,000 cash for two weeks' salary earned.
  24 Collected $9,800 cash for storage fees from customers.
  26 Paid another $1,000 cash for two weeks' salary earned by an employee.
  27 Paid $950 cash for minor repairs to a leaking roof.
  27 Paid $400 cash for this month's telephone bill.
  28 Plume withdrew $2,000 cash for personal use.

PRACTICE SET 2

Safe Storage Co.
Applying the accounting cycle
LO3   LO4   LO5

The company's chart of accounts follows:

101	Cash	401	Storage Fees Earned
106	Accounts Receivable	606	Depreciation Expense—Buildings
124	Office Supplies	622	Salaries Expense
128	Prepaid Insurance	637	Insurance Expense
173	Buildings	640	Rent Expense
174	Accumulated Depreciation—Buildings	650	Office Supplies Expense
209	Salaries Payable	684	Repairs Expense
301	L. Plume, Capital	688	Telephone Expense
302	L. Plume, Withdrawals	901	Income Summary

Required

1. Use the balance column format to set up each ledger account listed in the chart of accounts.
2. Prepare journal entries to record the transactions for July and post them to the ledger accounts.
3. Prepare an unadjusted trial balance as of July 31.
4. Use the following information to journalize and post adjusting entries for the month:
   a. Two-thirds of one month's insurance coverage has expired. (Round your answer to the nearest dollar).
   b. At the end of the month, $1,525 of office supplies are still available.
   c. This month's depreciation on the buildings is $1,500.
   d. An employee earned $100 of unpaid and unrecorded salary as of month-end.
5. Prepare the income statement and the statement of owner's equity for the month of July and the balance sheet at July 31, 2010.
6. Prepare journal entries to close the temporary accounts and post these entries to the ledger.
7. Prepare a post-closing trial balance.

Check   (3) Unadj. trial balance totals, $189,800

(4a) Dr. Insurance Expense, $400

(5) Net income, $1,575; L. Plume, Capital (7/31/2010), $179,575; Total assets, $179,675

(7) P-C trial balance totals, $181,175

SERIAL PROBLEM

Success Systems

LO3   LO4

(This serial problem began in Chapter 1 and continues through most of the book. If previous chapter segments were not completed, the serial problem can begin at this point. It is helpful, but not necessary, that you use the Working Papers that accompany the book.)

SP 6   The December 31, 2010, adjusted trial balance of Success Systems (reflecting its transactions from October through December of 2010) follows.

No.	Account Title	Debit	Credit
101	Cash	$ 80,260	
106	Accounts receivable	5,800	
126	Computer supplies	775	
128	Prepaid insurance	1,800	
131	Prepaid rent	875	
163	Office equipment	10,000	
164	Accumulated depreciation—Office equipment		$ 625
167	Computer equipment	25,000	
168	Accumulated depreciation—Computer equipment		1,250
201	Accounts payable		2,100
210	Wages payable		600
236	Unearned computer services revenue		2,500
301	A. Lopez, Capital		110,000
302	A. Lopez, Withdrawals	8,500	
403	Computer services revenue		36,170
612	Depreciation expense—Office equipment	625	
613	Depreciation expense—Computer equipment	1,250	
623	Wages expense	4,650	
637	Insurance expense	600	
640	Rent expense	2,625	
652	Computer supplies expense	4,675	
655	Advertising expense	2,990	
676	Mileage expense	1,120	
677	Miscellaneous expenses	300	
684	Repairs expense—Computer	1,400	
901	Income summary		0
	Totals	$153,245	$153,245

Required

1. Record and post the necessary closing entries for Success Systems.
2. Prepare a post-closing trial balance as of December 31, 2010.

Check Post-closing trial balance totals, $124,510

BEYOND THE NUMBERS

BTN 6-1   Refer to **Best Buy**'s financial statements in Appendix A to answer the following.

Required

1. For the fiscal year ended March 1, 2008, what amount is credited to Income Summary to summarize its revenues earned?
2. For the fiscal year ended March 1, 2008, what is the balance of its Income Summary account before it is closed?

REPORTING IN ACTION
L02 L03

BTN 6-2   On January 20, 2011, Tamira Nelson, the accountant for Picton Enterprises, is feeling pressure to complete the annual financial statements. The company president has said he needs up-to-date financial statements to share with the bank on January 21 at a dinner meeting that has been called to discuss Picton's obtaining loan financing for a special building project. Tamira knows that she will not be able to gather all the needed information in the next 24 hours to prepare the entire set of adjusting entries that must be posted before the financial statements accurately portray the company's performance and financial position for the fiscal period ended December 31, 2010. Tamira ultimately decides to estimate several expense accruals at the last minute. When deciding on estimates for the expenses, she uses low estimates because she does not want to make the financial statements look worse than they are. Tamira finishes the financial statements before the deadline and gives them to the president without mentioning that several account balances are estimates that she provided.

ETHICS CHALLENGE
L05

Required

1. Identify several courses of action that Tamira could have taken instead of the one she took.
2. If you were in Tamira's situation, what would you have done? Briefly justify your response.

BTN 6-3   Assume that one of your classmates states that a company's books should be ongoing and therefore not closed until that business is terminated. Write a one-half-page memo to this classmate explaining the concept of the closing process by drawing analogies between (1) a scoreboard for an athletic event and the revenue and expense accounts of a business or (2) a sports team's record book and the capital account. (*Hint:* Think about what would happen if the scoreboard is not cleared before the start of a new game.)

WORKPLACE COMMUNICATION
L02 L03

BTN 6-4   Go to the American institute of Professional Bookkeepers Website, located at <u>www.aipb.org</u>. Click on "certification" and then on "Certified Bookkeeper Survey." Using information from this survey, answer the following questions:

TAKING IT TO THE NET

1. What are the requirements for a bookkeeper to become a Certified Bookkeeper?
2. What are the six primary topics covered on the Certified Bookkeeper examination?
3. What percentage of Certified Bookkeepers recommend certification to other bookkeepers?

TEAMWORK IN
ACTION
L01   L03   L04

BTN 6-5   The unadjusted trial balance and information for the accounting adjustments of Noseworthy Investigators follow. Form teams of four members each. Then, within each four-person team, form two-person groups. Each group involved in this project is to assume two of the four responsibilities listed. After completing each of these responsibilities, the team should work together to prove the accounting equation.

Unadjusted Trial Balance		
Account Title	**Debit**	**Credit**
Cash	$16,000	
Supplies	12,000	
Prepaid insurance	3,000	
Equipment	25,000	
Accumulated depreciation—Equipment		$ 7,000
Accounts payable		3,000
D. Noseworthy, Capital		34,000
D. Noseworthy, Withdrawals	6,000	
Investigation fees earned		33,000
Rent expense	15,000	
Totals	$77,000	$77,000

Additional Year-End Information

a. Insurance that expired in the current period amounts to $2,200.
b. Equipment depreciation for the period is $4,000.
c. Unused supplies total $5,000 at period-end.

Responsibilities

Two team members work together to complete the following tasks:

1. Determine the necessary adjusting journal entries.
2. Use this adjusting information to determine the adjusted balances to extend to the balance sheet columns of a work sheet for Noseworthy. Also determine total assets and total liabilities.

Two other team members work together to complete the following tasks:

3. Using the adjusting information obtained from the other two team members, determine the adjusted balances of Noseworthy's revenue and expense accounts.
4. Prepare closing journal entries. Provide the other team members with the ending capital account balance.

The entire team should then prove the accounting equation using post-closing balances. If the equation does not balance, work as a team to resolve the error. The team's goal is to complete the task as quickly and accurately as possible.

ENTREPRENEURS
IN BUSINESS
L02   L03   L05

BTN 6-6   Review the chapter's opening feature on Kathryn Kerrigan and her shoe business.

1. Why is it important for Kathryn Kerrigan to match costs and revenues in a specific time period? How do closing entries help in this regard?
2. What objectives are met when Kathryn Kerrigan applies closing procedures at the end of each accounting period?

BTN 6-7   You make a printout of the electronic work sheet used to prepare financial statements. There is no depreciation adjustment, yet you own a large amount of equipment. Does the absence of depreciation adjustment concern you?

YOU CALL IT

1. e

2. c

3. e

4. a

5. c

ANSWERS TO MULTIPLE CHOICE QUIZ

A Look Back

Chapter 6 explained the final steps in the accounting cycle. We described the closing process and showed how a work sheet aids in preparing financial statements.

A Look at This Chapter

This chapter extends our study of accounting to fraud and internal control. We explain workplace fraud and describe internal control procedures that can help prevent it.

A Look Ahead

Chapter 8 focuses on cash and control of cash. We discuss control features of banking activities and petty cash systems.

Chapter 7

Fraud, Ethics, and Controls

Learning Objectives

LO 1   Define workplace fraud and explain the four elements common to all fraud schemes.

LO 2   Describe the three major types of workplace fraud.

LO 3   Define internal control and identify its purpose and principles.

LO 4   Explain how technology impacts an internal control system.

LO 5   Describe the limitations of internal control.

LO 6   Explain provisions of the Sarbanes-Oxley Act that are designed to detect and curtail fraud.

LO 7   *Appendix 7A*—Describe the use of documentation and verification to control cash disbursements.

"It's a creative outlet for me . . . it doesn't feel like work"—Dylan Lauren (Jeff Rubin on left)

Sweet Success

NEW YORK—A 10-foot chocolate bunny named Jeffrey greets you as you enter the store—that should be warning enough! This elite designer candy store, christened **Dylan's Candy Bar (DylansCandyBar.com),** is the brainchild of co-founders Dylan Lauren and Jeff Rubin (the bunny is named for him). This sweet-lovers heaven offers more than 5,000 different choices of sweets from all over the world. It has become a hip hangout for locals and tourists—and it has made candy cool. Says Lauren, "Park Avenue women come in, and the first thing they ask for is Gummi bears. They love that it's very childhood, nostalgic."

Although marketing is an important part of its success, Lauren and Rubin's management of internal controls and cash is equally impressive. Several control procedures monitor its business activities and safeguard its assets. An example is the biometric time and attendance control system using fingerprint characteristics. Says Rubin, "There's no fooling the system! It is going to help us remotely manage our employees while eliminating human error and dishonesty. [It] is a cost-effective and important business management tool." Similar controls are applied throughout the store. Rubin asserts that such controls raise productivity and cut expenses.

The store's cash management practices are equally impressive, including controls over cash receipts and payments. Internal controls are crucial when on a busy day its store brings in more than a thousand customers, and their cash. Moreover, expansion is already underway in Orlando and Houston. Through it all, Lauren says it is "totally fun."

[Sources: *Dylan's Candy Bar Website,* January 2009; *Entrepreneur,* June 2005; *USA Today,* October 26, 2001; *Duke Magazine,* January–February 2004; *CNN.com,* November 2005; *CandyAddict.com,* June 2007]

We all are aware of reports and experiences of theft and fraud. These affect us in several ways: We lock doors, chain bikes, review sales receipts, and buy alarm systems. A company also takes actions to safeguard, control, and manage what it owns. Experience tells us that small companies are most vulnerable, usually due to weak internal controls. This chapter discusses workplace fraud. Management must set up policies and procedures to safeguard a company's assets. To do so, management *and* employees must understand and apply principles of internal control. This chapter describes these principles and how to apply them.

Fraud, Ethics, and Controls

Workplace Fraud
- Characteristics of fraud
- Types of fraud
- Detecting fraud

Internal Control
- Purpose of controls
- Principles of controls
- Technology and controls
- Limitations of controls
- Voucher system

Sarbanes-Oxley
- Requirements
- Fraud detection

Workplace Fraud

LO1 Define workplace fraud and explain the four elements common to all fraud schemes.

Workplace fraud involves the use of one's job for personal gain, through the deliberate misuse of the employer's assets. Such fraud includes, for example, theft of the employer's cash or other assets, overstating reimbursable expenses, payroll schemes, and financial statement frauds. Workplace fraud affects all business and it is costly: A 2008 *Report to the Nation* from the Association of Certified Fraud Examiners estimates the average U.S. business loses 7% of its annual revenues to fraud. Fraud is particularly costly for small businesses because it can lead to the business's demise. The Association of Certified Fraud Examiners (acfe.com) estimates that employee fraud costs small companies more than $100,000 per incident.

Elements of Workplace Fraud Schemes

While there are many types of fraud schemes, all workplace fraud

- Is secret.
- Violates the employee's duties to his employer.
- Is done to provide direct or indirect benefit to the employee.
- Costs the employer money.

For example, in a billing fraud, an employee sets up a bogus supplier. The employee then secretly prepares bills from the supplier and pays these bills from the employer's checking account. The employee cashes the checks sent to the bogus supplier and uses them for his or her own personal benefit. Later in this chapter we discuss how a system of internal control can help the employer prevent this and other types of fraud schemes.

Major Types of Workplace Fraud

LO2 Describe the three major types of workplace fraud.

According to the Association of Certified Fraud Examiners' *2008 Report to the Nation*, most workplace frauds fall into three broad types:

1. **Asset misappropriation.** This type involves the theft or misuse of the employer's resources. For example, the employee might steal cash or inventory, disburse payroll checks to bogus employees, or pay invoices to phony suppliers. Other common schemes include accepting cash payments from customers but not recording sales, filing false expense reports, and claiming overtime for hours not worked.

2. **Corruption.** These schemes involve an employee's wrongful use of influence in a business transaction with the result that the employee receives financial gain at the expense of

the employer. Bribery is often part of corruption schemes; for example, an employee might bribe another party to take part in a fraudulent invoice scheme.

3. **Fraudulent financial statements.** Falsification of the employer's financial statements commonly includes recording fictitious revenues, overstating certain asset values, and hiding certain liabilities or expenses.

Exhibit 7.1 shows the percentage of reported frauds by type and their related losses. The percentages sum to more than 100 percent as a fraud occurrence might involve more than one type. Asset misappropriation is the most commonly reported fraud, but fraudulent financial statements cause the greatest losses in dollars.

Reported Frauds	Percentage of Reported Frauds	Loss per Occurrence
Asset misappropriation	88.7%	$ 150,000
Corruption	27.4%	$ 375,000
Fraudulent financial statements	10.3%	$2,000,000

Percentages in this chart sum to more than 100% as several cases involve more than one type of fraud.

Exhibit 7.1

Losses from Fraud

Detecting Fraud   Exhibit 7.2 provides information on the percentage of fraud cases detected by various methods. Tips, often received through anonymous hotlines, are the most common way frauds are detected. Most of these tips come from employees of the defrauded business, suggesting employee education might be useful in fighting fraud. Customers and suppliers are also good sources of tips. Many frauds are detected by internal controls and internal audits, which we discuss in detail in this chapter. About 9 percent of frauds are detected by external auditors, typically in the course of their testing the firm's internal controls and other processes. Still, many frauds are detected simply by accident.

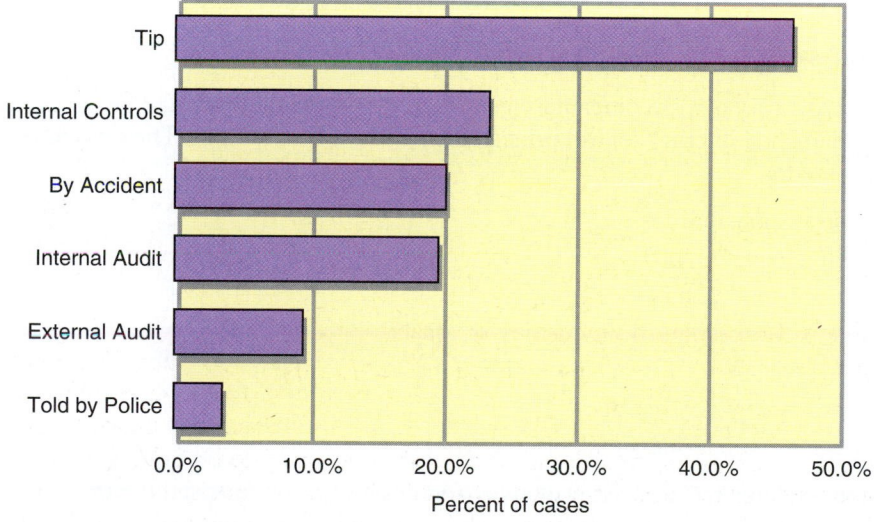

Exhibit 7.2

Methods of Fraud Detection

People committing fraud ("fraudsters") often leave behavioral clues. Knowledge of these clues can help employees identify suspicious behaviors that could indicate fraud. Common examples of red flags exhibited by fraudsters include:

- Employee paid an average salary buys fancy cars, clothes, boats, or homes.
- Employee is facing serious financial hardships, such as medical bills, loan or credit card payments.
- Employee won't share duties or take vacations—might indicate fear of fraud being uncovered.
- Employee is unusually irritable or defensive.
- Employee is too close with suppliers—might indicate they are a fraud "team."

Internal Control

This section describes internal control. We also discuss how technology impacts internal control and the limitations of control procedures.

Purpose of Internal Control

LO3 Define internal control and identify its purpose and principles.

Managers (or owners) of small businesses often control the entire operation. These managers usually purchase all assets, hire and manage employees, negotiate all contracts, and sign all checks. They know from personal contact and observation whether the business is actually receiving the assets and services paid for. Most companies, however, cannot maintain this close personal supervision. They must use formal procedures to control business activities.

Managers use an internal control system to monitor and control business activities. An **internal control system** is the policies and procedures managers use to:

- Protect assets.
- Ensure reliable accounting.
- Promote efficient operations.
- Urge adherence to company policies.

Managers like internal control systems because they can prevent avoidable losses, help managers plan operations, and monitor company and employee performance. Internal controls do not provide guarantees against loss, but they lower the company's risk of loss.

IN THE NEWS

What's the Password?   Good internal control prevents unauthorized access to assets and accounting records by requiring passwords. It takes a password, for instance, to boot up most office PCs, log onto a network, and access voice mail, e-mail, and most online services.

Principles of Internal Control

Internal controls vary across companies due to factors like the nature of the business and its size. Certain fundamental internal control principles apply to all companies. The **principles of internal control** are to

1. Establish responsibilities.
2. Maintain adequate records.
3. Insure assets and bond key employees.
4. Separate recordkeeping from custody of assets.
5. Divide responsibility for related transactions.
6. Apply technological controls.
7. Perform regular and independent reviews.

This section explains these seven principles and describes how internal control procedures reduce the risk of workplace fraud and theft. These procedures also increase the reliability and accuracy of accounting records.

Establish Responsibilities   Responsibility for a task should be clearly established and assigned to one person. When a problem occurs in a company where responsibility is not identified, determining who is at fault is difficult. For instance, if two salesclerks share the same cash register and there is a cash shortage, neither clerk can be held accountable. To prevent this problem, one clerk might be given responsibility for handling all cash sales. Alternately, a company can use a register with separate cash drawers for each clerk. Most of us have waited at a retail counter during a shift change while employees swap cash drawers. Many companies have a mandatory vacation policy for employees who handle cash. When another employee must cover for the one on vacation, it is more difficult to hide cash frauds.

Maintain Adequate Records Good recordkeeping helps protect assets and ensures that employees use prescribed procedures. Reliable records provide information that managers use to monitor company activities. When detailed records are kept, for instance, equipment is unlikely to be lost or stolen without detection. Similarly, transactions are less likely to be entered in wrong accounts if a chart of accounts is set up and carefully used. Preprinted forms and internal documents are also useful. When sales slips are properly designed, for instance, sales personnel can record needed information efficiently with less chance of errors or delays to customers. When sales slips are prenumbered and controlled, each one issued is the responsibility of one salesperson. This prevents the salesperson from pocketing cash by making a sale and destroying the sales slip. Computerized point-of-sale systems achieve the same control results.

Insure Assets and Bond Key Employees Assets should be adequately insured against loss. Employees handling large amounts of cash and easily transferable assets should be bonded. An employee is *bonded* when a company purchases an insurance policy, or a bond, against losses from theft by that employee. Bonding reduces the risk of loss and discourages theft. Bonded employees know an independent bonding company is unlikely to be sympathetic with an employee involved in theft.

Separate Recordkeeping from Custody of Assets A person who controls or has access to an asset must not keep that asset's accounting records. This reduces the risk of theft or waste of an asset because the person with control over it knows that another person keeps its records. Also, a recordkeeper who does not have access to the asset has no reason to falsify records. To steal an asset and hide the theft from the records, two or more people must *collude* (agree in secret to commit the fraud).

IN THE NEWS

Tag Control A novel technique exists for marking physical assets. It involves embedding a less than one-inch-square tag of fibers that creates a unique optical signature recordable by scanners. Manufacturers hope to embed tags in everything from compact discs and credit cards to designer clothes.

Divide Responsibility for Related Transactions Good internal control divides responsibility for a transaction or a series of related transactions between two or more individuals or departments. This ensures that the work of one individual acts as a check on the other. This *separation of duties* is not a call for duplication of work. Each employee or department should perform unduplicated work. Examples of transactions with divided responsibility are placing purchase orders, receiving merchandise, and paying **vendors** (sellers or suppliers). These tasks should not be given to one individual or department. Assigning responsibility for two or more of these tasks to one party increases mistakes and perhaps fraud. Having an independent person, for example, check incoming goods for quality and quantity encourages more care and attention to detail than having the person who placed the order do the checking. Added protection can result from having a third person approve payment of the invoice. A company can even designate a fourth person with authority to write checks as another protective measure.

Apply Technological Controls Cash registers, check protectors, time clocks, and personal identification scanners are examples of devices that can improve internal control. Technology often improves the effectiveness of controls. A cash register with a locked-in tape or electronic file makes a record of each cash sale. A check protector perforates the amount of a check into its face and makes it difficult to alter the amount. A time clock registers the exact time an employee both arrives at and leaves from the job. Personal scanners limit access to only authorized individuals. These and other technological controls are an effective part of many internal control systems.

IN THE NEWS

About Face Face-recognition software snaps a digital picture of a person's face and converts key facial features—say, the distance between the eyes—into a series of numerical values. These can be stored on an ID or ATM card as a simple bar code to prohibit unauthorized access.

Perform Regular and Independent Reviews   Personnel changes, time pressures, and technological advances present risks of errors or fraud. To counter these factors, regular reviews of internal control systems are needed to ensure that procedures are followed. These reviews are preferably done by internal auditors not directly involved in the activities. Many companies also pay for audits by independent, external auditors. Losses from fraud are lower in businesses with an internal audit department.

Technology and Internal Control

LO4   Explain how technology impacts an internal control system.

Technology impacts internal control systems in several important ways. Technology allows us quicker access to databases and information. Used effectively, this greatly improves managers' abilities to monitor and control business activities. This section also describes other technological impacts.

Information on Internet fraud can be found at these Websites:
• fraud.org
• sec.gov/investor/pubs/cyberfraud .htm
• ftc.gov/bcp/consumer/shtm

Reduced Processing Errors   Technology reduces errors in processing information. If the software and data entry are correct, the risk of mechanical and mathematical errors is nearly eliminated. However, less human involvement in data processing can cause data entry errors to go undiscovered. Also, errors in software can produce consistent but erroneous processing of transactions. Continually checking and monitoring all types of systems are important.

More Extensive Testing of Records   A company's review and audit of electronic records can include more extensive testing when information is easily and rapidly accessed. When accounting records are kept manually, auditors and others likely select only small samples of data to test. When data are accessible with computer technology, however, auditors can quickly analyze large samples or even the entire database.

IN THE NEWS

Identity Check   There's a new security device—a person's ECG (electrocardiogram) reading—that is as unique as a fingerprint and a lot harder to lose or steal than a PIN. ECGs can be read through fingertip touches. An ECG also shows that a living person is actually there, whereas fingerprint and facial recognition software can be fooled.

Limited Evidence of Processing   With computers, fewer hard-copy items of documentary evidence are available for review. Yet technologically advanced systems can provide new evidence. They can, for instance, record who made the entries, the date and time, the source of the entry, and so on. Technology can also be designed to require the use of passwords or other identification before access to the system is granted. This means that internal control depends more on the design and operation of the information system and less on the analysis of its resulting documents.

Crucial Separation of Duties   Technology often eliminates or consolidates some jobs. A company with a reduced workforce risks losing its crucial separation of duties. To minimize risk of error and fraud, the person who designs and programs the information system must not be the one who operates it. The company must also separate control over computer programs and files from the activities related to cash receipts and disbursements. For instance, a computer operator should not control check-writing activities. Separation of duties can be especially difficult and costly in small companies with few employees.

IN THE NEWS

Mystery Movie   The Association of Certified Fraud Examiners' Website reports: A movie theater manager stole $30,000. During slow times, when he thought he was not being observed, the manager would print a customer's ticket but keep it for himself and allow the customer to enter the movie without a ticket. During busy times, the manager would then resell the tickets he had withheld and pocket the cash. The manager was caught by an alert employee who happened to see what he was doing.

Increased E-Commerce   Technology has encouraged the growth of e-commerce. Amazon.com and eBay are examples of companies that successfully use e-commerce. Most companies have some e-commerce transactions. All such transactions involve at least three risks. (1) *Credit card number theft* is a risk of using, transmitting, and storing such data online. This increases the cost of e-commerce. (2) *Computer viruses* are harmful programs that attach themselves to innocent files for purposes of infecting other files and programs. (3) *Impersonation* online can result in charges of sales to bogus accounts, purchases of inappropriate materials, and the unknowing release of confidential information to hackers. Companies use both *firewalls* and *encryption* to combat some of these risks—firewalls are points of entry to a system that require passwords to continue, and encryption is a mathematical process to rearrange contents that cannot be read without the process code. Each year millions of Americans have their privacy compromised.

"Worst case of identity theft I've ever seen!"

Copyright 2004 by Randy Glasbergen. www.glasbergen.com

Limitations of Internal Control

All internal control policies and procedures have limitations which usually arise from either (1) the human element or (2) the cost-benefit principle.

Internal controls are applied by people. This human element creates several potential limitations that we can categorize as either (1) human error or (2) human fraud. *Human error* can occur from negligence, fatigue, misjudgment, or confusion. *Human fraud* involves intent by people to defeat internal controls, such as *management override*, for personal gain. Fraud also includes collusion to thwart the separation of duties. Dollar losses from fraud more than triple when two or more people collude. The human element highlights the importance of establishing an *internal control environment* to convey management's commitment to internal control policies and procedures.

The second major internal control is the *cost-benefit principle*. The costs of internal controls must not exceed their benefits. Analysis of costs and benefits must consider the impact on morale. Most companies, for instance, can legally read employees' e-mails, yet few do unless they have evidence of potential harm to the company. The same holds for drug testing, phone tapping, and hidden cameras. The bottom line is that managers must establish internal control policies and procedures with a net benefit to the company.

L05 Describe the limitations of internal control.

A Hacker's Guide to Cyberspace

A Hacker's Guide to Cyberspace

Pharming Viruses attached to e-mails and Websites load software onto your PC that monitors key strokes; when you sign on to financial Websites, it steals your passwords.

Phishing Hackers send e-mails to you posing as banks; you are asked for information using fake Websites where they reel in your passwords and personal data.

WI-Phishing Cybercrooks set up wireless networks hoping you use them to connect to the Web; your passwords and data are stolen as you use their network.

Bot-Networking Hackers send remote-control programs ("bots") to your PC that take control to send out spam and viruses; they then even rent your bot to other cybercrooks.

Typo-Squatting Hackers set up Websites with addresses similar to legit outfits; when you make a typo and hit their sites, they infect your PC with viruses or take them over as bots.

HOW YOU DOIN'?   Answers—p. 170

1. Principles of internal control suggest that (choose one): (*a*) Responsibility for a series of related transactions (such as placing orders, receiving and paying for merchandise) should be assigned to one employee; (*b*) Responsibility for individual tasks should be shared by more than one employee so that one serves as a check on the other; or (*c*) Employees who handle considerable cash and easily transferable assets should be bonded.

2. What are some impacts of computing technology on internal control?

Voucher System of Control

Most large thefts occur from payment of phony invoices. A **voucher system** is a set of procedures and approvals designed to control payments and the acceptance of obligations. A **voucher** is an internal document (or file). The voucher system of control establishes procedures for

- Verifying, approving, and recording obligations for eventual cash payment.
- Issuing checks for payment of verified, approved, and recorded obligations.

A reliable voucher system follows standard procedures for every transaction. This applies even when multiple purchases are made from the same supplier.

IN THE NEWS

Cyber Setup   The FTC is on the cutting edge of cybersleuthing. Opportunists in search of easy money are lured to **WeMarket4U.net/netops**. Take the bait and you get warned—and possibly targeted. The top 4 fraud complaints as compiled by the Internet Crime Complaint Center are shown to the right.

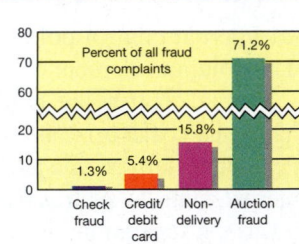

> Establish responsibilties

> Divide responsibility; separate recordkeeping from asset custody; bond key employees

> Maintain adequate records.

Voucher systems illustrate internal control principles. A voucher system often limits the type of obligations that a department or individual can incur. In a large retail store, for instance, only a purchasing department should be authorized to incur obligations for merchandise inventory. Another key factor is that procedures for purchasing, receiving, and paying for merchandise are divided among several departments (or individuals). These employees are often bonded to insure against loss from theft. These departments include the one requesting the purchase, the purchasing department, the receiving department, and the accounting department. To coordinate and control responsibilities of these departments, a company uses several different business documents. Exhibit 7.3 shows how documents are accumulated in a voucher. This specific example begins with a *purchase requisition* and concludes with a *check* drawn against cash. Appendix 7A describes each document entering and leaving a voucher system. It also describes the internal control objective served by each document.

A voucher system should be applied to all expenditures. To illustrate, when a company receives a monthly telephone bill, it should review and verify the charges, prepare a voucher (file), and insert the bill. This transaction is then recorded with a journal entry. If the amount is currently

Exhibit 7.3

Document Flow in a Voucher System

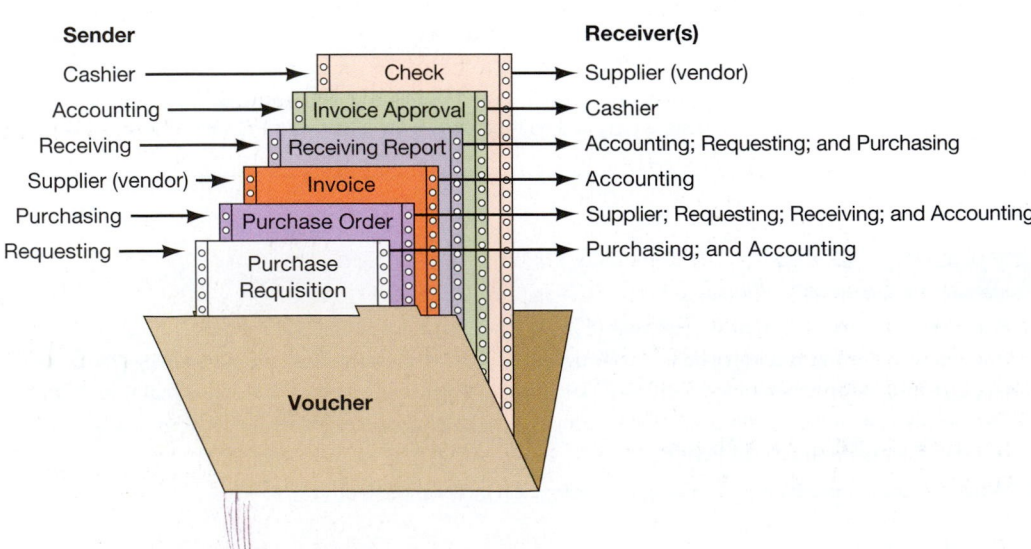

due, a check is issued. If not, the voucher is filed for payment on its due date. If no voucher is prepared, verifying the invoice and its amount after several days or weeks can be difficult. Also, without records, a dishonest employee could collude with a dishonest supplier to get more than one payment for an obligation, payment for excessive amounts, or payment for goods and services not received. An effective voucher system helps prevent such frauds.

IN THE NEWS

Phony Consulting   From the Association of Certified Fraud Examiners' Website: A purchasing agent for a large company set up a vendor file in his wife's maiden name, then approved more than $1 million in company payments to her. The supporting documentation consisted of the wife's invoices for "consulting services," but those services were never performed. A fellow employee, suspicious of the agent's recent purchase of a new boat and car, caught on to the scheme and turned him in.

The Sarbanes–Oxley Act

Congress passed the Sarbanes-Oxley Act in 2002. This act has several provisions designed to reduce financial fraud. Adherence to the act's provisions is required for U.S. public companies. However, privately held and small businesses can also benefit from many of the control features in the act. Next we discuss some of the act's provisions that might be useful as part of a system of internal control to reduce fraud.

LO6 Explain provisions of the Sarbanes-Oxley Act that are designed to detect and curtail fraud.

Requirements of the Sarbanes-Oxley Act

The act requires each annual report to include an *internal control* report, which must:

- State managers' responsibility for establishing and maintaining adequate internal controls for financial reporting.
- Assess the effectiveness of those controls.

In addition, the company's external auditor must test the company's internal control system with respect to financial reporting. This independent review provides an important external check on the company's financial statements.

Each company's chief executive officer (CEO) and chief financial officer (CFO) must certify that the financial statements fairly present the operations and financial condition of the company. This fixes responsibility for the company's financial reports with high-level executives who should have knowledge of the company's accounting.

The act also requires publicly traded companies to establish procedures for "the confidential, anonymous submission by employees of complaints regarding the company's accounting or internal controls."

Fraud Detection   Evidence in the Association of Certified Fraud Examiners 2008 *Report to the Nation* suggests anonymous tips are a company's best way to detect fraud. About 46% of all detected frauds were detected by tips, leading frauds detected by internal audit (about 19%), and frauds detected by accident (about 20%).

Evidence suggests that several of the Sarbanes-Oxley related controls are helpful in reducing fraud. Exhibit 7.4 compares average loss per fraud occurrence for public companies, based on whether they have anonymous fraud hotlines and whether management certifies the financial statements. Though not required, controls like these are also helpful in reducing fraud losses of private companies.

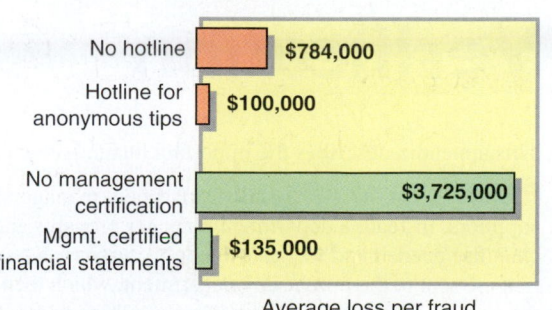

Exhibit 7.4

Sarbanes-Oxley Controls and Average Loss per Fraud

Answers—p. 170

HOW YOU DOIN'?

3. Should all companies require a voucher system? At what point in a company's growth would you recommend a voucher system?
4. What type of company must follow the provisions of the Sarbanes-Oxley Act?
5. What is a company's best way to detect fraud?

Demonstration Problem

Shaw Company applies the following practices for internal control purposes.

1. Each sales clerk uses his or her own cash drawer. The cash drawer can be opened only by swiping an employee identification card.
2. The company's cash registers keep a record of each transaction in an electronic file. The company's manager reviews these files daily.
3. The company's manager issues prenumbered sales slips to salespersons. Salespersons must submit their sales slips to the manager after making a sale. The manager verifies that all sales slips are accounted for each month.
4. The company buys goods for resale from a manufacturer. Each purchase must be approved by a manager. The company's receiving department employees check incoming goods for quantity and quality. The company purchases a bond on each of its receiving department employees. The manager cannot receive goods, and the receiving department employees cannot make purchase orders. Neither the manager nor any of the receiving department employees are allowed to make accounting journal entries.

Required

Identify which of the seven principles of internal control is being applied in each of the above scenarios. More than one principle of internal control might apply to a scenario.

Solution to Demonstration Problem

	Scenario Number			
	1	2	3	4
■ Establish responsibilities	x			
■ Maintain adequate records			x	
■ Insure assets and bond key employees				x
■ Separate recordkeeping from custody of assets				x
■ Divide responsibility for related transactions				x
■ Apply technological controls	x	x		
■ Perform regular and independent reviews		x	x	

APPENDIX 7A

Documentation and Verification

LO7 Describe the use of documentation and verification to control cash disbursements.

This appendix describes the important business documents of a voucher system of control.

Purchase Requisition   Department managers are usually not allowed to place orders directly with suppliers. Instead, a department manager prepares and signs a **purchase requisition,** which lists the merchandise needed and requests that it be purchased—see Exhibit 7A.1. Two copies of the purchase requisition are sent to the purchasing department, which then sends one copy to the accounting department. When the accounting department receives a purchase requisition, it creates and maintains a voucher for this transaction. The requesting department keeps a third copy.

```
 ○                     ┌─────────────────────┐                        ○
 ○                     │ Purchase Requisition│          No. 917       ○
 ○                     └─────────────────────┘                        ○
 ○                            Z-Mart                                  ○
 ○                                                                    ○
 ○   From ___ Sporting Goods Department ___   Date ___ October 28, 2010 ○
 ○   To ___ Purchasing Department ___   Preferred Vendor ___ Trex ___  ○
 ○                                                                    ○
 ○   Request purchase of the following item(s):                      ○
 ○   ┌──────────────┬──────────────────┬──────────────┐             ○
 ○   │ Model No.    │ Description       │ Quantity     │             ○
 ○   │ CH 015       │ Challenger X7     │ 1            │             ○
 ○   │ SD 099       │ SpeedDemon        │ 1            │             ○
 ○   └──────────────┴──────────────────┴──────────────┘             ○
 ○                                                                    ○
 ○   Reason for Request _____ Replenish inventory _____            ○
 ○   Approval for Request _____ T.Z. _____                         ○
 ○                                                                    ○
 ○                                                                    ○
 ○   For Purchasing Department use only: Order Date _10/30/10_  P.O. No. __P98__ ○
```

Exhibit 7A.1

Purchase Requisition

Purchase Order

A **purchase order** is a document the purchasing department uses to place an order with a vendor. A purchase order authorizes a vendor to ship ordered merchandise at the stated price and terms—see Exhibit 7A.2. When the purchasing department receives a purchase requisition, it prepares at least five copies of a purchase order. The copies are distributed as follows: *copy 1* to the vendor as a purchase request and as authority to ship merchandise; *copy 2*, along with a copy of the purchase requisition, to the accounting department, where it is entered in the voucher and used in approving payment of the invoice; *copy 3* to the requesting department to inform its manager that action is being taken; *copy 4* to the receiving department without order quantity so it can compare with goods received and provide independent count of goods received; and *copy 5* retained on file by the purchasing department.

> It is important to note that a voucher system is designed to uniquely meet the needs of a specific business. Thus, you should read this appendix as one example of a common voucher system design, but *not* the only design.

```
 ○                     ┌─────────────────┐                         ○
 ○                     │ Purchase Order  │          No. P98        ○
 ○                     └─────────────────┘                         ○
 ○                          Z-Mart                                 ○
 ○                    10 Michigan Street                           ○
 ○                   Chicago, Illinois 60521                       ○
 ○                                                                 ○
 ○   To:  Trex                      Date _____ 10/30/10 _____    ○
 ○        W9797 Cherry Road         FOB _____ Destination ___    ○
 ○        Antigo, Wisconsin 54409   Ship by _ As soon as possible _ ○
 ○                                  Terms _____ 2/15, n/30 ___   ○
 ○                                                                 ○
 ○   Request shipment of the following item(s):                    ○
 ○   ┌──────────┬────────────┬──────────┬────────┬─────────┐      ○
 ○   │ Model No.│ Description │ Quantity │ Price  │ Amount  │      ○
 ○   │ CH 015   │ Challenger X7│ 1       │ 490    │ 490     │      ○
 ○   │ SD 099   │ SpeedDemon  │ 1        │ 710    │ 710     │      ○
 ○   └──────────┴────────────┴──────────┴────────┴─────────┘      ○
 ○   All shipments and invoices must    Ordered by                ○
 ○   include purchase order number                                ○
 ○                                          J.W.                   ○
 ○                                                                 ○
```

Exhibit 7A.2

Purchase Order

Invoice

An **invoice** is an itemized statement of goods prepared by the vendor listing the customer's name, items sold, sales prices, and terms of sale. An invoice is also a bill sent to the buyer from the supplier. From the vendor's point of view, it is a *sales invoice*. The buyer, or **vendee**, treats it as a *purchase invoice*. When receiving a purchase order, the vendor ships the ordered merchandise to the buyer and includes or mails a copy of the invoice covering the shipment to the buyer. The invoice is sent to the buyer's accounting department where it is placed in the voucher.

Receiving Report

Many companies have a separate department to receive all merchandise and purchased assets. When each shipment arrives, this receiving department counts the goods and checks them for damage and agreement with the purchase order. It then prepares four or more copies of a **receiving report,** which is used within the company to notify the appropriate persons that ordered goods have been received and to describe the quantities and condition of the goods. One copy is sent to accounting and placed in the voucher. Copies are also sent to the requesting department and the purchasing department to notify them that the goods have arrived. The receiving department retains a copy in its files.

Invoice Approval When a receiving report arrives, the accounting department should have copies of the following documents in the voucher: purchase requisition, purchase order, and invoice. With the information in these documents, the accounting department can record the purchase and approve its payment. In approving an invoice for payment, it checks and compares information across all documents. To facilitate this checking and to ensure that no step is omitted, it often uses an **invoice approval,** also called *check authorization*—see Exhibit 7A.3. An invoice approval is a checklist of steps necessary for approving an invoice for recording and payment. It is a separate document either filed in the voucher or preprinted (or stamped) on the voucher.

Exhibit 7A.3

Invoice Approval

Invoice Approval			
Document		By	Date
Purchase requisition	917	72	10/28/10
Purchase order	P98	gw	10/30/10
Receiving report	R85	sk	11/3/10
Invoice:	4657		11/12/10
Price		9k	11/12/10
Calculations		9k	11/12/10
Terms		9k	11/12/10
Approved for payment		BC	

As each step in the checklist is approved, the person initials the invoice approval and records the current date. Final approval implies the following steps have occurred:

1. **Requisition check:** Items on invoice are requested per purchase requisition.
2. **Purchase order check:** Items on invoice are ordered per purchase order.
3. **Receiving report check:** Items on invoice are received, per receiving report.
4. **Invoice check: Price:** Invoice prices are as agreed with the vendor.
   Calculations: Invoice has no mathematical errors.
   Terms: Terms are as agreed with the vendor.

Voucher Once an invoice has been checked and approved, the voucher is complete. A complete voucher is a record summarizing a transaction. Once the voucher certifies a transaction, it authorizes recording an obligation. A voucher also contains approval for paying the obligation on an appropriate date. The physical form of a voucher varies across companies. Many are designed so that the invoice and other related source documents are placed inside the voucher, which can be a folder.

Completion of a voucher usually requires a person to enter certain information on both the inside and outside of the voucher. Typical information required on the inside of a voucher is shown in Exhibit 7A.4,

Exhibit 7A.4

Inside of a Voucher

		Z-Mart **Chicago, Illinois**	Voucher No. 5268
Date	Oct. 28, 2010		
Pay to	Trex		
City	Antigo	State	Wisconsin

For the following: (attach all invoices and supporting documents)

Date of Invoice	Terms	Invoice Number and Other Details	Terms
Nov. 2, 2010	2/15, n/30	Invoice No. 4657	1,200
		Less discount	24
		Net amount payable	1,176

Payment approved

N. O. Neal

Auditor

and that for the outside is shown in Exhibit 7A.5. This information is taken from the invoice and the supporting documents filed in the voucher. A complete voucher is sent to an authorized individual (often called an *auditor*). This person performs a final review, approves the accounts and amounts for debiting (called the *accounting distribution*), and authorizes recording of the voucher.

Exhibit 7A.5

Outside of a Voucher

Accounting Distribution

Account Debited	Amount
Purchases	1,200
Store Supplies	
Office Supplies	
Sales Salaries	
Other	
Total Vouch. Pay. Cr.	1,200

Voucher No. 5268

Due Date .... November 12, 2010
Pay to .... Trex
City .... Antigo
State .... Wisconsin

Summary of charges:
    Total charges 1,200
    Discount 24
    Net payment 1,176

Record of payment:
    Paid ....
    Check No. ....

After a voucher is approved and recorded (in a journal called a **voucher register**), it is filed by its due date. A check is then sent on the payment date from the cashier, the voucher is marked "paid," and the voucher is sent to the accounting department and recorded (in a journal called the **check register**). The person issuing checks relies on the approved voucher and its signed supporting documents as proof that an obligation has been incurred and must be paid. The purchase requisition and purchase order confirm the purchase was authorized. The receiving report shows that items have been received, and the invoice approval form verifies that the invoice has been checked for errors. There is little chance for error and even less chance for fraud without collusion unless all the documents and signatures are forged.

Summary

LO1 Define workplace fraud and explain the four elements common to all fraud schemes. Workplace fraud involves the use of one's job for personal gain, through deliberate misuse of the employer's assets. All workplace fraud is secret, violates the employee's job duties, provides financial benefit to the employee, and costs the employer money.

LO2 Describe the three major types of workplace fraud. Asset misappropriation, corruption, and fraudulent financial statements are the three major types of workplace fraud.

LO3 Define internal control and identify its purpose and principles. An internal control system consists of the policies and procedures managers use to protect assets, ensure reliable accounting, promote efficient operations, and urge adherence to company policies. It can prevent avoidable losses and help managers both plan operations and monitor company and human performance. Principles of good internal control include establishing responsibilities, maintaining adequate records, insuring assets and bonding employees, separating recordkeeping from custody of assets, dividing responsibilities for related transactions, applying technological controls, and performing regular independent reviews.

LO4 Explain how technology impacts an internal control system. Technology improves managers' abilities to monitor and control business activities. It also allows for more extensive testing of records. However, technological systems often produce less hard-copy evidence to review. Technology often eliminates jobs, making separation of duties more difficult, particularly in small companies.

LO5 Describe the limitations of internal control. Internal control systems are limited by the human element and the cost-benefit principle. Human error and/or human fraud, particularly collusion, limit the effectiveness of internal control systems. The cost-benefit principle states that the costs of internal controls must not exceed their benefits. In considering costs the employer must consider the effects of certain controls on employee morale.

LO6 Explain provisions of the Sarbanes-Oxley Act that are designed to detect and curtail fraud. The Sarbanes-Oxley Act requires each annual report to include an internal control report that states managers' responsibility for maintaining adequate internal controls for financial reporting. The company must also assess the effectiveness of its internal controls.

LO7^A Describe the use of documentation and verification to control cash disbursements. A voucher system is a set of procedures and approvals designed to control cash disbursements and acceptance of obligations. The voucher system of control relies on several important documents, including the voucher and its supporting files. A key factor in this system is that only approved departments and individuals are authorized to incur certain obligations.

Guidance Answers to HOW YOU DOIN'?

1. (*c*)

2. Technology reduces processing errors. It also allows more extensive testing of records, limits the amount of hard evidence, and highlights the importance of separation of duties.

3. Not all companies need a voucher system. A voucher system is used when an owner/manager can no longer control purchasing procedures through personal supervision and direct participation.

4. U.S. public companies.

5. Anonymous tips.

Key Terms

Check register (p. 169) Another name for a cash disbursements journal when the journal has a column for check numbers.

Internal control system (p. 160) All policies and procedures used to protect assets, ensure reliable accounting, promote efficient operations, and urge adherence to company policies.

Invoice (p. 167) Itemized record of goods, prepared by the vendor that lists the customer's name, items sold, sales prices, and terms of sale.

Invoice approval (p. 168) Document containing a checklist of steps necessary for approving the recording and payment of an invoice; also called *check authorization.*

Principles of internal control (p. 160) Principles prescribing management to establish responsibility, maintain records, insure assets, separate recordkeeping from custody of assets, divide responsibility for related transactions, apply technological controls, and perform reviews.

Purchase order (p. 168) Document used by the purchasing department to place an order with a seller (vendor).

Purchase requisition (p. 166) Document listing merchandise needed by a department and requesting it be purchased.

Receiving report (p. 167) Form used to report that ordered goods are received and to describe the quantity and condition.

Vendee (p. 167) Buyer of goods or services.

Vendor (p. 161) Seller of goods or services.

Voucher (p. 164) Internal file used to store documents and information to control cash disbursements and to ensure that a transaction is properly authorized and recorded.

Voucher register (p. 169) Journal (referred to as *book of original entry*) in which all vouchers are recorded after they have been approved.

Voucher system (p. 164) Procedures and approvals designed to control cash disbursements and acceptance of obligations.

Workplace fraud (p. 158) The deliberate misuse of an employer's assets for an employee's personal gain.

Multiple Choice Quiz   Answers on p. 175   mhhe.com/wildCA2e

Additional Multiple Choice Quizzes are available at the book's Website.

1. When two clerks share the same cash register, it is a violation of which internal control principle?
  a. Establish responsibilities.
  b. Maintain adequate records.
  c. Insure assets.
  d. Bond key employees.
  e. Apply technological controls.

2. The impact of technology on internal controls includes
  a. Reduced processing errors.
  b. Elimination of the need for regular audits.
  c. Elimination of the need to bond employees.
  d. More efficient separation of duties.
  e. Elimination of fraud.

3. The most serious limitation of internal control is
  a. Computer error.
  b. Human fraud or human error.
  c. Cost-benefit principle.
  d. Cybercrime.
  e. Management fraud.

4. A set of procedures and approvals that is designed to control cash disbursements and the acceptance of obligations is referred to as a(n):
  a. Internal cash system.
  b. Petty cash system.
  c. Cash disbursement system.
  d. Voucher system.
  e. Cash control system.

5. The source by which the greatest percentage of workplace fraud schemes is detected is
  a. Tips from customers and vendors.
  b. Internal auditors.
  c. Accident.
  d. Tips from employees.
  e. Independent auditors.

Discussion Questions

1. List the four common elements of all workplace frauds.
2. List the three major types of workplace frauds.
3. List the seven broad principles of internal control.
4. Internal control procedures are important in every business, but at what stage in the development of a business do they become especially critical?
5. Why should responsibility for related transactions be divided among different departments or individuals?
6. Why should the person who keeps the records of an asset not be the person responsible for its custody?
7. When a store purchases merchandise, why are individual departments not allowed to directly deal with suppliers?
8. What are the limitations of internal controls?
9. What are the three main methods of detecting workplace fraud?

connect

An internal control system consists of all policies and procedures used to protect assets, ensure reliable accounting, promote efficient operations, and urge adherence to company policies.

1. What is the main objective of internal control procedures? How is that objective achieved?
2. Why should recordkeeping for assets be separated from custody over those assets?
3. Why should the responsibility for a transaction be divided between two or more individuals or departments?

QUICK STUDY

QS 7–1
Internal control objectives   **LO3**

A good system of internal control separates the recordkeeping from the control of assets.

1. Explain why this separation of duties can be effective.
2. Which limitation of internal control might limit 'separation of duties' from preventing fraud?
3. How can technology impact a company's ability to separate duties?

QS 7–2
Internal control
LO3   LO4   LO5

For each of the independent cases below, identify the principle of internal control that is violated, and recommend what should be done to remedy the violation.

1. In order to save money, Regal Company has decided to drop its property insurance on assets and to stop bonding the cashiers who handle less than $10,000 in cash each day.
2. Wang Company records each sale on prenumbered invoices. These invoices are left in an open drawer for any employee to access. No employee at Wang Company examines whether all the invoices are accounted for after employees take them from the open drawer.
3. Gerald McNichols, the owner of McNichols Company, prides himself on hiring only the most competent employees. McNichols believes that since these employees are highly competent and that he trusts them completely and wants to keep employee morale high, there is no need for anyone to review the employees' performance.

QS 7–3
Internal control procedures   **LO3**

Management uses a voucher system to help control and monitor cash disbursements. Identify at least four key documents that are part of a voucher system of control.

QS 7–4^A
Documents in a voucher system
LO7

Identify and explain provisions of the Sarbanes-Oxley Act that are designed to prevent fraud.

QS 7–5
Sarbanes-Oxley   **LO6**

EXERCISES

Exercise 7-1
Analyzing internal control
LO2   LO3

Franco Company is a rapidly growing start-up business. Its recordkeeper, who was hired one year ago, left town after the company's manager discovered that a large sum of money had disappeared over the past six months. An audit disclosed that the recordkeeper had written and signed several checks made payable to her fiancé and then recorded the checks as salaries expense. The fiancé, who cashed the checks but never worked for the company, left town with the recordkeeper. As a result, the company incurred an uninsured loss of $184,000. Evaluate Franco's internal control system and indicate which principles of internal control appear to have been ignored. Which type of workplace fraud has been committed?

Exercise 7-2
Principles of internal control
LO3

Match each of the following transactions 1 through 10 with the applicable internal control principle A through G (some answers refer to more than one principle).

A. Establish responsibility.

B. Maintain adequate records.

C. Insure assets and bond employees.

D. Separate recordkeeping from custody of assets.

E. Divide responsibility for related transactions.

F. Apply technological controls.

G. Perform regular and independent reviews.

_____   **1.** Cashier does not have access to the cash register recorded tape or file.

_____   **2.** A company uses a voucher system.

_____   **3.** No two clerks share the same cash drawer.

_____   **4.** The bookkeeper prepares and signs checks.

_____   **5.** A company uses a computerized point of sale system.

_____   **6.** A company hires CPAs to perform an audit.

_____   **7.** A company buys an insurance policy to protect against employee theft.

_____   **8.** A company has separate departments for purchasing, receiving, and accounts payable.

_____   **9.** A company has an internal auditor on staff.

_____   **10.** A company uses a check protector.

Exercise 7-3ᴬ
Voucher system   **LO7**

The voucher system of control is designed to control cash disbursements and the acceptance of obligations.

1. The voucher system of control establishes procedures for what two processes?

2. What types of expenditures should be overseen by a voucher system of control?

3. When is the voucher initially prepared? Explain.

Exercise 7-4ᴬ
Documents in a voucher system
LO7

Match each document in a voucher system in column one with its description in column two.

Document

1. Purchase requisition

2. Purchase order

3. Invoice

4. Receiving report

5. Invoice approval

6. Voucher

Description

A. An itemized statement of goods prepared by the vendor listing the customer's name, items sold, sales prices, and terms of sale.

B. An internal file used to store documents and information to control cash disbursements and to ensure that a transaction is properly authorized and recorded.

C. A document used to place an order with a vendor that authorizes the vendor to ship ordered merchandise at the stated price and terms.

D. A checklist of steps necessary for the approval of an invoice for recording and payment; also known as a check authorization.

E. A document used by department managers to inform the purchasing department to place an order with a vendor.

F. A document used to notify the appropriate persons that ordered goods have arrived, including a description of the quantities and condition of goods.

connect

For each of these five separate cases, identify the principle(s) of internal control that is violated. Recommend what the business should do to ensure adherence to principles of internal control.

1. Halton Company records each sale on a preprinted invoice. Since sometimes invoices are spoiled when they are prepared, the invoices are not prenumbered, but the sales clerk writes the next number onto each invoice.

2. Julia and Justine are cashiers at Tico Company. Justine often processes transactions from Julia's cash drawer when Julia is at lunch.

3. Nori Nozumi posts all patient charges and payments at the Hopeville Medical Clinic. Each night Nori backs up the computerized accounting system to a tape and stores the tape in a locked file at her desk.

4. Benedict Shales prides himself on hiring quality workers who require little supervision. As office manager, Benedict gives his employees full discretion over their tasks and for years has seen no reason to perform independent reviews of their work.

5. Cala Farah's manager has told her to reduce costs. Cala decides to raise the deductible on the plant's property insurance from $5,000 to $10,000. This cuts the property insurance premium in half. In a related move, she decides that bonding the plant's employees is a waste of money since the company has not experienced any losses due to employee theft. Cala saves the entire amount of the bonding insurance premium by dropping the bonding insurance.

PROBLEM SET A

Problem 7–1A
Analyzing internal control **LO3**

It is important that companies assess their risks of workplace fraud. Managers must also possess the skills to identify workplace fraud and the skills to establish internal controls to effectively reduce the risks of such fraud.

Required

For each of the following five separate cases, identify which of the three major types of workplace fraud is likely to occur. Recommend internal controls that are effective in reducing the likelihood of such fraud.

1. As part of his computer programming duties, Martin Gomez adds new employees to his company's payroll system. Martin also manages the payroll and signs payroll checks. Martin recently added several fictitious employees to the payroll.

2. Green Oaks Racquet Club uses a manual system to record which member uses its tennis courts. Members often pay for their court times with cash, which is deposited nightly. The manager of Green Oaks notices that several nightly deposits are at unexpectedly low amounts.

3. Haynes Company pays its accountant a bonus based on its financial performance. The accountant overstated the company's revenues in its most recent income statement.

4. An accounts payable clerk has been processing invoices with inflated prices from a certain supplier. In return, the clerk receives 20% of the invoice price as a kickback.

5. Custom Electronics is a major wholesaler of computers, stereos, and other expensive electronic equipment. The inventory is stored in a warehouse that is often left unlocked. Its inventory manager notices that a large number of iPods are missing.

Problem 7–2A
Workplace fraud and internal controls
LO2 LO3 LO6

For each of these five separate cases, identify the principle(s) of internal control that is violated. Recommend what the business should do to ensure adherence to principles of internal control.

1. Latisha Tally is the company's computer specialist and oversees its computerized payroll system. Her boss recently asked her to put password protection on all office computers. Latisha has put a password in place that allows only the boss access to the file where pay rates are changed and personnel are added or deleted from the payroll.

2. Marker Theater has a computerized order-taking system for its tickets. The system is active all week and backed up every Friday night.

3. Sutton Company has two employees handling acquisitions of inventory. One employee places purchase orders and pays vendors. The second employee receives the merchandise.

4. The owner of Super Pharmacy uses a check protector to perforate checks, making it difficult for anyone to alter the amount of the check. The check protector is on the owner's desk in an office that contains company checks and is normally unlocked.

PROBLEM SET B

Problem 7–1B
Analyzing internal control **LO3**

5. Lavina Company is a small business that has separated the duties of cash receipts and cash disbursements. The employee responsible for data base programming and data entry also writes checks to pay for purchases.

Problem 7–2B
Workplace fraud and internal controls
LO2   LO3   LO6

It is important that companies assess their risks of workplace fraud. Managers must also possess the skills to identify workplace fraud and the skills to establish internal controls to effectively reduce the risks of such fraud.

Required

For each of the following five separate cases, identify which of the three major types of workplace fraud is likely to occur. Recommend internal controls that are effective in reducing the likelihood that such fraud occurs.

1. As part of her computer programming duties, Brandi Marks adds new suppliers to her company's accounts payable system. Brandi also manages accounts payable and signs checks payable to suppliers. Brandi recently added several new suppliers to the accounts payable system.

2. Peña Company has its employees write down their hours worked in a manual ledger. One employee consistently claims more unscheduled overtime hours than any other employee.

3. Gibson Company pays its accountant a bonus based on its financial performance. The accountant understated the company's expenses in its most recent income statement.

4. An employee refuses to buy goods from a potential supplier unless that supplier hires the employee's wife.

5. Ace Electronics is a major wholesaler of electronic equipment. The company's inventory manager is responsible for ordering inventory and paying suppliers. Recently, warehouse employees reported several large shipments of cell phones missing.

BEYOND THE NUMBERS

REPORTING IN ACTION
LO2   LO5

BTN 7–1   Workplace fraud affects **Best Buy**. Refer to Best Buy's financial statements in Appendix A to answer the following:

1. Explain how inventory losses (such as theft) impact how Best Buy reports merchandise inventory on its balance sheet.

2. In which income statement account does Best Buy report inventory losses?

ETHICS CHALLENGE
LO2   LO3

BTN 7–2   The owner of a start-up information services company requires all employees to take at least one week of vacation per year. Why does the employer require this "forced vacation" policy?

WORKPLACE COMMUNICATION
LO6

BTN 7–3   Assume you are the owner of a small business. You are planning on borrowing money from a local bank. What are some features of the Sarbanes-Oxley Act that you could adopt to help persuade the banker that your financial statements are not fraudulent?

TAKING IT TO THE NET
LO1   LO2   LO3

BTN 7–4   Visit the Association of Certified Fraud Examiners Website at acfe.com. Research the fraud facts (refer to the 2008 *Report to the Nation,* see fraud resource center—under publications—*Report to the Nation*) presented at this site and fill in the blanks in the following statements.

1. It is estimated that ____% of U.S. organizations' revenues are lost as a result of occupational fraud and abuse. Applied to the U.S. gross domestic product, this translates to losses of approximately $____ billion.

2. Small businesses are the most vulnerable to occupational fraud and abuse. The average scheme in a small business causes $_____ in losses. The average scheme in the largest companies costs $_____.

3. The most common method for detecting occupational fraud is through tips from _____, customers, vendors, and anonymous sources. The second most common method of discovery is _____.

4. The typical occupational fraud perpetrator is a first-time offender. Only _____% of occupational fraudsters in this study were known to have prior convictions for fraud-related offenses.

5. All occupational frauds fall into one of three categories: _____, corruption, or _____ statements.

6. Over _____% of occupational frauds involve asset misappropriations. Cash is the targeted asset _____% of the time.

7. Corruption schemes account for _____% of all occupational frauds, and they cause over $_____ in losses, on average.

8. Fraudulent statements are the most costly form of occupational fraud with median losses of $_____ million per scheme.

9. Frauds committed by employees cause median losses of $_____, while frauds committed by owners cause median losses of $_____.

10. Losses caused by perpetrators older than 60 are _____ times higher than losses caused by employees 25 and younger.

BTN 7-5   Organize the class into teams. Each team must prepare a list of 10 internal controls a consumer could observe in a typical retail department store. When called upon, the team's spokesperson must be prepared to share controls identified by the team that have not been shared by another team's spokesperson.

TEAMWORK IN ACTION
L03   L04

BTN 7-6   Review the opening feature of this chapter that highlights Dylan Lauren and Jeff Rubin and their company **Dylan's Candy Bar**.

ENTREPRENEURS IN BUSINESS
L03   L05

Required

1. List the seven principles of internal control and explain how Dylan and Jeff could implement each of them in their candy store.

2. Do you believe that they will need to add additional controls as their business expands? Explain.

---

1. a	**4.** d
2. a	**5.** d
3. b	

ANSWERS TO MULTIPLE CHOICE QUIZ

A Look Back

Chapter 7 focused on fraud, ethics, and controls. We described control procedures that can reduce fraud.

A Look at This Chapter

This chapter focuses on cash and its control. We explain the control of and accounting for cash receipts and payments. These controls include banking activities, petty cash funds, and bank reconciliations.

A Look Ahead

Chapter 9 focuses on employee payroll. We show how the employer records employee payroll and deductions.

Chapter 8

Cash and Cash Controls

Learning Objectives

LO 1	Define cash and describe three guidelines for control of cash.
LO 2	Describe controls for cash receipts.
LO 3	Describe controls for cash disbursements.
LO 4	Explain and record petty cash fund transactions.
LO 5	Identify banking activities as controls of cash.
LO 6	Describe a bank statement.
LO 7	Prepare and explain a bank reconciliation.

"You must follow through on your promises and do the best work you can"
—Youngsong Martin

Dressing Up for Business

BUENA PARK, CA—Youngsong Martin found the plain, dreary look of most social and business events extremely disappointing. She recalls, "I was too familiar with the institutional look of those metal-rimmed chairs in banquet halls and ballrooms, drab folding chairs at many outdoor events, and the rather ordinary tablecloths and napkins." Martin reacted by launching **Wildflower Linen** (**WildflowerLinens.com**) to provide custom table linens, chair covers, and sashes to dress up banquets, meetings, weddings, and special events of all sorts.

"I derive more pleasure than I had imagined," explains Martin. "It has been a dream come true to 'dress' entire events." Martin also enjoys the service side and getting "to know customers on a more personal level."

But the business side is where Martin needed the most help. "You don't really realize what's involved with running a business until you actually do it," says Martin. "I definitely needed help with the management and financial aspects." In particular, Martin needed help with internal controls, including controls over cash receipts, disbursements, petty cash, and bank reconciliations. The online order system is linked with cash and the banking system that requires careful management.

"It's one thing to think you know where your money's going," stresses Martin. "But it's quite another to actually write expenses down and see how they affect your operations." Martin says she must "analyze expenses and determine if they are necessary to help keep my business growing. It's almost like I'm getting an MBA." With nearly 40 employees and growing revenue, Martin has dressed up her business with more than just linens.

[Sources: *Wildflower Linen Website*, May 2009; *SCORE.org Website*, June 2009]

Cash is a necessary asset of every business. Cash is the most liquid of all assets and can be easily hidden or moved. Experience tells us that small businesses are most vulnerable, usually due to weak controls over cash. It is important that the business owner have a system of control over cash. This chapter describes controls to safeguard cash.

Cash and Cash Controls

- **Control of Cash**
  - Cash and liquidity
  - Control of receipts
  - Control of disbursements

- **Banking Activities as Controls**
  - Basic bank services
  - Bank statement
  - Bank reconciliation

Control of Cash

Cash and Liquidity

LO1 Define cash and describe three guidelines for control of cash.

Good accounting systems help manage cash and control access to it. **Liquidity** refers to a company's ability to pay its near-term obligations. Cash and similar assets are called **liquid assets** because they can be readily used to settle such obligations. A company needs liquid assets to effectively operate.

Cash includes currency and coins along with the amounts on deposit in bank accounts. Cash also includes items that are acceptable for deposit in bank accounts, such as checks and money orders. Cash is a business's most liquid asset. A system of cash control should meet three basic guidelines:

1. Handling cash is separate from recordkeeping of cash.
2. Cash receipts are promptly deposited in a bank.
3. Cash payments are made by check.

The first guideline separates duties to reduce errors and the potential for fraud. With duties separated, two or more people must work together to steal cash and hide this action in the accounting records. The second and third guidelines produce a timely, independent bank record of cash receipts and payments and reduce the chance of cash theft or loss. Independent bank records of cash receipts and cash payments are useful in controlling cash, as we discuss in the next two sections.

Control of Cash Receipts

LO2 Describe controls for cash receipts.

Control of cash receipts ensures that cash received is properly recorded and deposited. Cash receipts arise from cash sales, collections of customer accounts, receipts of interest earned, bank loans, sales of assets, and owner investments. This section explains control over two important types of cash receipts: over-the-counter and by mail.

Over-the-Counter Cash Receipts
Over-the-counter cash sales should be recorded on a cash register at the time of each sale. To help ensure that correct amounts are entered, each register should be located so customers can read the amounts entered. Clerks also should enter each sale before wrapping merchandise and give the customer a receipt for each sale. Each cash register should provide a permanent, locked-in record of each sale (sometimes referred to as a *cash register tape*).

Access to cash should be separate from its recordkeeping. For over-the-counter cash receipts, this separation begins with the cash sale. The clerk who has access to cash in the register should not have access to its locked-in record in the register. At the end of the clerk's work period, the

IN THE NEWS

Perpetual Accounting   Wal-Mart uses a network of information links with its point-of-sale cash registers to coordinate sales, purchases, and distribution. Its supercenters, for instance, ring up to 15,000 separate sales on heavy days. By using cash register information, the company can fix pricing mistakes quickly and capitalize on sales trends.

clerk should count the cash in the register, record the amount, and turn over the cash and a record of its amount to the company cashier. The cashier, like the clerk, has access to the cash but should not have access to accounting records (or the cash register tape). A third employee, often a supervisor, compares the record of total register transactions (or the cash register tape) with the cash receipts reported by the cashier. This record is the basis for a journal entry recording over-the-counter cash receipts. The third employee has access to the records for cash but not to the actual cash. The clerk and the cashier have access to cash but not to the accounting records. None of them can make a mistake or divert cash without the difference being revealed—see the following diagram.

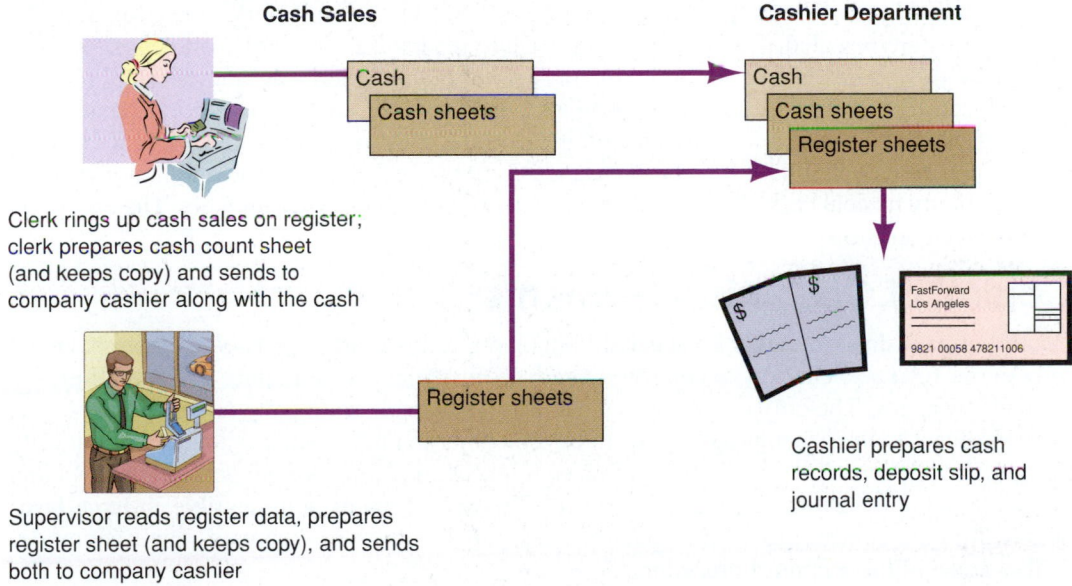

Cash Sales

Clerk rings up cash sales on register; clerk prepares cash count sheet (and keeps copy) and sends to company cashier along with the cash

Supervisor reads register data, prepares register sheet (and keeps copy), and sends both to company cashier

Cashier Department

Cashier prepares cash records, deposit slip, and journal entry

Cash over and short.   Although a clerk is careful, customers can be given the wrong change. This means that at the end of a work period, the cash in a cash register might not equal the record of cash receipts. This difference is reported in the **Cash Over and Short** account, which records the income statement effects of cash overages and cash shortages. A credit entry to Cash Over and Short increases income, while a debit to Cash Over and Short decreases income. To illustrate, if a cash register's record shows $550 but the count of cash in the register is $555, the entry to record cash sales and its overage is

				Assets = Liabilities + Equity
Cash	555			+555
Cash Over and Short		5		+ 5
Sales		550		+550
To record cash sales and a cash overage.				

Instead, if a cash register's record shows $625 but the count of cash in the register is $621, the entry to record cash sales and its shortage is:

Assets = Liabilities + Equity
+621   −   4
                   +625

Cash	621	
Cash Over and Short	**4**	
Sales		625
To record cash sales and a cash shortage.		

Since customers more often dispute being shortchanged than being given too much change, the Cash Over and Short account usually has a debit balance at the end of an accounting period. A debit balance reflects an expense.

Collusion implies that two or more individuals know of or are involved with the activities of the other(s).

Cash Receipts by Mail
Control of cash receipts that arrive by mail starts with opening the mail. Two people should be present for opening the mail. If so, theft of cash receipts by mail requires collusion between these two employees. The person(s) opening the mail enters a list (in triplicate) of money received. This list includes a record of each sender's name, the amount, and an explanation of why the money is sent. The first copy is sent with the money to the cashier. A second copy is sent to the recordkeeper. A third copy is kept by the clerks who opened the mail. The cashier deposits the money in a bank, and the recordkeeper records the amounts received in the accounting records.

This process reflects good cash control. When the bank balance is reconciled by another person (explained later in the chapter), errors or acts of fraud by the mail clerks, the cashier, or the recordkeeper are revealed. They are revealed because the bank's record of cash deposited must agree with the records from each of the three. Also, if the mail clerks do not report all receipts correctly, customers will question their account balances. If the cashier does not deposit all receipts, the bank balance does not agree with the recordkeeper's cash balance. The recordkeeper and the person who reconciles the bank balance do not have access to cash and therefore have no opportunity to steal cash. This system makes errors and fraud highly unlikely. The exception is employee collusion.

Control of Cash Disbursements

L03 Describe controls for cash disbursements.

Control of cash disbursements is especially important as most large thefts occur from payment of fictitious invoices. One key to controlling cash disbursements is to require all expenditures to be made by check. The only exception is small payments made from petty cash. Another key is to deny access to the accounting records to anyone other than the owner who has the authority to sign checks. A small business owner often signs checks and knows from personal contact that the items being paid for are actually received. This arrangement is impossible in large businesses. Instead, control procedures must be substituted for personal contact. This section describes some of these control procedures.

Petty Cash System of Control
A basic principle for controlling cash disbursements is that all payments must be made by check. An exception is made for **petty cash** disbursements, which are the small payments required for items such as postage, courier fees, minor repairs, and low-cost supplies. To avoid the time and cost of writing checks for small amounts, a company sets up a petty cash fund to make small payments. A petty cash fund is used only for business expenses.

Operating a petty cash fund. Establishing a petty cash fund requires estimating the total amount of small payments likely to be made during a short period such as a week or month. A check is then drawn by the company cashier for an amount slightly in excess of this estimate. This check is recorded with a debit to the Petty Cash account (an asset) and a credit to Cash. The check is cashed, and the cash is given to an employee designated as the *petty cashier*. The petty cashier keeps this cash safe, makes payments from the fund, and keeps records of it in a secure place called the *petty cashbox*.

L04 Explain and record petty cash fund transactions.

When each cash disbursement is made, the person receiving payment should sign a prenumbered *petty cash receipt*—see Exhibit 8.1. The petty cash receipt is then put in the petty cashbox with the remaining money. The sum of all receipts plus the remaining cash should always equal the total fund amount. A $100 petty cash fund, for instance, contains any combination of cash and petty cash receipts that totals $100 (examples are $80 cash plus $20 in receipts, or $10 cash plus $90 in receipts). Each disbursement reduces cash and increases the amount of receipts in the petty cashbox.

<table>
<tr><td colspan="4" align="center">**Petty Cash Receipt**   No. 9
Z-Mart</td></tr>
<tr><td>For</td><td>Freight charges</td><td>Date</td><td>11/5/10</td></tr>
<tr><td>Charge to</td><td>Transportation-In</td><td>Amount</td><td>$6.75</td></tr>
<tr><td>Approved by</td><td>Jim Gills</td><td>Received by</td><td>Dick Fitch</td></tr>
</table>

Exhibit 8.1

Petty Cash Receipt

Cash should be added to the petty cash fund when the fund nears zero and at the end of an accounting period when financial statements are prepared. The petty cashier sorts the paid receipts by the type of expense and then totals the receipts. The petty cashier gives all paid receipts to the company cashier, who stamps all receipts *paid* so they cannot be reused, files them for record-keeping, and gives the petty cashier a check for their total. When this check is cashed and the money placed in the petty cashbox, the total money in the petty cashbox equals its original amount. The fund is now ready for a new cycle of petty cash payments.

Illustrating a petty cash fund.   To illustrate, assume Z-Mart establishes a petty cash fund on November 1 and designates one of its office employees as the petty cashier. A $75 check is drawn, cashed, and the cash given to the petty cashier. The entry to record the setup of this petty cash fund is

Nov. 1	Petty Cash	75	
	Cash		75
	To establish a petty cash fund.		

Assets = Liabilities + Equity
+75
−75

After the petty cash fund is established, the *Petty Cash account is not debited or credited again unless the amount of the fund is changed. (Reducing the balance or eliminating a petty cash fund would require a credit to Petty Cash).*

Next, assume that Z-Mart's petty cashier makes several November payments from petty cash. Each person who received payment signs a receipt. On November 27, after making a $26.50 cash payment for tile cleaning, only $3.70 cash remains in the fund. The petty cashier summarizes and totals the petty cash receipts as shown in Exhibit 8.2. (This report can also include receipt number and names of those who approved and received cash payments.)

Z-MART **Petty Cash Payments Report**		
Miscellaneous Expenses		
Nov. 2 Washing windows	$20.00	
Nov. 27 Tile cleaning	26.50	$46.50
Transportation-In		
Nov. 5 Transport of merchandise purchased	6.75	
Nov. 20 Transport of merchandise purchased	8.30	15.05
Delivery Expense		
Nov. 18 Customer's package delivered		5.00
Office Supplies Expense		
Nov. 15 Purchase of office supplies immediately used		4.75
Total		**$71.30**

Exhibit 8.2

Petty Cash Payments Report

Transportation costs for inventory purchases are added to the Transportation-In account that becomes part of the merchandise inventory cost. The petty cash payments report and all receipts are given to the company cashier in exchange for a $71.30 check to reimburse the fund. The petty cashier cashes the check and puts the $71.30 cash in the petty cashbox. The recordkeeper makes this entry:

Assets = Liabilities + Equity			
−71.30	−46.50		
	−15.05		
	− 5.00		
	− 4.75		

Nov. 27	Miscellaneous Expenses..........................	46.50	
	Transportation-In...............................	15.05	
	Delivery Expense...............................	5.00	
	Office Supplies Expense.........................	4.75	
	Cash......................................		71.30
	To reimburse petty cash.		

Increasing or decreasing a petty cash fund. To illustrate, assume Z-Mart *increases* its petty cash fund from $75 to $100, after making the November 27 entry above. The entry to increase the fund is

Assets = Liabilities + Equity	
+25.00	
−25.00	

Nov. 27	Petty Cash	25	
	Cash......................................		25
	To increase the petty cash fund amount.		

Cash over and short. Sometimes a petty cashier fails to get a receipt for payment or over-pays for the amount due. When this occurs and the fund is later reimbursed, the petty cash payments report plus the cash remaining will not equal the fund balance. This mistake causes the fund to be *short*. This shortage is recorded as an expense in the reimbursing entry with a debit to the Cash Over and Short account. (An overage in the petty cash fund is recorded with a credit to Cash Over and Short in the reimbursing entry.) To illustrate, the entry to reimburse a $200 petty cash fund when its payments report shows $178 in miscellaneous expenses and $15 cash remains is:

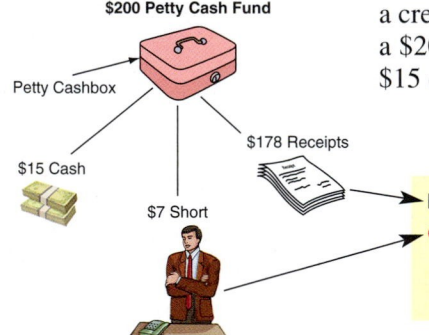

$200 Petty Cash Fund

Petty Cashbox

$15 Cash

$7 Short

$178 Receipts

	Miscellaneous Expenses	178	
	Cash Over and Short..	**7**	
	Cash		185
	To reimburse petty cash.		

Alternatively, if Z-Mart *decreases* the petty cash fund from $75 to $55 on November 27, the entry is to (1) credit Petty Cash for $20 (decreasing the fund from $75 to $55) and (2) debit Cash for $20 (reflecting the $20 transfer from Petty Cash to Cash).

In summary, to avoid errors in recording petty cash reimbursement, follow these steps:

Event	Petty Cash	Cash	Expenses
Set up fund	Dr.	Cr.	—
Reimburse fund ..	—	Cr.	Dr.
Increase fund	Dr.	Cr.	—
Decrease fund ...	Cr.	Dr.	—

1. Prepare petty cash payments report.
2. Compute cash needed by subtracting cash remaining from total fund amount.
3. Record journal entry.
4. Check to make sure "Dr. = Cr." in entry. Any difference is recorded in Cash Over and Short.

HOW YOU DOIN'? Answers—p. 192

1. Why are some cash payments made from a petty cash fund, and not by check?
2. Why should a petty cash fund be reimbursed at the end of an accounting period?
3. Identify at least two results of reimbursing a petty cash fund.

Banking Activities as Controls

Banks provide many services, including helping companies control cash. Banks safeguard cash and provide detailed and independent records of cash transactions. This section describes these services and the banking documents that help control cash.

Basic Bank Services

This section explains basic bank services—such as the bank account, the bank deposit, and checking—that help control cash.

LO5 Identify banking activities as controls of cash.

Bank Account, Deposit, and Check A *bank account* is a record set up by a bank for a customer. It permits a customer to deposit money for safekeeping and helps control withdrawals. To limit access to a bank account, all persons authorized to write checks on the account must sign a **signature card** (Exhibit 8.3), which bank employees use to verify signatures on checks. Many companies have more than one bank account to serve different needs and to handle special transactions such as payroll.

Exhibit 8.3

Signature Card

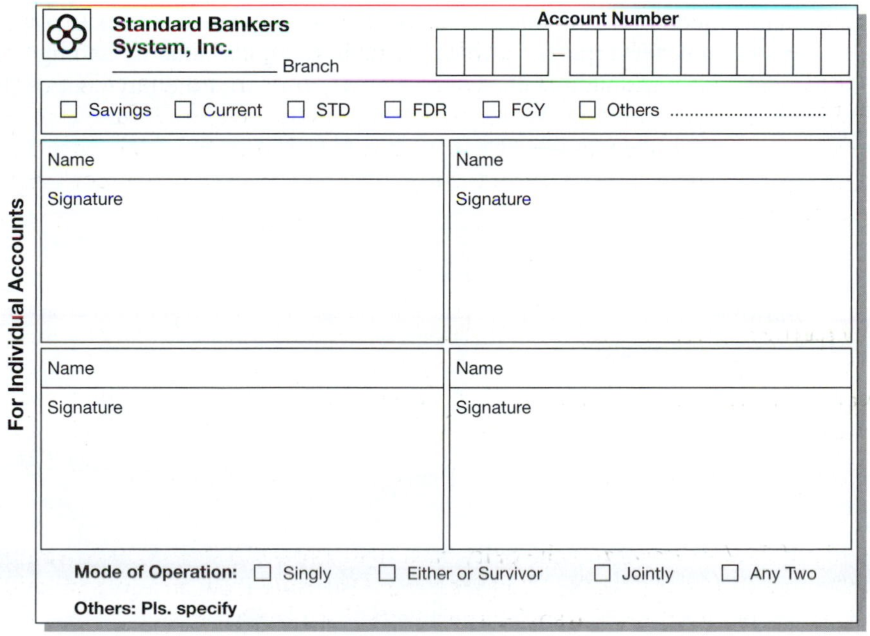

For Individual Accounts

Standard Bankers System, Inc.
_______ Branch
Account Number
☐ Savings ☐ Current ☐ STD ☐ FDR ☐ FCY ☐ Others ....

Name	Name
Signature	Signature
Name	Name
Signature	Signature

Mode of Operation: ☐ Singly ☐ Either or Survivor ☐ Jointly ☐ Any Two
Others: Pls. specify

Each bank deposit is supported by a **deposit ticket,** which lists items such as currency, coins, and checks deposited along with their dollar amounts. The bank gives the customer a copy of the deposit ticket or a deposit receipt as proof of the deposit. Exhibit 8.4 shows one type of deposit ticket.

Exhibit 8.4

Deposit Ticket

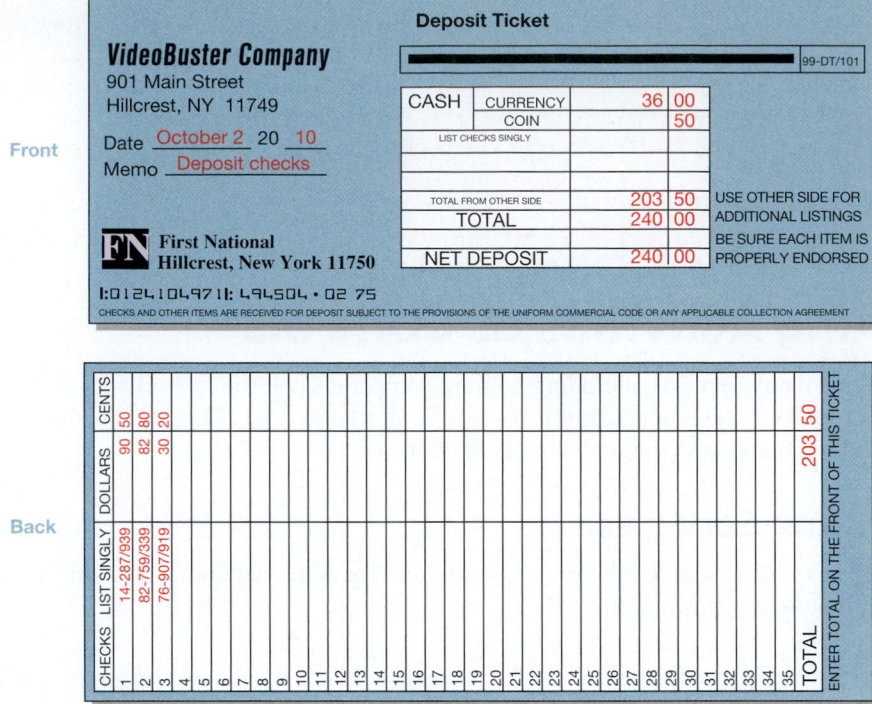

A check being deposited must be endorsed by the depositor. The **endorsement** is a written authorization transferring ownership of the check, generally to a bank. There are two basic types of endorsements:

1. **Blank endorsement**—the depositor signs the back of the check and the check is payable to the bearer of the check.
2. **Restrictive endorsement** (Exhibit 8.5)—the depositor transfers the check to a specific person, business, or bank for a specific purpose. This is generally done by adding words such as "For Deposit" or "Payable to James Myers only" to restrict the payment of the check.

Exhibit 8.5

Restrictive Endorsement

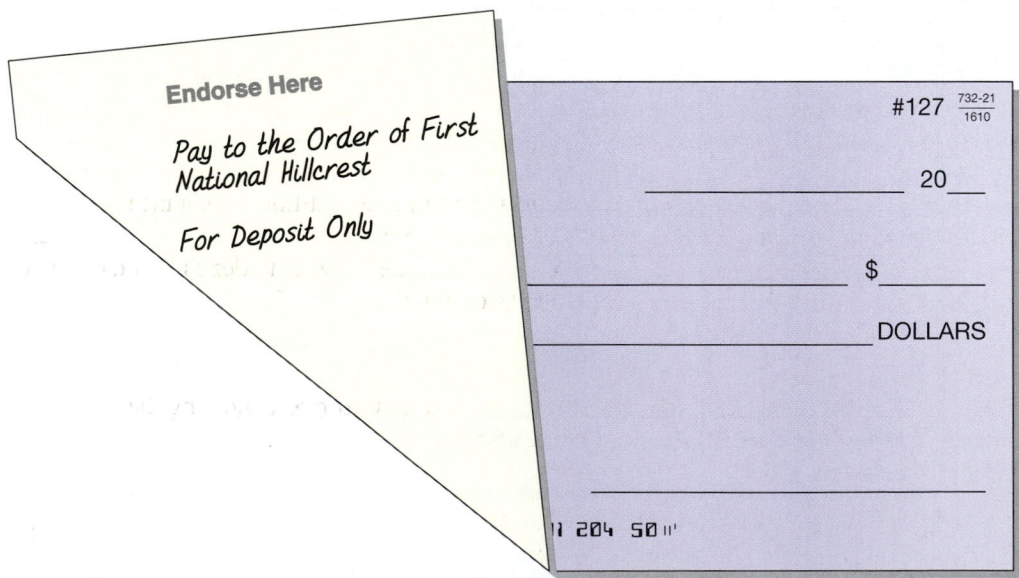

A **check** is used to withdraw money from a bank account. A check involves three parties: a *maker* who signs the check, a *payee* who receives the check, and a *bank* (or *payer*) on which the check is drawn. The bank provides a customer with checks that are numbered and imprinted

IN THE NEWS

Web-bank   Many companies balance checkbooks and pay bills online. Customers value the convenience of banking services anytime, anywhere. Services include the ability to stop payment on a check, move money between accounts, get up-to-date balances, and identify cleared checks and deposits.

with the name and address of both the customer and bank. Exhibit 8.6 shows one type of check, accompanied by an optional *remittance advice* explaining the payment. When a remittance advice is unavailable, the *memo* line is often used for a brief explanation.

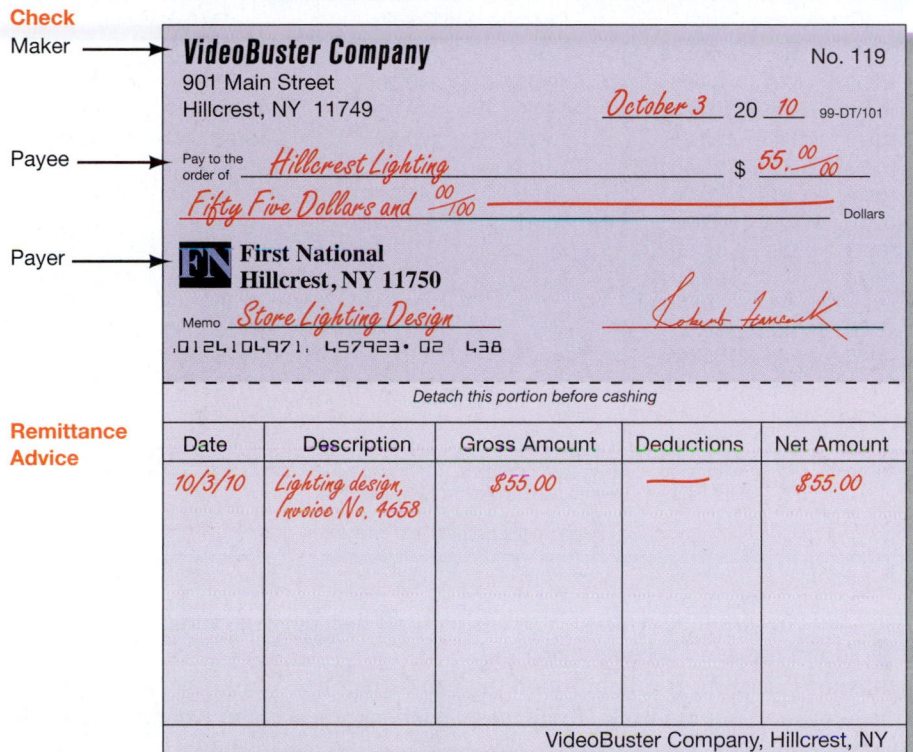

Check Maker →

Payee →

Payer →

Remittance Advice

Exhibit 8.6

Check with Remittance Advice

Electronic Funds Transfer   **Electronic funds transfer (EFT)** is the electronic transfer of cash from one party to another. No paper documents are used. Banks simply transfer cash from one account to another with a journal entry. Companies are increasingly using EFT because it is easy and low cost. For instance, it can cost up to 50 cents to process a check through the banking system, whereas EFT cost is near zero. Items such as payroll, rent, utilities, insurance, and interest payments are commonly handled by EFT. The bank statement lists cash withdrawals by EFT with the checks and other deductions. Cash receipts by EFT are listed with deposits and other additions. A bank statement is sometimes a depositor's only notice of an EFT.

Bank Statement

Usually once a month, the bank sends each depositor a **bank statement** showing the activity in the account. Different banks use different formats for their bank statements, but all include the following information:

1. Beginning-of-period balance of the depositor's account.
2. Checks and other debits decreasing the account during the period.
3. Deposits and other credits increasing the account during the period.
4. End-of-period balance of the depositor's account.

This information reflects the bank's records. Exhibit 8.7 shows a bank statement. Identify each of these four items in that statement. Part ❶ of Exhibit 8.7 summarizes changes in the account.

L06   Describe a bank statement.

Exhibit 8.7

Bank Statement

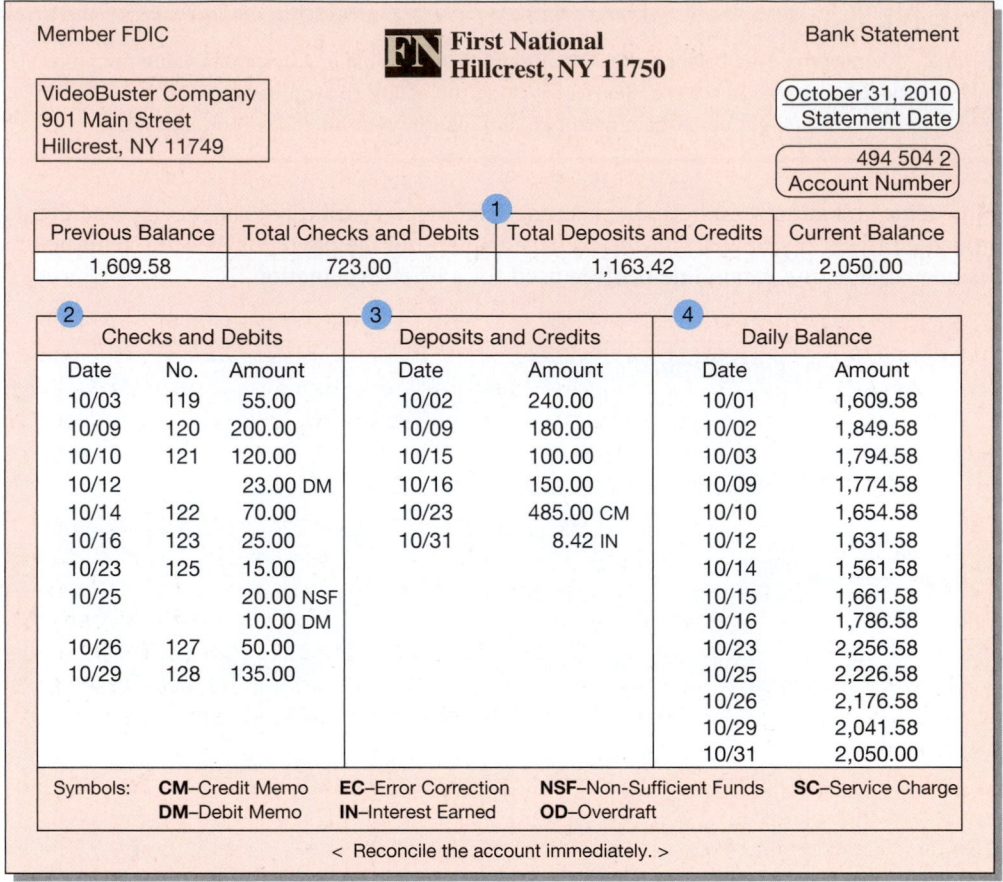

Part ② lists paid checks along with other debits. Part ③ lists deposits and credits to the account, and part ④ shows the daily account balances.

The depositor's account is a liability on the bank's records. This is because the money belongs to the depositor, not the bank. To increase a depositor's account balance, the bank *credits* that liability account. This means that debit memos from the bank produce *credits* on the depositor's books, and credit memos from the bank produce *debits* on the depositor's books.

The bank statement includes a list of the depositor's canceled checks (or the actual canceled checks) along with any debit or credit memoranda affecting the account. **Canceled checks** are checks the bank has paid and deducted from the customer's account during the period. Other deductions that can appear on a bank statement include (1) bank service charges and fees, (2) checks deposited that are uncollectible, (3) corrections of previous errors, (4) withdrawals through automated teller machines (ATMs), and (5) periodic payments set up in advance by a depositor. (Most company checking accounts do not allow ATM withdrawals because the company wants to make all disbursements by check.) Except for service charges, the bank notifies the depositor of each deduction with a debit memorandum when the bank reduces the balance. A copy of each debit memorandum is usually sent with the statement.

Transactions that increase the depositor's account include amounts the bank collects on behalf of the depositor and the corrections of previous errors. Credit memoranda notify the depositor of all increases when they are recorded. A copy of each credit memorandum is often sent with the bank statement. Banks that pay interest on checking accounts credit it to the depositor's account each period. In Exhibit 8.7, the bank credits $8.42 of interest to the account as shown at the bottom of the "Deposits and Credits" column.

Bank Reconciliation

LO7 Prepare and explain a bank reconciliation.

When a company deposits all cash receipts and makes all cash payments (except petty cash) by check, the bank statement helps prove the accuracy of its cash records. This is done using a **bank reconciliation,** which is a report explaining any differences between the checking account balance according to the depositor's records and the balance reported on the bank statement.

Purpose of Bank Reconciliation   The balance of a checking account reported on the bank statement rarely equals the balance in the depositor's accounting records. This is usually due to information that one party has that the other does not. We must therefore prove the accuracy of both the depositor's records and those of the bank. This means we must *reconcile* the two balances and explain or account for any differences in them. Among the reasons the bank statement balance might differ from the depositor's book balance are these:

■ **Outstanding checks. Outstanding checks** are checks written (or drawn) by the depositor, deducted on the depositor's records, and sent to payees, but not yet received by the bank for payment at the bank statement date.

■ **Deposits in transit** (also called **outstanding deposits**). **Deposits in transit** are deposits made and recorded by the depositor but not yet recorded on the bank statement. For example, companies can make deposits (in the night depository) at the end of a business day after the bank is closed. If such a deposit occurred on a bank statement date, it would not appear on this period's statement. The bank would record such a deposit on the next business day, and it would appear on the next period's bank statement.

■ **Deductions for uncollectible items and for services.** A company sometimes deposits another party's check that is uncollectible (usually meaning the balance in the other party's account is not large enough to cover the check). This is called a *non-sufficient funds (NSF)* check. The bank would have initially credited (increased) the depositor's account for the amount of the check. When the bank learns the check is uncollectible, it debits (reduces) the depositor's account for the amount of that check. Other possible bank charges to a depositor's account that are first reported on a bank statement include printing new checks and service fees.

■ **Additions for collections and for interest.** Banks sometimes act as collection agents for their depositors by collecting notes and other items. Banks can also receive electronic funds transfers to the depositor's account. When a bank collects an item, it is added to the depositor's account, less any service fee. The bank also sends a credit memorandum to notify the depositor of the transaction. When the memorandum is received, the depositor should record it; yet it sometimes remains unrecorded until the bank reconciliation is prepared. The bank statement also includes a credit for any interest earned.

■ **Errors.** Both banks and depositors can make errors. Bank errors might not be discovered until the depositor prepares the bank reconciliation. Also, depositor errors can be discovered when the bank balance is reconciled. Error testing includes: (a) comparing deposits on the bank statement with deposits in the accounting records and (b) comparing canceled checks on the bank statement with checks recorded in the accounting records.

> **Forms of Check Fraud (CkFraud.org)**
> • Forged signatures—legitimate blank checks with fake payer signature
> • Forged endorsements—stolen check that is endorsed and cashed by someone other than the payee
> • Counterfeit checks—fraudulent checks with fake payer signature
> • Altered checks—legitimate check altered (such as changed payee or amount) to benefit perpetrator
> • Check kiting—deposit check from one bank account (without sufficient funds) into a second bank account

Illustration of a Bank Reconciliation   We follow nine steps in preparing the bank reconciliation. It is helpful to refer to the bank reconciliation in Exhibit 8.8 when studying steps ① through ⑨.

Exhibit 8.8

Bank Reconciliation

VIDEOBUSTER Bank Reconciliation October 31, 2010						
① Bank statement balance		$ 2,050.00	⑤ Book balance			$ 1,404.58
② Add			⑥ Add			
Deposit of Oct. 31 in transit		145.00	Collect $500 note less $15 fee	$485.00		
		2,195.00	Interest earned	8.42		493.42
③ Deduct						1,898.00
Outstanding checks			⑦ Deduct			
No. 124	$150.00		Check printing charge		23.00	
No. 126	200.00	350.00	NSF check plus service fee		30.00	53.00
④ **Adjusted bank balance**		**$1,845.00**	⑧ **Adjusted book balance**			**$1,845.00**

⑨ Balances are equal (reconciled)

1 Identify the bank statement balance of the cash account (*balance per bank*). VideoBuster's bank balance is $2,050.

2 Identify and list any unrecorded deposits and any bank errors understating the bank balance. Add them to the bank balance. VideoBuster's $145 deposit placed in the bank's night depository on October 31 is not recorded on its bank statement.

3 Identify and list any outstanding checks and any bank errors overstating the bank balance. Outstanding checks are identified by comparing canceled checks on the bank statement with checks recorded. Deduct them from the bank balance. VideoBuster's comparison of canceled checks with its books shows two checks outstanding: No. 124 for $150 and No. 126 for $200.

4 Compute the *adjusted bank balance,* also called the *corrected* or *reconciled balance.*

5 Identify the company's book balance of the cash account (*balance per book*). VideoBuster's book balance is $1,404.58.

6 Identify and list any unrecorded credit memoranda from the bank, any interest earned, and errors understating the book balance. Add them to the book balance. Enclosed with VideoBuster's bank statement is a credit memorandum showing the bank collected a note receivable for the company on October 23. The note's proceeds of $500 (minus a $15 collection fee) are credited to the company's account. VideoBuster's bank statement also shows a credit of $8.42, not yet recorded, for interest earned on the average cash balance.

7 Identify and list any unrecorded debit memoranda from the bank, any service charges, and errors overstating the book balance. Deduct them from the book balance. Debits on VideoBuster's bank statement that are not yet recorded include (a) a $23 charge for check printing and (b) an NSF check for $20 plus a related $10 processing fee. (The NSF check is dated October 16 and was included in the book balance.)

8 Compute the *adjusted book balance,* also called *corrected* or *reconciled balance.*

9 Verify that the two adjusted balances from steps 4 and 8 are equal. If so, they are reconciled. If not, check for accuracy and missing data until the balances are equal.

IN THE NEWS

Not-So-Free Banking   **Bankrate.com** surveys indicate non-sufficient funds and overdraft program fees have risen significantly from 2005 to 2008, with the average fee now at $28.95 per transaction, an increase of more than 7% in the past three years. Bank and credit union income from non-sufficient funds and overdraft program fees exceed $34.7 billion in the United States. (**Bretton-woods.com**, 2009)

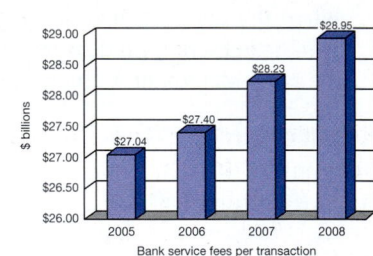

Bank service fees per transaction

Adjusting Entries from a Bank Reconciliation

A bank reconciliation often identifies unrecorded items that need recording by the company. In VideoBuster's reconciliation, the adjusted balance of $1,845 is the correct balance as of October 31. But the company's accounting records show a $1,404.58 balance. We must prepare journal entries to adjust the book balance to the correct balance. *It is important to remember that only the items reconciling the book balance require adjustment.* A review of Exhibit 8.8 indicates that four entries are required for VideoBuster. Adjusting entries could also be combined into one compound entry.

Collection of note.   The first entry records the proceeds of its note receivable collected by the bank and the expense of having the bank perform that service. A note receivable is a written promise to pay from a customer.

Oct. 31	Cash	485		Assets = Liabilities + Equity
	Collection Expense	15		+485 −15
	Notes Receivable.		500	−500
	To record the collection fee and proceeds			
	for a note collected by the bank.			

Interest earned. The second entry records interest credited to its account by the bank.

Oct. 31	Cash	8.42		Assets = Liabilities + Equity
	Interest Revenue		8.42	+8.42 +8.42
	To record interest earned on the cash			
	balance in the checking account.			

Check printing. The third entry records expenses for the check printing charge.

Oct. 31	Miscellaneous Expenses.	23		Assets = Liabilities + Equity
	Cash		23	−23 −23
	Check printing charge.			

NSF check. The fourth entry records the NSF check that is returned as uncollectible. The $20 check was originally received from T. Woods in payment of his account and then deposited. (The company debited Cash and credited Accounts Receivable.) The bank charged $10 for handling the NSF check and deducted $30 total from VideoBuster's account. The entry must reverse the effects of the original entry made when the check was received and must record (add) the $10 bank fee to the amount owed by T. Woods.

Oct. 31	Accounts Receivable—T. Woods	30		Assets = Liabilities + Equity
	Cash		30	+30
	To charge Woods' account for $20 NSF check			−30
	and $10 bank fee.			

After these four entries are recorded, the book balance of cash is adjusted to the correct amount of $1,845 (computed as $1,404.58 + $485 + $8.42 − $23 − $30). The Cash T-account to the side shows the same computation.

Cash			
Beg. bal.	1,404.58		
6	485.00	7	23.00
6	8.42	7	30.00
Adj. bal.	1,845.00		

HOW YOU DOIN'?   Answers—p. 192

4. What is a bank statement?
5. What is the meaning of the phrase *to reconcile a bank balance?*
6. Why do we reconcile the bank statement balance of cash and the depositor's book balance of cash?
7. List at least two items affecting the bank balance side of a bank reconciliation and indicate whether the items are added or subtracted.
8. List at least three items affecting the book balance side of a bank reconciliation and indicate whether the items are added or subtracted.

Demonstration Problem 1

Prepare a bank reconciliation for Jamboree Enterprises for the month ended November 30, 2010. The following information is available to reconcile Jamboree Enterprises' book balance of cash with its bank statement balance as of November 30, 2010:

a. After all posting is complete on November 30, the company's book balance of Cash has a $16,380 debit balance, but its bank statement shows a $38,520 balance.

b. Checks No. 2024 for $4,810 and No. 2026 for $5,000 are outstanding.

c. In comparing the canceled checks on the bank statement with the entries in the accounting records, it is found that Check No. 2025 in payment of rent is correctly drawn for $1,000 but is erroneously entered in the accounting records as $880.

d. The November 30 deposit of $17,150 was placed in the night depository after banking hours on that date, and this amount does not appear on the bank statement.

e. In reviewing the bank statement, a check written by Jumbo Enterprises in the amount of $160 was erroneously drawn against Jamboree's account.

f. A credit memorandum enclosed with the bank statement indicates that the bank collected a $30,000 note and $900 of related interest on Jamboree's behalf. This transaction was not recorded by Jamboree prior to receiving the statement.

g. A debit memorandum for $1,100 lists a $1,100 NSF check received from a customer, Marilyn Welch. Jamboree had not recorded the return of this check before receiving the statement.

h. Bank service charges for November total $40. These charges were not recorded by Jamboree before receiving the statement.

Planning the Solution

- Set up a bank reconciliation with a bank side and a book side (as in Exhibit 8.8). Leave room to both add and deduct items. Each column will result in a reconciled, equal balance.
- Examine each item *a* through *h* to determine whether it affects the book or the bank balance and whether it should be added or deducted from the bank or book balance.
- After all items are analyzed, complete the reconciliation and arrive at a reconciled balance between the bank side and the book side.
- For each reconciling item on the book side, prepare an adjusting entry. Additions to the book side require an adjusting entry that debits Cash. Deductions on the book side require an adjusting entry that credits Cash.

Solution to Demonstration Problem 1

JAMBOREE ENTERPRISES
Bank Reconciliation
November 30, 2010

Bank statement balance		$38,520	Book balance		$16,380
Add			Add		
Deposit of Nov. 30	$17,150		Collection of note	$30,000	
Bank error (Jumbo)	160	17,310	Interest earned	900	30,900
		55,830			47,280
Deduct			Deduct		
Outstanding checks			NSF check (M. Welch)	1,100	
No. 2024	4,810		Recording error (# 2025)	120	
No. 2026	5,000	9,810	Service charge	40	1,260
Adjusted bank balance		**$46,020**	**Adjusted book balance**		**$46,020**

REQUIRED ADJUSTING ENTRIES FOR JAMBOREE				
Nov.	30	Cash	30 9 0 0 00	
		Notes Receivable		30 0 0 0 00
		Interest Revenue		9 0 0 00
		To record collection of note with interest.		
Nov.	30	Accounts Receivable—M. Welch	1 1 0 0 00	
		Cash		1 1 0 0 00
		To reinstate account due from an NSF check.		
Nov.	30	Rent Expense	1 2 0 00	
		Cash		1 2 0 00
		To correct recording error on check no. 2025.		
Nov.	30	Bank Service Charges	4 0 00	
		Cash		4 0 00
		To record bank service charges.		

Demonstration Problem 2

Bacardi Company established a $150 petty cash fund with Dean Martin as the petty cashier. When the fund balance reached $19 cash, Martin prepared a petty cash payments report, which follows.

Petty Cash Payments Report				
Receipt No.	Account Charged		Approved by	Received by
12	Delivery Expense	$ 29	Martin	A. Smirnoff
13	Transportation-In	18	Martin	J. Daniels
15	(Omitted)	32	Martin	C. Carlsberg
16	Miscellaneous Expense	41	(Omitted)	J. Walker
	Total	$120		

Required

1. Identify four internal control weaknesses from the payments report.
2. Prepare general journal entries to record:
   a. Establishment of the petty cash fund.
   b. Reimbursement of the fund. (Assume for this part only that petty cash receipt no. 15 was issued for miscellaneous expenses.)
3. What is the Petty Cash account balance immediately before reimbursement? Immediately after reimbursement?

Solution to Demonstration Problem 2

1. Four internal control weaknesses are
   a. Petty cash ticket no. 14 is missing. Its omission raises questions about the petty cashier's management of the fund.
   b. The $19 cash balance means that $131 has been withdrawn ($150 − $19 = $131). However, the total amount of the petty cash receipts is only $120 ($29 + $18 + $32 + $41). The fund is $11 short of cash ($131 − $120 = $11). Was petty cash receipt no. 14 issued for $11? Management should investigate.
   c. The petty cashier (Martin) did not sign petty cash receipt no. 16. This omission could have been an oversight on his part or he might not have authorized the payment. Management should investigate.

d. Petty cash receipt no. 15 does not indicate which account to charge. This omission could have been an oversight on the petty cashier's part. Management could check with C. Carlsberg and the petty cashier (Martin) about the transaction. Without further information, debit Miscellaneous Expense.

2. Petty cash general journal entries.

a. Entry to establish the petty cash fund.

Petty Cash	150	
Cash		150

b. Entry to reimburse the fund.

Delivery Expense	29	
Transportation-In	18	
Miscellaneous Expense ($41 + $32)	73	
Cash Over and Short	11	
Cash		131

3. The Petty Cash account balance *always* equals its fund balance, in this case $150. This account balance does not change unless the fund is increased or decreased.

Summary

LO1 **Define cash and describe three guidelines for control of cash.** Cash includes currency, coins, amounts on deposit in bank accounts, and checks acceptable for deposit in bank accounts. Guidelines for control of cash include (1) separation of the handling of cash from its recordkeeping, (2) cash receipts should be promptly deposited in a bank, and (3) cash payments should be made by check.

LO2 **Describe controls for cash receipts.** Control of over-the-counter cash receipts includes use of a cash register, customer review, use of receipts, a permanent transaction record locked-in the cash register, and separation of access to cash from its recordkeeping. Control of cash receipts by mail includes at least two people assigned to open mail and a listing of each sender's name, amount paid, and an explanation.

LO3 **Describe controls for cash disbursements.** Except for very small dollar transactions, all expenditures should be made by check. A petty cash system is used to account for small dollar transactions. Employees who sign checks should not have access to accounting records.

LO4 **Explain and record petty cash fund transactions.** Petty cash payments are for amounts for items such as postage, delivery fees, minor repairs, and supplies. A petty cashier safeguards the petty cash, makes payments from the petty cash fund, and keeps petty cash receipts and records. A Petty Cash account is debited only when the fund is established or increased in amount. When the fund is replenished, petty cash disbursements are recorded with debits to expense (or asset) accounts and a credit to cash.

LO5 **Identify banking activities as controls of cash.** A bank account is a record set up by a bank, allowing a customer to endorse checks and to deposit money for safekeeping and to draw checks on it. A bank deposit ticket proves money was deposited into a bank account. A check tells the bank to pay money from a customer's (*maker*) account to a recipient (*payee*).

LO6 **Describe a bank statement.** A bank statement shows activity in a bank account. Each bank statements lists the beginning-of-period account balance, checks and other debits decreasing the account during the period, deposits and other credits increasing the account during the period, and the end-of-period account balance.

LO7 **Prepare and explain a bank reconciliation.** A bank reconciliation proves the accuracy of the customer's and the bank's records. The bank statement balance is adjusted for items such as outstanding checks and unrecorded deposits made on or before the bank statement date but not reflected on the bank statement. The book balance is adjusted for items like service charges, bank collections for the customer, and interest earned on the account.

Guidance Answers to HOW YOU DOIN'?

1. If all cash payments are made by check, numerous checks for small amounts must be written. Since this practice is expensive and time-consuming, a petty cash fund is often established for making small (immaterial) cash payments.

2. If the petty cash fund is not reimbursed at the end of an accounting period, the transactions involving petty cash are not yet recorded and the petty cash asset is overstated.

3. First, petty cash transactions are recorded when the petty cash fund is reimbursed. Second, reimbursement provides cash to allow the fund to continue being used. Third, reimbursement identifies any cash shortage or overage in the fund.

4. A bank statement is a report prepared by the bank describing the activities in a depositor's account.

5. To reconcile a bank balance means to explain the difference between the cash balance in the depositor's accounting records and the cash balance on the bank statement.

6. The purpose of the bank reconciliation is to determine whether the bank or the depositor has made any errors and whether the bank has entered any transactions affecting the account that the depositor has not recorded.

7. Unrecorded deposits—added
Outstanding checks—subtracted

8. Interest earned—added   Debit memos—subtracted
Credit memos—added   NSF checks—subtracted
                                Bank service charges—subtracted

Key Terms

Bank reconciliation (p. 186) Report that explains the difference between the book (company) balance of cash and the cash balance reported on the bank statement.

Bank statement (p. 185) Bank report on the depositor's beginning and ending cash balances, and a listing of its changes, for a period.

Blank endorsement (p. 184) Depositor signs the back of the check and the check is payable to the bearer of the check.

Canceled checks (p. 186) Checks that the bank has paid and deducted from the depositor's account.

Cash (p. 178) Includes currency, coins, and amounts on deposit in bank checking or savings accounts.

Cash Over and Short (p. 179) Income statement account used to record cash overages and cash shortages arising from errors in cash receipts or payments.

Check (p. 184) Document signed by a depositor instructing the bank to pay a specific amount to a designated recipient.

Deposits in transit (p. 187) Deposits recorded by the company but not yet recorded by its bank.

Deposit ticket (p. 183) Lists items such as currency, coins, and checks deposited and their corresponding dollar amounts.

Electronic funds transfer (EFT) (p. 185) Use of electronic communication to transfer cash from one party to another.

Endorsement (p. 184) A written authorization transferring ownership of a check.

Liquid assets (p. 178) Resources such as cash that are easily converted into other assets or used to pay for goods, services, or liabilities.

Liquidity (p. 178) Availability of resources to meet short-term cash requirements.

Outstanding checks (p. 187) Checks written and recorded by the depositor but not yet paid by the bank at the bank statement date.

Petty cash (p. 180) Small amount of cash in a fund to pay minor expenses.

Restrictive endorsement (p. 184) The depositor transfers the check to a specific person, business, or bank for a specific purpose.

Signature card (p. 183) Includes the signatures of each person authorized to sign checks on the bank account.

Multiple Choice Quiz   Answers on p. 203   mhhe.com/wildCA2e

Additional Multiple Choice Quizzes are available at the book's Website.

1. A company needs to replenish its $500 petty cash fund. Its petty cash box has $75 cash and petty cash receipts of $420. The journal entry to replenish the fund includes
   a. A debit to Cash for $75.
   b. A credit to Cash for $75.
   c. A credit to Petty Cash for $420.
   d. A credit to Cash Over and Short for $5.
   e. A debit to Cash Over and Short for $5.

2. The following information is available for Hapley Company:
   - The November 30 bank statement shows a $1,895 balance.
   - The general ledger shows a $1,742 balance at November 30.
   - A $795 deposit placed in the bank's night depository on November 30 does not appear on the November 30 bank statement.
   - Outstanding checks amount to $638 at November 30.
   - A customer's $335 note was collected by the bank in November. A collection fee of $15 was deducted by the bank and the difference deposited in Hapley's account.
   - A bank service charge of $10 is deducted by the bank and appears on the November 30 bank statement.

   How will the customer's note appear on Hapley's November 30 bank reconciliation?
   a. $320 appears as an addition to the book balance of cash.
   b. $320 appears as a deduction from the book balance of cash.
   c. $320 appears as an addition to the bank balance of cash.
   d. $320 appears as a deduction from the bank balance of cash.
   e. $335 appears as an addition to the bank balance of cash.

3. Using the information from question 2, what is the reconciled balance on Hapley's November 30 bank reconciliation?
   a. $2,052
   b. $1,895
   c. $1,742
   d. $2,201
   e. $1,184

4. Using the information from question 2, how will the $10 bank service charge appear on Hapley's November 30 bank reconciliation?
   a. $10 appears as an addition to the book balance of cash.
   b. $10 appears as an addition to the bank balance of cash.
   c. $10 appears as a deduction from the book balance of cash.
   d. $10 appears as a deduction from the bank balance of cash.
   e. The service charge will not appear on the November 30 bank reconciliation.

5. Using the information from question 2, the journal entries to adjust Hapley's book balance of cash to the bank's balance of cash on November 30 will include a
   a. Debit to Cash for the $10 bank service charge.
   b. Credit to Cash for $638 of outstanding checks.
   c. Debit to Cash for $795 of deposits in transit.
   d. Debit to Cash for $320 for collection of note, net of bank collection fees.
   e. Debit to Cash for the $153 difference between the bank's balance of Cash and the book balance of Cash.

Discussion Questions

1. Why should responsibility for related transactions be divided among different individuals?

2. Why should the person who keeps the cash records not have access to cash?

3. Which of the following assets is most liquid? Which is least liquid? Inventory, building, accounts receivable, or cash.

4. What is a petty cash receipt? Who should sign it?

5. Which type of endorsement should be used to entitle the check to be payable to the bearer of the check?

6. Why should cash receipts be deposited on the day of receipt?

7. **Best Buy**'s statement of cash flows in Appendix A describes changes in cash and cash equivalents for the year ended March 1, 2008. What amount is provided (used) by investing activities? What amount is provided (used) by financing activities?

8. Refer to **RadioShack**'s balance sheet in Appendix A. How does its cash compare with its other current assets (both in amount and percent) as of December 31, 2007. Compare and assess the cash amount at December 31, 2007, with its amount at December 31, 2006.

QUICK STUDY

QS 8–1
Cash and liquidity   **L01**

Good accounting systems help to manage cash and control access to it.

1. What items are included in the category of cash?

2. What does the term *liquidity* refer to?

QS 8–2
Control of cash
L01   L02   L03

A good system of cash control helps protect both cash receipts and cash disbursements.

1. What are three basic guidelines that help achieve this protection?

2. Identify a control system for cash disbursements.

QS 8–3
Petty cash accounting   **L04**

1. The petty cash fund of the Brooks Agency is established at $85. At the end of the current period, the fund contained $14.80 and had the following receipts: film rentals, $21.30, refreshments for meetings, $30.85 (both expenditures to be classified as Entertainment Expense); postage, $8.95; and printing, $9.10. Prepare journal entries to record (*a*) establishment of the fund and (*b*) reimbursement of the fund at the end of the current period.

2. Identify the two events that cause a Petty Cash account to be credited in a journal entry.

QS 8–4
Bank reconciliation   **L07**

1. For each of the following items, indicate whether its amount (i) affects the bank or book side of a bank reconciliation and (ii) represents an addition or a subtraction in a bank reconciliation.

   a. Interest on cash balance   **d.** Outstanding checks   **g.** Unrecorded deposits

   b. Bank service charges   **e.** Credit memos

   c. Debit memos   **f.** NSF checks

2. Which of the items in part 1 require an adjusting journal entry in the depositor's books?

QS 8–5
Petty cash accounting   **L04**

What are the four steps to avoid errors in recording petty cash reimbursement?

QS 8–6
Deposit ticket preparation   **L05**

Given the following facts, prepare a deposit ticket. Use Exhibit 8.4 as a guide.

Company Name:	Ned's Necklaces	
Date:	July 28, 2010	
Currency:	$35.00	
Coin:	$1.53	
Checks:	Account	Amount
	14-267	$13.50
	15-2263	$37.50
	4-98	$10.00

Given the following facts, prepare a check and check stub. Use Exhibit 8.6 as a guide.

Date:	August 25, 2010
Payee:	Tony's Pizza
Amount:	$53.33
Description:	Company Party
Signature:	Mark Ellingson, Ellingson Electronics

QS 8–7
Check and check stub preparation
LO5

connect

Franco Company is a rapidly growing start-up business. Its recordkeeper, who was hired one year ago, left town after the company's manager discovered that a large sum of money had disappeared over the past six months. An audit disclosed that the recordkeeper had written and signed several checks made payable to her fiancé and then recorded the checks as salaries expense. The fiancé, who cashed the checks but never worked for the company, left town with the recordkeeper. As a result, the company incurred an uninsured loss of $184,000. Evaluate Franco's cash control system and indicate which guidelines of cash control appear to have been ignored.

EXERCISES

Exercise 8–1
Analyzing cash control   **LO3**

Some of Crown Company's cash receipts from customers are received by the company with the regular mail. Crown's recordkeeper opens these letters and deposits the cash received each day. (a) Identify any internal control problem(s) in this arrangement. (b) What changes do you recommend?

Exercise 8–2
Control of cash receipts by mail
LO2

What control procedures would you recommend in each of the following situations?

1. A concession company has one employee who sells sunscreen, T-shirts, and sunglasses at the beach. Each day, the employee is given enough sunscreen, shirts, and sunglasses to last through the day and enough cash to make change. The money is kept in a box at the stand.

2. An antique store has one employee who is given cash and sent to garage sales each weekend. The employee pays cash for this merchandise that the antique store resells.

Exercise 8–3
Control recommendations   **LO1**

Palmona Co. establishes a $200 petty cash fund on January 1. On January 8, the fund shows $38 in cash along with receipts for the following expenditures: postage, $74; photocopy expenses, $29; delivery expenses, $16; and miscellaneous expenses, $43. Prepare journal entries to (1) establish the fund on January 1, (2) reimburse it on January 8, and (3) both reimburse the fund and increase it to $450 on January 8, assuming no entry in part 2. (*Hint:* Make two separate entries for part 3.)

Exercise 8–4
Petty cash fund accounting
LO4

Check   (2) Cr. Cash $162

Waupaca Company establishes a $350 petty cash fund on September 9. On September 30, the fund shows $104 in cash along with receipts for the following expenditures: printing expenses, $40; postage expenses, $123; and miscellaneous expenses, $80. The petty cashier could not account for a $3 shortage in the fund. Prepare (1) the September 9 entry to establish the fund, (2) the September 30 entry to reimburse the fund, and (3) an October 1 entry to increase the fund to $400.

Exercise 8–5
Petty cash fund with a shortage
LO4

Check   (2) Cr. Cash $246 and (3) Cr. Cash $50

Prepare a table with the following headings for a monthly bank reconciliation dated September 30.

Exercise 8–6
Bank reconciliation   **LO6   LO7**

Bank Balance		Book Balance		Not Shown on the Reconciliation
Add	Deduct	Add	Deduct	

For each item 1 through 10, place an x in the appropriate column to indicate whether the item should be added to or deducted from the book or bank balance, or whether it should not appear on the reconciliation. At the left side of your table, number the items to correspond to the following list.

1. NSF check from customer returned on September 25 but not yet recorded by this company.

2. Interest earned on the September cash balance in the bank.

3. Deposit made on September 5 and processed by the bank on September 6.

4. Checks written by another depositor but charged against this company's account.

5. Bank service charge for September.

6. Checks outstanding on August 31 that cleared the bank in September.

7. Check written against the company's account and cleared by the bank; erroneously not recorded on the company books.

8. Checks written and mailed to payees on October 2.

9. Checks written by the company and mailed to payees on September 30.

10. Night deposit made on September 30 after the bank closed.

Exercise 8–7
Adjusting entries for bank reconciliation   **LO7**

List the items in Exercise 8-6 that require adjusting journal entries and indicate whether the Cash balance should be debited or credited.

Exercise 8–8
Bank reconciliation   **LO7**

Del Gato Clinic deposits all cash receipts on the day they are received and it makes all cash payments by check. At the close of business on June 30, 2010, its Cash account shows an $11,589 debit balance. Del Gato Clinic's June 30 bank statement shows $10,555 on deposit in the bank. Prepare a bank reconciliation for Del Gato Clinic using the following information:

a. Outstanding checks as of June 30 total $1,829.

b. The June 30 bank statement included a $16 debit memorandum for bank services.

c. Check No. 919, listed with the canceled checks, was correctly drawn for $467 in payment of a utility bill on June 15. Del Gato Clinic mistakenly recorded it with a debit to Utilities Expense and a credit to Cash in the amount of $476.

Check   Reconciled bal., $11,582

d. The June 30 cash receipts of $2,856 were placed in the bank's night depository after banking hours and were not recorded on the June 30 bank statement.

Exercise 8–9
Adjusting entries from bank reconciliation   **LO7**

Prepare the adjusting journal entries that Del Gato Clinic must record as a result of preparing the bank reconciliation in Exercise 8-8.

---

connect™

PROBLEM SET A

Problem 8–1A
Analyzing cash control
LO1   LO2   LO3

For each of these five separate cases, identify the basic control guidelines(s) that is violated. Recommend what the business should do for better control.

1. Chi Han records all incoming customer cash receipts for his employer and posts the customer payments to their respective accounts.

2. At Tico Company, Julia and Justine alternate lunch hours. Julia is the petty cash cashier, but if someone needs petty cash when she is at lunch, Justine fills in as cashier.

3. Nori Nozumi personally opens all the mail for Hopeville Medical Clinic and performs monthly bank reconciliations.

4. Benedict Shales prides himself on hiring quality workers who require little supervision. As office manager, Benedict allows his bookkeeper to sign checks for the business.

5. Cala Farah deposits cash receipts for Green Meadows Video once each week.

Problem 8–2A
Establish, reimburse, and increase petty cash   **LO4**

Nakashima Gallery had the following petty cash transactions in February of the current year.

Feb. 2   Wrote a $400 check, cashed it, and gave the proceeds and the petty cashbox to Chloe Addison, the petty cashier.

     5   Purchased bond paper for the copier for $14.15 that is immediately used.

   12   Paid $7.95 postage to express mail a contract to a client.

   14   Reimbursed Adina Sharon, the manager, $68 for business mileage on her car.

   20   Purchased stationery for $67.77 that is immediately used.

   23   Paid a courier $20 to deliver merchandise sold to a customer, terms FOB destination.

   27   Paid $54 for postage expenses.

   28   The fund had $166.02 remaining in the petty cash box. Sorted the petty cash receipts by accounts affected and exchanged them for a check to reimburse the fund for expenditures.

   28   The petty cash fund amount is increased by $100 to a total of $500.

Required

1. Prepare the journal entry to establish the petty cash fund.

2. Prepare a petty cash payments report for February with these categories: delivery expense, mileage expense, postage expense, and office supplies expense. Sort the payments into the appropriate categories and total the expenditures in each category.

3. Prepare the journal entries for part 2 to both (a) reimburse and (b) increase the fund amount.

Check   (3a) Cr. Cash $233.98

Kiona Co. set up a petty cash fund for payments of small amounts. The following transactions involving the petty cash fund occurred in May (the last month of the company's fiscal year).

Problem 8–3A
Establish, reimburse, and adjust petty cash   **LO4**

QB

May   1   Prepared a company check for $300 to establish the petty cash fund.
15   Prepared a company check to replenish the fund for the following expenditures made since May 1.
    a.   Paid $88 for janitorial services.
    b.   Paid $53.68 for miscellaneous expenses.
    c.   Paid postage expenses of $53.50.
    d.   Paid $47.15 to *The County Gazette* (the local newspaper) for an advertisement.
    e.   Counted $62.15 remaining in the petty cash box.
16   Prepared a company check for $200 to increase the fund to $500.
31   The petty cashier reports that $288.20 cash remains in the fund. A company check is drawn to replenish the fund for the following expenditures made since May 15.
    f.   Paid postage expenses of $147.36.
    g.   Reimbursed the office manager for business mileage, $23.50.
    h.   Paid $34.75 to deliver merchandise to a customer.
31   The company decides that the May 16 increase in the fund was too large. It reduces the fund by $100, leaving a total of $400.

Required

1. Prepare journal entries to establish the fund on May 1, to replenish it on May 15 and on May 31, and to reflect any increase or decrease in the fund balance on May 16 and May 31.

Check   (1) Cr. to Cash: May 15, $237.85; May 16, $200

Analysis Component

2. Explain how the company's financial statements are affected if the petty cash fund is not replenished and no entry is made on May 31.

The following information is available to reconcile Branch Company's book balance of cash with its bank statement cash balance as of July 31, 2010.

Problem 8–4A
Prepare a bank reconciliation and record adjustments   **LO7**

a. After all posting is complete on July 31, the company's Cash account has a $27,497 debit balance, but its July bank statement shows a $27,233 cash balance.

b. Check No. 3031 for $1,482 and Check No. 3040 for $558 were outstanding on the June 30 bank reconciliation. Check No. 3040 is listed with the July canceled checks, but Check No. 3031 is not. Also, Check No. 3065 for $382 and Check No. 3069 for $2,281, both written in July, are not among the canceled checks on the July 31 statement.

c. In comparing the canceled checks on the bank statement with the entries in the accounting records, it is found that Check No. 3056 for July rent was correctly written and drawn for $1,270 but was erroneously entered in the accounting records as $1,250.

d. A credit memorandum enclosed with the July bank statement indicates the bank collected $8,000 cash on a noninterest-bearing note for Branch, deducted a $45 collection fee, and credited the remainder to its account. Branch had not recorded this event before receiving the statement.

e. A debit memorandum for $805 lists a $795 NSF check plus a $10 NSF charge. The check had been received from a customer, Evan Shaw. Branch has not yet recorded this check as NSF.

f. Enclosed with the July statement is a $25 debit memorandum for bank services. It has not yet been recorded because no previous notification had been received.

g. Branch's July 31 daily cash receipts of $11,514 were placed in the bank's night depository on that date, but do not appear on the July 31 bank statement.

Required

1. Prepare the bank reconciliation for this company as of July 31, 2010.

2. Prepare the journal entries necessary to bring the company's book balance of cash into conformity with the reconciled cash balance as of July 31, 2010.

Check   (1) Reconciled balance, $34,602; (2) Cr. Note Receivable $8,000

Analysis Component

3. Assume that the July 31, 2010, bank reconciliation for this company is prepared and some items are treated incorrectly. For each of the following errors, explain the effect of the error on (i) the adjusted bank statement cash balance and (ii) the adjusted cash account book balance.

    a. The company's unadjusted cash account balance of $27,497 is listed on the reconciliation as $27,947.

    b. The bank's collection of the $8,000 note less the $45 collection fee is added to the bank statement cash balance on the reconciliation.

Problem 8-5A

Prepare a bank reconciliation and record adjustments   **LO6**   **LO7**

mhhe.com/wildCA2e

Chavez Company most recently reconciled its bank statement and book balances of cash on August 31 and it reported two checks outstanding, No. 5888 for $1,028.05 and No. 5893 for $494.25. The following information is available for its September 30, 2010, reconciliation.

From the September 30 Bank Statement

Previous Balance	Total Checks and Debits	Total Deposits and Credits	Current Balance
16,800.45	9,620.05	11,272.85	18,453.25

Checks and Debits			Deposits and Credits		Daily Balance	
Date	No.	Amount	Date	Amount	Date	Amount
09/03	5888	1,028.05	09/05	1,103.75	08/31	16,800.45
09/04	5902	719.90	09/12	2,226.90	09/03	15,772.40
09/07	5901	1,824.25	09/21	4,093.00	09/04	15,052.50
09/17		600.25 NSF	09/25	2,351.70	09/05	16,156.25
09/20	5905	937.00	09/30	12.50 IN	09/07	14,332.00
09/22	5903	399.10	09/30	1,485.00 CM	09/12	16,558.90
09/22	5904	2,090.00			09/17	15,958.65
09/28	5907	213.85			09/20	15,021.65
09/29	5909	1,807.65			09/21	19,114.65
					09/22	16,625.55
					09/25	18,977.25
					09/28	18,763.40
					09/29	16,955.75
					09/30	18,453.25

From Chavez Company's Accounting Records

Cash Receipts Deposited				Cash Disbursements		
Date		Cash Debit		Check No.		Cash Credit
Sept.	5	1,103.75		5901		1,824.25
	12	2,226.90		5902		719.90
	21	4,093.00		5903		399.10
	25	2,351.70		5904		2,060.00
	30	1,682.75		5905		937.00
		11,458.10		5906		982.30
				5907		213.85
				5908		388.00
				5909		1,807.65
						9,332.05

Cash						Acct. No. 101
Date		Explanation	PR	Debit	Credit	Balance
Aug.	31	Balance				15,278.15
Sept.	30	Total receipts	R12	11,458.10		26,736.25
	30	Total disbursements	D23		9,332.05	17,404.20

Additional Information

Check No. 5904 is correctly drawn for $2,090 to pay for computer equipment; however, the recordkeeper misread the amount and entered it in the accounting records with a debit to Computer Equipment and a credit to Cash of $2,060. The NSF check shown in the statement was originally received from a customer, S. Nilson, in payment of her account. Its return has not yet been recorded by the company. The credit memorandum is from the collection of a $1,500 note for Chavez Company by the bank. The bank deducted a $15 collection fee. The collection and fee are not yet recorded.

Required

1. Prepare the September 30, 2010, bank reconciliation for this company.

2. Prepare the journal entries to adjust the book balance of cash to the reconciled balance.

Check (1) Reconciled balance, $18,271.45 (2) Cr. Note Receivable $1,500

Analysis Component

3. The bank statement reveals that some of the prenumbered checks in the sequence are missing. Describe three situations that could explain this.

For each of these five separate cases, identify the basic control guideline(s) that is violated. Recommend what the business should do for better control.

1. Lavina Company is a small business that has separated the duties of cash receipts and cash disbursements. The employee responsible for cash disbursements reconciles the bank account monthly.

2. Latisha Tally personally opens all the mail for Professional Systems and performs monthly bank reconciliations.

3. Jim Sutton prides himself on hiring quality workers who require little supervision. As office manager, Jim allows his bookkeeper to sign checks for the business.

4. Victor Vu deposits cash receipts for Quality Lawncare once each week.

5. Gates' Dog Salon uses a petty cash system. Jill is the petty cash cashier, but she allows other employees to access the petty cash drawer if she is away from her desk.

PROBLEM SET B

Problem 8–1B
Analyzing internal control   **LO1**

Blues Music Center had the following petty cash transactions in March of the current year.

March	5	Wrote a $250 check, cashed it, and gave the proceeds and the petty cashbox to Jen Rouse, the petty cashier.
	11	Paid $10.75 delivery charges on merchandise sold to a customer.
	12	Purchased file folders for $14.13 that are immediately used.
	14	Reimbursed Bob Geldof, the manager, $11.65 for office supplies purchased and used.
	18	Purchased printer paper for $20.54 that is immediately used.
	28	Paid postage expenses of $18.
	30	Reimbursed Geldof $56.80 for business car mileage.
	31	Cash of $119.13 remained in the fund. Sorted the petty cash receipts by accounts affected and exchanged them for a check to reimburse the fund for expenditures.
	31	The petty cash fund amount is increased by $50 to a total of $300.

Problem 8–2B
Establish, reimburse, and increase petty cash   **LO4**

Required

1. Prepare the journal entry to establish the petty cash fund.

2. Prepare a petty cash payments report for March with these categories: delivery expense, mileage expense, postage expense, and office supplies expense. Sort the payments into the appropriate categories and total the expenses in each category.

3. Prepare the journal entries for part 2 to both (*a*) reimburse and (*b*) increase the fund amount.

Check (2) Total expenses $131.87

(3a) Cr. Cash $130.87

Moya Co. establishes a petty cash fund for payments of small amounts. The following transactions involving the petty cash fund occurred in January (the last month of the company's fiscal year).

Jan.	3	A company check for $150 is written and made payable to the petty cashier to establish the petty cash fund.
	14	A company check is written to replenish the fund for the following expenditures made since January 3.

Problem 8–3B
Establishing, reimbursing, and adjusting petty cash   **LO4**

     a. Purchased office supplies for $14.29 that are immediately used up.

     b. Paid $19.60 COD shipping charges on merchandise purchased for resale. Hint: Debit "Transportation-In."

     c. Paid $38.57 to All-Tech for minor repairs to a computer.

     d. Paid $12.82 for items classified as miscellaneous expenses.

     e. Counted $62.28 remaining in the petty cash box.

15   Prepared a company check for $50 to increase the fund to $200.

31   The petty cashier reports that $17.35 remains in the fund. A company check is written to replenish the fund for the following expenditures made since January 14.

     f. Paid $50 to *The Smart Shopper* for an advertisement in January's newsletter.

     g. Paid $48.19 for postage expenses.

     h. Paid $78 to Smooth Delivery for delivery of merchandise.

31   The company decides that the January 15 increase in the fund was too little. It increases the fund by another $50, leaving a total of $250.

Required

Check (1) Cr. to Cash: Jan. 14, $87.72; Jan. 15, $50

1. Prepare journal entries to establish the fund on January 3, to replenish it on January 14 and January 31, and to reflect any increase or decrease in the fund balance on January 15 and 31.

Analysis Component

2. Explain how the company's financial statements are affected if the petty cash fund is not replenished and no entry is made on January 31.

Problem 8-4B

Prepare a bank reconciliation and record adjustments **LO7**

The following information is available to reconcile Severino Co.'s book balance of cash with its bank statement cash balance as of December 31, 2010.

a. After posting is complete, the December 31 cash balance according to the accounting records is $32,878.30, and the bank statement cash balance for that date is $46,822.40.

b. Check No. 1273 for $4,589.30 and Check No. 1282 for $400.00, both written and entered in the accounting records in December, are not among the canceled checks. Two checks, No. 1231 for $2,289.00 and No. 1242 for $410.40, were outstanding on the most recent November 30 reconciliation. Check No. 1231 is listed with the December canceled checks, but Check No. 1242 is not.

c. When the December checks are compared with entries in the accounting records, it is found that Check No. 1267 had been correctly drawn for $3,456 to pay for office supplies but was erroneously entered in the accounting records as $3,465.

d. Two debit memoranda are enclosed with the statement and are unrecorded at the time of the reconciliation. One debit memorandum is for $762.50 and dealt with an NSF check for $745 received from a customer, Titus Industries, in payment of its account. The bank assessed a $17.50 fee for processing it. The second debit memorandum is a $99.00 charge for check printing. Severino did not record these transactions before receiving the statement.

e. A credit memorandum indicates that the bank collected $19,000 cash on a note receivable for the company, deducted a $20 collection fee, and credited the balance to the company's Cash account. Severino did not record this transaction before receiving the statement.

f. Severino's December 31 daily cash receipts of $9,583.10 were placed in the bank's night depository on that date, but do not appear on the December 31 bank statement.

Required

Check (1) Reconciled balance, $51,005.80; (2) Cr. Note Receivable $19,000

1. Prepare the bank reconciliation for this company as of December 31, 2010.

2. Prepare the journal entries necessary to bring the company's book balance of cash into conformity with the reconciled cash balance as of December 31, 2010.

Analysis Component

3. Explain the nature of the communications conveyed by a bank when the bank sends the depositor (*a*) a debit memorandum and (*b*) a credit memorandum.

Problem 8-5B

Prepare a bank reconciliation and record adjustments **LO6 LO7**

Shamara Systems Co. most recently reconciled its bank balance on April 30 and reported two checks outstanding at that time, No. 1771 for $781.00 and No. 1780 for $1,425.90. The following information is available for its May 31, 2010, reconciliation.

From the May 31 Bank Statement

Previous Balance	Total Checks and Debits	Total Deposits and Credits	Current Balance
18,290.70	13,094.80	16,566.80	21,762.70

Checks and Debits			Deposits and Credits		Daily Balance	
Date	No.	Amount	Date	Amount	Date	Amount
05/01	1771	781.00	05/04	2,438.00	04/30	18,290.70
05/02	1783	382.50	05/14	2,898.00	05/01	17,509.70
05/04	1782	1,285.50	05/22	1,801.80	05/02	17,127.20
05/11	1784	1,449.60	05/25	7,350.00 CM	05/04	18,279.70
05/18		431.80 NSF	05/26	2,079.00	05/11	16,830.10
05/25	1787	8,032.50			05/14	19,728.10
05/26	1785	63.90			05/18	19,296.30
05/29	1788	654.00			05/22	21,098.10
05/31		14.00 SC			05/25	20,415.60
					05/26	22,430.70
					05/29	21,776.70
					05/31	21,762.70

From Shamara Systems' Accounting Records

Cash Receipts Deposited

Date		Cash Debit
May	4	2,438.00
	14	2,898.00
	22	1,801.80
	26	2,079.00
	31	2,727.30
		11,944.10

Cash Disbursements

Check No.		Cash Credit
1782		1,285.50
1783		382.50
1784		1,449.60
1785		63.90
1786		353.10
1787		8,032.50
1788		644.00
1789		639.50
		12,850.60

Cash **Acct. No. 101**

Date		Explanation	PR	Debit	Credit	Balance
Apr.	30	Balance				16,083.80
May	31	Total receipts	R7	11,944.10		28,027.90
	31	Total disbursements	D8		12,850.60	15,177.30

Additional Information

Check No. 1788 is correctly drawn for $654 to pay for May utilities; however, the recordkeeper misread the amount and entered it in the accounting records with a debit to Utilities Expense and a credit to Cash for $644. The bank paid and deducted the correct amount. The NSF check shown in the statement was originally received from a customer, W. Sox, in payment of her account. The company has not yet recorded its return. The credit memorandum is from a $7,400 note that the bank collected for the company. The bank deducted a $50 collection fee and deposited the remainder in the company's account. The collection and fee have not yet been recorded.

Required

1. Prepare the May 31, 2010, bank reconciliation for Shamara Systems.

2. Prepare the journal entries to adjust the book balance of cash to the reconciled balance.

Check   (1) Reconciled balance, $22,071.50; (2) Cr. Note Receivable $7,400

Analysis Component

3. The bank statement reveals that some of the prenumbered checks in the sequence are missing. Describe three possible situations to explain this.

SERIAL PROBLEM

Success Systems
L07

(This serial problem began in Chapter 1 and continues through most of the book. If previous chapter segments were not completed, the serial problem can begin at this point. It is helpful, but not necessary, that you use the Working Papers that accompany the book.)

SP 8   Adriana Lopez receives the March bank statement for Success Systems on April 11, 2011. The March 31 bank statement shows an ending cash balance of $86,896. A comparison of the bank statement with the general ledger Cash account, No. 101, reveals the following.

a. Lopez notices that the bank erroneously cleared a $470 check against her account that she did not issue. The check documentation included with the bank statement shows that this check was actually issued by a company named Sierra Systems.

b. On March 25, the bank issued a $50 debit memorandum for the safety deposit box that Success Systems agreed to rent from the bank beginning March 25.

c. On March 26, the bank issued a $75 debit memorandum for printed checks that Success Systems ordered from the bank.

d. On March 31, the bank issued a credit memorandum for $33 interest earned on Success Systems's checking account for the month of March.

e. Lopez notices that the check she issued for $192 on March 31, 2011, has not yet cleared the bank.

f. Lopez verifies that all deposits made in March do appear on the March bank statement.

g. The general ledger Cash account, No. 101, shows an ending cash balance per books as $87,266 (prior to any reconciliation).

Required

1. Prepare a bank reconciliation for Success Systems for the month ended March 31, 2011.

2. Prepare any necessary adjusting entries. Use Miscellaneous Expenses, No. 677, for any bank charges. Use Interest Revenue, No. 404, for any interest earned on the checking account for the month of March.

BEYOND THE NUMBERS

REPORTING IN ACTION
L01

BTN 8–1   Refer to **Best Buy**'s financial statements in Appendix A to answer the following.

1. For both fiscal year-ends March 1, 2008, and March 3, 2007, identify the total amount of cash and cash equivalents. Determine the percent this amount represents of total current assets, total current liabilities, total shareholders' equity, and total assets for both years. Comment on any trends.

2. For fiscal years ended March 1, 2008, and March 3, 2007, use the information in the statement of cash flows to determine the percent change between the beginning and ending year amounts of cash and cash equivalents.

ETHICS CHALLENGE
L01   L02   L03

BTN 8–2   Harriet Knox, Ralph Patton, and Marcia Diamond work for a family physician, Dr. Gwen Conrad, who is in private practice. Dr. Conrad is knowledgeable about office management practices and has segregated the cash receipt duties as follows. Knox opens the mail and prepares a triplicate list of money received. She sends one copy of the list to Patton, the cashier, who deposits the receipts daily in the bank. Diamond, the recordkeeper, receives a copy of the list and posts payments to patients' accounts. About once a month the office clerks have an expensive lunch they pay for as follows. First, Patton endorses a patient's check in Dr. Conrad's name and cashes it at the bank. Knox then destroys the remittance advice accompanying the check. Finally, Diamond posts payment to the customer's account as a miscellaneous credit. The three justify their actions by their relatively low pay and knowledge that Dr. Conrad will likely never miss the money.

Required

1. Who is the best person in Dr. Conrad's office to reconcile the bank statement?

2. Would a bank reconciliation uncover this office fraud?

3. What are some procedures to detect this type of fraud?

4. Suggest additional controls that Dr. Conrad could implement.

BTN 8-3   You make a surprise count of a $300 petty cash fund. You arrive at the petty cashier when she is on the telephone. She politely asks that you return after lunch so that she can finish her business on the telephone. You agree and return after lunch. In the petty cashbox, you find 14 new $20 bills with consecutive serial numbers plus receipts totaling $20. What is your evaluation?

WORKPLACE COMMUNICATION
LO4

Required

Explain your evaluation. Provide a response in memorandum format.

BTN 8-4   Visit the Association of Certified Fraud Examiners Website at acfe.com. Review the cash frauds (refer to the 2008 *Report to the Nation;* see Fraud resource center—under publications—and answer the following questions.

TAKING IT TO THE NET
LO1   LO2   LO3

Required

1. What percentage of asset misappropriation schemes involve cash?
2. Fraudsters who steal cash generally must access the money at one of three points within the victim's organization. What are the three points?
3. What are the five types of fraudulent disbursement schemes? What is the most common form of cash scheme? Which type of fraudulent disbursements has the high median dollar loss per occurrence?

BTN 8-5   Refer to the chapter opener on **Wildflower Linens**. Identify and describe several cash controls that Wildflower Linens likely uses.

ENTREPRENEURS IN BUSINESS
LO2   LO3

1. e; The entry follows.

Debits to expenses (or assets)	420
Cash Over and Short	5
Cash	425

4. c
5. d

ANSWERS TO MULTIPLE CHOICE QUIZ

2. a; recognizes cash collection of note by bank.
3. a; the bank reconciliation follows.

Bank Reconciliation November 30			
Balance per bank statement	$1,895	Balance per books	$1,742
Add: Deposit in transit	795	Add: Note collected (net fee)	320
Deduct: Outstanding checks	(638)	Deduct: Service charge	(10)
Reconciled balance	$2,052	Reconciled balance	$2,052

A Look Back

Chapter 8 focused on cash. We showed how petty cash systems, bank reconciliations, and banking activities can help the business owner control cash.

A Look at This Chapter

This chapter emphasizes employee payroll. We show how to compute payroll deductions to comply with laws. We also show how the employer uses a payroll register and employee earnings records to record and control its payroll.

A Look Ahead

Chapter 10 explains how the employer pays taxes. It also shows the tax documents the employer must file to comply with laws.

Chapter 9

Employee Earnings, Deductions, and Payroll

Learning Objectives

LO 1	Describe the laws that affect employee payroll.
LO 2	Compute employee gross pay.
LO 3	Compute employee deductions for taxes and net pay.
LO 4	Record employee payroll information in a payroll register.
LO 5	Journalize payroll transactions in a general journal.
LO 6	Prepare an earnings record for each employee.
LO 7	Explain how an employer can control payroll.

"Get a clear vision and stick to it"
—Jason Osborn

Granola Gurus

NEW YORK—Jason Osborn never planned to be an entrepreneur. "It was sort of an accident," explains Osborn. "I was looking for a healthy snack food as an alternative to cookies and brownies." Osborn started cooking with granola and his concoctions caught on. After sharing it with his buddy, Jason Wright, the two decided to launch **Feed Granola Company (FeedGranola.com),** a provider of granola snacks made with organic multi-grains.

"We started peddling it . . . to a few different coffee shops and one natural health food store," recalls Osborn. "That created a small demand and we realized we had a viable product." Adds Wright, "I had no idea that I would have a granola company one day!" Their commitment to healthy food carries over to the financial side. The two especially focus on the important task of managing liabilities for payroll, supplies, employee benefits, vacations, training, and taxes. Both insist that effective management of liabilities, especially payroll and employee benefits, is crucial to success. They stress that monitoring and controlling payroll costs are a must.

To help control costs, Osborn describes how they began by trading their granola products for kitchen space. "We partnered with a meal delivery service and bartered to use their kitchen space," explains Osborn. "We'd bake our granola during the night when they weren't using it and we paid for the usage in granola. That's how we paid rent."

The two continue to monitor liabilities and their payment patterns. "Trying to balance receivables versus payables is always a big challenge," explains Wright. "When you are a small, growing company, cash flow is always a problem." The two insist that accounting for and monitoring payroll costs, the labor laws, and payroll taxes are key to a successful startup. Their company now generates sufficient income to pay for liabilities and produces revenue growth for expansion. "We want to expand our product line," says Osborn. "[Soon] we'll be available in almost every region of the country."

[Sources: *Feed Granola Website,* January 2009; *BusinessWeek,* September 2007; *Inc.com,* July and October 2007; *The Wall Street Journal,* May 2008]

In this chapter we discuss the laws that require the employer to withhold amounts from employee pay for taxes. These amounts are additional liabilities in the journal entry to record wages. We also show how the employer can use payroll registers and employee earnings records to comply with laws and control payroll expenses.

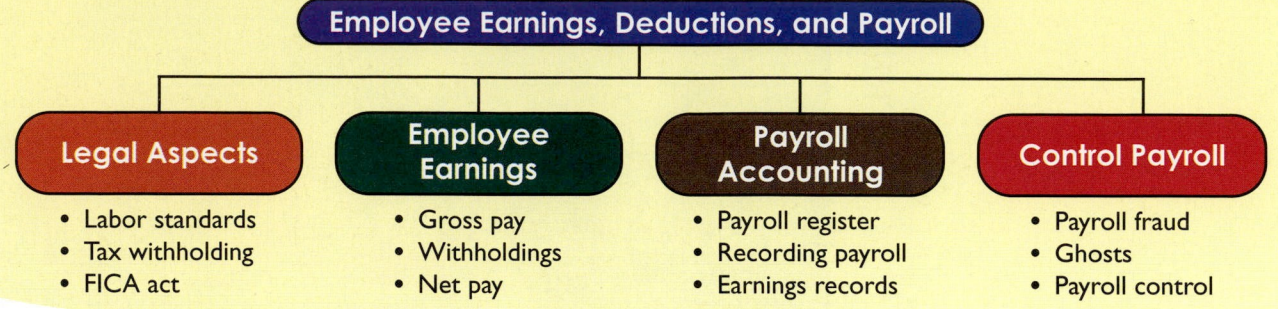

Employee Earnings, Deductions, and Payroll

Legal Aspects	Employee Earnings	Payroll Accounting	Control Payroll
• Labor standards • Tax withholding • FICA act	• Gross pay • Withholdings • Net pay	• Payroll register • Recording payroll • Earnings records	• Payroll fraud • Ghosts • Payroll control

Legal Aspects of Employee Payroll

Most employees and employers pay federal and state payroll taxes. Laws require employers to also prepare and submit reports that explain how they computed tax payments. Governments can impose penalties if the employer does not follow payroll tax laws. Law requires employers to withhold amounts from employees' pay for taxes. An **employee** is someone whose work is under the direction of the employer, such as a bookkeeper or secretary. The employer controls what work the employee is to do and how it should be done. For example, employees are typically trained to perform tasks a certain way. An **independent contractor** performs a job for the employer, but decides how to do the work. Independent contractors typically do not receive training from the employer. The employer does not withhold any money for taxes for independent contractors. Using independent contractors can help businesses lower their payroll costs. However, the employer must be careful in classifying employees as independent contractors to withstand potential audit by the Internal Revenue Service.

Fair Labor Standards Act

LO1 Describe the laws that affect employee payroll.

This law applies to firms engaged in business across states. It sets a minimum wage, currently $7.25 per hour (as of July 24, 2009), and sets 40 hours as the most an employee can be required to work in a week at the normal pay rate. Employees that work more than 40 hours in a week receive overtime pay. This pay is at least one and one-half times their normal pay rate for those overtime hours.

Federal and State Income Tax Withholding

Each employee fills out an **Employee's Withholding Allowance Certificate (Form W-4)** as shown in Exhibit 9.1. The employer withholds a different amount of federal taxes for each employee. These amounts depend on the employee's marital status, his or her **gross pay,** and the number of withholding allowances the employee claims. Gross pay is the total amount an employee earns before deductions such as taxes. A **withholding allowance** lowers the amount of an employee's gross pay that is taxed. Each employee gets one personal allowance, one for a spouse if they are married, and one for each child or dependent. The more allowances an employee claims, the less tax the employer withholds.

For example, Robert Austin is an employee of Phoenix Sales and Service, a landscape design company. He is single (box 3) and has no dependents. He chooses one withholding allowance (box 5) and elects to have no additional amounts withheld from his paycheck (box 6). Employees who did not pay any taxes in the previous year and do not expect to pay taxes in the current year do not have taxes withheld from their paychecks. They write "Exempt" in box 7 on their W-4.

Exhibit 9.1

Employee's Withholding
Allowance Certificate (W-4)

Form W-4 — Employee's Withholding Allowance Certificate

Cut here and give Form W-4 to your employer. Keep the top part for your records.

OMB No. 1545-0010

▶ Whether you are entitled to claim a certain number of allowances or exemption from withholding is subject to review by the IRS. Your employer may be required to send a copy of this form to the IRS.

1. Type or print your first name and middle initial: **Robert J.**   Last name: **Austin**
2. Your social security number: **333 22 9999**

3. ☑ Single ☐ Married ☐ Married, but withhold at higher Single rate.
Note. If married, but legally separated, or spouse is a nonresident alien, check the "Single" box.

Home address (number and street or rural route): **18 Roosevelt Blvd., Apt. C**

City or town, state, and ZIP code: **Tempe, AZ 86322**

4. If your last name differs from that shown on your social security card, check here. You must call 1-800-772-1213 for a new card. ▶ ☐

5. Total number of allowances you are claiming (from line H above or from the applicable worksheet on page 2) ... 5 | **1**
6. Additional amount, if any, you want withheld from each paycheck ... 6 | **$0**
7. I claim exemption from withholding for 2009, and I certify that I meet both of the following conditions for exemption.
   • Last year I had a right to a refund of all federal income tax withheld because I had no tax liability and
   • This year I expect a refund of all federal income tax withheld because I expect to have no tax liability.
   If you meet both conditions, write "Exempt" here ... ▶ 7

Under penalties of perjury, I declare that I have examined this certificate and to the best of my knowledge and belief, it is true, correct, and complete.

Employee's signature (Form is not valid unless you sign it.) ▶ **Robert J. Austin**   Date ▶ **01/01/09**

8. Employer's name and address [Employer. Complete lines 8 and 10 only if sending to the IRS.): **Phoenix Sales & Service, 1214 Mill Road, Phoenix, AZ 85621**
9. Office code (optional)
10. Employer identification number (EIN): **86 3214587**

For Privacy Act and Paperwork Reduction Act Notice, see page 2.   Cat. No. 102200   Form W-4 (2009)

Federal Insurance Contributions Act (FICA)

The federal Social Security system pays benefits to qualified workers. Employers usually separate **FICA** taxes into two groups: (1) retirement, disability, and survivors, and (2) medical. The first group is called *Social Security benefits* and it is paid for with *Social Security taxes*. The second group is called *Medicare benefits* and it is paid for with *Medicare taxes*.

Law requires employers to withhold FICA taxes from employees to pay for this system. For the year 2009, the amount withheld from each employee's pay for Social Security taxes is 6.2% of the first $106,800 the employee earns during the calendar year. The most an individual employee could pay for Social Security tax in 2009 is $6,621.60 (0.062 × $106,800). The Medicare tax for 2009 is 1.45% of *all* amounts the employee earns. There is no upper limit on the amount of Medicare tax an employee could pay. For any changes in tax rates or maximum earnings levels, check the IRS Website at **www.IRS.gov** or the Social Security Administration Website at **www.SSA.gov**.

To illustrate the calculation of the Social Security and Medicare (FICA) taxes, assume the following income for Kelly Wheeler:

	Gross Earnings	
Pay Period	Current	Year-to-Date
December 5–11, 2009	$2,100	$105,850
December 12–18, 2009	2,150	108,000

During the pay period December 12–18, 2009, Wheeler's earnings for the calendar year went over the $106,800 Social Security maximum earnings limit by $1,200:

Year-to-date earnings	$108,000
Social Security earnings maximum for 2009	106,800
Portion of Kelly's December 12–18, 2009, earnings not subject to Social Security tax......................	$ 1,200

Therefore, $1,200 of his earnings would not be subject to the Social Security tax. The Social Security tax on Wheeler's December 12–18, 2009, earnings would be:

Gross earnings.	$2,150.00
Portion of Kelly's earnings not subject to Social Security tax	1,200.00
Portion of Kelly's earnings subject to Social Security tax.	$ 950.00
Social Security tax rate	6.2%
Social Security tax.	$ 58.90

All earnings are subject to the Medicare tax. Therefore, the Social Security tax on Wheeler's December 12–18, 2009, earnings would be:

Gross earnings	$2,150.00
Medicare tax rate	1.45%
Medicare tax	$ 31.18

Kelly Wheeler's total Social Security and Medicare (FICA) taxes for the December 12–18, 2009, pay period would be:

Social Security tax.	$58.90
Medicare tax	31.18
Total Social Security and Medicare taxes	$90.08

Self–Employment Tax Persons who operate their own businesses as sole proprietors or independent contractors pay **self-employment tax.** A self-employed person must pay both the employee and employer FICA taxes. The self-employment tax rates are 12.4% (6.2% × 2) for Social Security and 2.9% (1.45% × 2) for Medicare. So, the most a self-employed person could pay for Social Security taxes in 2009 is $13,243.20 (2 × 0.062 × $106,800). There is no upper limit on the amount of Medicare tax a self-employed person could pay. Currently, people who earn $400 or more from self-employment must pay self-employment tax. This also applies to individuals who operate a part-time business in addition to a regular job.

Employee Earnings and Withholdings

Three steps are needed to determine how much to pay an employee each pay period:

1. Compute employee gross pay.
2. Determine the total amount of withholdings to deduct from gross pay.
3. Compute net pay by subtracting total withholdings from gross pay.

This section explains how we compute employee gross pay and net pay, and how withholdings impact employee pay.

Compute Employee Gross Pay

LO2 Compute employee gross pay.

Generally, management and administrative workers receive a salary. A **salary** is a fixed amount of compensation paid or received on a regular basis—every two weeks, monthly, or annually. Skilled or unskilled labor generally receive wages. **Wages** are money paid or received for work or services by the hour, day, or week or by the number of units produced.

Many employers pay wages for each hour worked. The employer must keep records of the number of hours each employee works on each day during a pay period. This can be done with a time sheet or a time clock. For example, see Exhibit 9.2 for Robert Austin's time sheet for the week ending January 7, 2009.

Exhibit 9.2

Employee Time Sheet

Time Sheet

EMPLOYEE ID No.	EMPLOYEE NAME	WEEK ENDING
AR101	Robert Austin	January 7, 2009

DAY	TIME IN	TIME OUT	TIME IN	TIME OUT	HOURS WORKED REGULAR	HOURS WORKED OVERTIME
Mon	7:30	11:30	12:30	4:30	8	
Tues	8:05	12:00	1:00	5:05	8	
Wed	8:00	12:00	12:30	4:30	8	
Thurs	7:45	11:45	12:45	4:45	8	
Fri	7:15	12:15	12:45	3:45	8	
				Total Hours	40	

Enter your time in HH:MM format

If Robert Austin earns a wage of $10 per hour worked, his gross pay for the week of January 7, 2009, is $400 (40 × $10). John Diaz, another employee of Phoenix Sales and Service, turns in a time card for the week of January 7, 2009, that shows he worked 40 regular hours and 2 overtime hours. If John Diaz's normal pay rate is $14 per hour, and he is paid one and one-half times his normal pay rate for overtime, his gross pay for the week ending January 7, 2009, is computed as:

Regular pay	40 hours × $14 per hour =	$560
Overtime premium	2 hours × $21 per hour =	42
Total gross pay		$602

Compute Withholdings from Employee Gross Pay

Payroll deductions, commonly called *withholdings,* are amounts withheld from an employee's gross pay. Required deductions result from law and include income taxes and Social Security taxes. Voluntary deductions, at an employee's option, include pension and health contributions, union dues, and charitable giving. Exhibit 9.3 summarizes the typical employee payroll deductions.

LO3 Compute employee deductions for taxes and net pay.

Exhibit 9.3

Payroll Deductions

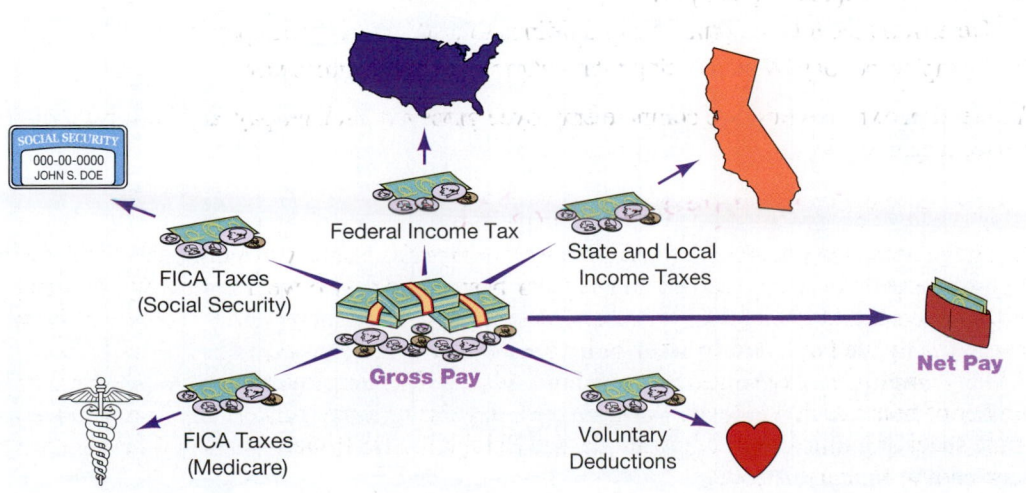

Federal Income Tax Withholding   The employer uses a withholding table (called **Circular E**) from the IRS to compute the amount of federal taxes to withhold. Circular E is available for free from **www.IRS.gov**. Separate withholding tables are provided for single or married persons, and for different pay periods (for example, weekly or monthly). Exhibit 9.4 provides a part of a

Exhibit 9.4

Withholding Table Example—
Single Persons Paid Weekly

SINGLE Persons—WEEKLY Payroll Period
(For Wages Paid Through December 2009)

If the wages are—		And the number of withholding allowances claimed is—										
At least	But less than	0	1	2	3	4	5	6	7	8	9	10
		The amount of income tax to be withheld is—										
$400	$410	$37	$26	$16	$6	$0	$0	$0	$0	$0	$0	$0
410	420	38	28	17	7	0	0	0	0	0	0	0
420	430	40	29	19	8	1	0	0	0	0	0	0
430	440	41	31	20	10	2	0	0	0	0	0	0
440	450	43	32	22	11	3	0	0	0	0	0	0
450	460	44	34	23	13	4	0	0	0	0	0	0
460	470	46	35	25	14	5	0	0	0	0	0	0
470	480	47	37	26	16	6	0	0	0	0	0	0
480	490	49	38	28	17	7	0	0	0	0	0	0
490	500	50	40	29	19	8	0	0	0	0	0	0
500	510	52	41	31	20	10	1	0	0	0	0	0
510	520	53	43	32	22	11	3	0	0	0	0	0
520	530	55	44	34	23	13	4	0	0	0	0	0
530	540	56	46	35	25	14	5	0	0	0	0	0
540	550	58	47	37	26	16	6	0	0	0	0	0
550	560	59	49	38	28	17	7	0	0	0	0	0
560	570	61	50	40	29	19	8	1	0	0	0	0
570	580	62	52	41	31	20	10	2	0	0	0	0
580	590	64	53	43	32	22	11	3	0	0	0	0
590	600	65	55	44	34	23	13	4	0	0	0	0
600	610	67	56	46	35	25	14	5	0	0	0	0
610	620	68	58	47	37	26	16	6	0	0	0	0
620	630	70	59	49	38	28	17	7	0	0	0	0
630	640	71	61	50	40	29	19	8	1	0	0	0
640	650	73	62	52	41	31	20	10	2	0	0	0
650	660	74	64	53	43	32	22	11	3	0	0	0
660	670	76	65	55	44	34	23	13	4	0	0	0
670	680	77	67	56	46	35	25	14	5	0	0	0
680	690	79	68	58	47	37	26	16	6	0	0	0
690	700	80	70	59	49	38	28	17	7	0	0	0
700	710	83	71	61	50	40	29	19	8	1	0	0
710	720	85	73	62	52	41	31	20	10	2	0	0
720	730	88	74	64	53	43	32	22	11	3	0	0
730	740	90	76	65	55	44	34	23	13	4	0	0
740	750	93	77	67	56	46	35	25	14	5	0	0
800	810	108	90	76	65	55	44	34	23	13	4	0
810	820	110	93	77	67	56	46	35	25	14	5	0
820	830	113	95	79	68	58	47	37	26	16	6	0
830	840	115	98	80	70	59	49	38	28	17	7	0
840	850	118	100	83	71	61	50	40	29	19	8	1
900	910	133	115	98	80	70	59	49	38	28	17	7
910	920	135	118	100	83	71	61	50	40	29	19	8
920	930	138	120	103	85	73	62	52	41	31	20	10
930	940	140	123	105	88	74	64	53	43	32	22	11
940	950	143	125	108	90	76	65	55	44	34	23	13
950	960	145	128	110	93	77	67	56	46	35	25	14
960	970	148	130	113	95	79	68	58	47	37	26	16
970	980	150	133	115	98	80	70	59	49	38	28	17
980	990	153	135	118	100	83	71	61	50	40	29	19
990	1,000	155	138	120	103	85	73	62	52	41	31	20
1,010	1,020	160	143	125	108	90	76	65	55	44	34	23
1,020	1,030	163	145	128	110	93	77	67	56	46	35	25
1,030	1,040	165	148	130	113	95	79	68	58	47	37	26
1,040	1,050	168	150	133	115	98	80	70	59	49	38	28
1,050	1,060	170	153	135	118	100	83	71	61	50	40	29
1,060	1,070	173	155	138	120	103	85	73	62	52	41	31
1,070	1,080	175	158	140	123	105	88	74	64	53	43	32
1,080	1,090	178	160	143	125	108	90	76	65	55	44	34
1,090	1,100	180	163	145	128	110	93	77	67	56	46	35
1,100	1,110	183	165	148	130	113	95	79	68	58	47	37
1,110	1,120	185	168	150	133	115	98	80	70	59	49	38
1,120	1,130	188	170	153	135	118	100	83	71	61	50	40
1,130	1,140	190	173	155	138	120	103	85	73	62	52	41
1,140	1,150	193	175	158	140	123	105	88	74	64	53	43
1,150	1,160	195	178	160	143	125	108	90	76	65	55	44
1,160	1,170	198	180	163	145	128	110	93	77	67	56	46
1,170	1,180	200	183	165	148	130	113	95	79	68	58	47
1,180	1,190	203	185	168	150	133	115	98	80	70	59	49
1,190	1,200	205	188	170	153	135	118	100	82	71	61	50
1,200	1,210	208	190	173	155	138	120	103	85	73	62	52
1,210	1,220	210	193	175	158	140	123	105	87	74	64	53
1,220	1,230	213	195	178	160	143	125	108	90	76	65	55
1,230	1,240	215	198	180	163	145	128	110	92	77	67	56
1,240	1,250	218	200	183	165	148	130	113	95	79	68	58

Exhibit 9.5

Withholding Table Example—
Married Persons Paid Weekly

MARRIED Persons—WEEKLY Payroll Period
(For Wages Paid Through December 2009)

If the wages are—		And the number of withholding allowances claimed is—										
At least	But less than	0	1	2	3	4	5	6	7	8	9	10
		The amount of income tax to be withheld is—										
$400	$410	$10	$3	$0	$0	$0	$0	$0	$0	$0	$0	$0
410	420	11	4	0	0	0	0	0	0	0	0	0
420	430	12	5	0	0	0	0	0	0	0	0	0
430	440	13	6	0	0	0	0	0	0	0	0	0
440	450	14	7	0	0	0	0	0	0	0	0	0
450	460	15	8	1	0	0	0	0	0	0	0	0
460	470	16	9	2	0	0	0	0	0	0	0	0
470	480	17	10	3	0	0	0	0	0	0	0	0
480	490	19	11	4	0	0	0	0	0	0	0	0
490	500	20	12	5	0	0	0	0	0	0	0	0
500	510	22	13	6	0	0	0	0	0	0	0	0
510	520	23	14	7	0	0	0	0	0	0	0	0
520	530	25	15	8	1	0	0	0	0	0	0	0
530	540	26	16	9	2	0	0	0	0	0	0	0
540	550	28	17	10	3	0	0	0	0	0	0	0
550	560	29	19	11	4	0	0	0	0	0	0	0
560	570	31	20	12	5	0	0	0	0	0	0	0
570	580	32	22	13	6	0	0	0	0	0	0	0
580	590	34	23	14	7	0	0	0	0	0	0	0
590	600	35	25	15	8	1	0	0	0	0	0	0
600	610	37	26	16	9	2	0	0	0	0	0	0
610	620	38	28	17	10	3	0	0	0	0	0	0
620	630	40	29	19	11	4	0	0	0	0	0	0
630	640	41	31	20	12	5	0	0	0	0	0	0
740	750	58	47	37	26	16	9	2	0	0	0	0
750	760	59	49	38	28	17	10	3	0	0	0	0
760	770	61	50	40	29	19	11	4	0	0	0	0
770	780	62	52	41	31	20	12	5	0	0	0	0
780	790	64	53	43	32	22	13	6	0	0	0	0
790	800	65	55	44	34	23	14	7	0	0	0	0
800	810	67	56	46	35	25	15	8	1	0	0	0
810	820	68	58	47	37	26	16	9	2	0	0	0
820	830	70	59	49	38	28	17	10	3	0	0	0
830	840	71	61	50	40	29	19	11	4	0	0	0
840	850	73	62	52	41	31	20	12	5	0	0	0
850	860	74	64	53	43	32	22	13	6	0	0	0
860	870	76	65	55	44	34	23	14	7	0	0	0
870	880	77	67	56	46	35	25	15	8	1	0	0
880	890	79	68	58	47	37	26	16	9	2	0	0
890	900	80	70	59	49	38	28	17	10	3	0	0
900	910	82	71	61	50	40	29	19	11	4	0	0
910	920	83	73	62	52	41	31	20	12	5	0	0
920	930	85	74	64	53	43	32	22	13	6	0	0
930	940	86	76	65	55	44	34	23	14	7	0	0
940	950	88	77	67	56	46	35	25	15	8	1	0
950	960	89	79	68	58	47	37	26	16	9	2	0
960	970	91	80	70	59	49	38	28	17	10	3	0
970	980	92	82	71	61	50	40	29	19	11	4	0
980	990	94	83	73	62	52	41	31	20	12	5	0
990	1,000	95	85	74	64	53	43	32	22	13	6	0
1,000	1,010	97	86	76	65	55	44	34	23	14	7	0
1,010	1,020	98	88	77	67	56	46	35	25	15	8	1
1,020	1,030	100	89	79	68	58	47	37	26	16	9	2
1,030	1,040	101	91	80	70	59	49	38	28	17	10	3
1,090	1,100	110	100	89	79	68	58	47	37	26	16	9
1,100	1,110	112	101	91	80	70	59	49	38	28	17	10
1,110	1,120	113	103	92	82	71	61	50	40	29	19	11
1,120	1,130	115	104	94	83	73	62	52	41	31	20	12
1,130	1,140	116	106	95	85	74	64	53	43	32	22	13
1,140	1,150	118	107	97	86	76	65	55	44	34	23	14
1,150	1,160	119	109	98	88	77	67	56	46	35	25	15
1,160	1,170	121	110	100	89	79	68	58	47	37	26	16
1,170	1,180	122	112	101	91	80	70	59	49	38	28	17
1,180	1,190	124	113	103	92	82	71	61	50	40	29	19
1,190	1,200	125	115	104	94	83	73	62	52	41	31	20
1,200	1,210	127	116	106	95	85	74	64	53	43	32	22
1,210	1,220	128	118	107	97	86	76	65	55	44	34	23
1,220	1,230	130	119	109	98	88	77	67	56	46	35	25
1,230	1,240	131	121	110	100	89	79	68	58	47	37	26

Circular E withholding table for single persons paid weekly. Exhibits 9.5, 9.6, and 9.7 show additional excerpts from the withholding table. IRS withholding tables are based on projecting weekly (or other period) pay into an annual amount.

From his W-4 form, Robert Austin is a single employee who claims one withholding allowance. He is paid each week. Robert's gross pay was $400 for the week ending January 7, 2009. To determine Robert's federal tax withholding, use the withholding table in Exhibit 9.4. Scan the "If wages are" columns until "at least $400 but less than $410" is found. This range includes the $400 of income Robert earned this week. Then find the column for 1 withholding allowance and scan down the table to the row found earlier. Based on Robert's gross pay of $400 and his one withholding

Exhibit 9.6

Withholding Table Example—
Single Persons Paid Monthly

SINGLE Persons—MONTHLY Payroll Period
(For Wages Paid Through December 2009)

At least	But less than	0	1	2	3	4	5	6	7	8	9	10
If the wages are—		And the number of withholding allowances claimed is—										
		The amount of income tax to be withheld is—										
1,840	1,880	176	130	85	39	5	0	0	0	0	0	0
1,880	1,920	182	136	91	45	9	0	0	0	0	0	0
1,920	1,960	188	142	97	51	13	0	0	0	0	0	0
1,960	2,000	194	148	103	57	17	0	0	0	0	0	0
2,000	2,040	200	154	109	63	21	0	0	0	0	0	0
2,040	2,080	206	160	115	69	25	0	0	0	0	0	0
2,080	2,120	212	166	121	75	29	0	0	0	0	0	0
2,120	2,160	218	172	127	81	35	2	0	0	0	0	0
2,160	2,200	224	178	133	87	41	6	0	0	0	0	0
2,200	2,240	230	184	139	93	47	10	0	0	0	0	0
2,240	2,280	236	190	145	99	53	14	0	0	0	0	0
2,280	2,320	242	196	151	105	59	18	0	0	0	0	0
2,320	2,360	248	202	157	111	65	22	0	0	0	0	0
2,360	2,400	254	208	163	117	71	26	0	0	0	0	0
2,400	2,440	260	214	169	123	77	32	0	0	0	0	0

Exhibit 9.7

Withholding Table Example—
Married Persons Paid Monthly

MARRIED Persons—MONTHLY Payroll Period
(For Wages Paid Through December 2009)

At least	But less than	0	1	2	3	4	5	6	7	8	9	10
If the wages are—		And the number of withholding allowances claimed is—										
		The amount of income tax to be withheld is—										
$0	$1,320	$0	$0	$0	$0	$0	$0	$0	$0	$0	$0	$0
1,320	1,360	3	0	0	0	0	0	0	0	0	0	0
1,360	1,400	7	0	0	0	0	0	0	0	0	0	0
1,400	1,440	11	0	0	0	0	0	0	0	0	0	0
1,440	1,480	15	0	0	0	0	0	0	0	0	0	0
1,480	1,520	19	0	0	0	0	0	0	0	0	0	0
1,520	1,560	23	0	0	0	0	0	0	0	0	0	0
1,560	1,600	27	0	0	0	0	0	0	0	0	0	0
1,600	1,640	31	0	0	0	0	0	0	0	0	0	0
1,640	1,680	35	4	0	0	0	0	0	0	0	0	0
1,680	1,720	39	8	0	0	0	0	0	0	0	0	0
4,800	4,840	490	444	399	353	307	262	216	171	125	79	47
4,840	4,880	496	450	405	359	313	268	222	177	131	85	51
4,880	4,920	502	456	411	365	319	274	228	183	137	91	55
4,920	4,960	508	462	417	371	325	280	234	189	143	97	59
4,960	5,000	514	468	423	377	331	286	240	195	149	103	63
5,000	5,040	520	474	429	383	337	292	246	201	155	109	67
5,040	5,080	526	480	435	389	343	298	252	207	161	115	71
5,080	5,120	532	486	441	395	349	304	258	213	167	121	76
5,120	5,160	538	492	447	401	355	310	264	219	173	127	82
5,160	5,200	544	498	453	407	361	316	270	225	179	133	88
5,200	5,240	550	504	459	413	367	322	276	231	185	139	94

allowance, Phoenix Sales and Service will withhold $26 for federal taxes from Robert's gross pay for the week of January 7, 2009.

State Income Tax Withholding   States withhold income taxes based on either withholding tables or a percentage of the amount withheld for federal taxes. In our examples we assume the state income tax withholding is 8 percent of the dollar amount withheld for federal income tax. Phoenix Sales and Service will withhold $2.08 (0.08 × $26) from Robert's pay for Arizona state income tax.

FICA Withholding   As of January 7, 2009, Robert Austin has earned less than the $106,800 annual maximum for Social Security taxes. Phoenix Sales and Service will withhold $24.80 (0.062 × $400) from his gross pay for FICA Social Security taxes. Phoenix Sales and Service will also withhold $5.80 (0.0145 × $400) from his gross pay for Medicare taxes.

Voluntary Deductions   The required deductions above result from laws. Employees can choose to have other amounts withheld from their pay. These voluntary deductions can include contributions for retirement and health plans, union dues, and gifts to charity. In this example Robert Austin has not chosen any voluntary deductions.

Compute Net Pay

An employee's **net pay,** also called *take-home pay,* is gross pay minus all withholdings. For the week of January 7, 2009, Robert Austin's net pay is computed as

Gross pay	$400.00
Minus deductions for:	
Federal income tax withholding	(26.00)
State income tax withholding	(2.08)
FICA—Social Security	(24.80)
FICA—Medicare	(5.80)
Net pay	$341.32

IN THE NEWS

A growing number of companies let employees collect their pay in "payroll cards." These cards are like debit cards and allow the employee to withdraw cash from ATMs or make purchases. They are particularly useful for employees who do not have bank accounts or whose small bank account balances would generate high fees. The use of "paperless" payroll can lower payroll processing costs by up to 75%.

HOW YOU DOIN'?   Answers—p. 219

1. A company pays its one employee $3,000 per month. This company's Social Security tax rate is 6.2% of the first $106,800; and its Medicare tax rate is 1.45% of all amounts earned. The company's March payroll will include what amount for employee Social Security and Medicare taxes?

2. Identify whether the employer or employee or both incur each of the following: (a) FICA taxes, and (b) withheld income taxes.

3. An employee worked 45 hours in a pay period. She earns $16 per hour and one and one-half her normal hourly wage for all overtime hours. What is her gross pay?

Payroll Accounting

This section describes payroll accounting, including the purpose and importance of a payroll register, the recording of payroll, and the use of banking services in dispensing payroll.

Payroll Register

A **payroll register** is often used to keep a record of pay period dates, hours worked, gross pay, deductions, and net pay of each employee for each pay period. Exhibit 9.8 shows the payroll register for Phoenix Sales and Service as of January 7, 2009. For each employee, the register includes whether they are single (S) or married (M) and the number of withholding allowances they chose on their Form W-4. This information is used with each employee's gross pay, and the withholding tables from Circular E, to determine the correct amount of tax to withhold for federal income taxes. This amount is reported in the "Federal Income Tax" column. In our example, withholdings for state purposes are 8% of the amount withheld for federal income tax; the amount is shown in the "State Income Tax" column in the payroll register.

Phoenix Sales and Service collects time sheets from each of its employees, verifies their accuracy, and records the number of hours worked in the "Hours Worked This Pay Period" column. Each employee's hourly wage is entered into the "Hourly Wage" column, and employee gross earnings (regular and overtime) are computed as we showed earlier for Robert Austin and John Diaz.

The payroll register also reports the gross pay used to compute Social Security, Medicare, and the employer's unemployment taxes (in the "Taxable Earnings For" columns). These amounts can be different. For example, once an employee has earned at least $7,000 during a year, the employer stops paying unemployment tax for that employee. (We discuss employer payroll taxes, including

LO4 Record employee payroll information in a payroll register.

Only employers pay unemployment taxes.

Exhibit 9.8

Phoenix Sales and Service Payroll Register for Week Ended January 7, 2009

Payroll Register

Employee Name	Marital Status and Allowances	Beginning Cumulative Gross Earnings	Hours Worked This Pay Period	Hourly Wage	EARNINGS THIS PERIOD			Ending Cumulative Gross Earnings
					Regular	Overtime	Gross	
Austin, Robert	S-1	0.00	40	10.00	400.00	00.00	400.00	400.00
Cross, Judy	S-2	0.00	41	14.00	560.00	21.00	581.00	581.00
Diaz, John	M-0	0.00	42	14.00	560.00	42.00	602.00	602.00
Kiefe, Kay	M-2	0.00	40	14.00	560.00	00.00	560.00	560.00
Miller, Lee	M-0	0.00	40	14.00	560.00	00.00	560.00	560.00
Sears, Dale	S-0	0.00	40	14.00	560.00	00.00	560.00	560.00
Total					3,200.00	63.00	3,263.00	3,263.00

TAXABLE EARNINGS FOR			EMPLOYEE DEDUCTIONS FOR				PAYMENT INFORMATION	
Social Security	Medicare	Unemployment	Social Security	Medicare	Federal Income Tax	State Income Tax	Net Pay	Check Number
400.00	400.00	400.00	24.80	5.80	26.00	2.08	341.32	9001
581.00	581.00	581.00	36.02	8.42	43.00	3.44	490.12	9002
602.00	602.00	602.00	37.32	8.73	37.00	2.96	515.99	9003
560.00	560.00	560.00	34.72	8.12	12.00	0.96	504.20	9004
560.00	560.00	560.00	34.72	8.12	31.00	2.48	483.68	9005
560.00	560.00	560.00	34.72	8.12	61.00	4.88	451.28	9006
3,263.00	3,263.00	3,263.00	202.30	47.31	210.00	16.80	2,786.59	

unemployment, in the next chapter.) The employer also stops withholding Social Security tax for any employee who has earned at least $106,800 during the year.

Since this is the first pay period of the year for Phoenix Sales and Service, none of its employees has reached these income maximums. Social Security taxes are entered for each employee in the "Social Security" column. Medicare taxes are entered for each employee in the "Medicare" column. Finally, each employee's net pay (gross pay minus all deductions) is computed and reported in the "Net Pay" column.

Recording and Settling Payroll

LO5 Journalize payroll transactions in a general journal.

The payroll register provides the data to prepare the journal entry to record the payroll in the general ledger accounts. For the pay period ending January 7, 2009, Phoenix Sales and Service records the following journal entry in the general journal.

Assets = Liabilities + Equity
+202.30   −3,263.00
+47.31
+210.00
+16.80
+2,786.59

Jan.	7	Wage Expense	3 2 6 3 00	
		FICA—Social Security Taxes Payable (6.2%)		2 0 2 30
		FICA—Medicare Taxes Payable (1.45%)		4 7 31
		Employee Federal Income Taxes Payable		2 1 0 00
		Employee State Income Taxes Payable		1 6 80
		Accrued Wages Payable		2 7 8 6 59
		To record payroll for week ending January 7.		

Paying Employees   To safeguard its cash, Phoenix Sales and Service should pay its employees by check or electronic funds transfer. Exhibit 9.9 shows the *payroll check* for Robert Austin. Included with the check is a detachable *statement of earnings* that shows Robert's gross pay, deductions, and net pay. Robert Austin should keep this statement of earnings for his records and deposit his paycheck in a bank. The payroll clerk enters the check number (9001) in the payroll register.

Companies with few employees often pay them with checks drawn on the company's regular bank account. Companies with many employees often use a special **payroll bank account** to pay employees. The payroll bank account is only used to pay employee payroll. If a payroll bank account is used, the company either (1) draws one check for the total payroll on the regular bank account and deposits it in the payroll bank account or (2) electronically transfers funds to the payroll bank account. Individual employee payroll checks are then drawn on the payroll bank account. This helps control the company's cash and helps in reconciling the regular bank account.

EMPLOYEE NO.	EMPLOYEE NAME		SOCIAL SECURITY NO.	PAY PERIOD END	CHECK DATE
AR101	Robert Austin		333-22-9999	1/7/09	1/7/09

ITEM	RATE	HOURS	TOTAL	ITEM	THIS CHECK	YEAR TO DATE
Regular	10.00	40.00	400.00	Gross	400.00	400.00
				Fed. Income tax	-26.00	-26.00
				FICA-Soc. Sec.	-24.80	-24.80
				FICA-Medicare	-5.80	-5.80
				State Income tax	-2.08	-2.08

HOURS WORKED	GROSS THIS PERIOD	GROSS YEAR TO DATE	NET CHECK	CHECK No.
40.00	400.00	400.00	$329.44	9001

(Detach and retain for your records)

PHOENIX SALES & SERVICE
1214 Mill Road
Phoenix, AZ 85621
602-555-8900

Phoenix Bank and Trust
Phoenix, AZ 85621
3312-87044

9001

CHECK NO.	DATE	AMOUNT
9001	Jan 7, 2009	***************$341.32*

Three Hundred Forty–One and 32/100 Dollars

PAY TO THE ORDER OF
Robert Austin
18 Roosevelt Blvd., Apt C
Tempe, AZ 86322

Mary Wills
AUTHORIZED SIGNATURE

Exhibit 9.9

Payroll Check and Statement of Earnings

Paying Employees from the Regular Bank Account

Each Phoenix Sales and Service employee will receive a check for net pay. If the employees are paid from the company's regular checking account, the company makes the following entry in the general journal.

Jan.	7	Accrued Wages Payable	2786 59		
		Cash—R. Austin		341 32
		Cash—J. Cross		490 12
		Cash—J. Diaz		515 99
		Cash—K. Kiefe		504 20
		Cash—L. Miller		483 68
		Cash—D. Sears		451 28
		To pay payroll for pay period ending January 7, 2009.		

Assets = Liabilities + Equity
−341.32   −2,786.59
−490.12
−515.99
−504.20
−483.68
−451.28

Paying Employees from a Special Payroll Bank Account

If instead Phoenix Sales and Service uses a special payroll bank account, the following journal entries will be made in the general journal.

Jan.	7	Cash—Payroll Bank Account	2786 59		
		Cash		2786 59
		To transfer cash to the payroll bank account.		
Jan.	7	Accrued Wages Payable	2786 59		
		Cash—Payroll Bank Account		2786 59
		To pay payroll for pay period ending January 7, 2009.		

Assets = Liabilities + Equity
+2,786.59
−2,786.59

Assets = Liabilities + Equity
−2,786.59   −2,786.59

HOW YOU DOIN'?   Answers—p. 219

4. What two items determine the amount deducted from an employee's wages for federal income taxes?

5. What amount of income tax is withheld from the salary of an employee who is single with three withholding allowances and earnings of $645 in a week? (*Hint:* Use the wage bracket withholding table from Exhibit 9.4.)

6. Which of the following steps are executed when a company draws one check for total payroll and deposits it in a special payroll bank account? (*a*) Write a check to the payroll bank account for the total payroll and record it with a debit to Accrued Wages Payable and a credit to Cash. (*b*) Deposit a check (or transfer funds) for the total payroll in the payroll bank account. (*c*) Issue individual payroll checks drawn on the payroll bank account. (*d*) All of the above.

Employee Earnings Records

LO6 Prepare an earnings record for each employee.

Law requires employers to maintain **employee earnings records.** These records summarize each employee's earnings, deductions, net pay, and total earnings during each calendar year. Information in these records is used to prepare quarterly and annual tax reports (discussed in the next chapter). Exhibit 9.10 provides an employee earnings record for Robert Austin for the month ended March 31, 2009. For this exhibit we assume Robert Austin works 40 hours in each of the 8 weeks from January 1, 2009, through February 24, 2009, and then works 40 hours in each of the four weeks in March. This means his gross pay is $400 each week. The next pay period ends on Sunday, April 1, 2009.

Exhibit 9.10

Employee Earnings Report

PHOENIX SALES AND SERVICE
Employee Earnings Report
For Month Ended March 31, 2009

EMPLOYEE ID No.	EMPLOYEE NAME	EMPLOYEE SS No.
AR101	Austin, Robert	333-22-9999

		EMPLOYEE DEDUCTIONS				
Date	Gross Pay	Federal Income Tax	State Income Tax	FICA-Social Security	FICA-Medicare	Net Pay
Beg. balance	3,200.00	208.00	16.64	198.40	46.40	2,730.56
3/4/2009	400.00	26.00	2.08	24.80	5.80	341.32
3/11/2009	400.00	26.00	2.08	24.80	5.80	341.32
3/18/2009	400.00	26.00	2.08	24.80	5.80	341.32
3/25/2009	400.00	26.00	2.08	24.80	5.80	341.32
Total: 3/4/09 through 3/25/09	1,600.00	104.00	8.32	99.20	23.20	1,365.28
Year-to-date total for Robert Austin	4,800.00	312.00	24.96	297.60	69.60	4,095.84

The amount in the year-to-date gross pay column in each individual employee earnings report is entered into the "Beginning Cumulative Gross Earnings" column of the payroll register in Exhibit 9.8 at the beginning of each pay period. This alerts the accountant of those employees with year-to-date income higher than the maximum amounts for Social Security or unemployment taxes. For example, $4,800 would be entered into the payroll register for the week ending April 1, 2009, for Robert Austin.

Control over Payroll

LO7 Explain how an employer can control payroll.

Payroll activities present important risks for the business owner. First, there are often fines and penalties for not following the many laws impacting payroll. For example, a 100% penalty can be levied, with interest, on any unpaid employee withholding taxes. The government can even close a company, take its assets, and pursue legal actions against those involved. Second, the employer must maintain confidential and sensitive data on employees; for example, their Social Security numbers. Employees can become victims of identity theft if this information falls into the wrong hands. Third, the employer must be careful not to pay employees for hours not worked or to pay fictitious employees. For example, poor controls led the United States Army to pay nearly $10 million to deserters, fictitious soldiers, and other unauthorized entities.

Payroll Fraud

Employee fraud is costly. The Association of Certified Fraud Examiners (**www.acfe.com**) estimates that employee fraud costs small companies more than $190,000 per incident. Many employee frauds involve payroll schemes. Joseph Wells discusses three common types of payroll fraud (*Occupational Fraud and Abuse,* Austin, TX (Obsidian Publishing Co., Inc., 1997) and "Keep Ghosts Off the Payroll," 2002 article at **www.acfe.com**.):

Ghost Employees   A ghost employee is a reference to a name of an individual included on the payroll register who is not an employee of the company. The ghost might be a former employee or a fictitious employee created by a payroll clerk. Wells estimates that the average loss to an employer victimized by a ghost employee payroll fraud is $275,000.

Overstated Hours Worked and Salary Rates   Employees might overstate the number of hours they worked on their time cards. Dishonest payroll clerks might inflate their own or other employees' pay rates. Wells estimates that the average loss to an employer victimized by a false hours or pay rate fraud is $30,000.

Overstated Salespersons' Commissions   Salespeople might overstate the amount of sales they made. Wells estimates that the average loss to an employer victimized by a commission payroll fraud is $200,000.

Payroll Control

Several procedures can help the employer reduce payroll risks. First, the employer must be careful in employee hiring and assign only the most-trusted employees to payroll activities. Second, the employer should review and verify all time sheets. Third, all employee payroll data should be kept in locked files. Only the payroll clerk and the employer should have access to these files. Fourth, any changes to employees' withholdings or voluntary deductions must be supported by authorization forms signed by the employee. The employer must keep these forms in locked files.

   The employer also must separate certain payroll duties. The signer of the payroll checks should verify the data for each employee in the payroll register. Payroll checks should not be distributed by the payroll clerk who prepared them. The payroll clerk should not reconcile the bank account.

HOW YOU DOIN'?   Answer—p. 219

7. What type of payroll fraud has the highest average dollar loss?

Demonstration Problem

A1 Lawns reports the information below related to its employees for the week ending June 7, 2009. A1 pays its employees one and one-half times their normal hourly wage for all hours worked beyond 40 hours per week. Each of A1 Lawns' employees is single.

Employee	Hours Worked	Hourly Wage	Withholding Allowances
S. House	40	$14.25	2
E. James	46	$15.00	2
R. Johnson	44	$12.13	1

Required

1. Compute each employee's gross pay for the week.
2. Compute the amounts A1 Lawns must withhold from its employees' pay for the week ending June 7, 2009, for
   a. Federal income taxes (use wage bracket withholding tables in Exhibit 9.4).
   b. State income taxes (assume A1 Lawns withholds 8% of the amount of federal income taxes withheld).

    c. Social Security taxes. Assume no employee's year-to-date earnings exceed the Social Security maximum.

    d. Medicare taxes.

3. Compute net pay for the week for each employee.

4. Prepare the journal entry to record the payroll for the week.

5. Prepare the journal entry to pay the payroll assuming two separate scenarios:

    a. A1 Lawns does not use a special payroll bank account, and

    b. A1 Lawns uses a special payroll bank account.

Planning the Solution

- For 1, multiply hours worked (up to 40) by the employee's hourly wage, and add to that the product of any hours worked over 40 multiplied by one and one-half times the employee's hourly wage.
- For 2, use wage bracket withholding tables and tax rules to compute each employee's deductions.
- For part 3, for each employee, subtract your answer in part 2 from your answer in part 1.
- For 4 and 5 determine the accounts affected and then record the entries.

Solution to Demonstration Problem

1. Gross pay for each employee is computed as:

S. House	$40 \times \$14.25$	$= \$570.00$
E. James	$(40 \times \$15.00) + (6 \times \$22.50)$	$= \$735.00$
R. Johnson	$(40 \times \$12.13) + (4 \times \$18.20)$	$= \$558.00$

2. Employee deductions:

    a. Withholdings

	Federal Income Tax[a]	State Income Tax[b]	Social Security[c]	Medicare[d]	Total
S. House	$41.00	$3.28	$35.34	$ 8.27	$ 87.89
E. James	65.00	5.20	45.57	10.66	126.43
R. Johnson	49.00	3.92	34.60	8.09	95.61

[a] From federal wage bracket withholding tables in Exhibit 9.4.

[b] Dollar amount withheld for federal income tax $\times$ 8%.

[c] Gross pay $\times$ 6.2%.

[d] Gross pay $\times$ 1.45%.

3. Net pay = Gross pay minus total deductions; computations follow:

S. House	$\$570.00 - \$ 87.89$	$= \$482.11$
E. James	$\$735.00 - \$126.43$	$= \$608.57$
R. Johnson	$\$558.00 - \$ 95.61$	$= \$462.39$

4.

June	7	Wage Expense	1 8 6 3 00	
		FICA—Social Security Taxes Payable (6.2%)		1 1 5 51
		FICA—Medicare Taxes Payable (1.45%)		2 7 02
		Employee Federal Income Taxes Payable		1 5 5 00
		Employee State Income Taxes Payable		1 2 40
		Accrued Wages Payable		1 5 5 3 07
		To record payroll for week ending June 7, 2009.		

5. a. Payroll paid from general bank account.

June	7	Accrued Wages Payable	1 5 5 3 07	
		Cash—S. House		4 8 2 11
		Cash—E. James		6 0 8 57
		Cash—R. Johnson		4 6 2 39
		To pay payroll for pay period ending June 7, 2009.		

b. Payroll paid from special payroll bank account.

June	7	Cash—Payroll Bank Account	1 5 5 3 07	
		Cash		1 5 5 3 07
		To transfer cash to the payroll bank account.		
June	7	Accrued Wages Payable	1 5 5 3 07	
		Cash—Payroll Bank Account.		1 5 5 3 07
		To pay payroll for pay period ending June 7, 2009.		

Summary

LO1 **Describe the laws that affect employee payroll.** Law requires employers to withhold amounts from employee pay for Social Security taxes, Medicare taxes, and for federal and state income taxes.

LO2 **Compute employee gross pay.** Gross pay is the amount of compensation the employee earned during the period before deductions for items like taxes. It is commonly computed as the employee's hourly wage rate multiplied by the number of hours the employee worked during the pay period.

LO3 **Compute employee deductions for taxes and net pay.** Employees pay 6.2% of their gross pay (up to $106,800) for Social Security taxes and 1.45% of their income for Medicare taxes. Based on the number of withholding allowances the employee chooses, the employee's marital status, and gross pay, the employer computes federal and state income tax withholdings from tax tables.

LO4 **Record employee payroll information in a payroll register.** A payroll register is often used to keep a record of pay period dates, hours worked, gross pay, deductions, and net pay of each

employee for each pay period. The payroll register provides information the accountant can use to make journal entries and prepare tax documents.

LO5 **Journalize payroll transactions in a general journal.** The accountant debits Wage Expense for the total gross pay and credits tax liability accounts for amounts owed, and Accrued Wages Payable for employees' net pay. Paying the payroll results in a debit to Accrued Wages Payable and a credit to Cash.

LO6 **Prepare an earnings record for each employee.** Employee earnings records summarize each employee's earnings, deductions, net pay, and total earnings during each calendar year. This information is used in computing taxes and in preparing tax documents required by law.

LO7 **Explain how an employer can control payroll.** The employer can control payroll by hiring trustworthy employees, maintaining confidential records in locked files, and by separating important payroll duties.

Guidance Answers to   HOW YOU DOIN'?

1. $(0.062 \times \$3,000) + (0.0145 \times \$3,000) = \underline{\$229.50}$

2. (*a*) FICA taxes are incurred by both employee and employer. (*b*) Withheld income taxes are incurred by the employee.

3. $(40 \times \$16) + (5 \times \$24) = \$760.$

4. An employee's gross earnings, number of withholding allowances, and marital status determine the deduction for federal income taxes.

5. $41

6. (*d*)

7. The ghost employee scheme, with an average loss of $275,000.

Key Terms

Circular E (p. 210) IRS federal income tax withholding tables.

Employee (p. 206) Someone whose work is under the direction of an employer.

Employee earnings records (p. 216) Record of an employee's net pay, gross pay, deductions, and year-to-date payroll information.

Employee's Withholding Allowance Certificate (Form W-4) (p. 206) A form which shows an employee's withholding allowances.

Federal Insurance Contributions Act (FICA) Taxes (p. 207) Taxes assessed on both employers and employees; for Social Security and Medicare programs.

Gross pay (p. 206) Total compensation earned by an employee.

Independent contractor (p. 206) Someone who does a job for an employer, but decides how to do the work.

Net pay (p. 213) Gross pay less all deductions; also called *take-home pay*.

Payroll bank account (p. 214) Bank account used solely for paying employees; each pay period an amount equal to the total

employees' net pay is deposited in it and the payroll checks are drawn on it.

Payroll deductions (p. 209) Amounts withheld from an employee's gross pay; also called *withholdings*.

Payroll register (p. 213) Record for a pay period that shows the pay period dates, regular and overtime hours worked, gross pay, net pay, and deductions.

Salary (p. 208) A fixed amount of compensation paid or received on a regular basis, such as every two weeks, monthly, or annually.

Self-employment tax (p. 208) Social Security and Medicare taxes for persons who operate their own businesses. Currently, the self-employment tax rates are 12.4% on the first $106,800 of income for Social Security and 2.9% on all income for Medicare.

Wages (p. 208) Money paid or received for work or services by the hour, day, or week or by the number of units produced.

Withholding allowance (p. 206) This determines the amount of federal income taxes to withhold from an employee's pay.

Multiple Choice Quiz   Answers on p. 229   mhhe.com/wildCA2e

Additional Multiple Choice Quizzes are available at the book's Website.

1. An employee earned $50,000 during the year. FICA tax for social security is 6.2% and FICA tax for Medicare is 1.45%. The employee's share of FICA taxes is
   a. Zero, since the employee's pay exceeds the FICA limit.
   b. Zero, since FICA is not an employee tax.
   c. $3,100
   d. $725
   e. $3,825

2. Which of the following taxes is not withheld from employee's pay?
   a. Social security taxes.
   b. Unemployment taxes.
   c. Federal income taxes.
   d. State income taxes.
   e. Medicare taxes.

3. An employee worked 48 hours in the last weekly pay period. She is paid a normal wage of $12 per hour and is paid one and one-half times her normal hourly wage for all hours worked beyond 40 hours. For this pay period her *gross pay* is
   a. $480
   b. $576
   c. $624
   d. $720
   e. $864

4. A single employee claiming 4 withholding allowances earns $710 per week. If she is paid weekly, what amount will be withheld from her pay for federal income tax withholdings? (Use the withholding table in Exhibit 9.4).
   a. $64
   b. $102
   c. $50
   d. $40
   e. $56

5. A company uses a special bank account to pay its payroll. If total gross pay for a pay period was $3,500 and total net pay for the same period was $2,750, the journal entry to pay the payroll will include a
   a. credit to Cash for $3,500.
   b. credit to Cash—Payroll Bank Account for $3,500.
   c. debit to Cash—Payroll Bank Account for $2,750 and a credit to Cash for $2,750.
   d. credit to Cash—Payroll Bank Account for $2,750.
   e. debit to Wage Expense for $2,750 and a credit to Cash for $2,750.

Discussion Questions

1. What is the combined amount (in percent) of the employee and employer Social Security tax rate?

2. What is the current maximum annual level of salary used to compute an employee's Social Security taxes?

3. What is the current Medicare tax rate? This rate is applied to what maximum level of salary and wages?

4. What determines the amount deducted from an employee's wages for federal income taxes?

5. Which payroll taxes are the employee's responsibility and which are the employer's responsibility?

6. What are examples of items employees might voluntarily choose to have deducted from their pay?

7. What is a tax withholding table?

8. What amount of income tax is withheld from the salary of an employee who is single with two withholding allowances and earns $725 per week? What if the employee earned $625 and has no withholding allowances? (Use Exhibit 9.4.)

9. What are employee earnings records? Why do employers maintain employee earnings records?

10. What risks do payroll activities pose for employers?

11. Give three examples of common payroll fraud schemes that are costly to employers.

12. What procedures can an employer use to control payroll fraud?

connect

Compute *gross pay* for each of the following employees. An overtime rate of one and one-half times the normal hourly wage is paid for each hour worked beyond 40 hours.

	Hourly Rate	No. of Hours Worked
Mike Mura	$11	42
Pedro Chavez	$14	50

QUICK STUDY

QS 9–1
Computing gross pay **LO2**

Nouri Hitzu's year-to-date earnings before this pay period were $45,000. Nouri's gross pay for this weekly pay period was $845. What amounts will be withheld from Nouri's pay for this period for federal income taxes? Nouri is married and claims a total of two withholding allowances. Nouri is paid weekly. (Use the tax withholding table in Exhibit 9.5).

QS 9–2
Computing tax withholdings **LO3**

Refer to QS 9-2. What amount must Nouri's employer withhold from Nouri's pay for Social Security (6.2%) taxes and Medicare (1.45%) taxes?

QS 9–3
Computing FICA taxes **LO3**

An employee earned $3,450 for the current period. Calculate the total and individual amounts to be withheld for Social Security (6.2%), Medicare (1.45%), and federal income tax (15%) assuming the entire employee's pay is subject to FICA taxes.

QS 9–4
Computing FICA taxes **LO3**

Dextra Computing's payroll register reports that Ramesh Jain's year-to-date earnings before this weekly pay period were $115,000. Ramesh earned $1,240 this weekly pay period. Ramesh is single and claims one withholding allowance. How much should be withheld from Ramesh's pay for federal income tax withholdings, Social Security taxes, and Medicare taxes? (Use the tax withholding table in Exhibit 9.4.)

QS 9–5
Computing withholdings **LO3**

Major Co. has five employees, each of whom earns $2,500 per month and have been employed since January 1. FICA Social Security taxes are 6.2% of the first $106,800 paid to each employee, and FICA Medicare taxes are 1.45% of gross pay. Federal income tax withholding is 15% of gross pay. State income tax withholding is 8% of the dollar amount withheld for federal income tax purposes. Prepare the March 31 journal entry to record the March wage expense and related liabilities.

QS 9–6
Record employer payroll taxes **LO2 LO3 LO5**

Refer to QS 9-6. Prepare the journal entries to pay the March 31 payroll, assuming Major Co. uses a special payroll bank account.

QS 9–7
Journalize payroll transactions **LO5**

A self-employed worker earned $47,000 during the year. The FICA tax for Social Security is 6.2% and the FICA tax for Medicare is 1.45%. How much should this worker pay for FICA taxes?

QS 9–8
Computing FICA taxes **LO3**

EXERCISES

Exercise 9-1
Computing payroll taxes and
income tax withholdings   **LO3**

BMX Co. has one employee, Keesha Parks, and the company is subject to the following taxes:

Tax	Rate	Applied To
FICA—Social Security	6.20%	First $106,800
FICA—Medicare	1.45	All gross pay

Compute BMX's amounts for FICA taxes and federal income tax withholdings as applied to Keesha's gross earnings for September under each of three separate situations (a), (b), and (c). (Use the withholding tables in Exhibit 9.6 and Exhibit 9.7.).

	Gross Pay through August	Gross Pay for September	Marital Status	Withholding Allowances
a.	$ 6,800	$ 900	M	2
b.	19,200	2,200	S	I
c.	104,800	5,000	M	4

Exercise 9-2
Payroll-related journal entries
LO5

Using the data in situation b of Exercise 9-1, prepare the employer's September 30 journal entries to record (1) salary expense and its related payroll liabilities for this employee and (2) payment of the payroll. BMX does not use a special payroll bank account.

Exercise 9-3
Computing federal tax
withholdings   **LO3**

Use withholding tables from Exhibits 9.4 and 9.5 to compute the amount of federal tax withheld from the weekly pay of the following employees:

Name	Gross Pay	Withholding Allowances	Marital Status
Keisha	$520	I	Single
James	600	3	Single
Tyrell	476	4	Married
Emily	817	2	Married

Exercise 9-4
Net pay and tax computations
LO3

The payroll records of One Click Software show the following information about Keisha LeShon, an employee, for the weekly pay period ending September 30, 2009. LeShon is single and claims one allowance. Compute her Social Security tax (6.2%), Medicare tax (1.45%), federal income tax withholding, state income tax (0.5%), and net pay for the current pay period. The state income tax is 0.5 percent on the first $9,000 earned. (Use the wage bracket withholding table in Exhibit 9.4 for the amount of federal income tax to withhold.)

Total (gross) earnings for current pay period	$ 725
Cumulative earnings of previous pay periods	9,600

Check   Net pay, $595.54

Exercise 9-5
Gross and net pay computation
LO2   LO3

Lucinda Florita, an unmarried employee, works 48 hours in the week ended January 12. Her pay rate is $14 per hour, and her wages are subject to no deductions other than FICA—Social Security, FICA—Medicare, and federal income taxes. She claims two withholding allowances. Compute her regular pay, overtime pay (overtime premium is 50% of the regular rate for hours in excess of 40 per week), and gross pay. Then compute her FICA tax deduction (use 6.2% for the Social Security portion and 1.45% for the Medicare portion), income tax deduction (use the wage bracket withholding table in Exhibit 9.4), total deductions, and net pay.

Check   Net Pay, $608.30

Exercise 9-6
Computing net pay   **LO3**

Phildell Phoenix is paid monthly. For the month of January of the current year, he earned gross pay of $8,288. FICA tax for Social Security is 6.2% and the FICA tax for Medicare is 1.45%. The amount of federal income tax withheld from his earnings was $1,375.17. Phildell contributes $125 of his monthly pay to a retirement plan and has $25 of union dues deducted from his monthly pay. Compute Phildell's net pay for the month.

Match each of the following terms A through G with the appropriate definitions 1 through 7.

A. FICA taxes

B. Payroll register

C. Withholding allowance

D. Gross pay

E. Wage bracket withholding table

F. Net pay

G. Payroll bank account

_____ **1.** A record for a pay period that shows the pay period dates, regular and overtime hours worked, gross pay, net pay, and deductions.

_____ **2.** A special bank account used solely for paying employees; each pay period an amount equal to the total employees' net pay is deposited and the employees' payroll checks are drawn on that account.

_____ **3.** Total compensation earned by an employee.

_____ **4.** Gross pay less all deductions.

_____ **5.** A number that is used to reduce the amount of federal income tax withheld from an employee's pay.

_____ **6.** A table of amounts of income tax to be withheld from employees' wages.

_____ **7.** Taxes assessed on both employer and employees under the Federal Insurance Contributions Act. These taxes fund Social Security and Medicare.

Exercise 9–7
Payroll terms   **L03   L04**

connect

Paloma Co. pays its employees each week. Its employees' gross pay is subject to these taxes:

Tax	Rate	Applied To
FICA—Social Security	6.20%	First $106,800
FICA—Medicare	1.45	All gross pay

The company is preparing its payroll calculations for the week ended August 25. Payroll records show the following information for the company's four employees.

PROBLEM SET A

Problem 9–1A
Payroll expenses, withholdings, and taxes   **L02   L03**

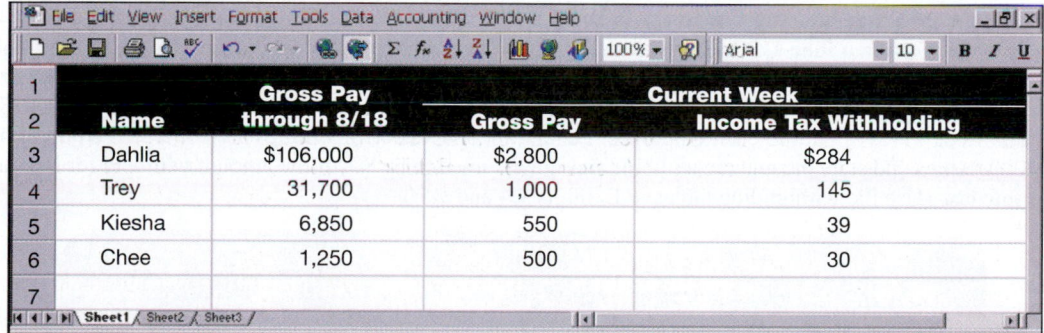

		Gross Pay	Current Week	
	Name	through 8/18	Gross Pay	Income Tax Withholding
3	Dahlia	$106,000	$2,800	$284
4	Trey	31,700	1,000	145
5	Kiesha	6,850	550	39
6	Chee	1,250	500	30

In addition to gross pay, each employee must pay one-half of the $34 per employee weekly health insurance premium. Dahlia contributes 5% of her weekly gross pay to a retirement plan. Trey and Chee each contribute $25 per week to the local United Way.

Required

Compute the following for the week ended August 25 (round amounts to the nearest cent):

1. Each employee's FICA withholdings for Social Security.

2. Each employee's FICA withholdings for Medicare.

3. Each employee's health insurance premium deduction.

4. Each employee's other voluntary deductions.

5. Each employee's net (take-home) pay.

Check   (5) Total net pay, $3,846.97

Problem 9-2A
Entries for payroll transactions
LO3 LO4

On January 8, the end of the first weekly pay period of the year, Regis Company's payroll register showed that its employees earned $22,760 of office salaries and $65,840 of sales salaries. Withholdings from the employees' salaries include FICA Social Security taxes at the rate of 6.2%, FICA Medicare taxes at the rate of 1.45%, $12,860 of federal income taxes, $1,340 of medical insurance deductions, and $840 of union dues.

Required

Check (1) Cr. Accrued Wages Payable, $66,782.10

1. Calculate FICA Social Security taxes payable and FICA Medicare taxes payable. Prepare the journal entry to record Regis Company's January 8 employee payroll expenses and liabilities.
2. Prepare the journal entry to pay the January 8 payroll. Regis uses a special payroll bank account.

Problem 9-3A
Payroll entries, deductions, and net pay
LO1 LO2 LO3 LO5

The payroll records of Swift Company provided the following data for the weekly pay period ended December 7:

Employee	Earnings to End of Previous Week	Gross Pay	Marital Status	No. of Allowances	Medical Insurance Deduction	Union Dues	United Way
Ronald Arthur ...	$54,000	$1,200	Married	3	$125	$15	$15
John Baines	40,500	900	Single	2	135	15	30
Ted Carter	45,000	1,000	Married	2	150	–0–	20

The FICA Social Security tax rate is 6.2% and the FICA Medicare tax rate is 1.45% on all of this week's wages paid to each employee. The state income tax equals 8 percent of the amount withheld for federal income tax purposes. (Use the withholding tables in Exhibits 9.4 and 9.5.)

Required

1. Prepare a payroll register similar to that in Exhibit 9.8 for Swift Company for the pay period ending December 7. Your payroll register should have columns for employee name, gross pay, federal income tax withheld, state income tax withheld, Social Security tax, Medicare tax, and deductions for medical insurance, union dues, and United Way contributions, and net pay.
2. Prepare the journal entry to record the December 7 payroll.
3. Prepare the journal entry to pay the December 7 payroll. Swift Company does not use a special payroll bank account.

Problem 9-4A
Payroll deductions, net pay, payroll register
LO2 LO3 LO4

Mackenzie Price operates Downtown Salon and Spa. Information on her three employees for the payroll period (week) ending June 1, 2009, is provided below. Each employee receives one and one-half times the normal hourly pay rate for any hour worked beyond 40 in a week. The FICA Social Security tax rate is 6.2% on the first $106,800 of each employee's gross pay and the FICA Medicare tax rate is 1.45% on all of this week's wages paid to each employee. Federal income tax withholdings are computed from withholding tables and state income tax withholdings are assumed to be 8% of the amount withheld for federal income tax. (Use the withholding tables in Exhibits 9.4 and 9.5.)

Employee	Earnings to End of Previous Week	Hours Worked	Regular Hourly Rate	Marital Status	No. of Allowances
Emily Jacobs	$20,800	46	$20.00	S	1
Shu Ming	14,560	40	14.00	M	5
Carter Johns	16,120	48	15.50	M	2

Required

1. Enter each employee's name, year-to-date earnings before this pay period, marital status, regular hourly rate, hours worked, and number of withholding allowances in a payroll register. Hours worked beyond 40 are considered overtime hours.
2. Compute the regular, overtime, and total gross pay for each employee for this pay period. Enter these amounts in the payroll register.
3. Compute the amounts of FICA taxes to be withheld from each employee's pay and enter these amounts in the payroll register.

4. Determine the amount of federal income tax to withhold from each employee's gross pay. Use the withholding tables in Exhibits 9.4 and 9.5. Enter these amounts in the payroll register.

5. Determine the amount of state income tax to withhold from each employee's gross pay. Enter these amounts in the payroll register.

6. Compute each employee's net pay and enter it into the payroll register.

7. Total the payroll register.

Refer to Problem 9-4A. Before the pay period ending June 1, 2009, the individual employee earnings record for Emily Jacobs reports the following:

Problem 9-5A

Payroll deductions, employee earnings records

LO2 LO3 LO6

DOWNTOWN SALON AND SPA
Employee Earnings Report
For Month Ended May 25, 2009

Employee

| Name | Jacobs, Emily |
| SS No. | 344-88-9999 |

| | | | Employee Deductions | | | | |
Reference	Date	Gross Pay	Federal Income Tax	State Income Tax	FICA—Social Security	FICA—Medicare	Net Pay
Beg. Balance		20,800	2,834	226.72	1,289.60	301.60	16,148.08
	6/01/2009						
	6/08/2009						
	6/15/2009						
	6/22/2009						
	6/29/2009						
Total of 6/01/2009 through 6/29/2009							
Year-to-date total for Emily Jacobs							

Social Security taxes of 6.2% and Medicare taxes of 1.45% are deducted from each employee's gross pay. Tax withholding tables are used to compute amounts to withhold for federal income taxes. State income tax withheld equals 8% of the dollar amount of federal income taxes withheld.

Required

1. Refer to Problem 9-4A and enter the payroll information for the pay period ending June 1, 2009, in an individual employee earnings record for Emily Jacobs.

2. Assume that Emily Jacobs works exactly 40 hours in each of the payroll periods ending June 8, June 15, June 22, and June 29 of 2009. Compute the amounts to withhold from Emily's weekly net pay for Social Security taxes, Medicare taxes, federal income tax withholdings, and state income tax withholdings.

3. Enter the amounts computed in requirement 2 in Emily Jacobs's individual employee earnings record.

4. Compute the total amounts of gross pay, federal income tax withholdings, state income tax withholdings, Social Security taxes, Medicare taxes, and net pay for Emily Jacobs for the month of June 1 through June 29, 2009. Enter these amounts in Emily Jacobs's individual employee earnings record.

5. Update the year-to-date totals of gross pay, federal income tax withholdings, state income tax withholdings, Social Security taxes, Medicare taxes, and net pay on Emily Jacobs's individual employee earnings record through June 29, 2009.

Fishing Guides Co. pays its employees each week. Employees' gross pay is subject to these taxes.

PROBLEM SET B

Problem 9-1B

Payroll expenses, withholdings, and taxes **LO2 LO3**

Tax	Rate	Applied To
FICA—Social Security	6.20%	First $106,800
FICA—Medicare	1.45%	All gross pay

The company is preparing its payroll calculations for the week ended September 30. Payroll records show the following information for the company's four employees.

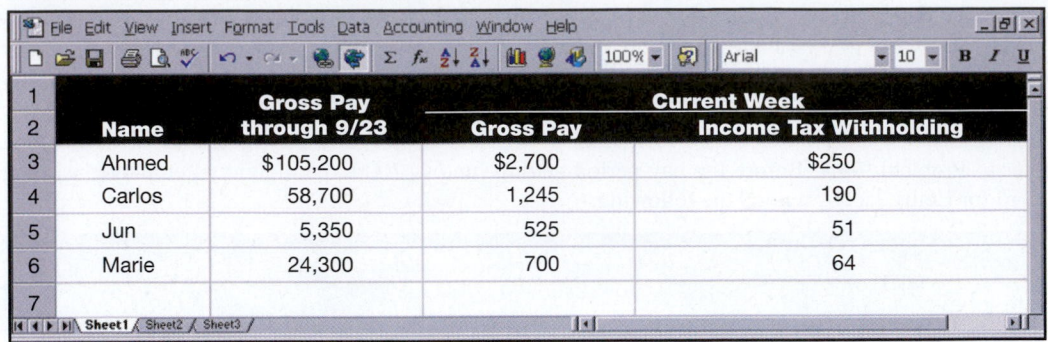

| | | Gross Pay | Current Week | |
	Name	through 9/23	Gross Pay	Income Tax Withholding
3	Ahmed	$105,200	$2,700	$250
4	Carlos	58,700	1,245	190
5	Jun	5,350	525	51
6	Marie	24,300	700	64

In addition to gross pay, each employee must pay one-half of the $40 per employee weekly health insurance premium. Ahmed contributes 5% of his weekly gross pay to a retirement plan. Carlos contributes $15 per week to charity. Jun pays $5 per week in union dues.

Required

Compute the following for the week ended September 30 (round amounts to the nearest cent):

1. Each employee's FICA withholdings for Social Security.

2. Each employee's FICA withholdings for Medicare.

3. Each employee's health insurance premium deduction.

4. Each employee's other voluntary deductions.

Check (5) Total net pay $4,052.70   **5.** Each employee's net (take-home) pay.

Problem 9–2B

Entries for payroll transactions
LO3   LO5

Tavella Company's first weekly pay period of the year ends on January 8. On that date, the column totals in Tavella's payroll register indicate its sales employees earned $34,745, its office employees earned $21,225, and its delivery employees earned $1,030. The employees are to have withheld from their wages FICA Social Security taxes at the rate of 6.2%, FICA Medicare taxes at the rate of 1.45%, $8,625 of federal income taxes, $1,160 of medical insurance deductions, and $138 of union dues.

Required

Check (1) Cr. Accrued Wages
            Payable, $42,716.50

1. Calculate FICA Social Security taxes payable and FICA Medicare taxes payable. Prepare the journal entry to record Tavella Company's January 8 employee payroll expenses and liabilities.

2. Prepare the journal entry to pay the January 8 payroll. Tavella uses a special payroll bank account.

Problem 9–3B

Payroll entries, deductions, net pay **LO3   LO4   LO5**

The payroll records of JK Landscape Design provided the following data for the weekly pay period ended October 7:

Employee	Earnings to End of Previous Week	Gross Pay	Marital Status	No. of Allowances	Medical Insurance Deduction	Union Dues	United Way
Roland Ames ...	$44,000	$1,100	Single	3	$ 85	$10	$25
Jan Barnes	30,500	780	Married	1	150	–0–	20
Todd Crane	35,000	985	Married	5	150	–0–	30

The FICA Social Security tax rate is 6.2% and the FICA Medicare tax rate is 1.45% on all of this week's wages paid to each employee. Use withholding tables in Exhibits 9.4 and 9.5 to find the amount of federal income tax to withhold and assume state income tax is 8% of the dollar amount of federal income tax withheld.

Required

1. Prepare a payroll register similar to that in Exhibit 9.8 for JK Landscape Design for the pay period ending October 7. Your payroll register should have columns for employee name, gross pay, federal income tax withheld, state income tax withheld, Social Security tax, Medicare tax, and deductions for medical insurance, union dues, and United Way contributions, and net pay.

2. Prepare the journal entry to record the October 7 payroll.

3. Prepare the journal entry to pay the October 7 payroll. JK Landscape Design does not use a special payroll bank account.

Merle Perkins operates A1 Auto Repair. Information on his three employees for the payroll period (week) ending June 1, 2009, is provided below. Each employee receives one and one-half times the normal hourly pay rate for any hour worked beyond 40 in a week. The FICA Social Security tax rate is 6.2% on the first $106,800 of each employee's gross pay and the FICA Medicare tax rate is 1.45% on all of this week's wages paid to each employee. Federal income tax withholdings are computed from withholding tables and state income tax withholdings are assumed to be 8% of the amount withheld for federal income tax. (Use the withholding tables in Exhibits 9.4 and 9.5.)

Problem 9–4B
Payroll deductions, net pay, payroll register **LO2 LO3 LO4**

Employee	Earnings to End of Previous Week	Hours Worked	Regular Hourly Rate	Marital Status	No. of Allowances
Andre Jones	$21,600	42	$21.00	S	2
Xiu Yi	12,480	35	15.00	M	3
Duane Wells	19,320	46	17.50	M	4

Required

1. Enter each employee's name, year-to-date earnings before this pay period, marital status, regular hourly rate, hours worked, and number of withholding allowances in a payroll register. Hours worked beyond 40 are considered overtime hours.

2. Compute the regular, overtime, and total gross pay for each employee for this pay period. Enter these amounts in the payroll register.

3. Compute the amounts of FICA taxes to be withheld from each employee's pay and enter these amounts in the payroll register.

4. Determine the amount of federal income tax to withhold from each employee's gross pay. Use the withholding tables in Exhibits 9.4 and 9.5. Enter these amounts in the payroll register.

5. Determine the amount of state income tax to withhold from each employee's gross pay. Enter these amounts in the payroll register.

6. Compute each employee's net pay and enter it into the payroll register.

7. Total the payroll register.

Refer to Problem 9-4B. Before the pay period ending June 1, 2009, the individual employee earnings record for Andre Jones reports the following:

Problem 9–5B
Payroll deductions, employee earnings records
LO2 LO3 LO6

A1 AUTO REPAIR
Employee Earnings Report
For Month Ended May 25, 2009

Employee
Name   Jones, Andre
SS No.   333-55-9999

			Employee Deductions				
Reference	Date	Gross Pay	Federal Income Tax	State Income Tax	FICA— Social Security	FICA— Medicare	Net Pay
Beg. Balance		21,600	2,943	235.44	1,339.20	313.20	16,769.16
	6/01/2009						
	6/08/2009						
	6/15/2009						
	6/22/2009						
	6/29/2009						
Total of 6/01/2009 through 6/29/2009							
Year-to-date total for Andre Jones							

Social Security taxes of 6.2% and Medicare taxes of 1.45% are deducted from each employee's gross pay. Tax withholding tables are used to compute amounts to withhold for federal income taxes. State income tax withheld equals 8% of the dollar amount of federal income taxes withheld.

Required

1. Refer to Problem 9-4B and enter the payroll information for the pay period ending June 1, 2009, in an individual employee earnings record for Andre Jones.

2. Assume that Andre Jones works exactly 40 hours in each of the payroll periods ending June 8, June 15, June 22, and June 29 of 2009. Compute the amounts to withhold from Andre's weekly net pay for Social Security taxes, Medicare taxes, federal income tax withholdings, and state income tax withholdings.

3. Enter the amounts computed in requirement 2 in Andre Jones's individual employee earnings record.

4. Compute the total amounts of gross pay, federal income tax withholdings, state income tax withholdings, Social Security taxes, Medicare taxes, and net pay for Andre Jones for the month of June 1 through June 29, 2009. Enter these amounts in Andre Jones's individual employee earnings record.

5. Update the year-to-date totals of gross pay, federal income tax withholdings, state income tax withholdings, Social Security taxes, Medicare taxes, and net pay on Andre Jones's individual employee earnings record through June 29, 2009.

SERIAL PROBLEM

Success Systems

(This serial problem began in Chapter 1 and continues through most of the book. If previous chapter segments were not completed, the serial problem can begin at this point. It is helpful, but not necessary, for you to use the Working Papers that accompany the book.)

SP 9   Michelle Jones earned $150 per day for the 8 days in the most recent pay period ending on February 26.

Required

1. Assume that Michelle Jones is an unmarried employee. Her wages are subject to no deductions other than FICA Social Security taxes, FICA Medicare taxes, and federal income taxes. Her federal income taxes for this pay period total $189. Compute her gross pay and net pay for the eight days' work paid on February 26.

2. Record the journal entry to reflect the payroll payment to Michelle Jones as computed in part 1. Success Systems does not use a payroll bank account.

BEYOND THE NUMBERS

REPORTING IN ACTION
LO5

BTN 9-1   Refer to the financial statements of **Best Buy** in Appendix A to answer the following:

Required

1. What payroll-related liability does Best Buy report at March 1, 2008?
2. In what income statement accounts does Best Buy report its payroll and benefit costs?

Fast Forward

3. Access Best Buy's financial statements for fiscal years ending after March 1, 2008, at its Website (www.BestBuy.com) or the SEC's EDGAR database (www.SEC.gov). What payroll-related liability does Best Buy report for years ending after March 1, 2008?

ETHICS CHALLENGE
LO1

BTN 9-2   You take a summer job working for a family friend as a Web page designer for a small information technology service. On your first payday, the owner slaps you on the back, gives you full payment in cash, winks, and adds: "No need to pay those high taxes, eh."

Required

What action, if any, do you take? Explain.

BTN 9-3   An owner of a growing business hires you as a consultant. He is concerned about rising payroll costs, and also concerned about payroll fraud. Currently, his payroll clerk collects time sheets and computes gross pay and deductions. The payroll clerk also adds new employees to the payroll system and makes all changes to employees' withholdings and voluntary deductions. Once the payroll is processed, the payroll clerk signs and distributes the payroll checks.

WORKPLACE COMMUNICATION
LO7

Required

Prepare a set of written recommendations to the business owner to strengthen the owner's control over payroll procedures. Your answer should be in a memorandum format.

BTN 9-4   Access the February 25, 2008, filing of the December 31, 2007, annual 10-K report of McDonald's Corporation (Ticker: MCD), which is available from **www.SEC.gov**.

TAKING IT TO THE NET
LO1

Required

1. Identify the amount of accrued payroll and other liabilities on McDonald's balance sheet as of December 31, 2007.
2. What amount does McDonald's report for payroll and other benefits costs for its company-operated restaurants on its 2007 income statement? Expressed as a percentage of sales, discuss how payroll and benefit costs for company-operated restaurants changed from the year ending 2006 to the year ending 2007.

BTN 9-5   Divide your team into four groups. Each group will select one employee for whom to calculate the Social Security Tax for the Zmud Company 11/30 weekly payroll. Recall that in 2009 there is a maximum earnings base of $106,800 per year for which the social security tax is assessed. Adi's gross weekly earnings are $2,700 with $104,200 earned through 11/23. Bob's gross weekly earnings are $1,445 with $59,700 earned through 11/23. Marcia's gross weekly earnings are $825 with $5,350 earned through 11/23. Gary's gross weekly earnings are $1,700 with $24,300 earned through 11/23.

Combine the social security tax from each group to arrive at a total social security tax for the Zmud company's 11/30 payroll.

TEAMWORK IN ACTION
LO2   LO3

BTN 9-6   Review the chapter's opening feature about Jason Osborn and Jason Wright and their start-up company, **Feed Granola Company**.

Both owners stress that controlling payroll liabilities is a must for success in business. What are some procedures both Jasons can use to reduce the chance that Feed Granola Company is hurt by a payroll fraud scheme?

ENTREPRENEURS IN BUSINESS
LO7

1. e; $50,000 × (.062 + .0145) = $3,825
2. b
3. c; (40 × $12) + (8 × $18) = $624
4. c
5. d

ANSWERS TO MULTIPLE CHOICE QUIZ

A Look Back

Chapter 9 focused on employee payroll and deductions. We showed how to compute employee tax deductions to comply with laws. We also showed how the employer records and controls its payroll.

A Look at This Chapter

This chapter emphasizes the employer's payroll reporting. We show how the employer computes and pays its payroll taxes and prepares tax documents to comply with laws.

A Look Ahead

Chapter 11 explains the accounting for merchandise sales and accounts receivable. We analyze and record merchandise sales transactions and explain the use of a sales and cash receipts journal.

Chapter 10

Employer Payroll Tax Reporting

Learning Objectives

LO 1 Describe laws that impact an employer's payroll obligations.

LO 2 Compute employer FICA taxes and record them in a general journal.

LO 3 Journalize an employer's deposit of federal income taxes and FICA taxes withheld, and prepare a deposit coupon.

LO 4 Prepare Form 941, Employer's Quarterly Federal Tax Return.

LO 5 Prepare Form W-2, Employee's Wage and Tax Statement, and Form W-3, Transmittal of Wage and Tax Statements.

LO 6 Compute an employer's state and federal unemployment taxes and record them in a general journal.

LO 7 Prepare unemployment tax returns.

LO 8 Compute and record workers' compensation insurance premiums for an employer.

"1-800-GOT-JUNK brings together great people to build a business that we can all be proud of"
—CEO, Brian Scudamore

One Man's Junk

Brian Scudamore was waiting in a McDonald's drive-thru when he realized his future was junk. With his last $700, Brian bought a used pickup truck and began hauling junk—old couches, appliances, household clutter—any nonhazardous material that two people can lift. "With a vision of creating the 'FedEx' of junk removal, I became a fulltime JUNKMAN," explains Brian. "My father was not impressed in the least."

He is now. Brian's vision resulted in him starting **1-800-GOT-JUNK (1800gotjunk.com),** the world's largest junk removal service. The company's approach is simple: Use clean, shiny trucks that serve as mobile billboards and employ professional, courteous drivers who are always on time. Develop a culture that is young, fun, and focused on employee growth, and "build a business that we can be proud of." With revenues of over $100 million in 2007, multiple "Best Company to Work For" awards, and a presence in 47 of North America's 50 top cities, the company has much to be proud of.

Unlike many entrepreneurs who attempt to minimize risk by outsourcing to independent contractors, Scudamore took a different approach. "I hired my first employee, a good friend of mine, a week after I started. I always believed in hiring people versus contract or consultants. I felt that if I wasn't willing to make the investment then I was questioning my own faith in the business."

Brian's investments in his 2,600 employees include five weeks of vacation per year, full health benefits, flex time, and a generous profit-sharing program that pays out 25% of company profits. While these employer-provided benefits are costly, Brian believes they help drive his company's success. "I've always said a great company is all about people."

Brian's goal is $1 billion in revenues by the end of 2012. Not bad for his initial investment of $700.

[Sources: *1-800-GOT-JUNK Website*, February 2009; *Wikipedia*, February 2009]

Keeping accurate payroll records and reports is essential to a company's success. Many laws impact the employer's payroll obligations. The employer can be assessed large penalties for not complying with these laws. This chapter shows how the employer computes its tax liabilities and prepares necessary tax documents to comply with laws.

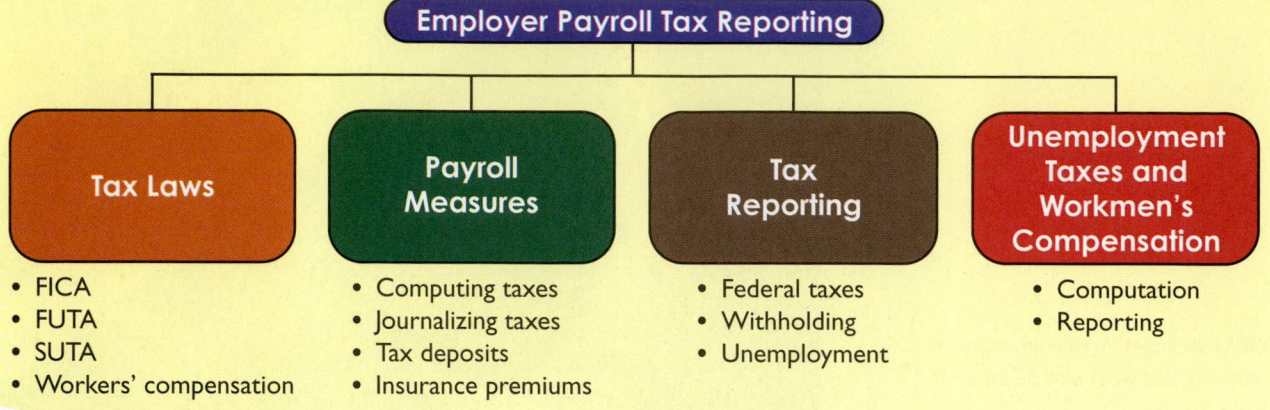

Employer Payroll Tax Reporting

Tax Laws	Payroll Measures	Tax Reporting	Unemployment Taxes and Workmen's Compensation
• FICA • FUTA • SUTA • Workers' compensation	• Computing taxes • Journalizing taxes • Tax deposits • Insurance premiums	• Federal taxes • Withholding • Unemployment	• Computation • Reporting

Laws Impacting Employer's Payroll Tax

Employer Identification Number

Each employee of a business has a unique Social Security number. Likewise, each business has its own **employer identification number (EIN).** The business uses its EIN for reporting its income and taxes. The business obtains its EIN by completing **Form SS-4,** available from **www.IRS.gov**. Form SS-4 is an Internal Revenue Service form that asks for general information about the business, including its name, location, main activity, and estimated number of employees.

Employer FICA Tax

LO1 Describe laws that impact an employer's payroll obligations.

Under the **Federal Insurance Contributions Act (FICA),** the employer must pay the same amounts as its employees do for Social Security and Medicare taxes. For 2009 the employer pays 6.2% of each employee's annual gross pay, up to a maximum annual gross pay of $106,800, for Social Security taxes. The employer also pays 1.45% of each employee's annual gross pay for Medicare taxes. There is no limit on Medicare taxes. Remember that self-employed persons pay both the employee and employer FICA taxes. This means the total FICA tax rate for self-employed individuals is 15.3%.

Federal and State Unemployment Tax Acts

The federal government works with states to provide a joint federal and state unemployment insurance program. These programs pay unemployment benefits to qualified workers. Each state runs its own program. The employer pays for the cost of this program. No amounts are withheld from employees.

Federal Unemployment Taxes (FUTA) For 2009, employers pay FUTA taxes of as much as 6.2% of the first $7,000 earned by each employee in that year. This amount can be reduced by a credit of up to 5.4% of unemployment taxes paid to a state program. So, the net federal unemployment tax is often only 0.8% (gross FUTA rate of 6.2% less credit for state unemployment tax of 5.4%) of the first $7,000 of each employee's annual gross pay.

State Unemployment Taxes (SUTA) In most states, the base rate for SUTA taxes is 5.4% of the first $7,000 paid to each employee during the year. For example, an employer with 50 employees who each earns more than $7,000 per year will pay $18,900 (0.054 × 50 × $7,000) of SUTA taxes. This base rate is adjusted for the employer's **merit rating.** The state assigns a merit rating that reflects the company's stability in employing workers. A company with low employee turnover receives a high merit rating and pays less than 5.4%. For example, the company with the same 50 employees from above might get a high merit rating and pay SUTA taxes of only 1%. This company would pay a total of only $3,500 (0.01 × 50 × $7,000) for SUTA taxes. This unemployment tax savings of $15,400 ($18,900 − $3,500) results from having a stable workforce with low employee turnover.

Workers' Compensation Insurance

Most states require employers to provide **workers' compensation insurance** for their employees. Workers' compensation provides benefits for employees who are injured on the job. The employer pays a premium, either to the state or to private insurance companies. The premium depends on the type of work the employees perform. Since construction work is considered more risky than secretarial work, an employer would pay a higher premium on its construction workers than on its secretaries. For example, the employer might pay a premium of $0.15 per each $100 of wages for a secretary, but pay $4 per each $100 of wages for a construction worker.

Employers with a small number of employees pay an estimated premium at the beginning of the year. This estimated premium is based on the company's estimated total wages for the upcoming year. At the end of the year, the actual premium is computed based on that year's total wages. The employer then either receives a refund or pays an additional premium.

HOW YOU DOIN'?   Answers—p. 247

1. What are the limits on an employee's annual pay for computing the employer's *(a)* Social Security tax; *(b)* Medicare tax; *(c)* federal unemployment tax; and *(d)* state unemployment tax?

2. Indicate whether the employer or employee or both incur each of the following: *(a)* FICA taxes; *(b)* FUTA taxes; *(c)* SUTA taxes; and *(d)* withheld income taxes.

3. A company pays its one employee $3,000 per month. The company's FUTA rate is 0.8% on the first $7,000 earned; its SUTA rate is 4.0% on the first $7,000; its Social Security tax rate is 6.2% of the first $106,800; and its Medicare tax rate is 1.45% of all amounts earned. What is the employer's total payroll tax expense for March?

Employer's Payroll Taxes

Computing Employer's FICA Tax

We return to our example of Phoenix Sales and Service, begun in Chapter 9. Phoenix Sales and Service must pay the same FICA tax amount it withholds from its employees' pay. For Robert Austin, and the week ending January 7, 2009, Phoenix Sales and Service must pay $24.80 for Social Security taxes and $5.80 for Medicare taxes. A partial payroll register for Phoenix Sales and Service is shown in Exhibit 10.1. From its payroll register, the total amounts Phoenix Sales and Service owes for FICA taxes for all of its employees for the period ending January 7, 2009, are $202.30 (Social Security) and $47.31 (Medicare).

LO2 Compute employer FICA taxes and record them in a general journal.

General Journal Entry to Record Employer FICA Tax

The general journal entry to record Phoenix Sales and Service Social Security and Medicare payroll taxes for the week ending January 7, 2009, is:

Jan.	09	Payroll Tax Expense	2 4 9 61	
		Employer FICA—Social Security Taxes Payable		2 0 2 30
		Employer FICA—Medicare Taxes Payable		4 7 31
		To record employer Social Security and Medicare payroll taxes.		

Assets = Liabilities + Equity
+202.30   −249.61
+47.31

Exhibit 10.1

Phoenix Sales and Service Partial Payroll Register

(continued across top of next page)

Partial Payroll Register

Employee Name	Marital Status and Allowances	Beginning Cumulative Gross Earnings	Hours Worked This Pay Period	Hourly Wage	EARNINGS			Ending Cumulative Gross Earnings
					Regular	Overtime	Gross	
Austin, Robert	S-1	0.00	40	10.00	400.00	00.00	400.00	400.00
Cross, Judy	S-2	0.00	41	14.00	560.00	21.00	581.00	581.00
Diaz, John	M-0	0.00	42	14.00	560.00	42.00	602.00	602.00
Keife, Kay	M-2	0.00	40	14.00	560.00	00.00	560.00	560.00
Miller, Lee	M-0	0.00	40	14.00	560.00	00.00	560.00	560.00
Sears, Dale	S-0	0.00	40	14.00	560.00	00.00	560.00	560.00
Total	Week of January 7, 2009				3,200.00	63.00	3,263.00	3,263.00
Total	Month of January 2009				12,800.00	252.00	13,052.00	13,052.00
Total	First Quarter of 2009				41,600.00	819.00	42,419.00	42,419.00
Total	Year Ending December 31, 2009				166,400.00	3,276.00	169,676.00	169,676.00

Payroll Tax Deposits

Timing of Payroll Tax Deposits   The Internal Revenue Service (IRS) requires employers to deposit payroll taxes either monthly or semiweekly (once or twice each week). New companies deposit monthly. For other companies, the IRS has a **look-back rule** to classify depositors. The IRS looks back to a one-year period that begins on July 1 and ends on June 30. To determine an employer's status for 2009, the IRS looks back to find the total amount of Social Security, Medicare, and federal income taxes the business paid from July 1, 2007, through June 30, 2008. If this amount is less than $50,000, the IRS classifies the business as a monthly depositor. If this amount is more than $50,000, the IRS classifies the business as a semiweekly depositor. A company's depositor status is reevaluated every year. In our example, Phoenix Sales and Service is classified as a monthly depositor. A monthly depositor must deposit its employee and employer FICA taxes and employees' federal income tax withholdings by the 15th of the next month.

If the employers' total tax liability is less than $2,500 in a quarter, no deposit is required for that quarter. In this case the employer includes a check for its tax liabilities with its tax returns.

IN THE NEWS

A company's delay or failure to pay withholding taxes to the government has severe consequences. For example, a 100% penalty can be levied, with interest, on the unpaid balance. The government can even close a company, take its assets, and pursue legal action against those involved.

Computing and Recording Payroll Tax Deposits

Federal tax withholdings.   By law, the employer must deposit federal tax withholdings on a timely basis in a **federal depository bank.** A federal depository bank is authorized to accept deposits of amounts payable to the federal government. These banks can either be **Federal Reserve Banks** or **authorized depositories.** A Federal Reserve Bank can accept payroll deposits from any business. An authorized depository can accept payroll deposits from its own checking account customers.

The company uses information from its payroll register to make tax deposits. Assume that Phoenix Sales and Service employee wages and deductions for the remaining three weekly

TAXABLE EARNINGS FOR			EMPLOYEE DEDUCTIONS FOR				PAYMENT INFORMATION	
Social Security	Medicare	Unemployment	Social Security	Medicare	Federal Income Tax	State Income Tax	Net Pay	Check Number
400.00	400.00	400.00	24.80	5.80	26.00	2.08	341.32	9001
581.00	581.00	581.00	36.02	8.42	43.00	3.44	490.12	9002
602.00	602.00	602.00	37.32	8.73	37.00	2.96	515.99	9003
560.00	560.00	560.00	34.72	8.12	12.00	0.96	504.20	9004
560.00	560.00	560.00	34.72	8.12	31.00	2.48	483.68	9005
560.00	560.00	560.00	34.72	8.12	61.00	4.88	451.28	9006
3,263.00	3,263.00	3,263.00	202.30	47.31	210.00	16.80	2,786.59	
13,052.00	13,052.00	13,052.00	809.20	189.24	840.00	67.20	11,146.36	
42,419.00	42,419.00	40,200.00	2,629.90	615.03	2,730.00	218.40	36,225.67	
169,676.00	169,676.00	42,000.00	10,519.60	2,460.12	10,920.00	873.60	144,902.68	

payroll periods in January are exactly the same as those for the week of January 7, 2009. The "Total Month of January 2009" row in Exhibit 10.1 reports the following withholdings:

Employees' federal income taxes	$ 840.00
Employee FICA—Social Security taxes	809.20
Employee FICA—Medicare taxes	189.24
Employer FICA—Social Security taxes (match employee amount)	809.20
Employer FICA—Medicare taxes (match employee amount)	189.24
Total	$2,836.88

Form 8109.   The total of $2,836.88 must be deposited in a federal depository bank. The company can make the tax payment either by electronic funds transfer or by check. Companies with annual federal tax deposits above $200,000 must use electronic funds transfers. If the tax payment is made by check, the accountant prepares a **Form 8109,** Federal Tax Deposit Coupon. These preprinted deposit coupons are obtained from the Internal Revenue Service.

If the company does not have a current supply of Forms 8109 or is a new entity, it completes **Form 8109-B.** Exhibit 10.2 presents Form 8109-B for Phoenix Sales and Service for the month

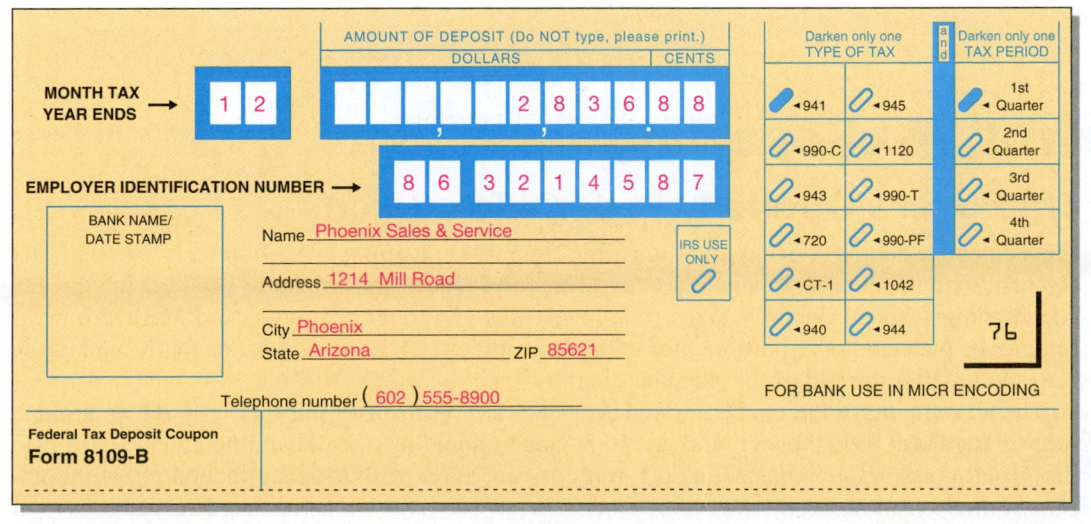

Exhibit 10.2

Form 8109-B, Federal Tax Deposit Coupon

LO3 Journalize an employer's deposit of federal income taxes and FICA taxes withheld, and prepare a deposit coupon.

of January. The company has a calendar year-end, so the accountant writes "12" in the "Month Tax Year Ends" box. The accountant also enters the company's EIN and the dollar amount ($2,836.88) of the tax deposit. Finally, the accountant darkens the "941" and "1st quarter" ovals, since the company is depositing federal taxes it will report on Form 941 (see below) and the deposit is for a month in the first quarter of the year.

General Journal Entry to Record Payroll Tax Deposit
Phoenix Sales and Service's accountant then makes the following entry in its general journal.

Assets = Liabilities + Equity
−2,836.88   −840.00
            −809.20
            −189.24
            −809.20
            −189.24

Jan.	31	Employee Federal Income Taxes Payable	840 00	
		Employee FICA—Social Security Taxes Payable	809 20	
		Employee FICA—Medicare Taxes Payable	189 24	
		Employer FICA—Social Security Taxes Payable	809 20	
		Employer FICA—Medicare Taxes Payable	189 24	
		Cash		2836 88
		Deposit January payroll tax withholdings.		

February and March Payroll Records
Assume that February has four weekly payroll periods and March has five weekly payroll periods. Also assume that employee wages and deductions for each weekly payroll period in February and March are exactly the same as those reported in the payroll register for the week ending January 7, 2009. The accountant for Phoenix Sales and Service has updated the company's payroll register and individual employee earnings records and made all the necessary journal entries for payroll. Then, the "Total First Quarter of 2009" row in Exhibit 10.1 reports the following withholdings:

Employees' federal income taxes	$2,730.00
Employee FICA—Social Security taxes	2,629.90
Employee FICA—Medicare taxes	615.03
Employer FICA—Social Security taxes (match employee amount)	2,629.90
Employer FICA—Medicare taxes (match employee amount)	615.03
Total	$9,219.86

Employer's Payroll Tax Reporting

Employer's Quarterly Federal Tax Return

LO4 Prepare Form 941, Employer's Quarterly Federal Tax Return.

Each calendar quarter the employer must file **Form 941, Employer's Quarterly Federal Tax Return,** with the Internal Revenue Service. This form reports the employer's federal income tax withholdings, Social Security taxes (employee plus employer portions), and Medicare taxes (employee plus employer portions) for the quarter just ended. Form 941 is due by the end of the next month after the end of the calendar quarter.

The accountant for Phoenix Sales and Service, Mary Wills, uses this quarterly information to prepare the Form 941, shown in Exhibit 10.3. Due to rounding, the dollar amount ($9,220.11) in the "Total taxes before adjustment" column does not agree with the total federal tax withholdings in the payroll register ($9,219.86). This difference is adjusted by adding $0.25 in box 7a of Form 941.

Form 941   **Employer's Quarterly Federal Tax Return**

9901

Department of the Treasury — Internal Revenue Service

OMB No. 1545-0029

Employer identification number   8 6 – 3 2 1 4 5 8 7

Name (not your trade name)   Mary Wills

Trade name (if any)   Phoenix Sales & Service

Address   1214   Mill Road
Number   Street   Suite or room number

Phoenix   AZ   85621
City   State   ZIP code

Read the seperate instructions before you fill out this form. Please type or print within the boxes.

Report for this Quarter ...
(Check one.)

- ✓ 1: January, February, March
- ☐ 2: April, May, June
- ☐ 3: July, August, September
- ☐ 4: October, November, December

Part 1: Answer these questions for this quarter.

1 Number of employees who received wages, tips, or other compensation for the pay period including: *Mar. 12* (Quarter 1), *June 12* (Quarter 2), *Sept. 12* (Quarter 3), *Dec. 12* (Quarter 4)	1	6
2 Wages, tips, and other compensation	2	42,419.00
3 Total income tax withheld from wages, tips, and other compensation	3	2,730.00

4 If no wages, tips, and other compensation are subject to social security or Medicare tax   ☐ Check and go to line 6.

5 Taxable social security and Medicare wages and tips:

	Column 1		Column 2	
5a Taxable social security wages	42,419.00	× .124 =	5,259.96	
5b Taxable social security tips	0.00	× .124 =	0.00	
5c Taxable Medicare wages & tips	42,419.00	× .029 =	1,230.15	

5d Total social security and Medicare taxes (*Column 2*, lines 5a + 5b + 5c = line 5d)	5d	6,490.11
6 Total taxes before adjustments (lines 3 + 5d = line 6)	6	9,220.11

7 Tax adjustments (If your answer is a negative number, write it in brackets.):

7a Current quarter's fractions of cents	(.25)
7b Current quarter's sick pay	.
7c Current quarter's adjustments for tips and group-term life insurance	.
7d Current year's income tax withholding (Attach Form 941c)	.
7e Prior quarters' social security and Medicare taxes (Attach Form 941c)	.
7f Special additions to federal income tax (reserved use)	.
7g Special additions to social security and Medicare (reserved use)	.

7h Total adjustments (Combine all amounts: lines 7a through 7g.)	7h	(.25)
8 Total taxes after adjustments (Combine lines 6 and 7h.)	8	9,219.86
9 Advance earned income credit (EIC) payments made to employees	9	0.00
10 Total taxes after adjustment for advance EIC (lines 8 – 9 = line 10)	10	9,219.86
11 Total deposits for this quarter, including overpayment applied from a prior quarter	11	9,219.86
12 Balance due (lines 10 – 11 = line 12) Make checks payable to the *United States Treasury*	12	0.00

13 Overpayment (If line 11 is more than line 10, write the difference here.)   0.00   Check one ☐ Apply to next return.   ☐ Send a refund.

Next →

(continued)

Exhibit 10.3

Form 941, Employer's Quarterly Federal Tax Return

Refer to www.IRS.gov for revised versions of this form.

Exhibit 10.3

(concluded)

9902

Name *(not your trade name)*
Mary Wills

Employer identification number
86-3214587

Part 2: Tell us about your deposit schedule for this quarter.

If you are unsure about whether you are a monthly schedule depositor or a semiweekly schedule depositor, see *Pub. 15 (Circular E), section 11.*

14 | A | Z | Write the state abbreviation for the state where you made your deposits OR write "MU" if you made your deposits in *multiple* states.

15   Check one: ☐ Line 10 is less than $2,500. Go to Part 3.

☑ You were a monthly schedule depositor for the entire quarter. Fill out your tax liability for each month. Then go to Part 3.

Tax liability:	Month 1	2,836.88
	Month 2	2,836.88
	Month 3	3,546.10
	Total	9,219.86	Total must equal line 10.

☐ You were a semiweekly schedule depositor for any part of this quarter. Fill out *Schedule B (Form 941): Report of Tax Liability for Semiweekly Schedule Depositors,* and attach it to this form.

Part 3: Tell us about your business. If a question does NOT apply to your business, leave it blank.

16   If your business has closed and you do not have to file returns in the future . . . . . .   ☐ Check here, and

enter the final date you paid wages   [/ /] .

17   If you are a seasonal employer and you do not have to file a return for every quarter of the year . . ☐ Check here.

Part 4: May we contact your third-party designee?

Do you want to allow an employee, a paid tax preparer, or another person to discuss this return with the IRS? See the instructions for details.

☐ Yes. Designee's name [   ]

Phone ( ) – [   ]   Personal Identification Number (PIN) [ ][ ][ ][ ][ ]

☑ No.

Part 5: Sign here

Under penalties of perjury, I declare that I have examined this return, including accompanying schedules and statements, and to the best of my knowledge and belief, it is true, correct, and complete.

✗ Sign your name here   *Mary Wills*

Print name and title   Mary Wills, Accountant

Date   04 / 30 /2009   Phone (602) 555 – 8900

Part 6: For paid preparers only *(optional)*

Preparer's signature [   ]

Firm's name [   ]

Address [   ]   EIN [   ]

[   ]   ZIP Code [   ]

Date [/ /]   Phone ( ) –   SSN/PTIN [   ]

☐ Check if you are self-employed.

Employer's Annual Withholding Reporting

L05 Prepare Form W-2, Employee's Wage and Tax Statement, and Form W-3, Transmittal of Wage and Tax Statements.

Form W-2   The employer must provide a **Form W-2, Wage and Tax Statement,** to each employee by January 31 after the calendar year ends. Form W-2 reports each employee's total earnings and deductions for the year just ended. This information comes from each employee's individual earnings record, shown in Chapter 9.

Exhibit 10.4 shows a Form W-2 for 2009 for Robert Austin. The amounts in Exhibit 10.4 assume Robert Austin's payroll information is exactly the same for each of the 52 weeks in 2009. For example, his total "wages, tips, and other compensation" of $20,800 (box 1) equals $400 (his weekly wage from Exhibit 10.1) times 52 weeks. The employer prepares several copies of Form W-2 for each employee. The employer sends one copy of Form W-2 for each employee to the Social Security Administration, one copy to the state tax department, and several copies to the employee for his or her federal and state tax returns. The employer also keeps a copy of Form W-2 for each employee.

Exhibit 10.4

Form W-2, Wage and Tax Statement

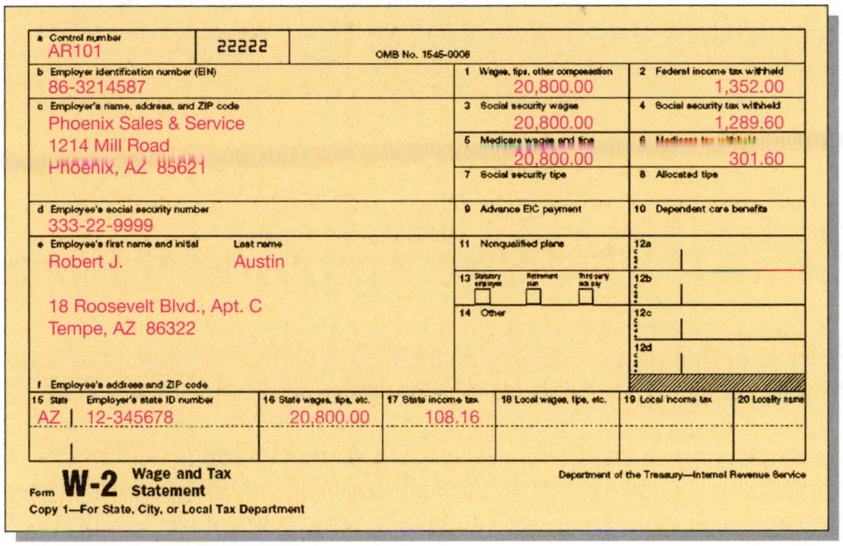
a Control number AR101 | 22222 | OMB No. 1545-0008
b Employer identification number (EIN) 86-3214587
c Employer's name, address, and ZIP code
Phoenix Sales & Service
1214 Mill Road
Phoenix, AZ 85621
1 Wages, tips, other compensation 20,800.00
2 Federal income tax withheld 1,352.00
3 Social security wages 20,800.00
4 Social security tax withheld 1,289.60
5 Medicare wages and tips 20,800.00
6 Medicare tax withheld 301.60
7 Social security tips
8 Allocated tips
d Employee's social security number 333-22-9999
9 Advance EIC payment
10 Dependent care benefits
e Employee's first name and initial Robert J. Last name Austin
18 Roosevelt Blvd., Apt. C
Tempe, AZ 86322
f Employee's address and ZIP code
11 Nonqualified plans
12a
13 Statutory employee / Retirement plan / Third-party sick pay
12b
14 Other
12c
12d
15 State AZ | Employer's state ID number 12-345678
16 State wages, tips, etc. 20,800.00
17 State income tax 108.16
18 Local wages, tips, etc.
19 Local income tax
20 Locality name
Form W-2 Wage and Tax Statement
Department of the Treasury—Internal Revenue Service
Copy 1—For State, City, or Local Tax Department

Form W-3 The employer also submits **Form W-3, Transmittal of Wage and Tax Statements,** with the W-2 Forms it sends to the Social Security Administration. Form W-3 reports the total wage and withholding information for all of the company's employees. Form W-3 is due by the last day of February after each calendar year-end. Exhibit 10.5 presents the Form W-3 for Phoenix Sales and Service for 2009.

Exhibit 10.5

Form W-3, Transmittal of Wage and Tax Statements

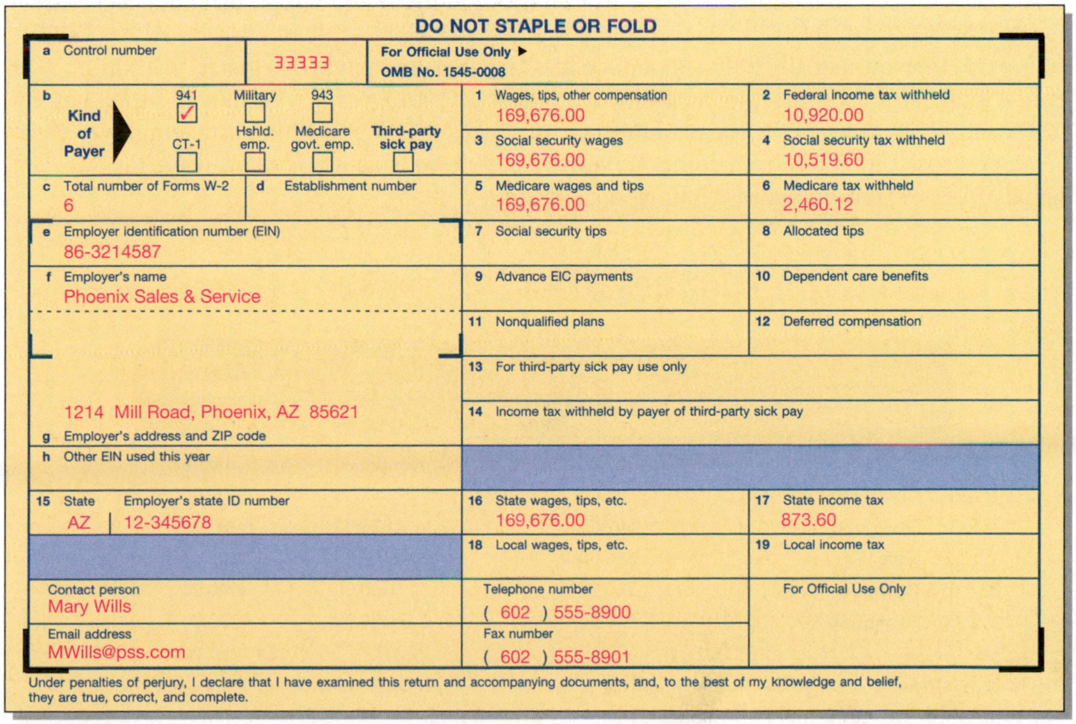
DO NOT STAPLE OR FOLD
a Control number | 33333 | For Official Use Only ▶ OMB No. 1545-0008
b Kind of Payer: 941 ✓ | Military | 943 | CT-1 | Hshld. emp. | Medicare govt. emp. | Third-party sick pay
1 Wages, tips, other compensation 169,676.00
2 Federal income tax withheld 10,920.00
3 Social security wages 169,676.00
4 Social security tax withheld 10,519.60
c Total number of Forms W-2 6
d Establishment number
5 Medicare wages and tips 169,676.00
6 Medicare tax withheld 2,460.12
e Employer identification number (EIN) 86-3214587
7 Social security tips
8 Allocated tips
f Employer's name Phoenix Sales & Service
9 Advance EIC payments
10 Dependent care benefits
11 Nonqualified plans
12 Deferred compensation
13 For third-party sick pay use only
1214 Mill Road, Phoenix, AZ 85621
g Employer's address and ZIP code
14 Income tax withheld by payer of third-party sick pay
h Other EIN used this year
15 State AZ | Employer's state ID number 12-345678
16 State wages, tips, etc. 169,676.00
17 State income tax 873.60
18 Local wages, tips, etc.
19 Local income tax
Contact person Mary Wills
Telephone number (602) 555-8900
For Official Use Only
Email address MWills@pss.com
Fax number (602) 555-8901
Under penalties of perjury, I declare that I have examined this return and accompanying documents, and, to the best of my knowledge and belief, they are true, correct, and complete.

HOW YOU DOIN'?   Answers—p. 247

4. For each of the following separate cases, determine how frequently (monthly or semiweekly) the employer must deposit payroll taxes for 2010: (a) a new business expects to pay $55,000 in payroll taxes during 2010; (b) a business had payroll taxes of $42,000 during the period July 1, 2008, through June 30, 2009; (c) a business had payroll taxes of $91,500 during the period July 1, 2008, through June 30, 2009

5. How frequently does the employer report federal payroll taxes? What tax form is used?

6. What is a Form W-2? A Form W-3?

Federal (FUTA) and State (SUTA) Unemployment Taxes

Federal and state unemployment taxes are computed at the end of each quarter. Deposits for FUTA taxes are due on the last day of the next month after the end of a quarter. The company uses either electronic funds transfer or prepares a Form 8109, Federal Tax Deposit coupon.

It is important to remember three points regarding unemployment taxes. First, unemployment taxes usually apply to only the first $7,000 of each employee's earnings during a year. The payroll clerk must keep individual employee earnings records up-to-date and be alert to employees' earnings passing this limit. Second, companies with a relatively stable employment history can pay a lower SUTA tax rate. Third, the employer receives a credit for SUTA taxes paid, and this lowers the employer's FUTA tax rate.

Computing Employer's Unemployment Taxes

L06 Compute an employer's state and federal unemployment taxes and record them in a general journal.

Phoenix Sales and Service has a good merit rating, so it pays 2.7% of the first $7,000 earned by each employee for SUTA taxes. It receives a credit for these payments and so pays only 0.8% of the first $7,000 earned by each employee for FUTA taxes. Note that the company's FUTA tax rate is reduced by the full credit of 5.4%, even though its actual SUTA rate was only 2.7%.

For the first quarter of 2009, Phoenix Sales and Service payroll register in Exhibit 10.1 reports total earnings subject to unemployment taxes of $40,200. Each employee's total pay for FUTA and SUTA taxes is the lesser of their gross pay or $7,000. Assuming each employee earns the same gross pay in the remaining 12 weekly pay periods as he or she did for the week of January 7, 2009, this amount is computed as follows:

Employee	Weekly Gross Pay	× 13 =	Total Quarterly Gross Pay	Total Pay for FUTA and SUTA
Austin, Robert	$400.00		$5,200.00	$ 5,200.00
Cross, Judy	581.00		7,553.00	7,000.00
Diaz, John	602.00		7,826.00	7,000.00
Keife, Kay	560.00		7,280.00	7,000.00
Miller, Lee	560.00		7,280.00	7,000.00
Sears, Dale	560.00		7,280.00	7,000.00
				$40,200.00

Chapter 10 Employer Payroll Tax Reporting

Phoenix Sales and Service computes the total amounts it owes for FUTA and SUTA taxes for the first quarter of 2009 as:

Federal Unemployment Taxes: 0.008 × $40,200.00 =	$ 321.60
State Unemployment Taxes: 0.027 × $40,200.00 =	1,085.40
Total Unemployment Tax Expense	$1,407.00

General Journal Entry to Record Unemployment Taxes   The accountant then makes the following two general entries in the general journal.

Apr.	10	Payroll Tax Expense	3 2 1	60		
		Federal Unemployment Taxes Payable			3 2 1	60
		Employer's federal unemployment taxes for first quarter.				
Apr.	10	Payroll Tax Expense	1 0 8 5	40		
		State Unemployment Taxes Payable			1 0 8 5	40
		Employer's state unemployment taxes for the first quarter.				

Assets = Liabilities + Equity
+321.60   −321.60

Assets = Liabilities + Equity
+1,085.40   −1,085.40

Reporting Employer's Unemployment Taxes

FUTA and SUTA taxes are typically due by the end of the next month following the end of the quarter.

LO7 Prepare unemployment tax returns.

Reporting State Unemployment Taxes   Phoenix Sales and Service must now do two things to meet the SUTA deadline. First, it files an **Employer's Quarterly Unemployment Tax Report** for unemployment taxes owed the state of Arizona and includes a check for $1,085.40. This report is shown in Exhibit 10.6. The dollar amounts in boxes 1, 3, and 4 all agree with amounts in the company's payroll register and individual employee earnings records. Phoenix Sales and Service did not owe any additional amounts for interest, penalties, or job training taxes. Second, it deposits $321.60 in a federal depository bank, as we showed earlier.

Reporting Federal Unemployment Taxes   The employer files **Form 940,** or **Form 940-EZ, Employer's Annual Federal Unemployment Tax Return** by January 31 after the year ends. This deadline is extended to February 10 if the employer has made all tax deposits during the year on time. The employer uses Form 940-EZ if it pays unemployment taxes to only one state.

Assume that Phoenix Sales and Service hires no new workers during 2009. As we illustrated earlier, five of the company's six employees' gross pay exceeds the $7,000 annual limit by the end of the first quarter of 2009. Robert Austin's gross pay also passes this limit during 2009. So, for 2009 Phoenix Sales and Service has total wages subject to FUTA tax of $42,000 (6 × $7,000). The company pays a total of $336 in FUTA taxes for the year

Exhibit 10.6

Employer's Quarterly Unemployment Tax Report

These forms vary by state, and are available through state governments.

ARIZONA DEPARTMENT OF ECONOMIC SECURITY
PO BOX 52027
PHOENIX, AZ 85072-2027
Telephone (602) 248-9354

ARIZONA ACCOUNT NUMBER
CALENDAR QUARTER ENDING
TO AVOID PENALTY MAIL BY
FEDERAL ID NO.

For Online Filling: **www.azui.com**

PLEASE RETURN ORIGINAL

UNEMPLOYMENT TAX AND WAGE REPORT

A. NUMBER OF EMPLOYEES -
Report for each month, the number of full and part-time covered workers who worked during or received pay subject to UI Taxes for the payroll period which includes the 12th of the month.

6

6

6

B. WAGES - List all employees in Social Security Number order, or alphabetically by last name. Please use white paper in the same format for additional employees. If you have six or more employees, consider reporting via magnetic media. Ask for "Arizona Magnetic Media Reporting" (PAU-430). We support diskette and cartridge media. Or consider online reporting at **www.azui.com**.

USE BLACK INK ONLY

C. WAGE SUMMARY - See Reverse For Instructions

1.	**TOTAL WAGES PAID IN QUARTER** From Section B. Wage Listing	42,419 . 00
2.	**SUBTRACT EXCESS WAGES** Cannot exceed Line 1 - see instructions	2,219 . 00
3.	**TAXABLE WAGES PAID** Up to $7000 per Employee - Line 1 minus line 2	40,200 . 00
4.	**TAX DUE** Line 3 × Tax Rate of The decimal equivalant = .027	1,085 . 40
5.	**ADD INTEREST DUE** 1% of Tax Due for each month payment is late	0 . 00
6.	**ADD PENALTY FOR LATE REPORT** 0.10% of Line 1 ($35 min / $200 max)	0 . 00
7.	**ADD JOB TRAINING TAX DUE** 0.10% of Line 3	0 . 00
8.	**TOTAL PAYMENT DUE** If the sum of lines 4 & 7 is equal to or less than $9.99, payment of the taxes due is not required.	1,085 . 40
9.	**SUBTRACT ANY CREDIT BALANCE** If a balance is listed, subtract from Line 8.	
10.	**AMOUNT PAID** Make check Payable to DES-Unemployment Tax	1,085 . 40

LIEN MAY BE FILED WITHOUT FURTHER NOTICE ON DELINQUENT TAXES.

1. Employee Social Security Number	2. Employee Name (*Last, First*)	3. Total Wages Paid in Quarter
333 - 22 - 9999	Austin, Robert	5,200.00
299 - 11 - 9201	Cross, Judy	7,553.00
444 - 11 - 9090	Diaz, John	7,826.00
909 - 11 - 3344	Keife, Kay	7,280.00
444 - 56 - 3211	Miller, Lee	7,280.00
	TOTAL WAGES THIS PAGE	35,139.00
Signature *Mary Wills*	TOTAL WAGES ALL PAGES	42,419.00*
Title: Accountant	Prepared by: Mary Wills	
Date: 04/10/2009	Telephone: (602) 555-8900	

PHOTO COPY FOR YOUR RECORDS

*Dale Sears' wages of $7,280.00 would be reported on a separate page.

($42,000 × 0.008). The company pays a total of $1,134 in SUTA taxes for the year ($42,000 × 0.027). By no later than January 31, 2010, the accountant files the Form 940-EZ shown in Exhibit 10.7.

General Journal Entry to Record Employer's Payment of Unemployment Taxes

After these tasks are done, the following entry is made in Phoenix Sales and Service's general journal. The employer does not file quarterly tax reports for FUTA taxes. These taxes are reported only annually. We show an example for Phoenix Sales and Service for 2009 next.

Apr.	10	Federal Unemployment Taxes Payable	3 2 1 60		
		Cash		3 2 1 60	
		Remit employer's federal unemployment taxes for the first quarter.			
Apr.	10	State Unemployment Taxes Payable	1 0 8 5 40		
		Cash		1 0 8 5 40	
		Remit employer's state unemployment taxes for the first quarter.			

Assets = Liabilities + Equity
−321.60   −321.60

Assets = Liabilities + Equity
−1,085.40   −1,085.40

HOW YOU DOIN'?   Answers—p. 247

7. A company has 10 employees. This company's FUTA rate is 0.8% on the first $7,000 earned; its SUTA rate is 2.5% on the first $7,000. Each employee earns over $7,000 in 2009, and the employer's total gross pay is $200,000. What amount of (*a*) FUTA taxes and (*b*) SUTA taxes will the employer pay in 2010?

8. How frequently does an employer report state and federal unemployment taxes?

Exhibit 10.7

Form 940-EZ, Employer's Annual Federal Unemployment (FUTA) Tax Return

Refer to www.IRS.gov for revised versions of this form.

Form **940-EZ**

Department of the Treasury
Internal Revenue Service

Employer's Annual Federal Unemployment (FUTA) Tax Return

▶ See the separate Instructions for Form 940-EZ for information on completing this form.

OMB No. 1545-1110

T	
FF	
FD	
FP	
I	
T	

You must complete this section. ▶

Name (as distinguished from trade name)
Mary Wills

Trade name, if any
Phoenix Sales & Service

Address (number and street)
1214 Mill Road

Calendar year
2009

Employer identification number (EIN)
86-3214587

City, state, and ZIP code
Phoenix, AZ 85621

*Answer the questions under **Who May Use Form 940-EZ** on page 2. If you cannot use Form 940-EZ, you must use Form 940.*

A Enter the amount of contributions paid to your state unemployment fund (see the separate instructions) . . ▶ $ 1,134 | 00

B (1) Enter the name of the state where you have to pay contributions . . . . ▶ Arizona

(2) Enter your state reporting number as shown on your state unemployment tax return. ▶ 12-345678

If you will not have to file returns in the future, check here (see **Who Must File** in separate instructions) and complete and sign the return. ▶ ☐

If this is an Amended Return, check here (see **Amended Returns** in the separate instructions) . . . . ▶ ☐

Part I   **Taxable Wages and FUTA Tax**

1	Total payments (including payments shown on lines 2 and 3) during the calendar year for services of employees	**1**	169,676 00
2	Exempt payments. (Explain all exempt payments, attaching additional sheets if necessary.) ▶	**2**	
3	Payments of more than $7,000 for services. Enter only amounts over the first $7,000 paid to each employee (see the separate instructions)	**3**	127,676 00
4	Add lines 2 and 3 . . . . ▶	**4**	127,676 00
5	Total taxable wages (subtract line 4 from line 1) . . . . ▶	**5**	42,000 00
6	FUTA tax. Multiply the wages on line 5 by .008 and enter here. (If the result is over $500, also complete Part II.)	**6**	336 00
7	Total FUTA tax deposited for the year, including any overpayment applied from a prior year	**7**	336 00
8	**Balance due** (subtract line 7 from line 6). Pay to the "United States Treasury." . . . . ▶	**8**	0 00
	If you owe more than $500, see **Depositing FUTA tax** in the separate instructions.		
9	Overpayment (subtract line 6 from line 7). Check if it is to be: ☐ Applied to next return or ☐ Refunded ▶	**9**	

Part II   **Record of Quarterly Federal Unemployment Tax Liability** (Do not include state liability.) **Complete only if line 6 is over $500.**

Quarter	First (Jan. 1 – Mar. 31)	Second (Apr. 1 – June 30)	Third (July 1 – Sept. 30)	Fourth (Oct. 1 – Dec. 31)	Total for year
Liability for quarter	321.60	14.40			336.00

Third-Party Designee

Do you want to allow another person to discuss this return with the IRS (see the separate instructions)? ☐ **Yes.** Complete the following. ☑ **No**

Designee's name ▶   Phone no. ▶ ( )   Personal identification number (PIN) ▶

Under penalties of perjury, I declare that I have examined this return, including accompanying schedules and statements, and, to the best of my knowledge and belief, it is true, correct, and complete, and that no part of any payment made to a state unemployment fund claimed as a credit was, or is to be, deducted from the payments to employees.

Signature ▶ *Mary Wills*   Title (Owner, etc.) ▶ Accountant   Date ▶ 01/14/2010

For Privacy Act and Paperwork Reduction Act Notice, see the separate instructions.   ▼ **DETACH HERE** ▼   Cat. No. 10983G   Form **940-EZ**

Workers' Compensation Insurance

Computing Estimated Workers' Compensation Insurance Premium

LO8 Compute and record workers' compensation insurance premiums for an employer.

Phoenix Sales and Service has two types of workers: office workers and landscapers. The company pays a workers' compensation premium of $0.30 per $100 of office worker wages and $2.50 per $100 of landscapers' wages. Based on previous experience at the beginning of 2009, Phoenix Sales and Service estimates its total wages in 2009 will be $160,000. The company also estimates $53,000 of its total wages will be paid to office workers, and $107,000 will be paid to landscapers. It computes estimated workers' compensation insurance premiums for 2009 as follows:

Office workers ($53,000/100) × $0.30 =	$ 159.00
Landscapers ($107,000/100) × $2.50 =	2,675.00
Total	$2,834.00

General Journal Entry to Record Estimated Workers' Compensation Insurance Premium   Phoenix Sales and Service pays this premium in January 2009. The company makes the following entry in the general journal.

Assets = Liabilities + Equity
−2,834.00   −2,834.00

Jan.	14	Workers' Compensation Insurance Expense	2 8 3 4 00	
		Cash		2 8 3 4 00
		Estimated workers' compensation insurance premium for 2009.		

Computing Actual Workers' Compensation Insurance Premium

After the end of 2009, the payroll clerk updates the individual employee earnings records, as we showed in Chapter 9. Assume that these records show the following actual total wages for Phoenix Sales and Service employees for the year ending December 31, 2009.

Office workers	$ 49,920
Landscapers	119,756

The actual workers' compensation insurance premium for Phoenix Sales and Service for 2009 is

Office workers ($49,920/100) × $0.30 =	$ 149.76
Landscapers ($119,756/100) × $2.50 =	2,993.90
Total	$3,143.66

General Journal Entry to Adjust Workers' Compensation Insurance Premium for Actual Wages   The company's estimated workers' compensation insurance premium for 2009 ($2,834.00) was too low. It pays the difference of $309.66 ($3,143.66 − $2,834.00) and makes the following journal entry.

Assets = Liabilities + Equity
−309.66   −309.66

Dec.	31	Workers' Compensation Insurance Expense	3 0 9 66	
		Cash		3 0 9 66
		Pay additional workers' compensation insurance premium		
		based on actual wages paid in 2009.		

HOW YOU DOIN'?   Answers—p. 247

9. A company has office staff and construction workers. The company pays workers' compensation insurance premiums of $0.20 per $100 of office staff wages and $3.00 per $100 of construction worker wages. The company estimates it will pay $65,000 in total pay to office workers and $218,000 in total pay to construction workers in 2009. What amount of estimated workers' compensation insurance premium will the company pay at the beginning of 2009?

10. What journal entry will the company in question 9 make to record the payment of its estimated workers' compensation insurance premium at the beginning of 2009?

11. Assume the company in question 9 actually pays $66,000 in total pay to office staff and $209,400 in total pay to construction workers during 2009. What journal entry will the company make to adjust its 2009 workers' compensation expense for actual 2009 wages?

Demonstration Problem

The Cutting Edge hair salon pays its employees monthly. Employees' gross pay is subject to the following taxes.

Tax	Rate	Applied to
FICA—Social Security	6.20%	First $106,800
FICA—Medicare	1.45	All gross pay
FUTA	0.80	First $7,000
SUTA	2.00	First $7,000

The company reports the following in its payroll register for its three employees for the month ending September 30, 2009.

	Gross Pay through 8/31	Current Month Gross Pay	Federal Income Tax Withholding
Brianna	$17,940	$1,840	$298
Juan	4,625	1,500	243
Shi	5,600	1,680	272
Total	$28,165	$5,020	$813

Required

1. Compute the following employer payroll taxes for the month ending September 30, 2009: (a) FICA—Social Security, (b) FICA—Medicare, (c) FUTA, and (d) SUTA.

2. Prepare the journal entries to record The Cutting Edge's payroll taxes for the month ending September 30, 2009. Assume $813 of federal income tax withheld has already been recorded with a debit to Payroll Taxes Expense and a credit to Employee Federal Income Taxes Payable.

3. The Cutting Edge deposits its payroll taxes monthly. Prepare the journal entry to record the company's payroll tax deposit for September.

4. Assume The Cutting Edge pays its FUTA and SUTA taxes monthly. Prepare the journal entry to record the payment of the company's FUTA and SUTA taxes for September.

Planning the Solution

- For 1, determine if any employee's gross pay through 8/31 is above the annual limits for any of the payroll taxes. Determine the amount of total income for the month subject to each tax. Multiply this income amount by the appropriate tax rate.
- For parts 2, 3, and 4, determine the accounts affected and then record the entries.

Solution to Demonstration Problem

1. No employee's gross pay through 8/31 exceeds the limit ($106,800) for FICA—Social Security tax. Brianna's gross pay through 8/31 does exceed the limit for FUTA and SUTA taxes, so The Cutting Edge does not owe FUTA or SUTA taxes on her pay for September. Shi's gross pay for September, when added to her gross pay through 8/31, causes her to exceed the FUTA and SUTA limit. The Cutting Edge pays FUTA and SUTA taxes on only $1,400 of Shi's September gross pay. The September payroll taxes are:

   a. FICA—Social Security $5,020 \times 6.2\% = \$311.24$
   b. FICA—Medicare $5,020 \times 1.45\% = \$72.79$
   c. FUTA $2,900^* \times 0.8\% = \$23.20$
   d. SUTA $2,900 \times 2.0\% = \$58.00$

   *Juan's gross pay of $1,500 + $1,400 of Shi's gross pay.

2.

Payroll Tax Expense	465.23	
Employer FICA—Social Security Taxes Payable . . .		311.24
Employer FICA—Medicare Taxes Payable.		72.79
Federal Unemployment Taxes Payable.		23.20
State Unemployment Taxes Payable		58.00

3.

Employee Federal Income Taxes Payable.	813.00	
Employer FICA—Social Security Taxes Payable	311.24	
Employer FICA—Medicare Taxes Payable.	72.79	
Cash		1,197.03

4.

Federal Unemployment Taxes Payable.	23.20	
State Unemployment Taxes Payable	58.00	
Cash		81.20

Summary

LO1 Describe laws that impact employer's payroll obligations.
Law requires employers to match their employees' Social Security and Medicare taxes. Employers must also pay federal and state unemployment taxes and workers' compensation insurance premiums.

LO2 Compute employer FICA taxes and record them in a general journal. The employer pays 6.2% of each employee's annual gross pay (up to $106,800) for Social Security taxes and 1.45% of their annual gross pay for Medicare taxes. The accountant debits Payroll Tax Expense and credits Employer FICA—Social Security Tax Payable and Employer—FICA Medicare Tax Payable.

LO3 Journalize an employer's deposit of federal income taxes and FICA taxes withheld and prepare a deposit coupon.
The employer must periodically deposit amounts withheld from employee pay in a federal depository. This is done by either electronic funds transfer or by completing a Form 8109. The accountant debits Employer FICA—Social Security Tax Payable and Employer FICA—Medicare Tax Payable and credits Cash.

LO4 Prepare Form 941, Employer's Quarterly Federal Tax Return. The accountant files this federal tax form within one month after each quarter ends. It reports on the employer's Federal Unemployment Taxes for the quarter.

LO5 Prepare Form W-2, Employee's Wage and Tax Statement, and Form W-3, Transmittal of Wage and Tax Statements.

After each calendar year-end the employer sends each employee a Form W-2, which summarizes the employee's wages and deductions for the year just ended. The employer transmits copies of these W-2's to the Social Security Administration and includes a Form W-3 that summarizes all the individual W-2's.

LO6 Compute an employer's state and federal unemployment taxes and record them in a general journal. The employer pays unemployment taxes of up to 6.2% of employee gross pay. Employers with stable employment histories and low turnover typically pay lower SUTA rates. Employers also receive credits for SUTA taxes and often pay FUTA taxes of only 0.8% of their employee's annual gross pay. The accountant debits Payroll Tax Expense and credits Federal Unemployment Taxes Payable and State Unemployment Taxes Payable.

LO7 Prepare unemployment tax returns. The employer files a quarterly state unemployment tax return. Federal unemployment taxes are reported annually on Form 940, the Employer's Federal Unemployment Tax Return.

LO8 Compute and record workers' compensation insurance premiums for an employer. Most states require the employer to provide benefits or pay insurance premiums for employees injured while on the job. Premium amounts are based on total estimated salary amounts and how hazardous the job is.

1. The annual limits are: (a) $106,800, (b) none, (c) $7,000, and (d) $7,000.

2. (a) FICA taxes are incurred by both employee and employer. (b) FUTA taxes are incurred by the employer. (c) SUTA taxes are incurred by the employer. (d) Withheld income taxes are incurred by the employee.

3. ($1,000 × 0.8%) + ($1,000 × 4%) + ($3,000 × 6.2%) + ($3,000 × 1.45%) = $277.50. $1,000 of the $3,000 March pay is subject to FUTA and SUTA—the entire $6,000 pay from January and February was subject to them.

4. (a) New businesses make monthly payroll tax deposits. (b) The company had less than $50,000 in payroll taxes in the "look-back" period (July 1, 2008, through June 30, 2009), so it makes monthly payroll tax deposits. (c) The company had more than $50,000 in payroll taxes in the "look-back" period (July 1, 2008, through June 30, 2009), so it makes semiweekly payroll tax deposits.

5. Federal payroll taxes are reported quarterly on Form 941.

6. A W-2 is an annual statement sent to each employee that reports the employee's total earnings and deductions for the year just ended. Form W-3 reports the total wage and withholding information for all of the company's employees.

7. (a) FUTA = 10 × $7,000 × 0.8% = $560. (b) SUTA = 10 × $7,000 × 2.5% = $1,750.

8. The employer files *quarterly* reports for state unemployment taxes and *annual* reports for federal unemployment taxes.

9. [($65,000 / $100) × $0.20] + [($218,000 / $100) × $3.00] = $6,670.

10.

Workers' Compensation Insurance Expense ...	6,670	
Cash		6,670

11. The company's actual workers' compensation insurance premium for 2009 is: [($66,000 / $100) × $0.20] + [($209,400 / $100) × $3.00] = $6,414. The company is entitled to a refund of $256 ($6,670 − $6,414), which is recorded as:

Workers' Compensation Insurance Refund Receivable	256	
Workers' Compensation Insurance Expense ..		256

Key Terms

Authorized depository (p. 234) A bank that can accept payroll deposits from its own checking account customers.

Employer identification number (EIN) (p. 232) A number issued by the federal government that uniquely identifies a business.

Employer's Quarterly Unemployment Tax Report (p. 241) A report filed with the state that shows an employer's unemployment taxes owed.

Federal depository bank (p. 234) Bank authorized to accept deposits of amounts payable to the federal government.

Federal Insurance Contributions Act (FICA) taxes (p. 232) Taxes assessed on both employers and employees; for Social Security and Medicare programs.

Federal Reserve Bank (p. 234) A bank that can accept payroll deposits from any business.

Federal unemployment taxes (FUTA) (p. 232) Payroll taxes on employers assessed by the federal government to support its unemployment insurance program.

Form 940 (p. 241) IRS form used to report an employer's federal unemployment taxes (FUTA) on an annual filing basis.

Form 940-EZ (p. 241) The Employer's Annual Federal Unemployment Tax Return. This shows the amount of FUTA tax the employer owes for the year.

Form 941 (p. 236) IRS form filed to report FICA taxes owed and remitted.

Form 8109 (p. 235) A preprinted Federal Tax Deposit Coupon. It is used when an employer deposits money into a federal depository bank.

Form 8109-B (p. 235) A Federal Tax Deposit Coupon used by new businesses or when the business does not have a supply of preprinted Forms 8109.

Form SS-4 (p. 232) An Internal Revenue Service form filed by a business in order to receive an employer identification number.

Form W-2 (p. 238) Annual report by an employer to each employee showing the employee's wages subject to FICA and federal income taxes along with amounts withheld.

Form W-3 (p. 239) The Transmittal of Wage and Tax Statements form. This form reports the total wages and tax withholding information for all the employer's employees for the year.

Look-back rule (p. 234) A rule used to classify business as monthly or semiweekly depositors.

Merit rating (p. 232) Rating assigned to an employer by a state based on the employer's record of employment.

State unemployment taxes (SUTA) (p. 232) State payroll taxes on employers to support its unemployment programs.

Workers' compensation insurance (p. 233) An insurance program that provides benefits to workers who are injured on the job.

Multiple Choice Quiz

Answers on p. 259   mhhe.com/wildCA2e

Additional Multiple Choice Quizzes are available at the book's Website.

1. An employee earned $50,000 during the year. FICA tax for social security is 6.2% and FICA tax for Medicare is 1.45%. The employer's share of FICA taxes is
   a. Zero, since the employee's pay exceeds the FICA limit.
   b. Zero, since FICA is not an employer tax.
   c. $3,100
   d. $725
   e. $3,825

2. Assume the FUTA tax rate is 0.8% and the SUTA tax rate is 5.4%. Both taxes are applied to the first $7,000 of an employee's pay. What is the total unemployment tax an employer must pay on an employee's annual wages of $40,000?
   a. $2,480
   b. $434
   c. $56
   d. $378
   e. Zero; the employee's wages exceed the $7,000 maximum.

3. A company estimates that its office employees will earn $70,000 next year and its construction employees will earn $145,000 next year. The company pays for workers' compensation insurance for all of its employees. The rates for this insurance are $0.40 per $100 of wages for office employees and $6.00 per $100 of wages for construction workers. The company's estimated workers' compensation insurance premium for the year is
   a. $4,780
   b. $8,980

   c. $898
   d. Zero; the company pays based on actual, not estimated, wages
   e. $13,760

4. A company's payroll register reports total employee gross pay of $16,200 for a recent pay period. A total of $14,000 of this amount is subject to Social Security tax. Only one of the company's employees has total gross pay for the year less than $7,000; this employee earned gross pay of $1,150 during the recent pay period. Assume a Social Security tax rate of 6.2%, a Medicare tax rate of 1.45%, a SUTA rate of 1.5%, and a FUTA rate of 0.8%. The employer's payroll tax expense for this pay period is
   a. $113.85
   b. $1,088.45
   c. $1,611.90
   d. $1,129.35
   e. $1,256.75

5. The Federal Insurance Contributions Act (FICA) requires that each employer file a
   a. W-4.
   b. Form 941.
   c. Form 1040.
   d. Form 1099.
   e. All of the above.

Discussion Questions

1. What is the combined amount (in percent) of the employee and employer Social Security tax rate?

2. What is the current Medicare tax rate? This rate is applied to what maximum level of salary and wages?

3. Which payroll taxes are the employee's responsibility and which are the employer's responsibility?

4. What is an employer's unemployment merit rating? How are these ratings assigned to employers?

5. What is a federal depository bank?

6. What is a Form W-2? To whom is Form W-2 sent?

7. What is a Form W-3? To whom is a Form W-3 sent?

8. How does an employer report its state and federal unemployment taxes?

9. When does an employer typically pay premiums for workers' compensation insurance?

10. How often must an employer deposit federal income tax withholdings?

11. How does an employer make federal income tax withholding deposits?

connect

QUICK STUDY

QS 10-1

Employer's payroll obligations

L01

Match each of the following terms A through H with the appropriate definitions 1 through 8.

A. EFTPS   **D.** FICA taxes   **G.** FUTA taxes
B. Form 941   **E.** Form 940   **H.** Federal depository bank
C. Merit rating   **F.** Form W-2

_____ **1.** A rating assigned to an employer by a state based on the employer's past record regarding stable employment.

_____ **2.** Taxes assessed on both employer and employees under the Federal Insurance Contributions Act. These taxes fund Social Security and Medicare.

_____ **3.** Payroll taxes on employers assessed by the federal government to support the federal unemployment insurance program.

_____ **4.** A bank authorized to accept deposits of amounts payable to the federal government, including payroll taxes.

_____ **5.** A system for depositing payroll taxes via computer or telephone.

_____ **6.** A statement that reports an individual employee's total earnings and deductions for the year.

_____ **7.** A form that reports an employer's federal tax withholdings for a quarter.

_____ **8.** A form that reports an employer's annual federal unemployment taxes.

Major Co. has five employees, each of whom earns $2,500 per month and has been employed since January 1. FICA Social Security taxes are 6.2% of the first $106,800 paid to each employee, and FICA Medicare taxes are 1.45% of gross pay. FUTA taxes are 0.8% and SUTA taxes are 2.8% of the first $7,000 paid to each employee. Prepare the March 31 journal entry to record the March payroll tax expense.

QS 10-2

Record employer payroll taxes

LO2   LO6

A company's employees had the following earnings records at the close of the weekly payroll period ending August 7, 2009.

QS 10-3

Employer's payroll tax expenses

LO2   LO6

Employees	Earnings through Prior Pay Period	Earnings This Pay Period
D. Adams	$11,300	$3,900
J. Hess	6,100	2,500
R. Lui	9,500	3,100
T. Morales	4,800	1,400
L. Vang	10,000	3,000

The company's payroll taxes expense on each employee's earnings includes: FICA Social Security taxes of 6.2% on the first $106,800 plus 1.45% FICA Medicare on all wages; 0.8% federal unemployment taxes on the first $7,000; and 2.5% state unemployment taxes on the first $7,000. Compute the employer's total payroll tax expense for the current pay period.

Refer to QS 10-3. Prepare the August 7, 2009, entry in the company's general journal to record the employer's payroll taxes for the current pay period.

QS 10-4

Recording employer payroll taxes

LO2   LO6

A company's employer payroll taxes are 0.8% for federal unemployment taxes, 5.4% for state unemployment taxes, 6.2% for FICA Social Security taxes on earnings up to $106,800, and 1.45% for FICA Medicare taxes on all earnings. Compute the Form W-2 Wage and Tax Statement information required below for the following employees:

QS 10-5

Preparing Form W-2   **LO5**

Employee	Gross Earnings	Federal Income Taxes Withheld
A. Baker	$84,000	$17,600
C. Dirkson	52,000	8,200

W-2 Information	A. Baker	C. Dirkson
Federal income tax withheld	_____	_____
Wages, tips, other compensation	_____	_____
Social Security tax withheld	_____	_____
Social Security wages	_____	_____
Medicare tax withheld	_____	_____
Medicare wages	_____	_____

QS 10–6
Preparing Form W-3   **LO5**

Refer to the data in QS 10-5. Compute the company's Form W-3 Transmittal of Wage and Tax Statements information required below.

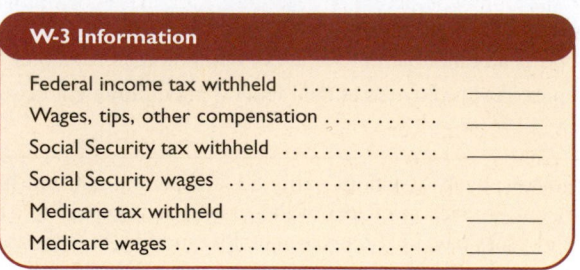

W-3 Information	
Federal income tax withheld	_____
Wages, tips, other compensation	_____
Social Security tax withheld	_____
Social Security wages	_____
Medicare tax withheld	_____
Medicare wages	_____

QS 10–7
Employer's payroll taxes
LO2   LO6

A company's payroll information for the month of May follows:

Administrative salaries	$2,000
Sales salaries	3,500
Shop wages	4,000
FICA taxes withheld	700
Federal income taxes withheld	1,300
Medical insurance premiums withheld	415
Union dues withheld	205

On May 31 the company issued Check No. 335 payable to the Payroll Bank Account to pay for the May payroll. It issued payroll checks to the employees after depositing the check. (1) Prepare the journal entry to record (accrue) the employer's payroll for May. (2) Prepare the journal entry to pay the May payroll. The federal and state unemployment tax rates are 0.8% and 5.4%, respectively, on the first $7,000 paid to each employee; the wages and salaries subject to these taxes were $6,000. (3) Prepare the journal entry to record the employer's payroll taxes. (Refer to Chapter 9 if necessary in answering questions 1 and 2.)

QS 10–8
Computing employer taxes
LO1   LO2   LO6

An employee earned $62,500 during the year working for an employer. The FICA tax for Social Security is 6.2% and the FICA tax for Medicare is 1.45%. The current FUTA tax rate is 0.8%, and the SUTA tax rate is 5.4%. Both unemployment taxes are applied to the first $7,000 of an employee's pay. What is the amount of total unemployment taxes the employer will pay for this employee?

connect

EXERCISES

Exercise 10–1
Computing payroll taxes
LO2   LO6

BMX Co. has one employee, and the company is subject to the following taxes:

Tax	Rate	Applied to
FICA—Social Security	6.20%	First $106,800
FICA—Medicare	1.45	All gross pay
FUTA	0.80	First $7,000
SUTA	2.90	First $7,000

Compute BMX's amounts for each of these four taxes as applied to the employee's gross earnings for September under each of three separate situations (*a*), (*b*), and (*c*).

	Gross Pay through August	Gross Pay for September
a.	$ 6,800	$ 900
b.	19,200	2,200
c.	101,800	8,000

Check   (a) FUTA, $1.60; SUTA, $5.80

Using the data in situation *a* of Exercise 10-1, prepare the employer's September 30 journal entries to record (1) the employer's payroll tax expense and its related liabilities and (2) its tax deposits. In preparing the tax deposit entry assume that the employer has already recorded liabilities for employee payroll taxes and withholdings. The employee's federal income taxes withheld by the employer are $150 for this pay period.

Exercise 10-2
Payroll-related journal entries
LO2   LO3

Metro Express has five sales employees, each of whom earns $4,000 per month and is paid on the last working day of the month. Each employee's wages are subject to FICA Social Security taxes of 6.2% and Medicare taxes of 1.45% on all wages. Withholding for each employee also includes federal income tax of 16%. Each employee's monthly medical insurance premium of $110 is also withheld from their paychecks. Metro Express also pays federal unemployment taxes of 0.8% of the first $7,000 paid each employee, and state unemployment taxes of 4.0% of the first $7,000 paid to each employee.

Prepare the journal entries to record (1) the employee's wages and payroll taxes at January 31, (2) the employer's payroll taxes at January 31, and (3) payment of the employer's payroll tax liabilities at January 31 for Metro Express. Metro Express deposits taxes monthly.

Exercise 10-3
Employer's payroll taxes
LO2   LO3   LO6

Premier Landscaping reports the following in its payroll register for August. The company makes monthly tax deposits.

Exercise 10-4
Employer's tax deposits   **LO3**

	Employee Deductions for		
Pay Period End	Federal Income Tax	Social Security	Medicare
Aug. 7	$1,530.00	$632.40	$147.90
Aug. 14	1,447.50	598.30	139.93
Aug. 21	1,563.00	646.04	151.09
Aug. 28	1,620.00	669.60	156.60

Prepare the general journal entry to record Premier Landscaping's deposit of its federal income tax withholdings and FICA taxes (employee and employer portions) for August.

Ideal Systems' employees had the following earnings records at the close of the first quarter:

Exercise 10-5
Computing and reporting unemployment taxes   **LO6   LO7**

Employee	Gross Pay for First Quarter
A. Poe	$8,200
B. Rye	7,450
C. Sims	6,770

The state unemployment tax is 5.4%, but Ideal Systems pays only 2% due to its high merit rating. Ideal Systems also pays 0.8% for federal unemployment taxes. Unemployment taxes are based on the first $7,000 of each employee's earnings during the year.

1. Compute Ideal Systems' SUTA and FUTA tax liabilities for the first quarter.
2. Prepare the general journal entry to record Ideal Systems' SUTA and FUTA tax liabilities for the first quarter.
3. Prepare the general journal entry to record Ideal Systems' payment of its SUTA and FUTA tax liabilities for the first quarter.
4. Explain how Ideal Systems will report its unemployment taxes to the state and federal governments.

A1 Construction began operations on January 1, 2009. The company pays workers' compensation insurance premiums for its employees. The company's accountant assembled the data below for 2009:

Exercise 10-6
Computing workers' compensation insurance premiums   **LO8**

Classification	Estimated Wages	Rate per $100 of Wages
Office workers	$ 60,000	0.25
Construction	320,000	4.20

1. Compute A1 Construction's estimated workers' compensation insurance premium for 2009.
2. Prepare the general journal entry to record A1 Construction's payment of its 2009 workers' compensation insurance premium on January 9, 2009.

Exercise 10–7
Employer's tax deposits   **LO3**

Jim Phillips Consulting reports the following in his payroll register for December 2009. The company makes monthly tax deposits.

| Pay Period End | Employee Deductions for | | |
	Social Security	Medicare	Federal Income Tax
Dec. 6	$552.13	$129.13	$1,380.33
Dec. 13	623.87	145.91	1,559.68
Dec. 20	453.16	105.98	1,132.90
Dec. 27	527.76	123.43	1,319.40

Prepare the general journal entry to record Jim Phillips' deposit of its federal income tax withholdings and FICA taxes (employee and employer portions) for the month of December 2009.

---

connect™

PROBLEM SET A

Problem 10–1A
Payroll expenses, withholdings, and taxes   **LO2 LO6**

mhhe.com/wildCA2e

Paloma Co. pays its employees each week. Its employees' gross pay is subject to these taxes:

Tax	Rate	Applied to
FICA—Social Security	6.20%	First $106,800
FICA—Medicare	1.45	All gross pay
FUTA	0.80	First $7,000
SUTA	2.15	First $7,000

The company is preparing its payroll calculations for the week ended August 25. Payroll records show the following information for the company's four employees.

| Name | Gross Pay through 8/18 | Current Week | |
		Gross Pay	Income Tax Withholding
Dahlia	$106,000	$2,800	$284
Trey	31,700	1,000	145
Kiesha	6,850	550	39
Chee	1,250	500	30

In addition to gross pay, the company must pay one-half of the $34 per employee weekly health insurance; each employee pays the remaining one-half. The company also contributes an extra 8% of each employee's gross pay (at no cost to employees) to a pension fund.

Required
Compute the following for the week ended August 25 (round amounts to the nearest cent):

Check (1) $176.70
(2) $70.33
(3) $5.20

1. Employer's FICA taxes for Social Security.
2. Employer's FICA taxes for Medicare.
3. Employer's FUTA taxes.
4. Employer's SUTA taxes.
5. Employer's total payroll-related expense for each employee.

On January 8, the end of the first weekly pay period of the year, Regis Company's payroll register showed that its employees earned $22,760 of office salaries and $65,840 of sales salaries. Withholdings from the employees' salaries include FICA Social Security taxes at the rate of 6.2%, FICA Medicare taxes at the rate of 1.45%, $12,860 of federal income taxes, $1,340 of medical insurance deductions, and $840 of union dues. No employee earned more than $7,000 in this pay period. Regis Company does not pay for its employees' medical insurance premiums or union dues.

Problem 10-2A

Entries for payroll transactions

L02   L06

Required

1. Calculate Regis Company's FICA Social Security taxes payable and FICA Medicare taxes payable (employer portion). Prepare the journal entry to record Regis Company's January 8 (employer) payroll expenses and liabilities.

2. Prepare the journal entry to record Regis's (employer) unemployment taxes resulting from the January 8 payroll. Regis's merit rating reduces its state unemployment tax rate to 4.0% of the first $7,000 paid each employee. The federal unemployment tax rate is 0.8%.

Check   (1) Cr. Social Security Taxes
Payable, $5,493.20
(2) Dr. Payroll Taxes Expense,
$4,252.80

Francisco Company has 10 employees, each of whom earns $2,800 per month and is paid on the last day of each month. All 10 have been employed continuously at this amount since January 1. Francisco uses a payroll bank account and special payroll checks to pay its employees. On March 1, the following accounts and balances exist in its general ledger:

Problem 10-3A

Entries for payroll transactions

L02   L03   L06

a. FICA—Social Security Taxes Payable, $3,472; FICA—Medicare Taxes Payable, $812. (The balances of these accounts represent total liabilities for *both* the employer's and employees' FICA taxes for the February payroll only.)

b. Employees' Federal Income Taxes Payable, $4,000 (liability for February only).

c. Federal Unemployment Taxes Payable, $448 (liability for January and February together).

d. State Unemployment Taxes Payable, $2,240 (liability for January and February together).

During March and April, the company had the following payroll transactions.

Mar. 15   Issued check payable to Swift Bank, a federal depository bank authorized to accept employers' payments of FICA taxes and employee income tax withholdings. The $8,284 check is in payment of the February FICA and employee income taxes.

31   Recorded the March payroll and transferred funds from the regular bank account to the payroll bank account. Issued checks payable to each employee in payment of the March payroll. The payroll register shows the following summary totals for the March pay period.

Check   March 31: Cr. Accrued Wages
Payable, $21,858

| Salaries and Wages | | | | Federal | |
Office Salaries	Shop Wages	Gross Pay	FICA Taxes*	Income Taxes	Net Pay
$11,200	$16,800	$28,000	$1,736	$4,000	$21,858
			$ 406		

*FICA taxes are Social Security and Medicare, respectively.

31   Recorded the employer's payroll taxes resulting from the March payroll. The company has a merit rating that reduces its state unemployment tax rate to 4.0% of the first $7,000 paid each employee. The federal rate is 0.8%.

March 31: Dr. Payroll Taxes Expenses,
$2,814

Apr. 15   Issued check to Swift Bank in payment of the March FICA and employee income taxes.

April 15: Cr. Cash, $8,284

15   Issued check to the State Tax Commission for the January, February, and March state unemployment taxes. Mailed the check and the first quarter tax return to the Commission.

30   Issued check payable to Swift Bank in payment of the employer's FUTA taxes for the first quarter of the year.

30   Mailed Form 941 to the IRS, reporting the FICA taxes and the employees' federal income tax withholdings for the first quarter.

Required

Prepare journal entries to record the transactions and events for both March and April.

Problem 10-4A
Preparing deposit coupons and
Form 941   **LO3   LO4**

Refer to Problem 10-3A. Francisco Company's tax year ends on December 31 and its Employer Identification Number is 851435867. It is located at 12 Round Rock Road, Santa Fe, New Mexico 87501.

Required

1. Prepare a Form 8109-B for Francisco Company's April 15 deposit of its March FICA and employee income taxes.

2. Prepare Francisco Company's Form 941 for the first quarter. Assume that January's and February's payroll taxes and withholdings were identical to March.

Problem 10-5A
Employer's payroll taxes,
unemployment tax returns
LO3   LO6   LO7

Warner Co. pays state unemployment tax of 2.0% of each employee's first $7,000 of annual gross pay. It also pays federal unemployment tax of 0.8% of each employee's first $7,000 of annual gross pay. Warner Co.'s Employer Identification Number is 778125398, its state taxpayer identification number is 13-458232, and it is located at 605 Main Street, Dallas, Texas 75201. Warner Co. reports the following summary information in its payroll register for 2009.

Quarter Ended	Total Gross Pay	Total Gross Pay for FUTA and SUTA
March 31	$32,310.00	31,340.70
June 30	29,675.00	24,333.50
September 30	31,274.00	7,818.50
December 31	27,420.00	1,096.80

Required

1. Compute the amounts of FUTA and SUTA taxes Warner Co. owes for each quarter in 2009.

2. Prepare the general journal entry to record Warner Co.'s FUTA and SUTA taxes for the second quarter (ending on June 30) of 2009. This journal entry is made on June 30, 2009.

3. Prepare the general journal entry to record Warner Co.'s deposit of its second quarter FUTA and SUTA taxes. This journal entry is made on June 30, 2009.

4. Prepare a Form 940-EZ for Warner Co. for the year 2009.

Problem 10-6A
Workers' compensation
insurance premiums   **LO8**

Precision Tool began operations on January 1, 2009. Precision Tool pays workers' compensation insurance premiums for its employees. The company's accountant assembled the data below for Precision Tool for 2009:

Classification	Estimated Wages	Rate per $100 of Wages
Office workers	$ 90,000	0.15
Machine operators	292,500	3.20
Warehouse workers	67,500	1.75

Classification	Actual Wages Situation A	Actual Wages Situation B
Office workers	$ 86,469	$ 99,834
Machine operators	281,024	294,748
Warehouse workers	64,852	80,818

Required

1. Prepare the general journal entry to record Precision Tool's payment of its estimated 2009 workers' compensation insurance premium on January 5, 2009.

2. For each of the two separate situations (A) and (B) prepare the general journal entry to adjust Precision Tool's 2009 workers' compensation insurance premium for its actual wages during 2009. Assume this entry is made on January 15, 2010.

Fishing Guides Co. pays its employees each week. Employees' gross pay is subject to these taxes.

Tax	Rate	Applied to
FICA—Social Security	6.20%	First $106,800
FICA—Medicare	1.45	All gross pay
FUTA	0.80	First $7,000
SUTA	1.75	First $7,000

PROBLEM SET B

Problem 10-1B
Payroll expenses, withholdings, and taxes **LO2 LO6**

The company is preparing its payroll calculations for the week ended September 30. Payroll records show the following information for the company's four employees.

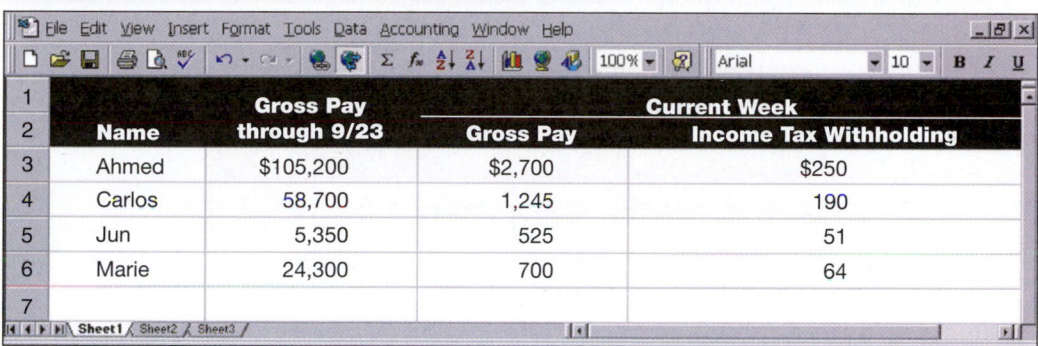

Name	Gross Pay through 9/23	Current Week Gross Pay	Current Week Income Tax Withholding
Ahmed	$105,200	$2,700	$250
Carlos	58,700	1,245	190
Jun	5,350	525	51
Marie	24,300	700	64

In addition to gross pay, the company must pay one-half of the $40 per employee weekly health insurance; each employee pays the remaining one-half. The company also contributes an extra 5% of each employee's gross pay (at no cost to employees) to a pension fund.

Required

Compute the following for the week ended September 30 (round amounts to the nearest cent):

1. Employer's FICA taxes for Social Security.
2. Employer's FICA taxes for Medicare.
3. Employer's FUTA taxes.
4. Employer's SUTA taxes.
5. Employer's total payroll-related expense for each employee.

Check (1) $252.34
(2) $74.96
(3) $4.20

Tavella Company's first weekly pay period of the year ends on January 8. On that date, the column totals in Tavella's payroll register indicate its sales employees earned $34,745, its office employees earned $21,225, and its delivery employees earned $1,030. The employees are to have withheld from their wages FICA Social Security taxes at the rate of 6.2%, FICA Medicare taxes at the rate of 1.45%, $8,625 of federal income taxes, $1,160 of medical insurance deductions, and $138 of union dues. No employee earned more than $7,000 in the first pay period. Tavella Company does not pay medical insurance premiums or union dues for its employees.

Problem 10-2B
Entries for payroll transactions **LO2 LO6**

Required

1. Compute Tavella Company's FICA Social Security taxes payable and FICA Medicare taxes payable. Prepare the journal entry to record Tavella Company's January 8 (employer) payroll expenses and liabilities.

2. Prepare the journal entry to record Tavella's (employer) unemployment taxes resulting from the January 8 payroll. Tavella's merit rating reduces its state unemployment tax rate to 3.4% of the first $7,000 paid each employee. The federal unemployment tax rate is 0.8%.

Check (1) Cr. FICA—Social Security Taxes Payable, $3,534
(2) Dr. Payroll Taxes Expense, $2,394

MLS Company has five employees, each of whom earns $1,600 per month and is paid on the last day of each month. All five have been employed continuously at this amount since January 1. MLS uses a payroll bank account and special payroll checks to pay its employees. On June 1, the following accounts and balances exist in its general ledger:

Problem 10-3B
Entries for payroll transactions **LO2 LO3 LO6**

a. FICA—Social Security Taxes Payable, $992; FICA—Medicare Taxes Payable, $232. (The balances of these accounts represent total liabilities for *both* the employer's and employees' FICA taxes for the May payroll only.)

b. Employees' Federal Income Taxes Payable, $1,050 (liability for May only).

c. Federal Unemployment Taxes Payable, $88 (liability for April and May together).

d. State Unemployment Taxes Payable, $440 (liability for April and May together).

During June and July, the company had the following payroll transactions.

June 15   Issued check payable to Security Bank, a federal depository bank authorized to accept employers' payments of FICA taxes and employee income tax withholdings. The $2,274 check is in payment of the May FICA and employee income taxes.

Check June 30: Cr. Accrued Payroll Payable, $6,338

      30   Recorded the June payroll and transferred funds from the regular bank account to the payroll bank account. Issued checks payable to each employee in payment of the June payroll. The payroll register shows the following summary totals for the June pay period.

| Salaries and Wages | | | | | |
Office Salaries	Shop Wages	Gross Pay	FICA Taxes*	Federal Income Taxes	Net Pay
$3,800	$4,200	$8,000	$496 $116	$1,050	$6,338

*FICA taxes are Social Security and Medicare, respectively.

Check June 30: Dr. Payroll Taxes Expenses, $612

July 15: Cr. Cash $2,274

      30   Recorded the employer's payroll taxes resulting from the June payroll. The company has a merit rating that reduces its state unemployment tax rate to 4.0% of the first $7,000 paid each employee. The federal rate is 0.8%.

July 15   Issued check payable to Security Bank in payment of the June FICA and employee income taxes.

      15   Issued check to the State Tax Commission for the April, May, and June state unemployment taxes. Mailed the check and the second quarter tax return to the State Tax Commission.

      31   Issued check payable to Security Bank in payment of the employer's FUTA taxes for the second quarter of the year.

      31   Mailed Form 941 to the IRS, reporting the FICA taxes and the employees' federal income tax withholdings for the second quarter.

Required

Prepare journal entries to record the transactions and events for both June and July.

Problem 10-4B

Preparing deposit coupons and Form 941   **LO3   LO4**

Refer to Problem 10-3B. MLS Company's tax year ends on December 31 and its federal Employer Identification Number is 548932154. It is located at 102 Grindstone Way, Columbus, Ohio 43085.

Required

1. Prepare a Form 8109 for MLS Company's July 15 deposit of its June FICA and employee income taxes.

2. Prepare MLS Company's Form 941 for the second quarter.

Problem 10-5B

Employer's payroll taxes, unemployment tax returns   **LO3   LO6   LO7**

Prestige Travel reports the following summary information in its payroll register for 2009. Prestige Travel pays state unemployment tax of 2.0% of each employee's first $7,000 of annual gross pay. Prestige Travel also pays federal unemployment tax of 0.8% of each employee's first $7,000 of annual gross pay. Prestige Travel's Employer Identification Number is 845699482. It is located at 11 Coral Lane, Miami, Florida 33101.

Quarter Ended	Total Gross Pay	Total Gross Pay for FUTA and SUTA
March 31	35,310.00	31,900.00
June 30	39,675.00	31,344.50
September 30	41,274.00	3,714.66
December 31	37,420.00	1,683.90

Required

1. Compute the amounts of FUTA and SUTA taxes Prestige Travel owes for each quarter in 2009.

2. Prepare the general journal entry to record Prestige Travel's FUTA and SUTA taxes for the third quarter (ending on September 30) of 2009. This journal entry is made on September 30, 2009.

3. Prepare the general entry to record Prestige Travel's deposit of its fourth quarter FUTA and SUTA taxes. This journal entry is made on September 30, 2009.

4. Prepare a Form 940-EZ for Prestige Travel for the year 2009.

Landmark Homes began operations on January 1, 2009. The company pays workers' compensation insurance premiums for its employees. The company's accountant assembled the data below for Landmark Homes for 2009:

Problem 10-6B
Workers' compensation
insurance premiums   **LO8**

Classification	Estimated Wages	Rate per $100 of Wages
Clerical office	$ 65,000	0.21
Carpentry	175,000	5.82
Electricians	100,000	3.07

Classification	Actual Wages Situation A	Actual Wages Situation B
Clerical office	$ 66,262	$ 59,834
Carpentry	186,410	171,211
Electricians	97,312	98,247

Required

1. Prepare the general journal entry to record Landmark Homes' payment of its estimated 2009 workers' compensation insurance premium on January 5, 2009.

2. For each of the two separate situations (A) and (B) prepare the general journal entry to adjust Landmark Homes' 2009 workers' compensation insurance premium for its actual wages during 2009. Assume this entry is made on January 15, 2010.

(This serial problem began in Chapter 1 and continues through most of the book. If previous chapter segments were not completed, the serial problem can begin at this point. It is helpful, but not necessary, for you to use the Working Papers that accompany the book.)

SERIAL PROBLEM

Success Systems

SP 10   Refer to the serial problem from Chapter 9. Michelle Jones' gross pay for the February 26 payroll equals $1,200.

1. Record the journal entry to reflect the employer payroll tax expenses for the February 26 payroll payment. Assume Michelle Jones has not met earnings limits for FUTA and SUTA—the FUTA rate is 0.8% and the SUTA rate is 4% for Success Systems. FICA taxes are 6.2% and 1.45% for Social Security and Medicare, respectively.

BEYOND THE NUMBERS

BTN 10-1   Refer to the financial statements of **Best Buy** in Appendix A to answer the following:

REPORTING IN ACTION
LO1

Required

1. In what income statement account(s) does Best Buy report its payroll and benefit costs?

2. Does Best Buy sponsor any retirement savings plans? (*Hint:* See footnote 7 Appendix A.) If so, what dollar amounts did Best Buy contribute to these plans during fiscal year 2008? What amounts did Best Buy's employees contribute to these plans in fiscal year 2008?

Fast Forward

3. Access Best Buy's financial statements for fiscal years ending after March 1, 2008, at its Website (www.BestBuy.com) or the SEC's EDGAR database (www.SEC.gov). What dollar amounts did Best Buy and its employees contribute to retirement savings plans for years ending after March 1, 2008?

ETHICS CHALLENGE
LO3 LO4

BTN 10-2 As ZTech's accountant you make payroll tax deposits. Recently ZTech has experienced financial distress. Your boss suggests that the company skip its upcoming quarterly tax deposit, and make the amount up at the end of the year "after business improves."

Required

1. Is your boss's suggestion ethical?

2. Is it a sound business decision?

WORKPLACE COMMUNICATIONS
LO8

BTN 10-3 As the accountant for Prestige Home Construction you record your employer's workers' compensation costs. At a meeting discussing the year-end financial statements, your boss, Dusty Haynes, says, "We paid over $15,000 for workers' compensation insurance at the beginning of the year. We didn't file any workers' compensation claims this year, so we should get a refund this year. But you tell me we have to pay another $2,000 to our insurer. What is going on here?"

Required

Write a one-page memorandum to your boss explaining this situation.

TAKING IT TO THE NET
LO1

BTN 10-4 Many employers are switching to payroll cards instead of issuing paper payroll checks to employees. Go to the **American Payroll Association** Website (www.americanpayroll.org) and select "PaycardPortal" and then select "Advantages."

Required

1. Discuss at least three cost savings an employer can expect from using payroll cards instead of paper paychecks.

2. How do payroll cards help minimize the employer's risk of paycheck fraud?

3. How do payroll cards reduce employees' chances of being harmed by identity theft?

TEAMWORK IN ACTION
LO2 LO6 LO8

BTN 10-5 Form learning teams of three members each. Each team member is to become an expert on one of the types of employer payroll tax listed below:

a. FICA (Social Security and Medicare)

b. Unemployment (State and Federal)

c. Worker's Compensation

Using the following data, teams are to develop a presentation answering requirements 1 through 4.

Background

Superior Stone Company designs and installs stone walls for homes and businesses. At the beginning of the year it employed two office workers and seven stone installers. During 2009 one office worker quit and was not replaced. Due to strong demand Superior Stone's stone installers worked a lot of overtime during 2009. It reports the following data for 2009 (the state unemployment tax rate is 1%; the federal unemployment tax rate is 0.8%).

Type of Employee	Estimated 2009 Wages	Actual 2009 Wages	Workers' Compensation Rate per $100 of Wages	2009 Wages Subject to FICA, FUTA, and SUTA	
				Estimated	Actual
Office worker	$ 77,500	$ 46,500	$0.20	$14,000	$14,000
Stone installer	232,500	263,500	2.50	49,000	49,000
Total	$310,000	$310,000		$63,000	$63,000

Required

1. Each team member computes the estimated amount of one employer payroll tax for 2009.
2. Each team member computes the actual amount of one employer payroll tax for 2009.
3. Team members share their computations and compute the total estimated and actual payroll tax and workers compensation insurance amounts for 2009.
4. Team members discuss differences between estimated and actual payroll tax and workers compensation insurance amounts for 2009. Round calculations to the nearest dollar.

BTN 10–6   Review the chapter's opening feature about Brian Scudamore and **1-800-GOT-JUNK**. To build a successful business, Scudamore had to attend to payroll, employee benefits, and taxes, among other issues, in getting his company where it is today.

ENTREPRENEURS IN BUSINESS

LO1

Required

Prepare a one-page memorandum that summarizes the types of employer payroll taxes and how they are reported. To the extent possible, reference the form to be filed for each tax.

1. e; $50,000 \times (.062 + .0145) = \underline{\$3,825}$
2. b; $7,000 \times (.054 + .008) = \underline{\$434}$
3. b; $((\$70,000/100) \times \$0.40) + ((\$145,000/100) \times \$6.00) = \underline{\$8,980}$
4. d; $(\$14,000 \times 0.062) + (\$16,200 \times 0.0145) + (\$1,150 \times 0.015) + (\$1,150 \times 0.008) = \underline{\$1,129.35}$
5. b

ANSWERS TO MULTIPLE CHOICE QUIZ

A Look Back

Chapter 10 focused on employer payroll taxes and reporting. We showed how payroll taxes are computed and paid. We also showed how to account for workers' compensation programs.

A Look at This Chapter

This chapter emphasizes merchandise activities. We analyze merchandise sales transactions, sales discounts, and sales returns and allowances. We show how special journals, sales journals, cash receipts journals, and accounts receivable subsidiary ledgers help in accounting for merchandise activities.

A Look Ahead

Chapter 12 extends our coverage of merchandising activities, with emphasis on accounting for merchandise purchases and accounts payable. We also explain the use of a cash disbursements journal.

Chapter

Merchandise Sales and Accounts Receivable

Learning Objectives

LO 1	Analyze and record transactions for merchandise sales.
LO 2	Describe how to compute and record sales discounts.
LO 3	Explain how to record sales returns and allowances.
LO 4	Describe the use of special journals and subsidiary ledgers.
LO 5	Journalize and post transactions using a sales journal.
LO 6	Prepare and prove the accuracy of the accounts receivable subsidiary ledger.
LO 7	Journalize and post transactions using a cash receipts journal.

"Celebrate today, don't wait until tomorrow"
—Bert and John Jacobs

The Good Life!

HUDSON, NEW HAMPSHIRE—For five years, brothers Bert and John Jacobs, owners of **Life is good** (**Lifeisgood.com**), hawked tee shirts door-to-door at college dorms up and down the east coast. They lived on peanut butter and jelly and slept in their van. After heading home from a long, less-than-fruitful road trip, they brainstormed how to keep their dreams alive. The result was "Jake," a new logo with an optimistic message. They began by printing up 48 Jake tee shirts for a street fair and all 48 tee shirts sold within hours. Once Jake was introduced to local retailers, the market embraced his positive message and the company took off. In 2007, the company sold 4.2 million of its $25 T-shirts and had sales of roughly $107 million.

As a wholesaler, Life is good must ensure that its distributors have the right product mix (colors, styles and sizes), with the right volume at the right price. Bert and John use accounting and inventory systems to set the sales price, monitor costs, and establish inventory levels to avoid costs of out-of-stock and excess inventory. When told by consultants that they could make $3 more on every tee shirt by skimping on quality, John countered, "We want this to be people's favorite shirt and we want it to still be their favorite shirt 10 years from now. It won't be if it's got holes and the collar's stretched out." The inventory system captures merchandising sales information to help with these and other business decisions.

Life is good's optimism is contagious as they now sell a full range of clothing for men, women, and children, in addition to jewelry, bags and headwear. Despite the challenges from competition, copycats, and knock-off products, Life is good continues to look at the cup as half full. Bert and John Jacobs suggest that we "appreciate everything." They add, "Celebrate today, don't wait until tomorrow."

[Sources: *LifeisGood.com Website,* March 2009; *Inc.,* October 2006; *Wikipedia,* October 2006; *The New York Times,* July 2008]

Merchandising activities are a major part of modern business. Consumers expect a wealth of products, discount prices, and inventory on demand. This chapter introduces the business and accounting practices used by companies engaged in merchandising activities. We show how to account for merchandise sales, sales discounts, and sales returns. We also show how to use special journals and subsidiary ledgers to make the accounting more efficient.

Merchandise Sales and Accounts Receivable

Merchandising Sales
- Sales of merchandise
- Sales discounts
- Sales returns and allowances
- Recording and posting

Special Journals and Subsidiary Ledgers
- Sales journal
- Accounts receivable subsidiary ledger
- Cash receipts journal

Merchandising Sales

LO1 Analyze and record transactions for merchandise sales.

Previous chapters emphasized the accounting and reporting activities of service companies. The company described in Chapters 2 through 6, FastForward, is an example of a service business. A merchandising company's activities differ from those of a service company. **Merchandise** consists of products, also called *goods,* that a company acquires to resell to customers. A **merchandiser** earns net income by buying and selling merchandise. Merchandisers are often identified as either wholesalers or retailers. A **wholesaler** is an *intermediary* that buys products from manufacturers or other wholesalers and sells them to retailers or other wholesalers. Examples of wholesalers are Fleming, SUPERVALU, and SYSCO. A **retailer** is an intermediary that buys products from manufacturers or wholesalers and sells them to consumers. Many retailers sell both products and services. The Gap, Best Buy, RadioShack and Wal-Mart are examples of retailers.

In this chapter we show how to account for merchandise sales. In the next chapter, we will show how to account for merchandise purchases and accounts payable. To illustrate, we use the transactions of Z-Mart, a merchandiser. Merchandising companies must account for sales, sales discounts, and sales returns and allowances.

Sales of Merchandise

Merchandisers can have credit sales (sales on account) and cash sales. To illustrate the accounting for credit sales, the following general journal entry records Z-Mart's $2,400 sale of merchandise on credit on November 3.

Assets = Liabilities + Equity
+2,400   +2,400

Nov.	3	Accounts Receivable	2 4 0 0 00	
		Sales		2 4 0 0 00
		Sold merchandise on credit.		

This entry reflects an increase in Z-Mart's assets in the form of an account receivable. It also shows the increase in revenue (Sales). If the sale is for cash, the debit is to Cash instead of Accounts Receivable.

Sales Discounts

LO2 Describe how to compute and record sales discounts.

To encourage timely payment from its customers that buy merchandise on credit, companies often offer **sales** (or cash) **discounts.** Sales discounts on credit sales can benefit a seller by decreasing the delay in receiving cash and reducing future collection efforts and default.

Credit Terms **Credit terms** for a sale include the amounts and timing of payments from a buyer to a seller. Credit terms usually reflect an industry's practices. To illustrate, when sellers require payment within 10 days after the end of the month of the invoice date, the invoice will show credit terms as "n/10 EOM," which stands for net 10 days after end of month (**EOM**). When sellers require payment within 30 days after the invoice date, the invoice shows credit terms of "n/30," which stands for *net 30 days*.

Exhibit 11.1 portrays credit terms. The amount of time allowed before full payment is due is called the **credit period.** Sellers can grant a **cash discount** to encourage buyers to pay earlier. Any cash discounts are described in the credit terms on the invoice. For example, credit terms of "2/10, n/60" mean that full payment is due within a 60-day credit period, but the buyer can deduct 2% of the invoice amount if payment is made within 10 days of the invoice date. This reduced payment applies only for the **discount period.** (Sellers sometimes charge fees if the full invoice price is not paid by the end of the credit period.)

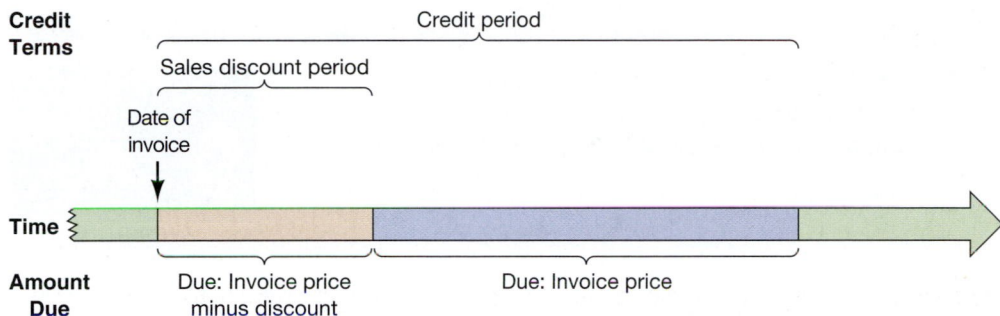

Exhibit 11.1
Credit Terms

Credit Sales Entries At the time of a credit sale, a seller does not know whether a customer will pay within the discount period and take advantage of a purchases discount. This means the seller usually does not record a sales discount until a customer actually pays within the discount period. To illustrate, Z-Mart completes a credit sale for $1,000 on November 12 with terms of 2/10, n/60. The following entry records this sale.

Nov.	12	Accounts Receivable	1000 00	
		Sales		1000 00
		Sold merchandise under terms of 2/10, n/60.		

Assets = Liabilities + Equity
+1,000   +1,000

This entry records the receivable and the revenue as if the customer will pay the full amount. The customer has two options, however. One option is to wait 60 days until January 11 and pay the full $1,000. In this case, Z-Mart records that receipt as:

Jan.	11	Cash	1000 00	
		Accounts Receivable		1000 00
		Received payment for Nov. 12 sale		

Assets = Liabilities + Equity
+1,000
−1,000

The customer's other option is to pay within the 10-day discount period ending November 22 and receive the cash discount. The cash discount is computed by multiplying the sales price by the discount percentage. In this case, the discount is $20, computed as the $1,000 sales price multiplied by 2%. If the customer pays on (or before) November 22, Z-Mart records the receipt as:

Nov.	22	Cash	980 00	
		Sales Discounts	20 00	
		Accounts Receivable		1000 00
		Received payment for Nov. 12 sale less discount.		

Assets = Liabilities + Equity
+980   −20
−1,000

Sales Discounts is a contra revenue account, meaning it is deducted from the Sales account when computing a company's net sales (see Exhibit 11.2). Management monitors Sales Discounts to assess the effectiveness and cost of its discount policy.

Exhibit 11.2

Net Sales Computation

Z-MART		
Computation of Net Sales		
For Year Ended December 31, 2010		
Sales		$321,000
Less: Sales discounts	$4,300	
Sales returns and allowances	2,000	6,300
Net sales		$314,700

IN THE NEWS

Return to Sender   Book merchandisers such as **Barnes & Noble** and **Borders Books** can return unsold books to publishers at their purchase price. Publishers say returns of new hardcover books run between 35% and 50% of sales.

Sales Returns and Allowances

LO3 Explain how to record sales returns and allowances.

Sales returns refer to merchandise that customers return to the seller after a sale. Many companies allow customers to return merchandise for a full refund. *Sales allowances* refer to reductions in the selling price of merchandise sold to customers. This can occur with damaged or defective merchandise that a customer is willing to purchase with a reduction in selling price. Sales returns and allowances usually involve dissatisfied customers, and managers need information about returns and allowances to monitor these problems.

Sales Returns   To illustrate, recall Z-Mart's sale of merchandise on November 3 for $2,400. Assume that the customer returns $800 of this merchandise on November 6. The journal entry for this transaction must reflect the decrease in sales and accounts receivable from the customer's return of merchandise as follows:

Assets = Liabilities + Equity
−800   −800

Nov.	6	Sales Returns and Allowances	800 00	
		Accounts Receivable		800 00
		Customer returns merchandise from Nov. 3 sale.		

Sales Returns and Allowances is also a contra revenue account, meaning it is deducted from the Sales account when computing net sales (see Exhibit 11.2). The Sales Returns and Allowances account is kept separate from the Sales account so the company can monitor the extent of sales returns and allowances.

Sales Allowances   To illustrate sales allowances, assume that $800 of the merchandise Z-Mart sold on November 3 is defective but the buyer decides to keep it because Z-Mart offers a $100 price reduction. Z-Mart records this transaction as:

Assets = Liabilities + Equity
−100   −100

Nov.	6	Sales Returns and Allowances	100 00	
		Accounts Receivable		100 00
		To record sales allowance on Nov. 3 sale.		

The seller usually prepares a credit memorandum to confirm a buyer's return or allowance. A seller's **credit memorandum** informs a buyer of the seller's credit to the buyer's Account Receivable (on the seller's books). The sender (maker) of a credit memorandum will *credit* the account of the receiver. The receiver of a credit memorandum will *debit* the account of the sender.

HOW YOU DOIN'? Answers—p. 274

1. Why are sales discounts and sales returns and allowances recorded in contra revenue accounts instead of directly in the Sales account?
2. When merchandise is sold on credit and the seller notifies the buyer of a price allowance, does the seller create and send a credit memorandum or a debit memorandum?

Recording and Posting Merchandise Sales

Companies also must collect state and local government sales tax on retail sales of certain goods and services and send them to the government on a regular basis. When goods or services are sold on credit, the sales tax is recorded as sales tax payable even though the cash has not yet been collected. Sales Tax Payable is a liability account.

To illustrate the accounting (both journal entries and posting to the general ledger) for sales and sales taxes, we consider Z-Mart's following transactions during November.

Nov. 3 Sold merchandise on credit to Bradford Inc.; Sales Invoice No. 145 for $2,400 plus $144 sales tax

5 Sold merchandise on credit to Smith Inc.; Sales Invoice No. 146 for $1,050 plus $63 sales tax

8 Sold merchandise on credit to Cluff Inc.; Sales Invoice No. 147 for $250 plus $15 sales tax

11 Sold merchandise on credit to Dobson Inc.; Sales Invoice No. 148 for $550 plus $33 sales tax

The general journal entries are in Exhibit 11.3. The journal entries are then posted to the general ledger as shown in Exhibit 11.4.

GENERAL JOURNAL				Page 17	
Date	Description	PR	Debit	Credit	
Nov 3	Accounts Receivable	106	2 5 4 4 00		
	Sales Tax Payable	232		1 4 4 00	
	Sales	401		2 4 0 0 00	
	Sold merchandise on credit to Bradford Inc.; Invoice No. 145				
5	Accounts Receivable	106	1 1 1 3 00		
	Sales Tax Payable	232		6 3 00	
	Sales	401		1 0 5 0 00	
	Sold merchandise on credit to Smith Inc.; Invoice No. 146				
8	Accounts Receivable	106	2 6 5 00		
	Sales Tax Payable	232		1 5 00	
	Sales	401		2 5 0 00	
	Sold merchandise on credit to Cluff Inc.; Invoice No. 147				
11	Accounts Receivable	106	5 8 3 00		
	Sales Tax Payable	232		3 3 00	
	Sales	401		5 5 0 00	
	Sold merchandise on credit to Dobson Inc.; Invoice No. 148				

Exhibit 11.3

General Journal Entries of November Sales for Z-Mart

Assets = Liabilities + Equity
+2,544   +144   +2,400

Assets = Liabilities + Equity
+1,113   +63   +1,050

Assets = Liabilities + Equity
+265   +15   +250

Assets = Liabilities + Equity
+583   +33   +550

Exhibit 11.4

Posting of Journal Entries for November Sales of Z-Mart

General Ledger

Accounts Receivable　　　　　　　　　　Acct. No. 106

Date		Item	PR	Debit	Credit	Balance
Nov.	1	Balance	✓			3,152
	3		G17	2,544		5,696
	5		G17	1,113		6,809
	8		G17	265		7,074
	11		G17	583		7,657

Sales　　　　　　　　　　　　　　　　Acct. No. 401

Date		Item	PR	Debit	Credit	Balance
Nov.	3		G17		2,400	2,400
	5		G17		1,050	3,450
	8		G17		250	3,700
	11		G17		550	4,250

Sales Tax Payable　　　　　　　　　　Acct. No. 232

Date		Item	PR	Debit	Credit	Balance
Nov.	1	Balance	✓			967
	3		G17		144	1,111
	5		G17		63	1,174
	8		G17		15	1,189
	11		G17		33	1,222

Special Journals and Subsidiary Ledgers

LO4　Describe the use of special journals and subsidiary ledgers.

Exhibit 11.3 shows that entering a journal entry each time there is a credit sale is a tedious, repetitive task. Writing descriptions of each sale and posting each transaction to the general ledger takes considerable effort. To make this process more efficient, special journals are used. While a **general journal** is an all-purpose journal where we can record any transaction, a **special journal** is used to record and post transactions of a similar type. Most transactions of a merchandiser, for instance, can be categorized into the journals shown below. Special journals are efficient tools in helping journalize and post transactions. This is done by accumulating debits and credits of similar transactions.

Sales Journal

For recording credit sales

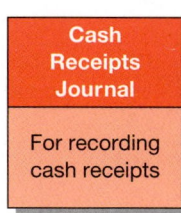

Cash Receipts Journal

For recording cash receipts

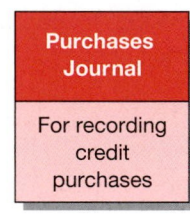

Purchases Journal

For recording credit purchases

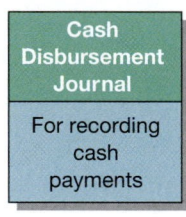

Cash Disbursement Journal

For recording cash payments

General Journal

For transactions not in special journals

Sales Journal

A typical **sales journal** is used to record sales of inventory *on credit*. Sales of inventory for cash are not recorded in a sales journal but in a cash receipts journal. Sales of noninventory assets on credit are recorded in the general journal.

LO5　Journalize and post transactions using a sales journal.

Journalizing　Credit sale transactions are recorded with information about each sale entered separately in a sales journal. This information is often taken from a copy of the sales ticket or invoice prepared at the time of sale (as shown in Exhibit 11.5). Exhibit 11.6 shows a typical sales journal from a merchandiser. It has columns for recording the date, customer's name, invoice number, posting reference, and the amount of each credit sale. The sales journal in this exhibit is called a **columnar journal,** which is any journal with more than one column. Each transaction recorded in the sales journal yields an entry in the Accounts Receivable, Sales Tax Payable, and Sales columns. Exhibit 11.6 shows the credit sales transactions that Z-Mart experienced in November.

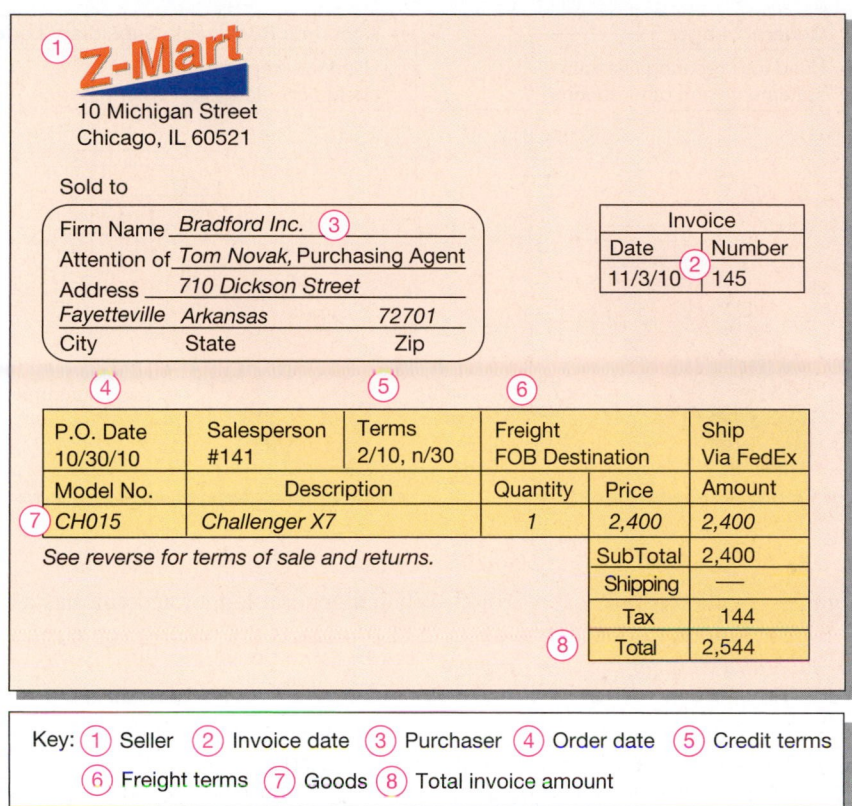

Exhibit 11.5

Sales Invoice

Sales Journal						Page 3
Date	**Account Debited**	**Invoice Number**	**PR**	**Accounts Receivable Dr.**	**Sales Tax Payable Cr.**	**Sales Cr.**
Nov. 3	Bradford Inc.	145		2,544	144	2,400
5	Smith Inc.	146		1,113	63	1,050
8	Cluff Inc.	147		265	15	250
11	Dobson Inc.	148		583	33	550
12	Taylor Inc.	149		1,431	81	1,350
15	Burns Inc.	150		636	36	600
17	Smith Inc.	151		1,484	84	1,400
23	Dobson Inc.	152		1,272	72	1,200
27	Taylor Inc.	153		318	18	300

Exhibit 11.6

Sales Journal Example

Accounts Receivable Subsidiary Ledger

A **subsidiary ledger** contains detailed information on a specific account in the general ledger. Many general ledger accounts have subsidiary ledgers. The **accounts receivable ledger** stores transaction data of individual customers. (The accounts payable ledger is presented in the next chapter.) The accounts receivable ledger shows how much each customer purchased, paid, and has yet to pay. Usually, the general ledger has a single Accounts Receivable account and the accounts receivable ledger keeps a separate account for each customer.

Controlling Account and Subsidiary Ledger Exhibit 11.7 shows the relation between the Accounts Receivable general ledger account and the individual customer accounts in the subsidiary ledger. After all items are posted, the balance in the Accounts Receivable account must equal the sum of all balances of its customers' accounts. The Accounts Receivable account is said to control the accounts receivable ledger and is called a **controlling account.** Since the accounts receivable ledger is a supplementary record controlled by an account in the

L06 Prepare and prove the accuracy of the accounts receivable subsidiary ledger.

Exhibit 11.7

Accounts Receivable Controlling
Account and Its Subsidiary Ledger

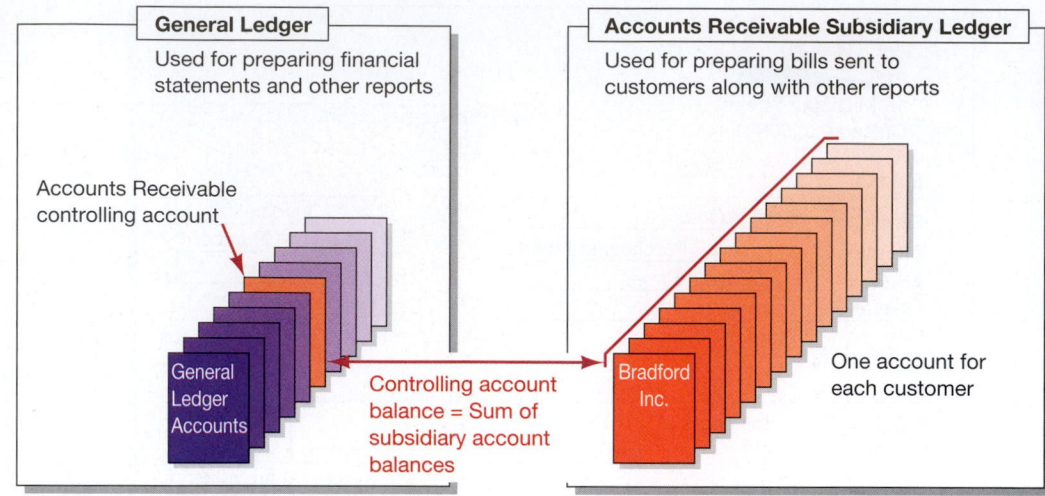

general ledger, it is called a *subsidiary* ledger. When a general ledger account has a subsidiary ledger, any transaction that impacts one of them also impacts the other—some refer to this as *general and subsidiary ledgers kept in tandem.*

Posting   A sales journal is posted as reflected in the arrow lines of Exhibit 11.8. Two types of posting are shown: (1) posting to the subsidiary ledger(s) and (2) posting to the general ledger.

Posting to subsidiary ledger.   Individual transactions in the sales journal are posted regularly to customer accounts in the accounts receivable ledger. These postings keep customer accounts up-to-date, which is important for the person granting credit to customers. When sales recorded in the sales journal are individually posted to customer accounts in the accounts receivable ledger, check marks are entered in the sales journal's PR column. Check marks are used rather than account numbers because customer accounts usually are arranged alphabetically in the accounts receivable ledger. Note that posting debits to Accounts Receivable twice—once to Accounts Receivable and once to the customer's subsidiary ledger account—does not violate the accounting equation of debits equal credits. The equality of debits and credits is always maintained in the general ledger. Postings are automatic in a computerized system, which are done when an entry is made.

Posting to general ledger.   The sales journal's account columns are totaled at the end of each period (the month of November in this case). In this example, the total accounts receivable from credit sales for the month of November of $9,646 is posted to the general ledger. The total sales tax payable for the month of $546 is also posted to the general ledger. The total sales for the month of $9,100 is posted to the general ledger. When totals are posted to accounts in the general ledger, the account numbers are entered below the column total in the sales journal for cross referencing. For example, we enter (106) below the account receivable column, (232) below the sales tax payable, and (401) below the sales column in the sales journal.

A company identifies in the PR column of its subsidiary ledgers the journal and page number from which an amount is taken. We identify a journal by using an initial. Items posted from the sales journal carry the initial *S* before their journal page numbers in a PR column. PR column is only checked *after* the amount(s) is posted.

LO6 Prepare and prove the accuracy of the accounts receivable subsidiary ledger.

Proving the Ledgers   Account balances in the general ledger and subsidiary ledgers are periodically proved (or reviewed) for accuracy after posting. To do this we first prepare a trial balance of the general ledger to confirm that debits equal credits. Second, we test a subsidiary ledger by preparing a *schedule* of individual accounts and amounts. A **schedule of accounts**

Exhibit 11.8

Sales Journal with Posting

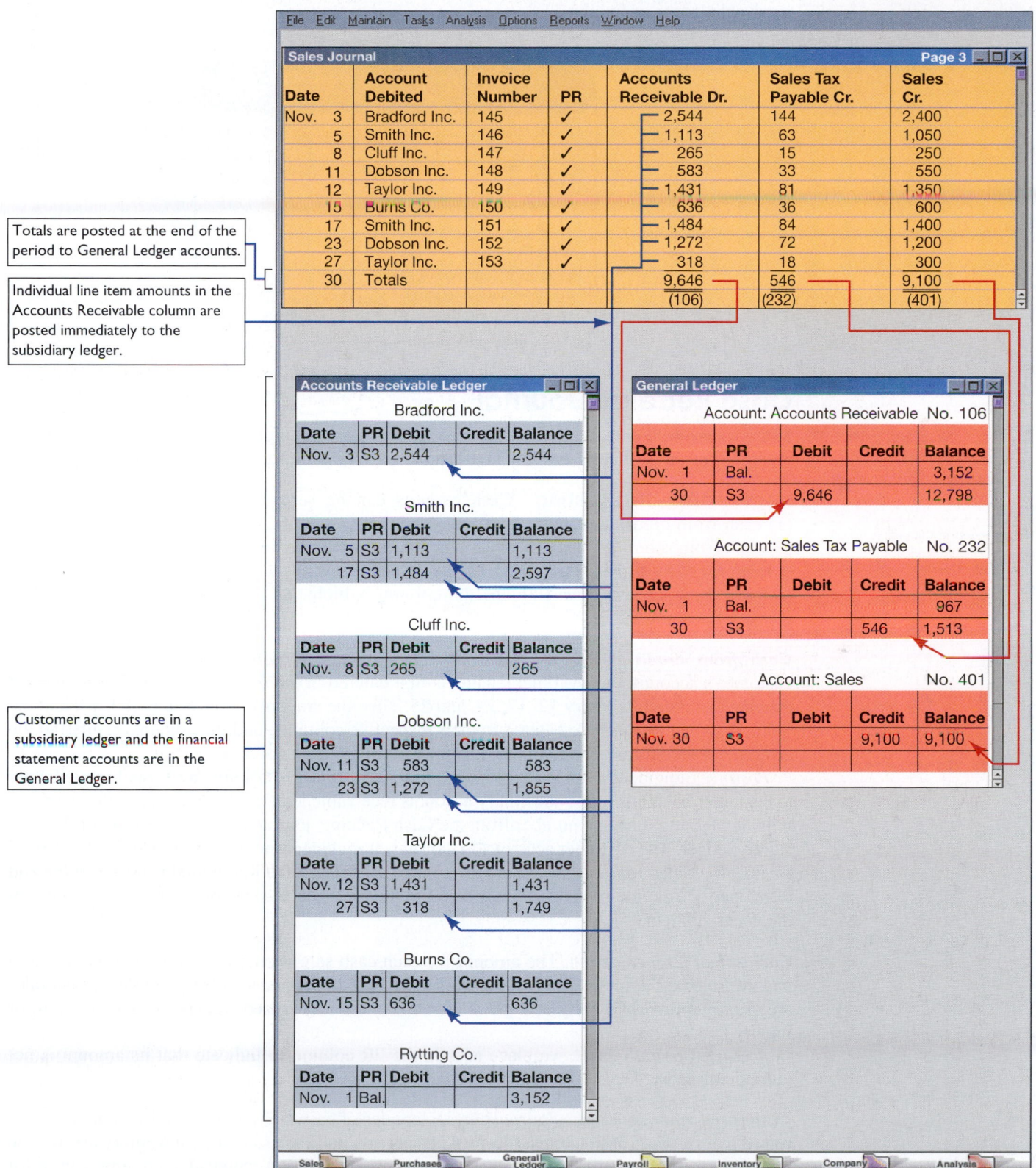

Totals are posted at the end of the period to General Ledger accounts.

Individual line item amounts in the Accounts Receivable column are posted immediately to the subsidiary ledger.

Customer accounts are in a subsidiary ledger and the financial statement accounts are in the General Ledger.

File Edit Maintain Tasks Analysis Options Reports Window Help

Sales Journal   Page 3

Date	Account Debited	Invoice Number	PR	Accounts Receivable Dr.	Sales Tax Payable Cr.	Sales Cr.
Nov. 3	Bradford Inc.	145	✓	2,544	144	2,400
5	Smith Inc.	146	✓	1,113	63	1,050
8	Cluff Inc.	147	✓	265	15	250
11	Dobson Inc.	148	✓	583	33	550
12	Taylor Inc.	149	✓	1,431	81	1,350
15	Burns Co.	150	✓	636	36	600
17	Smith Inc.	151	✓	1,484	84	1,400
23	Dobson Inc.	152	✓	1,272	72	1,200
27	Taylor Inc.	153	✓	318	18	300
30	Totals			9,646	546	9,100
				(106)	(232)	(401)

Accounts Receivable Ledger

Bradford Inc.

Date	PR	Debit	Credit	Balance
Nov. 3	S3	2,544		2,544

Smith Inc.

Date	PR	Debit	Credit	Balance
Nov. 5	S3	1,113		1,113
17	S3	1,484		2,597

Cluff Inc.

Date	PR	Debit	Credit	Balance
Nov. 8	S3	265		265

Dobson Inc.

Date	PR	Debit	Credit	Balance
Nov. 11	S3	583		583
23	S3	1,272		1,855

Taylor Inc.

Date	PR	Debit	Credit	Balance
Nov. 12	S3	1,431		1,431
27	S3	318		1,749

Burns Co.

Date	PR	Debit	Credit	Balance
Nov. 15	S3	636		636

Rytting Co.

Date	PR	Debit	Credit	Balance
Nov. 1	Bal.			3,152

General Ledger

Account: Accounts Receivable   No. 106

Date	PR	Debit	Credit	Balance
Nov. 1	Bal.			3,152
30	S3	9,646		12,798

Account: Sales Tax Payable   No. 232

Date	PR	Debit	Credit	Balance
Nov. 1	Bal.			967
30	S3		546	1,513

Account: Sales   No. 401

Date	PR	Debit	Credit	Balance
Nov. 30	S3		9,100	9,100

Sales   Purchases   General Ledger   Payroll   Inventory   Company   Analysis

receivable lists each customer and the balance owed. If this total equals the balance of the Accounts Receivable controlling account, the accounts in the accounts receivable ledger are assumed correct. Exhibit 11.9 shows a schedule of accounts receivable drawn from the accounts receivable ledger of Exhibit 11.8.

Exhibit 11.9

Schedule of Accounts Receivable

Schedule of Accounts Receivable November 30	
Bradford Inc.	$ 2,544
Smith Inc.	2,597
Cluff Inc.	265
Dobson Inc.	1,855
Taylor Inc.	1,749
Burns Co.	636
Rytting Co. (outstanding balance from pre-November sales)	3,152
Total accounts receivable	$12,798

Cash Receipts Journal

L07 Journalize and post transactions using a cash receipts journal.

Many transactions involving cash are repetitive. A **cash receipts journal** is typically used to record all receipts of cash. Exhibit 11.10 shows one common form of the cash receipts journal.

Each transaction in the cash receipts journal involves a debit to Cash. Credit accounts will vary.

Journalizing and Posting Cash receipts can be separated into one of three types: (1) cash from credit customers in payment of their accounts, (2) cash from cash sales, and (3) cash from other sources. The cash receipts journal in Exhibit 11.10 has a separate credit column for each of these three sources. We describe how to journalize transactions from each of these three sources. (An Explanation column is included in the cash receipts journal to identify the source.)

Cash from credit customers. *Journalizing.* To record cash received in payment of a customer's account, the customer's name is first entered in the Account Credited column—see transactions dated February 12, 17, 23, and 25. Then the amounts debited to both Cash and the Sales Discount (if any) are entered in their respective columns, and the amount credited to the customer's account is entered in the Accounts Receivable Cr. column.

Posting. Individual amounts in the Accounts Receivable Cr. column are posted immediately to customer accounts in the subsidiary accounts receivable ledger. These postings are identified with an "R" and the page number from the Cash Receipts journal in the PR column of the subsidiary ledger. The customer accounts in the subsidiary ledger include some postings from page three of the Sales Journal ('S3' in the PR column). The $1,500 column total is posted at the end of the period (month in this case) as a credit to the Accounts Receivable controlling account in the general ledger.

Cash sales. *Journalizing.* The amount for each cash sale is entered in the Cash Dr. column and the Sales Cr. column. The February 7, 14, 21, and 28 transactions are examples. (Cash sales are usually journalized daily or at point of sale, but are journalized weekly in Exhibit 11.10 for brevity.)

Posting. For cash sales, we place an *x* in the PR column to indicate that its amount is not individually posted. We do post the $17,300 Sales Cr. total.

Cash from other sources. *Journalizing.* Examples of cash from other sources are money borrowed from a bank, cash interest received on account, and cash sale of noninventory assets. The transactions of February 20 and 22 are illustrative. The Other Accounts Cr. column is used for these transactions.

Posting. Amounts from these transactions are immediately posted to their general ledger accounts and the PR column identifies those accounts.

Exhibit 11.10

Cash Receipts Journal with Posting

Individual line item amounts in the Other Accounts Cr. column and the Accounts Receivable Cr. column are posted immediately.

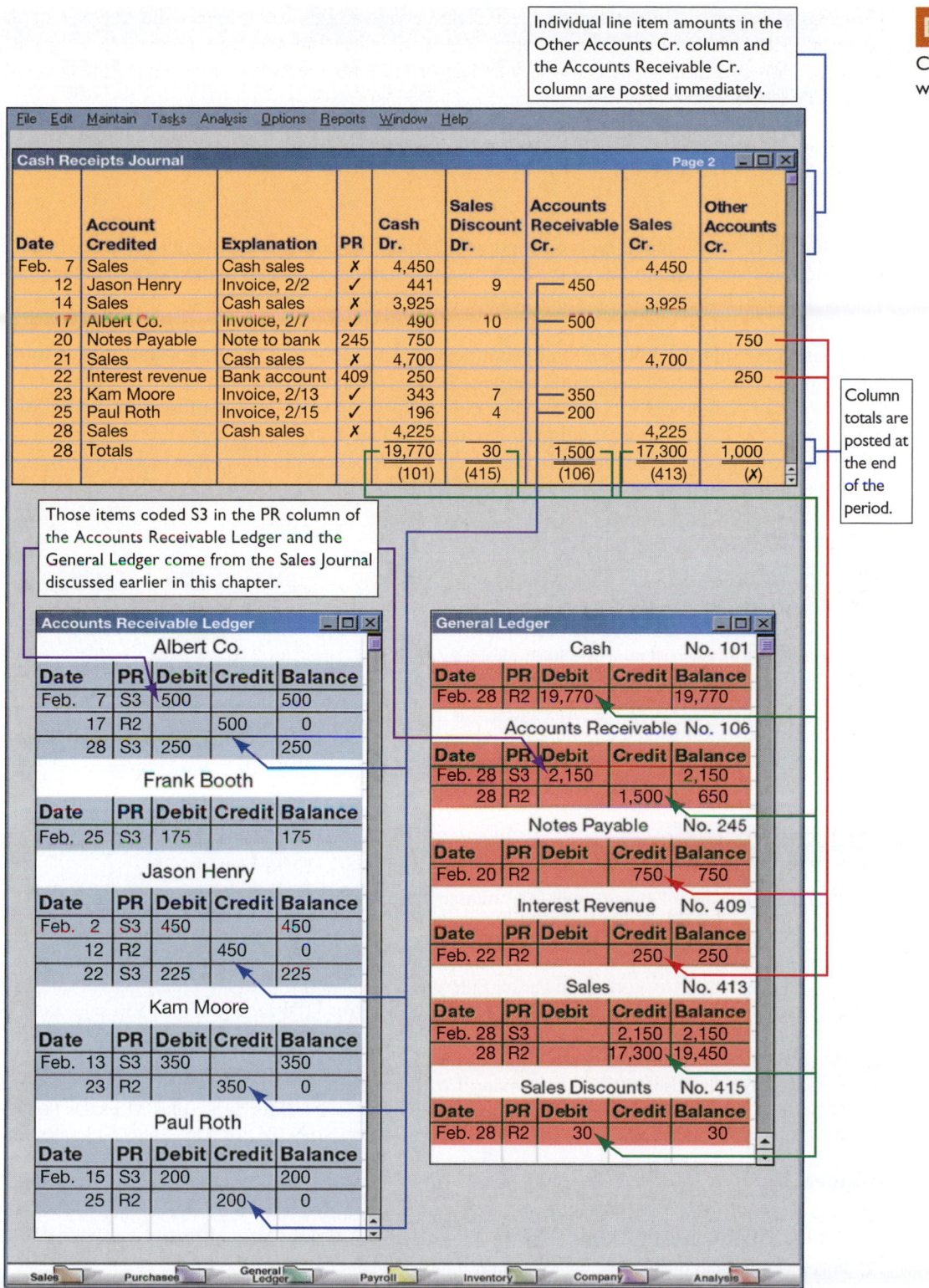

Column totals are posted at the end of the period.

Those items coded S3 in the PR column of the Accounts Receivable Ledger and the General Ledger come from the Sales Journal discussed earlier in this chapter.

Footing, Crossfooting, and Posting To be sure that total debits and credits in a columnar journal are equal, we often crossfoot column totals before posting them. To *foot* a column of numbers is to add it. To *crossfoot* in this case is to add the Debit column totals, then add the Credit column totals, and compare the two sums for equality. Footing and crossfooting of the numbers in Exhibit 11.10 results in the report in Exhibit 11.11.

Subsidiary ledgers and their controlling accounts are *in balance* only after all posting is complete.

Exhibit 11.11

Footing and Crossfooting
Journal Totals

Debit Columns		Credit Columns	
Cash Dr.	$19,770	Accounts Receivable Cr.	$ 1,500
Sales Discounts Dr.	30	Sales Cr.	17,300
		Other Accounts Cr.	1,000
Total	$19,800	Total	$19,800

At the end of the period, after crossfooting the journal to confirm that debits equal credits, the total amounts from the columns of the cash receipts journal are posted to their general ledger accounts. The Other Accounts Cr. column total is not posted because the individual amounts are directly posted to their general ledger accounts. We place an *x* below the Other Accounts Cr. column to indicate that this column total is not posted. The account numbers for the column totals that are posted are entered in parentheses below each column. (*Note:* Posting items immediately from the Other Accounts Cr. column with a delayed posting of their offsetting items in the Cash column total causes the general ledger to be out of balance during the period. Posting the Cash Dr. column total at the end of the period corrects this imbalance in the general ledger before the trial balance and financial statements are prepared.)

HOW YOU DOIN'?   Answers—p. 274

3. How do debits and credits remain equal when credit sales are posted twice (once to Accounts Receivable and once to the customer's subsidiary account)?

4. How do we identify the journal from which an amount in a ledger account was posted?

5. How are sales taxes recorded in the context of special journals?

Demonstration Problem

Perry Company has the following credit sales transactions for January.

Jan. 4   Sold merchandise on credit to Hinckley Inc., Invoice No. 1123 for $2,015, plus $161 sales tax.
Jan. 7   Sold merchandise on credit to Bednar Co., Invoice No. 1124 for $1,616, plus $129 sales tax.
Jan. 9   Sold merchandise on credit to Packer Enterprises, Invoice No. 1125 for $222, plus $18 sales tax.
Jan. 13   Sold merchandise on credit to Nelson Inc., Invoice No. 1126 for $456, plus $36 sales tax.
Jan. 14   Sold merchandise on credit to Packer Enterprises, Invoice No. 1127 for $16, plus $1 sales tax.
Jan. 19   Sold merchandise on credit to Hinckley Inc., Invoice No. 1128 for $1,732, plus $139 sales tax.
Jan. 22   Sold merchandise on credit to Uchtdorf Co., Invoice No. 1129 for $1,819, plus $145 sales tax.
Jan. 27   Sold merchandise on credit to Nelson Inc., Invoice No. 1130 for $152, plus $12 sales tax.
Jan. 30   Sold merchandise on credit to Ballard Corp., Invoice No. 1131 for $157, plus $13 sales tax.

Required

1. Record these sales in a sales journal using Accounts Receivable (#106), Sales Tax Payable (#232), and Sales (#401). Assume these accounts have zero balances at the beginning of January.
2. Post these sales to the general ledger and post the references.
3. Post these sales to the accounts receivable subsidiary ledger.

Planning the Solution

- Set up the sales journal using the template from Exhibit 11.6 or Exhibit 11.8 with a debit entry column for Accounts Receivable and credit entry columns for Sales Tax Payable and Sales.
- Record each sale, with each transaction taking one line in the sales journal.
- Post each transaction to the appropriate account in the accounts receivable subsidiary ledger. Posting to the subsidiary ledger should be done daily, not at the end of the month.
- Sum the columns in the special journal to prepare to post totals to the general ledger accounts.

Solution to Demonstration Problem

1.

Sales Journal						Page 1
Date	Account Debited	Invoice Number	PR	Accounts Receivable Dr.	Sales Tax Payable Cr.	Sales Cr.
Jan. 4	Hinckley Inc.	1123		2,176	161	2,015
7	Bednar Co.	1124		1,745	129	1,616
9	Packer Enterprises	1125		240	18	222
13	Nelson Inc.	1126		492	36	456
14	Packer Enterprises	1127		17	1	16
19	Hinckley Inc.	1128		1,871	139	1,732
22	Uchtdorf Co.	1129		1,964	145	1,819
27	Nelson Inc.	1130		164	12	152
30	Ballard Corp.	1131		170	13	157

2. and **3.**

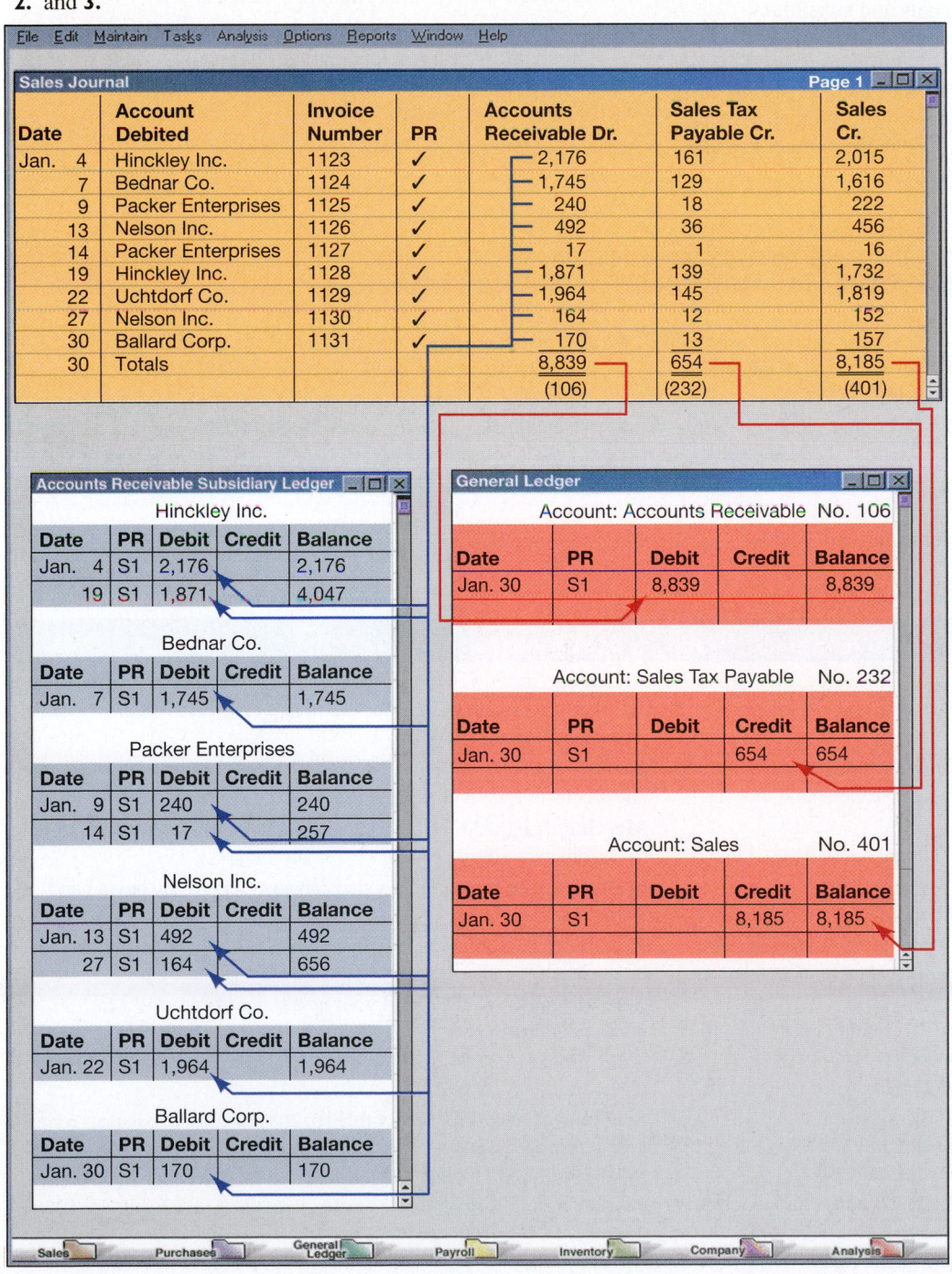

Summary

LO1 **Analyze and record transactions for merchandise sales.** A merchandiser records sales at the invoice price of the sale. The sale may be for cash or on credit.

LO2 **Describe how to compute and record sales discounts.** When cash discounts from the sales price are offered and customers pay within the discount period, the seller debits Sales Discounts, a contra account to Sales.

LO3 **Explain how to record sales returns and allowances.** Refunds or credits given to customers for unsatisfactory merchandise are recorded as debits to Sales Returns and Allowances, a contra account to Sales.

LO4 **Describe the use of special journals and subsidiary ledgers.** Special journals are used for recording transactions of similar type, each meant to cover one kind of transaction. Four of the most common special journals are the sales journal, cash receipts journal, purchases journal, and cash disbursements journal. Special journals are efficient and cost-effective tools in the journalizing and posting process.

LO5 **Journalize and post transactions using a sales journal.** The sales journal is an efficient means to record sales of inventory on credit. The sales journal will typically debit Accounts Receivable and credit Sales and Sales Tax Payable (if applicable).

LO6 **Prepare and prove the accuracy of the accounts receivable subsidiary ledger.** Account balances in the general ledger and the accounts receivable subsidiary ledger are tested for accuracy after posting is complete. This procedure is twofold: (1) prepare a trial balance of the general ledger to confirm that debits equal credits and (2) prepare a schedule of accounts receivable to confirm that the controlling account's balance equals the subsidiary ledger's balance.

LO7 **Journalize and post transactions using a cash receipts journal.** A cash receipts journal is typically used to record cash receipts from credit customers, cash from cash sales, and cash received from other sources.

Guidance Answers to HOW YOU DOIN'?

1. Recording sales discounts and sales returns and allowances separately from sales gives useful information to managers for internal monitoring and decision making.

2. Credit memorandum—seller credits accounts receivable from buyer.

3. The equality of debits and credits is kept within the general ledger. The subsidiary ledger keeps the customer's individual account and is used only for supplementary information.

4. An initial and the page number of the journal from which the amount was posted are entered in the PR column next to the amount.

5. A separate column for Sales Taxes Payable can be included in the sales journal.

Key Terms

Accounts receivable ledger (p. 267) Subsidiary ledger listing individual customer accounts.

Cash discount (p. 263) Reduction in the price of merchandise granted by a seller to a buyer when payment is made within the discount period.

Cash Receipts Journal (p. 270) Special journal normally used to record all receipts of cash.

Columnar journal (p. 266) Journal with more than one column.

Controlling account (p. 267) General ledger account, the balance of which (after posting) equals the sum of the balances in its related subsidiary ledger.

Credit memorandum (p. 265) Notification that the sender has credited the recipient's account in the sender's records.

Credit period (p. 263) Time period that can pass before a customer's payment is due.

Credit terms (p. 263) Description of the amounts and timing of payments that a buyer (debtor) agrees to make in the future.

Discount period (p. 263) Time period in which a cash discount is available and the buyer can make a reduced payment.

EOM (p. 263) Abbreviation for *end of month;* used to describe credit terms for credit transactions.

General journal (p. 266) All-purpose journal for recording the debits and credits of transactions and events.

Merchandise (p. 262) Goods that a company owns and expects to sell to customers; also called *merchandise inventory*.

Merchandiser (p. 262) Entity that earns net income by buying and selling merchandise.

Retailer (p. 262) Intermediary that buys products from manufacturers or wholesalers and sells them to consumers.

Sales discount (p. 262) Term used by a seller to describe a cash discount granted to buyers who pay within the discount period.

Sales journal (p. 266) Journal normally used to record sales of goods on credit.

Schedule of accounts receivable (p. 268) List of the balances for all accounts in the accounts receivable ledger and their total.

Special journal (p. 266) Any journal used for recording and posting transactions of a similar type.

Subsidiary ledger (p. 267) List of individual sub-accounts and amounts with a common characteristic; linked to a controlling account in the general ledger.

Wholesaler (p. 262) Intermediary that buys products from manufacturers or other wholesalers and sells them to retailers or other wholesalers.

Multiple Choice Quiz   Answers on p. 283   mhhe.com/wildCA2e

Additional Multiple Choice Quizzes are available at the book's Website.

1. A company has cash sales of $75,000, credit sales of $320,000, sales returns and allowances of $13,700, and sales discounts of $6,000. Its net sales equal
   a. $395,000
   b. $375,300
   c. $300,300
   d. $339,700
   e. $414,700

2. The sales journal is used to record
   a. Credit sales
   b. Cash sales
   c. Cash receipts
   d. Cash purchases
   e. Credit purchases

3. The ledger that contains the financial statement accounts of a company is the
   a. General journal
   b. Column balance journal
   c. Special ledger
   d. General ledger
   e. Special journal

4. A subsidiary ledger that contains a separate account for each customer to the company is the
   a. Controlling account
   b. Accounts payable ledger
   c. Accounts receivable ledger
   d. General ledger
   e. Special journal

5. A company sells $1,000 worth of goods to a customer on July 19 with credit terms of 2/10 net 30. If the customer pays on July 28, they would pay
   a. $1,000
   b. $1,020
   c. $983
   d. $980
   e. Cannot be determined

Discussion Questions

1. Why do companies offer cash discounts?
2. How is net sales computed?
3. What account is used to show that a company has collected sales tax but has not yet remitted it to the state or local government? Is this account an asset, a liability, or an equity account?
4. Why do businesses monitor the amount of sales returns and allowances?
5. Why would one merchandising company use a sales journal, but another merchandising company would not?
6. Why does a company maintain an accounts receivable subsidiary ledger?
7. What type of account is Sales Discounts? What is its normal balance?

8. When a company uses an accounts receivable subsidiary ledger, it must make one entry into the individual account of the subsidiary ledger and another entry into the accounts receivable account of the general ledger. If two entries are made, will the debits equal the credits in the trial balance? Why or why not?
9. Refer to the income statement for **Best Buy** in Appendix A. How does Best Buy title its net sales revenue account? Does it disclose sales returns and allowances separately?
10. Refer to the income statement for **RadioShack** in Appendix A. How does RadioShack title its net sales revenue account? ®RadioShack®

connect

Show the general journal entries for the following sales transactions for Martindale Company from June 2010. Sales tax equals 8% of sales price.

June	2	Sold merchandise on credit to A. Fullmer, $3,300 plus tax.
	9	Sold merchandise on credit to B. Olson, $2,600 plus tax.
	13	Sold merchandise on credit to P. Bleak, $1,200 plus tax.
	27	Sold merchandise on credit to B. Taysom, $4,100 plus tax.

QUICK STUDY

QS 11–1
Journalizing credit sales
LO1

QS 11-2

Interpreting credit terms   **LO2**

Interpret the meaning of the following credit terms.

a. 2/10, n/60   **c.** 3/10, n/30

b. 2/EOM, n/60   **d.** 2/10, n/30

QS 11-3

Identifying special journals   **LO4**

Steele Manufacturing uses special journals in its accounting system. Indicate the journal that would be used for each of the following transactions. (Use the illustration below Exhibit 11.4 as a guide.)

A. Sales Journal   **C.** Cash Receipt Journal   **E.** Purchases Journal

B. Cash Disbursement Journal   **D.** General Journal

_____ **1.** Purchased merchandise for cash.

_____ **2.** Sold merchandise for cash.

_____ **3.** Purchased merchandise on credit.

_____ **4.** Gave $700 credit for returned merchandise.

_____ **5.** Sold merchandise on credit.

_____ **6.** Paid cash for merchandise previously purchased on credit.

_____ **7.** Purchased merchandise on credit.

_____ **8.** Sold merchandise for cash.

QS 11-4

Journalizing credit sales in a sales journal   **LO5**

Refer to the transactions in QS 11-1. Show how these transactions would be entered in a sales journal. (*Hint:* Use Exhibit 11.6 as a guide.)

QS 11-5

Computing net sales

LO1   LO2   LO3

Compute net sales for 2010 for Snedigar Company given the following information.

Sales (Gross)	43,251
Sales Discounts	757
Sales Returns and Allowances	2,253

QS 11-6

Journalizing cash receipts   **LO7**

Show the general journal entries for the following transactions which involved cash receipts at Alan Lawson Nursing Supplies. (*Hint:* Only journalize transactions that involve a receipt of cash).

Jul.   4   Sold $4,200 of merchandise on credit from Foxworth Co., terms n/20.

7   Sold merchandise costing $940 on credit to Cassell Co. for $1,000, subject to a $20 sales discount if paid by the end of the month.

9   Borrowed $9,500 cash by signing a note payable to the bank.

13   A. Lawson, the owner, contributed $5,000 cash to the company.

20   Received $4,200 cash from Foxworth Co. on account.

28   Received $920 cash from Cassell Co. on account within the discount period.

QS 11-7

Journalizing cash receipts in a cash receipts journal   **LO7**

Refer to the transactions in QS 11-6. Show how these transactions would be entered in a cash receipts journal.

---

connect

EXERCISES

Exercise 11-1

Recording sales returns and allowances   **LO3**

Check   (c) Dr. Sales Returns and Allowances $680

Allied Parts, a wholesaler, was organized on May 1, 2010, and made its first purchase of merchandise on May 3. The purchase was for 2,000 units at a price of $10 per unit. On May 5, Allied Parts sold 1,500 of the units for $14 per unit to Baker Co. Terms of the sale were 2/10, n/60. Ignore sales taxes. Prepare entries for Allied Parts to record the May 5 sale and each of the following separate transactions *a* through *c*.

a. On May 7, Baker returns 200 units because they did not fit its customer's needs.

b. On May 8, Baker discovers that 300 units are damaged but are still of some use and, therefore, keeps the units. Allied Parts sends Baker a credit memorandum for $600 to compensate for the damage.

c. On May 15, Baker discovers that 100 units are the wrong color. Baker keeps 60 of these units because Allied sends a $120 credit memorandum to compensate. However, Baker returns the remaining 40 units to Allied.

Business decision makers desire information on sales returns and allowances. (1) Explain why a company's manager wants the accounting system to record customers' returns of unsatisfactory goods in the Sales Returns and Allowances account instead of the Sales account. (2) Explain whether this information would be useful for external decision makers.

Exercise 11–2
Sales returns and allowances
LO3

Wilcox Electronics uses a sales journal, a purchases journal, a cash receipts journal, a cash disbursements journal, and a general journal. Wilcox recently completed the following transactions *a* through *h*. Identify the journal in which each transaction should be recorded.

Exercise 11–3
Identifying the special journal of entry   **LO4**

a. Sold merchandise on credit.
b. Purchased shop supplies on credit.
c. Paid an employee's salary in cash.
d. Borrowed cash from the bank.

e. Sold merchandise for cash.
f. Purchased merchandise on credit.
g. Purchased inventory for cash.
h. Paid cash to a creditor.

At the end of May, the sales journal of Mountain View appears as follows. (There are no sales taxes on Mountain View's sales.)

Exercise 11–4
Posting to subsidiary ledger accounts; preparing a schedule of accounts receivable   **LO4**

Sales Journal					
Date	Account Debited	Invoice Number	PR	Accounts Receivable Dr.	Sales Cr.
May 6	Aaron Reckers	190		3,880	3,880
10	Sara Reed	191		2,940	2,940
17	Anna Page	192		1,850	1,850
25	Sara Reed	193		1,340	1,340
31	Totals			10,010	10,010

Mountain View also recorded the return of defective merchandise with the following entry.

May	20	Sales Returns and Allowances		3 5 0 00	
		Accounts Receivable—Anna Page			3 5 0 00
		Customer returned (worthless) merchandise.			

Required

1. Open an accounts receivable subsidiary ledger that has a T-account for each customer listed in the sales journal. Post to the customer accounts the entries in the sales journal and any portion of the general journal entry that affects a customer's account. Ignore sales tax. Assume that these accounts have zero balances at the beginning of May.

2. Open a general ledger that has T-accounts for Accounts Receivable, Sales, and Sales Returns and Allowances. Assume that these accounts have zero balances at the beginning of May. Post the sales journal and any portion of the general journal entry that affects these accounts.

3. Prepare a schedule of accounts receivable as of May 31 and prove that its total equals the balance in the Accounts Receivable controlling account at May 31.

Check   (3) Accounts Receivable, $9,660

Keeler Company had the following credit sales to its customers during June.

Exercise 11–5
Accounts receivable ledger; posting from sales journal   **LO4**

Date	Customer	Sales Price
June 2	Joe Mack	$ 4,600
8	Eric Horner	7,100
10	Tess Cox	14,400
14	Hong Jiang	21,500
20	Tess Cox	12,200
29	Joe Mack	8,300
	Total credit sales	$68,100

Required

1. Open an accounts receivable subsidiary ledger having a T-account for each customer. Post the invoices to the subsidiary ledger. Ignore sales tax.

2. Open an Accounts Receivable controlling T-account and a Sales T-account to reflect general ledger accounts. The Accounts Receivable controlling account has a zero balance on June 1. Post the end-of-month total from the sales journal to these accounts.

3. Prepare a schedule of accounts receivable as of June 30 and prove that its total equals the Accounts Receivable controlling account balance on June 30.

Exercise 11-6
Cash receipts journal   **LO7**

Assume the transactions in Exercise 11-5 involve cash sales instead of credit sales. Also assume that the Keeler company receives interest revenue on June 17 of $350 from the bank and receives a loan of $2,000 on June 23 from the bank. Prepare headings for a cash receipts journal like the one in Exhibit 11.10. Prepare a cash receipts journal for these cash receipts during the month of June.

Exercise 11-7
Cash receipts journal   **LO5 LO7**

Ali Co. uses a general journal and several special journals. The following transactions occur in the month of November.

Nov. 3 Purchased $3,200 of merchandise on credit from Hart Co., terms n/20.
　　 7 Sold merchandise costing $840 on credit to J. Than for $1,000, subject to a $20 sales discount if paid by the end of the month.
　　 9 Borrowed $3,750 cash by signing a note payable to the bank.
　　 13 J. Ali, the owner, contributed $5,000 cash to the company.
　　 18 Sold merchandise costing $250 to B. Cox for $330 cash.
　　 22 Paid Hart Co. $3,200 cash for the merchandise purchased on November 3.
　　 27 Received $980 cash from J. Than in payment of the November 7 purchase.
　　 30 Paid salaries of $1,650 in cash.

Prepare headings for a cash receipts journal like the one in Exhibit 11.10. Journalize the November transactions that should be recorded in the cash receipts journal.

Exercise 11-8
Sales and cash receipts journals
LO7

The Sun Company completed the following sales and cash receipts transactions during the first week of December. The Sun Company uses the periodic inventory system.

Dec. 1 Sold merchandise for $6,700 on credit to the Two Rivers Co., terms 2/10, n/30. Invoice Number 1455.
　　 1 Sold merchandise for $3,400 on credit to the Berlin Co., terms 2/10, n/30. Invoice Number 1456.
　　 2 Sold merchandise for $590 cash to the Ellison Co. Invoice Number 1457.
　　 3 Borrowed $10,000 from Custer Bank on a long-term note payable.
　　 3 Sold merchandise for $7,200 on credit to the Amherst Co., terms 2/10, n/30. Invoice Number 1458.
　　 5 Received the amount due from the Two Rivers Co. from the sale on December 1.
　　 6 Sold merchandise on credit for $950 to the Waupaca Co., terms 2/10, n/30. Invoice Number 1459.
　　 6 Received the amount due from the Berlin Co. from the sale on December 1.

Required

a. Prepare headings for a sales journal like the one in Exhibit 11.6. Prepare headings for a cash receipts journal like the one in Exhibit 11.10. Journalize the transactions that should be recorded in the sales and cash receipts journals.

b. Prepare a schedule of accounts receivable as of December 31. There were no accounts receivable as of December 1.

---

connect™

PROBLEM SET A

Problem 11-1A
Sales journal and accounts receivable subsidiary ledger

LO5 LO6

QB

Wiset Company completes the following transactions during April, its first month of operations. A tax rate of 8% applies to all sales.

Apr. 3 Sold $4,000 of merchandise on credit to Page Alistair, Invoice No. 760.
　　 5 Sold $8,000 of merchandise on credit to Paula Kohr, Invoice No. 761.
　　 11 Sold $10,500 of merchandise on credit to Nic Nelson, Invoice No. 762.
　　 13 Sold $5,100 of merchandise on credit to Page Alistair, Invoice No. 763.
　　 27 Sold $3,170 of merchandise on credit to Paula Kohr, Invoice No. 764.
　　 27 Sold $6,700 of merchandise on credit to Nic Nelson, Invoice No. 765.

Required

1. Prepare a sales journal like that in Exhibit 11.6. Number the sales journal page as page 3. Enter the transactions in the sales journal.

2. Open the following general ledger accounts: Accounts Receivable (#106), Sales Tax Payable (#205), and Sales (#400). Also open accounts receivable subsidiary ledger accounts for Paula Kohr, Page Alistair, and Nic Nelson. Post the transactions to the subsidiary ledger accounts. Prepare the month-end postings to the general ledger accounts.

Using your solution to Problem 11-1A, prove the accuracy of the accounts receivable subsidiary ledger by preparing a schedule of accounts receivable as of April 30.

Problem 11-2A

Schedule of Accounts Receivable
L06

Church Company completes the following transactions during March, its first month of operations (terms for all its credit sales are 2/10, n/30).

Mar. 2 Sold merchandise on credit to Min Cho, Invoice No. 854, for $16,800 plus sales tax of $1,176.
 3 Sold merchandise on credit to Linda Witt, Invoice No. 855, for $10,200 plus sales tax of $714.
 10 Sold merchandise on credit to Jovita Albany, Invoice No. 856, for $5,600 plus sales tax of $392.
 27 Sold merchandise on credit to Jovita Albany, Invoice No. 857, for $14,910 plus sales tax of $1,044.
 28 Sold merchandise on credit to Linda Witt, Invoice No. 858, for $4,315 plus sales tax of $302.

Problem 11-3A

Sales journal, subsidiary ledger, and schedule of accounts receivable **L05 L06**

mhhe.com/wildCA2e

Required

1. Open the following general ledger accounts: Accounts Receivable (#106), Sales (#400), and Sales Tax Payable (#205). Open the following accounts receivable subsidiary ledger accounts: Jovita Albany, Min Cho, and Linda Witt.

2. Enter the transactions in a sales journal like Exhibit 11.6. Number all journal pages as page 2.

3. Post all transactions to the accounts receivable subsidiary ledger and its month-end totals to the general ledger.

4. Prove the accuracy of the subsidiary ledger by preparing a schedule of accounts receivable as of March 31.

Check (4) Total accounts receivable, $55,453

The March sales transactions of Church Company are described in Problem 11-3A. In addition to those transactions, Church has the following nonsales transactions.

Mar. 12 Received cash payment from Min Cho for the March 2 sale less the 2% cash discount.
 13 Received cash payment from Linda Witt for the March 3 sale less the 2% cash discount.
 20 Received cash payment from Jovita Albany for the March 10 sale less the 2% cash discount.
 30 Issued a credit memorandum of $500 (plus a $35 sales tax refund) for damaged goods from the sale to Linda Witt made on March 28.

Problem 11-4A

Journal entries for cash receipts, sales discounts, and sales returns and allowances
L01 L02 L03

Required

Record each cash receipt (less any cash discount) as a general journal entry. Also, record any sales return as a general journal entry.

Wiset Company completes these transactions during April of the current year (the terms of all its credit sales are 2/10, n/30).

Apr. 2 Purchased $14,300 of merchandise on credit from Noth Company, invoice dated April 2, terms 2/10, n/60.
 3 Sold merchandise on credit to Page Alistair, Invoice No. 760, for $4,000.
 3 Purchased $1,480 of office supplies on credit from Custer, Inc. Invoice dated April 2, terms n/10 EOM.
 4 Issued Check No. 587 to *World View* for advertising expense, $899.
 5 Sold merchandise on credit to Paula Kohr, Invoice No. 761, for $8,000.
 6 Received an $80 credit memorandum from Custer, Inc., for the return of some of the office supplies received on April 3.
 9 Purchased $12,125 of store equipment on credit from Hal's Supply, invoice dated April 9, terms n/10 EOM.

Problem 11-5A

Special journals, subsidiary ledgers, and schedule of accounts receivable **L05 L06 L07**

11   Sold merchandise on credit to Nic Nelson, Invoice No. 762, for $10,500.

12   Issued Check No. 588 to Noth Company in payment of its April 2 invoice, less the discount.

13   Received payment from Page Alistair for the April 3 sale, less the discount.

13   Sold $5,100 of merchandise on credit to Page Alistair, Invoice No. 763.

14   Received payment from Paula Kohr for the April 5 sale, less the discount.

16   Issued Check No. 589, payable to Payroll, in payment of sales salaries expense for the first half of the month, $10,750. Cashed the check and paid employees.

16   Cash sales for the first half of the month are $52,840. (Cash sales are recorded daily from cash register data but are recorded only twice in this problem to reduce repetitive entries.)

17   Purchased $13,750 of merchandise on credit from Grant Company, invoice dated April 17, terms 2/10, n/30.

18   Borrowed $60,000 cash from First State Bank by signing a long-term note payable.

20   Received payment from Nic Nelson for the April 11 sale, less the discount.

20   Purchased $830 of store supplies on credit from Hal's Supply, invoice dated April 19, terms n/10 EOM.

23   Received a $750 credit memorandum from Grant Company for the return of defective merchandise received on April 17.

23   Received payment from Page Alistair for the April 13 sale, less the discount.

25   Purchased $11,375 of merchandise on credit from Noth Company, invoice dated April 24, terms 2/10, n/60.

26   Issued Check No. 590 to Grant Company in payment of its April 17 invoice, less the return and the discount.

27   Sold $3,170 of merchandise on credit to Paula Kohr, Invoice No. 764.

27   Sold $6,700 of merchandise on credit to Nic Nelson, Invoice No. 765.

30   Issued Check No. 591, payable to Payroll, in payment of the sales salaries expense for the last half of the month, $10,750.

30   Cash sales for the last half of the month are $73,975.

Required

1. Prepare a sales journal like that in Exhibit 11.6 and a cash receipts journal like that in Exhibit 11.10. Number both journal pages as page 3. Then review the transactions of Wiset Company and enter those that should be journalized in the sales journal and those that should be journalized in the cash receipts journal. Ignore any transactions that should be journalized in a purchases journal, a cash disbursements journal, or a general journal.

2. Open the following general ledger accounts: Cash, Accounts Receivable, Inventory, Long-Term Notes Payable, Sales, and Sales Discounts. Enter the March 31 balances for Cash ($85,000), Inventory ($125,000), and Long-Term Notes Payable ($210,000). Also open accounts receivable subsidiary ledger accounts for Paula Kohr, Page Alistair, and Nic Nelson.

3. Verify that amounts that should be posted as individual amounts from the journals have been posted. (Such items are immediately posted.) Foot and crossfoot the journals and make the month-end postings.

Check   Trial balance totals, $434,285

4. Prepare a trial balance of the general ledger and prove the accuracy of the subsidiary ledger by preparing a schedule of accounts receivable.

PROBLEM SET B

Problem 11–1B
Sales journal and accounts receivable subsidiary ledger
LO5   LO6

Acorn Industries completes the following transactions during July, its first month of operations (the terms of all its credit sales are 2/10, n/30). A tax rate of 10% applies to all sales.

July   5   Sold merchandise on credit to Kim Nettle, Invoice No. 918, for $19,200.

6   Sold merchandise on credit to Ruth Blake, Invoice No. 919, for $7,500.

13   Sold merchandise on credit to Ashton Moore, Invoice No. 920, for $8,550.

14   Sold merchandise on credit to Kim Nettle, Invoice No. 921, for $5,100.

29   Sold merchandise on credit to Ruth Blake, Invoice No. 922, for $17,500.

30   Sold merchandise on credit to Ashton Moore, Invoice No. 923, for $16,820.

Required

1. Prepare a sales journal like that in Exhibit 11.6. Number the sales journal as page 3.

2. Open the following general ledger accounts: Accounts Receivable (#106), Sales Tax Payable (#205), and Sales (#400). Also open accounts receivable subsidiary ledger accounts for Kim Nettle, Ashton Moore, and Ruth Blake. Post the transactions to the subsidiary ledger accounts. Prepare the month-end postings to the general ledger accounts.

Problem 11–2B
Schedule of Accounts Receivable
LO6

Using your solution to 11-1B, prove the accuracy of the accounts receivable subsidiary ledger by preparing a schedule of accounts receivable as of July 31.

Problem 11–3B
Sales journal, subsidiary ledger, and schedule of accounts receivable   **LO5   LO6**

Grassley Company completes the following transactions during November, its first month of operations (terms for all its credit sales are 2/10, n/30).

Nov. 8   Sold merchandise on credit to Cyd Rounder, Invoice No. 439, for $6,550 plus sales tax of $524.
10   Sold merchandise on credit to Carlos Mantel, Invoice No. 440, for $13,500 plus sales tax of $1,080.
15   Sold merchandise on credit to Tori Tripp, Invoice No. 441, for $5,250 plus sales tax of $420.
22   Sold merchandise on credit to Carlos Mantel, Invoice No. 442, for $3,695 plus sales tax of $296.
24   Sold merchandise on credit to Tori Tripp, Invoice No. 443, for $4,280 plus sales tax of $342.

Required

1. Open the following general ledger accounts: Accounts Receivable (#106), Sales (#400), and Sales Tax Payable (#205). Open the following accounts receivable subsidiary ledger accounts: Carlos Mantel, Tori Tripp, and Cyd Rounder.
2. Enter the transactions in a sales journal like that in Exhibit 11.6. Number the journal page as page 2.
3. Post all transactions to the accounts receivable subsidiary ledger and its month-end totals to the general ledger.
4. Prove the accuracy of the subsidiary ledger by preparing a schedule of accounts receivable as of November 30.

Check   (4) Total accounts receivable, $35,937

Problem 11–4B
Journal entries for sales discounts and sales returns and allowances
LO1   LO2   LO3

The November sales transactions of Grassley Company are described in Problem 11-3B. In addition to those transactions, Grassley has the following nonsales transactions.

Nov. 18   Received cash payment from Cyd Rounder for the November 8 sale less the 2% cash discount.
19   Received cash payment from Carlos Mantel for the November 10 sale less the 2% cash discount.
25   Received cash payment from Tori Tripp for the November 15 sale less the 2% cash discount.
29   Issued a credit memorandum of $675 (plus a $54 sales tax refund) for damaged goods from the sale to Carlos Mantel made on November 22.

Required

Record each cash receipt (less any cash discount) as a general journal entry. Also, record any sales return as a general journal entry.

Problem 11–5B
Special journals, subsidiary ledgers, schedule of accounts receivable   **LO5   LO6   LO7**

Acorn Industries completes these transactions during July of the current year (the terms of all its credit sales are 2/10, n/30).

July 1   Purchased $6,500 of merchandise on credit from Teton Company, invoice dated June 30, terms 2/10, n/30.
3   Issued Check No. 300 to *The Weekly* for advertising expense, $625.
5   Sold merchandise on credit to Kim Nettle, Invoice No. 918, for $19,200.
6   Sold merchandise on credit to Ruth Blake, Invoice No. 919, for $7,500.
7   Purchased $1,250 of store supplies on credit from Plaine, Inc., invoice dated July 7, terms n/10 EOM.
8   Received a $250 credit memorandum from Plaine, Inc., for the return of store supplies received on July 7.
9   Purchased $38,220 of store equipment on credit from Charm's Supply, invoice dated July 8, terms n/10 EOM.
10   Issued Check No. 301 to Teton Company in payment of its June 30 invoice, less the discount.

13   Sold merchandise on credit to Ashton Moore, Invoice No. 920, for $8,550.

14   Sold merchandise on credit to Kim Nettle, Invoice No. 921, for $5,100.

15   Received payment from Kim Nettle for the July 5 sale, less the discount.

15   Issued Check No. 302, payable to Payroll, in payment of sales salaries expense for the first half of the month, $31,850. Cashed the check and paid employees.

15   Cash sales for the first half of the month are $118,350. (Cash sales are recorded daily using data from the cash registers but are recorded only twice in this problem to reduce repetitive entries.)

16   Received payment from Ruth Blake for the July 6 sale, less the discount.

17   Purchased $7,200 of merchandise on credit from Drake Company, invoice dated July 17, terms 2/10, n/30.

20   Purchased $650 of office supplies on credit from Charm's Supply, invoice dated July 19, terms n/10 EOM.

21   Borrowed $15,000 cash from College Bank by signing a long-term note payable.

23   Received payment from Ashton Moore for the July 13 sale, less the discount.

24   Received payment from Kim Nettle for the July 14 sale, less the discount.

24   Received a $2,400 credit memorandum from Drake Company for the return of defective merchandise received on July 17.

26   Purchased $9,770 of merchandise on credit from Teton Company, invoice dated July 26, terms 2/10, n/30.

27   Issued Check No. 303 to Drake Company in payment of its July 17 invoice, less the return and the discount.

29   Sold merchandise on credit to Ruth Blake, Invoice No. 922, for $17,500.

30   Sold merchandise on credit to Ashton Moore, Invoice No. 923, for $16,820.

31   Issued Check No. 304, payable to Payroll, in payment of the sales salaries expense for the last half of the month, $31,850.

31   Cash sales for the last half of the month are $80,244.

Required

1. Prepare a sales journal like that in Exhibit 11.6 and a cash receipts journal like that in Exhibit 11.10. Number both journals as page 3. Then review the transactions of Acorn Industries and enter those transactions that should be journalized in the sales journal and those that should be journalized in the cash receipts journal. Ignore any transactions that should be journalized in a purchases journal, a cash disbursements journal, or a general journal.

2. Open the following general ledger accounts: Cash, Accounts Receivable, Inventory, Long-Term Notes Payable, Sales, and Sales Discounts. Enter the June 30 balances for Cash ($100,000), Inventory ($200,000), and Long-Term Notes Payable ($300,000). Also open accounts receivable subsidiary ledger accounts for Kim Nettle, Ashton Moore, and Ruth Blake.

3. Verify that amounts that should be posted as individual amounts from the journals have been posted. (Such items are immediately posted.) Foot and crossfoot the journals and make the month-end postings.

Check   Trial balance totals, $588,264

4. Prepare a trial balance of the general ledger and prove the accuracy of the subsidiary ledger by preparing a schedule of accounts receivable.

BEYOND THE NUMBERS

REPORTING IN ACTION

L07

BTN 11–1   Refer to **Best Buy**'s financial statements in Appendix A to answer the following.

Required

1. Identify and total the inventory assets as of March 1, 2008, and March 3, 2007, for Best Buy. Compute the percentage of inventory assets relative to current assets.

Fast Forward

2. Access Best Buy's financial statements (form 10-K) for fiscal years ending after March 1, 2008, from its Website (**BestBuy.com**) or the SEC's EDGAR database (**www.sec.gov**). Recompute and interpret the percentage of inventory assets relative to current assets for these current fiscal years.

BTN 11-2 Amy Martin is a student who plans to attend approximately four professional events a year at her college. Each event necessitates a financial outlay of $100–$200 for a new suit and accessories. After incurring a major hit to her savings for the first event, Amy developed a different approach. She buys the suit on credit the week before the event, wears it to the event, and returns it the next week to the store for a full refund on her charge card.

ETHICS CHALLENGE
LO1 LO3 LO4

Required

1. Comment on the ethics exhibited by Amy and possible consequences of her actions.
2. How does the merchandising company account for the suits that Amy returns?
3. How can an accounts receivable subsidiary ledger alert the store's manager to Amy's behavior?

BTN 11-3 Your friend, Wendy Geiger, owns a small retail store that sells candies and nuts. Geiger acquires her goods from a few select vendors. She generally makes purchase orders by phone and on credit. Sales are primarily for cash. Geiger keeps her own manual accounting system using a general journal and a general ledger. At the end of each business day, she records one summary entry for cash sales. Geiger recently began offering items in creative gift packages. This has increased sales substantially, and she is now receiving orders from corporate and other clients who order large quantities and prefer to buy on credit. As a result of increased credit transactions in both purchases and sales, keeping the accounting records has become extremely time consuming. Geiger wants to continue to maintain her own manual system and calls you for advice. Write a memo to her advising how she might modify her current manual accounting system to accommodate the expanded business activities. Geiger is accustomed to checking her ledger by using a trial balance. Your memo should explain the advantages of what you propose and of any other verification techniques you recommend.

WORKPLACE COMMUNICATION
LO4 LO5 LO6 LO7

BTN 11-4 William Fuerst Company completes the following transactions during July of the current year. A tax rate of 8% applies to all sales.

TEAMWORK IN ACTION
LO1 LO5

July	3	Sold $6,000 of merchandise on credit to Susan Scholz, Invoice No. 1060.
	7	Sold $4,500 of merchandise on credit to Mike Ettredge, Invoice No. 1061.
	9	Sold $7,700 of merchandise on credit to Mark Hirschey, Invoice No. 1062.
	13	Sold $1,600 of merchandise on credit to Susan Scholz, Invoice No. 1063.
	24	Sold $5,300 of merchandise on credit to Gilbert Karuga, Invoice No. 1064.
	29	Sold $7,100 of merchandise on credit to Mark Hirschey, Invoice No. 1065.

Required

Divide your team into two groups. Have one group prepare the general journal entries for each sale. Have the other group prepare a sales journal like that in Exhibit 11.6. Compare and contrast the advantages and disadvantages of each approach.

BTN 11-5 Refer to the opening feature about Bert and John Jacobs and their **Life is good** company.

ENTREPRENEURS IN BUSINESS
LO4

Required

1. Identify the special journals that Life is good would likely use in its operations.
2. Identify any subsidiary ledgers that Life is good would likely use.

BTN 11-6 You want to know how promptly customers are paying their bills. This information can help you plan your cash payments and decide whether to extend credit. Where do you find this information?

YOU CALL IT— ENTREPRENEUR
LO5 LO6

---

1. b; Net sales = $75,000 + $320,000 − $13,700 −
   $6,000 = $375,300

2. a

3. d

4. c

5. d; $1,000 less $20 (.02 × $1,000) discount

ANSWERS TO MULTIPLE CHOICE QUIZ

A Look Back

Chapter 11 emphasized merchandise sales transactions, sales discounts, and sales returns and allowances. We also explained the use of a sales journal, cash receipts journal, and an accounts receivable subsidiary ledger.

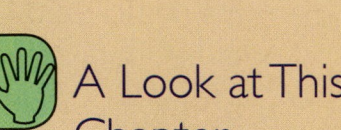

A Look at This Chapter

Chapter 12 extends our coverage of merchandising activities, with emphasis on accounting for merchandise purchases and accounts payable. We also explain the use of a cash disbursements journal.

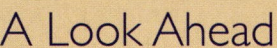

A Look Ahead

Chapter 13 provides a summary of accrual accounting. We emphasize the matching of expenses with the revenues generated.

Chapter 12

Merchandise Purchases and Accounts Payable

Learning Objectives

LO 1 Analyze and record transactions for merchandise purchases.

LO 2 Journalize and post transactions using a purchases journal.

LO 3 Prepare and prove the accuracy of an accounts payable subsidiary ledger.

LO 4 Journalize and post transactions using a cash disbursements journal.

"We're selling a feeling to the consumer"
—Renee Pepys Lowe

CoCaLo Creates Sweet Dreams

COSTA MESA, CA—"I always had my mother to lean on," admits Renee Pepys Lowe. But when her mother decided to sell her small business in which Renee worked, Renee lost her job. "That was a big change," recalls Renee. "I did a lot of soul-searching."

Renee rebounded by starting an infant bedding and nursery accessories company, **CoCaLo** (**CoCaLo.com**)—named after her daughters, Courtenay and Catherine Lowe. Renee envisioned a company with fashionable, high-quality products at affordable prices. Fortunately, she says her designers have "a remarkable talent for seeing what fabrics, colors, and textures can look like in combination."

Although CoCaLo is now profiting in the infant bedding industry, the early days were not easy. "You really have to take a lot of risks," says Renee. "It's all about allowing everyone to have a bedding collection with style, without having to spend a thousand dollars to get it." Adds Renee, "The scariest part for me is that I'm responsible for . . . finances, loans [and all aspects of accounting]."

To succeed, Renee needed to make smart business decisions. She set up an accounting system to capture and communicate costs and sales information. Effectively tracking merchandising activities is needed to set prices and create policies for discounts and allowances, returns on sales, and purchases. An inventory system enabled CoCaLo to stock the right type and amount of merchandise and to avoid the costs of out-of-stock and excess inventory. And with an estimated $20 million in annual sales to stores like Babies "R" Us and J.C. Penney, keeping track of merchandise is a critical job.

Mastering accounting for merchandising is a means to an end for Renee. "I love this business," she says. "There's something about giving new parents the tools to create a room they can feel proud of." Judging by CoCaLo's sales, there are plenty of proud parents out there.

[Sources: *CoCaLo Website,* March 2009; *Orange County Business Journal,* March 2009]

Merchandising companies purchase inventory to resell to their customers. This chapter introduces the accounting for inventory purchases by merchandising companies and the use of the purchases journal and an accounts payable subsidiary ledger to further enhance this process.

Merchandise Purchases and Accounts Payable

Merchandising Purchases
- Purchasing procedures
- Trade and purchase discounts
- Purchase returns and allowances
- Transportation costs

Journals and Subsidiary Ledgers
- Purchases journal
- Accounts payable subsidiary ledger
- Cash disbursements journal

Accounting for Merchandise Purchases

A **merchandiser** buys and sells products. Merchandising companies must account for purchases, inventory, cost of goods sold, trade and purchase discounts, and purchase returns and allowances.

L01 Analyze and record transactions for merchandise purchases.

Purchasing Procedures

Most merchandisers need inventory in their stores or warehouses to sell to customers. **Merchandise inventory,** or simply **inventory,** refers to products that a company owns and intends to sell. Inventory represents a current asset of the firm. For a large firm, a central purchasing department will locate potential suppliers and negotiate prices and credit terms and ultimately place orders for inventory. In a small retail store, the owner or manager of the store will perform all of these purchasing tasks.

When a department needs products to sell, the department (or sales) manager will prepare and sign a **purchase requisition** listing the merchandise needed (see Exhibit 12.1) and send it to the purchasing department.

Exhibit 12.1

Purchase Requisition

Purchase Requisition			No. 917
Z-Mart			

From ___ Sporting Goods Department ___ Date ___ October 28, 2010 ___
To ___ Purchasing Department ___ Preferred Vendor ___ Trex ___

Request purchase of the following item(s):

Model No.	Description	Quantity
CH 015	Challenger X7	1
SD 099	SpeedDemon	1

Reason for Request ___ Replenish inventory ___
Approval for Request ___ J.Z. ___

For Purchasing Department use only: Order Date __10/30/10__ P.O. No. ___P98___

The purchasing department then selects a **vendor** (also called a supplier) that can supply the goods, and places a **purchase order.** A purchase order authorizes a vendor to ship ordered merchandise at the stated price and credit terms (see Exhibit 12.2). Someone with authority to approve purchases signs the purchase order (sometimes abbreviated as P.O.) and sends it to the vendor.

Exhibit 12.2

Purchase Order

	Purchase Order		No. P98
	Z-Mart		
	10 Michigan Street		
	Chicago, Illinois 60521		

To: Trex
W9797 Cherry Road
Antigo, Wisconsin 54409

Date _____ 10/30/10 _____
FOB _____ Destination _____
Ship by __As soon as possible__
Terms _____ 2/15, n/30 _____

Request shipment of the following item(s):

Model No.	Description	Quantity	Price	Amount
CH 015	Challenger X7	1	490	490
SD 099	SpeedDemon	1	710	710

All shipments and invoices must include purchase order number

Ordered by

T. N.

Upon receipt of the purchase order, the vendor ships the ordered merchandise to the buyer. Many companies maintain a separate department to receive all merchandise and purchased assets. When each shipment arrives, a receiving department employee counts the goods and checks them for damage and agreement with the purchase order. This person then prepares a **receiving report,** which is used within the company to notify the appropriate persons that ordered goods have been received and to describe the quantities and condition of the goods.

The seller sends an invoice when the ordered merchandise is shipped. The **invoice** is an itemized statement of goods sent by the vendor listing the customer's name, items sold, sales prices, and terms of sale. As shown in Exhibit 12.3, an invoice is also a bill sent to the buyer from the vendor. From the vendor's point of view, it is a *sales invoice*. The buyer treats it as a *purchase invoice.*

Accounting for Purchases and Freight Charges

Shortly before the invoice (or bill) is due, the accounting department will make payment. Under the periodic system of inventory accounting, the cost of merchandise purchased for resale is recorded in the Purchases account. The Purchases account is a temporary account that is closed to Cost of Goods Sold at the end of the accounting period. The normal balance for the Purchases account is a debit.

The cost of shipping the goods from the vendor to the buyer is called **transportation-in.** This freight charge is accounted for separately from the purchases account as a debit. To illustrate, Z-Mart purchases $1,200 of merchandise on credit and incurs $96 of freight charges. The journal entry to record this credit purchase is:

Nov.	2	Purchases		1 2 0 0 00	
		Transportation-In		9 6 00	
		Accounts Payable			1 2 9 6 00

Assets = Liabilities + Equity
+1,296   −1,200
−96

Trade Discounts

When a manufacturer or wholesaler prepares a catalog of items it has for sale, it usually gives each item a **list price,** also called a *catalog price*. However, an item's intended *selling price*

Exhibit 12.3

Invoice

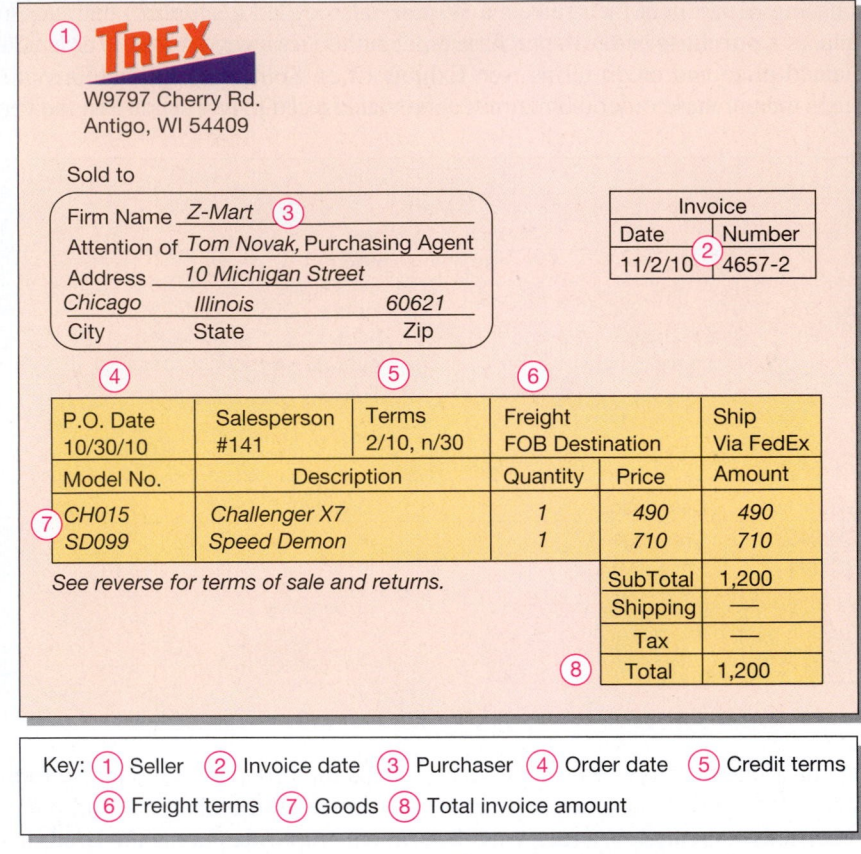

Exhibit 12.4

Credit Terms

equals list price minus a given percent called a **trade discount.** The amount of trade discount usually depends on whether a buyer is a wholesaler, retailer, or final consumer. A wholesaler buying in large quantities is often granted a larger discount than a retailer buying in smaller quantities. A buyer records the net amount of list price minus trade discount. For example, in the November 2 purchase of merchandise by Z-Mart, the merchandise was listed in the seller's catalog at $2,000 and Z-Mart received a 40% trade discount. This meant that Z-Mart's purchase price was $1,200, computed as $2,000 − (40% × $2,000).

Purchase Discounts

A buyer can receive a **purchase discount** if timely payment is made. Any purchase (cash) discount is described in the **credit terms** on the invoice. Exhibit 12.4 portrays the credit terms.

Since both the buyer and seller know the invoice date, this date is used in determining the discount and credit periods.

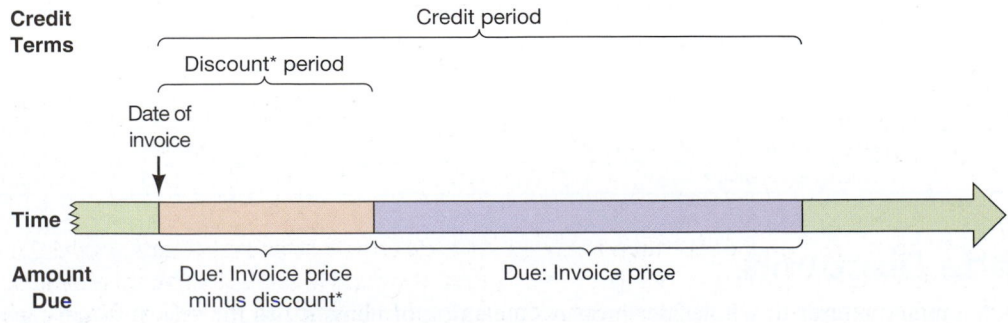

Recall from Chapter 11, credit terms of "2/10, n/30" mean that full payment is due within a 30-day **credit period,** but the buyer can deduct 2% of the invoice amount if payment is made within 10 days of the invoice date. This reduced payment applies only in the **discount period.**

Purchase discounts are recorded in a contra-purchases account that normally carries a credit balance. The entry to record the merchandise purchase under a periodic inventory system is

Nov.	2	Purchases	1 2 0 0 00	
		Accounts Payable		1 2 0 0 00
		Purchased merchandise on credit, invoice		
		dated Nov. 2, terms 2/10, n/30.		

Assets = Liabilities + Equity
+1,200   −1,200

If Z-Mart pays the amount due on (or before) November 12, the entry is

Nov.	12	Accounts Payable	1 2 0 0 00	
		Purchase Discounts		2 4 00
		Cash		1 1 7 6 00
		Paid for the $1,200 purchase of Nov. 2 less the		
		discount of $24 (2% × $1,200).		

Assets = Liabilities + Equity
−1,176   −1,200   +24

After these entries are posted, the net cost of merchandise purchased is reflected in Purchases minus Purchase Discounts. The Accounts Payable account shows a zero balance. The ledger accounts, in T-account form, follow:

Accounts Payable				Purchases			Purchase Discounts	
Nov. 12	1,200	Nov. 2	1,200	Nov. 2	1,200			Nov. 12	24
		Balance	0	Balance	1,200			Balance	24

Purchase Returns and Allowances

Purchase returns refer to merchandise a buyer acquires but then returns to the seller. A *purchase allowance* is a reduction in the cost of defective or unacceptable merchandise that a buyer acquires. Buyers often keep defective but still marketable merchandise if the seller grants an acceptable allowance.

When a buyer returns or takes an allowance on merchandise, the buyer issues a **debit memorandum** to inform the seller of a debit made to the seller's account in the buyer's records. To illustrate, on November 15 Z-Mart (buyer) issues a $300 debit memorandum for an allowance from Trex for defective merchandise. Z-Mart's November 15 entry to record the purchase allowance is

Nov.	15	Accounts Payable	3 0 0 00	
		Purchase Returns and Allowances		3 0 0 00
		Allowance for defective merchandise.		

Assets = Liabilities + Equity
−300   +300

If this had been a return, then the total *recorded cost* (all costs less any discounts) of the defective merchandise would be entered. The buyer's cost of returned and defective merchandise is usually offset against the buyer's current account payable balance to the seller. When cash is refunded, the Cash account is debited instead of Accounts Payable.

Transportation Costs and Ownership Transfer

The buyer and seller must agree on who is responsible for paying any freight costs and who bears the risk of loss during transit for merchandising transactions. This determines the point when ownership transfers from the seller to the buyer. The point of transfer is called the **FOB** (*free on board*) point, which determines who pays transportation costs (and often other incidental costs of transit such as insurance).

Exhibit 12.5 identifies two alternative points of transfer. (1) *FOB shipping point,* also called *FOB factory,* means the buyer accepts ownership when the goods leave the seller's place of business. The buyer is then responsible for paying shipping costs and bearing the risk of damage or loss when goods are in transit. The goods are part of the buyer's inventory when they are in transit since ownership has transferred to the buyer. **Cannondale**, a major bike manufacturer, uses FOB shipping point. (2) *FOB destination* means ownership of goods transfers to the buyer when the goods arrive at the buyer's place of business. The seller is responsible for paying shipping charges and bears the risk of damage or loss in transit. The seller does not record revenue from this sale until the goods arrive at the destination because this transaction is not complete before that point. The buyer does not record the purchase until the goods arrive at the buyer's place of business.

Exhibit 12.5

Ownership Transfer and Transportation Costs

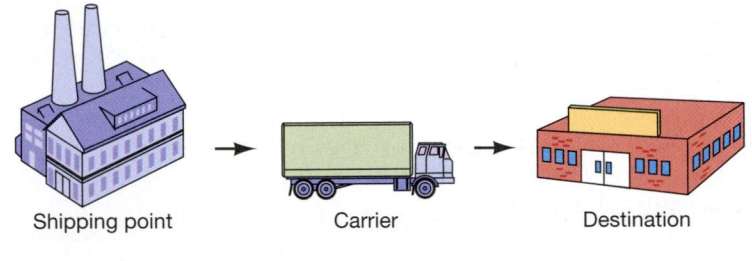

	Shipping point	Carrier	Destination

	Ownership Transfers When Goods Passed to	Transportation Costs Paid by
FOB shipping point	Carrier	Buyer
FOB destination	Buyer	Seller

Z-Mart's $1,200 purchase on November 2 is on terms of FOB destination. This means Z-Mart does not pay transportation costs. When a buyer is responsible for paying transportation costs, the payment is made to a carrier or directly to the seller depending on the agreement. The cost principle requires that any necessary transportation costs of a buyer (often called *transportation-in* or *freight-in*) be included as part of the cost of purchased merchandise. To illustrate, Z-Mart's entry to record a $75 freight charge from an independent carrier for merchandise purchased FOB shipping point is

Assets = Liabilities + Equity
−75   −75

Nov.	24	Transportation-In		7 5 00	
		Cash			7 5 00
		Paid freight costs on purchased merchandise.			

A seller records the costs of shipping goods to customers in a Delivery Expense account when the seller is responsible for these costs. Delivery Expense, also called *transportation-out* or *freight-out,* is reported as a selling expense in the seller's income statement.

In sum, purchases are recorded as debits to the Purchases account. Any purchase discounts or returns and allowances are credited to the Purchase Discounts and Purchases Returns and Allowances accounts, respectively. Freight charges are debited to Transportation-In. These items are used to compute **net purchases.** Z-Mart's itemized cost of net merchandise purchases for year 2010 are shown in Exhibit 12.6.

Z-MART Itemized Costs of Net Merchandise Purchases For Year Ended December 31, 2010	
Purchases	$235,800
Less: Purchase discounts	(4,200)
Purchase returns and allowances	(1,500)
Add: Transportation-In	2,300
Net purchases	**$232,400**

Exhibit 12.6

Itemized Costs of Net Merchandise Purchases

HOW YOU DOIN'?

Answers—p. 302

1. How long are the credit and discount periods when credit terms are 2/10, n/60?

2. Identify which items are subtracted from the *list* amount and not recorded when computing purchase price: (*a*) transportation-in; (*b*) trade discount; (*c*) purchase discount; (*d*) purchase return.

3. What does *FOB* mean? What does *FOB destination* mean?

Purchases Journal and Accounts Payable Subsidiary Ledger

Exhibit 12.7 illustrates the accounting for several February merchandise purchases on credit by Z-Mart. The journal entries are entered in the general journal and then posted to the general ledger. As you can see from Exhibit 12.7, entering a journal entry each time there is a credit

GENERAL JOURNAL				Page 1	
Date	Description	PR	Debit		Credit
Feb. 3	Purchases	502	325 00		
	Transportation-In	503	25 00		
	Accounts Payable	207			350 00
	Purchased Merchandise from Horning Supply Co.,				
	Invoice 337, terms n/30				
5	Purchases	502	177 00		
	Transportation-In	503	23 00		
	Accounts Payable	207			200 00
	Purchased Merchandise from Ace Mfg Co.,				
	Invoice 4242, terms 2/10, n/30				
13	Purchases	502	135 00		
	Transportation-In	503	15 00		
	Accounts Payable	207			150 00
	Purchased Merchandise from Wynet & Co.,				
	Invoice 667, terms 2/10, n/30				
20	Purchases	502	283 00		
	Transportation-In	503	17 00		
	Accounts Payable	207			300 00
	Purchased Merchandise from Smite Co.,				
	Invoice 2333, terms 2/10, n/30				

Exhibit 12.7

General Journal Entries and Posting of February Purchases for Z-Mart

[continued on next page]

[continued from previous page]

25	Purchases	502	9 2 00		
	Transportation-In	503	8 00		
	Accounts Payable	207		1 0 0 00
	Purchased Merchandise from Ace Mfg. Co.,			
	Invoice 4295, terms 2/10, n/30			
28	Purchases	502	2 0 7 00		
	Transportation-In	503	1 8 00		
	Accounts Payable	207		2 2 5 00
	Purchased Merchandise from ITT Co.,			
	Invoice 3367, terms n/30			

Account

Accounts Payable — Account No. 207

Date	Item	PR	Debit	Credit	Balance
Feb. 1	Balance				0
3		G1		350	350
5		G1		200	550
13		G1		150	700
20		G1		300	1,000
25		G1		100	1,100
28		G1		225	1,325

Transportation-In — Account No. 503

Date	Item	PR	Debit	Credit	Balance
Feb. 3		G1	25		25
5		G1	23		48
13		G1	15		63
20		G1	17		80
25		G1	8		88
28		G1	18		106

Purchases — Account No. 502

Date	Item	PR	Debit	Credit	Balance
Feb. 3		G1	325		325
5		G1	177		502
13		G1	135		637
20		G1	283		920
25		G1	92		1,012
28		G1	207		1,219

purchase is a tedious, repetitive task. Writing descriptions of each purchase and posting each transaction to the general ledger represent significant effort. To make this process more efficient, a purchases journal is used.

Purchases Journal

LO2 Journalize and post transactions using a purchases journal.

A **purchases journal** is typically used to record all credit purchases. Cash purchases are typically recorded in the cash disbursements journal or general journal. We illustrate all credit merchandise purchases for Z-Mart in the month of February in Exhibit 12.8. To record transactions in a purchases journal, use the information on the purchase invoice.

1. Enter the date of the journal entry, the invoice date, and credit terms.
2. In the Accounts Payable Credit column, enter the total owed to the supplier.
3. In the Purchases Debit column, enter the total amount of purchases bought.
4. In the Transportation-In Debit column, enter the freight charges.

Once the journal entries are entered in the purchases journal, totals are posted to the general ledger. As illustrated in Exhibit 12.8, compute totals for the Accounts Payable Credit column

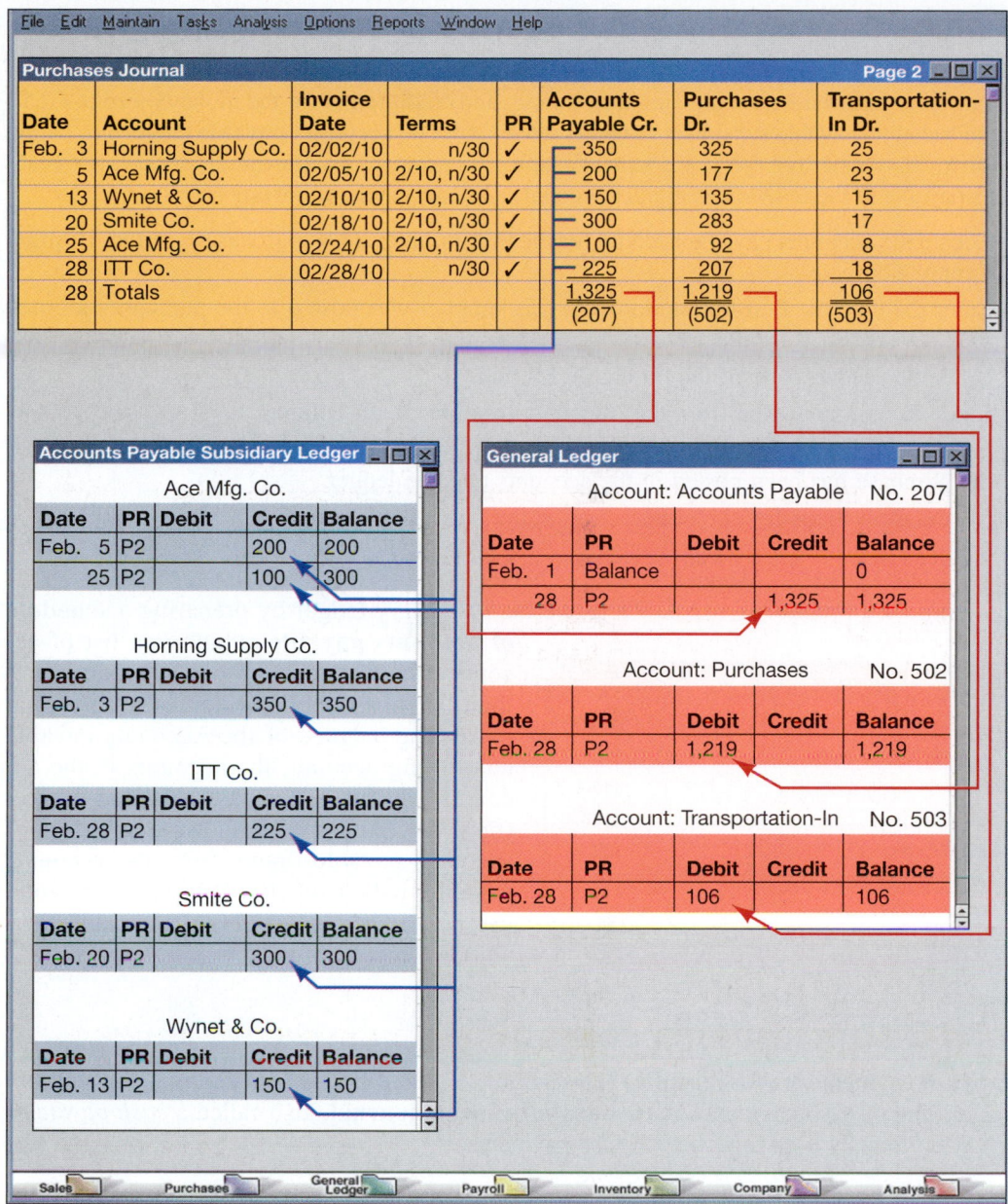

Exhibit 12.8

Purchases Journal with Posting

($1,325) and for the Purchases Debit ($1,219) and Transportation-In Debit ($106) columns. Before posting, we must ensure the debits (Purchases and Transportation-In) equal the credits (Accounts Payable). Then we post the column totals from the Purchases journal to the general ledger as follows:

1. Locate the general ledger accounts needed: Accounts Payable (207), Purchases (502), and Transportation-In (503).

2. Enter the date of the posting.

3. Post the reference. In this case, we post P2. **P** is for purchases journal. The number **2** denotes the second page of the purchases journal.

4. Post the total from the Accounts Payable Credit column. Compute the new balance.

5. Post the total from the Purchases Debit column. Compute the new balance.

6. Post the total from the Transportation-In Debit column. Compute the new balance.

Posting to the Accounts Payable Subsidiary Ledger

Once the purchases journal is posted to the general ledger, the ledger accounts are up to date. To keep accurate information on the amounts, timing, and credit terms for the money owed to creditors, an accounts payable subsidiary ledger is often kept. The **accounts payable ledger** is a listing of individual supplier (creditor) accounts. Exhibit 12.8 provides an illustration of posting the accounts payable to the individual supplier accounts. We suggest the following steps:

1. Locate the accounts payable account for the first supplier in the purchases journal, Horning Supply Company.
2. Enter the date the first transaction with this supplier was posted to the purchases journal.
3. Post the reference. In this case, we post P2. **P** is for purchases journal. The number **2** denotes the second page of the purchases journal.
4. Enter the amount owed from the Accounts Payable Credit column.
5. Enter a checkmark in the Post Reference column in the Purchases journal to indicate that the purchase has been posted in the accounts payable ledger.
6. Repeat these steps for each transaction in the purchases journal.

LO3 Prepare and prove the accuracy of an accounts payable subsidiary ledger

Proving the Ledger Accounts payable balances in the subsidiary ledger are proved after posting the purchases journal. We prove the subsidiary ledger by preparing a **schedule of accounts payable,** which is a list of accounts from the accounts payable ledger with their balances and the total. If this total equals the balance of the Accounts Payable controlling account, the accounts in the accounts payable ledger are assumed correct (proved). Exhibit 12.9 shows a schedule of accounts payable drawn from the accounts payable ledger of Exhibit 12.8. Its total ($1,325) equals the balance of Accounts Payable in the general ledger.

Exhibit 12.9

Schedule of Accounts Payable

Schedule of Accounts Payable February 28	
Ace Mfg. Company	$ 300
Horning Supply Company	350
ITT Company	225
Smite Company	300
Wynet & Company	150
Total accounts payable	$1,325

Cash Disbursements Journal

LO4 Journalize and post transactions using a cash disbursements journal.

Many cash payments are for repetitive transactions. A cash disbursements journal can simplify the recording of cash payments. A **cash disbursements journal,** also called a *cash payments journal,* is typically used to record all cash payments.

Journalizing The cash disbursements journal shown in Exhibit 12.10 illustrates repetitive entries to the Cash Cr. column of this journal (reflecting cash payments). Also note the frequent credits to Inventory (which reflect purchase discounts) and the debits to Accounts Payable. For example, on February 15, the company pays Ace on account (credit terms of 2/10, n/30). Since payment occurs in the discount period, the company pays $196 ($200 invoice less $4 discount). The $4 discount is credited to Purchase Discounts. Note that when this company purchases inventory for cash, it is recorded using the Other Accounts Dr. column and the Cash Cr. column as illustrated in the February 3 and 12 transactions. Generally, the Other Accounts column is used to record cash payments on items for which no column exists. For example, on February 15, the company pays salaries expense of $250. The title of the account debited (Salaries Expense) is entered in the Account Debited column.

Each transaction in the cash disbursements journal involves a credit to Cash. Debit accounts will vary.

The cash disbursements journal has a column titled Ck. No. (check number). For control over cash disbursements, all payments except for those of small amounts are made by check. Checks should be prenumbered and each check's number entered in the journal in numerical order in the column headed Ck. No. This makes it possible to scan the numbers in the column for omitted checks. When a cash disbursements journal has a column for check numbers, it is sometimes called a **check register.**

Exhibit 12.10

Cash Disbursements Journal with Posting

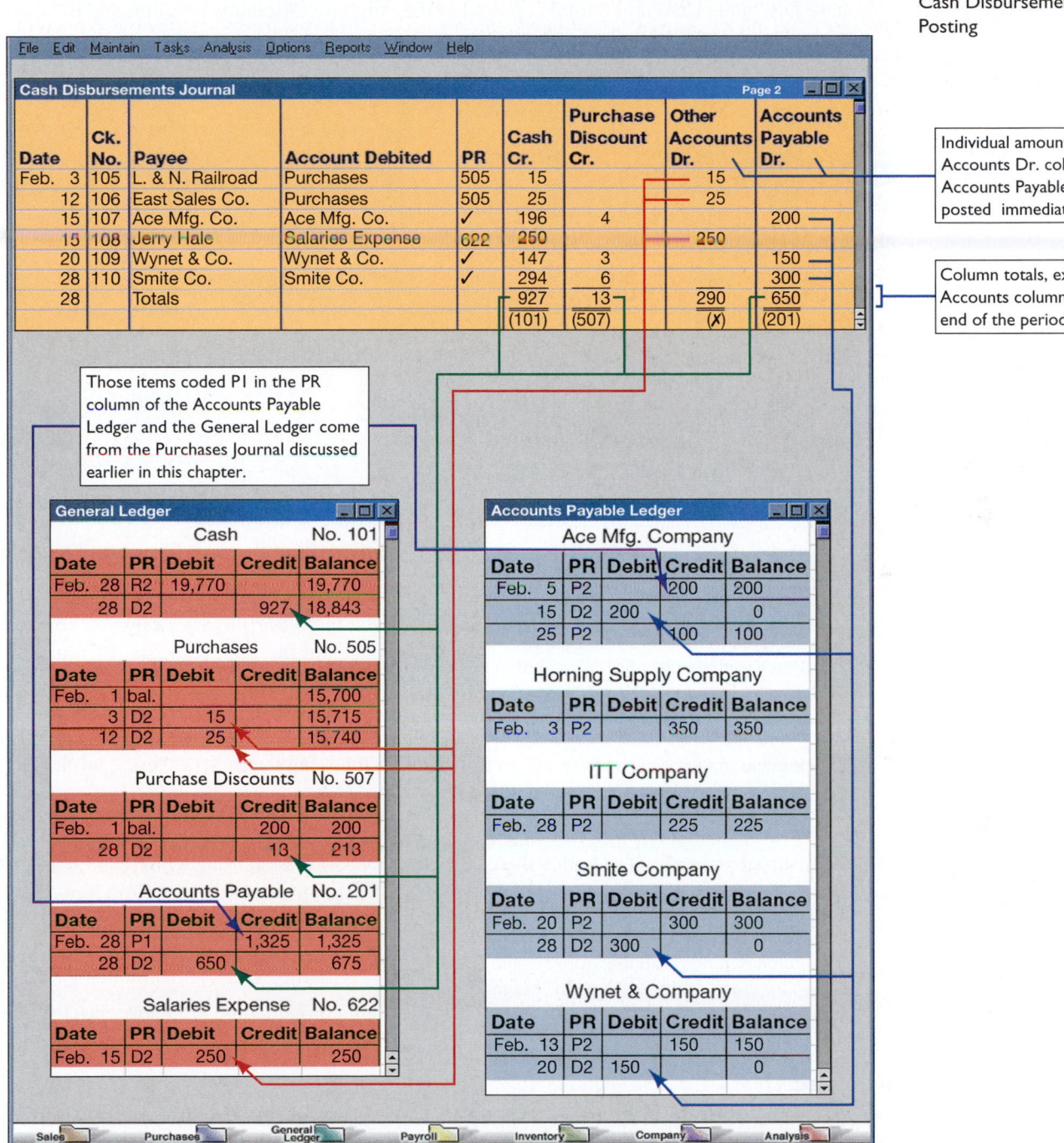

Posting Individual amounts in the Other Accounts Dr. column of a cash disbursements journal are immediately posted to their general ledger accounts. Individual amounts in the Accounts Payable Dr. column are also immediately posted to creditors' accounts in the subsidiary Accounts Payable ledger. These postings are identified with a "D" along with a page number from the cash disbursements journal in the PR column of the subsidiary ledger. The customer accounts in the subsidiary ledger include some postings from page two of the purchases journal (coded 'P2' in the PR column). At the end of the period, we crossfoot column totals and post the Accounts Payable Dr. column total to the Accounts Payable controlling account. Also, the Purchase Discounts Cr. column total is posted to the Purchase Discounts account, and the Cash Cr. column total is posted to the Cash account.

HOW YOU DOIN'?   Answers—p. 302

4. What are the normal recording and posting procedures when using special journals and controlling accounts with subsidiary ledgers?

5. What is the process for posting to a subsidiary ledger and its controlling account?

6. How do we prove the accuracy of account balances in the general ledger and subsidiary ledgers after posting?

Demonstration Problem 1

Connie Company has the following credit merchandise purchase transactions in the month of July. All goods are shipped FOB shipping point.

July 3   Purchased merchandise from Alison Inc. under the following terms: $750 price, invoice date 7/2, credit terms n/30, freight $62.

     7   Purchased merchandise from Hyrum Inc. under the following terms: $1,500 price, invoice date 7/5, credit terms 2/10, n/30, freight $92.

     9   Purchased merchandise from Melissa Inc. under the following terms: $75 price, invoice date 7/8, credit terms n/30, freight $5.

   13   Purchased merchandise from Alison Inc. under the following terms: $1,750 price, invoice date 7/12, credit terms n/30, freight $117.

   14   Purchased merchandise from Joseph Inc. under the following terms: $152 price, invoice date 7/14, credit terms 2/10, n/30, freight $23.

   19   Purchased merchandise from Rebecca Supply Inc. under the following terms: $866 price, invoice date 7/19, credit terms 2/10, n/30, freight $57.

   22   Purchased merchandise from Melissa Inc. under the following terms: $7,502 price, invoice date 7/19, credit terms n/30, freight $215.

   27   Purchased merchandise from Hyrum Inc. under the following terms: $117 price, invoice date 7/26, credit terms 2/10, n/30, freight $14.

   30   Purchased merchandise from Alison Inc. under the following terms: $750 price, invoice date 7/28, credit terms n/30, freight $62.

Required

1. Account for these purchases in a purchases journal using Accounts Payable (acct. #207), Purchases (acct. #502), and Transportation-In (acct. #503). The purchase journal page is page 3. Remember to include the invoice date and credit terms.

2. Post these accounts to the general ledger and post the references.

3. Post these transactions to the accounts payable subsidiary ledger.

Planning the Solution

1. Set up the purchases journal using the template from Exhibit 12.8 with a credit column for Accounts Payable and debit entry columns for Purchases and Transportation-In.

2. Record each credit purchase, with each transaction taking one line in the purchases journal.

3. When complete, sum the columns in the purchase journal to prepare to post totals to the general ledger accounts.

4. Post the column totals in Accounts Payable Credit, Purchases Debit, and Transportation-In Debit to their general ledger accounts.

5. Post each transaction from the purchases journal to the appropriate account in the accounts payable subsidiary ledger.

Solution to Demonstration Problem 1

1. and 2. Account for the purchases of Connie Company using a purchases journal.

Purchases Journal   Page 3

Date	Account	Invoice Date	Terms	PR	Accounts Payable Cr.	Purchases Dr.	Transportation-In Dr.
Jul. 3	Alison Inc.	July 2	n/30		812	750	62
7	Hyrum Inc.	July 5	2/10, n/30		1,592	1,500	92
9	Melissa Inc.	July 8	n/30		80	75	5
13	Alison Inc.	July 12	n/30		1,867	1,750	117
14	Joseph Inc.	July 14	2/10, n/30		175	152	23
19	Rebecca Supply Inc.	July 19	2/10, n/30		923	866	57
22	Melissa Inc.	July 19	n/30		7,717	7,502	215
27	Hyrum Inc.	July 26	2/10, n/30		131	117	14
30	Alison Inc.	July 28	n/30		812	750	62

3. and 4. Post the totals from the purchases journal to the general ledger.

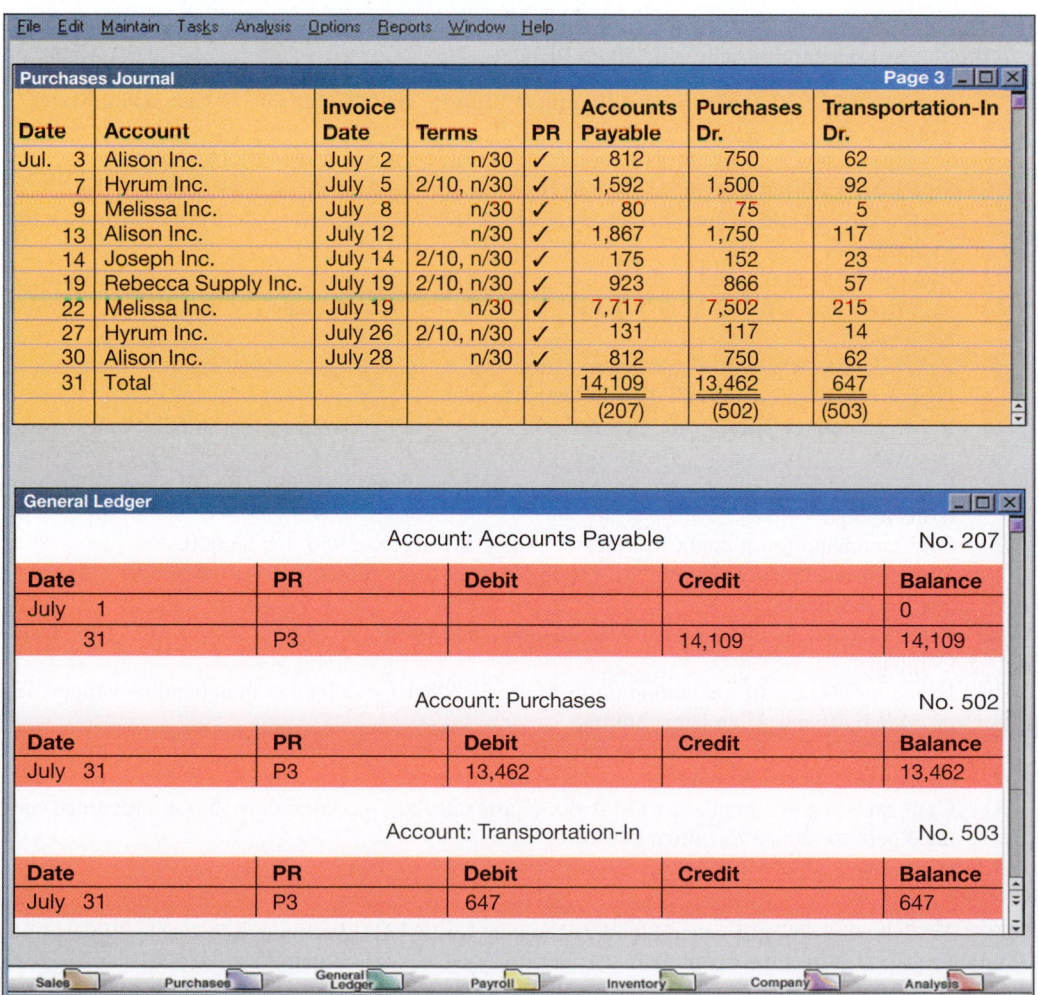

File Edit Maintain Tasks Analysis Options Reports Window Help

Purchases Journal   Page 3

Date	Account	Invoice Date	Terms	PR	Accounts Payable	Purchases Dr.	Transportation-In Dr.
Jul. 3	Alison Inc.	July 2	n/30	✓	812	750	62
7	Hyrum Inc.	July 5	2/10, n/30	✓	1,592	1,500	92
9	Melissa Inc.	July 8	n/30	✓	80	75	5
13	Alison Inc.	July 12	n/30	✓	1,867	1,750	117
14	Joseph Inc.	July 14	2/10, n/30	✓	175	152	23
19	Rebecca Supply Inc.	July 19	2/10, n/30	✓	923	866	57
22	Melissa Inc.	July 19	n/30	✓	7,717	7,502	215
27	Hyrum Inc.	July 26	2/10, n/30	✓	131	117	14
30	Alison Inc.	July 28	n/30	✓	812	750	62
31	Total				14,109	13,462	647
					(207)	(502)	(503)

General Ledger

Account: Accounts Payable   No. 207

Date	PR	Debit	Credit	Balance
July 1				0
31	P3		14,109	14,109

Account: Purchases   No. 502

Date	PR	Debit	Credit	Balance
July 31	P3	13,462		13,462

Account: Transportation-In   No. 503

Date	PR	Debit	Credit	Balance
July 31	P3	647		647

Sales   Purchases   General Ledger   Payroll   Inventory   Company   Analysis

5. Posting the accounts payable balances to the accounts payable subsidiary ledger.

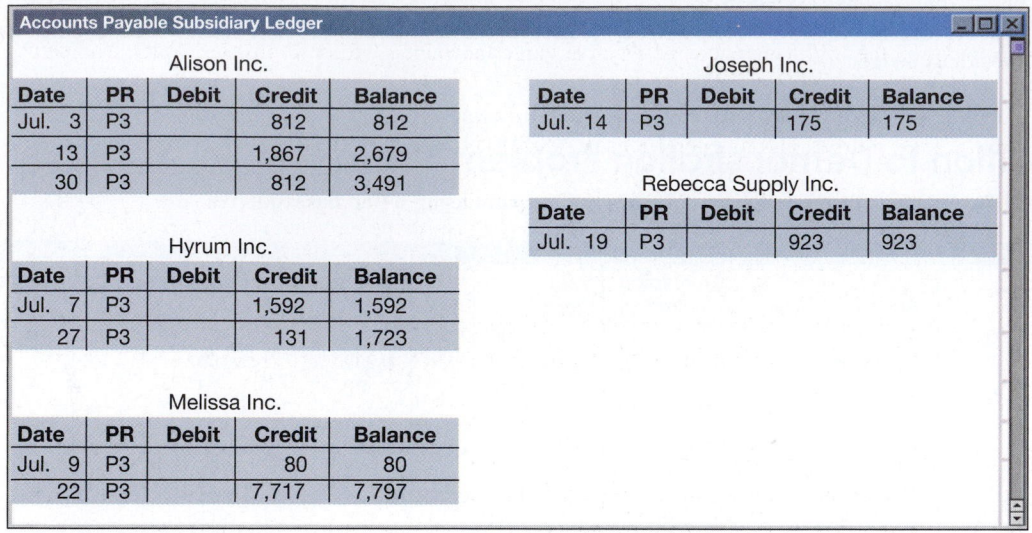

Accounts Payable Subsidiary Ledger

Alison Inc.

Date	PR	Debit	Credit	Balance
Jul. 3	P3		812	812
13	P3		1,867	2,679
30	P3		812	3,491

Hyrum Inc.

Date	PR	Debit	Credit	Balance
Jul. 7	P3		1,592	1,592
27	P3		131	1,723

Melissa Inc.

Date	PR	Debit	Credit	Balance
Jul. 9	P3		80	80
22	P3		7,717	7,797

Joseph Inc.

Date	PR	Debit	Credit	Balance
Jul. 14	P3		175	175

Rebecca Supply Inc.

Date	PR	Debit	Credit	Balance
Jul. 19	P3		923	923

Demonstration Problem 2

Pepper Company completed the following selected transactions and events during March of this year. (Terms of all credit sales for the company are 2/10, n/30.)

Mar. 4   Purchased $1,220 of office supplies on credit from Mack Company. Invoice dated March 3, terms n/30.

       5   Sold merchandise on credit to Jennifer Nelson, Invoice No. 954, for $16,800.

       6   Sold merchandise on credit to Dennie Hoskins, Invoice No. 955, for $10,200.

    11   Purchased $52,600 of merchandise, invoice dated March 6, terms 2/10, n/30, from Defore Industries.

    12   Borrowed $26,000 cash by giving Commerce Bank a long-term promissory note payable.

    14   Received cash payment from Jennifer Nelson for the March 4 sale less the discount (Invoice No. 954).

    16   Received a $200 credit memorandum from Defore Industries for unsatisfactory merchandise Pepper purchased on March 11 and later returned.

    16   Received cash payment from Dennie Hoskins for the March 6 sale less the discount (Invoice No. 955).

    18   Purchased $22,850 of store equipment on credit from Schmidt Supply, invoice dated March 15, terms n/30.

    20   Sold merchandise on credit to Marjorie Allen, Invoice No. 956, for $5,600.

    21   Sent Defore Industries Check No. 516 in payment of its March 6 dated invoice less the return and the discount.

    22   Purchased $41,625 of merchandise, invoice dated March 18, terms 2/10, n/30, from Welch Company.

    26   Issued a $600 credit memorandum to Marjorie Allen for defective merchandise Pepper sold on March 20 and Allen later returned.

    31   Issued Check No. 517, payable to Payroll, in payment of $15,900 sales salaries for the month. Cashed the check and paid the employees.

    31   Cash sales for the month are $134,680. (Cash sales are recorded daily but are recorded only once here to reduce repetitive entries.)

Required

1. Open the following selected general ledger accounts: Cash (101), Accounts Receivable (106), Office Supplies (124), Store Equipment (165), Accounts Payable (201), Long-Term Notes Payable (251),

Sales (413), Sales Returns and Allowances (414), Sales Discounts (415), Purchases (505), Purchases Returns and Allowances (506), Purchases Discounts (507), and Sales Salaries Expense (621). Open the following accounts receivable ledger accounts: Marjorie Allen, Dennie Hoskins, and Jennifer Nelson. Open the following accounts payable ledger accounts: Defore Industries, Mack Company, Schmidt Supply, and Welch Company.

2. Enter the transactions using a sales journal, a purchases journal, a cash receipts journal, a cash disbursements journal, and a general journal. Regularly post to the individual customer and creditor accounts. Also, post any amounts that should be posted as individual amounts to general ledger accounts. Foot and crossfoot the journals and make the month-end postings. *Pepper Co. uses the periodic inventory system in this problem.* (Refer to Chapter 11 for an example of a sales journal and cash receipts journal and to Chapter 12 for an example of a purchases journal and cash disbursements journal.)

3. Prepare a trial balance for the selected general ledger accounts in part 1 and prove the accuracy of subsidiary ledgers by preparing schedules of accounts receivable and accounts payable.

Planning the Solution

- Set up the required general ledger, subsidiary ledger accounts, the sales journal, the cash receipts journal, the purchases journal, the cash disbursements journal, and the general journal.
- Read and analyze each transaction and decide in which special journal (or general journal) the transaction is recorded.
- Record each transaction in the proper journal (and post the appropriate individual amounts).
- Once you have recorded all transactions, total the journal columns. Post from each journal to the appropriate ledger accounts.
- Prepare a trial balance to prove the equality of the debit and credit balances in your general ledger.
- Prepare schedules of accounts receivable and accounts payable as of March 31. Compare the totals of these schedules to the Accounts Receivable and Accounts Payable controlling account balances, making sure that they agree.

Solution to Demonstration Problem 2

Sales Journal — Page 2

Date	Account Debited	Invoice Number	PR	Accounts Receivable Dr. Sales Cr.
Mar. 5	Jennifer Nelson	954	✓	16,800
6	Dennie Hoskins	955	✓	10,200
20	Marjorie Allen	956	✓	5,600
31	Totals			32,600
				(106/413)

Cash Receipts Journal — Page 3

Date	Account Credited	Explanation	PR	Cash Dr.	Sales Discount Dr.	Accounts Receivable Cr.	Sales Cr.	Other Accounts Cr.
Mar. 12	L.T. Notes Payable	Note to bank	251	26,000				26,000
14	Jennifer Nelson	Invoice 954, 3/5	✓	16,464	336	16,800		
16	Dennie Hoskins	Invoice 955, 3/6	✓	9,996	204	10,200		
31	Sales	Cash sales	x	134,680			134,680	
31	Totals			187,140	540	27,000	134,680	26,000
				(101)	(415)	(106)	(413)	(x)

Purchases Journal   Page 3

Date	Account	Date of Invoice	Terms	PR	Accounts Payable Cr.	Purchases Dr.	Office Supplies Dr.	Other Accounts Dr.
Mar. 4	Office Supplies/Mack Co.	3/3	n/30	✓	1,220		1,220	
11	Defore Industries	3/6	2/10, n/30	✓	52,600	52,600		
18	Store Equipment/Schmidt Supp.	3/15	n/30	165/✓	22,850			22,850
22	Welch Company	3/18	2/10, n/30	✓	41,625	41,625		
31	Totals				118,295	94,225	1,220	22,850
					(201)	(505)	(124)	(x)

Cash Disbursements Journal   Page 3

Date	Ck. No.	Payee	Account Debited	PR	Cash Cr.	Purch. Discount Cr.	Other Accounts Dr.	Accounts Payable Dr.
Mar. 21	516	Defore Industries	Defore Industries	✓	51,352	1,048		52,400
31	517	Payroll	Sales Salaries Expense	621	15,900		15,900	
31		Totals			67,252	1,048	15,900	52,400
					(101)	(507)	(x)	(201)

General Journal   Page 2

Mar. 16	Accounts Payable—Defore Industries	201/✓	200	
	Purchases Returns and Allowances.............	506		200
	To record credit memorandum received.			
26	Sales Returns and Allowances.....................	414	600	
	Accounts Receivable—Marjorie Allen	106/✓		600
	To record credit memorandum issued.			

Accounts Receivable Ledger

Marjorie Allen

Date	PR	Debit	Credit	Balance
Mar. 20	S2	5,600		5,600
26	G2		600	5,000

Dennie Hoskins

Date	PR	Debit	Credit	Balance
Mar. 6	S2	10,200		10,200
16	R3		10,200	0

Jennifer Nelson

Date	PR	Debit	Credit	Balance
Mar. 5	S2	16,800		16,800
14	R3		16,800	0

Accounts Payable Ledger

Defore Industries

Date	PR	Debit	Credit	Balance
Mar. 11	P3		52,600	52,600
16	G2	200		52,400
21	D3	52,400		0

Mack Company

Date	PR	Debit	Credit	Balance
Mar. 4	P3		1,220	1,220

Schmidt Supply

Date	PR	Debit	Credit	Balance
Mar. 18	P3		22,850	22,850

Welch Company

Date	PR	Debit	Credit	Balance
Mar. 22	P3		41,625	41,625

General Ledger (Partial Listing)

Cash   **Acct. No. 101**

Date	PR	Debit	Credit	Balance
Mar. 31	R3	187,140		187,140
31	D3		67,252	119,888

Accounts Receivable   **Acct. No. 106**

Date	PR	Debit	Credit	Balance
Mar. 26	G2		600	(600)
31	S2	32,600		32,000
31	R3		27,000	5,000

Office Supplies   **Acct. No. 124**

Date	PR	Debit	Credit	Balance
Mar. 31	P3	1,220		1,220

Store Equipment   **Acct. No. 165**

Date	PR	Debit	Credit	Balance
Mar. 18	P3	22,850		22,850

Accounts Payable   **Acct. No. 201**

Date	PR	Debit	Credit	Balance
Mar. 16	G2	200		(200)
31	P3		118,295	118,095
31	D3	52,400		65,695

Long-Term Notes Payable   **Acct. No. 251**

Date	PR	Debit	Credit	Balance
Mar. 12	R3		26,000	26,000

Sales   **Acct. No. 413**

Date	PR	Debit	Credit	Balance
Mar. 31	S2		32,600	32,600
31	R3		134,680	167,280

Sales Returns and Allowances   **Acct. No. 414**

Date	PR	Debit	Credit	Balance
Mar. 26	G2	600		600

Sales Discounts   **Acct. No. 415**

Date	PR	Debit	Credit	Balance
Mar. 31	R3	540		540

Purchases   **Acct. No. 505**

Date	PR	Debit	Credit	Balance
Mar. 31	P3	94,225		94,225

Purchases Returns and Allowances   **Acct. No. 506**

Date	PR	Debit	Credit	Balance
Mar. 16	G2		200	200

Purchases Discounts   **Acct. No. 507**

Date	PR	Debit	Credit	Balance
Mar. 31	D3		1,048	1,048

Sales Salaries Expense   **Acct. No. 621**

Date	PR	Debit	Credit	Balance
Mar. 31	D3	15,900		15,900

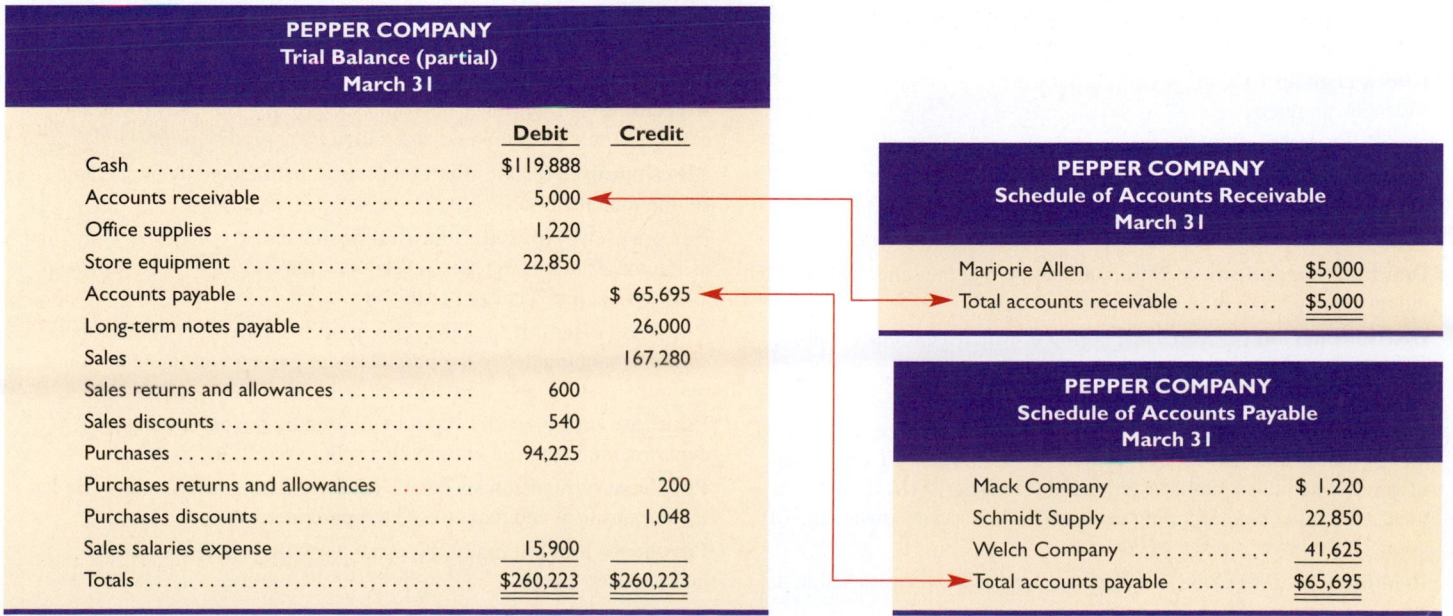

PEPPER COMPANY
Trial Balance (partial)
March 31

	Debit	Credit
Cash	$119,888	
Accounts receivable	5,000	
Office supplies	1,220	
Store equipment	22,850	
Accounts payable		$ 65,695
Long-term notes payable		26,000
Sales		167,280
Sales returns and allowances	600	
Sales discounts	540	
Purchases	94,225	
Purchases returns and allowances		200
Purchases discounts		1,048
Sales salaries expense	15,900	
Totals	$260,223	$260,223

PEPPER COMPANY
Schedule of Accounts Receivable
March 31

Marjorie Allen	$5,000
Total accounts receivable	$5,000

PEPPER COMPANY
Schedule of Accounts Payable
March 31

Mack Company	$ 1,220
Schmidt Supply	22,850
Welch Company	41,625
Total accounts payable	$65,695

Summary

LO1 Analyze and record transactions for merchandise purchases. A merchandiser records sales at list price less any trade discounts. The merchandiser records applicable purchase discounts for cash payment within the discount period as well as applicable purchase returns and freight charges.

LO2 Journalize and post transactions using a purchases journal. The purchases journal is an efficient means to record the purchase of inventory on credit. The purchases journal will typically debit merchandise inventory (and transportation-in if applicable) and credit accounts payable.

LO3 Prepare and prove the accuracy of an accounts payable subsidiary ledger. Account balances in the general ledger and the accounts payable subsidiary ledger are tested for accuracy after posting is complete. This procedure is twofold: (1) prepare a trial balance of the general ledger to confirm that debits equal credits and (2) prepare a schedule to confirm that the controlling account's balance equals the subsidiary ledger's balance.

LO4 Journalize and post transactions using a cash disbursements journal. This journal, also called a cash payments journal, is used to record cash payments for purchases, expenses, and other items.

Guidance Answers to   HOW YOU DOIN'?

1. Under credit terms of 2/10, n/60, the credit period is 60 days and the discount period is 10 days.

2. (b) trade discount.

3. *FOB* means "free on board." It is used in identifying the point when ownership transfers from seller to buyer. *FOB destination* means that the seller transfers ownership of goods to the buyer when they arrive at the buyer's place of business. It also means that the seller is responsible for paying shipping charges and bears the risk of damage or loss during shipment.

4. The normal recording and posting procedures are threefold. First, transactions are entered in a special journal if applicable. Second, individual amounts are posted to any subsidiary ledger

accounts. Third, column totals are posted to general ledger accounts if not already individually posted.

5. Individual amounts in the Accounts Payable Dr. column are posted immediately to creditor's accounts in the Accounts Payable subsidiary ledger. After crossfooting column totals at the end of the month, the Accounts Payable Dr. column is posted to the controlling account in the general ledger.

6. Tests for accuracy of account balances in the general ledger and subsidiary ledgers are twofold. First, we prepare a trial balance of the general ledger to confirm that debits equal credits. Second, we prove the subsidiary ledgers by preparing schedules of accounts receivable and accounts payable.

Key Terms

Accounts payable ledger (p. 294) Subsidiary ledger listing individual creditor (supplier) accounts.

Cash disbursements journal (p. 294) Special journal normally used to record all payments of cash; also called *cash payments journal.*

Check register (p. 294) A cash disbursements journal with a column for check numbers.

Credit period (p. 289) Time period that can pass before a customer's payment is due.

Credit terms (p. 288) Description of the amounts and timing of payments that a buyer (debtor) agrees to make in the future.

Debit memorandum (p. 289) Notification that the sender has debited the recipient's account in the sender's records.

Discount period (p. 289) Time period in which a cash discount is available and the buyer can make a reduced payment.

FOB (p. 290) Abbreviation for *free on board;* the point when ownership of goods passes to the buyer; *FOB shipping point* (or *factory*) means the buyer pays shipping costs and accepts ownership of goods when the seller transfers goods to carrier; *FOB destination* means the seller pays shipping costs and buyer accepts ownership of goods at the buyer's place of business.

Inventory (p. 286) Goods a company owns and expects to sell in its normal operations.

Invoice (p. 287) Itemized record of goods prepared by the vendor that lists the customer's name, items sold, sales prices, and terms of sale.

List price (p. 287) Catalog (full) price of an item before any trade discount is deducted.

Merchandise inventory (p. 286) Goods that a company owns and expects to sell to customers; also called *merchandise* or *inventory.*

Merchandiser (p. 286) Entity that earns net income by buying and selling merchandise.

Net purchases (p. 290) Net cost of merchandise purchased; computed as Purchases minus Purchase Discounts, minus Purchase Returns and Allowances, plus Transportation-In.

Purchase discount (p. 288) Term used by a purchaser to describe a cash discount granted to the purchaser for paying within the discount period.

Purchase order (p. 287) Document used by the purchasing department to place an order with a seller (vendor).

Purchase requisition (p. 286) Document listing merchandise needed by a department and requesting it be purchased.

Purchases journal (p. 292) Journal normally used to record all purchases on credit.

Receiving report (p. 287) Form used to report that ordered goods are received and to describe their quantity and condition.

Schedule of accounts payable (p. 294) List of the balances of all accounts in the accounts payable ledger and their total.

Trade discount (p. 288) Reduction from a list or catalog price that can vary for wholesalers, retailers, and consumers.

Transportation-In (p. 287) Freight costs paid by the buyer.

Vendor (p. 287) Seller of goods or services.

Multiple Choice Quiz   Answers on p. 313   mhhe.com/wildCA2e

Additional Multiple Choice Quizzes are available at the book's Website.

1. In the purchases journal, the _____ account is credited.
   a. Purchases
   b. Accounts Receivable
   c. Transportation-In
   d. Accounts Payable

2. A company purchased $4,500 of merchandise on May 1 with terms of 2/10, n/30. On May 6, it returned $250 of that merchandise. On May 8, it paid the balance owed for merchandise, taking any discount it is entitled to. The cash paid on May 8 is
   a. $4,500
   b. $4,250
   c. $4,160
   d. $4,165
   e. $4,410

3. Merchandise inventory
   a. Is a long-term asset account.
   b. Is a current asset account.
   c. Includes supplies.
   d. Is classified with investments on the balance sheet.
   e. Must be sold within one month.

4. Net purchases includes
   a. Any purchase discounts.
   b. Any returns and allowances.
   c. Any necessary transportation-in costs.
   d. Any trade discounts.
   e. All of the above.

5. In the cash disbursements journal, the _____ account is credited.
   a. Cash
   b. Accounts Receivable
   c. Transportation-In
   d. Accounts Payable

Discussion Questions

1. In comparing the accounts of a merchandising company with those of a service company, what additional accounts would the merchandising company likely use?

2. What items appear in financial statements of merchandising companies but not in the statements of service companies?

3. Why do companies offer cash discounts?

4. Distinguish between cash discounts and trade discounts. Is the amount of a trade discount on purchased merchandise recorded in the accounts?

5. What is the difference between a sales discount and a purchase discount?

6. Why would a company's manager be concerned about the quantity of its purchase returns if its suppliers allow unlimited returns?

7. Refer to the balance sheet and income statement for Best Buy in Appendix A. What does the company title its inventory account?

8. Refer to the income statement for RadioShack in Appendix A. What does RadioShack title its accounts payable account?

connect

Prepare journal entries to record each of the following purchases transactions of a merchandising company.

QUICK STUDY

QS 12–1
Recording purchases LO1

Mar. 5   Purchased 600 units of product with a list price of $10 per unit. The purchaser is granted a trade discount of 20%; terms of the sale are 2/10, n/60; invoice is dated March 5.

Mar. 7   Returned 25 defective units from the March 5 purchase and received full credit.

Mar. 15 Paid the amount due from the March 5 purchase, less the return on March 7.

QS 12–2
Special Journals   LO2   LO4

Wagstaff Electronics uses a sales journal, a purchases journal, a cash receipts journal, and a cash disbursements journal. Wagstaff recently completed the following transactions *a* through *d*. Identify the journal in which each transaction should be recorded.

a. Sold merchandise for cash.

b. Purchased merchandise on account.

c. Purchased inventory for cash.

d. Paid cash to a creditor.

QS 12–3
Special Journals   LO2   LO4

Beach Electronics uses a sales journal, a purchases journal, a cash receipts journal, and a cash disbursements journal. Beach recently completed the following transactions *a* through *d*. Identify the journal in which each transaction should be recorded.

a. Sold merchandise on credit.

b. Purchased shop supplies on credit.

c. Paid an employee's salary in cash.

d. Borrowed cash from a bank.

QS 12–4
Recording purchases in a purchases journal   LO2

Account for the following purchases in a purchases journal using Accounts Payable (acct. #207), Purchases (acct. #502), and Transportation-In (acct. #503). (*Hint:* Use the chapter demonstration problem as a guide.)

Dec. 3   Purchased $850 in merchandise from Camille Inc., credit terms n/30; invoice date 12/2, freight $72.
       7   Purchased $1,600 in merchandise from Travis Inc., credit terms 2/10, n/30; invoice date 12/5, freight $162.
       9   Purchased $65 in merchandise from Braden Inc., credit terms n/30; invoice date 12/8, freight $9.

QS 12–5
Recording purchases in a purchases journal   LO2

Account for the following purchases in a purchases journal using Accounts Payable (acct. #207), Purchases (acct. #502), and Transportation-In (acct. #503). (*Hint:* Use the chapter demonstration problem as a guide.)

Mar. 13   Purchased $2,750 in merchandise from Kaitlyn Supply Co., credit terms n/30; invoice date 12/12, freight $117.
      14   Purchased $162 in merchandise from Ashley Inc., credit terms 2/10, n/30; invoice date 12/14, freight $33.
      19   Purchased $966 in merchandise from Kaitlyn Supply Co., credit terms n/30; invoice date 12/19, freight $67.

QS 12–6
Cash disbursements journal   LO4

Ziebart uses a cash disbursements journal. Please record the following April cash payments in a cash disbursements journal.

Apr. 9   Issued check no. 520 to Muller Corp. to buy store supplies for $650.
      12   Issued check no. 521 to Hinkle Bank for note payable of $900.

QS 12–7
Cash disbursements journal   LO4

Sougiannis uses a cash disbursements journal. Prepare a cash disbursements journal using the following July cash payments.

July 8   Issued check no. 522 to Hammersley Corp. to pay for gardening for $1,400.
      28   Issued check no. 523 to Comprix Corp. pay for April Janitorial Services for $1,200.

---

connect

EXERCISES

Prepare journal entries to record the following transactions for a retail store.

Exercise 12–1
Recording entries for merchandise purchases   LO1

Apr. 2   Purchased merchandise from Lyon Company under the following terms: $4,600 price, invoice dated April 2, credit terms of 2/15, n/60, and FOB shipping point.
       3   Paid $300 for shipping charges on the April 2 purchase.
       4   Returned to Lyon Company unacceptable merchandise that had an invoice price of $600.

17   Sent a check to Lyon Company for the April 2 purchase, net of the discount and the returned merchandise.

18   Purchased merchandise from Frist Corp. under the following terms: $8,500 price, invoice dated April 18, credit terms of 2/10, n/30, and FOB destination.

21   After negotiations, received from Frist a $1,100 allowance on the April 18 purchase.

28   Sent check to Frist paying for the April 18 purchase, net of the discount and allowance.

Check April 28, Cr. Cash $7,252

Santa Fe Company purchased merchandise for resale from Mesa Company with an invoice price of $24,000 and credit terms of 3/10, n/60. The merchandise had cost Mesa $16,000. Santa Fe paid within the discount period. Prepare entries that Santa Fe Company should record for the merchandise purchase and the cash payment.

Exercise 12-2
Analyzing and recording merchandise transactions **LO1**

Insert the letter for each term in the blank space beside the definition that it most closely matches.

A. Cash discount   **E.** FOB shipping point   **H.** Purchase discount

B. Credit period   **F.** Trade discount   **I.** Sales discount

C. Discount period   **G.** Merchandise inventory

D. FOB destination

_____ **1.** Reduction below list or catalog price that is negotiated in setting the price of goods.

_____ **2.** Reduction in a receivable or payable if it is paid within the discount period.

_____ **3.** Time period that can pass before a customer's payment is due.

_____ **4.** Time period in which a cash discount is available.

_____ **5.** Ownership of goods is transferred when the seller delivers goods to the carrier.

_____ **6.** Ownership of goods is transferred when delivered to the buyer's place of business.

_____ **7.** Goods a company owns and expects to sell to its customers.

_____ **8.** Purchaser's description of a cash discount received from a supplier of goods.

_____ **9.** Seller's description of a cash discount granted to buyers in return for early payment.

Exercise 12-3
Applying merchandising terms
LO1

On May 5, Baker purchases 1,500 units of merchandise from Allied Parts for $14 per unit. Baker is a retailer and purchases the units for resale. Three separate transactions *a* through *c* also occur.

a. On May 7, Baker returns 200 units because they did not fit the customer's needs.

b. On May 8, Baker discovers that 300 units are damaged but are still of some use and, therefore, keeps the units. Allied Parts sends Baker a credit memorandum for $600 to compensate for the damage.

c. On May 15, Baker discovers that 100 units are the wrong color. Baker keeps 60 of these units because Allied sends a $120 credit memorandum to compensate. However, Baker returns the remaining 40 units to Allied.

Prepare the appropriate journal entries for Baker Co. to record the May 5 purchase and each of the three separate transactions *a* through *c*.

Exercise 12-4
Recording purchase returns and allowances **LO1**

On May 11, Sydney Co. accepts delivery of $40,000 of merchandise it purchases for resale from Troy Corporation. With the merchandise is an invoice dated May 11, with terms of 3/10, n/90, FOB shipping point. When the goods are delivered, Sydney pays $345 to Express Shipping for delivery charges on the merchandise. On May 12, Sydney returns $1,400 of goods to Troy, who receives them one day later. On May 20, Sydney mails a check to Troy Corporation for the amount owed. Troy receives it the following day.

1. Prepare journal entries that Sydney Co. records for these transactions.

2. Prepare journal entries that Troy Corporation records for these transactions.

Exercise 12-5
Analyzing and recording merchandise transactions—both buyer and seller **LO1**

Check (1) May 20, Cr. Cash $37,442

Exercise 12–6

Preparing journal entries for inventory purchases and sales
LO1

Journalize the following merchandising transactions for Chilton Systems.

1. On November 1, Chilton Systems purchases merchandise for $1,500 on credit with terms of 2/5, n/30, FOB shipping point; invoice dated November 1.

2. On November 5, Chilton Systems pays cash for the November 1 purchase.

3. On November 7, Chilton Systems discovers and returns $200 of defective merchandise purchased on November 1 for a cash refund.

4. On November 10, Chilton Systems pays $90 cash for transportation costs for the November 1 purchase.

5. On November 13, Chilton Systems sells merchandise for $1,600 on credit. The cost of the merchandise is $800.

6. On November 16, the customer returns merchandise from the November 13 transaction. The returned items sell for $300 and cost $150.

Exercise 12–7

Cash disbursements journal
LO4

Ziegler Inc. has the following cash disbursements in April.

Apr. 2   Issued check no. 210 to Curington Corp. to buy store supplies for $650.
     7   Issued check no. 211 for $1,400 to pay off a note payable to First Savings Bank.
   20   Purchased merchandise for $4,500 on credit from O'Leary-Kelly, terms 2/10, net 30.
   28   Issued check no. 212 to O'Leary-Kelly to pay the amount due for the purchase of April 20, less the discount.

Prepare headings for a cash disbursements journal like the one in Exhibit 12.10. Journalize the April transactions that should be recorded in the cash disbursements journal.

Exercise 12–8

Cash disbursements journal   **LO4**

Marx Supply uses a sales journal, a purchases journal, a cash receipts journal, a cash disbursements journal, and a general journal. The following transactions occur in the month of April.

Apr. 3   Purchased merchandise for $2,950 on credit from Seth, Inc., terms 2/10, n/30.
     9   Issued check no. 210 to Kitt Corp. to buy store supplies for $650.
   12   Sold merchandise on credit to C. Myers for $770, terms n/30.
   17   Issued check no. 211 for $1,400 to pay off a note payable to City Bank.
   20   Purchased merchandise for $4,500 on credit from Lite, terms 2/10, n/30.
   28   Issued check no. 212 to Lite to pay the amount due for the purchase of April 20, less the discount.
   29   Paid salary of $1,800 to B. Dock by issuing check no. 213.
   30   Issued check no. 214 to Seth, Inc., to pay the amount due for the purchase of April 3.

Prepare headings for a cash disbursements journal like the one in Exhibit 12.10. Journalize the April transactions that should be recorded in the cash disbursements journal.

Exercise 12–9

Cash disbursements and purchases journal   **LO2**   **LO4**

Williams Company began business on May 1. The following transactions involving purchases and cash disbursements occurred during the first week of May.

May 2   Purchased $25,000 of merchandise inventory on credit from the Sioux City Company, terms 2/10, n/30. Invoice dated May 1.
     3   Purchased $12,000 of merchandise inventory on credit from the Wichita Company, terms 2/10, n/30. Invoice dated May 2.
     3   Purchased $3,000 of office supplies for cash from Bettendorf Co. Check no. 1267.
     4   Purchased $36,000 of office equipment on credit from Office Outfitters, terms n/60. Invoice dated May 3.
     6   Paid the amount due for the merchandise purchased from Sioux City Company. Check no. 1268.
     6   Purchased $14,500 of merchandise inventory for cash from the Davenport Co. Check no. 1269.

Required

a. Prepare a purchases journal like that in Exhibit 12.8 and a cash disbursements journal like that in Exhibit 12.10. Number all journal pages as page 20.

b. Prepare a schedule of accounts payable as of May 31. There were no accounts payable on May 1.

connect™

Prepare journal entries to record the following merchandising transactions of Blink Company.

July   1   Purchased merchandise from Boden Company for $6,000 under credit terms of 1/15, n/30, FOB shipping point, invoice dated July 1.
3   Paid $125 cash for freight charges on the purchase of July 1.
9   Purchased merchandise from Leight Co. for $2,200 under credit terms of 2/15, n/60, FOB destination, invoice dated July 9.
11   Received a $200 credit memorandum from Leight Co. for the return of part of the merchandise purchased on July 9.
16   Paid the balance due to Boden Company within the discount period.
24   Paid Leight Co. the balance due within the discount period.

PROBLEM SET A

Problem 12–1A
Preparing journal entries for merchandising activities   **LO1**

Check   July 16, Cr. Cash $5,940
July 24, Cr. Cash $1,960

Prepare journal entries to record the following merchandising transactions of Sheng Company.

Aug.   1   Purchased merchandise from Arotek Company for $7,500 under credit terms of 1/10, n/30, invoice dated August 1.
8   Purchased merchandise from Waters Corporation for $5,400 under credit terms of 1/10, n/45, FOB shipping point, invoice dated August 8. The invoice showed that at Sheng's request, Waters paid the $140 shipping charges and added that amount to the bill. (*Recall:* Discounts are not applied to freight and shipping charges.)
12   After negotiations with Waters Corporation concerning problems with the merchandise purchased on August 8, Sheng received a credit memorandum from Waters granting a price reduction of $700.
18   Paid the amount due Waters Corporation for the August 8 purchase less the price reduction granted.
30   Paid Arotek Company the amount due from the August 1 purchase.

Problem 12–2A
Preparing journal entries for merchandising activities   **LO1**

Check   Aug. 18, Cr. Cash $4,793

Gomez Corp. has the following credit purchase transactions in the month of October.

Oct.   4   Purchased merchandise from Benjamin Inc. under the following terms, $950 price, invoice date 10/2, credit terms n/30, freight $62.
7   Purchased merchandise from Rachel Inc. under the following terms: $1,350, invoice date 10/5, credit terms 2/10, n/30, freight $92.
9   Purchased merchandise from Bethany Co. under the following terms: $725, invoice date 10/8, credit terms n/30, freight $65.
13   Purchased merchandise from Benjamin Inc. under the following terms: $1,350, invoice date 10/12, credit terms n/30, freight $117.
14   Purchased merchandise from Matthew Inc. under the following terms: $657, invoice date 10/14, credit terms 2/10, n/30, freight $23.

Required

1. Account for these purchases in a purchases journal using Accounts Payable (acct. #207), Purchases (acct. #502) and Transportation-In (acct. #503). The purchases journal page is page 4. Include the invoice date and credit terms.

2. Post these accounts to the general ledger (including the references).

3. Post these accounts to the accounts payable subsidiary ledger.

Problem 12–3A
Purchases journal and accounts payable subsidiary ledger
LO2   LO3

Prepare journal entries to record the following merchandising transactions of Yarvelle Company.

May   2   Purchased merchandise from Havel Co. for $10,000 under credit terms of 1/15, n/30, FOB shipping point, invoice dated May 2.
5   Paid $250 cash for freight charges on the purchase of May 2.
10   Purchased merchandise from Duke Co. for $3,650 under credit terms of 2/15, n/60, FOB destination, invoice dated May 10.
12   Received a $400 credit memorandum from Duke Co. for the return of part of the merchandise purchased on May 10.
17   Paid the balance due to Havel Co. within the discount period.
25   Paid Duke Co. the balance due within the discount period.

PROBLEM SET B

Problem 12–1B
Preparing journal entries for merchandising activities
LO1

Check   May 25, Cr. Cash $3,185

Problem 12-2B

Preparing journal entries for merchandising activities **LO1**

Prepare journal entries to record the following merchandising transactions of Mason Company.

July 3   Purchased merchandise from OLB Corp. for $15,000 under credit terms of 1/10, n/30, FOB destination, invoice dated July 3.

10   Purchased merchandise from Rupert Corporation for $14,200 under credit terms of 1/10, n/45, FOB shipping point, invoice dated July 10. The invoice showed that at Mason's request, Rupert paid the $500 shipping charges and added that amount to the bill. (*Recall:* Discounts are not applied to freight and shipping charges.)

14   After negotiations with Rupert Corporation concerning problems with the merchandise purchased on July 10, Mason received a credit memorandum from Rupert granting a price reduction of $2,000.

20   Paid the amount due Rupert Corporation for the July 10 purchase less the price reduction granted.

31   Paid OLB Corp. the amount due from the July 3 purchase.

Check   July 20, Cr. Cash, $12,578
       July 31, Cr. Cash, $15,000

Problem 12-3B

Purchases journal and accounts payable subsidiary ledger
LO2   LO3

Beach Corp. has the following credit purchase transactions in the month of January.

Jan. 5   Purchased merchandise from Bethany Inc. under the following terms: $725, invoice date 1/4, credit terms 2/10, n/30, freight $65.

9   Purchased merchandise from Daniel Inc. under the following terms: $1,650, invoice date 1/8, credit terms n/30, freight $109.

14   Purchased merchandise from David Co. under the following terms: $673, invoice date 1/12, credit terms n/30, freight $57.

22   Purchased merchandise from Bethany Inc. under the following terms: $675, invoice date 1/21, credit terms 2/10, n/30, freight $123.

28   Purchased merchandise from Mason Inc. under the following terms: $553, invoice date 1/28, credit terms 2/10, n/30, freight $52.

Required

1.   Account for these purchases in a purchases journal using Accounts Payable (acct. #207), Purchases (acct. #502), and Transportation-In (acct. #503). The purchases journal page is page 3. Include the invoice date and credit terms.

2.   Post these accounts to the general ledger (including the references).

3.   Post these accounts to the accounts payable subsidiary ledger.

---

connect™

PRACTICE SET 1

Wiset Corp.

Special journals, subsidiary ledgers, and schedule of accounts receivable
LO2   LO3   LO4

Wiset Company completes these transactions during April of the current year (the terms of all its credit sales are 2/10, n/30).

Apr. 2   Purchased $14,300 of merchandise on credit from Noth Company, invoice dated April 2, terms 2/10, n/60.

3   Sold merchandise on credit to Page Alistair, Invoice No. 760, for $4,000.

3   Purchased $1,480 of office supplies on credit from Custer, Inc., invoice dated April 2, terms n/10 EOM.

4   Issued Check No. 587 to *World View* for advertising expense, $899.

5   Sold merchandise on credit to Paula Kohr, Invoice No. 761, for $8,000.

6   Received an $80 credit memorandum from Custer, Inc., for the return of some of the office supplies received on April 3.

9   Purchased $12,125 of store equipment on credit from Hal's Supply, invoice dated April 9, terms n/10 EOM.

11   Sold merchandise on credit to Nic Nelson, Invoice No. 762, for $10,500.

12   Issued Check No. 588 to Noth Company in payment of its April 2 invoice, less the discount.

13   Received payment from Page Alistair for the April 3 sale, less the discount.

13   Sold $5,100 of merchandise on credit to Page Alistair, Invoice No. 763.

14   Received payment from Paula Kohr for the April 5 sale, less the discount.

16 Issued Check No. 589, payable to Payroll, in payment of sales salaries expense for the first half of the month, $10,750. Cashed the check and paid employees.

16 Cash sales for the first half of the month are $52,840. (Cash sales are recorded daily from cash register data but are recorded only twice in this problem to reduce repetitive entries.)

17 Purchased $13,750 of merchandise on credit from Grant Company, invoice dated April 17, terms 2/10, n/30.

18 Borrowed $60,000 cash from First State Bank by signing a long-term note payable.

20 Received payment from Nic Nelson for the April 11 sale, less the discount.

20 Purchased $830 of store supplies on credit from Hal's Supply, invoice dated April 19, terms n/10 EOM.

23 Received a $750 credit memorandum from Grant Company for the return of defective merchandise received on April 17.

23 Received payment from Page Alistair for the April 13 sale, less the discount.

25 Purchased $11,375 of merchandise on credit from Noth Company, invoice dated April 24, terms 2/10, n/60.

26 Issued Check No. 590 to Grant Company in payment of its April 17 invoice, less the return and the discount.

27 Sold $3,170 of merchandise on credit to Paula Kohr, Invoice No. 764.

27 Sold $6,700 of merchandise on credit to Nic Nelson, Invoice No. 765.

30 Issued Check No. 591, payable to Payroll, in payment of the sales salaries expense for the last half of the month, $10,750.

30 Cash sales for the last half of the month are $73,975.

Required

1. Prepare a general journal, a purchases journal like that in Exhibit 12.8, and a cash disbursements journal like that in Exhibit 12.10. Number all journal pages as page 3. Review the April transactions of Wiset Company and enter those transactions that should be journalized in the general journal, the purchases journal, or the cash disbursements journal. Ignore any transactions that should be journalized in a sales journal or cash receipts journal.

2. Open the following general ledger accounts: Cash, Inventory, Office Supplies, Store Supplies, Store Equipment, Accounts Payable, Long-Term Notes Payable, Purchases, Purchases Returns and Allowances, Purchases Discounts, Sales Salaries Expense, and Advertising Expense. Enter the March 31 balances of Cash ($85,000), Inventory ($125,000), and Long-Term Notes Payable ($210,000). Also open accounts payable subsidiary ledger accounts for Hal's Supply, Noth Company, Grant Company, and Custer, Inc.

3. Verify that amounts that should be posted as individual amounts from the journals have been posted. (Such items are immediately posted.) Foot and crossfoot the journals and make the month-end postings.

4. Prepare a trial balance of the general ledger and a schedule of accounts payable as of April 30.

Check Trial balance totals, $237,026

Acorn Industries completes these transactions during July of the current year (the terms of all its credit sales are 2/10, n/30).

July 1 Purchased $6,500 of merchandise on credit from Teton Company, invoice dated June 30, terms 2/10, n/30.

3 Issued Check No. 300 to *The Weekly* for advertising expense, $625.

5 Sold merchandise on credit to Kim Nettle, Invoice No. 918, for $19,200.

6 Sold merchandise on credit to Ruth Blake, Invoice No. 919, for $7,500.

7 Purchased $1,250 of store supplies on credit from Plaine, Inc., invoice dated July 7, terms n/10 EOM.

8 Received a $250 credit memorandum from Plaine, Inc., for the return of store supplies received on July 7.

9 Purchased $38,220 of store equipment on credit from Charm's Supply, invoice dated July 8, terms n/10 EOM.

10 Issued Check No. 301 to Teton Company in payment of its June 30 invoice, less the discount.

13 Sold merchandise on credit to Ashton Moore, Invoice No. 920, for $8,550.

14 Sold merchandise on credit to Kim Nettle, Invoice No. 921, for $5,100.

PRACTICE SET 2

Acorn Co.

Special journals, subsidiary ledgers, schedule of accounts receivable **LO2 LO3 LO4**

15   Received payment from Kim Nettle for the July 5 sale, less the discount.

15   Issued Check No. 302, payable to Payroll, in payment of sales salaries expense for the first half of the month, $31,850. Cashed the check and paid employees.

15   Cash sales for the first half of the month are $118,350 (cost is $76,330). (Cash sales are recorded daily using data from the cash registers but are recorded only twice in this problem to reduce repetitive entries.)

16   Received payment from Ruth Blake for the July 6 sale, less the discount.

17   Purchased $7,200 of merchandise on credit from Drake Company, invoice dated July 17, terms 2/10, n/30.

20   Purchased $650 of office supplies on credit from Charm's Supply, invoice dated July 19, terms n/10 EOM.

21   Borrowed $15,000 cash from College Bank by signing a long-term note payable.

23   Received payment from Ashton Moore for the July 13 sale, less the discount.

24   Received payment from Kim Nettle for the July 14 sale, less the discount.

24   Received a $2,400 credit memorandum from Drake Company for the return of defective merchandise received on July 17.

26   Purchased $9,770 of merchandise on credit from Teton Company, invoice dated July 26, terms 2/10, n/30.

27   Issued Check No. 303 to Drake Company in payment of its July 17 invoice, less the return and the discount.

29   Sold merchandise on credit to Ruth Blake, Invoice No. 922, for $17,500.

30   Sold merchandise on credit to Ashton Moore, Invoice No. 923, for $16,820.

31   Issued Check No. 304, payable to Payroll, in payment of the sales salaries expense for the last half of the month, $31,850.

31   Cash sales for the last half of the month are $80,244.

Required

1. Prepare a general journal, a purchases journal like that in Exhibit 12.8, and a cash disbursements journal like that in Exhibit 12.10. Number all journal pages as page 3. Review the July transactions of Acorn Company and enter those transactions that should be journalized in the general journal, the purchases journal, or the cash disbursements journal. Ignore any transaction that should be journalized in a sales journal or cash receipts journal.

2. Open the following general ledger accounts: Cash, Inventory, Office Supplies, Store Supplies, Store Equipment, Accounts Payable, Long-Term Notes Payable, Purchases, Purchases Returns and Allowances, Purchases Discounts, Sales Salaries Expense, and Advertising Expense. Enter the June 30 balances of Cash ($100,000), Inventory ($200,000), and Long-Term Notes Payable ($300,000). Also open accounts payable subsidiary ledger accounts for Teton Company, Plaine, Inc., Charm's Supply, and Drake Company.

3. Verify that amounts that should be posted as individual amounts from the journals have been posted. (Such items are immediately posted.) Foot and crossfoot the journals and make the month-end postings.

Check   Trial balance totals, $352,266

4. Prepare a trial balance of the general ledger and a schedule of accounts payable.

SERIAL PROBLEM

Success Systems

(This serial problem began in Chapter 1 and continues through most of the book. If previous chapter segments were not completed, the serial problem can begin at this point. It is helpful, but not necessary, that you use the Working Papers that accompany the book.)

SP 12   Adriana Lopez created Success Systems on October 1, 2010. The company has been successful, and its list of customers has grown. To accommodate the growth, the accounting system is modified to set up separate accounts for each customer. The following chart of accounts includes the account number used for each account and any balance as of December 31, 2010. These balances are taken from SP 5. Lopez decided to add a fourth digit with a decimal point to the 106 account number that had been used for the single Accounts Receivable account. This modification allows the company to continue using the existing chart of accounts. For simplicity, ignore payroll taxes and sales taxes in this problem.

No.	Account Title	Dr.	Cr.
101	Cash	$80,260	
106.1	Alex's Engineering Co.	0	
106.2	Wildcat Services	0	
106.3	Easy Leasing	0	
106.4	Clark Co........................	2,300	
106.5	Chang Corp.	0	
106.6	Gomez Co.	3,500	
106.7	Delta Co........................	0	
106.8	KC, Inc........................	0	
106.9	Dream, Inc.	0	
106.10	Bob Building Co.	0	
119	Merchandise inventory	0	
126	Computer supplies	775	
128	Prepaid insurance	1,800	
131	Prepaid rent	875	
163	Office equipment	10,000	
164	Accumulated depreciation—		
	Office equipment		625
167	Computer equipment	25,000	
168	Accumulated depreciation—		
	Computer equipment		1,250
201	Accounts payable		2,100

No.	Account Title	Dr.	Cr.
210	Wages payable		600
236	Unearned computer services revenue		2,500
301	A. Lopez, Capital		117,435
302	A. Lopez, Withdrawals	0	
403	Computer services revenue		0
413	Sales		0
414	Sales returns and allowances	0	
415	Sales discounts	0	
505	Purchases	0	
506	Purchase returns and allowances		0
507	Purchase discounts		0
508	Transportation-In	0	
612	Depreciation expense—Office equipment	0	
613	Depreciation expense—		
	Computer equipment	0	
623	Wages expense	0	
637	Insurance expense	0	
640	Rent expense	0	
652	Computer supplies expense	0	
655	Advertising expense	0	
676	Mileage expense	0	
677	Miscellaneous expenses	0	
684	Repairs expense—Computer	0	

In response to requests from customers, Lopez will begin selling computer software. The company will extend credit terms of 1/10, n/30, FOB shipping point, to all customers who purchase this merchandise. However, no cash discount is available on consulting fees. Additional accounts (Nos. 119, 413, 414, 415, 505, 506, 507, and 508) are added to its general ledger to accommodate the company's new merchandising activities. All revenue and expense accounts have zero balances as of January 1, 2011. Its transactions for January through March follow:

Jan. 4 Paid cash to Michelle Jones for five days' work at the rate of $150 per day. Four of the five days relate to wages payable that were accrued in the prior year.
5 Adriana Lopez invested an additional $10,000 cash in the business.
7 Purchased $5,700 of merchandise from Kansas Corp. with terms of 1/10, n/30, FOB shipping point, invoice dated January 7.
9 Received $3,500 cash from Gomez Co. as full payment on its account.
11 Completed a five-day project for Bob's Building Co. and billed it $6,500.
13 Sold merchandise with a retail value of $6,000 to Chang Corp., invoice dated January 13.
15 Paid $400 cash for freight charges on the merchandise purchased on January 7.
16 Received $5,600 cash from Delta Co. for computer services provided.
17 Paid Kansas Corp. for the invoice dated January 7, net of the discount.
20 Chang Corp. returned $500 of defective merchandise from its invoice dated January 13. The returned merchandise is discarded. (The policy of Success Systems is to not adjust its accounts for returned merchandise.)
22 Received the balance due from Chang Corp., net of both the discount and the credit for the returned merchandise.
24 Returned defective merchandise to Kansas Corp. and accepted a credit against future purchases. The defective merchandise invoice cost, net of the discount, was $496.
26 Purchased $9,500 of merchandise from Kansas Corp. with terms of 1/10, n/30, FOB destination, invoice dated January 26.
26 Sold merchandise for $4,700 on credit to KC, Inc., invoice dated January 26.
29 Received a $496 credit memorandum from Kansas Corp. concerning the merchandise returned on January 24.
31 Paid cash to Michelle Jones for 10 days' work at $150 per day.

Feb. 1 Paid $2,625 cash to Summit Mall for another three months' rent in advance. (Debit Prepaid Rent, an asset.)

       3 Paid Kansas Corp. for the balance due, net of the cash discount, less the $496 amount in the credit memorandum.

       5 Paid $800 cash to the local newspaper for an advertising insert in today's paper.

     11 Received the balance due from Bob's Building Co. for fees billed on January 11.

     15 Adriana Lopez withdrew $5,200 cash for personal use.

     23 Sold merchandise for $3,800 on credit to Delta Co., invoice dated February 23.

     26 Paid cash to Michelle Jones for eight days' work at $150 per day.

     27 Reimbursed Adriana Lopez for business automobile mileage (1,000 miles at $0.32 per mile).

Mar. 8 Purchased $3,250 of computer supplies from Cain Office Products on credit, invoice dated March 8.

      9 Received the balance due from Delta Co. for merchandise sold on February 23.

     11 Paid $1,200 cash for minor repairs to the company's computer.

     16 Received $6,250 cash from Dream, Inc., for computing services provided.

     19 Paid the full amount due to Cain Office Products, including amounts created on December 15 (of $2,100) and March 8.

     24 Billed Easy Leasing for $11,000 of computing services provided.

     25 Sold merchandise for $3,900 on credit to Wildcat Services, invoice dated March 25.

     30 Sold merchandise for $2,500 on credit to Clark Company, invoice dated March 30.

     31 Reimbursed Adriana Lopez for business automobile mileage (600 miles at $0.32 per mile).

Required

1. Prepare journal entries to record each of the January through March transactions.

2. Post the journal entries in part 1 to the accounts in the company's general ledger. (*Note:* Begin with the ledger's post-closing adjusted balances as of December 31, 2010.)

3. Prepare the unadjusted trial balance.

Check (2) Ending balances: Cash, $87,266; Sales, $20,900;

        (3) Unadj. totals, $182,708

BEYOND THE NUMBERS

REPORTING IN ACTION
LO1

BTN 12-1 Refer to **Best Buy**'s financial statements in Appendix A to answer the following.

Best Buy includes freight costs in the merchandise inventory account. List three such costs, using information in footnote 1 for the fiscal year ended March 1, 2008.

ETHICS CHALLENGE
LO1

BTN 12-2 As the new credit manager, you are being trained by the outgoing manager. She explains that the system prepares checks for amounts net of favorable cash discounts, and the checks are dated the last day of the discount period. She also tells you that checks are not mailed until five days later, adding that "the company gets free use of cash for an extra five days, and our department looks better. When a supplier complains, we blame the computer system and the mailroom."

Required

1. In your view, is the company currently abusing its suppliers' cash discount policy? Explain.

2. Is it appropriate to indicate that the late payments are due to computer or mail problems? Explain.

3. Assume you feel uncomfortable with your company taking the suppliers' cash discounts. What steps could you take to remedy the situation?

TAKING IT TO THE NET
LO1

BTN 12-3 Access the Association of Certified Fraud Examiner's website (http://www.acfe.com/).

Required

Use the search terms "fraud and purchases" and find the discussion on fraud that can occur associated with purchases. List and explain three types of fraud associated with purchases.

BTN 12-4   Refer to the opening feature about **CoCaLo**. Assume that Renee Pepys Lowe considers using a purchases journal for its purchases.

In a brief memo, in your role as accountant for CoCaLo, explain the costs and benefits of using a purchases journal instead of a general journal.

1. d.

2. d; ($4,500 − $250) × (100% − 2%) = $4,165

3. b.

4. e.

5. a.

A Look Back

Chapter 12 considered the accounting for merchandise purchases. We also explained the use of the purchases journal, the cash disbursements journal, and the accounts payable subsidiary ledger.

A Look at This Chapter

Chapter 13 shows adjusting entries for a merchandising business. We present the adjustments needed for inventory and show how a trial balance is useful in organizing information for a merchandiser. We also show the adjustments for accrued revenues and unearned revenues.

A Look Ahead

In Chapter 14 we show how to prepare classified income statements and balance sheets for a merchandiser. We also explain the closing process for the merchandiser.

Chapter 13

Merchandiser's Adjustments and Trial Balance

Learning Objectives

LO 1	Use a trial balance for a merchandiser.
LO 2	Prepare the adjusting entries for inventory.
LO 3	Prepare adjusting entries for prepaid and accrued expenses.
LO 4	Compute net sales and net purchases.
LO 5	Compute cost of goods sold.
LO 6	Compute gross profit.
LO 7	Prepare the adjusting entry for accrued revenue.
LO 8	Prepare the adjusting entry for unearned revenue.
LO 9	*Appendix* 13A—Describe the alternatives in accounting for prepayments.

New Nightmare Freddy

"I've always been a gambler . . . but we were also growing exponentially the first few years"
—Joel Boblit

Toy Story

SOMERSET, WI—Joel Boblit says his first and greatest business challenge was "being teased by my friends." But now Joel is having the time of his life. His retail business, **BigBadToyStore** (**BigBadToyStore.com**), deals in new and old action figures. Launched from his parents' basement, the store now projects over $15 million in annual sales.

But the early years were not easy. "I mortgaged everything I owned for the first two years," explains Joel. The business required a merchandising accounting system that Joel says needed to account for purchases and sales transactions. Inventory was especially important to account for. "Many of the store's customers offered inventory suggestions," explains Joel.

To succeed, Joel needed to make smart business decisions. He set up an accounting system to capture and communicate costs and sales information.

Tracking merchandising activities was necessary to set prices and to manage discounts, allowances, and returns of both sales and purchases. Joel's inventory system enabled him to stock the right type and amount of merchandise and to avoid the costs of out-of-stock and excess inventory. "We're [now] able to make much more efficient use of the space we have," recounts Joel.

Mastering accounting for merchandising is a means to an end for Joel. He says he loves his business and enjoys the nostalgia of childhood toys. Joel insists, however, that he will continue to take risks. "I've always been a gambler," insists Joel, and "I've always [believed] . . . that the harder you work, the more you'll be paid."

[Sources: *BigBadToyStore Website*, January 2009; *Entrepreneur*, December and October 2005; *St. Croix Chronicle*, March–April 2005; *Alma Matters*, Fall 2005; *YouMakeMillions.blogspot.com*, May 2007]

Previous chapters showed how a merchandising business records sales and purchases. In this chapter we show how the merchandiser can use a trial balance to summarize the results of sale and purchase transactions. We then show how the merchandiser adjusts its Merchandise Inventory account. The chapter also reviews the adjusting entries for prepaid and accrued expenses and shows the adjusting entries for accrued and unearned revenues.

Merchandiser's Adjustments and Trial Balance

Merchandiser's Trial Balance	Expense Adjustments	Partial Work Sheet	Revenue Adjustments
• Using a trial balance • Inventory adjustments	• Adjusting process • Prepaid expenses • Accrued expenses	• Adjusted trial balance • Net sales and net purchases • Cost of goods sold • Gross profit	• Accrued revenues • Unearned revenues

Merchandiser's Trial Balance

In Chapter 11 we showed how to record individual sales transactions for Z-Mart, a merchandiser. In Chapter 12 we showed how to record Z-Mart's individual purchase transactions. After recording all of its sales and purchase transactions, and other transactions for the year ending December 31, 2010, Z-Mart reports the unadjusted trial balance shown in Exhibit 13.1.

Exhibit 13.1

Unadjusted Trial Balance for a Merchandiser

Under a periodic system, the unadjusted balance in the Merchandise Inventory account is its balance as of the end of the previous accounting period.

Chapter 11 shows how to record sales transactions.

Chapter 12 shows how to record purchase transactions.

Z-MART
Unadjusted Trial Balance
December 31, 2010

No.	Account	Debit	Credit
101	Cash	8,200	
106	Accounts receivable	11,200	
119	Merchandise Inventory	19,000	
126	Supplies	3,800	
128	Prepaid insurance	900	
167	Equipment	34,200	
168	Accumulated depr.—Equip.		3,700
201	Accounts payable		16,000
301	K. Marty, Capital		42,600
302	K. Marty, Withdrawals	4,000	
413	Sales		321,000
414	Sales returns and allowances	2,000	
415	Sales discounts	4,300	
505	Purchases	235,800	
506	Purchases returns and allowance		1,500
507	Purchases discounts		4,200
508	Transportation-in	2,300	
622	Salaries expense	43,000	
640	Rent expense	9,000	
655	Advertising expense	11,300	
	Totals	389,000	389,000

Using a Trial Balance

Z-Mart's unadjusted trial balance in Exhibit 13.1 shows several items important for a merchandiser. First, Z-Mart reports $19,000 of merchandise inventory. **Merchandise inventory,** or simply **inventory,** refers to products that a merchandiser owns and intends to sell. Since Z-Mart uses a periodic inventory system, this $19,000 is the cost of inventory as of the end of the previous accounting period. As we showed in Chapters 11 and 12, Z-Mart has made no journal entries involving the Merchandise Inventory account during the year. Second, the trial balance reports Z-Mart's total sales ($321,000), sales returns and allowances ($2,000), and sales discounts ($4,300). Third, the trial balance reports Z-Mart's total purchases of inventory ($235,800), purchases returns and allowances ($1,500), purchase discounts ($4,200), and transportation-in ($2,300). These additional accounts are not found in a service company's trial balance. We show how a merchandiser adjusts its Merchandise Inventory account next.

LO1 Use a trial balance for a merchandiser.

Adjusting Entries for Merchandise Inventory

The December 31, 2010, balance in Merchandise Inventory ($19,000) on Z-Mart's unadjusted trial balance in Exhibit 13.1 has not changed since the beginning of the year. However, a physical count shows $21,000 of inventory in Z-Mart's warehouse at the end of the year. Z-Mart now needs to prepare two adjusting entries using this account. These entries will:

LO2 Prepare the adjusting entries for inventory.

1. Replace the beginning inventory balance with its correct ending balance.
2. Aid in reflecting cost of goods sold in the Income Summary account.

As we show later in this chapter, beginning and ending inventory amounts are used in computing cost of goods sold. As part of the closing process (described in Chapter 6 and reviewed in Chapter 14), the temporary account Income Summary is used to close temporary accounts. The Income Summary account is also used to adjust the Merchandise Inventory balance under a periodic system. We show Z-Mart's inventory adjusting entries, with T-account postings, next. We label these entries with BI (for beginning inventory) or EI (for ending inventory).

Entry 1: Transfer beginning inventory balance to Income Summary

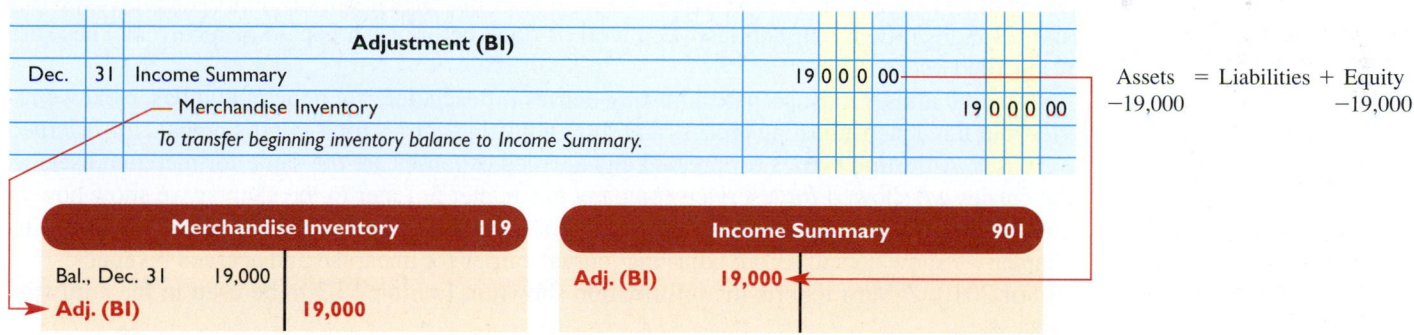

Entry 2: Record ending inventory balance

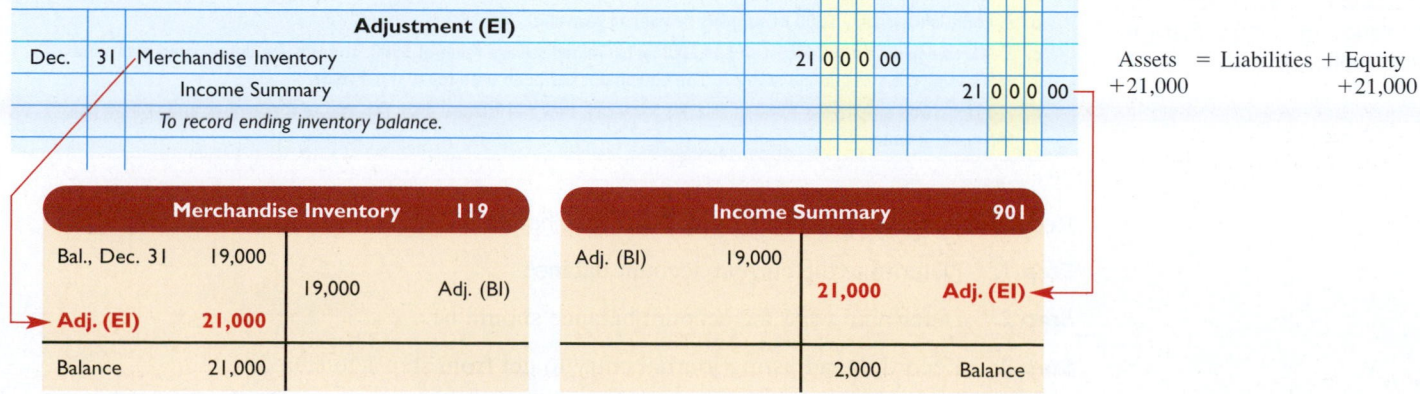

After posting entries BI and EI, the Income Summary account has a $2,000 credit balance. In Chapter 14 we illustrate the closing process for the merchandiser's Income Summary account.

Expense Adjustments

Adjusting Process

LO3 Prepare adjusting entries for prepaid and accrued expenses.

Exhibit 13.2 revisits a summary of the types of adjustments. Accrual basis accounting requires adjustments for transactions where cash receipts or payments do not occur in the same accounting period as work performed. Recall that these adjusting entries will always involve at least one income statement account and at least one balance sheet account. The cash account never appears in an adjusting entry.

Exhibit 13.2

Types of Adjustments

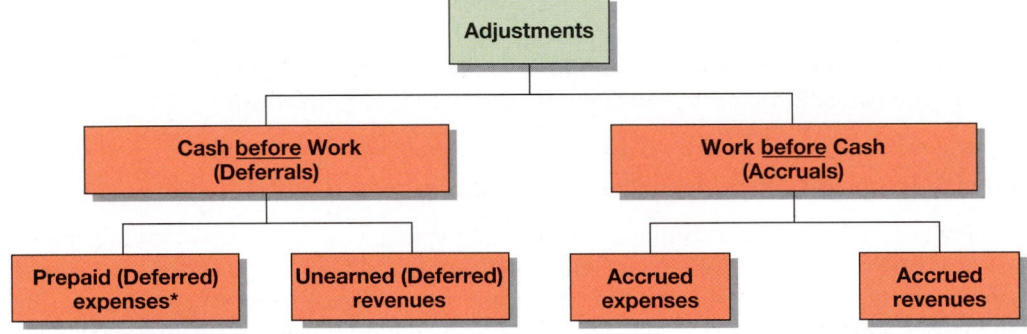

*Includes depreciation.

Prepaid expenses and unearned revenues reflect transactions where cash is paid or received before a related expense or revenue is recognized. They are also called *deferrals* because the recognition of an expense or revenue is *deferred* until after the related work is done. Accrued expenses and revenues reflect transactions when work is done before cash is paid or received. These are also called *accruals*.

A merchandiser must prepare adjusting entries for each deferral or accrual it has. Next we review our three-step adjusting process and show adjusting entries for Z-Mart's prepaid and accrued expenses. Adjusting entries for prepaid and accrued expenses are the same for merchandisers as the entries we showed for a service company in Chapter 5. Later in the chapter we show how to enter those adjusting entries on a (partial) work sheet for a merchandiser. Near the end of this chapter we show how to record adjusting journal entries for unearned and accrued revenues.

For 2010, Z-Mart reports the information shown in Exhibit 13.3 to be used in the adjusting process.

Exhibit 13.3

Information for Z-Mart's Expense Adjustments

> **a.** A review shows that $300 of insurance policies remain unexpired at year-end.
>
> **b.** A count shows that $800 of supplies remain at year-end.
>
> **c.** Z-Mart's equipment has a cost of $34,200, an estimated salvage value of $900, and is being depreciated over nine years using the straight-line method. The equipment has been used for two full years.
>
> **d.** Z-Mart owes employees $800 in salaries for work they performed near the end of December and will be paid for in early January.

Recall our three-step adjusting process from Chapter 5:

Step 1:   Determine the current account balance.

Step 2:   Determine what the account balance should be.

Step 3:   Record the adjusting journal entry to get from step 1 to step 2.

We apply this three-step process below to Z-Mart's information in Exhibit 13.3.

Adjusting Prepaid Expenses (Including Depreciation)

Prepaid Insurance

Step 1: Z-Mart's trial balance in Exhibit 13.1 shows the Prepaid Insurance account has an unadjusted balance of $900.

Step 2: As time passes, the benefits of the insurance gradually expire and some of the Prepaid Insurance asset becomes expense. At December 31, 2010, only $300 of the Prepaid Insurance asset has a future benefit to Z-Mart. The $600 difference ($900 − $300) should be recorded as insurance expense for the year.

Step 3: The adjusting entry to record this expense and reduce the asset, along with postings to T-accounts, follows:

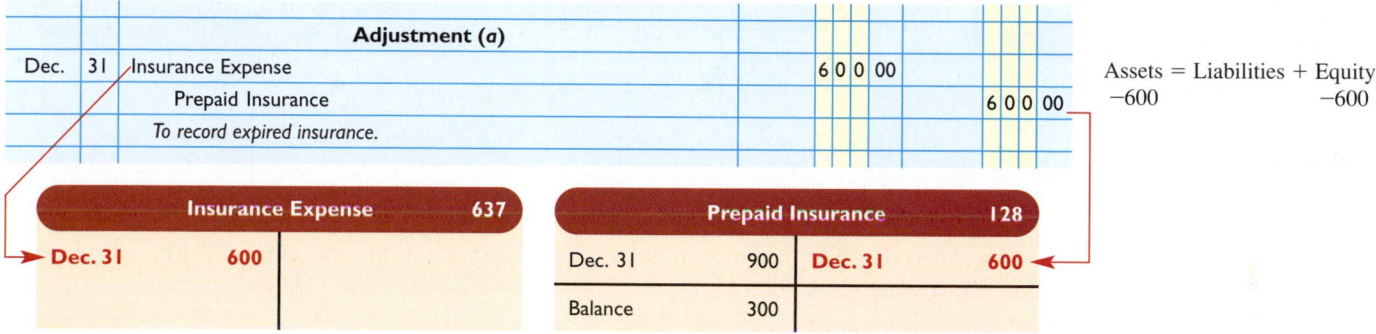

Supplies

Step 1: Z-Mart's trial balance in Exhibit 13.1 shows the Supplies account has an unadjusted balance of $3,800.

Step 2: On December 31, Z-Mart counts its *unused* supplies and finds $800 remaining. The $3,000 difference between these two amounts ($3,800 − $800) is the year's supplies expense.

Step 3: The adjusting entry to record this expense and reduce the Supplies asset account, along with T-account postings, follows:

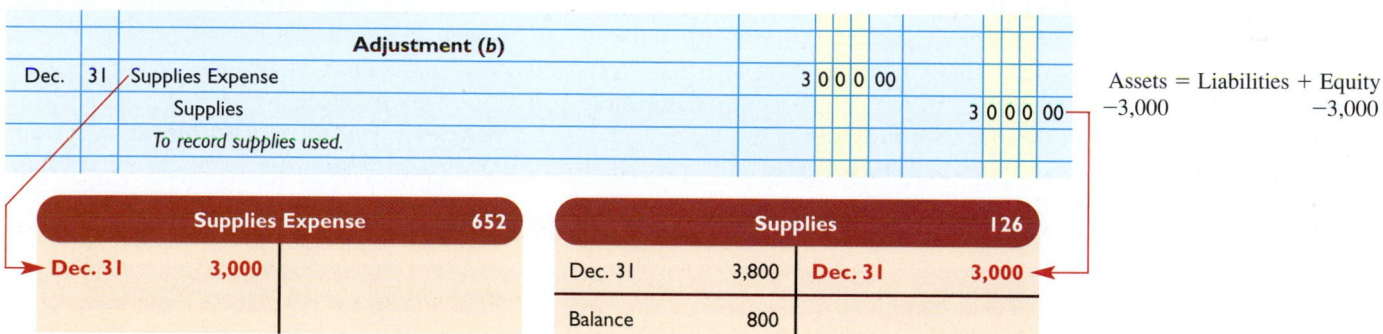

Equipment

Step 1: From the trial balance in Exhibit 13.1, Z-Mart's equipment cost $34,200, and its related Accumulated Depreciation account has an unadjusted balance of $3,700 on December 31, 2010.

Step 2: Since Z-Mart has used the equipment for two full years, the Accumulated Depreciation account, after adjustment, should equal two full years of depreciation. The equipment is expected to have a useful life (benefit period) of nine years. Using straight-line depreciation, Z-Mart's annual depreciation expense is:

$$\text{Annual depreciation expense} = \frac{\text{Cost} - \text{Salvage value}}{\text{Useful life}}$$

$$= \frac{(\$34,200 - 900)}{9 \text{ years}} = \$3,700 \text{ per year}$$

Thus, Z-Mart should record $3,700 of depreciation expense and increase the balance in its Accumulated Depreciation account by $3,700.

Step 3:   The adjusting entry to record depreciation expense, along with T-account postings follows:

Assets = Liabilities + Equity
−3,700   −3,700

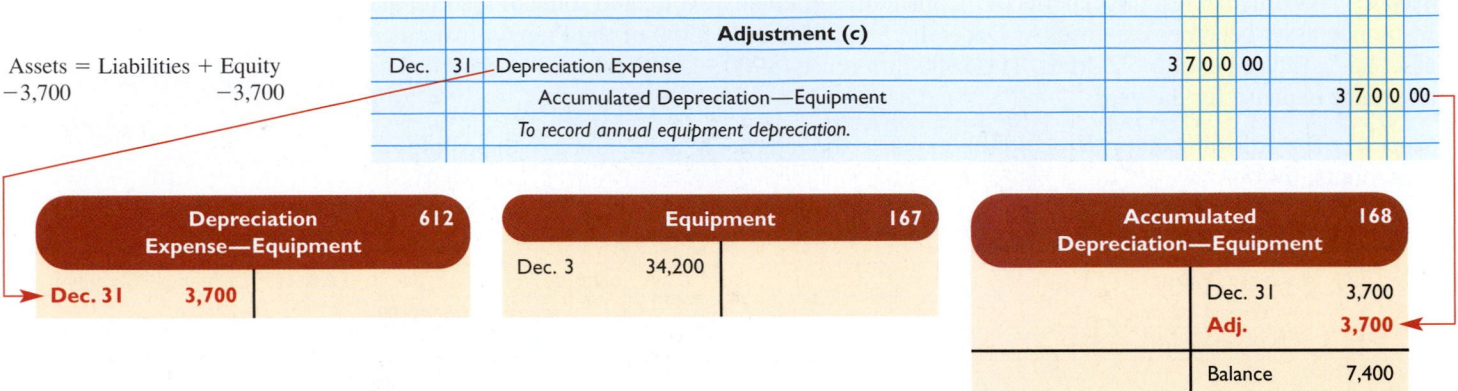

The December 31, 2010, balance in Accumulated Depreciation now equals $7,400, or two years of straight-line depreciation.

Adjusting Accrued Expenses

Accrued Salaries

Step 1:   Z-Mart owes its employees $800 for work they performed just before the end of the year. Z-Mart will pay the employees in early January of the next year. Z-Mart's balance in Salaries Payable is $0.

Step 2:   Z-Mart owes its employees $800 and thus needs to record a liability of $800 and increase its salaries expense by $800.

Step 3:   The adjusting entry to record accrued salaries, along with T-account postings, follows:

Assets = Liabilities + Equity
            +800   −800

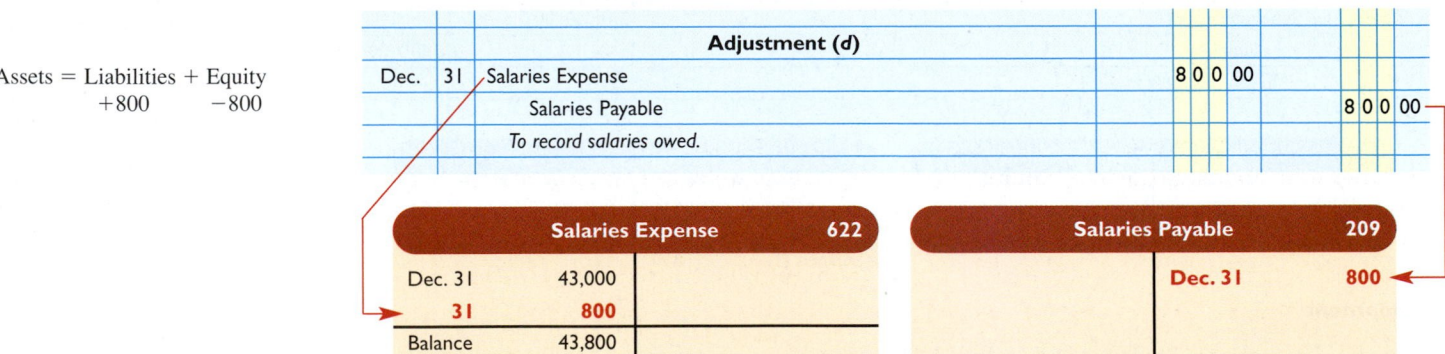

Partial Work Sheet

Adjusted Trial Balance

After journalizing and posting the adjusting entries above, Z-Mart's partial work sheet (through the Adjusted Trial Balance columns) appears in Exhibit 13.4. As we discussed earlier, this (partial) work sheet includes accounts, such as Merchandise Inventory, Sales, and Purchases, that did not apply to the service company we studied earlier. In addition, this work sheet adds a row for

Income Summary so that we can include the adjusting entries for Merchandise Inventory. Recall from Chapter 6 that Income Summary is primarily used in the closing process (which we revisit in Chapter 14). If a business uses a periodic inventory system, like Z-Mart, then the Income Summary account is also used in the adjusting process. We also add a row for the accounts that appeared in our adjusting journal entries, including Salaries Payable, Depreciation Expense–Equipment, Insurance Expense, and Advertising Expense.

Exhibit 13.4

Z-Mart Adjusted Trial Balance and Partial Work Sheet

	No.	Account	Unadjusted Trial Balance Dr.	Unadjusted Trial Balance Cr.	Adjustments Dr.	Adjustments Cr.	Adjusted Trial Balance Dr.	Adjusted Trial Balance Cr.
3	101	Cash	8,200				8,200	
4	106	Accounts receivable	11,200				11,200	
5	119	Merchandise Inventory	19,000		(EI) 21,000	(BI) 19,000	21,000	
6	126	Supplies	3,800			(b) 3,000	800	
7	128	Prepaid insurance	900			(a) 600	300	
8	167	Equipment	34,200				34,200	
9	168	Accumulated depr.—Equip.		3,700		(c) 3,700		7,400
10	201	Accounts payable		16,000				16,000
11	209	Salaries payable		0		(d) 800		800
12	301	K. Marty, Capital		42,600				42,600
13	302	K. Marty, Withdrawals	4,000				4,000	
14	901	Income summary			(BI) 19,000	(EI) 21,000	19,000	21,000
15	413	Sales		321,000				321,000
16a	414	Sales returns and allowances	2,000				2,000	
16b	415	Sales discounts	4,300				4,300	
16c	505	Purchases	235,800				235,800	
16d	506	Purchases returns & allowance		1,500				1,500
17	507	Purchases discounts		4,200				4,200
18	508	Transportation-in	2,300				2,300	
19	612	Depreciation expense—Equip.	0		(c) 3,700		3,700	
20	622	Salaries expense	43,000		(d) 800		43,800	
21	637	Insurance expense	0		(a) 600		600	
22	640	Rent expense	9,000				9,000	
23	652	Supplies expense	0		(b) 3,000		3,000	
24	655	Advertising expense	11,300				11,300	
25		Totals	389,000	389,000	48,100	48,100	414,500	414,500
26		Net income						

Note that the debit and credit adjustment amounts for Income Summary are *both* extended into the Adjusted Trial Balance columns. This is helpful in preparing financial statements from the work sheet. In the next chapter we show how to extend this work sheet to prepare financial statements and prepare the closing entries for a merchandiser. Next we show how to use the adjusted trial balance in this partial work sheet to compute key summary measures for a merchandiser.

HOW YOU DOIN'?

Answers—p. 332

1. If the Prepaid Insurance account has an unadjusted balance of $3,200, and $2,000 of insurance policies remain unexpired at the end of the year, what is the amount of Insurance Expense for the year?

2. If the Supplies account has an unadjusted balance of $1,400 and a count shows that $620 of supplies remain at the end of the year, what is the amount of Supplies Expense for the year?

3. A machine with a four-year useful life and $2,000 salvage value was purchased for $22,000. Using the straight-line method, what is the annual depreciation expense on this machine?

Computing Net Sales and Net Purchases for a Merchandiser

LO4 Compute net sales and net purchases.

Net income to a merchandiser equals revenues from selling merchandise minus both the cost of merchandise sold during the period and the amount of other expenses for the period (see Exhibit 13.5). The usual accounting term for revenues from selling merchandise is *sales,* and the term used for the expense of buying and preparing that merchandise is **cost of goods sold** (also called *cost of sales*). Cost of goods sold is often the largest single expense on a merchandiser's income statement. **Gross profit,** also called *gross margin,* equals net sales minus the cost of goods sold, and it is used to assess a merchandiser's performance. We show how to compute net sales and net purchases next. In the next section we show to use these items to compute cost of goods sold and gross profit.

Exhibit 13.5

Computing Income for a Merchandising Company versus a Service Company

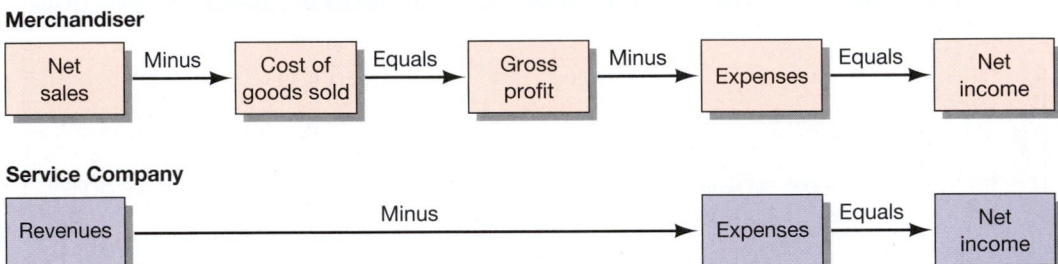

Computing Net Sales   **Net sales** is defined as sales minus sales discounts and minus sales returns and allowances. For Z-Mart for the year ending December 31, 2010, net sales is computed from its adjusted trial balance in Exhibit 13.4 as:

$$\text{Net sales} = \text{Sales} - \text{Sales discounts} - \text{Sales returns and allowances}$$

Sales		$ 321,000
Less: Sales discounts	$4,300	
Sales returns and allowances	2,000	6,300
Net sales		**$314,700**

Computing Net Purchases   We can also use Z-Mart's adjusted trial balance to compute net purchases. **Net purchases** is defined as purchases minus purchase discounts and purchase returns and allowances, plus the cost of transportation-in. For Z-Mart for the year ending December 31, 2010, net purchases is computed as:

Purchases		$235,800
Less: Purchase discounts	$4,200	
Purchase returns and allowances	1,500	(5,700)
Add: Cost of transportation-in		2,300
Net purchases		**$232,400**

Computing Cost of Goods Sold

LO5 Compute cost of goods sold.

Under a periodic inventory system, a merchandiser physically counts the number of inventory items remaining (unsold) at the end of the period, and assigns them a total cost. This information is then used along with information on beginning inventory and the net cost of purchases to compute cost of goods sold, as we show in Exhibit 13.6.

Exhibit 13.6 shows that the cost of *merchandise available for sale* equals the cost of beginning inventory plus the net purchases for the period. We obtain the cost of beginning merchandise inventory ($19,000) from the work sheet and compute net purchases ($232,400) as we showed above. So, Z-Mart had a total of $251,400 (computed as $19,000 plus $232,400) of merchandise available for sale during 2010.

As Exhibit 13.6 shows, merchandise available for sale is either sold (cost of goods sold) or not sold (ending inventory) during the period. After Z-Mart counts and assigns a cost to its ending inventory, it computes cost of goods sold for 2010 as follows:

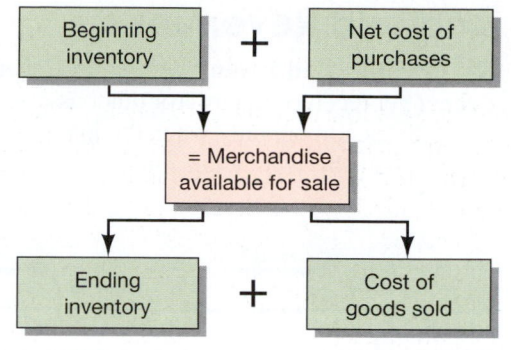

Exhibit 13.6

Merchandiser's Cost Flow for a Single Time Period

Beginning inventory	$ 19,000
Plus: Net purchases	232,400
Merchandise available for sale	$251,400
Less: Cost of ending inventory	(21,000)
Cost of goods sold	**$230,400**

Computing Gross Profit

A merchandiser is very interested in generating gross profit by selling products at prices above their costs. We compute gross profit for Z-Mart for 2010 as:

LO6 Compute gross profit.

$$\text{Gross profit} = \text{Net sales} - \text{Cost of goods sold}$$

Net sales	$314,700
Less: Cost of goods sold	230,400
Gross profit	**$84,300**

HOW YOU DOIN'?

Answers—p. 332

4. A merchandiser reports sales of $450,000, sales returns and allowances of $4,000, and sales discounts of $7,000. What is the merchandiser's net sales for the period?

5. A merchandiser reports purchases of $325,000, purchase returns and allowances of $7,000, transportation-in of $1,000, and purchase discounts of $8,000. What is the merchandiser's net purchases for the period?

6. A merchandiser reports beginning inventory of $75,000. A physical inventory count shows $42,000 of inventory remains at the end of the year. If net purchases during the year were $220,000, what is the cost of goods sold for the year? If net sales were $303,000 during the year, what is gross profit?

Revenue Adjustments

We now discuss and show how to record adjusting entries involving revenues. A business can receive cash before work is performed. As Exhibit 13.2 shows, this requires an adjustment for unearned revenue. Also, a business can have performed work for a customer, but not yet billed or received cash. As Exhibit 13.2 shows, this requires an adjustment for accrued revenue. We show each of these adjustments below for SuperSub, a sandwich shop.

LO7 Prepare the adjusting entry for accrued revenue.

Accrued Revenues

The term **accrued revenues** refers to revenues earned in a period that are both unrecorded and not yet received in cash (or other assets) at the end of the period. An example is a technician who bills customers only when the job is done. If one-third of a job is complete by the end of a period, then the technician must record one-third of the expected billing as revenue in that

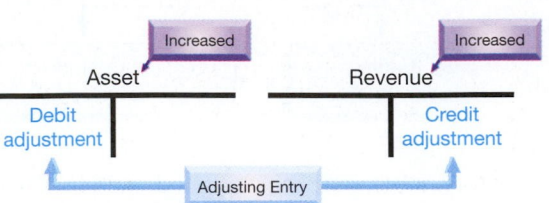

period—even though there is no billing or collection. The adjusting entries for accrued revenues increase assets and increase revenues as shown in Exhibit 13.7. Accrued revenues commonly arise from services, products, interest, and rent. We use service fees to show how to adjust for accrued revenues.

Exhibit 13.7

Adjusting for Accrued Revenues

Accrued Services Revenue Accrued revenues are not recorded until adjusting entries are made at the end of the accounting period. These accrued revenues are earned but unrecorded because either the buyer has not yet paid for them or the seller has not yet billed the buyer. SuperSub, a submarine sandwich shop, provides an example. SuperSub has received an agreement to cater a New Year's Eve party for a group of anesthesiologists for a fixed fee of $1,800. SuperSub caters the party and then later bills for its sandwiches. The revenue recognition principle suggests that since the goods have been provided, that revenue should be recognized on SuperSub's December income statement. These $1,800 of revenues are added to the other sales SuperSub recorded during December ($9,050) as we show in the T-account below. The balance sheet also must report that the group of anesthesiologists owes SuperSub $1,800. The year-end adjusting entry to account for accrued sales revenue is

Assets = Liabilities + Equity
+1,800   +1,800

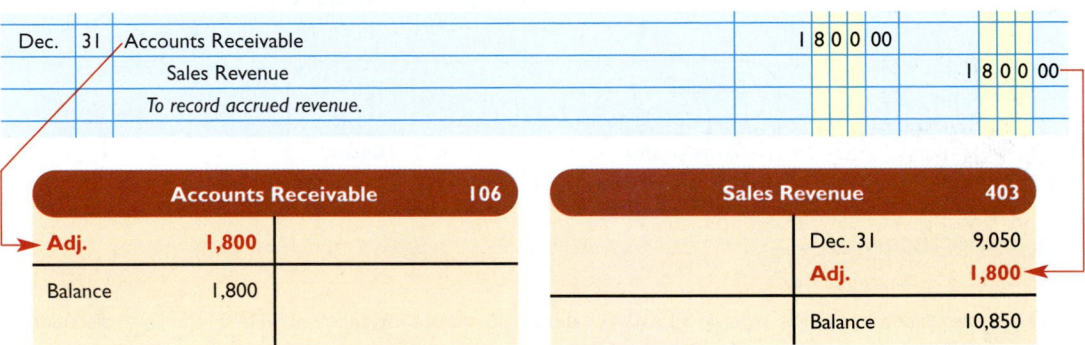

Accounts receivable are reported on the year-end balance sheet at $1,800, and an additional $1,800 of sales revenue is reported on the income statement. *Not* making the adjustment would understate (1) both sales revenue and net income by $1,800 in the December income statement and (2) both accounts receivable (assets) and equity by $1,800 on the December 31 balance sheet.

Unearned (Deferred) Revenues

LO8 Prepare the adjusting entry for unearned revenue.

The term **unearned revenues** refers to cash received in advance of providing products and services. Unearned revenues, also called *deferred revenues,* are liabilities. When cash is received in advance, an obligation to provide products or services is accepted. As products or services are provided, the unearned revenues become *earned* revenues, in line with the revenue recognition principle. Adjusting entries for unearned revenues involve increasing revenues and decreasing unearned revenues, as shown in Exhibit 13.8.

An example of unearned revenues comes from the **Boston Celtics**. When the Celtics receive cash from advance ticket sales and broadcast fees, they record it in an unearned revenue account called *Deferred Game Revenues*. The Celtics recognize this unearned revenue with adjusting entries on a game-by-game basis. Since the NBA regular season begins in October and ends in April, revenue recognition is mainly limited to this period. For a recent season, the Celtics' quarterly revenues were $0 million for July–September; $34 million for October–December; $48 million for January–March; and $17 million for April–June.

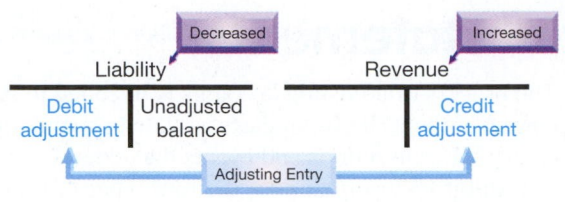

Exhibit 13.8

Adjusting for Unearned Revenues

SuperSub has unearned revenues. It agreed on December 1 to provide catered lunches once a week for the local Bikers' Club for the next 10 weeks. On that same day, the Bikers' Club paid SuperSub the $3,000 fee covering the entire 10-week period. The entry to record the cash received in advance is

Dec.	1	Cash	3 0 0 0 00	
		Unearned Sales Revenue		3 0 0 0 00
		Received advance payment for catering.		

Assets = Liabilities + Equity
+3,000   +3,000

This advance payment increases cash and creates an obligation to cater the lunches for the next 10 weeks. Unearned Sales Revenue is a liability because, if SuperSub does not provide the catered lunches, the bikers will expect their money back. As time passes, SuperSub will earn revenue by catering lunches. By December 31, it has provided four weeks of lunches and earned 4/10 of the $3,000 unearned revenue. This amounts to $1,200 ($3,000 × 4/10). The revenue recognition principle implies that $1,200 of the advance payment be reported as revenue on the December income statement. The adjusting entry to reduce the liability account and recognize earned revenue, along with T-account postings, is

		Adjustment		
Dec.	31	Unearned Sales Revenue	1 2 0 0 00	
		Sales Revenue		1 2 0 0 00
		To record earned revenue that was received in		
		advance ($3,000 × 4/10).		

Assets = Liabilities + Equity
          −1,200   +1,200

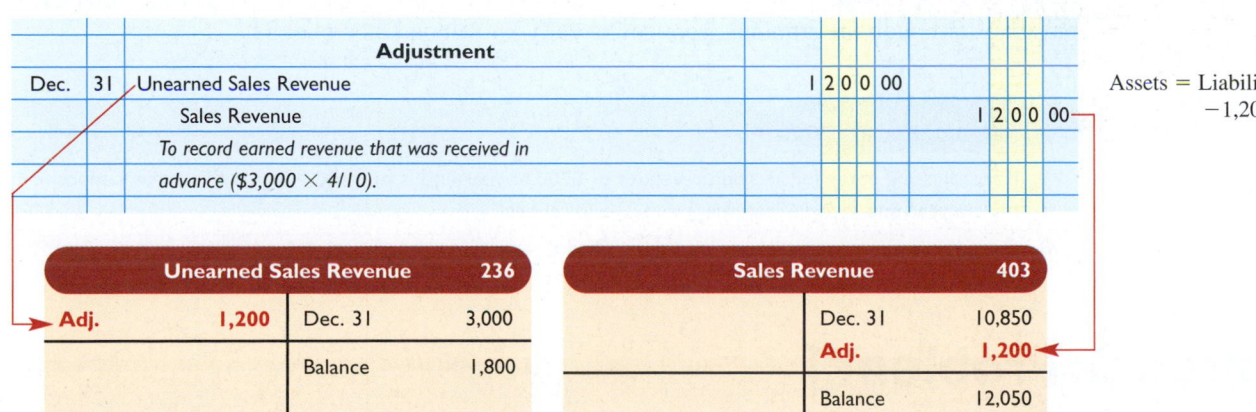

The adjusting entry transfers $1,200 from unearned revenue (a liability account) to a revenue account. *Not* making the adjustment (1) understates revenue and net income by $1,200 in the December income statement and (2) overstates unearned revenue and understates equity by $1,200 on the December 31 balance sheet.

Accounting for unearned revenues is crucial to many companies. For example, the **National Retail Federation** reports that gift card sales, which are unearned revenues for sellers, are more than $20 billion annually. Gift cards are now a top-selling holiday gift. (An alternate method of accounting for unearned revenues is presented in Appendix 13A.)

Links to Financial Statements

The process of adjusting accounts is intended to bring an asset or liability account balance to its correct amount. It also updates a related expense or revenue account. These adjustments are necessary for transactions and events that extend over more than one period.

Exhibit 13.9 summarizes the four types of transactions requiring adjustment. Understanding this exhibit is important to understanding the adjusting process and its importance to financial statements. Remember that each adjusting entry affects one or more income statement accounts *and* one or more balance sheet accounts (but not cash).

Exhibit 13.9

Summary of Adjustments and Financial Statement Links

| Category | BEFORE Adjusting Entry | | Adjusting Entry |
	Balance Sheet	Income Statement	
Prepaid expenses[†]	Asset overstated	Expense understated	**Dr. Expense**
	Equity overstated		**Cr. Asset***
Unearned revenues[†]	Liability overstated	Revenue understated	**Dr. Liability**
	Equity understated		**Cr. Revenue**
Accrued expenses	Liability understated	Expense understated	**Dr. Expense**
	Equity overstated		**Cr. Liability**
Accrued revenues	Asset understated	Revenue understated	**Dr. Asset**
	Equity understated		**Cr. Revenue**

* For depreciation, the credit is to Accumulated Depreciation (contra asset).

[†] Exhibit 13.9 assumes that Prepaid Expenses are initially recorded as assets and that Unearned Revenues are initially recorded as liabilities.

Information about some adjustments is not always available until several days or even weeks after the period-end. This means that some adjusting and closing entries are recorded later than, but dated as of, the last day of the period. One example is a company that receives a utility bill on January 10 for costs incurred for the month of December. When it receives the bill, the company records the expense and the payable as of December 31. Other examples include long-distance phone usage and costs of many service billings. The December income statement reflects these additional expenses incurred, and the December 31 balance sheet includes these payables, although the amounts were not actually known on December 31.

HOW YOU DOIN'?   Answers—p. 332

7. If an adjusting entry for accrued revenues of $200 at year-end is omitted, what is this error's effect on the year-end income statement and balance sheet?

8. Describe how an accrued revenue arises. Give an example.

Demonstration Problem 1

At December 31, 2010, SuperSub reports the following unadjusted balances as part of its unadjusted trial balance:

Merchandise inventory	$2,000
Sales	7,225
Sales returns and allowances	150
Sales discounts	200
Purchases	6,950
Purchase returns and allowances	75
Purchase discounts	175
Transportation-in	50

SuperSub uses a periodic inventory system. In addition, an inventory count shows that $3,200 of merchandise inventory remains unsold on December 31, 2010.

Required

1. Prepare the adjusting entries for SuperSub's merchandise inventory on December 31, 2010.
2. Compute net sales.
3. Compute net purchases.
4. Compute cost of goods sold.
5. Compute gross profit.

Planning the Solution

- Determine the adjustments to replace the beginning merchandise inventory balance with the amount of inventory remaining unsold at year-end.
- Recall the formulas to compute net sales and net purchases and compute these amounts.
- Use the inventory equation to compute the cost of goods sold. Subtract cost of goods sold from net sales to compute gross profit.

Solution to Demonstration Problem 1

1. Inventory adjusting entries

(BI)	Dec. 31	Income Summary		2 0 0 0 00	
		Merchandise Inventory			2 0 0 0 00
(EI)	Dec. 31	Merchandise Inventory		3 2 0 0 00	
		Income Summary			3 2 0 0 00

2. Net sales = Sales − Sales returns and allowances − Sales discounts
   = $7,225 − $150 − $200 = $6,875.
3. Net purchases = Purchases − Purchase returns and allowances − Purchase discounts
   + Transportation-in
   = $6,950 − $75 − $175 + $50 = $6,750.
4. The inventory equation is: Beginning inventory + Net purchases − Ending inventory = Cost of goods sold.
   For SuperSub, Cost of goods sold = $2,000 + $6,750 − $3,200 = $5,550.
5. Gross profit = Net sales − cost of goods sold = $6,875 − $5,550 = $1,325.

Demonstration Problem 2

The following information relates to Joel's Alarm Services on December 31, 2010. The company, which uses the calendar year as its annual reporting period, initially records prepaid and unearned items in balance sheet accounts (assets and liabilities, respectively).

a. The company's weekly payroll is $8,750, paid each Friday for a five-day workweek. Assume December 31, 2010, falls on a Monday, but the employees will not be paid their wages until Friday, January 4, 2011. (For simplicity, ignore payroll taxes for this problem).

b. Eighteen months earlier, on July 1, 2008, the company purchased equipment that cost $20,000. Its useful life is predicted to be five years, at which time the equipment is expected to be worthless (zero salvage value).

c. On October 1, 2010, the company agreed to work on a new housing development. The company is paid $120,000 on October 1 in advance of future installation of alarm systems in 24 new homes. That amount was credited to the Unearned Services Revenue account. Between October 1 and December 31, work on 20 homes was completed.

d. On September 1, 2010, the company purchased a 12-month insurance policy for $2,400. The transaction was recorded with a $2,400 debit to Prepaid Insurance.

e. On December 29, 2010, the company completed a $7,000 alarm installation service that has not been billed and not recorded as of December 31, 2010.

Required

1. Prepare any necessary adjusting entries on December 31, 2010, in relation to transactions and events *a* through *e*.

2. Prepare T-accounts for the accounts affected by adjusting entries, and post the adjusting entries. Determine the adjusted balances for the Unearned Revenue and the Prepaid Insurance accounts.

3. Complete the following table and determine the amounts and effects of your adjusting entries on the year 2010 income statement and the December 31, 2010, balance sheet. Use up (down) arrows to indicate an increase (decrease) in the Effect columns.

Entry	Amount in the Entry	Effect on Net Income	Effect on Total Assets	Effect on Total Liabilities	Effect on Total Equity

Planning the Solution

- Analyze each situation to determine which accounts need to be updated with an adjustment.
- Calculate the amount of each adjustment and prepare the necessary journal entries.
- Show the amount of each adjustment in the designated accounts, determine the adjusted balance, and identify the balance sheet classification of the account.
- Determine each entry's effect on net income for the year and on total assets, total liabilities, and total equity at the end of the year.

Solution to Demonstration Problem 2

1. Adjusting journal entries.

				Debit	Credit
(a)	Dec.	31	Wages Expense	1 750 00	
			Wages Payable		1 750 00
			To accrue wages for the last day of the year		
			($8,750 × 1/5).		
(b)	Dec.	31	Depreciation Expense—Equipment	4 000 00	
			Accumulated Depreciation—Equipment		4 000 00
			To record depreciation expense for the year		
			($20,000/5 years = $4,000 per year).		
(c)	Dec.	31	Unearned Services Revenue	100 000 00	
			Services Revenue		100 000 00
			To recognize services revenue earned		
			($120,000 × 20/24).		
(d)	Dec.	31	Insurance Expense	800 00	
			Prepaid Insurance		800 00
			To adjust for expired portion of insurance		
			($2,400 × 4/12).		
(e)	Dec.	31	Accounts Receivable	7 000 00	
			Services Revenue		7 000 00
			To record services revenue earned.		

2. T-accounts for adjusting journal entries *a* through *e*.

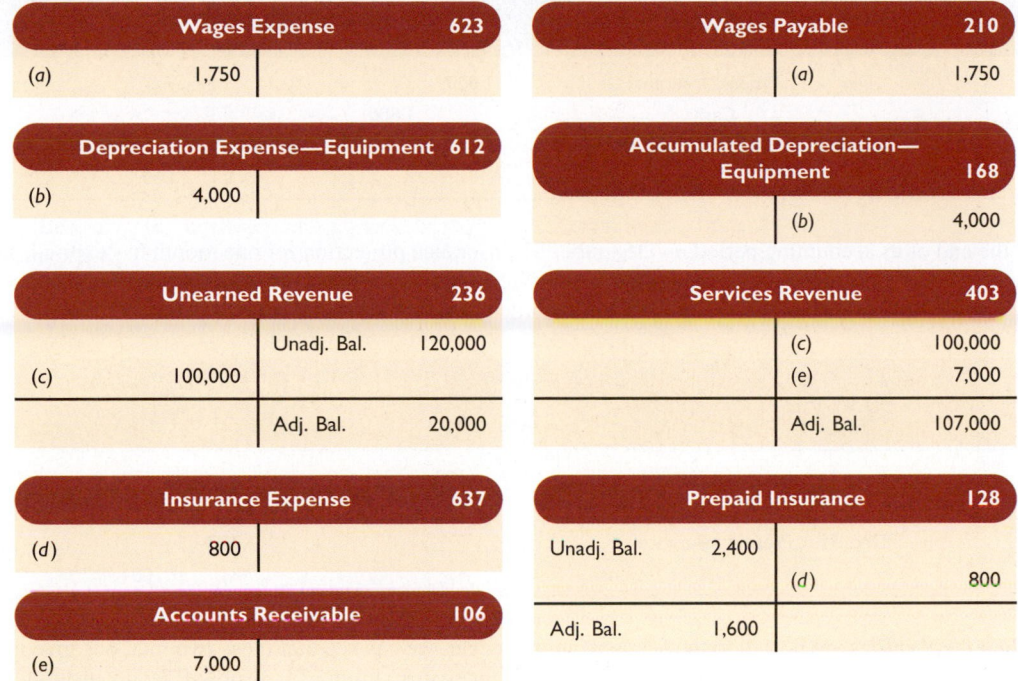

		Wages Expense	623
(a)	1,750		

		Wages Payable	210
		(a)	1,750

		Depreciation Expense—Equipment	612
(b)	4,000		

		Accumulated Depreciation—Equipment	168
		(b)	4,000

	Unearned Revenue		236
		Unadj. Bal.	120,000
(c)	100,000		
		Adj. Bal.	20,000

		Services Revenue	403
		(c)	100,000
		(e)	7,000
		Adj. Bal.	107,000

	Insurance Expense	637
(d)	800	

Prepaid Insurance		128
Unadj. Bal.	2,400	
		(d)	800
Adj. Bal.	1,600	

	Accounts Receivable	106
(e)	7,000	

3. Financial statement effects of adjusting journal entries.

Entry	Amount in the Entry	Effect on Net Income	Effect on Total Assets	Effect on Total Liabilities	Effect on Total Equity
a	$ 1,750	$ 1,750 ↓	No effect	$ 1,750 ↑	$ 1,750 ↓
b	4,000	4,000 ↓	$4,000 ↓	No effect	4,000 ↓
c	100,000	100,000 ↑	No effect	$100,000 ↓	100,000 ↑
d	800	800 ↓	$ 800 ↓	No effect	800 ↓
e	7,000	7,000 ↑	$7,000 ↑	No effect	7,000 ↑

Alternative Accounting for Prepayments

APPENDIX
13A

This appendix explains an alternative in accounting for prepaid expenses and unearned revenues.

Recording the Prepayment of Expenses in Expense Accounts

An alternative method is to record *all* prepaid expenses with debits to expense accounts. If any prepaids remain unused or unexpired at the end of an accounting period, then adjusting entries must transfer the cost of the unused portions from expense accounts to prepaid expense (asset) accounts. This alternative method is acceptable. The financial statements are identical under either method, but the adjusting entries are different. To illustrate the differences between these two methods, let's look at SuperSub's cash payment of $1,800 on December 1 for 18 months of insurance coverage beginning on December 1. SuperSub recorded that payment with a debit to an asset account, but it could have recorded a debit to an expense account. These alternatives are shown in Exhibit 13A.1.

LO9 Describe the alternatives in accounting for prepayments.

Exhibit 13A.1

Alternative Initial Entries for Prepaid Expenses

			Payment Initially Recorded as	
			Asset	Expense
Dec. 1	Prepaid Insurance		1,800	
	Cash			1,800	
Dec. 1	Insurance Expense			1,800
	Cash				1,800

At the end of its accounting period on December 31, insurance protection for one month has expired. This means $100 ($1,800/18) of insurance coverage expired and is an expense for December. The adjusting entry depends on how the original payment was recorded. This is shown in Exhibit 13A.2.

Exhibit 13A.2

Adjusting Entry for Prepaid Expenses for the Two Alternatives

			Payment Initially Recorded as	
			Asset	Expense
Dec. 31	Insurance Expense		100	
	Prepaid Insurance		100	
Dec. 31	Prepaid Insurance			1,700
	Insurance Expense			1,700

When these entries are posted to the accounts in the ledger, we can see that these two methods give identical results. The December 31 adjusted account balances in Exhibit 13A.3 show Prepaid Insurance of $1,700 and Insurance Expense of $100 for both methods.

Exhibit 13A.3

Account Balances under Two Alternatives for Recording Prepaid Expenses

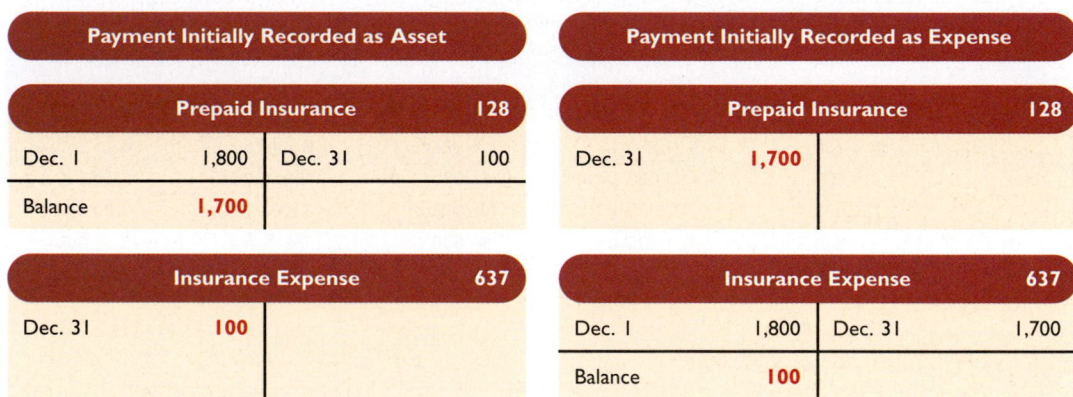

Payment Initially Recorded as Asset				Payment Initially Recorded as Expense			
Prepaid Insurance			128	**Prepaid Insurance**			128
Dec. 1	1,800	Dec. 31	100	Dec. 31	1,700		
Balance	1,700						
Insurance Expense			637	**Insurance Expense**			637
Dec. 31	100			Dec. 1	1,800	Dec. 31	1,700
				Balance	100		

Recording the Prepayment of Revenues in Revenue Accounts

As with prepaid expenses, an alternative method is to record *all* unearned revenues with credits to revenue accounts. If any revenues are unearned at the end of an accounting period, then adjusting entries must transfer the unearned portions from revenue accounts to unearned revenue (liability) accounts. The adjusting entries are different for these two alternatives, but the financial statements are identical. To illustrate the accounting differences between these two methods, let's look at SuperSub's December 1 receipt of $3,000 for services covering 10 weekly lunches. SuperSub recorded this transaction with a credit to a liability account. The alternative is to record it with a credit to a revenue account, as shown in Exhibit 13A.4.

Exhibit 13A.4

Alternative Initial Entries for Unearned Revenues

			Receipt Initially Recorded as	
			Liability	Revenue
Dec. 1	Cash		3,000	
	Unearned Sales Revenue		3,000	
Dec. 1	Cash			3,000
	Sales Revenue			3,000

By the end of its accounting period on December 31, SuperSub has earned $1,200 of this revenue. This means $1,200 of the liability has been satisfied. Depending on how the initial receipt is recorded, the adjusting entry is as shown in Exhibit 13A.5.

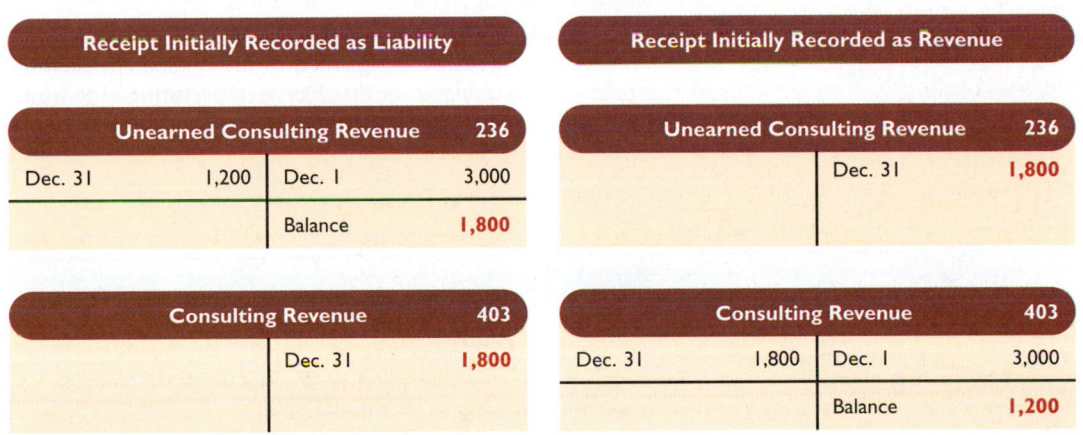

		Receipt Initially Recorded as	
		Liability	Revenue
Dec. 31	Unearned Sales Revenue	1,200	
	Sales Revenue		1,200
Dec. 31	Sales Revenue		1,800
	Unearned Sales Revenue		1,800

Exhibit 13A.5

Adjusting Entry for Unearned Revenues for the Two Alternatives

After adjusting entries are posted, the two alternatives give identical results. The December 31 adjusted account balances in Exhibit 13A.6 show unearned revenue of $1,800 and sales revenue of $1,200 for both methods.

Exhibit 13A.6

Account Balances under Two Alternatives for Recording Unearned Revenues

Receipt Initially Recorded as Liability

Unearned Consulting Revenue			236
Dec. 31	1,200	Dec. 1	3,000
		Balance	**1,800**

Consulting Revenue			403
		Dec. 31	**1,800**

Receipt Initially Recorded as Revenue

Unearned Consulting Revenue			236
		Dec. 31	**1,800**

Consulting Revenue			403
Dec. 31	1,800	Dec. 1	3,000
		Balance	**1,200**

Summary

LO1 Use a trial balance for a merchandiser. The merchandiser's trial balance includes accounts for merchandise inventory, sales, and purchases. Under a periodic inventory system the unadjusted merchandise inventory balance is its balance as of the beginning of the period.

LO2 Prepare the adjusting entries for inventory. Two entries are needed to adjust inventory. First, debit Income Summary and credit Merchandise Inventory for the beginning balance of merchandise inventory from the unadjusted trial balance. Second, debit Merchandise Inventory and credit Income Summary for the ending balance of inventory, determined by a physical count.

LO3 Prepare adjusting entries for prepaid and accrued expenses. Prepaid assets, like prepaid insurance or supplies, are used during a period. An adjusting entry records the amount used as expense and reduces the related asset to the amount that remains for future use. Depreciation is a special case of prepaid expenses. Accrued expenses are costs, like employee salaries, that occur before the end of an accounting period but that won't be paid until the next

period. An adjusting entry records these expenses and creates a liability for the amount owed.

LO4 Compute net sales and net purchases. Net sales is computed as: sales minus sales returns and allowances minus sales discounts. Net purchases is computed as purchases plus transportation-in minus purchase returns and allowances minus purchase discounts. Balances for each of these accounts come from the ending unadjusted trial balance.

LO5 Compute cost of goods sold. The inventory equation is used to compute cost of goods sold: Beginning inventory plus net purchases minus ending inventory equals cost of goods sold. Ending inventory is determined from a physical count of the inventory that remains unsold at the end of the period.

LO6 Compute gross profit. Gross profit is computed as net sales minus cost of goods sold. It is an important measure of performance for a merchandiser.

LO7 Prepare the adjusting entry for accrued revenue. Accrued revenue is revenue earned for work performed before the end of a period, but amounts won't be collected until the next period. An adjusting entry is recorded with a debit to Accounts Receivable and a credit to Sales (or Revenue).

LO8 **Prepare the adjusting entry for unearned revenue.** When a business receives cash before it performs work, it has a liability to perform that future work. When the work is performed, Unearned Revenue (a liability) is reduced with a debit and Revenue is increased with a credit.

LO9 **Appendix 13A—Describe the alternatives in accounting for prepayments.** Debiting all prepaid expenses to expense accounts when they are purchased is acceptable. When this is done, adjusting entries must transfer any unexpired amounts from expense accounts to asset accounts. Crediting all unearned revenues to revenue accounts when cash is received is also acceptable. In this case, the adjusting entries must transfer any unearned amounts from revenue accounts to unearned revenue accounts.

Guidance Answers to **HOW YOU DOIN'?**

1. Insurance expense = $3,200 − $2,000 = $1,200.

2. Supplies expense = $1,400 − $620 = $780.

3. Annual depreciation expense = ($22,000 − $2,000)/4 = $5,000.

4. Net sales = Sales − Sales returns and allowances − Sales discounts, or, $450,000 − $4,000 − $7,000 = $439,000.

5. Net purchases = Purchases − Purchase returns and allowances − Purchase discounts + Transportation-in, or $325,000 − $7,000 − $8,000 + $1,000 = $311,000.

6. Cost of goods sold = Beginning inventory + Net purchases − Ending inventory, or $75,000 + $220,000 − $42,000 = $253,000. Gross profit = Net sales − Cost of goods sold, or $303,000 − $253,000 = $50,000.

7. If the accrued revenues adjustment of $200 is not made, then both revenues and net income are understated by $200 on the current year's income statement, and both assets and equity are understated by $200 on the balance sheet.

8. An accrued revenue arises when revenue is earned but not yet received in cash nor recorded in the books. An example would be consulting work that has been performed for which payment has not yet been received.

Key Terms

Accrued revenues (p. 324) Revenues earned in a period that are both unrecorded and not yet received in cash (or other assets); adjusting entries for recording accrued revenues involve increasing assets and increasing revenues.

Cost of goods sold (p. 322) Cost of inventory sold to customers during a period; also called *cost of sales*.

Gross profit (p. 322) Net sales minus cost of goods sold; also called *gross margin*.

Merchandise inventory (p. 317) Goods that a company owns and expects to sell to customers; also called *merchandise* or *inventory*.

Net purchases (p. 322) Net cost of merchandise purchased; computed as purchases minus purchase discounts, minus purchase returns and allowances, plus transportation-in.

Net sales (p. 322) Net amount of merchandise sold; computed as sales minus sales returns and allowances minus sales discounts.

Unearned revenues (p. 324) Liability created when customers pay in advance for products or services; earned when the products or services are later delivered.

Multiple Choice Quiz   Answers on p. 343   mhhe.com/wildCA2e

Additional Multiple Choice Quizzes are available at the book's Website.

1. The accounting principle that requires revenue to be reported when earned is the
   a. Matching principle.
   b. Revenue recognition principle.
   c. Time period principle.
   d. Accrual reporting principle.
   e. Going-concern principle.

2. Adjusting entries
   a. Affect only income statement accounts.
   b. Affect only balance sheet accounts.
   c. Affect both income statement and balance sheet accounts.
   d. Affect only cash flow statement accounts.
   e. Affect only equity accounts.

3. On May 1, 2010, a two-year insurance policy was purchased for $12,000 with coverage to begin immediately. What is the amount of insurance expense that appears on the company's income statement for the year ended December 31, 2010?
   a. $2,000
   b. $4,000
   c. $6,000
   d. $10,000
   e. $12,000

4. On November 1, 2010, Stockton Co. receives $3,600 cash from Hans Co. for consulting services to be provided evenly over the period November 1, 2010, to April 30, 2011—at which time Stockton credited $3,600 to Unearned Consulting Fees. The adjusting entry on December 31, 2010 (Stockton's year-end) would include a
  a. Debit to Unearned Consulting Fees for $1,200.
  b. Debit to Unearned Consulting Fees for $2,400.
  c. Credit to Consulting Fees Earned for $2,400.
  d. Debit to Consulting Fees Earned for $1,200.
  e. Credit to Cash for $3,600.

5. Employees at Guthrie Co. worked three days at the end of 2010 and earned $5,400. They will be paid for this work at the next payroll date on January 9, 2011. What is the adjusting entry that Guthrie must make for the year ending December 31, 2010?
  a. Debit Wages Expense $5,400, Credit Prepaid Wages $5,400.
  b. Debit Wages Payable $5,400, Credit Wages Expense $5,400.
  c. Debit Prepaid Wages $5,400, Credit Wages Payable $5,400.
  d. Debit Wages Expense $5,400, Credit Wages Payable $5,400.

Superscript letter ^{A} denotes assignments based on Appendix 13A.

Discussion Questions

1. How does a merchandiser compute net sales?

2. How does a merchandiser compute cost of goods sold?

3. What is an accrued expense and where is it reported in the financial statements?

4. What is unearned revenue and where is it reported in financial statements?

5. What is an accrued revenue? Give an example.

6. ^{A}If a company initially records prepaid expenses with debits to expense accounts, what type of account is debited in the adjusting entries for those prepaid expenses?

7. Review the balance sheet of **Best Buy** in Appendix A. Identify the liability accounts that require adjustment before annual financial statements can be prepared. What would be the effect on the income statement if these liability accounts were not adjusted?

8. Review the balance sheet of Best Buy in Appendix A. What amount does Best Buy report for Merchandise Inventories on its most recent balance sheet?

---

connect

Compute net sales and gross profit from the adjusted trial balance information below.

Sales	$150,000
Sales discounts	5,200
Sales returns and allowances	20,000
Cost of goods sold	79,600

QUICK STUDY

QS 13-1
Computing net sales and gross profit **L04 L06**

Compute net purchases and cost of goods sold from the adjusted trial balance information below.

Beginning inventory	50,000
Ending inventory	42,000
Purchases	143,000
Purchase discounts	18,000
Purchase returns	16,000
Net sales	200,000

QS 13-2
Computing net purchases and cost of goods sold **L04 L05**

Refer to the data in QS 13-2. Prepare the necessary adjusting entries for merchandise inventory at the end of the year. The company uses a periodic inventory system. Use December 31 for the date of the entries.

QS 13-3
Adjusting entries for inventory **L02**

QS 13-4

Identifying accounting adjustments

LO5 LO7 LO8

Classify the following adjusting entries as involving prepaid expenses (PE), unearned revenues (UR), accrued expenses (AE), or accrued revenues (AR).

a. _____ To record revenue earned that was previously received as cash in advance.

b. _____ To record wages expense incurred but not yet paid (nor recorded).

c. _____ To record revenue earned but not yet billed (nor recorded).

d. _____ To record expiration of prepaid insurance.

e. _____ To record annual depreciation expense.

QS 13-5

Preparing adjusting entries for prepaid and accrued expenses

LO3

Check (b) Dr. Insurance Expense, $2,100

Prepare adjusting journal entries for the year ended December 31, 2010, for each of these separate situations. Assume that prepaid expenses are initially recorded in asset accounts.

a. Depreciation on the company's equipment for 2010 is computed to be $23,000.

b. The Prepaid Insurance account had a $2,600 debit balance at December 31, 2010, before adjusting for the costs of any expired coverage. An analysis of insurance policies showed that $2,100 of coverage had expired as of December 31, 2010.

c. Wage expenses of $6,700 have been incurred but are not paid as of December 31, 2010.

QS 13-6

Preparing adjusting entries for unearned revenues **LO8**

One-third of the work related to $15,000 cash received in advance is performed this period. Prepare the adjusting entry needed at year-end, assuming fees collected in advance of work are initially recorded as liabilities.

QS 13-7

Adjusting entry for accrued revenue **LO7**

Premier Lawn has earned but unbilled (and unrecorded) mowing fees of $1,200 at the end of its first accounting period. What journal entry is needed?

QS 13-8

Adjusting for unearned revenues **LO8**

Tao receives $10,000 cash in advance for four months of legal services on October 1, 2010, and records it by debiting Cash and crediting Unearned Revenue both for $10,000. It is now December 31, 2010, and Tao has provided legal services as planned. What adjusting entry should Tao make to account for the work performed from October 1 through December 31, 2010?

QS 13-9

Preparing adjusting entries

LO3 LO7 LO8

During the year, Sereno Co. recorded prepayments of expenses in asset accounts, and cash receipts of unearned revenues in liability accounts. At the end of its annual accounting period, the company must make three adjusting entries: (1) accrue salaries expense, (2) adjust the Unearned Services Revenue account to recognize earned revenue, and (3) record services revenue earned for which cash will be received the following period. For each of these adjusting entries (1), (2), and (3), indicate the account from *a* through *i* to be debited and the account to be credited.

a. Prepaid Salaries   **d.** Unearned Services Revenue   **g.** Accounts Receivable

b. Cash   **e.** Salaries Expense   **h.** Accounts Payable

c. Salaries Payable   **f.** Services Revenue   **i.** Equipment

QS 13-10

Interpreting adjusting entries

LO3

The following information is taken from Brooke Company's unadjusted and adjusted trial balances.

	Unadjusted		Adjusted	
	Debit	Credit	Debit	Credit
Prepaid insurance	$4,100		$3,700	
Wages payable		$ 0		$800

Given this information, which of the following is likely included among its adjusting entries?

a. A $400 debit to Insurance Expense and an $800 debit to Wages Payable.

b. A $400 debit to Insurance Expense and an $800 debit to Wages Expense.

c. A $400 credit to Prepaid Insurance and an $800 debit to Wages Payable.

In making adjusting entries at the end of its accounting period, Chao Consulting failed to record $1,600 of insurance coverage that had expired. This $1,600 cost had been initially debited to the Prepaid Insurance account. The company also failed to record accrued salaries expense of $1,000. As a result of these two oversights, the financial statements for the reporting period will [choose one] (1) understate assets by $1,600; (2) understate expenses by $2,600; (3) understate net income by $1,000; or (4) overstate liabilities by $1,000.

QS 13-11
Determining effects of adjusting entries   **LO3**

Calvin Consulting initially records prepaid and unearned items in income statement accounts. Given Calvin Consulting's accounting practices, which of the following applies to the preparation of adjusting entries at the end of its first accounting period?

a. Earned but unbilled (and unrecorded) consulting fees are recorded with a debit to Unearned Consulting Fees and a credit to Consulting Fees Earned.

b. Unpaid salaries are recorded with a debit to Prepaid Salaries and a credit to Salaries Expense.

c. The cost of unused office supplies is recorded with a debit to Supplies Expense and a credit to Office Supplies.

d. Unearned fees (on which cash was received in advance earlier in the period) are recorded with a debit to Consulting Fees Earned and a credit to Unearned Consulting Fees.

QS 13-12ᴬ
Preparing adjusting entries
LO9

connect

Compute net sales and gross profit for each separate case *a* through *c*.

EXERCISES

Exercise 13-1
Computing net sales and gross profit   **LO3   LO6**

	a	b	c
Sales	$550,000	$38,700	$255,700
Sales discounts	17,500	600	4,200
Sales returns and allowances	6,000	5,300	900
Cost of goods sold	329,700	24,300	126,900

Following are financial figures for three companies. Compute net purchases, cost of goods sold, and gross profit for each company.

Exercise 13-2
Computing net purchases, cost of goods sold, and gross profit
LO4   LO5   LO6

	Company a	Company b	Company c
Beginning inventory	$ 75,000	$ 18,000	$ 25,000
Ending inventory	98,000	16,000	28,000
Purchases	177,000	86,000	110,000
Purchase discounts	23,000	16,000	0
Purchase returns	12,000	7,000	8,000
Net sales	188,000	119,000	152,000

Refer to Exercise 13-2. For each of the three companies, prepare the necessary adjusting entries for merchandise inventory at the end of the accounting period. Each company uses the periodic inventory method.

Exercise 13-3
Adjusting entries for inventory
LO2

In the blank space beside each adjusting entry that follows, enter the letter of the explanation *A* through *E* that most closely describes the entry.

A. To record this period's depreciation expense.

B. To record accrued salaries expense.

C. To record this period's use of a prepaid expense.

D. To record accrued consulting fee revenue.

E. To record the earning of previously unearned income.

Exercise 13-4
Classifying adjusting entries
LO3   LO7   LO8

___	1.	Insurance Expense	1,653	
		Prepaid Insurance		1,653
___	2.	Unearned Professional Fees	19,250	
		Professional Fees Earned		19,250
___	3.	Consulting Fee Receivable	3,300	
		Consulting Fee Revenue		3,300
___	4.	Depreciation Expense	12,413	
		Accumulated Depreciation		12,413
___	5.	Salaries Expense	6,250	
		Salaries Payable		6,250

Exercise 13-5

Adjusting and paying accrued wages   LO3

Reese Management has four part-time employees, each of whom earns $300 per day. They are normally paid on Fridays for work completed Monday through Friday of the same week. They were paid in full on Friday, December 28, 2010. The next week, the five employees worked only four days because New Year's Day was an unpaid holiday. Show (*a*) the adjusting entry that would be recorded on Monday, December 31, 2010, and (*b*) the journal entry that would be made to record payment of the employees' wages on Friday, January 4, 2011. (For simplicity, ignore payroll taxes.)

Exercise 13-6

Adjusting for accrued expenses and accrued revenues

LO3   LO7

The following two separate situations require adjusting journal entries to prepare financial statements as of April 30. For each situation, present both the April 30 adjusting entry and the subsequent entry during May to record the payment of the accrued expenses or collection of the accrued revenue.

a. On April 1, the company retained an attorney at a flat monthly fee of $3,500. This amount is payable on the 12th of May.

b. On April 30 the company has earned $7,500 of design fees, which it has yet to bill or record. This amount is collected on May 28.

Exercise 13-7

Computing cost of goods sold and gross profit   LO5   LO6

Following are financial figures for five companies. Solve for the missing items a through e.

	Company 1	Company 2	Company 3	Company 4	Company 5
Beginning inventory	$ 57,000	$ 63,000	$ 97,000	$ 30,000	$ e
Purchases	150,000	173,000	92,000	115,000	255,000
Purchase discounts	17,000	21,000	15,000	12,000	23,000
Purchase returns	17,000	13,000	8,000	7,000	15,000
Cost of goods available for sale	a	202,000	166,000	126,000	329,000
Ending inventory	56,000	69,000	72,000	d	130,000
Cost of goods sold	117,000	133,000	c	110,000	199,000
Sales	200,000	b	119,000	152,000	313,000
Gross profit	83,000	55,000	25,000	42,000	114,000

Exercise 13-8

Preparing adjusting entries

LO3   LO8

The following information is available for Goode Company. Assume that December 31 is the end of its annual accounting period.

a. The Prepaid Insurance account shows a debit balance of $2,340, representing the cost of a three-year fire insurance policy that was purchased on October 1 of the current year.

b. The Office Supplies account has a debit balance of $400; a year-end count reveals $80 of supplies still available.

c. On November 1 of the current year, Unearned Rent was credited for $1,500. This amount represented a prepayment received for a three-month period beginning November 1.

d. Depreciation on office equipment is $600.

Required

Record the December 31 adjusting entries for the transactions and events *a* through *d*.

The following information is available for Blassie Company. Assume that December 31 is the end of the annual accounting period.

a. The Prepaid Insurance account shows a debit balance of $3,600, representing the cost of a three-year fire insurance policy that was purchased on October 1 of the current year.

b. The Office Supplies account has a debit balance of $800; a year-end count reveals $90 of supplies still available.

c. On November 1 of the current year, Unearned Rent was credited for $3,300. This amount represented a prepayment received for a three-month period beginning November 1.

d. Depreciation on office equipment is $900.

Required

Record the December 31 adjusting entries for the transactions and events *a* through *d*.

Exercise 13-9
Preparing adjusting entries
LO3   LO8

Following are two income statements for Alexis Co. for the year ended December 31. The left column is prepared before any adjusting entries are recorded, and the right column includes the effects of adjusting entries. The company records cash receipts and payments related to unearned and prepaid items in balance sheet accounts. Analyze the statements and prepare the eight adjusting entries that likely were recorded. (*Note:* 30% of the $7,000 adjustment for Fees Earned has been earned but not billed, and the other 70% has been earned by performing services that were paid for in advance.)

Exercise 13-10
Analyzing and preparing adjusting entries   LO3   LO7

ALEXIS CO. Income Statements For Year Ended December 31		
	Unadjusted	**Adjusted**
Revenues		
Fees earned	$18,000	$25,000
Commissions earned	36,500	36,500
Total revenues	$54,500	$61,500
Expenses		
Depreciation expense—Computers	0	1,600
Depreciation expense—Office furniture	0	1,850
Salaries expense	13,500	15,750
Insurance expense	0	1,400
Rent expense	3,800	3,800
Office supplies expense	0	580
Advertising expense	2,500	2,500
Utilities expense	1,245	1,335
Total expenses	21,045	28,815
Net income	$33,455	$32,685

Ricardo Construction began operations on December 1. In setting up its accounting procedures, the company decided to debit expense accounts when it prepays its expenses and to credit revenue accounts when customers pay for services in advance. Prepare journal entries for items *a* through *d* and the adjusting entries as of its December 31 period-end for items *e* through *g*.

a. Supplies are purchased on December 1 for $2,000 cash.

b. The company prepaid its insurance premiums for $1,540 cash on December 2.

c. On December 15, the company receives an advance payment of $13,000 cash from customers for remodeling work.

d. On December 28, the company receives $3,700 cash from another customer for remodeling work to be performed in January.

e. A physical count on December 31 indicates that Ricardo has $1,840 of supplies available.

Exercise 13-11[A]
Adjusting for prepaids recorded as expenses and unearned revenues recorded as revenues   LO9

f. An analysis of the insurance policies in effect on December 31 shows that $340 of insurance coverage had expired.

g. As of December 31, one remodeling project has been worked on and completed. The $5,570 fee for this project had been received in advance.

connect™

PROBLEM SET A

Problem 13–1A
Merchandiser's partial work sheet, adjusting entries, and gross profit
LO1   LO2   LO3   LO4
LO5   LO6   LO7

The following unadjusted trial balance is prepared at fiscal year-end for Helix Company.

File Edit View Insert Format Tools Data Accounting Window Help

HELIX COMPANY
Unadjusted Trial Balance
January 31, 2010

		Debit	Credit
2	Cash	$ 28,750	
3	Merchandise inventory	13,000	
4	Store supplies	5,500	
5	Prepaid insurance	2,400	
6	Store equipment	42,600	
7	Accumulated depreciation—Store equipment		$ 19,750
8	Accounts payable		14,000
9	A. Helix, Capital		39,000
10	A. Helix, Withdrawals	2,000	
11	Income summary	0	0
12	Sales		115,800
13	Sales discounts	1,900	
14	Sales returns and allowances	2,300	
15	Purchases	37,750	
16	Purchase discounts		400
17	Purchase returns and allowances		350
18	Transportation-in	1,000	
19	Depreciation expense—Store equipment	0	
20	Salaries expense	27,400	
21	Insurance expense	0	
22	Rent expense	15,000	
23	Store supplies expense	0	
24	Advertising expense	9,700	
25	Totals	$189,300	$189,300

Sheet1 / Sheet2 / Sheet3 /

Helix Company uses a periodic inventory system.

Required

1. Prepare adjusting journal entries to reflect each of the items below. Record your entries on a (partial) work sheet, using Exhibit 13.4 as a guide.

    a. Store supplies still available at year-end amount to $2,550.

    b. Expired insurance for the year is $1,450.

    c. Depreciation expense on store equipment is $1,975 for the year.

    d. $10,300 of inventory is still available at fiscal year-end.

2. Complete the (partial) worksheet through the Adjusted Trial Balance columns.

3. Compute net sales.
4. Compute net purchases.
5. Compute cost of goods sold.
6. Compute gross profit.

For each of the following entries, enter the letter of the explanation that most closely describes it in the space beside each entry. (You can use letters more than once.)

Problem 13-2A
Identifying adjusting entries with explanations   LO3   LO7

A. To record receipt of unearned revenue.
B. To record this period's earning of prior unearned revenue.
C. To record payment of an accrued expense.
D. To record receipt of an accrued revenue.
E. To record an accrued expense.

F. To record an accrued revenue.
G. To record this period's use of a prepaid expense.
H. To record payment of a prepaid expense.
I. To record this period's depreciation expense.

____ 1.	Salaries Expense	1,000	
	Salaries Payable		1,000
____ 2.	Depreciation Expense	4,000	
	Accumulated Depreciation		4,000
____ 3.	Unearned Professional Fees	3,000	
	Professional Fees Earned		3,000
____ 4.	Insurance Expense	4,200	
	Prepaid Insurance		4,200
____ 5.	Salaries Payable	1,400	
	Cash		1,400
____ 6.	Prepaid Rent	4,500	
	Cash		4,500
____ 7.	Salaries Expense	6,000	
	Salaries Payable		6,000
____ 8.	Accounts Receivable	5,000	
	Sales		5,000
____ 9.	Cash	9,000	
	Accounts Receivable		9,000
____ 10.	Cash	7,500	
	Unearned Professional Fees		7,500
____ 11.	Rent Expense	2,000	
	Prepaid Rent		2,000

Gomez Co. had the following transactions in the last two months of its year ended December 31.

Problem 13-3A^A
Recording prepaid expenses and unearned revenues
LO6   LO8   LO9

Nov. 1 Paid $1,800 cash for future newspaper advertising.
    1 Paid $2,460 cash for 12 months of insurance through October 31 of the next year.
   30 Received $3,600 cash for future services to be provided to a customer.
Dec. 1 Paid $3,000 cash for a consultant's services to be received over the next three months.
   15 Received $7,950 cash for future services to be provided to a customer.
   31 Of the advertising paid for on November 1, $1,200 worth is not yet used.
   31 A portion of the insurance paid for on November 1 has expired. No adjustment was made in November to Prepaid Insurance.
   31 Services worth $1,500 are not yet provided to the customer who paid on November 30.
   31 One-third of the consulting services paid for on December 1 have been received.
   31 The company has performed $3,300 of services that the customer paid for on December 15.

Required

1. Prepare entries for these transactions under the method that records prepaid expenses as assets and records unearned revenues as liabilities. Also prepare adjusting entries at the end of the year.

2. Prepare entries for these transactions under the method that records prepaid expenses as expenses and records unearned revenues as revenues. Also prepare adjusting entries at the end of the year. (*Hint:* Refer to Appendix 13A).

PROBLEM SET B

Problem 13-1B

Merchandiser's partial work sheet, adjusting entries, and gross profit
LO1 LO2 LO3 LO4
LO5 LO6 LO7

The following unadjusted trial balance is prepared at fiscal year-end for Giaccio Products Company.

File Edit View Insert Format Tools Data Accounting Window Help

GIACCIO PRODUCTS COMPANY
Unadjusted Trial Balance
October 31, 2010

		Debit	Credit
2	Cash	$ 30,150	
3	Merchandise inventory	13,000	
4	Store supplies	5,300	
5	Prepaid insurance	2,700	
6	Store equipment	42,900	
7	Accumulated depreciation—Store equipment		$ 19,900
8	Accounts payable		15,000
9	G. Giaccio, Capital		38,000
10	G. Giaccio, Withdrawals	2,050	
11	Income summary	0	0
12	Sales		116,250
13	Sales discounts	1,950	
14	Sales returns and allowances	2,300	
15	Purchases	38,000	
16	Purchase returns and allowances		1,200
17	Purchase discounts		800
18	Transportation-in	3,000	
19	Depreciation expense—Store equipment	0	
20	Salaries expense	26,000	
21	Insurance expense	0	
22	Rent expense	14,000	
23	Store supplies expense	0	
24	Advertising expense	9,800	
25	Totals	$191,150	$191,150
26			

Sheet1 Sheet2 Sheet3

Giaccio Products Company uses a periodic inventory system.

Required

1. Prepare adjusting journal entries to reflect each of the items below. Record your entries on a (partial) work sheet, using Exhibit 13.4 as a guide.

   a. Store supplies still available at year-end amount to $1,650.

   b. Expired insurance for the year is $1,300.

   c. Depreciation expense on store equipment is $1,990 for the year.

   d. $11,600 of inventory is still available at fiscal year-end.

2. Complete the (partial) worksheet through the Adjusted Trial Balance columns.

3. Compute net sales.

4. Compute net purchases.

5. Compute cost of goods sold.

6. Compute gross profit.

For each of the following entries, enter the letter of the explanation that most closely describes it in the space beside each entry. (You can use letters more than once.)

Problem 13-2B
Identifying adjusting entries with explanations   **LO7   LO8**

A. To record payment of a prepaid expense.

B. To record this period's use of a prepaid expense.

C. To record this period's depreciation expense.

D. To record receipt of unearned revenue.

E. To record this period's earning of prior unearned revenue.

F. To record an accrued expense.

G. To record payment of an accrued expense.

H. To record an accrued revenue.

I. To record receipt of accrued revenue.

____ 1.	Accounts Receivable	3,500	
	Sales		3,500
____ 2.	Salaries Payable	9,000	
	Cash		9,000
____ 3.	Depreciation Expense	8,000	
	Accumulated Depreciation		8,000
____ 4.	Cash	9,000	
	Unearned Professional Fees		9,000
____ 5.	Insurance Expense	4,000	
	Prepaid Insurance		4,000
____ 6.	Salaries Expense	5,000	
	Salaries Payable		5,000
____ 7.	Cash	1,500	
	Accounts Receivable		1,500
____ 8.	Salaries Expense	7,000	
	Salaries Payable		7,000
____ 9.	Prepaid Rent	3,000	
	Cash		3,000
____ 10.	Rent Expense	7,500	
	Prepaid Rent		7,500
____ 11.	Unearned Professional Fees	6,000	
	Professional Fees Earned		6,000

Tremor Co. had the following transactions in the last two months of its fiscal year ended May 31.

Problem 13-3B[A]
Recording prepaid expenses and unearned revenues   **LO9**

Apr. 1   Paid $2,450 cash to an accounting firm for future consulting services.
  1   Paid $3,600 cash for 12 months of insurance through March 31 of the next year.
  30   Received $8,500 cash for future services to be provided to a customer.
May 1   Paid $4,450 cash for future newspaper advertising.
  23   Received $10,450 cash for future services to be provided to a customer.
  31   Of the consulting services paid for on April 1, $2,000 worth has been received.
  31   A portion of the insurance paid for on April 1 has expired. No adjustment was made in April to Prepaid Insurance.
  31   Services worth $4,600 are not yet provided to the customer who paid on April 30.
  31   Of the advertising paid for on May 1, $2,050 worth is not yet used.
  31   The company has performed $5,500 of services that the customer paid for on May 23.

Required

1. Prepare entries for these transactions under the method that records prepaid expenses and unearned revenues in balance sheet accounts. Also prepare adjusting entries at the end of the year.

2. Prepare entries for these transactions under the method that records prepaid expenses and unearned revenues in income statement accounts. Also prepare adjusting entries at the end of the year. (*Hint:* Refer to Appendix 13A).

(This serial problem began in Chapter 1 and continues through most of the book. If previous chapter segments were not completed, the serial problem can begin at this point. It is helpful, but not necessary, that you use the Working Papers that accompany the book.)

SERIAL PROBLEM

Success Systems

SP 13   Adriana Lopez created Success Systems on October 1, 2010. Below is a list of the company's (unadjusted) general ledger account balances as of March 31, 2011 and additional facts needed to prepare adjusting entries on March 31, 2011.

No.	Account Title	Dr.	Cr.
101	Cash	$87,266	
106.1	Alex's Engineering Co.	0	
106.2	Wildcat Services	3,900	
106.3	Easy Leasing	11,000	
106.4	Clark Co.	4,800	
106.5	Chang Corp.	0	
106.6	Gomez Co.	0	
106.7	Delta Co.	0	
106.8	KC, Inc.	4,700	
106.9	Dream, Inc.	0	
106.10	Bob's Building Co.	0	
119	Merchandise inventory	0	
126	Computer supplies	4,025	
128	Prepaid insurance	1,800	
131	Prepaid rent	3,500	
163	Office equipment	10,000	
164	Accumulated depreciation— Office equipment		625
167	Computer equipment	25,000	
168	Accumulated depreciation— Computer equipment		1,250
201	Accounts payable		0

No.	Account Title	Dr.	Cr.
210	Wages payable		0
236	Unearned computer services revenue		2,500
301	A. Lopez, Capital		127,435
302	A. Lopez, Withdrawals	5,200	
403	Computer services revenue		29,350
413	Sales		20,900
414	Sales returns and allowances	500	
415	Sales discounts	55	
505	Purchases	15,200	
506	Purchase returns and allowances		496
507	Purchase discounts		152
508	Transportation-In	400	
612	Depreciation expense—Office equipment	0	
613	Depreciation expense—Computer equipment	0	
623	Wages expense	2,850	
637	Insurance expense	0	
640	Rent expense	0	
652	Computer supplies expense	0	
655	Advertising expense	800	
676	Mileage expense	512	
677	Miscellaneous expenses	0	
684	Repairs expense—Computer	1,200	

The following additional facts are available for preparing adjustments on March 31:

a. The March 31 amount of computer supplies still available totals $1,950.

b. Three more months have expired since the company purchased its annual insurance policy at a $2,400 cost for 12 months of coverage.

c. Michelle Jones has not been paid for seven days of work at the rate of $150 per day.

d. Three months have passed since any prepaid rent has been transferred to expense. The monthly rent expense is $875.

e. Depreciation on the computer equipment for January 1 through March 31 is $1,250.

f. Depreciation on the office equipment for January 1 through March 31 is $625.

g. An inventory count shows that $680 of merchandise remains unsold on March 31.

h. Success Systems completed a project for Alex's Engineering Co., thereby earning the $2,500 advance cash payment previously paid by Alex.

Required

1. Using Exhibit 13.4 as a guide, enter the account numbers, account titles, and unadjusted balances in a partial worksheet. Include a row for the Income Summary account directly after the A. Lopez, Withdrawals account.

2. Enter the necessary adjusting journal entries for March 31 in the adjustments columns of your partial worksheet. *Hint:* No entry "BI" is needed since the beginning inventory balance is zero.

3. Prepare an adjusted trial balance.

4. From the adjusted trial balance, compute the following for the quarter ended March 31:
(*a*) Net sales, (*b*) Net purchases, (*c*) Cost of goods sold, and (*d*) Gross profit.

BEYOND THE NUMBERS

REPORTING IN ACTION
LO4 LO5 LO6

BTN 13–1   Refer to **Best Buy**'s financial statements in Appendix A to answer the following.

1. What were the amounts of Best Buy's cost of goods sold and gross profit for the year ended March 1, 2008?

2. Assume that the amounts for inventories and cost of sales reflect items purchased in a form ready for resale. Compute the net cost of goods purchased for the year ended March 1, 2008.

BTN 13-2   At year-end, the president instructs you, the financial officer, not to record accrued expenses until next year because they will not be paid until then. The president also directs you to record in current-year sales a recent purchase order from a customer that requires merchandise to be delivered two weeks after the year-end. Your company would report a net income instead of a net loss if you carry out these instructions.

ETHICS CHALLENGE

LO3   LO7

Required

1. Relying on the matching principle, discuss the rationale for revenue recognition. Explain why the delayed recognition of accrued expense and the early recognition of revenue would violate GAAP.

2. If the president insists on such accounting treatment, what would you do to remedy this ethical situation?

BTN 13-3   Best Buy sells gift cards to generate future revenues.

TAKING IT TO THE NET

LO8

Required

Obtain Best Buy's 2008 financial statements from its website (**BestBuy.com**) or the SEC (**sec.gov**) and answer the following questions:

1. When does Best Buy recognize revenue from gift cards? (*Hint:* Refer to footnote 1).

2. Explain what Best Buy means by "gift card breakage."

3. What is the amount of Best Buy's gift card breakage revenue for the year ending March 1, 2008?

BTN 13-4   Official Brands' general ledger and supplementary records at the end of its current period reveal the following.

TEAMWORK IN ACTION

LO4   LO5   LO6

Sales	$600,000	Merchandise inventory (beginning of period)	$ 98,000
Sales returns	20,000	Invoice cost of merchandise purchases	360,000
Sales discounts	13,000	Purchase discounts	9,000
Cost of transportation-in	22,000	Purchase returns and allowances	11,000
		Merchandise inventory (end of period)	84,000

Required

1. *Each* member of the team is to assume responsibility for computing *one* of the following items. You are not to duplicate your teammates' work. Get any necessary amounts to compute your item from the appropriate teammate. Each member is to explain his or her computation to the team in preparation for reporting to the class.

    a. Net sales   **c.** Cost of goods sold

    b. Total cost of merchandise purchases   **d.** Gross profit

BTN 13-5   Refer to the chapter's opening feature about Joel Boblit and his **BigBadToyStore** company. Assume that Joel's business currently pays for costs of delivery of goods to customers, and that customers can receive a 1% discount for quick payment. Joel is considering offering customers a 3% discount for quick payment but also having customers pay for the costs of delivery. If Joel implements this proposal, he expects his net income to increase by more than 10%.

ENTREPRENEURS IN BUSINESS

Required

1. Based on the predicted change in net income alone, should Joel implement the proposal?

2. What other factors (beside the predicted change in net income) should Joel consider before he implements the proposal? Explain.

BTN 13-6   The owner of an electronics store applies for a business loan. The store's financial statements reveal large increases in current-year revenues and income. Analysis shows that these increases are due to a promotion that lets consumers buy now and pay nothing until January 1 of next year. The store recorded these sales as accrued revenue. Does your analysis raise any concerns?

YOU CALL IT

LO7

ANSWERS TO MULTIPLE CHOICE QUIZ

1. b

2. c

3. b; Insurance expense = $12,000 \times (8/24) = $4,000; adjusting entry is: *dr.* Insurance Expense for $4,000, *cr.* Prepaid Insurance for $4,000.

4. a; Consulting fees earned = $3,600 \times (2/6) = $1,200; adjusting entry is: *dr.* Unearned Consulting Fee for $1,200, *cr.* Consulting Fees Earned for $1,200.

5. d

A Look Back

Chapter 13 showed how to compute net sales, net purchases, and cost of goods sold for a merchandiser. It also showed common adjusting entries for a merchandiser.

A Look at This Chapter

This chapter shows how to prepare financial statements for a merchandiser. These financial statements include multiple-step and single-step income statements, the statement of owner's equity, and a classified balance sheet. The chapter also illustrates the closing process for a merchandiser.

A Look Ahead

Chapter 15 describes how companies account for and report accounts receivable. It also explains how to account for receivables that are uncollectible.

Chapter 14

Merchandiser's Financial Statements and the Closing Process

Learning Objectives

LO 1	Prepare a work sheet for a merchandising business.
LO 2	Define and prepare multiple-step and single-step income statements.
LO 3	Prepare a statement of owner's equity.
LO 4	Explain and prepare a classified balance sheet.
LO 5	Prepare journal entries to close temporary accounts.
LO 6	Prepare a post-closing trial balance.
LO 7	Prepare reversing entries and explain their purpose.

"The more clicks we can get, the better our future"
—Todd Rath

On the Green

ROCHESTER, NY—Brothers Tom and Todd Rath paid their college tuition by diving for lost golf balls and then reselling them. Today, their company RockBottomGolf.com applies a similar strategy of buying leftover products and reselling them. "Some of our critics refer to us as the 'graveyard of golf,'" explains Tom. "Oftentimes, we may be selling the last 3,000 drivers a manufacturer has ever made. If anyone can find a home for it, we can." The company boasts over 500,000 customers, affectionately referred to as "Rock Heads."

RockBottom's warehouse sports signs with "Scratch," the company's cartoonish, red-bearded caveman mascot. Scratch is surrounded with slogans such as: "A Clean Cave Is a Happy Cave" and "A Happy Rock Head Stays a Rock Head." Though Scratch is goofy, the company is all business. Offering a wide inventory of well-known brands of golf clubs, bags, balls, apparel, and accessories, this merchandising company buys in large lots and strives to keep costs low. For example, they located their distribution center in Virginia—enabling them to ship to over 60% of the U.S. population within two days. Also, they pack items in small, uniformly-sized boxes to lower costs.

Multiple-step income statements allow the company's managers to tell if sales are high enough above costs of goods sold, or if the company is paying too much for the items it sells. These income statements also give details on the company's other costs, for example shipping costs, to help managers make decisions. Classified balance sheets help company managers assess financial position.

In addition to financial statements, the company tracks "checkout flow," providing details on the point at which potential customers drop out of the checkout process and how many drop out. "If I had a 50% checkout success rate one day and 23% the next day, this lets me see that," explains Todd. This helps Todd steer more customers through the checkout process. He also tracks customer approval ratings, currently above 99%, as a performance measure.

As Todd says, the company plans to expand "as long as there are customers to win." Their expansion plans do not stop with golf. RockBottomGolf wants to become RockBottomSports, with many other sporting goods products available. With its fast-paced growth and position as the top golf retailer on the Internet, RockBottomGolf is "on the green."

[Sources: *RockBottomGolf.com Website*, January 2009; *Internet Retailer*, July 2007; *Inside Business-Hampton Roads*, October 2006.]

Once we make all necessary adjustments to the trial balance, we are ready to produce financial statements. Different financial statement formats can provide useful information to different financial statement users. We describe alternative formats for both income statements and balance sheets. We also describe the closing processes necessary to prepare for the next period's transactions.

Merchandiser's Financial Statements and the Closing Process

Work Sheet
- Preparing the work sheet for a merchandising business

Financial Statement Formats
- Multiple-step income statement
- Single-step income statement
- Statement of owner's equity
- Classified balance sheet

Completing the Accounting Cycle
- Closing entries
- Post-closing trial balance
- Reversing entries

The Work Sheet

Preparing the Work Sheet

LO1 Prepare a work sheet for a merchandising business.

Preparing the work sheet for a merchandiser follows the steps we showed for a service business in Chapter 6. Below we list the five steps in preparing the work sheet.

Step 1: Enter unadjusted trial balance.

Step 2: Enter adjustments.

Step 3: Prepare adjusted trial balance.

Step 4: Sort adjusted trial balance amounts to financial statement columns.

Step 5: Total statement columns, compute income or loss, and balance columns.

Exhibit 14.1 presents a completed work sheet for Z-Mart as of December 31, 2010. Steps 1 through 3 were completed in Chapter 13. In completing step 4, note that we extend the ending balance of merchandise inventory, obtained from a count of the items remaining unsold, to the balance sheet debit column. In addition, a merchandiser typically uses several detailed accounts to record sales and purchases. All of these accounts are temporary accounts, and thus they are extended into the income statement columns.

In completing step 5, we compute the total of each financial statement column. Z-Mart's income statement debit column totals $334,800, and its income statement credit column totals $347,700. The difference between these two totals ($12,900) is Z-Mart's net income for the period. This amount is added to the income statement debit column. Likewise, this $12,900 is added to the balance sheet credit column so that the two balance sheet column totals equal.

In the next section we show how to prepare the merchandiser's financial statements from work sheet information.

Exhibit 14.1

10-Column Work Sheet

File Edit View Insert Format Tools Data Accounting Window Help

	No.	Account	Unadjusted Trial Balance Dr.	Cr.	Adjustments Dr.	Cr.	Adjusted Trial Balance Dr.	Cr.	Income Statement Dr.	Cr.	Balance Sheet Dr.	Cr.
3	101	Cash	8,200				8,200				8,200	
4	106	Accounts receivable	11,200				11,200				11,200	
5	119	Merchandise Inventory	19,000		(EI) 21,000	(BI) 19,000	21,000				21,000	
6	126	Supplies	3,800			(b) 3,000	800				800	
7	128	Prepaid insurance	900			(a) 600	300				300	
8	167	Equipment	34,200				34,200				34,200	
9	168	Accumulated depr.—Equip.		3,700		(c) 3,700		7,400				7,400
10	201	Accounts payable		16,000				16,000				16,000
11	209	Salaries payable				(d) 800		800				800
12	301	K. Marty, Capital		42,600				42,600				42,600
13	302	K. Marty, Withdrawals	4,000				4,000				4,000	
14	901	Income Summary			(BI) 19,000	(EI) 21,000	19,000	21,000	19,000	21,000		
15	413	Sales		321,000				321,000		321,000		
16a	414	Sales returns and allowances	2,000				2,000		2,000			
16b	415	Sales discounts	4,300				4,300		4,300			
16c	505	Purchases	235,800				235,800		235,800			
16d	506	Purchases returns & allowance		1,500				1,500		1,500		
17	507	Purchases discounts		4,200				4,200		4,200		
18	508	Transportation-in	2,300				2,300		2,300			
19	612	Depreciation expense—Equip.			(c) 3,700		3,700		3,700			
20	622	Salaries expense	43,000		(d) 800		43,800		43,800			
21	637	Insurance expense			(a) 600		600		600			
22	640	Rent expense	9,000				9,000		9,000			
23	652	Supplies expense			(b) 3,000		3,000		3,000			
24	655	Advertising expense	11,300				11,300		11,300			
25		Totals	389,000	389,000	48,100	48,100	414,500	414,500	334,800	347,700	79,700	66,800
26		Net income							12,900			12,900
27		Totals							347,700	347,700	79,700	79,700

Sheet1 Sheet2 Sheet3

Financial Statement Formats

Generally accepted accounting principles do not require companies to use any one presentation format for financial statements. This section describes formats for multiple-step and single-step income statements, a statement of owner's equity, and a classified balance sheet.

Multiple-Step Income Statement

A **multiple-step income statement** format shows detailed computations of net sales and other costs and expenses, and reports subtotals for various classes of items. Exhibit 14.2 shows a multiple-step income statement for Z-Mart. The statement has three main parts: (1) *gross profit,* determined by net sales less cost of goods sold, (2) *income from operations,* determined by gross profit less operating expenses, and (3) *net income,* determined by income from operations adjusted for nonoperating items. The gross profit section includes a detailed cost of goods computation. Also, Z-Mart does not report any nonoperating items.

Some companies further classify operating expenses into two sections. **Selling expenses** include the expenses of promoting sales by displaying and advertising merchandise, making sales, and delivering goods to customers. Depreciation expense on store equipment is included since

LO2 Define and prepare multiple-step and single-step income statements.

Exhibit 14.2

Multiple-Step Income Statement

Z-MART
Income Statement
For Year Ended December 31, 2010

Sales			$321,000
Less: Sales discounts		$ 4,300	
Sales returns and allowances		2,000	6,300
Net sales			$314,700
Cost of goods sold:			
Merchandise inventory, January 1, 2010			$19,000
Purchases		$235,800	
Less: Purchase returns and allowances	($1,500)		
Purchase discounts	(4,200)		
Plus: Transportation-in	2,300	($3,400)	
Net purchases		$232,400	
Goods available for sale		$251,400	
Less: Merchandise inventory, December 31, 2010		21,000	
Cost of goods sold			$230,400
Gross profit			$ 84,300
Operating expenses			
Depreciation expense-Equipment		$ 3,700	
Salaries expense		43,800	
Insurance expense		600	
Rent expense		9,000	
Supplies expense		3,000	
Advertising expense		11,300	
Total operating expenses			71,400
Net income			$ 12,900

Gross profit computation

Income from operations computation

this equipment is used to generate sales. **General and administrative expenses** support a company's overall operations and include expenses related to accounting, human resource management, and financial management. These expenses are not directly related to the sales function of the business. If a company further classifies its operating expenses this way, the multiple-step income statement will include subtotals for the total selling expenses and the total general and administrative expenses.

Nonoperating activities consist of other expenses, revenues, losses, and gains that are unrelated to a company's operations. They are reported in two sections: (1) *other revenues and gains,* which often include interest revenue, dividend revenue, rent revenue, and gains from asset disposals, and (2) *other expenses and losses,* which often include interest expense, losses from asset disposals, and casualty losses. When a company has no reportable nonoperating activities, its income from operations is simply labeled net income. A partial income statement for a company with nonoperating activities might look like the following:

Income from operations		12,900
Other revenues and gains (expenses and losses)		
Interest revenue	1,000	
Gain on sale of building	2,500	
Interest expense	(1,500)	
Total other revenue and gains (expenses and losses)		2,000
Net income		$14,900

Nonoperating activities computation

Single-Step Income Statement

A **single-step income statement** is another widely used format. An example is shown in Exhibit 14.3 for Z-Mart. It lists cost of goods sold as another expense and shows only one subtotal for total expenses. Expenses are grouped into very few, if any, categories. Many companies use formats that combine features of both the single- and multiple-step statements. Provided that income statement items are shown sensibly, management can choose the format. (In later chapters, we describe some items, such as extraordinary gains and losses, that must be reported in certain locations on the income statement.)

Z-MART Income Statement For Year Ended December 31, 2010		
Revenues		
Net sales		$314,700
Expenses		
Cost of goods sold	$230,400	
Operating expenses	71,400	
Total expenses		301,800
Net income		$ 12,900

Exhibit 14.3

Single-Step Income Statement

Statement of Owner's Equity

The statement of owner's equity summarizes changes in the owner's equity account during the year due to:

LO3 Prepare a statement of owner's equity.

Item	Source of information
Net income or loss for the year	Income statement
Owner investments during the year	Owner, Capital, general ledger account
Owner withdrawals during the year	Work sheet

The Owner, Capital, account is updated during the year only for additional owner investments. Thus, for Z-Mart, the ending balance in K. Marty, Capital, on the work sheet ($42,600) must be increased for 2010's net income of $12,900 and decreased by K. Marty's withdrawals ($4,000) during the year. If K. Marty made no additional investments in Z-Mart during the year, Z-Mart's statement of owner's equity for 2010 would appear as in Exhibit 14.4 below.

Z-MART Statement of Owner's Equity For Year Ended December 31, 2010	
K. Marty, Capital, January 1, 2010	$42,600
Add: Net income	12,900
	55,500
Less: Withdrawals by owner	4,000
K. Marty, Capital, December 31, 2010	$51,500

Exhibit 14.4

Statement of Owner's Equity

Classified Balance Sheet

This section describes a classified balance sheet. An **unclassified balance sheet** is one whose items are broadly grouped into assets, liabilities, and equity. A **classified balance sheet** organizes assets and liabilities into important subgroups that provide more information to decision makers.

LO4 Explain and prepare a classified balance sheet.

Exhibit 14.5

Typical Categories in a Classified Balance Sheet

Assets	Liabilities and Equity
Current assets	Current liabilities
Noncurrent assets	Noncurrent liabilities
Long-term investments	Equity
Plant assets	
Intangible assets	

Classification Structure A classified balance sheet has no required layout, but it usually contains the categories in Exhibit 14.5. One of the more important classifications is the separation between current and noncurrent items for both assets and liabilities. Current items are those expected to come due (either collected or owed) within one year or the company's operating cycle, whichever is longer. The **operating cycle** is the time span from when *cash is used* to acquire goods and services until *cash is received* from the sale of goods and services. "Operating" refers to company operations and "cycle" refers to the circular flow of cash used for company inputs and then cash received from its outputs. The length of a company's operating cycle depends on its activities. For a service company, the operating cycle is the time span between (1) paying employees who perform the services and (2) receiving cash from customers. For a merchandiser selling products, the operating cycle is the time span between (1) paying suppliers for merchandise and (2) receiving cash from customers.

Current is also called *short-term*, and noncurrent is also called *long-term*.

Most operating cycles are less than one year. This means most companies use a one-year period in deciding which assets and liabilities are current. A few companies have an operating cycle longer than one year. For instance, producers of certain beverages (wine) and products (ginseng) that require aging for several years have operating cycles longer than one year. A classified balance sheet lists current assets before noncurrent assets and current liabilities before noncurrent liabilities. This consistency in presentation allows users to quickly identify current assets that are most easily converted to cash and current liabilities that are shortly coming due. Items in current assets and current liabilities are listed in the order of how quickly they will be converted to, or paid in, cash.

Classification Categories This section describes the most common categories in a classified balance sheet. The balance sheet for Z-Mart in Exhibit 14.6 shows some of these typical categories. Its assets are classified as either current or noncurrent. Its liabilities are all classified as current. Not all companies use the same categories of assets and liabilities for their balance

Exhibit 14.6

Example of a Classified Balance Sheet

Z-MART		
Balance Sheet		
December 31, 2010		
Assets		
Current assets		
Cash		$ 8,200
Accounts receivable		11,200
Merchandise inventory		21,000
Prepaid expenses		
Prepaid insurance	$ 300	
Supplies	800	1,100
Total current assets		41,500
Noncurrent assets		
Equipment	34,200	
Less: Accumulated depreciation	7,400	26,800
Total assets		$68,300
Liabilities and Owner's Equity		
Current liabilities		
Accounts payable		$16,000
Salaries payable		800
Total current liabilities		$16,800
Owner's equity		
K. Marty, Capital		51,500
Total liabilities and owner's equity		$68,300

sheets. **K2 Inc.**'s balance sheet lists only three asset classes: current assets; property, plant, and equipment; and other assets.

Current assets   Current assets are cash and other resources that are expected to be sold, collected, or used within one year or the company's operating cycle, whichever is longer. Examples are cash, short-term investments, accounts receivable, short-term notes receivable, merchandise inventory, and prepaid expenses. Current assets are usually listed according to the ease with which they can be converted to cash. Contra-assets, like Accumulated Depreciation, are listed in the assets section, even though they have credit balances. Prepaid expenses are usually listed last because they will not be converted to cash (instead, they are used).

Long-term investments   A second major balance sheet classification is **long-term** (or *noncurrent*) **investments.** Notes receivable and investments in stocks and bonds are long-term assets when they are expected to be held for more than the longer of one year or the operating cycle. Land held for future expansion is a long-term investment because it is *not* used in operations.

Plant assets   Plant assets are tangible assets that are both *long lived* and *used to produce* or *sell products and services.* Examples are equipment, machinery, buildings, and land used to produce or sell products and services. Plant assets are also called *fixed assets; property, plant, and equipment;* or *long-lived assets.*

Intangible assets   Intangible assets are long-term resources that benefit business operations. They usually lack physical form and have uncertain benefits. Examples are patents, trademarks, copyrights, franchises, and goodwill. Their value comes from the privileges or rights granted to or held by the owner. **K2, Inc.,** reports intangible assets of $228 million, which is nearly 20 percent of its total assets. Its intangibles include trademarks, patents, and licensing agreements.

Current liabilities   Current liabilities are obligations due to be paid or settled within one year or the operating cycle, whichever is longer. They are usually settled by paying out current assets such as cash. Current liabilities often include accounts payable, notes payable, wages payable, taxes payable, interest payable, and unearned revenues. Also, any portion of a long-term liability due to be paid within one year or the operating cycle, whichever is longer, is a current liability. Unearned revenues are current liabilities when they will be settled by delivering products or services within one year or the operating cycle, whichever is longer. Current liabilities are reported in the order of those to be settled first.

Long-term liabilities   Long-term liabilities are obligations *not* due within one year or the operating cycle, whichever is longer. Notes payable, mortgages payable, bonds payable, and lease obligations are common long-term liabilities. If a company has both short- and long-term items in any of these categories, they are commonly reported in both sections of the classified balance sheet. For example, assume a company owes $20,000 on a note payable, $2,000 of which is due next year. The company would include $2,000 for notes payable in the current liabilities section and $18,000 for notes payable in the noncurrent liabilities section.

Equity   Equity is the owner's claim on assets. For a proprietorship, this claim is reported in the equity section with an owner's capital account. (For a partnership, the equity section reports a capital account for each partner. For a corporation, the equity section is divided into two main subsections, common stock and retained earnings. We discuss accounting for partnerships and corporations in later chapters.)

HOW YOU DOIN'?   Answers—p. 358

1. Classify the following assets as (1) current assets, (2) plant assets, or (3) intangible assets:
   (a) land used in operations, (b) office supplies, (c) receivables from customers due in 10 months,
   (d) insurance protection for the next nine months, (e) trucks used to provide services to customers,
   (f) trademarks.
2. Cite two examples of assets classified as investments on the balance sheet.
3. Explain the operating cycle for a service company.

Completing the Accounting Cycle

After journalizing and posting the adjusting entries and preparing financial statements, the accountant completes the accounting cycle by journalizing and posting closing entries and preparing a post-closing trial balance. We illustrate these steps next.

Closing Entries

L05

Prepare journal entries to close temporary accounts.

There are four necessary steps to record and post the closing entries for a merchandiser.

Step 1: Close revenue accounts and those accounts used in computing cost of goods sold having credit balances to Income Summary.

Step 2: Close expense accounts and those accounts used in computing cost of goods sold having debit balances to Income Summary.

Step 3: Close the Income Summary account to the owner's capital account.

Step 4: Close the Withdrawals account to the owner's capital account.

Like service companies, merchandisers follow these four steps in closing temporary accounts. However, merchandisers typically have additional temporary accounts related to the recording of sales and purchases.

We illustrate the closing entries for Z-Mart, using information from Z-Mart's partial work sheet (from Exhibit 14.1) in Exhibit 14.7. The dollar amount for step 3 is obtained from a review of the postings to the Income Summary account, shown in Exhibit 14.8.

Exhibit 14.7

Closing Journal Entries for a Merchandiser

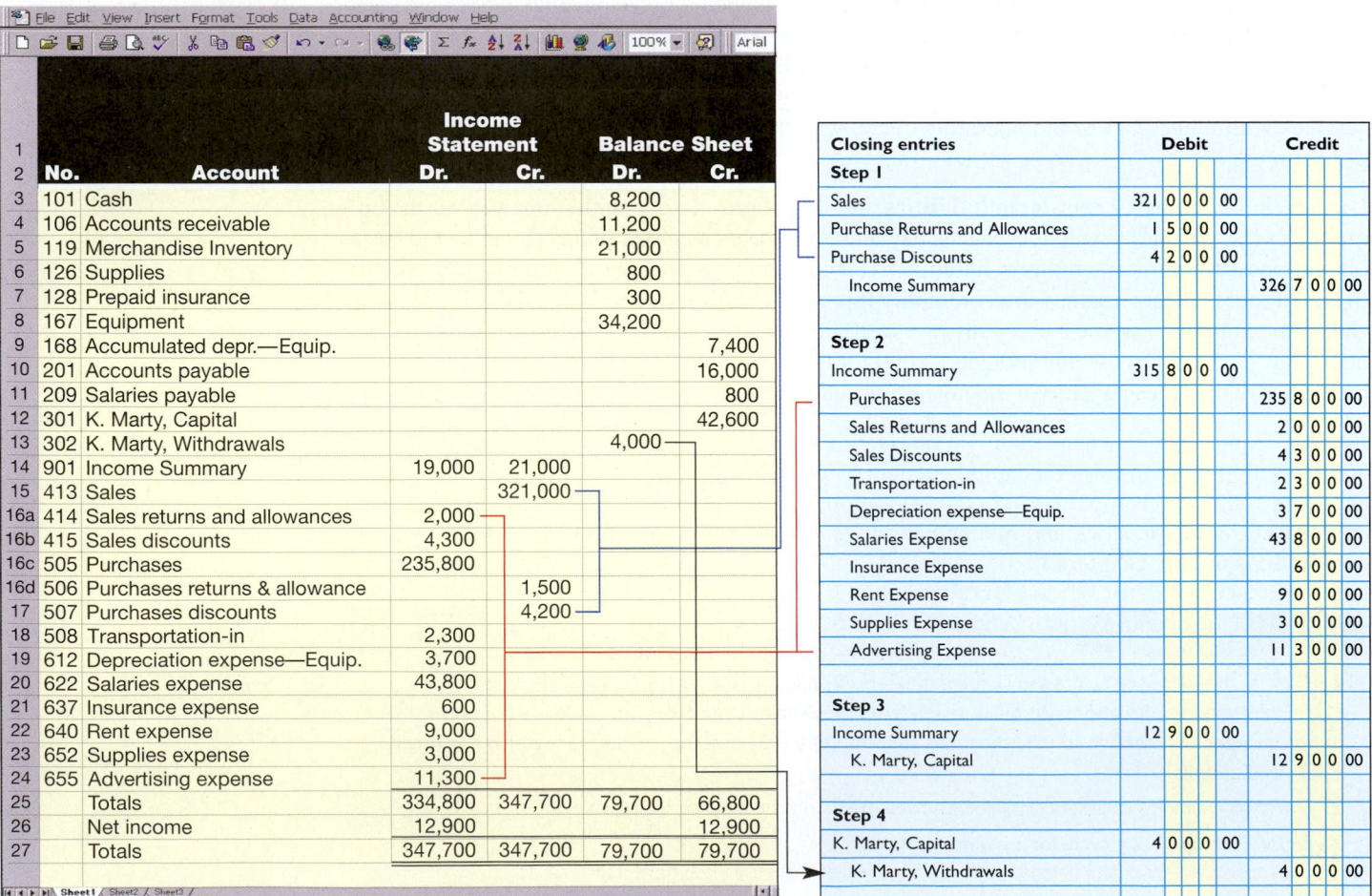

The closing entries are all posted to general ledger accounts as we showed in Chapter 6. In Exhibit 14.8 below we show the posting of closing entries to just the Income Summary account. In addition, we post the adjusting entries to Income Summary for the beginning and ending merchandise inventory balances (from Chapter 13). After posting these adjusting and closing entries, the Income Summary account should have a zero balance, as we show in Exhibit 14.8.

Income Summary				Account No. 901
Date	Explanation	Debit	Credit	Balance
2010 Dec. 31	Adjusting (BI)	19,000		19,000
Dec. 31	Adjusting (EI)		21,000	(2,000)
Dec. 31	Closing (Step 1)		326,700	(328,700)
Dec. 31	Closing (Step 2)	315,800		(12,900)
Dec. 31	Closing (Step 3)	12,900		-0-

Exhibit 14.8

Postings to Income Summary Account

Post-Closing Trial Balance

After journalizing and posting the closing entries a post-closing trial balance is prepared using the balances in the **permanent** accounts from the work sheet. Since all the temporary accounts have been closed, they have zero balances and do not appear on the post-closing trial balance. Recall that the work sheet does not have an updated balance for the owner's capital account; this can be obtained from the statement of owner's equity (see Exhibit 14.4) or from the general ledger.

The post-closing trial balance is used to prove that total debits equal total credits in the permanent accounts in the general ledger. Exhibit 14.9 presents Z-Mart's post-closing trial balance at December 31, 2010.

LO6 Prepare a post-closing trial balance.

Z-MART Post-Closing Trial Balance December 31, 2010		
Account	**Debit**	**Credit**
Cash	$ 8,200	
Accounts receivable	11,200	
Merchandise inventory	21,000	
Supplies	800	
Prepaid insurance	300	
Equipment	34,200	
Accumulated depreciation—Equipment		$ 7,400
Accounts payable		16,000
Salaries payable		800
K. Marty, Capital		51,500
Totals	$75,700	$75,700

Exhibit 14.9

Z-Mart Post-Closing Trial Balance

The final optional step in the accounting cycle is to prepare reversing entries. Some companies use reversing entries in preparation for the next accounting period. Reversing entries are discussed in the appendix to this chapter.

HOW YOU DOIN'?   Answers—p. 358

4. What temporary accounts do you expect to find in a merchandising business but not in a service business?

5. Describe the closing entries normally made by a merchandising company.

Demonstration Problem

Presented below is the adjusted trial balance for Worker Products Company as of December 31, 2010. The company started the year with a balance of $24,000 in Merchandise Inventory.

WORKER PRODUCTS COMPANY Adjusted Trial Balance December 31, 2010		
	Debit	**Credit**
Cash	$ 9,400	
Accounts receivable	25,000	
Merchandise inventory	36,000	
Office supplies	900	
Store equipment	75,000	
Accumulated depreciation—store equipment		$ 22,000
Office equipment	60,000	
Accumulated depreciation—office equipment		15,000
Accounts payable		42,000
Notes payable		10,000
F. Worker, Capital		110,700
F. Worker, Withdrawals	48,000	
Income Summary		12,000
Sales		325,000
Sales discounts	6,000	
Sales returns and allowances	16,500	
Purchases	210,000	
Purchase discounts		2,500
Purchase returns and allowances		1,500
Transportation-in	1,000	
Sales salaries expense	32,500	
Depreciation expense—store equipment	11,000	
Depreciation expense—office equipment	7,500	
Office supplies expense	1,300	
Interest expense	600	
Totals	$540,700	$540,700

Required

1. Prepare a multiple-step income statement in good form.
2. Prepare the necessary closing entries.

Planning the Solution

- Classify each income statement item as either a component of (1) gross profit, (2) income from operations, or (3) net income.
- Classify operating expenses into either selling or general and administrative.
- Use Exhibit 14.2 as a guide for the format of a multiple-step income statement.
- Follow the four steps for recording the closing entries.

Solution to Demonstration Problem

1. Multiple-step income statement

WORKER PRODUCTS COMPANY			
Income Statement			
For the Year Ended December 31, 2010			
Sales			$325,000
Less: Sales discounts		$ 6,000	
Sales returns and allowances		16,500	22,500
Net sales			$302,500
Merchandise inventory, 12/31/09		24,000	
Purchases	210,000		
Transportation-in	1,000		
Less: Purchase discounts	(2,500)		
Purchase returns and allowances	(1,500)		
Net purchases		207,000	
Goods available for sale		231,000	
Less: Merchandise inventory, 12/31/10		(36,000)	
Cost of goods sold			195,000
Gross profit			107,500
Operating expenses			
Selling expenses			
Sales salaries expense		32,500	
Depreciation expense—store equipment		11,000	
Total selling expenses		43,500	
General and administrative expenses			
Depreciation expense—office equipment		7,500	
Office supplies expense		1,300	
Total general and administrative expenses		8,800	
Total operating expenses			52,300
Income from operations			55,200
Other expenses			
Interest expense			600
Net income			$ 54,600

2. Closing journal entries

	Debit	Credit
Sales	325 0 0 0 00	
Purchase Returns and Allowances	1 5 0 0 00	
Purchase Discounts	2 5 0 0 00	
Income Summary		329 0 0 0 00
To close temporary accounts having credit balances		
Income Summary	286 4 0 0 00	
Purchases		210 0 0 0 00
Sales Returns and Allowances		16 5 0 0 00
Sales Discounts		6 0 0 0 00
Transportation-In		1 0 0 0 00
Depreciation Expense—Store Equipment		11 0 0 0 00
Depreciation Expense—Office Equipment		7 5 0 0 00
Sales Salaries Expense		32 5 0 0 00
Office Supplies Expense		1 3 0 0 00
Interest Expense		6 0 0 00
To close temporary accounts having debit balances		
Income Summary	54 6 0 0 00	
F. Worker, Capital		54 6 0 0 00
To close Income Summary		
F. Worker, Capital	48 0 0 0 00	
F. Worker, Withdrawals		48 0 0 0 00
To close owner withdrawals		

APPENDIX 14A

Reversing Entries

Reversing entries are optional. They are recorded in response to accrued assets and accrued liabilities that were created by adjusting entries at the end of a reporting period. The purpose of reversing entries is to simplify a company's recordkeeping. Exhibit 14A.1 shows an example of FastForward's (a company

Exhibit 14A.1

Reversing Entries for an Accrued Expense

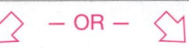

Accrue salaries expense on December 31, 2010

| Salaries Expense | 210 | |
| Salaries Payable | | 210 |

Salaries Expense

Date	Expl.	Debit	Credit	Balance
2010				
Dec. 12		700		700
26		700		1,400
31		210		1,610

Salaries Payable

Date	Expl.	Debit	Credit	Balance
2010				
Dec. 31			210	210

— OR —

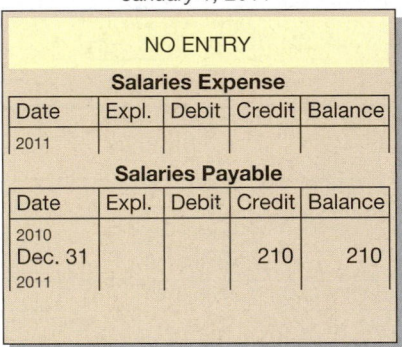

No reversing entry recorded on January 1, 2011

| NO ENTRY | | | | |

Salaries Expense

Date	Expl.	Debit	Credit	Balance
2011				

Salaries Payable

Date	Expl.	Debit	Credit	Balance
2010				
Dec. 31			210	210
2011				

Reversing entry recorded on January 1, 2011

| Salaries Payable | 210 | |
| Salaries Expense | | 210 |

Salaries Expense*

Date	Expl.	Debit	Credit	Balance
2011				
Jan. 1			210	(210)

Salaries Payable

Date	Expl.	Debit	Credit	Balance
2010				
Dec. 31			210	210
2011				
Jan. 1		210		0

Pay the accrued and current salaries on January 9, the first payday in 2011

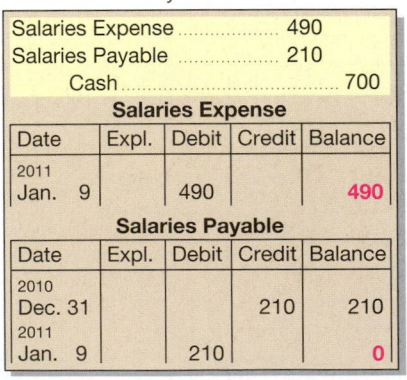

Salaries Expense	490	
Salaries Payable	210	
Cash		700

Salaries Expense

Date	Expl.	Debit	Credit	Balance
2011				
Jan. 9		490		**490**

Salaries Payable

Date	Expl.	Debit	Credit	Balance
2010				
Dec. 31			210	210
2011				
Jan. 9		210		**0**

| Salaries Expense | 700 | |
| Cash | | 700 |

Salaries Expense*

Date	Expl.	Debit	Credit	Balance
2011				
Jan. 1			210	(210)
Jan. 9		700		**490**

Salaries Payable

Date	Expl.	Debit	Credit	Balance
2010				
Dec. 31			210	210
2011				
Jan. 1		210		**0**

Under both approaches, the expense and liability accounts have identical balances after the cash payment on January 9.

| Salaries Expense | $490 |
| Salaries Payable | $ 0 |

*Circled numbers in the *Balance* column indicate abnormal balances.

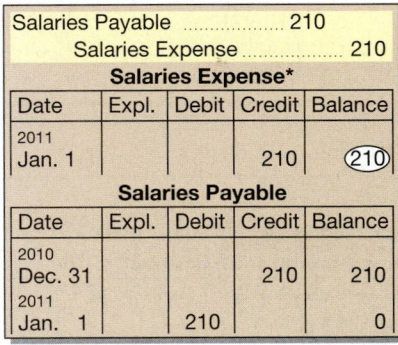

whose transactions we examined in detail in Chapters 2 through 6) reversing entries. The top of the exhibit shows the adjusting entry FastForward recorded on December 31 for its employee's earned but unpaid salary. We explained this entry in Chapter 5. The entry recorded three days' salary of $210, which increased December's total salary expense to $1,610. The entry also recognized a liability of $210. The expense is reported on December's income statement. The expense account is then closed. The ledger on January 1, 2010, shows a $210 liability and a zero balance in the Salaries Expense account. At this point, the choice is made between using or not using reversing entries.

> As a general rule, adjusting entries that create new asset or liability accounts are likely candidates for reversing.

Accounting *without* Reversing Entries

The path down the left side of Exhibit 14A.1 is described in the chapter. To summarize here, when the next payday occurs on January 9, we record payment with a compound entry that debits both the expense and liability accounts and credits Cash. Posting that entry creates a $490 balance in the expense account and reduces the liability account balance to zero because the payable has been settled. The disadvantage of this approach is the slightly more complex entry required on January 9. Paying the accrued liability means that this entry differs from the routine entries made on all other paydays. To construct the proper entry on January 9, we must recall the effect of the December 31 adjusting entry. Reversing entries overcome this disadvantage.

Accounting *with* Reversing Entries

The right side of Exhibit 14A.1 shows how reversing entries can be helpful. *A reversing entry is the exact opposite of an adjusting entry.* For FastForward, the Salaries Payable liability account is debited for $210, meaning that this account now has a zero balance after the entry is posted. The Salaries Payable account temporarily understates the liability, but this is not a problem since financial statements are not prepared before the liability is settled on January 9. The credit to the Salaries Expense account is unusual because it gives the account an *abnormal credit balance*. We highlight an abnormal balance by circling it. Because of the reversing entry, the January 9 entry to record payment is straightforward. This entry debits the Salaries Expense account and credits Cash for the full $700 paid. It is the same as all other entries made to record 10 days' salary for the employee. Notice that after the payment entry is posted, the Salaries Expense account has a $490 balance that reflects seven days' salary of $70 per day (see the lower right side of Exhibit 14A.1). The zero balance in the Salaries Payable account is now correct. The lower section of Exhibit 14A.1 shows that the expense and liability accounts have exactly the same balances whether reversing entries are used or not. This means that both approaches yield identical results.

LO7 Prepare reversing entries and explain their purpose.

Summary

LO1 **Prepare a work sheet for a merchandising business.** A work sheet can be useful in organizing data, preparing financial statements, and preparing closing entries. The work sheet includes columns for the unadjusted trial balance, the adjusting entries, and the adjusted trial balance. Balances in the adjusted trial balance columns are then extended into either income statement or balance sheet columns.

LO2 **Define and prepare multiple-step and single-step income statements.** Multiple-step income statements include greater detail for sales, purchases, and expenses than do single-step income statements. Multiple-step income statements often report expenses in categories reflecting different activities.

LO3 **Prepare a statement of owner's equity.** The statement of owner's equity is used to summarize changes in the owner's capital account during the year. The beginning balance of owner's capital is updated for the net income or loss for the period, additional owner investments during the period, and any owner withdrawals during the period. The ending balance of owner's capital is included on the end of period balance sheet.

LO4 **Explain and prepare a classified balance sheet.** Classified balance sheets report assets and liabilities in two categories: current and noncurrent. Current assets often include cash, accounts receivable, and merchandise inventory. Noncurrent assets often include long-term investments, plant assets, and intangible assets. Current liabilities often include accounts payable and wages payable. Noncurrent liabilities often include notes payable, bonds payable, and leases.

LO5 **Prepare journal entries to close temporary accounts.** Closing entries involve four steps: (1) close temporary accounts having credit balances to Income Summary, (2) close temporary accounts having debit balances to Income Summary, (3) close Income Summary to the owner's capital account, and (4) close the owner withdrawals account to the owner's capital account.

LO6 **Prepare a post-closing trial balance.** After journalizing and posting the closing entries, a trial balance is prepared using the ending balances in the permanent accounts. This post-closing trial balance proves the equality of debits and credits in the general ledger.

LO7 **Prepare reversing entries and explain their purpose.** Reversing entries are an optional step in the accounting cycle. They are applied to accrued expenses and revenues. The purpose of reversing entries is to simplify subsequent journal entries. Financial statements are not affected by the choice to use or not use reversing entries.

Guidance Answers to HOW YOU DOIN'?

1. Current assets: (*b*), (*c*), (*d*). Plant assets: (*a*), (*e*). Item (*f*) is an intangible asset.

2. Investment in common stock, investment in bonds, and land held for future expansion.

3. For a service company, the operating cycle is the usual time between (1) paying employees who do the services and (2) receiving cash from customers for services provided.

4. Purchase Discounts, Purchase Returns and Allowances, Transportation-in, Sales, Sales Returns and Allowances, and Sales Discounts.

5. Four closing entries: (1) close temporary accounts with credit balances to Income Summary, (2) close temporary accounts with debit balances to Income Summary, (3) close Income Summary to owner's capital, and (4) close withdrawals account to owner's capital.

Key Terms

Classified balance sheet (p. 349) Balance sheet that presents assets and liabilities in relevant subgroups, including current and noncurrent classifications.

Current assets (p. 351) Cash and other assets expected to be sold, collected, or used within one year or the company's operating cycle, whichever is longer.

Current liabilities (p. 351) Obligations due to be paid or settled within one year or the company's operating cycle, whichever is longer.

General and administrative expenses (p. 348) Expenses that support the operating activities of a business.

Intangible assets (p. 351) Long-term assets (resources) used to produce or sell products or services; usually lack physical form and have uncertain benefits.

Long-term investments (p. 351) Long-term assets not used in operating activities such as notes receivable and investments in stocks and bonds.

Long-term liabilities (p. 351) Obligations not due to be paid within one year or the operating cycle, whichever is longer.

Multiple-step income statement (p. 347) Income statement format that shows subtotals between sales and net income, categorizes expenses, and often reports the details of net sales and expenses.

Operating cycle (p. 350) Normal time between paying cash for merchandise or employee services and receiving cash from customers.

Reversing entries (p. 356) Optional entries recorded at the beginning of a period that prepare the accounts for the usual journal entries as if adjusting entries had not occurred in the prior period.

Selling expenses (p. 347) Expenses of promoting sales, such as displaying and advertising merchandise, making sales, and delivering goods to customers.

Single-step income statement (p. 349) Income statement format that includes cost of goods sold as an expense and shows only one subtotal for total expenses.

Unclassified balance sheet (p. 349) Balance sheet that broadly groups assets, liabilities, and equity accounts.

Multiple Choice Quiz   Answers on p. 367   mhhe.com/wildCA2e

Additional Multiple Choice Quizzes are available at the book's Website.

1. A company has $550,000 in net sales and $123,000 in gross profit. Its cost of goods sold equals
  a. $427,000   **d.** $123,000
  b. $673,000   **e.** ($123,000)
  c. $550,000

2. J. Awn, the proprietor of Awn Services, withdrew $8,700 from the business during the current year. The entry to close the withdrawals account at the end of the year is

a.	J. Awn, Withdrawals	8,700	
	Cash		8,700
b.	J. Awn, Capital	8,700	
	J. Awn, Withdrawals		8,700
c.	J. Awn, Withdrawals	8,700	
	J. Awn, Capital		8,700
d.	J. Awn, Capital	8,700	
	Salary Expense		8,700
e.	Income Summary	8,700	
	J. Awn, Capital		8,700

3. An income statement that includes cost of goods sold as another expense and shows only one subtotal for total expenses is a

  a. Balanced income statement.
  b. Single-step income statement.
  c. Multiple-step income statement.
  d. Combined income statement.
  e. Simplified income statement.

4. A classified balance sheet
  a. Measures a company's ability to pay its bills on time.
  b. Organizes assets and liabilities into important subgroups.
  c. Presents revenues, expenses, and net income.
  d. Reports operating, investing, and financing activities.
  e. Reports the effect of profit and withdrawals on owner's capital.

5. A company shows a $60,000 debit balance in Merchandise Inventory in the Unadjusted Trial Balance columns of the work sheet. The company uses a periodic inventory system. This $60,000 balance represents
  a. The amount of inventory at the beginning of the year.
  b. Cost of goods sold for the year.
  c. The cost of merchandise purchased during the year.
  d. The amount of inventory at the end of the year.
  e. Sales returns and allowances.

Superscript letter ^A denotes assignments based on Appendix 14A.

Discussion Questions

1. What is a company's operating cycle?

2. What classes of assets and liabilities are shown on a typical classified balance sheet?

3. How is unearned revenue classified on the balance sheet?

4. What are the characteristics of plant assets?

5. What is the difference between the single-step and multiple-step income statement formats?

6.^AHow do reversing entries simplify recordkeeping?

7.^AIf a company recorded accrued salaries expense of $500 at the end of its fiscal year, what reversing entry could be made? When would it be made?

8. Refer to the balance sheet for **Best Buy** in Appendix A. What five noncurrent asset categories are used on its classified balance sheet?

9. Refer to Best Buy's balance sheet in Appendix A. Identify the accounts listed as current liabilities.

---

connect

The following are common categories on a classified balance sheet.

A. Current assets   **D.** Intangible assets

B. Long-term investments   **E.** Current liabilities

C. Plant assets   **F.** Long-term liabilities

For each of the following items, select the letter that identifies the balance sheet category where the item typically would appear. Some letters are used more than once.

_____ **1.** Land not currently used in operations

_____ **2.** Notes payable (due in three years)

_____ **3.** Accounts receivable

_____ **4.** Trademarks

_____ **5.** Accounts payable

_____ **6.** Store equipment

_____ **7.** Wages payable

_____ **8.** Cash

QUICK STUDY

QS 14–1
Classifying balance sheet items
LO4

List the following steps in preparing a work sheet in their proper order by writing numbers 1–5 in the blank spaces provided.

a. _____ Total the statement columns, compute net income (loss), and complete work sheet.

b. _____ Extend adjusted balances to appropriate financial statement columns.

c. _____ Prepare an unadjusted trial balance on the work sheet.

d. _____ Prepare an adjusted trial balance on the work sheet.

e. _____ Enter adjustments data on the work sheet.

QS 14–2
Ordering work sheet steps
LO1

Match the following terms A through J with the appropriate definitions 1 through 10.

A. Plant assets   **F.** Closing entries

B. Owner's capital   **G.** Current liabilities

C. Classified balance sheet   **H.** Long-term investments

D. Intangible assets   **I.** Current assets

E. Operating cycle   **J.** Unclassified balance sheet

_____ **1.** The owner's claim on the assets of a company.

_____ **2.** Tangible long-lived assets used to produce or sell products or services.

_____ **3.** Cash or other assets that are expected to be sold, collected, or used within one year or the company's operating cycle, whichever is longer.

_____ **4.** Entries recorded at the end of each accounting period to transfer end-of-period balances in revenue, expense, and withdrawals accounts to the permanent owner's capital account.

_____ **5.** Long-term assets used to produce or sell products or services; these assets usually lack physical form and their benefits are uncertain.

_____ **6.** Assets such as notes receivable or investments in stocks which are held for the longer of one year or the operating cycle of the company.

_____ **7.** A balance sheet that organizes the assets and liabilities into important subgroups.

_____ **8.** Obligations that are due to be paid or settled within one year or the operating cycle of a business, whichever is longer.

QS 14–3
Balance sheet classifications
LO4

_____ **9.** A balance sheet that broadly groups assets, liabilities, and equity items.

_____ **10.** The time it takes a merchandiser to go from paying cash to buy goods to receiving cash from selling those goods.

QS 14-4

Income statement terms **LO2**

Match the following terms **A** through **E** with the appropriate definitions 1 through 5.

A. Merchandise inventory
D. Multiple-step income statement
B. Single-step income statement
E. General and administrative expenses
C. Selling expenses

_____ **1.** An income statement format that shows only one subtotal for total expenses.

_____ **2.** Products a company owns and intends to sell.

_____ **3.** Expenses that support overall operations and includes expenses related to accounting, human resource management, and financial management.

_____ **4.** An income statement format that shows detailed computations of net sales and other costs and expenses, and reports subtotals for various classes of items.

_____ **5.** The expenses of promoting sales by displaying and advertising merchandise, making sales, and delivering goods to customers.

QS 14-5

Net sales section of the income statement **LO2**

EL Merchandising reports the (partial) adjusted trial balance information below for the year ending December 31, 2010. Prepare the net sales section of a multiple-step income statement for EL Merchandising for 2010.

Merchandise inventory	$ 25,000
E. Lynn, Capital, ...	70,000
E. Lynn, Withdrawals	33,000
Operating expenses	150,000
Purchases	208,500
Purchase discounts	4,250
Purchase returns and allowances	6,250
Sales	384,250
Sales discounts	7,750
Sales returns and allowances	1,500
Transportation-in	2,000

QS 14-6

Cost of goods sold section of the income statement **LO2**

Refer to the data in Quick Study 14-5. In addition, EL Merchandising reports an inventory balance of $30,000 on January 1, 2010. Prepare the cost of goods sold section of a multiple-step income statement for EL Merchandising for 2010.

QS 14-7

Statement of owner's equity

LO3

Refer to the data in Quick Study 14-5. EL Merchandising reports net income of $120,000 for 2010. Prepare the statement of owner's equity for 2010.

QS 14-8

Post-closing trial balance **LO6**

Refer to the data in Quick Study 14-5. What accounts would appear on EL Merchandising's December 31, 2010, post-closing trial balance?

QS 14-9

Closing entries **LO5**

Refer to the data in Quick Study 14-5. Prepare the journal entries to close EL Merchandising's temporary accounts on December 31, 2010.

QS 14-10[A]

Reversing entries **LO7**

On December 31, 2010, Yates Co. prepared an adjusting entry for $12,000 of earned but unrecorded management fees. On January 16, 2011, Yates received $26,700 cash in management fees, which included the accrued fees earned in 2010. Assuming the company uses reversing entries, prepare the January 1, 2011, reversing entry and the January 16, 2011, cash receipt entry.

connect

Use the following post-closing trial balance of Jones Merchandising Company to prepare a statement of owner's equity for 2010. Net income for 2010 was $25,500. K. Jones withdrew $20,000 during the year. (*Hint:* Solve for beginning K. Jones, Capital).

Account Title	Debit	Credit
Cash	$ 18,000	
Accounts receivable	17,500	
Merchandise inventory	85,000	
Office supplies	3,000	
Trucks	172,000	
Accumulated depreciation—Trucks		$ 36,000
Accounts payable		37,500
Interest payable		4,000
Long-term notes payable (all due in 2014)		53,000
K. Jones, Capital		165,000
Totals	$295,500	$295,500

Use the information in the post-closing trial balance reported in Exercise 14-1 to prepare Jones Merchandising Company's classified balance sheet as of December 31, 2010.

Listed below are a number of accounts. Use the table to classify each account. Indicate whether it is a temporary or permanent account (T or P), whether it is included in the income statement or balance sheet (IS or BS), whether it is closed at the end of the accounting period, and if so, how it is closed (Dr. or Cr. entry). The first one is done as an example.

Account	Permanent (P) or Temporary (T)	Income Statement (IS) or Balance Sheet (BS)	Closed (C) or Not Closed (NC)	Closed with a Debit (Dr) or Credit (CR)
a. Accounts payable	P	BS	NC	—
b. Accounts receivable				
c. Accumulated depreciation—equipment				
d. Advertising expense				
e. Cash				
f. Depreciation expense—equipment				
g. Equipment				
h. Insurance expense				
i. Interest expense				
j. Merchandise inventory (ending balance)				
k. Notes payable				
l. Office supplies				
m. Office supplies expense				
n. Purchases				
o. Purchase returns				
p. Owner, capital				
q. Owner, withdrawals				
r. Salaries expense				
s. Sales				
t. Sales discounts				
u. Transportation-in				

EXERCISES

Exercise 14-1
Preparing a statement of owner's equity **L03**

Exercise 14-2
Preparing a classified balance sheet **L04**

Check   Total assets, $259,500; K. Jones, Capital, $165,000

Exercise 14-3
L01   L05

Exercise 14-4
Preparing classified balance sheets
LO4

Based on the post-closing trial balance shown below, prepare a classified balance sheet for J-Mart as of December 31. Net income for 2010 was $63,700.

J-MART Post-Closing Trial Balance December 31		
	Debit	**Credit**
Cash	$ 18,200	
Accounts receivable	34,200	
Supplies	2,100	
Merchandise inventory	25,000	
Delivery equipment	45,000	
Accumulated depreciation—delivery equipment		$ 11,080
Intangible assets	16,000	
Accounts payable		16,200
Wages payable		4,120
Long-term notes payable*		20,000
Emily Jacobs, Capital		89,100
Totals	$140,500	$140,500

* $2,000 of the long-term note payable is due during the next year.

Exercise 14-5
Preparing the multiple-step income statement   **LO2**

JK Products reports the following adjusted trial balance at December 31, 2010, the end of its first year of operations. Prepare a multiple-step income statement for the year ending December 31, 2010.

JK PRODUCTS Adjusted Trial Balance December 31, 2010		
Account	**Debit**	**Credit**
Cash	$ 8,250	
Accounts receivable	12,400	
Merchandise inventory	17,650	
Office equipment	90,000	
Less: Accumulated depreciation		$ 22,500
Accounts payable		8,500
Salaries payable		4,250
Notes payable (long-term)		60,000
J. Kwon, Capital		59,250
J. Kwon, Withdrawals	30,000	
Income summary	40,000	17,650
Sales		433,500
Sales discounts	41,250	
Sales returns and allowances	12,250	
Purchases	285,000	
Purchase discounts		32,500
Purchase returns and allowances		15,250
Transportation-in	22,750	
Advertising expense	21,000	
Depreciation expense—office equipment	22,500	
Interest expense	8,000	
Rent expense	12,000	
Sales salaries expense	30,350	
Total	$653,400	$653,400

Check   Net income, $3,800

Refer to the data in Exercise 14-5. JK Products' cost of goods sold was $282,350 for 2010. Prepare a single-step income statement for the year ending December 31, 2010.

Exercise 14-6
Preparing the single-step income statement   **LO2**

Refer to the data in Exercise 14-5. JK's net income for 2010 was $3,800. Prepare the statement of owner's equity for 2010.

Exercise 14-7
Preparing the statement of owner's equity   **LO3**

Refer to the data in Exercise 14-5. The December 31, 2010, ending balance in the J. Kwon capital account after closing entries have been posted is $33,050. Prepare a classified balance sheet as of December 31, 2010.

Exercise 14-8
Preparing the classified balance sheet   **LO4**

Check   Total assets, $105,800

Refer to the data in Exercise 14-5. The December 31, 2010, ending balance in the J. Kwon capital account after closing entries have been posted is $33,050. Prepare a post-closing trial balance as of December 31, 2010.

Exercise 14-9
Post-closing trial balance   **LO6**

Check   T.B. totals $128,300

Hawk Company records prepaid assets and unearned revenues in balance sheet accounts. The following information was used to prepare adjusting entries for Hawk Company as of August 31, the end of the company's fiscal year.

a. The company has earned $6,000 in unrecorded service fees.

b. The expired portion of prepaid insurance is $3,700.

c. The company has earned $2,900 of its Unearned Service Fees account balance.

d. Depreciation expense for office equipment is $3,300.

e. Employees have earned but have not been paid salaries of $3,400.

Prepare any necessary reversing entries for the accounting adjustments *a* through *e* assuming that Hawk uses reversing entries in its accounting system.

Exercise 14-10ᴬ
Preparing reversing entries   **LO7**

connect

In the blank space beside each numbered balance sheet item, enter the letter of its balance sheet classification. If the item should not appear on the balance sheet, enter a *Z* in the blank.

PROBLEM SET A

Problem 14-1A
Determining balance sheet classifications   **LO4**

A. Current assets   **D.** Intangible assets   **F.** Long-term liabilities
B. Long-term investments   **E.** Current liabilities   **G.** Equity
C. Plant assets

_____ **1.** Long-term investment in stock
_____ **2.** Sales
_____ **3.** Merchandise inventory
_____ **4.** Interest receivable
_____ **5.** Sales discounts
_____ **6.** Automobiles
_____ **7.** Notes payable (due in 3 years)
_____ **8.** Accounts payable
_____ **9.** Prepaid insurance
_____ **10.** Owner, Capital
_____ **11.** Unearned revenue

_____ **12.** Accumulated depreciation—Trucks
_____ **13.** Cash
_____ **14.** Buildings
_____ **15.** Store supplies
_____ **16.** Office equipment
_____ **17.** Land (used in operations)
_____ **18.** Purchases
_____ **19.** Office supplies
_____ **20.** Current portion of long-term note payable

Problem 14-2A
Computing merchandising amounts and formatting income statements
LO1　LO2

Cacuango Company's adjusted trial balance on August 31, 2010, its fiscal year-end, follows.

	Debit	Credit
Merchandise inventory	$ 41,000	
Other (noninventory) assets	130,400	
Total liabilities		$ 25,000
C. Cacuango, Capital		104,550
C. Cacuango, Withdrawals	8,000	
Income summary	25,400	41,000
Sales		225,600
Sales discounts	2,250	
Sales returns and allowances	12,000	
Purchases	92,000	
Purchase discounts		2,000
Purchase returns and allowances		4,500
Transportation-in	4,600	
Sales salaries expense	32,000	
Rent expense—Selling space	8,000	
Store supplies expense	1,500	
Advertising expense	13,000	
Office salaries expense	28,500	
Rent expense—Office space	3,600	
Office supplies expense	400	
Totals	$402,650	$402,650

On August 31, 2009, merchandise inventory was $25,400.

Required

1. Compute the company's net sales for the year.

2. Compute the company's total cost of net purchases for the year.

3. Prepare a multiple-step income statement that includes separate categories for selling expenses and for general and administrative expenses.

4. Prepare a single-step income statement that includes these expense categories: cost of goods sold, selling expenses, and general and administrative expenses.

Problem 14-3A
Preparing closing entries
LO5

Use the data for Cacuango Company in Problem 14-2A to complete the following requirements.

Required

Prepare closing entries as of August 31, 2010.

In the blank space beside each numbered balance sheet item, enter the letter of its balance sheet classification. If the item should not appear on the balance sheet, enter a Z in the blank.

A. Current assets
B. Long-term investments
C. Plant assets
D. Intangible assets

E. Current liabilities
F. Long-term liabilities
G. Equity

_____ **1.** Sales
_____ **2.** Interest receivable
_____ **3.** Long-term investment in stock
_____ **4.** Merchandise inventory
_____ **5.** Machinery
_____ **6.** Notes payable (due in 15 years)
_____ **7.** Copyrights
_____ **8.** Current portion of long-term note payable
_____ **9.** Accumulated depreciation—Trucks
_____ **10.** Office equipment
_____ **11.** Rent receivable
_____ **12.** Salaries payable
_____ **13.** Purchase discounts
_____ **14.** Owner, Capital
_____ **15.** Office supplies
_____ **16.** Interest payable
_____ **17.** Rent expense
_____ **18.** Notes receivable (due in 120 days)
_____ **19.** Land (used in operations)
_____ **20.** Transportation-in

White Company's adjusted trial balance on March 31, 2010, its fiscal year-end, follows.

	Debit	Credit
Merchandise inventory	$ 56,500	
Other (noninventory) assets	202,600	
Total liabilities		$ 42,500
J. White, Capital		164,425
J. White, Withdrawals	3,000	
Income summary	37,500	56,500
Sales		332,650
Sales discounts	5,875	
Sales returns and allowances	20,000	
Purchases	138,500	
Purchase discounts		2,950
Purchase returns and allowances		6,700
Transportation-in	5,750	
Sales salaries expense	44,500	
Rent expense—Selling space	16,000	
Store supplies expense	3,850	
Advertising expense	26,000	
Office salaries expense	40,750	
Rent expense—Office space	3,800	
Office supplies expense	1,100	
Totals	$605,725	$605,725

On March 31, 2009, merchandise inventory was $37,500.

Required

1. Calculate the company's net sales for the year.
2. Calculate the company's total cost of net purchases for the year.
3. Prepare a multiple-step income statement that includes separate categories for selling expenses and for general and administrative expenses.
4. Prepare a single-step income statement that includes these expense categories: cost of goods sold, selling expenses, and general and administrative expenses.

Problem 14-3B
Preparing closing entries
LO5

Use the data for White Company in Problem 14-2B to complete the following requirements:

Required

Prepare closing entries as of March 31, 2010.

SERIAL PROBLEM

Success Systems

(This serial problem began in Chapter 1 and continues through most of the book. If previous chapter segments were not completed, the serial problem can begin at this point. It is helpful, but not necessary, that you use the Working Papers that accompany the book.)

SP 14 The March 31, 2011, adjusted trial balance of Success Systems (reflecting its transactions from October 2010 through March of 2011) follows.

No.	Account Title	Dr.	Cr.
101	Cash	$ 87,266	
106.1	Alex's Engineering Co.	0	
106.2	Wildcat Services	3,900	
106.3	Easy Leasing	11,000	
106.4	Clark Co.	4,800	
106.5	Chang Corporation	0	
106.6	Gomez Co.	0	
106.7	Delta Co.	0	
106.8	KC, Inc.	4,700	
106.9	Dream, Inc.	0	
106.10	Bob's Building Co.	0	
119	Merchandise inventory	680	
126	Computer supplies	1,950	
128	Prepaid insurance	1,200	
131	Prepaid rent	875	
163	Office equipment	10,000	
164	Accumulated depreciation—Office equipment		$ 1,250
167	Computer equipment	25,000	
168	Accumulated depreciation—Computer equip.		2,500
201	Accounts payable		0
210	Wages payable		1,050

No.	Account Title	Dr.	Cr.
236	Unearned computer services revenue		$ 0
301	A. Lopez, Capital		127,435
302	A. Lopez, Withdrawals	$ 5,200	
901	Income Summary		680
403	Computer services revenue		31,850
413	Sales		20,900
414	Sales returns and allowances	500	
415	Sales discounts	55	
505	Purchases	15,200	
506	Purchase returns and allowances		496
507	Purchase discounts		152
508	Transportation-in	400	
612	Depreciation expense—Office equipment	625	
613	Depreciation expense—Computer equipment	1,250	
623	Wages expense	3,900	
637	Insurance expense	600	
640	Rent expense	2,625	
652	Computer supplies expense	2,075	
655	Advertising expense	800	
676	Mileage expense	512	
677	Miscellaneous expenses	0	
684	Repairs expense—Computer	1,200	
	Totals	$186,313	$186,313

Required

1. Record the necessary closing entries at March 31, 2011.
2. Prepare a single-step income statement for the three months ended March 31, 2011.
3. Prepare a statement of owner's equity for the three months ended March 31, 2011.
4. Prepare a classified balance sheet as of March 31, 2011.

BTN 14-1   Refer to **Best Buy**'s financial statements in Appendix A to answer the following.

Required

1. In its first footnote, Best Buy lists the primary costs classified in both costs of goods sold and selling, general, and administrative expenses. Give some examples of the primary costs included in each category.

REPORTING IN ACTION
LO2

BEST BUY

BTN 14-2   Access the SEC's EDGAR database (www.sec.gov) and obtain the March 23, 2009, filing of its fiscal 2008 10-K report (for year ended January 31, 2009) for **J. Crew Group, Inc**.

Required

Prepare a table that reports the gross profit amounts for J. Crew using the revenues and cost of goods sold data from J. Crew's income statement for each of its most recent three years. Analyze and comment on the trend in its gross profit amounts.

TAKING IT TO THE NET
LO4

BTN 14-3   Review this chapter's opening feature involving **RockBottomGolf.com**. Assume that Todd and Tom Rath want to expand their business to sell apparel for high-altitude camping. They plan on meeting with a bank for potential funding and have been asked by its loan officers for their financial statements.

Required

1. What type of financial statement information will the loan officers consider?
2. What information on the classified balance sheet would help the loan officers assess whether RockBottomGolf.com will be able to repay its loans?

ENTREPRENEURS IN BUSINESS
LO4

BTN 14-4   The controller of Orvil Corporation is contemplating a balance sheet which offers few details. He reasons that this will cause less questions from the company's shareholders. Does your analysis of this situation raise any concerns?

YOU CALL IT
LO4

1. a; $550,000 − $123,000 = $427,000
2. b
3. b
4. b
5. a

ANSWERS TO MULTIPLE CHOICE QUIZ

Appendix A

Financial Statement Information

This appendix includes financial information for (1) **Best Buy** and (2) **RadioShack**. This information is taken from their annual 10-K reports filed with the SEC. An **annual report** is a summary of a company's financial results for the year along with its current financial condition and future plans. This report is directed to external users of financial information, but it also affects the actions and decisions of internal users.

A company uses an annual report to showcase itself and its products. Many annual reports include attractive photos, diagrams, and illustrations related to the company. The primary objective of annual reports, however, is the *financial section,* which communicates much information about a company, with most data drawn from the accounting information system. The layout of an annual report's financial section is fairly established and typically includes the following:

- ■ Letter to Shareholders
- ■ Financial History and Highlights
- ■ Management Discussion and Analysis
- ■ Management's Report on Financial Statements and on Internal Controls
- ■ Report of Independent Accountants (Auditor's Report) and on Internal Controls
- ■ Financial Statements
- ■ Notes to Financial Statements
- ■ List of Directors and Officers

This appendix provides the financial statements for Best Buy (plus selected notes) and RadioShack. The appendix is organized as follows:

- ■ **Best Buy** **A-2** through **A-20**   ■ **RadioShack** **A-21** through **A-26**

Many assignments at the end of each chapter refer to information in this appendix. We encourage readers to spend time with these assignments; they are especially useful in showing the relevance and diversity of financial accounting and reporting.

> *Special note:* The SEC maintains the EDGAR (**E**lectronic **D**ata **G**athering, **A**nalysis, and **R**etrieval) database at **www.sec.gov**. The **Form 10-K** is the annual report form for most companies. It provides electronically accessible information. The **Form 10-KSB** is the annual report form filed by "small businesses." It requires slightly less information than the Form 10-K. One of these forms must be filed within 90 days after the company's fiscal year-end. (Forms 10-K405, 10-KT, 10-KT405, and 10-KSB405 are slight variations of the usual form due to certain regulations or rules.)

Financial Report

Selected Financial Data

The following table presents our selected financial data. Certain prior-year amounts have been reclassified to conform to the current-year presentation. In fiscal 2004, we sold our interest in Musicland. All fiscal years presented reflect the classification of Musicland's financial results as discontinued operations.

Five-Year Financial Highlights

$ in millions, except per share amounts

Fiscal Year	2008	2007	2006	2005	2004
Consolidated Statements of Earnings Data					
Revenue	$40,023	$35,934	$30,848	$27,433	$24,548
Operating income	2,161	1,999	1,644	1,442	1,304
Earnings from continuing operations	1,407	1,377	1,140	934	800
Loss from discontinued operations, net of tax	—	—	—	—	(29)
Gain (loss) on disposal of discontinued operations, net of tax	—	—	—	50	(66)
Net earnings	1,407	1,377	1,140	984	705
Per Share Data					
Continuing operations	$3.12	$2.79	$2.27	$1.86	$1.61
Discontinued operations	—	—	—	—	(0.06)
Gain (loss) on disposal of discontinued operations	—	—	—	0.10	(0.13)
Net earnings	3.12	2.79	2.27	1.96	1.42
Cash dividends declared and paid	0.46	0.36	0.31	0.28	0.27
Common stock price:					
High	53.90	59.50	56.00	41.47	41.80
Low	41.85	43.51	31.93	29.25	17.03
Operating Statistics					
Comparable store sales gain	2.9%	5.0%	4.9%	4.3%	7.1%
Gross profit rate	23.9%	24.4%	25.0%	23.7%	23.9%
Selling, general and administrative expenses rate	18.5%	18.8%	19.7%	18.4%	18.6 %
Operating income rate	5.4%	5.6%	5.3%	5.3%	5.3%
Year-End Data					
Current ratio	1.1	1.4	1.3	1.4	1.3
Total assets	$12,758	$13,570	$11,864	$10,294	$8,652
Debt, including current portion	816	650	596	600	850
Total shareholders' equity	4,484	6,201	5,257	4,449	3,422
Number of stores					
Domestic	971	873	774	694	631
International	343	304	167	144	127
Total	1,314	1,177	941	838	758
Retail square footage (000s)					
Domestic	37,511	34,092	30,874	28,513	26,699
International	11,069	9,419	4,652	4,057	3,587
Total	48,580	43,511	35,526	32,570	30,286

Fiscal 2007 included 53 weeks. All other periods presented included 52 weeks.

BEST BUY

Consolidated Balance Sheets

$ in millions, except per share amounts

	March 1, 2008	March 3, 2007
Assets		
Current Assets		
Cash and cash equivalents	$ 1,438	$ 1,205
Short-term investments	64	2,588
Receivables	549	548
Merchandise inventories	4,708	4,028
Other current assets	583	712
Total current assets	7,342	9,081
Property and Equipment		
Land and buildings	732	705
Leasehold improvements	1,752	1,540
Fixtures and equipment	3,057	2,627
Property under capital lease	67	32
	5,608	4,904
Less accumulated depreciation	2,302	1,966
Net property and equipment	3,306	2,938
Goodwill	1,088	919
Tradenames	97	81
Equity and Other Investments	605	338
Other Assets	320	213
Total Assets	$12,758	$13,570
Liabilities and Shareholders' Equity		
Current Liabilities		
Accounts payable	$ 4,297	$ 3,934
Unredeemed gift card liabilities	531	496
Accrued compensation and related expenses	373	332
Accrued liabilities	975	990
Accrued income taxes	404	489
Short-term debt	156	41
Current portion of long-term debt	33	19
Total current liabilities	6,769	6,301
Long-Term Liabilities	838	443
Long-Term Debt	627	590
Minority Interests	40	35
Shareholders' Equity		
Preferred stock, $1.00 par value: Authorized — 400,000 shares; Issued and outstanding — none	—	—
Common stock, $.10 par value: Authorized — 1.0 billion shares; Issued and outstanding — 410,578,000 and 480,655,000 shares, respectively	41	48
Additional paid-in capital	8	430
Retained earnings	3,933	5,507
Accumulated other comprehensive income	502	216
Total shareholders' equity	4,484	6,201
Total Liabilities and Shareholders' Equity	$12,758	$13,570

See Notes to Consolidated Financial Statements.

Consolidated Statements of Earnings
$ in millions, except per share amounts

For the Fiscal Years Ended	March 1, 2008	March 3, 2007	February 25, 2006
Revenue	$40,023	$35,934	$30,848
Cost of goods sold	30,477	27,165	23,122
Gross profit	9,546	8,769	7,726
Selling, general and administrative expenses	7,385	6,770	6,082
Operating income	2,161	1,999	1,644
Other income (expense)			
Investment income and other	129	162	107
Interest expense	(62)	(31)	(30)
Earnings before income tax expense, minority interest			
and equity in loss of affiliates	2,228	2,130	1,721
Income tax expense	815	752	581
Minority interest in earnings	(3)	(1)	—
Equity in loss of affiliates	(3)	—	—
Net earnings	$ 1,407	$ 1,377	$ 1,140
Earnings per share			
Basic	$ 3.20	$ 2.86	$ 2.33
Diluted	$ 3.12	$ 2.79	$ 2.27
Weighted-average common shares outstanding (in millions)			
Basic	439.9	482.1	490.3
Diluted	452.9	496.2	504.8

See Notes to Consolidated Financial Statements.

BEST BUY

Consolidated Statements of Cash Flows
$ in millions

For the Fiscal Years Ended	March 1, 2008	March 3, 2007	February 25, 2006
Operating Activities			
Net earnings	$1,407	$1,377	$1,140
Adjustments to reconcile net earnings to total cash provided by operating activities:			
Depreciation	580	509	456
Stock-based compensation	105	121	132
Deferred income taxes	74	82	(151)
Excess tax benefits from stock-based compensation	(24)	(50)	(55)
Other, net	(3)	21	1
Changes in operating assets and liabilities, net of acquired assets and liabilities:			
Receivables	12	(70)	(43)
Merchandise inventories	(562)	(550)	(457)
Other assets	42	(47)	(11)
Accounts payable	221	320	385
Other liabilities	74	185	165
Income taxes	99	(136)	178
Total cash provided by operating activities	2,025	1,762	1,740
Investing Activities			
Additions to property and equipment, net of $80, and $75 non-cash capital expenditures in fiscal 2008 and 2006, respectively	(797)	(733)	(648)
Purchases of investments	(8,501)	(4,789)	(4,561)
Sales of investments	10,935	5,095	4,362
Acquisitions of businesses, net of cash acquired	(89)	(421)	—
Change in restricted assets	(85)	63	47
Other, net	1	5	46
Total cash provided by (used in) investing activities	1,464	(780)	(754)
Financing Activities			
Repurchase of common stock	(3,461)	(599)	(772)
Issuance of common stock under employee stock purchase plan and for the exercise of stock options	146	217	292
Dividends paid	(204)	(174)	(151)
Repayments of debt	(4,353)	(84)	(69)
Proceeds from issuance of debt	4,486	96	36
Excess tax benefits from stock-based compensation	24	50	55
Other, net	(16)	(19)	(10)
Total cash used in financing activities	(3,378)	(513)	(619)
Effect of Exchange Rate Changes on Cash	122	(12)	27
Increase in Cash and Cash Equivalents	233	457	394
Cash and Cash Equivalents at Beginning of Year	1,205	748	354
Cash and Cash Equivalents at End of Year	$1,438	$1,205	$ 748
Supplemental Disclosure of Cash Flow Information			
Income taxes paid	$ 644	$ 804	$ 547
Interest paid	49	14	16

See Notes to Consolidated Financial Statements.

Consolidated Statements of Changes in Shareholders' Equity
$ and shares in millions

	Common Shares	Common Stock	Additional Paid-In Capital	Retained Earnings	Accumulated Other Comprehensive Income	Total
Balances at February 26, 2005	**493**	**$49**	**$936**	**$3,315**	**$149**	**$4,449**
Net earnings	—	—	—	1,140	—	1,140
Other comprehensive income, net of tax:						
Foreign currency translation adjustments	—	—	—	—	101	101
Unrealized gains on available-for-sale investments	—	—	—	—	11	11
Total comprehensive income						1,252
Stock options exercised	9	1	256	—	—	257
Tax benefit from stock options exercised and employee stock purchase plan	—	—	55	—	—	55
Issuance of common stock under employee stock purchase plan	1	—	35	—	—	35
Stock-based compensation	—	—	132	—	—	132
Common stock dividends, $0.31 per share	—	—	—	(151)	—	(151)
Repurchase of common stock	(18)	(1)	(771)	—	—	(772)
Balances at February 25, 2006	**485**	**49**	**643**	**4,304**	**261**	**5,257**
Net earnings	—	—	—	1,377	—	1,377
Other comprehensive loss, net of tax:						
Foreign currency translation adjustments	—	—	—	—	(33)	(33)
Unrealized losses on available-for-sale investments	—	—	—	—	(12)	(12)
Total comprehensive income						1,332
Stock options exercised	7	1	167	—	—	168
Tax benefit from stock options exercised and employee stock purchase plan	—	—	47	—	—	47
Issuance of common stock under employee stock purchase plan	1	—	49	—	—	49
Stock-based compensation	—	—	121	—	—	121
Common stock dividends, $0.36 per share	—	—	—	(174)	—	(174)
Repurchase of common stock	(12)	(2)	(597)	—	—	(599)
Balances at March 3, 2007	**481**	**48**	**430**	**5,507**	**216**	**6,201**
Net earnings	—	—	—	1,407	—	1,407
Other comprehensive income (loss), net of tax:						
Foreign currency translation adjustments	—	—	—	—	311	311
Unrealized losses on available-for-sale investments	—	—	—	—	(25)	(25)
Total comprehensive income						1,693
Cumulative effect of adopting a new accounting standard (Note 8)	—	—	—	(13)	—	(13)
Stock options exercised	4	—	93	—	—	93
Tax benefit from stock options exercised and employee stock purchase plan	—	—	17	—	—	17
Issuance of common stock under employee stock purchase plan	1	—	53	—	—	53
Stock-based compensation	—	—	105	—	—	105
Common stock dividends, $0.46 per share	—	—	—	(204)	—	(204)
Repurchase of common stock	(75)	(7)	(690)	(2,764)	—	(3,461)
Balances at March 1, 2008	**411**	**$41**	**$ 8**	**$3,933**	**$502**	**$4,484**

See Notes to Consolidated Financial Statements.

Notes to Consolidated Financial Statements

$ in millions, except per share amounts or as otherwise noted

1. Summary of Significant Accounting Policies

Description of Business

Best Buy is a specialty retailer of consumer electronics, home office products, entertainment software, appliances and related services, with fiscal 2008 revenue of $40.0 billion.

We operate two reportable segments: Domestic and International. The Domestic segment is comprised of all states, districts and territories of the U.S. and includes store, call center and online operations of Best Buy, Best Buy Mobile, Geek Squad, Magnolia Audio Video, Pacific Sales Kitchen and Bath Centers ("Pacific Sales") and Speakeasy ("Speakeasy").

The International segment is comprised of all Canada store, call center and online operations, including Best Buy, Future Shop and Geek Squad; all China store, call center and online operations, including Best Buy, Geek Squad and Jiangsu Five Star Appliance Co. ("Five Star"). The International segment offers products and services similar to those offered by our Domestic segment. However, Canada Best Buy stores do not carry appliances. Further, our China Best Buy store and Five Star stores do not carry entertainment software. At the end of fiscal 2008, the International segment operated 131 Future Shop stores and 51 Best Buy stores in Canada, and 160 Five Star stores and one Best Buy store in China.

In support of our retail store operations, we also maintain Web sites for each of our brands (BestBuy.com, BestBuy.ca, BestBuy.com.cn, BestBuyMobile.com, FiveStar.cn, FutureShop.ca, GeekSquad.com, GeekSquad.ca, MagnoliaAV.com, PacificSales.com, and Speakeasy.net).

Use of Estimates in the Preparation of Financial Statements

The preparation of financial statements in conformity with accounting principles generally accepted in the United States ("GAAP") requires us to make estimates and assumptions. These estimates and assumptions affect the reported amounts in the consolidated balance sheets and statements of earnings, as well as the disclosure of contingent liabilities. Future results could be materially affected if actual results were to differ from these estimates and assumptions.

Fiscal Year

Our fiscal year ends on the Saturday nearest the end of February. Fiscal 2008 and 2006 each included 52 weeks, and fiscal 2007 included 53 weeks.

Cash and Cash Equivalents

Cash primarily consists of cash on hand and bank deposits. Cash equivalents primarily consist of money market accounts and other highly liquid investments with an original maturity of three months or less when purchased. The amounts of cash equivalents at March 1, 2008, and March 3, 2007, were $871 and $695, respectively, and the weighted-average interest rates were 4.1% and 4.8%, respectively.

Outstanding checks in excess of funds on deposit (book overdrafts) totaled $159 and $183 at March 1, 2008, and March 3, 2007, respectively, and are reflected as current liabilities in our consolidated balance sheets.

Merchandise Inventories

Merchandise inventories are recorded at the lower of cost, using either the average cost or first-in, first-out method, or market. Inbound freight-related costs from our vendors are included as part of the net cost of merchandise inventories. Also included in the cost of inventory are certain vendor allowances that are not a reimbursement of specific, incremental and identifiable costs to promote a vendor's products. Other costs associated with acquiring, storing and transporting merchandise inventories to our retail stores are expensed as incurred and included in cost of goods sold.

Our inventory loss reserve represents anticipated physical inventory losses (e.g., theft) that have occurred since the last physical inventory date. Independent physical inventory

$ in millions, except per share amounts or as otherwise noted

counts are taken on a regular basis to ensure that the inventory reported in our consolidated financial statements is properly stated. During the interim period between physical inventory counts, we reserve for anticipated physical inventory losses on a location-by-location basis.

Our markdown reserve represents the excess of the carrying value, typically average cost, over the amount we expect to realize from the ultimate sale or other disposal of the inventory. Markdowns establish a new cost basis for our inventory. Subsequent changes in facts or circumstances do not result in the reversal of previously recorded markdowns or an increase in that newly established cost basis.

Restricted Assets

Restricted cash and investments in debt securities totaled $408 and $382, at March 1, 2008, and March 3, 2007, respectively, and are included in other current assets or equity and other investments in our consolidated balance sheets. Such balances are pledged as collateral or restricted to use for vendor payables, general liability insurance, workers' compensation insurance and warranty programs.

Property and Equipment

Property and equipment are recorded at cost. We compute depreciation using the straight-line method over the estimated useful lives of the assets. Leasehold improvements are depreciated over the shorter of their estimated useful lives or the period from the date the assets are placed in service to the end of the initial lease term. Leasehold improvements made significantly after the initial lease term are depreciated over the shorter of their estimated useful lives or the remaining lease term, including renewal periods, if reasonably assured. Accelerated depreciation methods are generally used for income tax purposes.

When property is fully depreciated, retired or otherwise disposed of, the cost and accumulated depreciation are removed from the accounts and any resulting gain or loss is reflected in the consolidated statement of earnings.

Repairs and maintenance costs are charged directly to expense as incurred. Major renewals or replacements that substantially extend the useful life of an asset are capitalized and depreciated.

Costs associated with the acquisition or development of software for internal use are capitalized and amortized over the expected useful life of the software, from three to seven years. A subsequent addition, modification or upgrade to internal-use software is capitalized only to the extent that it enables the software to perform a task it previously did not perform. Capitalized software is included in fixtures and equipment. Software maintenance and training costs are expensed in the period incurred.

Property under capital lease is comprised of buildings and equipment used in our retail operations and corporate support functions. The related depreciation for capital lease assets is included in depreciation expense. The carrying value of property under capital lease was $54 and $26 at March 1, 2008, and March 3, 2007, respectively, net of accumulated depreciation of $13 and $6, respectively.

During the fourth quarter of fiscal 2007, we removed from our fixed asset balance $621 of fully depreciated assets that were no longer in service. This asset adjustment was based primarily on an analysis of our fixed asset records and certain other validation procedures and had no net impact on our fiscal 2007 consolidated balance sheet, statement of earnings or statement of cash flows.

Goodwill and Intangible Assets

Goodwill

Goodwill is the excess of the purchase price over the fair value of identifiable net assets acquired in business combinations accounted for under the purchase method. We do not amortize goodwill but test it for impairment annually, or when indications of potential impairment exist, utilizing a fair value approach at the reporting unit level. A reporting unit is the operating segment, or a business unit one level below that operating segment, for which discrete financial information is prepared and regularly reviewed by segment management.

$ in millions, except per share amounts or as otherwise noted

Tradenames

We have indefinite-lived intangible assets related to our Pacific Sales and Speakeasy tradenames which are included in the Domestic segment. We also have indefinite-lived intangible assets related to our Future Shop and Five Star tradenames, which are included in the International segment.

We determine fair values utilizing widely accepted valuation techniques, including discounted cash flows and market multiple analyses. During the fourth quarter of fiscal 2008, we completed our annual impairment testing of our goodwill and tradenames, using the valuation techniques as described above, and determined there was no impairment.

Investments

Debt Securities

Short-term and long-term investments in debt securities are comprised of auction-rate securities, variable-rate demand notes, asset-backed securities, municipal debt securities and commercial paper. In accordance with SFAS No. 115, *Accounting for Certain Investments in Debt and Equity Securities,* and based on our ability to market and sell these instruments, we classify auction-rate securities and other investments in debt securities as available-for-sale and carry them at fair value. Auction-rate securities are intended to behave like short-term debt instruments because their interest rates are reset periodically through an auction process, typically at intervals of 7, 28 and 35 days. Investments in these securities can be sold for cash at par value on the auction date if the auction is successful. Substantially all of our auction-rate securities are AAA/Aaa-rated and collateralized by student loans, which are guaranteed 95% to 100% by the U.S. government. We also hold auction-rate securities that are in the form of municipal revenue bonds, the vast majority of which are AAA/Aaa-rated and insured by bond insurers. We do not have any investments in securities that are collateralized by assets that include mortgages or subprime debt. Our intent with these investments is not to hold these securities to maturity, but to use the periodic

auction feature to provide liquidity as needed. See Note 3, *Investments,* for further information.

In accordance with our investment policy, we place our investments in debt securities with issuers who have high-quality credit and limit the amount of investment exposure to any one issuer. The primary objective of our investment activities is to preserve principal and maintain a desired level of liquidity to meet working capital needs. We seek to preserve principal and minimize exposure to interest-rate fluctuations by limiting default risk, market risk and reinvestment risk.

Marketable Equity Securities

We also invest in marketable equity securities and classify them as available-for-sale. Investments in marketable equity securities are included in equity and other investments in our consolidated balance sheets, and are reported at fair value based on quoted market prices. All unrealized holding gains and losses are reflected net of tax in accumulated other comprehensive income in shareholders' equity.

Other Investments

We also have investments that are accounted for on either the cost method or the equity method that we include in equity and other investments in our consolidated balance sheets.

We review the key characteristics of our debt, marketable equity securities and other investments portfolio and their classification in accordance with GAAP on an annual basis, or when indications of potential impairment exist. If a decline in the fair value of a security is deemed by management to be other-than-temporary, we write down the cost basis of the investment to fair value, and the amount of the write-down is included in net earnings.

Income Taxes

We account for income taxes using the asset and liability method. Under this method, deferred tax assets and liabilities are recognized for the estimated future tax consequences attributable to differences between the

$ in millions, except per share amounts or as otherwise noted

financial statement carrying amounts of existing assets and liabilities and their respective tax bases, and operating loss and tax credit carryforwards. Deferred tax assets and liabilities are measured pursuant to tax laws using rates we expect to apply to taxable income in the years in which we expect those temporary differences to be recovered or settled. We recognize the effect of a change in income tax rates on deferred tax assets and liabilities in our consolidated statement of earnings in the period that includes the enactment date. We record a valuation allowance to reduce the carrying amounts of deferred tax assets if it is more likely than not that such assets will not be realized.

Long-Term Liabilities

The major components of long-term liabilities at March 1, 2008, and March 3, 2007, included long-term rent-related liabilities, unrecognized tax benefits recorded pursuant to FIN No. 48, deferred compensation plan liabilities, advances received under vendor alliance programs and self-insurance reserves.

Revenue Recognition

We recognize revenue when the sales price is fixed or determinable, collectibility is reasonably assured and the customer takes possession of the merchandise, or in the case of services, at the time the service is provided. Revenue is recognized for store sales when the customer receives and pays for the merchandise at the point of sale. For online sales, we estimate and defer revenue and the related product costs for shipments that are in-transit to the customer. Revenue is recognized at the time we estimate the customer receives the product. Customers typically receive goods within a few days of shipment. Such amounts were immaterial at March 1, 2008, and March 3, 2007. Amounts billed to customers for shipping and handling are included in revenue.

Revenue is reported net of estimated sales returns and excludes sales taxes. We estimate our sales returns reserve based on historical return rates. Our sales returns reserve was $101 and $104, at March 1, 2008, and March 3, 2007, respectively.

Gift Cards

We sell gift cards to our customers in our retail stores, through our Web sites, and through selected third parties. We do not charge administrative fees on unused gift cards, and our gift cards do not have an expiration date. We recognize revenue from gift cards when: (i) the gift card is redeemed by the customer, or (ii) the likelihood of the gift card being redeemed by the customer is remote ("gift card breakage"), and we determine that we do not have a legal obligation to remit the value of unredeemed gift cards to the relevant jurisdictions. We determine our gift card breakage rate based upon historical redemption patterns. Based on our historical information, the likelihood of a gift card remaining unredeemed can be determined 24 months after the gift card is issued. At that time, we recognize breakage income for those cards for which the likelihood of redemption is deemed remote and we do not have a legal obligation to remit the value of such unredeemed gift cards to the relevant jurisdictions. Gift card breakage income is included in revenue in our consolidated statements of earnings.

We began recognizing gift card breakage income during the third quarter of fiscal 2006. Gift card breakage income was as follows in fiscal 2008, 2007 and 2006:

	2008	2007	2006
Gift card breakage income	$34	$46	$43

Due to the resolution of certain legal matters associated with gift card liabilities, we recognized $19 and $27 of gift card breakage income in fiscal 2007 and 2006, respectively, that related to prior fiscal years.

$ in millions, except per share amounts or as otherwise noted

Cost of Goods Sold and Selling, General and Administrative Expenses

The following table illustrates the primary costs classified in each major expense category:

Cost of Goods Sold	SG&A
• Total cost of products sold including: — Freight expenses associated with moving merchandise inventories from our vendors to our distribution centers; — Vendor allowances that are not a reimbursement of specific, incremental and identifiable costs to promote a vendor's products; and — Cash discounts on payments to merchandise vendors; • Cost of services provided including; — Payroll and benefits costs for services employees; and — Cost of replacement parts and related freight expenses; • Physical inventory losses; • Markdowns; • Customer shipping and handling expenses; • Costs associated with operating our distribution network, including payroll and benefit costs, occupancy costs, and depreciation; • Freight expenses associated with moving merchandise inventories from our distribution centers to our retail stores; and • Promotional financing costs.	• Payroll and benefit costs for retail and corporate employees; • Occupancy costs of retail, services and corporate facilities; • Depreciation related to retail, services and corporate assets; • Advertising; • Vendor allowances that are a reimbursement of specific, incremental and identifiable costs to promote a vendor's products; • Charitable contributions; • Outside service fees; • Long-lived asset impairment charges; and • Other administrative costs, such as credit card service fees, supplies, and travel and lodging.

Advertising Costs

Advertising costs, which are included in SG&A, are expensed the first time the advertisement runs. Advertising costs consist primarily of print and television advertisements as well as promotional events. Net advertising expenses were $684, $692 and $644 in fiscal 2008, 2007 and 2006, respectively. Allowances received from vendors for advertising of $156, $140 and $123, in fiscal 2008, 2007 and 2006, respectively, were classified as reductions of advertising expenses.

Stock-Based Compensation

At the beginning of fiscal 2006, we early-adopted the fair value recognition provisions of SFAS No. 123 (revised 2004), *Share-Based Payment* (123(R)), requiring us to recognize expense related to the fair value of our stock-based compensation awards. We elected the modified prospective transition method as permitted by SFAS No. 123(R). Under this transition method, stock-based compensation expense in fiscal 2008, 2007 and 2006 included: (i) compensation expense for all

$ in millions, except per share amounts or as otherwise noted

stock-based compensation awards granted prior to, but not yet vested as of February 26, 2005, based on the grant date fair value estimated in accordance with the original provisions of SFAS No. 123, *Accounting for Stock-Based Compensation;* and (ii) compensation expense for all stock-based compensation awards granted subsequent to February 26, 2005, based on the grant-date fair value estimated in accordance with the provisions of SFAS No. 123(R). We recognize compensation expense on a straight-line basis over the requisite service period of the award (or to an employee's eligible retirement date, if earlier). Total stock-based compensation expense included in our consolidated statements of earnings for fiscal 2008, 2007 and 2006 was $105 ($72, net of tax), $121 ($82, net of tax) and $132 ($87, net of tax), respectively. In accordance with the modified prospective transition method of SFAS No. 123(R), financial results for prior periods have not been restated.

2.   Acquisitions

Speakeasy, Inc.

On May 1, 2007, we acquired Speakeasy for $103 in cash, or $89 net of cash acquired, which included transaction costs and the repayment of $5 of Speakeasy's debt. We acquired Speakeasy, an independent U.S. broadband, voice, data and information technology services provider, to strengthen our portfolio of technology solutions. We accounted for the acquisition using the purchase method in accordance with SFAS No. 141, *Business Combinations.* Accordingly, we recorded the net assets at their estimated fair values, and included operating results in our Domestic segment from the date of acquisition. We allocated the purchase price on a preliminary basis using information then available. The allocation of the purchase price to the assets and liabilities acquired will be finalized no later than the first quarter of fiscal 2009. The premium we paid in excess of the fair value of the net assets acquired was primarily

for the expected synergies we believe Speakeasy will generate by providing new technology solutions for our existing and future customers, as well as to obtain Speakeasy's skilled, established workforce. None of the goodwill is deductible for tax purposes.

The preliminary purchase price allocation, net of cash acquired, was as follows:

Receivables	$ 8
Property and equipment	7
Other assets	25
Tradename	6
Goodwill	74
Current liabilities	(31)
Total	$ 89

Jiangsu Five Star Appliance Co., Ltd.

On June 8, 2006, we acquired a 75% interest in Five Star for $184, which included a working capital injection of $122 and transaction costs. Five Star is an appliance and consumer electronics retailer and had 131 stores located in eight of China's 34 provinces on the date of acquisition. We made the investment in Five Star to further our international growth plans, to increase our knowledge of Chinese customers and to obtain an immediate retail presence in China. We have a contractual commitment to acquire the remaining 25% interest within the next several years, subject to Chinese government approval. The acquisition was accounted for using the purchase method in accordance with SFAS No. 141. Accordingly, we recorded the net assets at their estimated fair values, and included operating results in our International segment from the date of acquisition. We allocated the purchase price on a preliminary basis using information then available. The allocation of the purchase price to the assets and liabilities acquired was finalized in the first quarter of fiscal 2008. There was no significant adjustment to the preliminary purchase price allocation. None of the goodwill is deductible for tax purposes.

$ in millions, except per share amounts or as otherwise noted

The final purchase price allocation, net of cash acquired, was as follows:

Restricted cash	$ 204
Merchandise inventories	109
Property and equipment	78
Other assets	80
Tradename	21
Goodwill	22
Accounts payable	(368)
Other current liabilities	(35)
Debt	(64)
Long-term liabilities	(1)
Minority interests [1]	(33)
Total	$ 13

[1]   The minority owners' proportionate share of assets and liabilities were recorded at historical carrying values.

The minority owners' proportionate share of net earnings was $3 and $1 in fiscal 2008 and 2007, respectively.

Five Star owns a 40% interest in, and purchases appliances from, Jiangsu Heng Xin Ge Li Air Conditioner Sales Co., Ltd. Purchases from this affiliate were $65 and $43 in fiscal 2008 and 2007, respectively. At March 1, 2008, and March 3, 2007, $22 and less than $1, respectively, was due to this affiliate for the purchase of appliances.

3. Investments

Investments were comprised of the following:

	March 1, 2008	March 3, 2007
Short-term investments		
Debt securities	$ 64	$2,588
Equity and other investments		
Debt securities	$417	$ 318
Marketable equity securities	172	4
Other investments	16	16
Total equity and other investments	$605	$ 338

Debt Securities

The following table presents the fair values, related weighted-average interest rates (taxable equivalent) and major security types for our investments:

	March 1, 2008		March 3, 2007	
	Fair Value	Weighted-Average Interest Rate	Fair Value	Weighted-Average Interest Rate
Short-term investments	$ 64	4.94%	$2,588	5.68%
Long-term investments	417	7.60%	318	5.68%
Total	$481		$2,906	
Auction-rate securities	$417		$2,377	
Municipal debt securities	—		506	
Commercial paper	64		—	
Variable-rate demand notes and asset-backed securities	—		23	
Total	$481		$2,906	

The carrying values of our investments were at fair value at March 1, 2008, and March 3, 2007. As discussed in Note 1, our investments include auction-rate securities, the interest rates of which are reset through an auction process, most commonly at intervals of 7, 28 and 35 days. The same auction process has historically provided a means by which we may rollover the investment or sell these securities at par in order to provide us with liquidity as needed. At March 1, 2008, we had $417 (par value) of auction-rate securities.

Marketable Equity Securities

The carrying values of our investments in marketable equity securities at March 1, 2008, and March 3, 2007,

$ in millions, except per share amounts or as otherwise noted

were $172 and $4, respectively. The increase in marketable equity securities since March 3, 2007, was primarily due to our investment in The Carphone Warehouse Group PLC ("CPW"), Europe's leading independent retailer of mobile phones and services. During the second quarter of fiscal 2008, we purchased in the open market 26.1 million shares of CPW common stock for $183, representing nearly 3% of CPW's outstanding shares.

Net unrealized losses, net of tax, included in accumulated other comprehensive income were ($25) and ($1) at March 1, 2008, and March 3, 2007, respectively.

Other Investments

The aggregate carrying values of investments accounted for on either the cost method or the equity method, at March 1, 2008, and March 3, 2007, were $16 and $16, respectively.

4.   Debt

Short-term debt consisted of the following:

	March 1, 2008	March 3, 2007
Revolving credit facilities, secured and unsecured, variable interest rates ranging from 3.5% to 8.0% at March 1, 2008	$ 156	$ 20
Notes payable to banks, secured, paid October 2007	—	21
Total short-term debt	$ 156	$ 41

Fiscal Year	2008	2007
Maximum month-end outstanding during the year	$1,955	$ 78
Average amount outstanding during the year	$ 655	$ 57
Weighted-average interest rate	4.5%	5.3%

Long-term debt consisted of the following:

	March 1, 2008	March 3, 2007
Convertible subordinated debentures, unsecured, due 2022, interest rate 2.25%	$ 402	$402
Financing lease obligations, due 2009 to 2023, interest rates ranging from 3.0% to 6.5%	197	171
Capital lease obligations, due 2010 to 2026, interest rates ranging from 5.1% to 8.8%	51	24
Other debt, due 2010 to 2022, interest rates ranging from 2.6% to 8.8%	10	12
Total long-term debt	660	609
Less: current portion	(33)	(19)
Total long-term debt, less current portion	$ 627	$590

Certain debt is secured by property and equipment with a net book value of $87 and $80 at March 1, 2008, and March 3, 2007, respectively.

Credit Facilities

On June 26, 2007, we entered into a $3,000 bridge loan facility with Goldman Sachs Credit Partners L.P. (the "Bridge Facility"), concurrent with the execution of

agreements to purchase $3,000 of shares of our common stock in the aggregate pursuant to our ASR program. See Note 5, *Shareholders' Equity*, for further information on the ASR program. We initially borrowed $2,500 under the Bridge Facility and used $500 of our existing cash and investments to fund the ASR program. Effective July 11, 2007, we reduced the amount we could borrow under the Bridge Facility to $2,500.

$ in millions, except per share amounts or as otherwise noted

Effective July 2, 2007, we terminated our previous $200 revolving credit facility that was scheduled to expire on December 22, 2009.

On September 19, 2007, we entered into a $2,500 five-year unsecured revolving credit agreement (the "Credit Agreement") with JPMorgan Chase Bank, N.A. ("JPMorgan"), as administrative agent, and a syndication of banks (the "Lenders"). The Credit Agreement permits borrowings up to $2,500, which may be increased up to $3,000 at our option and upon the consent of JPMorgan and each of the Lenders providing an incremental credit commitment. The Credit Agreement includes a $300 letter of credit sub-limit and a $200 foreign currency sub-limit. The Credit Agreement expires in September 2012.

Convertible Debentures

In January 2002, we sold convertible subordinated debentures having an aggregate principal amount of $402. The proceeds from the offering, net of $6 in offering expenses, were $396. The debentures mature in 2022 and are callable at par, at our option, for cash on or after January 15, 2007.

Holders may require us to purchase all or a portion of their debentures on January 15, 2012, and January 15, 2017, at a purchase price equal to 100% of the principal amount of the debentures plus accrued and unpaid interest up to but not including the date of purchase. We have the option to settle the purchase price in cash, stock, or a combination of cash and stock. On January 15, 2007, holders had the option to require us to purchase all or a portion of their debentures, at a purchase price equal to 100% of the principal amount of the debentures plus accrued and unpaid interest up to but not including the date of purchase. However, no debentures were so purchased.

The debentures become convertible into shares of our common stock at a conversion rate of 21.7391 shares per $0.001 principal amount of debentures, equivalent to an initial conversion price of $46.00 per share, if the closing price of our common stock exceeds a specified price for 20 consecutive trading days in a 30-trading day period preceding the date of conversion, if our credit rating falls below specified levels, if the debentures are called for redemption or if certain specified corporate transactions occur. During a portion of fiscal 2007, our closing stock price exceeded the specified stock price for more than 20 trading days in a 30-day trading period. Therefore, debenture holders had the option to convert their debentures into shares of our common stock. However, no debentures were so converted. Due to changes in the price of our common stock, the debentures were no longer convertible at March 3, 2007, and have not been convertible at the holders' option through April 25, 2008.

The debentures have an interest rate of 2.25% per annum. The interest rate may be reset, but not below 2.25% or above 3.25%, on July 15, 2011, and July 15, 2016. One of our subsidiaries has guaranteed the convertible debentures.

5.   Shareholders' Equity
Stock Compensation Plans

Our outstanding stock options have a 10-year term. Outstanding stock options issued to employees generally vest over a four-year period, and outstanding stock options issued to directors vest immediately upon grant.

Earnings per Share

Our basic earnings per share calculation is based on the weighted-average number of common shares outstanding. Our diluted earnings per share calculation is based on the weighted-average number of common shares outstanding adjusted by the number of additional shares that would have been outstanding had the potentially dilutive common shares been issued. Potentially dilutive shares of common stock include stock options, nonvested share awards and shares issuable under our ESPP, as well as common shares that would have resulted from the assumed conversion of our convertible debentures (see Note 4, *Debt*). Since the potentially dilutive shares related to the convertible debentures are included in the calculation, the related interest expense, net of tax, is added back to earnings from continuing operations, as the interest would not have been paid if the convertible debentures had been converted

$ in millions, except per share amounts or as otherwise noted

to common stock. Nonvested market-based share awards and nonvested performance-based share awards are included in the average diluted shares outstanding each period if established market or performance criteria have been met at the end of the respective periods.

At March 1, 2008, stock options to purchase 28.8 million shares of common stock were outstanding as follows (shares in millions):

| | Exercisable | | | Unexercisable | | | Total | | |
	Shares	%	Weighted Average Price per Share	Shares	%	Weighted Average Price per Share	Shares	%	Weighted Average Price per Share
In-the-money	16.5	93	$32.49	2.7	24	$43.60	19.2	67	$34.05
Out-of-the-money	1.2	7	54.65	8.4	76	50.53	9.6	33	51.04
Total	17.7	100	$34.00	11.1	100	$48.84	28.8	100	$39.73

The computation of dilutive shares outstanding excludes the out-of-the-money stock options because such outstanding options' exercise prices were greater than the average market price of our common shares and, therefore, the effect would be antidilutive (i.e., including such options would result in higher earnings per share). The following table presents a reconciliation of the numerators and denominators of basic and diluted earnings per share in fiscal 2008, 2007 and 2006:

	2008	2007	2006
Numerator:			
Net earnings, basic	$1,407	$1,377	$1,140
Adjustment for assumed dilution:			
Interest on convertible debentures due in 2022, net of tax	6	7	7
Net earnings, diluted	$1,413	$1,384	$1,147
Denominator (in millions):			
Weighted-average common shares outstanding	439.9	482.1	490.3
Effect of potentially dilutive securities:			
Shares from assumed conversion of convertible debentures	8.8	8.8	8.8
Stock options and other	4.2	5.3	5.7
Weighted-average common shares outstanding, assuming dilution	452.9	496.2	504.8
Basic earnings per share	$ 3.20	$ 2.86	$ 2.33
Diluted earnings per share	$ 3.12	$ 2.79	$ 2.27

Repurchase of Common Stock

On June 26, 2007, our Board of Directors ("Board") authorized a new $5,500 share repurchase program. The new program terminated and replaced our prior $1,500 share repurchase program authorized by our Board in June 2006. The June 2006 program terminated and replaced a $1,500 share repurchase program authorized by the Board in April 2005. There is no expiration date governing the period over which we can make our share repurchases under the June 2007 share repurchase program. At March 1, 2008, $2,500 remains available for future purchases under the June 2007 share repurchase program. Repurchased shares have been retired and constitute authorized but unissued shares.

$ in millions, except per share amounts or as otherwise noted

Open Market Repurchases

The following table presents open market share repurchases in fiscal 2008, 2007 and 2006 (shares in millions):

	2008	2007	2006
Total number of shares repurchased	9.8	11.8	18.3
Total cost of shares repurchased	$461	$599	$772

During fiscal 2008, we purchased and retired 9.8 million shares at a cost of $461 under our June 2006 share repurchase program. During fiscal 2008, we made no open market repurchases under our June 2007 share repurchase program.

Comprehensive Income

Comprehensive income is computed as net earnings plus certain other items that are recorded directly to shareholders' equity. In addition to net earnings, the significant components of comprehensive income include foreign currency translation adjustments and unrealized gains and losses, net of tax, on available-for-sale marketable equity securities. Foreign currency translation adjustments do not include a provision for income tax expense when earnings from foreign operations are considered to be indefinitely reinvested outside the U.S. Comprehensive income was $1,693, $1,332 and $1,252 in fiscal 2008, 2007 and 2006, respectively.

The components of accumulated other comprehensive income, net of tax, were as follows:

	March 1, 2008	March 3, 2007
Foreign currency translation	$527	$217
Unrealized losses on available-for-sale investments	(25)	(1)
Total	$502	$216

6.   Leases

The composition of net rent expense for all operating leases, including leases of property and equipment, was as follows in fiscal 2008, 2007 and 2006:

	2008	2007	2006
Minimum rentals	$757	$679	$569
Contingent rentals	1	1	1
Total rent expense	758	680	570
Less: sublease income	(22)	(20)	(18)
Net rent expense	$736	$660	$552

The future minimum lease payments under our capital, financing and operating leases by fiscal year (not including contingent rentals) at March 1, 2008, were as follows:

Fiscal Year	Capital Leases	Financing Leases	Operating Leases
2009	$ 16	$ 29	$ 772
2010	16	29	761
2011	8	29	716
2012	2	28	666
2013	2	28	635
Thereafter	19	115	3,282
Subtotal	63	258	$6,832
Less: imputed interest	(12)	(61)	
Present value of lease obligations	$ 51	$197	

$ in millions, except per share amounts or as otherwise noted

Total minimum lease payments have not been reduced by minimum sublease rent income of approximately $99 due under future noncancelable subleases.

During fiscal 2008, we entered into agreements totaling $35 related to various information system capital leases. These leases were noncash transactions and have been eliminated from our consolidated statements of cash flows.

7. Benefit Plans

We sponsor retirement savings plans for employees meeting certain age and service requirements. Participants may choose from various investment options including a fund comprised of our company stock. The total matching contributions, net of forfeitures, were $53, $26 and $19 in fiscal 2008, 2007 and 2006, respectively.

8.   Income Taxes

The following is a reconciliation of the federal statutory income tax rate to income tax expense in fiscal 2008, 2007 and 2006:

	2008	2007	2006
Federal income tax at the statutory rate	$780	$747	$603
State income taxes, net of federal benefit	67	38	34
Benefit from foreign operations	(25)	(36)	(37)
Non-taxable interest income	(17)	(34)	(28)
Other	10	37	9
Income tax expense	$815	$752	$581
Effective income tax rate	36.6%	35.3%	33.7%

9.   Segments

We operate two reportable segments: Domestic and International. The Domestic segment is comprised of all U.S. store, call center and online operations. The International segment is comprised of all store, call center and online operations outside the U.S. We have included Speakeasy, which we acquired on May 1, 2007, in the Domestic segment. Our segments are evaluated on an operating income basis, and a stand-alone tax provision is not calculated for each segment. The other accounting policies of the segments are the same as those described in Note 1, *Summary of Significant Accounting Policies*. The following tables present our business segment information for fiscal 2008, 2007 and 2006:

$ in millions, except per share amounts or as otherwise noted

	2008	2007	2006
Revenue			
Domestic	$33,328	$31,031	$27,380
International	6,695	4,903	3,468
Total revenue	$40,023	$35,934	$30,848
Operating Income			
Domestic	$ 1,999	$ 1,900	$ 1,588
International	162	99	56
Total operating income	2,161	1,999	1,644
Other income (expense)			
Investment income and other	129	162	107
Interest expense	(62)	(31)	(30)
Earnings from operations before income tax expense, minority interest and equity in loss of affiliates	$ 2,228	$ 2,130	$ 1,721
Assets			
Domestic	$ 8,194	$10,614	$ 9,722
International	4,564	2,956	2,142
Total assets	$12,758	$13,570	$11,864

10. Contingencies and Commitments

Contingencies

We are involved in various other legal proceedings arising in the normal course of conducting business. We believe the amounts provided in our consolidated financial statements, as prescribed by GAAP, are adequate in light of the probable and estimable liabilities. The resolution of those other proceedings is not expected to have a material impact on our results of operations or financial condition.

Commitments

We engage Accenture LLP ("Accenture") to assist us with improving our operational capabilities and reducing our costs in the information systems, procurement and human resources areas. Our future contractual obligations to Accenture are expected to range from $76 to $272 per year through 2012, the end of the periods under contract. Prior to our engagement of Accenture, a significant portion of these costs were incurred as part of normal operations.

We had outstanding letters of credit for purchase obligations with a fair value of $90 at March 1, 2008.

At March 1, 2008, we had commitments for the purchase and construction of facilities valued at approximately $45. Also, at March 1, 2008, we had entered into lease commitments for land and buildings for 104 future locations. These lease commitments with real estate developers provide for minimum rentals ranging from 5 to 20 years, which if consummated based on current cost estimates, will approximate $72 annually over the initial lease terms. These minimum rentals are reported in the future minimum lease payments included in Note 6, *Leases*.

In April 2008, CompUSA, Inc. accepted our offer to acquire the rights to 17 leases for $13.5. Pending approval from the landlords, we expect to take possession of all sites by June 2008. The total square footage related to these leases is approximately 453,000 square feet, or an average of approximately 27,000 square feet per site. The remaining minimum lease terms range from 3 to 14 years, however, all leases include renewal options for an additional 5 to 20 years. The sites are located throughout the U.S., primarily in western states, and we anticipate utilizing these sites over the next two fiscal years for planned new stores for both Best Buy and Pacific Sales.

Alabama Albertville, Alexander City, Andalusia, Arab, Ardmore, Athens, Atmore, Attalla, Bay Minette, Bayou La Batre, Bessemer, Birmingham, Butler, Calera, Camden, Center Point, Centre, Childersburg, Clanton, Cullman, Daphne, Decatur, Demopolis, Dothan, Enterprise, Fairfield, Fairhope, Florence, Foley, Fort Payne, Gadsden, Gardendale, Gulf Shores, Guntersville, Haleyville, Hamilton, Hartselle, Hoover, Huntsville, Jackson, Jasper, Leeds, Linden, Luverne, Madison, Marion, Mobile, Montgomery, Moulton, Northport, Opelika, Opp, Oxford, Pelham, Pell City, Phenix City, Piedmont, Prattville, Robertsdale, Rogersville, Russellville, Saraland, Scottsboro, Selma, Sumiton, Sylacauga, Tallassee, Thomasville, Troy, Tuscaloosa *Alaska* Anchorage, Bethel, Cordova, Craig, Eagle River, Fairbanks, Glennallen, Haines, Homer, Juneau, Kenai, Ketchikan, Kodiak, Petersburg, Seward, Sitka, Skagway, Soldotna, Valdez, Wasilla *Arizona* Ajo, Apache Junction, Avondale, Benson, Bullhead City, Camp Verde, Casa Grande, Chandler, Chino Valley, Colorado City, Coolidge, Cottonwood, Douglas, Flagstaff, Florence, Fort Mohave, Fountain Hills, Gilbert, Glendale, Greenvalley, Heber, Holbrook, Kayenta, Kingman, Lake Havasu, Lakeside, Maricopa, Mesa, Miami, Morenci, New River, Nogales, Oro Valley, Parker, Payson, Peoria, Phoenix, Prescott, Prescott Valley, Quartzsite, Safford, San Manuel, Scottsdale, Sedona, Show Low, Sierra Vista, Springerville, St. Johns, Sun City, Surprise, Taylor, Tempe, Thatcher, Tuba City, Tucson, Wickenburg, Willcox, Yuma *Arkansas* Arkadelphia, Ash Flat, Batesville, Beebe, Benton, Bentonville, Berryville, Brinkley, Bryant, Cabot, Camden, Cave City, Clarksville, Clinton, Conway, Danville, De Queen, De Witt, Dumas, El Dorado, Fayetteville, Flippin, Forrest City, Fort Smith, Glenwood, Harrison, Heber Springs, Hope, Hot Springs, Jacksonville, Jasper, Jonesboro, Little Rock, Magnolia, Malvern, Mammoth Springs, Marshall, Melbourne, Mena, Mountain Home, Mountain View, North Little Rock, Nashville, Newport, Paragould, Paris, Pine Bluff, Prescott, Rogers, Russellville, Salem, Searcy, Sheridan, Siloam Springs, Springdale, Star City, Stuttgart, Van Buren, West Helena, West Memphis, Wynne *California* Agoura, Alameda, Albany, Alhambra, Alta Loma, Alturas, American Canyon, Anaheim, Anaheim Hills, Anderson, Angels Camp, Antioch, Apple Valley, Arcadia, Arcata, Arnold, Arroyo Grande, Atascadero, Atwater, Auburn, Avalon, Azusa, Bakersfield, Baldwin Park, Barstow, Beaumont, Bell, Belmont, Benicia, Berkeley, Beverly Hills, Big Bear Lake, Bishop, Blue Jay, Blythe, Brawley, Brea, Buellton, Buena Park, Burbank, Burlingame, Calexico, California City, Camarillo, Canoga Park, Canyon Country, Capitola, Carlsbad, Carmichael, Carpinteria, Carson, Castro Valley, Cathedral City, Cerritos, Chatsworth, Chico, Chino, Chino Hills, Chula Vista, Citrus Heights, City of Industry, Clearlake, Cloverdale, Clovis, Coachella, Coalinga, Colton, Colusa, Compton, Concord, Corcoran, Corning, Corona, Corte Madera, Costa Mesa, Covina, Crescent City, Crestline, Culver City, Cupertino, Cypress, Daly City, Dana Point, Danville, Davis, Del Mar, Delano, Desert Hot Springs, Diamond Bar, Dinuba, Downey, Duarte, Dublin, E Los Angeles, El Cajon, El Centro, El Cerrito, El Monte, Elk Grove, Emeryville, Encinitas, Encino, Escondido, Eureka, Fairfield, Fall River Mills, Fallbrook, Folsom, Fontana, Foothill Ranch, Fortuna, Foster City, Fountain Valley, Freedom, Fremont, Fresno, Fort Bragg, Fullerton, Garberville, Garden Grove, Gardena, Gilroy, Glendale, Glendora, Goleta, Gonzales, Granada Hills, Grass Valley, Greenfield, Grover Beach, Hanford, Harbor City, Hawthorne, Hayward, Hemet, Hercules, Hesperia, Highland, Hollister, Hollywood, Huntington Beach, Huntington Park, Indio, Inglewood, Irvine, Jackson, King City, La Habra, La Jolla, La Mesa, La Mirada, La Puente, La Quinta, La Verne, Lafayette, Laguna Hills, Laguna Niguel, Lake Elsinore, Lake Isabella, Lakeport, Lakewood, Lancaster, Lawndale, Lemoore, Lincoln Heights, Livermore, Lodi, Lompoc, Long Beach, Los Alamitos, Los Angeles, Los Banos, Los Gatos, Los Osos, Lynwood, Madera, Malibu, Mammoth Lakes, Manhattan Beach, Manteca, Marina Del Rey, Martinez, Marysville, Maywood, Merced, Milpitas, Mission Hills, Modesto, Mojave, Monrovia, Montclair, Montebello, Monterey, Monterey Park, Montrose, Moorpark, Moreno Valley, Morgan Hill, Morro Bay, Mountain View, Mount Shasta, Murrieta, Napa, National City, Newbury Park, Newhall, Newport Beach, North Highlands, North Hollywood, Northridge, Norwalk, Novato, Oakdale, Oakhurst, Oakland, Oakley, Oceanside, Ojai, Ontario, Orange, Orangevale, Orland, Oroville, Oxnard, Pacifica, Palm Desert, Palm Springs, Palmdale, Palo Alto, Panorama City, Paradise, Paramount, Pasadena, Paso Robles, Patterson, Perris, Petaluma, Phelan, Pico Rivera, Pinole, Pittsburg, Placentia, Placerville, Pleasant Hill, Pleasanton, Pollock Pines, Pomona, Porterville, Poway, Quincy, Ramona, Rancho Cordova, Rancho Cucamonga, Rancho Santa Margarita, Red Bluff, Redding, Redlands, Redondo Beach, Redwood City, Reedley, Rialto, Ridgecrest, Rio Vista, Riverbank, Riverside, Rocklin, Rohnert Park, Rolling Hills, Rosamond, Rosemead, Roseville, Rowland Heights, Sacramento, Salinas, San Bernardino, San Bruno, San Clemente, San Diego, San Dimas, San Francisco, San Jose, San Leandro, San Luis Obispo, San Marcos, San Mateo, San Pablo, San Pedro, San Rafael, San Ramon, Sanger, Santa Ana, Santa Barbara, Santa Clara, Santa Cruz, Santa Maria, Santa Monica, Santa Paula, Santa Rosa, Santee, Saugus, Scotts Valley, Seal Beach, Seaside, Sebastopol, Selma, Sherman Oaks, Signal Hill, Simi, San Juan Capistrano, Soledad, Sonoma, Sonora, South Gate, South Lake Tahoe, South Pasadena, South San Francisco, Spring Valley, Stockton, Studio City, Sun Valley, Sunnyvale, Susanville, Sylmar, Taft, Tehachapi, Temecula, Temple City, Thousand Oaks, Torrance, Tracy, Truckee, Tujunga, Tulare, Turlock, Tustin, Twentynine Palms, Ukiah, Union City, Upland, Vacaville, Valencia, Vallejo, Valley Springs, Van Nuys, Venice, Ventura, Victorville, Visalia, Vista, Walnut Creek, Wasco, Watsonville, Weaverville, West Covina, West Hollywood, West Los Angeles, West Sacramento, Westchester, Westminster, Whittier, Willits, Willows, Wilmington, Windsor, Woodland, Woodland Hills, Yorba Linda, Yreka, Yuba City, Yucaipa, Yucca Valley *Colorado* Alamosa, Arvada, Aspen, Aurora, Avon, Bayfield, Bennett, Boulder, Brighton, Broomfield, Buena Vista, Burlington, Canon City, Castle Rock, Castle Rock, Centennial, Center, Colorado Springs, Conifer, Cortez, Craig, Crested Butte, Denver, Durango, Elizabeth, Englewood, Estes Park, Evergreen, Flagler, Fort Collins, Fountain, Fraser, Frisco, Glenwood Spring, Golden, Grand Junction, Greeley, Greenwood Village, Gunnison, Highlands Ranch, Holyoke, Idaho Springs, La Junta, Lafayette, Lakewood, Lamar, Limon, Littleton, Longmont, Loveland, Meeker, Monte Vista, Montrose, Monument, Northglenn, Pagosa Springs, Paonia, Parachute, Parker, Pueblo, Rifle, Salida, Springfield, Steamboat Springs, Sterling, Thornton, Westminster, Woodland Park, Wray, Yuma *Connecticut* Avon, Barkhamsted, Bloomfield, Branford, Bridgeport, Bristol, Canaan, Cheshire, Clinton, Cos Cob, Cromwell, Danbury, Derby, East Haven, Enfield, Fairfield, Farmington, Glastonbury, Groton, Guilford, Hamden, Hartford, Manchester, Meriden, Middletown, Milford, Naugatuck, New Britain, New Canaan, New Haven, New London, New Milford, Newington, Newtown, North Haven, Norwalk, Norwich, Old Saybrook, Orange, Plainfield, Putnam, Ridgefield, Riverside, Southbury, Southington, Stamford, Torrington, Trumbull, Vernon, Wallingford, Waterbury, Waterford, Watertown, West Hartford, Westport, Wethersfield, Willimantic, Wilton, Windsor, *D.C.* Washington *Delaware* Bear, Claymont, Dover, Georgetown, Middletown, Milford, New Castle, Newark, Rehoboth Beach, Seaford, Smyrna, Wilmington *Florida* Alachua, Altamonte, Altamonte Springs, Apopka, Arcadia, Atlantic Beach, Auburndale, Avon Park, Bartow, Bayonet Point, Belle Glade, Belleview, Big Pine Key, Boca Raton, Bonita Springs, Boynton Beach, Bradenton, Brandon, Branford, Brooksville, Callaway, Cape Coral, Casselberry, Century, Chiefland, Chipley, Clearwater, Clermont, Clewiston, Cocoa, Cocoa Beach, Cooper City, Coral Gables, Coral Springs, Crawfordville, Crestview, Crystal River, Davie, Daytona Beach, Deerfield, Deerfield Beach, Defuniak Springs, Deland, Delray Beach, Deltona, Destin, Dunnellon, Englewood, Fernandina Beach, Florida City, Fort Lauderdale, Fort Myers, Fort Pierce, Fort Walton Beach, Gainesville, Greenacres, Gulf Breeze, Haines City, Hialeah, Hilliard, Holiday, Hollywood, Homestead, Homosassa, Immokalee, Indiantown, Inverness, Jacksonville, Jensen Beach, Jupiter, Key Largo, Key West, Keystone Heights, Kissimmee, Lady Lake, Lake City, Lake Mary, Lake Placid, Lake Wales, Lake Worth, Lakeland, Lantana, Largo, Lauderdale Lakes, Lauderhill, Leesburg, Lehigh Acres, Live Oak, Longwood, Lutz, Macclenny, Madison, Marathon, Marco Island, Margate, Marianna, Mary Esther, Melbourne, Merritt Island, Miami, Miami Beach, Milton, Miramar, Monticello, Mount Dora, North Fort Myers, North Miami Beach, Naples, Navarre, New Port Richey, New Smyrna Beach, Niceville, Oakland Park, Ocala, Ocoee, Okeechobee, Orange City, Orange Park, Orlando, Ormond Beach, Oviedo, Palatka, Palm Bay, Palm Beach Garden, Palm Coast, Palm Harbor, Panama City, Pembroke Pines, Pensacola, Perry, Plant City, Plantation, Pompano Beach, Port Charlotte, Port Orange, Port Richey, Port St. Joe, Port St. Lucie, Punta Gorda, Riverview, Royal Palm Beach, Ruskin, Sanford, Santa Rosa Beach, Sarasota, Satellite Beach, Sebastian, Sebring, Seffner, Seminole, South Daytona, Spring Hill, St. Augustine, St. Cloud, St. Petersburg, Starke, Stuart, Sunrise, Tallahassee, Tampa, Tarpon Springs, Temple Terrace, Tequesta, Titusville, Venice, Vero Beach, Wauchula, Wellington, West Palm Beach, Weston, Wildwood, Wilton Manors, Winter Haven, Winter Park, Winter Springs, Zephyrhills *Georgia* Adel, Albany, Alpharetta, Americus, Athens, Atlanta, Augusta, Austell, Bainbridge, Barnesville, Baxley, Blairsville, Blakely, Blue Ridge, Brunswick, Buford, Cairo, Calhoun, Canton, Carrollton, Cartersville, Cedartown, Centerville, Chamblee, Chatsworth, Clayton, Cleveland, Columbus, Commerce, Conyers, Cordele, Cornelia, Covington, Cumming, Cuthbert, Dahlonega, Dalton, Dawson, Dawsonville, Decatur, Donalsonville, Douglas, Douglasville, Dublin, Duluth, East Ellijay, Elberton, Fayetteville, Fitzgerald, Folkston, Forest Park, Forsyth, Fort Gaines, Fort Oglethorpe, Fort Valley, Gainesville, Griffin, Hampton, Hartwell, Hazlehurst, Hiawassee, Hinesville, Hiram, Homerville, Jackson, Jasper, Jesup, Kennesaw, Lafayette, Lagrange, Lawrenceville, Lilburn, Lincolnton, Lithonia, Macon, Madison, Marietta, Martinez, Mc Rae, McDonough, Metter, Milledgeville, Monroe, Monticello, Morrow, Moultrie, Nashville, Newnan, Norcross, Oakwood, Peachtree City, Perry, Quitman, Richmond Hill, Riverdale, Rockmart, Rome, Roswell, Royston, Savannah, Smyrna, Snellville, St. Marys, St. Simons Island, Statesboro, Stockbridge, Stone Mountain, Summerville, Suwanee, Sylvania, Sylvester, Thomaston, Thomasville, Thomson, Tifton, Toccoa, Trenton, Union City, Valdosta, Vidalia, Villa Rica, Warner Robins, Washington, Waycross, Winder, Woodbury, Woodstock *Hawaii* Aiea, Ewa Beach, Haleiwa, Hilo, Honolulu, Kahului, Kailua, Kailua-Kona, Kamuela, Kaneohe, Kapolei, Kihei, Lahaina, Lihue, Mililani, Wahiawa, Waianae, Waipahu *Idaho* American Falls, Blackfoot, Boise, Bonners Ferry, Buhl, Burley, Caldwell, Chubbuck, Coeur d'Alene, Cottonwood, Driggs, Emmett, Grangeville, Hailey, Idaho Falls, Lewiston, McCall, Meridian, Montpelier, Moscow, Mountain Home, Nampa, Orofino, Pocatello, Post Falls, Rexburg, Rigby, Salmon, Sandpoint, Twin Falls, Wendell *Illinois* Aledo, Alton, Anna, Antioch, Arcola, Arlington Heights, Arthur, Aurora, Bartlett, Batavia, Belleville, Belvidere, Bensenville, Benton, Berwyn, Bloomingdale, Bloomington, Blue Island, Bolingbrook, Bourbonnais, Burbank, Calumet City, Canton, Carbondale, Carlinville, Carmi, Centralia, Champaign, Channahon, Chester, Chicago, Chicago Heights, Cicero, Collinsville, Crystal Lake, Danville, Decatur, Des Plaines, Dixon, Dolton, Downers Grove, Du Quoin, Dwight, East Peoria, East St Louis, Effingham, El Paso, Elgin, Elk Grove Village, Eureka, Evanston, Fairbury, Fairfield, Fairview Heights, Flora, Fox Lake, Frankfort, Freeport, Galesburg, Geneseo, Gibson City, Glen Carbon, Glen Ellyn, Glencoe, Glenview, Granite City, Greenville, Gurnee, Harrisburg, Havana, Highland, Highland Park, Hoffman Estates, Homer Glen, Homewood, Hoopeston, Jacksonville, Jerseyville, Joliet, Kankakee, Kewanee, La Grange, Lake Zurich, Lansing, Lemont, Lincoln, Litchfield, Lake in the Hills, Lombard, Machesney Park, Macomb, Marengo, Marion, Markham, Mascoutah, Matteson, Mattoon, McHenry, Melrose Park, Mendota, Midlothian, Moline, Montgomery, Morris, Mount Vernon, Mundelein, Naperville, Nashville, Niles, Norridge, North Riverside, Oak Lawn, Oak Park, Olney, Ottawa, Palatine, Palos Heights, Paris, Pekin, Peoria, Peru, Petersburg, Pontiac, Princeton, Quincy, Robinson, Rochelle, Rockford, Round Lake Beach, Salem, Sandwich, Savanna, Savoy, Schaumburg, Seneca, Shiloh, Skokie, South Elgin, South Holland, Sparta, Springfield, St. Charles, Staunton, Sterling, Streator, Sullivan, Sycamore, Tinley Park, Tuscola, Urbana, Vernon Hills, Villa Park, Virden, Waterloo, Watseka, Waukegan, West Dundee, Wheaton, Wheeling, Willowbrook, Wilmington, Wood River, Yorkville, Zion *Indiana* Anderson, Angola, Argos, Auburn, Aurora, Avon, Batesville, Bedford, Berne, Bicknell, Bloomington, Bluffton, Brazil, Bremen, Brook, Brookville, Brownsburg, Brownstown, Cannelton, Carmel, Clarksville, Columbia City, Columbus, Corydon, Covington, Crawfordsville, Crown Point, Decatur, Demotte, Elkhart, Elwood, Evansville, Fishers, Fort Wayne, Fowler, Frankfort, Franklin, Gary, Goshen, Greencastle, Greenfield, Greensburg, Greenwood, Griffith, Hammond, Hobart, Huntington, Indianapolis, Jasper, Kendallville, Knox, Kokomo, La Porte, Lafayette, Lagrange, Lebanon, Ligonier, Linton, Madison, Marion, Martinsville, Merrillville, Michigan City, Mishawaka, Monticello, Mooresville, Muncie, Munster, Nappanee, New Albany, New Carlisle, New Castle, New Haven, Noblesville, North Manchester, North Vernon, Paoli, Peru, Petersburg, Plainfield, Plymouth, Portage, Portland, Princeton, Rensselaer, Richmond, Rising Sun, Rochester, Rockport, Rockville, Rushville, Schererville, Seymour, Shelbyville, South Bend, Syracuse, Terre Haute, Tipton, Valparaiso, Vincennes, W Lafayette, Wabash, Warsaw, Washington, Winamac, Winchester *Iowa* Adel, Altoona, Ames, Ankeny, Atlantic, Belle Plaine, Boone, Carroll, Cedar Falls, Cedar Rapids, Chariton, Charles City, Cherokee, Clarinda, Clinton, Coralville, Council Bluffs, Cresco, Creston, Davenport, Decorah, Denison, Des Moines, Dubuque, Dyersville, Eagle Grove, Estherville, Fairfield, Fort Dodge, Fort Madison, Garner, Glenwood, Greenfield, Grinnell, Hampton, Harlan, Humboldt, Independence, Iowa City, Iowa Falls, Jefferson, Keokuk, Knoxville, Le Mars, Logan, Manchester, Maquoketa, Marengo, Marshalltown, Mason City, Mount Pleasant, Muscatine, New Hampton, Newton, Orange City, Osage, Osceola, Ottumwa, Pella, Perry, Pocahontas, Red Oak, Rock Valley, Sac City, Sheldon, Sioux Center, Sioux City, Spencer, Spirit Lake, Stuart, Vinton, Washington, Waterloo, Webster City, West Burlington, West Des Moines, West Union, Winterset *Kansas* Abilene, Anthony, Arkansas City, Atchison, Atwood, Bonner Springs, Burlington, Chanute, Clay Center, Colby, Columbus, Concordia, Derby, Dodge City, El Dorado, Ellsworth, Emporia, Fort Scott, Garden City, Garnett, Girard, Goodland, Great Bend, Hays, Hillsboro, Horton, Hutchinson, Independence, Iola, Junction City, Kansas City, Lawrence ... Lenexa, Liberal, Manhattan, McPherson, Mission, Newton, Oakley, Olathe, Osage City, Osawatomie, Ottawa, Overland Park, Parsons, Pittsburg, Pratt, Salina, Scott City, Seneca, Shawnee Mission ... Wellington, Wichita, Winfield *Kentucky* Alexandria, Ashland, Barbourville, Bardstown, Bardwell, Beaver Dam, Berea, Bowling Green, Brandenburg, Cadiz, Campbellsville, Campton, Carrollt... ...al City, Columbia, ...a, Danville, Dry Ridge, Elizabethtown, Erlanger, Falmouth, Flemingsburg, Florence, Frankfort, Franklin, Georgetown, Glasgow, Grayson, Hazard, Henderson, Hopkinsville, Jackson, ...er, La Grange, Latonia, Leba... ...exington, London, Louisville, Madisonville, Mayfield, Maysville, Middlesboro, Monticello, Morehead, Morgantown, Mount Sterling, Mount Vernon, Murray, Newport, Nichol... ...e, Owensboro, Paducah, Paris, Pike... Pineville, Prestonsburg, Princeton, Radcliff, Richmond, Russell Springs, Russellville, Salyersville, Scottsville, Shelbyville, Somerset, South Williamson, Stanton, Taylorsvil... ...arsaw, West Liberty, Whitley City, Williams... Winchester *Louisiana* Abbeville, Alexandria, Bastrop, Baton Rouge, Bogalusa, Bossier City, Boutte, Crowley, Cut Off, Denham Springs, Deridder, Eunice, Franklinton, G... ...ies, Hammond, Harahan, Harvey, Houma, Jea... ...te, Jena, Jennings, Kenner, Kentwood, La Place, Lafayette, Lake Charles, Leesville, Mandeville, Mansfield, Many, Metairie, Minden, Monroe, Morgan City, Natchit... ...s, New Iberia, New Orleans, New Roads, Oakdale, ...elousas, Pineville, Plaquemine, Rayne, Ruston, Shreveport, Slidell, Springhill, St. Francisville, Sulphur, Thibodaux, Ville Platte, West Monroe, Westwego, Winfiel... ...innsboro, Zachary *Maine* Auburn, Augusta, Bangor, B... ...arbor, Belfast, Biddeford, Boothbay Harbor, Brunswick, Bucksport, Damariscotta, Dover-Foxcroft, Ellsworth, Falmouth, Farmington, Fort Kent, Lewiston, Mac... ...s, Madawaska, Mexico, Millinocket, Oxford, Portland, P... ...ue Isle, Rockland, Sanford, Skowhegan, South Portland, Standish, Topsham, Waterville, Wells, Windham *Maryland* Aberdeen, Annapolis, Baltimore, Bel... Beltsville. Bethesda. Bowie. Burtonsville, Cambridge, Cator... ...le, Charlotte Hall, Chestertown, Clinton, Cockeysville, College Park, Columbia, Denton, Derwood, Dunkirk, Easton, Edgewood, Eldersburg, Elkton, Ellicot... ...y, F... ...rederick, Gaithersburg, Gan... ...lls, Germantown, Glen Burnie, Greenbelt, Hagerstown, Hampstead, Hanover, Hyattsville, Kensington, La Plata, La Vale, Largo, Laurel, Leonardtown, Lexi... ...on Park, M... ...ights, M... ...Mount Airy, Oakland, Ocea... ...ity, Odenton, Olney, Owings Mills, Oxon Hill, Oxon Hill, Pasadena, Pocomoke City, Potomac, Prince Fredrick, Randallstown, Reisterstown, Rockville, S... ...bury, Seat... Severna ...er Spring, Stevensville, ...oma Park, Towson, Waldorf, Westminster, Wheaton *Massachusetts* Acton, Andover, Ashland, Athol, Auburn, Bedford, Beverly, Billerica, Boston, Bra... ...ee, Bridge... ...ckton, Br... ...rlington, Cambridge, Che... ...sford, Chicopee, Danvers, Dedham, Dorchester, East Boston, East Walpole, East Wareham, Fairhaven, Fall River, Falmouth, Fitchburg, Foxboro, Frar... ...n, Gardner, ...r, Greenfi... Barrington, Hadley, Hano... Haverhill, Holyoke, Hyannis, Kingston, Lanesborough, Lenox, Leominster, Lowell, Lynn, Malden, Marlborough, Marshfield, Medford, Milford, Nan... ...ket, Natick, ...ford, New... Newton, North Adams, N... ...h Attleboro, North Dartmouth, Northampton, Orleans, Peabody, Pittsfield, Plymouth, Quincy, Raynham, Revere, Roslindale, Saugus, South Attle... ...o, South Bo... ...uth Denni... Easton, South Lawrence, ...uth Yarmouth, Southbridge, Springfield, Stoneham, Stoughton, Sudbury, Swampscott, Swansea, Taunton, Vineyard Haven, Waltham, Watertown... Webster, We... ...field, We... ...n, Westfield, Westford, Whi... ...sville, Wilmington, Woburn, Worcester *Michigan* Adrian, Albion, Allegan, Alpena, Ann Arbor, Auburn Hills, Bad Axe, Battle Creek, Bay City, Bellaire ...elleville, Ben... ...ig Rapids, Birmingham, Bloomfie... Boyne City, Brighton, Brooklyn, Brown City, Burton, Byron Center, Cadillac, Canton, Caro, Carson City, Cass City, Center Line, Charlevoix, Cheboygan ...esaning, Cl... ...n Township, Clio, Coldwater, Co... ...erce, Davison, Dearborn, Dearborn Heights, Detroit, Dowagiac, Eastpointe, Eaton Rapids, Escanaba, Evart, Farmington Hills, Farmington, Fenton, Fe... ...dale, Flint, F... ...t, Fran... Fremont, Gaylord, Grand Bla... Grand Haven, Grand Rapids, Grayling, Greenville, Grosse Pointe, Hastings, Hemlock, Highland Park, Holland, Houghton Lake, Howell, Imlay City, Ion... ...ron Mount... ...ood, Ish... ...ackson, Jenison, Jonesville ...lamazoo, Kalkaska, Kentwood, Lake Orion, L'Anse, Lansing, Lapeer, Lincoln Park, Livonia, Ludington, Madison Heights, Manistee, Manistique, Marin... ...ty, Marque... ...hall, Mi... ...ord, Monroe, Mount Pleas... ..., Munising, Muskegon, Newberry, Niles, Novi, Oak Park, Okemos, Oscoda, Owosso, Petoskey, Pinconning, Plainwell, Pontiac, Port Huron, Portage, Re... ...d, Reed C... ...ond, Roc... ...s, Rogers City, Roseville, ...al Oak, Saginaw, Sandusky, Sault St. Marie, Shelby, South Haven, Southfield, Southgate, St. Ignace, St. Johns, Standish, Stanton, Sturgis, Suttons Bay, ...as City, ...ee Oaks, ...rs, Traverse City, Troy, ...a, Vassar, Washington Township, Waterford, Wayne, Westland, White Cloud, White Pigeon, Whitehall, Woodhaven, Wyoming, Ypsilanti *Minnesota* Ada, ...in, Alba... Lea, Alex... ...ple Valley, Austin, Ba... ...te, Baxter, Bemidji, Benson, Blaine, Bloomington, Brooklyn Center, Burnsville, Cambridge, Chanhassen, Coon Rapids, Cottage Grove, Crystal, Detroit Lakes, ...uth, Du... ...gan, Eden... ...na, Elk River, Erskine ...irmont, Faribault, Fergus Falls, Forest Lake, Golden Valley, Grand Marais, Grand Rapids, Hibbing, Hilltop, Hutchinson, International Falls, Jackson, Lake City, L... ...ueur ... Little Fall... ...airie, Mankato, Ma... Grove, Marshall, Minneapolis, Minnetonka, Montevideo, Monticello, Moorhead, Moose Lake, Mora, Morris, New Ulm, North Branch, Ortonville, Owatonna, Pa... ...pids, Pi... ...eton, Red W... Redwood Falls, Richfield, Rochester, Roseau, Roseville, Saint Cloud, Saint Paul, Savage, Shakopee, Sleepy Eye, St. Cloud, St. James, St. Louis Park, St. Paul, S... ...ter, Stillwater, Thief River Falls, Vadnais Height... ...rginia, Walker, Warroad, Waseca, Wayzata, Willmar, Windom, Winona, Woodbury, Worthington, Young America *Mississippi* Amory, Batesville, Biloxi, Booneville, Bro... ...ven, Canton, Carthage, Clarksdale, Clevel... Clinton, Columbia, Columbus, Corinth, Crystal Springs, D'Iberville, Flora, Greenville, Greenwood, Grenada, Gulfport, Hattiesburg, Houston, Jackson, Laurel, Lucedale, Mag... McComb, Mendenhall, Meridian, Mont... , Morton, Natchez, New Albany, Ocean Springs, Olive Branch, Oxford, Pascagoula, Pearl, Philadelphia, Picayune, Pontotoc, Poplarville, Prentiss, Purvis, Quitman, Ridgeland, Se... ...c, Southaven, Starkville, Tupel... ...rtown, Vicksburg, Waynesboro, West Point, Wiggins, Yazoo City *Missouri* Alton, Arnold,

RADIOSHACK

RadioShack.

CONSOLIDATED BALANCE SHEETS
RadioShack Corporation and Subsidiaries

(In millions, except for share amounts)	December 31, 2007	December 31, 2006
Assets		
Current assets:		
Cash and cash equivalents	$ 509.7	$ 472.0
Accounts and notes receivable, net	256.0	247.9
Inventories	705.4	752.1
Other current assets	95.7	127.6
Total current assets	1,566.8	1,599.6
Property, plant and equipment, net	317.1	386.3
Other assets, net	105.7	84.1
Total assets	$ 1,989.6	$ 2,070.0
Liabilities and Stockholders' Equity		
Current liabilities:		
Short-term debt, including current maturities of long-term debt	$ 61.2	$ 194.9
Accounts payable	257.6	254.5
Accrued expenses and other current liabilities	393.5	442.2
Income taxes payable	35.7	92.6
Total current liabilities	748.0	984.2
Long-term debt, excluding current maturities	348.2	345.8
Other non-current liabilities	123.7	86.2
Total liabilities	1,219.9	1,416.2
Commitments and contingent liabilities		
Stockholders' equity:		
Preferred stock, no par value, 1,000,000 shares authorized:		
Series A junior participating, 300,000 shares designated and none issued	—	—
Common stock, $1 par value, 650,000,000 shares authorized; 191,033,000 shares issued	191.0	191.0
Additional paid-in capital	108.4	92.6
Retained earnings	1,992.1	1,780.9
Treasury stock, at cost; 59,940,000 and 55,196,000 shares, respectively	(1,516.5)	(1,409.1)
Accumulated other comprehensive loss	(5.3)	(1.6)
Total stockholders' equity	769.7	653.8
Total liabilities and stockholders' equity	$ 1,989.6	$ 2,070.0

CONSOLIDATED STATEMENTS OF INCOME
RadioShack Corporation and Subsidiaries

| (In millions, except per share amounts) | Year Ended December 31, | | | | | |
| | 2007 | | 2006 | | 2005 | |
	Dollars	% of Revenues	Dollars	% of Revenues	Dollars	% of Revenues
Net sales and operating revenues	$4,251.7	100.0%	$4,777.5	100.0%	$5,081.7	100.0%
Cost of products sold (includes depreciation amounts of $10.0 million, $10.7 million and $10.3 million, respectively)	2,225.9	52.4	2,648.1	55.4	2,815.0	55.4
Gross profit	2,025.8	47.6	2,129.4	44.6	2,266.7	44.6
Operating expenses:						
Selling, general and administrative	1,538.5	36.2	1,810.7	37.9	1,803.3	35.5
Depreciation and amortization	102.7	2.4	117.5	2.5	113.5	2.2
Impairment of long-lived assets and other charges	2.7	—	44.3	0.9	—	—
Total operating expenses	1,643.9	38.6	1,972.5	41.3	1,916.8	37.7
Operating income	381.9	9.0	156.9	3.3	349.9	6.9
Interest income	22.6	0.5	7.4	0.1	5.9	0.1
Interest expense	(38.8)	(0.9)	(44.3)	(0.9)	(44.5)	(0.8)
Other income (loss)	0.9	—	(8.6)	(0.2)	10.2	0.2
Income before income taxes	366.6	8.6	111.4	2.3	321.5	6.4
Income tax provision	129.8	3.0	38.0	0.8	51.6	1.0
Income before cumulative effect of change in accounting principle	236.8	5.6	73.4	1.5	269.9	5.4
Cumulative effect of change in accounting principle, net of $1.8 million tax benefit in 2005	—	—	—	—	(2.9)	(0.1)
Net income	$ 236.8	5.6%	$ 73.4	1.5%	$ 267.0	5.3%3

Net income per share

Basic:

Income before cumulative effect of change in accounting principle	$	1.76	$	0.54	$	1.82
Cumulative effect of change in accounting principle, net of taxes		—		—		(0.02)
Basic income per share	$	1.76	$	0.54	$	1.80

Assuming dilution:

Income before cumulative effect of change in accounting principle	$	1.74	$	0.54	$	1.81
Cumulative effect of change in accounting principle, net of taxes		—		—		(0.02)
Diluted income per share	$	1.74	$	0.54	$	1.79

Shares used in computing income per share:

Basic	134.6	136.2	148.1
Diluted	135.9	136.2	148.8

CONSOLIDATED STATEMENTS OF STOCKHOLDERS' EQUITY AND COMPREHENSIVE INCOME
RadioShack Corporation and Subsidiaries

(In millions)	Shares at December 31,			Dollars at December 31,		
	2007	2006	2005	2007	2006	2005
Common stock						
Beginning and end of year	191.0	191.0	191.0	$ 191.0	$ 191.0	$ 191.0
Treasury stock						
Beginning of year	(55.2)	(56.0)	(32.8)	$(1,409.1)	$(1,431.6)	$ (859.4)
Purchase of treasury stock	(8.7)	—	(25.3)	(208.5)	—	(625.8)
Issuance of common stock	0.5	0.6	1.2	12.8	18.6	31.8
Exercise of stock options and grant of stock awards	3.5	0.2	0.9	88.3	3.9	21.8
End of year	(59.9)	(55.2)	(56.0)	$(1,516.5)	$(1,409.1)	$(1,431.6)
Additional paid-in capital						
Beginning of year				$ 92.6	$ 87.7	$ 82.7
Issuance of common stock				6.2	(5.7)	3.5
Excercise of stock options and grant of stock awards				(8.4)	(1.7)	(5.0)
Stock option compensation				10.7	12.0	—
Net stock-based compensation income tax benefits				7.3	0.3	6.5
End of year				$ 108.4	$ 92.6	$ 87.7
Retained earnings						
Beginning of year				$ 1,780.9	$ 1,741.4	$1,508.1
Net income				236.8	73.4	267.0
Implementation of FIN 48				7.2	—	—
Common stock cash dividends declared				(32.8)	(33.9)	(33.7)
End of year				$ 1,992.1	$ 1,780.9	$1,741.4
Accumulated other comprehensive (loss) income						
Beginning of year				$ (1.6)	$ 0.3	$ (0.3)
Pension adjustments, net of tax				0.4	(1.0)	—
Other comprehensive (loss) income				(4.1)	(0.9)	0.6
End of year				$ (5.3)	$ (1.6)	$ 0.3
Total stockholders' equity				$ 769.7	$ 653.8	$ 588.8
Comprehensive income						
Net income				$ 236.8	$ 73.4	$ 267.0
Other comprehensive (loss) income, net of tax:						
Foreign currency translation adjustments				(4.0)	0.3	(0.4)
Amortization of gain on cash flow hedge				(0.1)	(0.1)	(0.1)
Unrealized (loss) gain on securities				—	(1.1)	1.1
Other comprehensive (loss) income				(4.1)	(0.9)	0.6
Comprehensive income				$ 232.7	$ 72.5	$ 267.6

CONSOLIDATED STATEMENTS OF CASH FLOWS
RadioShack Corporation and Subsidiaries

(In millions)	Year Ended December 31,		
	2007	2006	2005
Cash flows from operating activities:			
Net income	$ 236.8	$ 73.4	$ 267.0
Adjustments to reconcile net income to net cash provided by operating activities:			
Depreciation and amortization	112.7	128.2	123.8
Cumulative effect of change in accounting principle	—	—	4.7
Impairment of long-lived assets and other charges	2.7	44.3	—
Stock option compensation	10.7	12.0	—
Reversal of unrecognized tax benefits	(11.9)	—	—
Deferred income taxes	16.5	(32.7)	(74.0)
Other non-cash items	(9.0)	5.1	(2.9)
Provision for credit losses and bad debts	0.4	0.4	0.1
Changes in operating assets and liabilities:			
Accounts and notes receivable	(0.7)	61.8	(68.2)
Inventories	46.8	212.8	38.8
Other current assets	5.3	2.5	28.5
Accounts payable, accrued expenses, income taxes payable and other	(31.3)	(193.0)	45.1
Net cash provided by operating activities	379.0	314.8	362.9
Cash flows from investing activities:			
Additions to property, plant and equipment	(45.3)	(91.0)	(170.7)
Proceeds from sale of property, plant and equipment	1.5	11.1	226.0
Other investing activities	1.8	0.6	(16.0)
Net cash (used in) provided by investing activities	(42.0)	(79.3)	39.3
Cash flows from financing activities:			
Purchases of treasury stock	(208.5)	—	(625.8)
Sale of treasury stock to employee benefit plans	—	10.5	30.1
Proceeds from exercise of stock options	81.3	1.7	17.4
Payments of dividends	(32.8)	(33.9)	(33.7)
Changes in short-term borrowings and outsanding checks in excess of cash balances, net	10.7	42.2	(4.0)
Reductions of long-term borrowings	(150.0)	(8.0)	(0.1)
Net cash (used in) provided by financing activities	(299.3)	12.5	(616.1)
Net increase (decrease) in cash and cash equivalents	37.7	248.0	(213.9)
Cash and cash equivalents, beginning of period	472.0	224.0	437.9
Cash and cash equivalents, end of period	$ 509.7	$ 472.0	$ 224.0
Supplemental cash flow information:			
Interest paid	$ 42.6	$ 44.0	$ 43.4
Income taxes paid	112.2	52.9	158.5

RADIOSHACK

Appendix B

Accounting Principles

Learning Objectives

LO 1 Describe a rules-based and a principles-based approach toward accounting standards.

LO 2 Define the primary objective of financial reporting.

LO 3 Discuss qualitative characteristics of useful accounting information.

LO 4 Describe assumptions underlying useful accounting information.

LO 5 Explain principles of useful accounting information.

LO 6 Describe constraints on useful accounting information.

For accounting information to be useful, it must possess certain qualitative characteristics. The purpose of this appendix is to provide a conceptual framework for accounting principles that is desirable for accounting information.

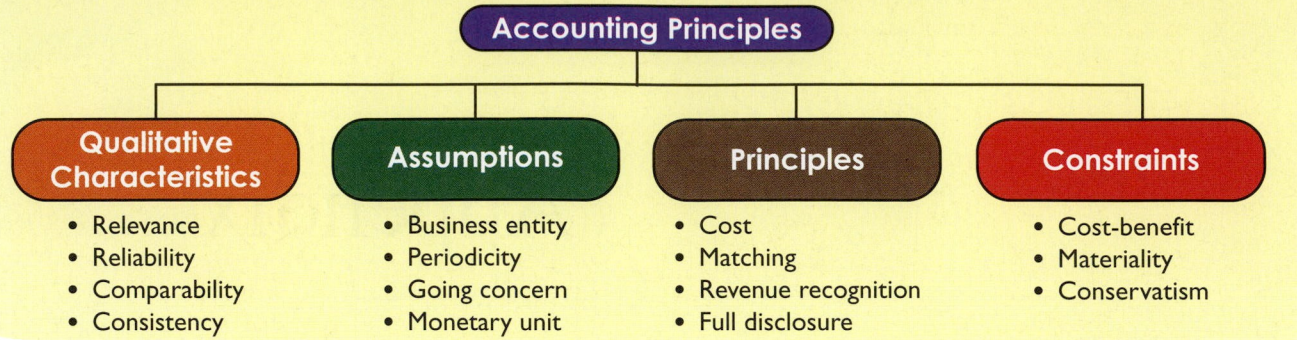

Rules–Based versus Principles–Based Accounting

LO1 Describe a rules-based and a principles-based approach toward accounting standards.

U.S. accounting practices are often viewed as *rules-based* (as mentioned in Chapter 1). This means that companies are required to apply technical, specific, and detailed rules in preparing financial statements and reports. A *principles-based* approach is sometimes argued as preferable. A principles-based system would develop and apply broad, fundamental concepts for accounting. Companies would have more flexibility in preparing principles-based financial statements to meet the intent of the accounting principle rather than just the specific accounting rule.

For example, a broad accounting principle might be that a company must report all debt it might have to repay. Certain executives of **Enron** were able to mislead investors by not reporting some of its debt. While many of Enron's reports technically followed rules-based standards, the reports failed to adequately disclose all of its debts. As another example, a broad principle might be that a company must report all of its building leases that it is contractually obligated to pay as a liability on its balance sheet. Executives of many retail companies (such as **Wal-Mart** and **Payless Shoe Source**) follow the rules-based standards of accounting for leases. Their balance sheets generally fail to comprehensively report all of the leases that each company is required to pay. In both instances, while the rules are technically followed, the accounting has not achieved the intent of the standards.

Sarbanes-Oxley Act and Principles-Based Accounting

As a result of the Enron scandal and other abuses of rules-based accounting practices, the **Sarbanes-Oxley Act** requires the **Securities and Exchange Commission,** the government group that establishes financial reporting requirements, to study the feasibility of shifting to a more "principles-based" approach. The **Financial Accounting Standards Board,** the private group that sets standards for accounting practice, has also proposed changes designed to create a more principles-based approach to accounting standards. Many accounting experts believe that a change to principles-based standards will force companies preparing financial statements to focus on the intent of accounting standards rather than just technical compliance with the rules. On the other side of the debate, some accounting experts worry that a shift to principles-based standards will lead to lawsuits as shareholders and companies fight over the true intent of the standards.

A principles-based system requires a sound conceptual framework. To more fully understand the principles-based approach, the existing conceptual framework of accounting principles is presented in this appendix.

Objectives of Financial Reporting

LO2 Define the primary objective of financial reporting.

External financial statements users, such as investors and creditors, use accounting information in financial reports to make decisions (such as whether to buy or sell a stock or extend a loan). To assist in decision making, accounting reports must possess useful information.

The primary objective of financial reporting is to provide useful economic information to assist decision makers. There are many elements of accounting information. Exhibit B.1 provides a pyramid detailing the framework of qualitative characteristics, assumptions, principles, and constraints for providing useful accounting information.

The objective of financial reporting is to provide useful accounting information to decision makers.

Qualitative Characteristics of Accounting Information
To be useful to decision makers, accounting information should have the following characteristics:

1. Relevance
a. Predictive Value (helps with forecasts)
b. Feedback Value (corrects or confirms forecasts)
c. Timely (available when needed)

2. Reliability
a. Verifiable (can be verified by an independent party)
b. Representational Faithfulness (reports what happened)
c. Neutrality (information is not biased)

3. Comparability
(Different companies use similar accounting principles and methods)

4. Consistency
(Same company uses the same accounting principles and methods each year)

Assumptions	**Principles**	**Constraints**
1. Business Entity (business is accounted for separately from its owner and other business entities)	**1. Cost** (accounting information is based on cash or equal-to-cash basis)	**1. Cost-Benefit** (benefits to accounting information users is greater than the cost to prepare it)
2. Periodicity (the life of a company can be divided up into smaller reportable time periods)	**2. Matching** (expenses are recorded as incurred to generate revenues)	**2. Materiality** (transactions too small to make an impact on a decision maker are recorded in the most cost-beneficial way)
3. Going Concern (entity will continue operating instead of being closed or sold)	**3. Revenue Recognition** (revenue recorded when earned and realizable)	**3. Conservatism** (select accounting methods that are least likely to overstate assets and income)
4. Monetary Unit (transactions expressed in monetary units)	**4. Full Disclosure** (any information that can influence the judgment of a decision maker is reported)	

Qualitative Characteristics of Useful Accounting Information

As noted in Exhibit B.1, to be useful, accounting information must be relevant, reliable, comparable, and consistent across time. Exhibit B.2 provides an illustration of these qualitative characteristics.

Relevance

To provide useful information, that information must be **relevant** to the decision maker. Information is relevant if it would make a difference in a business decision. Information is relevant when it helps users predict the future (*predictive value*) or evaluate the past (*feedback value*) and is received in time to affect their decisions (*timeliness*).

LO3 Discuss qualitative characteristics of useful accounting information.

Reliability

Information is **reliable** if users can depend on it to be free from bias and error. Reliable information is *verifiable* and *faithfully represents* the substance of the underlying economic transaction. If **Best Buy** sold a television for $4,000, it should be reported in its sales revenue as

Qualitative Characteristics of Useful Accounting Information

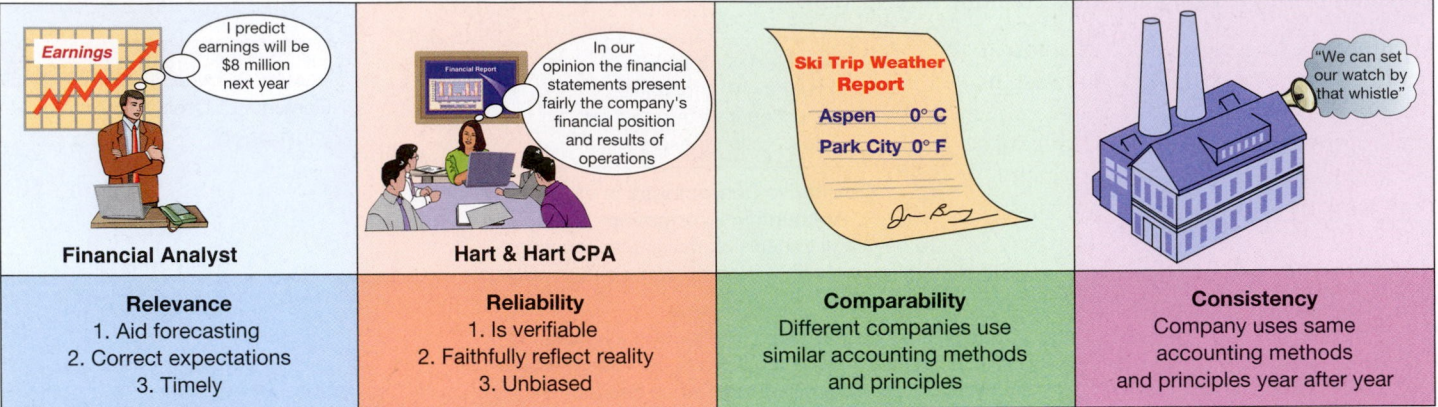

$4,000. Reliable accounting information is neutral, or free from bias. In other words, accounting information should not be designed to lead accounting information users to accept or reject any specific decision alternative.

Comparability

Information is **comparable** if it helps users to identify differences and similarities between companies. Comparability is possible only if companies follow similar accounting methods and practices. However, even if all companies uniformly follow the same accounting practices, comparable reports do not result if the practices are not appropriate. For example, comparable information would not be provided if all companies were to ignore the useful lives of their assets and depreciate all assets over two years.

Comparability is often harder for cross-country comparisons. Suppose we want to make an investment in an automobile manufacturer such as **Daimler Chrysler**, a German company, or **Toyota**, a Japanese company. Since each of these countries has its own set of accounting rules and methods, a direct comparison will be difficult. The **International Accounting Standards Board** has been established to help harmonize accounting practices across countries.

Consistency

Accounting information users generally look at multiple time periods of a company's financial statements to see if there are any noticeable trends. To make this comparison over multiple periods, the same accounting principles and methods should be used in each period. Otherwise, it is hard to know if changes over time are due to real fundamental changes in financial performance or are simply because the company changed the way it accounted for certain items. Applying the same accounting information methods and practices over time is known as **consistency**.

Underlying Accounting Assumptions

LO4 Describe assumptions underlying useful accounting information.

Four assumptions underlie the overall objective of providing useful information to decision makers. These are the business entity assumption, the periodicity assumption, the going concern assumption, and the monetary unit assumption.

Business Entity Assumption

The **business entity assumption** means that a business is accounted for separately from other business entities, including its owner. The reason for this principle is that separate information about each business is necessary for good decisions. A business entity can take one of three legal forms: *proprietorship, partnership,* or *corporation.*

Abuse of the business entity assumption was a main culprit in the collapse of **Enron.**

Periodicity Assumption

A component of providing relevant and useful information is that it must be timely. Useful information must reach decision makers frequently and promptly. To provide timely information, accounting systems prepare reports at regular intervals. This results in an accounting process impacted by the periodicity (or time period) principle. The **periodicity assumption** is that an organization's activities can be divided into specific time periods such as a month, a three-month quarter, a six-month interval, or a year.

"RadioShack announces earnings per share of . . ."

Going-Concern Assumption

The **going-concern assumption** means that accounting information reflects an assumption that the business will continue operating instead of being closed or sold. This implies, for example, that a factory facility is reported at cost instead of, say, liquidation values that assume immediate, involuntary closure.

IN THE NEWS

Principles and Scruples   Auditors, directors, and lawyers are using principles to improve accounting reports. Examples include financial restatements at **Delphi**, accounting reviews at **Echostar**, and expense adjustments at **Electronic Data Systems**. Principles-based accounting has led accounting firms to drop clients deemed too risky.

Monetary Unit Assumption

The **monetary unit assumption** means that we can express transactions and events in monetary, or money, units. Money is the common denominator in business. Examples of monetary units are the dollar in the United States, Canada, Australia, and Singapore; the pound sterling in the United Kingdom; and the peso in Mexico, the Philippines, and Chile. The monetary unit assumption also means that financial statement amounts are typically not adjusted for the effects of inflation.

> For currency conversion:
> **www.xe.com**

HOW YOU DOIN'?   Answers—p. B-8

1. Why is it important to have comparable accounting methods between companies?
2. Why is the business entity assumption important?
3. Why is the going-concern assumption important?

Accounting Principles

Accounting relies on four key principles (as illustrated in Exhibit B.1): cost, matching, revenue recognition, and full disclosure.

LO5 Explain principles of useful accounting information.

Cost Principle

The **cost principle** means that accounting information is based on actual cost. Cost is measured on a cash or equal-to-cash basis. This means if cash is given for a service, the transaction's cost is measured as the amount of cash paid. If something besides cash is exchanged (such as a car traded for a truck), the transaction's cost is measured as the cash value of what is given up or received. The cost principle emphasizes reliability, and information based on cost is considered objective. To illustrate, suppose a company pays $5,000 for equipment. The cost principle requires that this purchase be recorded at a cost of $5,000. It makes no difference if the owner thinks this equipment is now worth $7,000.

> The cost principle is also called the *historical cost principle*.

Matching Principle

The **matching principle** prescribes that expenses be reported in the same period and on the same income statement as the revenues that were earned as a result of those expenses. To illustrate, suppose a business provides traffic consulting services to a municipal client. All of the expenses (consultant labor, computer use, copies, travel, presentation preparation, use of office space) incurred to complete those consulting services should be recorded in the same period as the consulting services.

Sometimes, it is difficult to match each expense with its related revenue. There are three general guidelines that are used in applying the matching principle (with examples):

Guideline	Example
• Cause and effect	Expenses directly incurred to generate revenue such as consultant labor
• Systematic and rational allocation	Depreciation of office equipment and office space
• Immediate recognition of some costs with uncertain future benefits	Advertising, salary of consultant's supervisor

Revenue Recognition Principle

Revenue (sales) is the amount received from selling products and services. The **revenue recognition principle** provides guidance on when a company must recognize revenue. To *recognize* revenue means to record it. If revenue is recognized too early, a company would look more profitable than it is. If revenue is recognized too late, a company would look less profitable than it is. The following three concepts are important to revenue recognition. (1) *Revenue is recognized when earned.* The earnings process is normally complete when services are performed or a seller transfers ownership of products to the buyer. (2) *Proceeds from selling products and services need not be in cash.* A common noncash proceed received by a seller is a customer's promise to pay at a future date, called *credit sales*. (3) *Revenue is measured by the cash received plus the cash value of any other items received.*

> When a bookstore sells a textbook on credit is its earnings process complete? *Answer:* The bookstore can record sales for these books minus an amount expected for book returns.

IN THE NEWS

Revenues for the **New England Patriots** football team include ticket sales, television and cable broadcasts, radio rights, concessions, and advertising. Revenues from ticket sales are earned when the Patriots play each game. Advance ticket sales are not revenues; instead, they represent a liability until the Patriots play the game for which the ticket was sold.

Full Disclosure Principle

Companies have many choices on what information to report. The **full disclosure principle** requires that all accounting information important enough to affect a decision be presented. Such accounting information may be disclosed in the financial statements, footnotes to the financial statements, or as supplementary information. There is always the possibility that too much information or too much detail will overwhelm the user. Therefore, companies try to be clear but concise.

Accounting Constraints

LO6 Describe constraints on useful accounting information.

All of the assumptions and principles discussed thus far help accountants provide useful information to decision makers. However, providing all of this quality information can be too costly to the company. There is a balance between providing sufficient information to the decision maker without being too costly to the company preparing the accounting information. There are three constraints to providing useful information to the decision maker: cost-benefit, materiality, and conservatism.

Cost-Benefit

The benefit to decision makers of receiving accounting information must be worth the cost of providing it. The **cost-benefit** trade-off suggests that information will be provided only if the benefits to users outweigh the costs of preparing and disclosing it.

However, the costs and benefits are not always easy to compute. Moreover, the costs are usually borne by the company, and the benefits are received by a diverse set of decision makers across the world. Still, it is useful to try to carefully consider the costs and benefits before producing or requiring the disclosure of additional accounting information.

Materiality

Materiality asks the question: Is the item big enough to make an impact on the decision maker? If the item is not big enough to make a difference, then **generally accepted accounting principles (GAAP)** do not have to be followed. To illustrate, if **RadioShack** makes a $10 mistake in recording an expense when its overall expenses are $10 billion, the $10 error is most likely not a material item and GAAP need not be followed.

Conservatism

Conservatism suggests that when faced with two equally plausible accounting method choices (or estimates), the company should choose the accounting method (or estimate) that is least likely to overstate assets and income or to understate liabilities and expenses. Managers are generally optimistic, and this constraint offsets that optimism to help present a more conservative view of a company's financial position. The general concept can be summarized in this way: if in doubt, recognize all losses but do not recognize any gains.

A common example of conservatism is in the valuation of inventory. Inventories are usually recorded at their cost. However, if the market value of the inventory falls below its cost, conservatism requires that inventories be written down to the market value. To illustrate, consider a company that sells computer systems. Due to the quick technology advances and declining prices of new computer hardware, if a computer does not sell relatively quickly, the market value can fall below the cost to manufacture and sell it. Due to conservatism, the computer is written down to its market value.

HOW YOU DOIN'?   Answers—p. B-8

4. Why is the revenue recognition principle important?

5. Do you think a $10 million error would be material in a company with $100 million in sales?

Summary

LO1 **Describe a rules-based and a principles-based approach toward accounting standards.** The rules-based approach implies that companies are required to apply technical, specific, and detailed rules in preparing financial statements and reports. The principles-based approach develops and applies broad, overarching, and fundamental concepts for accounting.

LO2 **Define the primary objective of financial reporting.** The primary objective of accounting is to provide useful economic information to assist decision makers to make decisions.

LO3 **Discuss qualitative characteristics of useful accounting information.** The qualitative characteristics of useful accounting information are that the information must be relevant, reliable, comparable, and consistent. Information is relevant if it would make a difference in a decision. Reliable information is information that can be depended on. Companies can be compared to each other if they use the same accounting methods and principles. Consistency

is met when firms apply the same accounting methods and principles year after year.

LO4 **Describe assumptions underlying useful accounting information.** There are several underlying assumptions to support the overall objective of providing useful information to decision makers including the business entity assumption, the periodicity assumption, the going concern assumption, and the monetary unit assumption.

LO5 **Explain principles of useful accounting information.** Accounting principles help make accounting information useful to decision makers. They include the cost, matching, revenue recognition, and full disclosure principles.

LO6 **Describe constraints on useful accounting information.** There are three constraints to providing useful information to decision makers. The benefits of the accounting information must be greater than the costs, the accounting information must be material, and the accounting choices must be conservative.

Guidance Answers to HOW YOU DOIN'?

1. Comparable accounting information provides a similar measuring stick for both companies to assess their relative financial performance. If companies have different accounting methods, there is no way to compare them. It would be like comparing apples to oranges.

2. Users desire information about the performance of a specific entity. If information is mixed between two or more entities, its usefulness decreases.

3. Many of the elements of the financial statements assume that company will continue in operation. This allows them to be valued at cost on the balance sheet rather than being sold at liquidation prices.

4. The revenue recognition principle gives guidelines of when to recognize (record) revenue. This is important; for example, if revenue is recognized too early, the financial statements report revenue sooner than it should and the business looks more profitable than it is. The reverse is also true.

5. Yes, this would be considered to be a material item since it represents 10% of the firm's sales, suggesting it would make a difference on a decision maker's decisions.

Key Terms

Business entity assumption (p. B-4) Concept that assumes a business will be accounted for separately from its owner(s) and any other entity.

Comparability (p. B-4) A qualitative characteristic of accounting information suggesting that information is more useful if it can be related to an industry or competitor benchmark.

Conservatism (p. B-7) Concept that prescribes use of the less optimistic estimate when two estimates are about equally likely.

Consistency (p. B-4) A qualitative characteristic of accounting information that prescribes use of the same accounting method(s) and practice(s) over time so that financial statements are comparable across periods.

Cost-benefit (p. B-7) A constraint of useful accounting information prescribing that information will be provided only if the benefits to users outweigh the costs of preparation.

Cost principle (p. B-5) Accounting principle that prescribes financial statement information to be based on actual costs incurred in business transactions.

Financial Accounting Standards Board (FASB) (p. B-2) Independent group of full-time members responsible for setting accounting rules.

Full disclosure principle (p. B-6) Principle that prescribes financial statements (including notes) to report all relevant information about an entity's operations and financial condition.

Generally Accepted Accounting Principles (GAAP) (p. B-7) Rules that specify acceptable accounting practices.

Going-concern assumption (p. B-5) Concept that prescribes financial statements to reflect the assumption that the business will continue operating indefinitely.

International Accounting Standards Board (IASB) (p. B-4) Group that identifies preferred accounting practices and encourages global acceptance; issues International Financial Reporting Standards (IFRS).

Matching principle (p. B-6) Prescribes expenses to be reported in the same period as the revenues that were earned as a result of the expenses.

Materiality (p. B-7) Prescribes that accounting for items that markedly impact financial statements, and any inferences drawn from them, adhere to GAAP.

Monetary unit assumption (p. B-5) Concept that assumes transactions and events can be expressed in money units.

Periodicity assumption (p. B-5) The life of a company can be divided up into smaller, reportable time periods.

Relevance (p. B-3) A qualitative characteristic of accounting information that prescribes that information be useful, understandable, timely, and pertinent for decision making.

Reliability (p. B-3) The principle that information is verifiable and faithfully represents the substance of the underlying economic transaction.

Revenue recognition principle (p. B-6) The principle prescribing that revenue is recognized when earned.

Sarbanes-Oxley Act (p. B-2) Created the *Public Company Accounting Oversight Board,* regulates analyst conflicts, imposes corporate governance requirements, enhances accounting and control disclosures, impacts insider transactions and executive loans, establishes new types of criminal conduct, and expands penalties for violations of federal securities laws.

Securities and Exchange Commission (SEC) (p. B-2) Federal agency Congress has charged to set reporting rules for organizations that sell ownership shares to the public.

Multiple Choice Quiz   Answers on p. B-12   mhhe.com/wildCA2e

Additional Multiple Choice Quizzes are available at the book's Website.

1. The principle that prescribes that a business be accounted for separately and distinctly from its owner or owners is known as the:
   a. Matching principle.
   b. Business entity assumption.
   c. Going-concern assumption.
   d. Revenue recognition principle.
   e. Cost principle.

2. The rule that prescribes financial statements reflect the assumption that the business will continue operating instead of being closed or sold, unless evidence shows that it will not continue, is the:
   a. Going-concern assumption.
   b. Business entity assumption.
   c. Matching principle.
   d. Cost Principle.
   e. Monetary unit assumption.

3. To include the personal assets and transactions of a business's owner in the records and reports of the business would conflict with the:
  a. Matching principle.
  b. Realization principle.
  c. Business entity assumption.
  d. Going-concern assumption.
  e. Revenue recognition principle.

4. The accounting principle that prescribes accounting information be based on actual cost and requires assets and services to be recorded initially at the cash or cash-equivalent amount given in exchange, is the:
  a. Accounting equation.
  b. Cost principle.

  c. Going-concern assumption.
  d. Revenue recognition principle.
  e. Business entity assumption.

5. The qualitative characteristic of reliability:
  a. Means that information is supported by independent, unbiased evidence.
  b. Means that information can be based on what the preparer thinks is true.
  c. Means that financial statements should contain information that is optimistic.
  d. Means that a business may not reorganize revenue until cash is received.
  e. All of the above.

Discussion Questions

1. Describe the four key qualitative characteristics of useful accounting information.
2. Why is the business entity assumption important?
3. Why is the matching principle important?
4. What are the three basic forms of business organization?
5. What does the reliability characteristic imply for information reported in financial statements?
6. A business reports its own office stationery on the balance sheet at its $400 cost, although it cannot be sold for more than

$10 as scrap paper. Which accounting principle(s) justifies this treatment?
7. What is **Best Buy**'s revenue recognition policy (as detailed in the footnotes to its financial statements [page A-11])?
8. By examining **RadioShack**'s financial statements in Appendix A, what  evidence is there that the company follows the matching principle?

connect

Identify the following characteristics of useful accounting information as being a component of either Relevant (R) or Reliable (L). (*Hint:* Refer to Exhibit B.1.)
1. Timeliness
2. Verifiable
3. Representational Faithfulness
4. Predictive Value
5. Feedback Value
6. Neutrality

QUICK STUDY

QS B–1
Identifying characteristics of accounting information **L03**

Fill in the blanks with appropriate accounting terminology.
1. Accounting information is _____ if different companies use similar accounting principles.
2. Information is _____ if it would make a difference in a business decision.
3. Accounting information is _____ if the same company uses the same accounting methods year after year.
4. Information is reliable if users can depend on it to be free from _____ and error.

QS B–2
Terminology of the characteristics of accounting information   **L03**

Identify the appropriate assumption underlying useful accounting information for each description 1 through 4.
1. Hancock Hats reports its sales on a monthly basis.
2. Joann Hancock, owner of Hancock Hats, keeps the accounting records of her business separate from her personal accounts.
3. Hancock Hats reports its financial statements assuming it will continue to be in business for the foreseeable future.
4. Hancock Hats expresses its financial statements using the U.S. dollar.

QS B–3
Assumptions underlying useful accounting information   **L04**

Identify the appropriate accounting principle for each description 1 through 4.
1. Callahan's Castles records expenses incurred to produce revenues in the accounting period.
2. Callahan's Castles discloses all information about pension expenses that can influence the decision maker.
3. Callahan's Castles records sales on its toy castles when they are delivered to the customer.
4. Callahan's Castles records its computer equipment at its acquisition cost.

QS B–4
Principles of useful accounting information **L05**

QS B-5
Constraints of useful accounting
information   **LO6**

Fill in the blanks with appropriate accounting terminology.

1. _____ suggests that transactions that are too small to make an impact on a decision maker are recorded in the most cost beneficial way.

2. Conservatism suggests that accounting methods be selected that are least likely to _____ assets and income.

3. The _____-benefit constraint suggests that the benefits to receiving accounting information than the costs to prepare it.

---

connect

EXERCISES

Exercise B-1
Identifying accounting principles
or assumptions   **LO4   LO5**

Identify which general accounting principle best describes each of the following practices.

a. In December 2009, Chavez Landscaping received a customer's order and cash prepayment to install sod at a new house that would not be ready for installation until March 2010. Chavez should record the revenue from the customer order in March 2010, not in December 2009.

b. If $51,000 cash is paid to buy land, the land is reported on the buyer's balance sheet at $51,000.

c. Jo Keene owns both Sailing Passions and Dockside Supplies. In preparing financial statements for Dockside Supplies, Keene makes sure that the expense transactions of Sailing Passions are kept separate from Dockside's statements.

Exercise B-2
Rules-based vs. principles-based
accounting   **LO1   LO3**

Target Corporation follows accounting rules in reporting its lease obligations. However, the vast majority of Target's obligations for its store leases are not reported as liabilities on Target's balance sheet. Similar to other retail establishments, Target structures its leases to avoid reporting lease liabilities on the balance sheet.

1. Why does Target Corp. wish to avoid reporting its store leases on the balance sheet?

2. Would a principles-based approach continue to allow Target Corp. to avoid reporting its store leases on the balance sheet?

3. Which qualitative characteristic(s) of accounting information is violated when Target Corp. avoids reporting its store leases on the balance sheet?

Exercise B-3
Identifying accounting principles
LO4   LO5

Match each of the numbered descriptions with the principle it best reflects. Indicate your answer by writing the letter for the appropriate principle in the blank space next to each description.

A. Cost principle
B. Business entity principle
C. Revenue recognition principle
D. Going-concern principle

_____ **1.** Financial statements reflect the assumption that the business continues operating.
_____ **2.** Every business is accounted for separately from its owner or owners.
_____ **3.** Revenue is recorded only when the earnings process is complete.
_____ **4.** Information is based on actual costs incurred in transactions.

Exercise B-4
Identifying accounting principles
and assumptions   **LO4   LO5**

You are reviewing the accounting records of Cathy's Antiques, owned by Cathy Miller. You have uncovered the following situations. Cite the appropriate accounting principle or assumption and suggest an action for each separate item.

1. In August, a check for $500 was written to Wee Day Care Center; this amount represents child care for her son Brandon.

2. Cathy plans a Going Out of Business Sale for May, since she will be closing her business for a month-long vacation in June. She plans to reopen July 1 and will continue operating Cathy's Antiques indefinitely.

3. Cathy received a shipment of pine furniture from Quebec, Canada; the invoice was stated in Canadian dollars.

4. Joseph Clark paid $1,500 for a dining table; the amount was recorded as revenue. The table will be delivered to Mr. Clark in six weeks.

Match each of the numbered transactions to the accounting terms A through E applicable to recording and reporting them.

A. Business entity assumption

B. Reliability

C. Cost principle

D. Monetary unit assumption

E. Revenue recognition principle

_____ **1.** An insurance company receives insurance premiums for six future months' worth of coverage.

_____ **2.** A building is for sale at $480,000; an appraisal is given for $450,000.

_____ **3.** Helen Cho, a sole proprietor, pays for her daughter's preschool out-of-business funds.

_____ **4.** Mayan Imports receives a shipment from Mexico; the invoice is stated in pesos.

_____ **5.** To make the balance sheet look better, Helen Cho added several thousand dollars to the Equipment account that she believed was undervalued.

Exercise B-5
Identifying accounting principles and assumptions
LO3   LO4   LO5

Fill in the blanks with the appropriate accounting terms or phrases.

1. _____ means that a company applies the same concept year after year.

2. For information to be relevant, it should have predictive or feedback _____, and it must be presented in a _____ manner.

3. _____ is the quality of information that suggests it can be depended on to represent reality, be verifiable and not be biased.

4. _____ means that two companies can be assessed relative to each other.

Exercise B-6
Identifying qualitative characteristics   **LO3**

---

1. Pagnozzi Properties is trying to decide if it needs to install a new accounting system to keep track of every detailed construction cost. The cost of the system will be $20,000 and the benefits are uncertain.

2. Gary Peters makes a $20 mistake when accounting for travel expenses. He has a question of whether this mistake needs to be corrected since it is relatively small.

3. Manuel Sanchez wants to know which accounting choice to make when accounting for consulting expenses at the end of the year. He decides that when in doubt, it would be better to understate rather than overstate net income.

In each case 1 through 3, identify the constraint that each of these statements addresses.

Exercise B-7
Identifying constraints of providing useful information   **LO6**

---

1. Inventory is reported at market value when cost is lower.

2. Computers costing less than $1,000 are immediately expensed even though their useful life is three years.

3. The auditors of Dietrich Co. found an error of $50 in its financial statements and decide to restate their financial statements; Dietrich has sales revenue of $15 million.

4. To appropriately account for the pension liability, Ziebart Co. installs an abnormally expensive system to track employees, their health, and their pension status. Ziebart argues that this system is necessary to comply with accounting guidelines.

Indicate the accounting constraint, if any, that is violated by each practice.

Exercise B-8
Identifying constraints violated   **LO6**

---

connect

Identify the accounting assumption, principle, or constraint that best describes the accounting practices at Ben Wallace Company.

1. Land is valued at its original purchase price rather than its appraised value.

2. Ben Wallace Company issues financial statements every three months.

3. Expenses are allocated to the appropriate revenues each accounting period.

4. All relevant financial information is disclosed in the financial reports.

PROBLEM SET A

Problem B-1A
Identify accounting assumptions, principles, or constraints
LO4   LO5   LO6

5. Personal computers costing less than $1,000 are expensed in the current period even though their useful life is three years.

6. The CEO's personal business records are kept separate from the company's records.

7. The U.S. dollar is the unit of currency used in financial reports.

Problem B-2A
Identifying assumptions, principles, or constraints violated
LO4   LO5   LO6

Presented below are transactions that occurred during 2010.

1. Susan Scholz, the president of Lake of the Ozarks cabin properties, buys a computer for personal use and charges it to her company's expense account.

2. In preparation of its financial statements, Ettredge Inc. omitted information about its method of accounting for accounts receivable.

3. To make its profits look better, Shanghai Automotive booked sales before its cars were shipped.

4. Jose Martinez reports all of its assets and liabilities at liquidation value, even though the company does not expect to go out of business in the foreseeable future.

5. Tom Hapgood writes up his inventory on the balance sheet since its market value is higher than its cost.

Required

For each of the above transactions, identify the assumption, principle, or constraint that has been violated.

PROBLEM SET B

Problem B-1B
Identify accounting assumptions, principles, or constraints
LO4   LO5   LO6

Identify the accounting assumption, principle, or constraint that best describes the accounting practices at Steve Hill Company.

1. Financial statements are prepared each year.

2. Market value changes after an asset's purchase are not recorded in the accounts.

3. Notes and supplementary information are included with the financial statements.

4. The factory is not reported at liquidation value. (Do not use the cost principle.)

5. Manufactured toys are not recorded as revenues until they have been sold and shipped.

6. Requires that generally accepted accounting principles be followed for all material items.

Problem B-2B
Identifying assumptions, principles, or constraints violated
LO4   LO5   LO6

Danny Manning and Larry Brown are accountants for the Engineering Institute. They disagree over the following transactions that occurred during 2010. Larry disagrees with Danny on each of the transactions below.

1. The Engineering Institute finds a bargain for a commercial-grade plotter and pays $3,000. Danny argues that if they had bought it from the dealer, they would have paid $4,000. Danny suggests they record the plotter for $4,000.

2. Timothy West, president of the Engineering Institute, used his company expense account to purchase a new BMW for his personal use. Danny argues that since the president is also the owner of the Engineering Institute, it really does not matter who paid for it.

3. Depreciation for the year was $114,000. Danny argues that since net income is expected to be lower in the current fiscal year, they should just charge it as an expense next year.

4. Danny suggests that the Engineering Institute value its equipment on its balance sheet at its liquidation value, which is $50,000 less than cost.

5. The Engineering Institute signed a lease on its offices for the next five years. A lease liability is not included on the company's balance sheet. Danny doesn't think such information needs to be disclosed.

Required

For each of the above transactions, identify why Larry disagrees. Also identify the assumption, principle, or constraint that has been violated.

ANSWERS TO MULTIPLE CHOICE QUIZ

1. b   **4.** b
2. a   **5.** a
3. c

Glossary

Accelerated depreciation method Method that produces larger depreciation charges in the early years of an asset's life and smaller charges in its later years. *(p. 452)*

Account Record within an accounting system in which increases and decreases are entered and stored in a specific asset, liability, equity, revenue, or expense. *(pp. 23 & 44)*

Account balance Difference between total debits and total credits (including the beginning balance) for an account. *(p. 47)*

Accounting Information and measurement system that identifies, records, and communicates relevant information about a company's business activities. *(p. 4)*

Accounting cycle Recurring steps performed each accounting period, starting with analyzing transactions and continuing through the post-closing trial balance (or reversing entries). *(p. 137)*

Accounting equation Equality involving a company's assets, liabilities, and equity; Assets = Liabilities + Equity; also called *balance sheet equation*. *(p. 22)*

Accounts payable ledger Subsidiary ledger listing individual creditor (supplier) accounts. *(p. 294)*

Accounts receivable Amounts due from customers for credit sales; backed by the customer's general credit standing. *(p. 370)*

Accounts receivable ledger Subsidiary ledger listing individual customer accounts. *(p. 267)*

Accounts receivable turnover Measure of both the quality and liquidity of accounts receivable; indicates how often receivables are received and collected during the period; computed by dividing net sales by average accounts receivable. *(p. 380)*

Accrual basis accounting Accounting system that recognizes revenues when earned and expenses when incurred; the basis for GAAP. *(p. 104)*

Accrued expenses Costs incurred in a period that are both unpaid and unrecorded; adjusting entries for recording accrued expenses involve increasing expenses and increasing liabilities. *(p. 109)*

Accrued revenues Revenues earned in a period that are both unrecorded and not yet received in cash (or other assets); adjusting entries for recording accrued revenues involve increasing assets and increasing revenues. *(p. 324)*

Adjusted trial balance List of accounts and balances prepared after period-end adjustments are recorded and posted. *(p. 110)*

Adjusting entry Journal entry at the end of an accounting period to bring an asset or liability account to its proper amount and update the related expense or revenue account. *(p. 106)*

Aging of accounts receivable Process of classifying accounts receivable by how long they are past due for purposes of estimating uncollectible accounts. *(p. 378)*

Allowance for Doubtful Accounts Contra asset account with a balance approximating uncollectible accounts receivable; also called *Allowance for Uncollectible Accounts*. *(p. 375)*

Allowance method Procedure that (a) estimates and matches bad debts expense with its sales for the period and/or (b) reports accounts receivable at estimated realizable value. *(p. 374)*

Amortization Process of allocating the cost of an intangible asset to expense over its estimated useful life. *(p. 460)*

Annual financial statements Financial statements covering a one-year period; often based on a calendar year, but any consecutive 12-month (or 52-week) period is acceptable. *(p. 105)*

Appropriated retained earnings Retained earnings separately reported to inform stockholders of funding needs. *(p. 548)*

Assets Resources a business owns or controls that are expected to provide current and future benefits to the business. *(p. 22)*

Authorized depository A bank that can accept payroll deposits from its own checking account customers. *(p. 234)*

Authorized stock Total amount of stock that a corporation's charter authorizes it to issue. *(p. 518)*

Average cost See *weighted average*. *(p. 428)*

Avoidable expense Expense (or cost) that is relevant for decision making; expense that is not incurred if a department, product, or service is eliminated. *(p. 817)*

Bad debts Accounts of customers who do not pay what they have promised to pay; an expense of selling on credit; also called *uncollectible accounts*. *(p. 373)*

Balance column account Account with debit and credit columns for recording entries and another column for showing the balance of the account after each entry. *(p. 80)*

Balance sheet Financial statement that lists types and dollar amounts of assets, liabilities, and equity at a specific date. *(p. 29)*

Bank reconciliation Report that explains the difference between the book (company) balance of cash and the cash balance reported on the bank statement. *(p. 186)*

Bank statement Bank report on the depositor's beginning and ending cash balances, and a listing of its changes, for a period. *(p. 185)*

Basic earnings per share Net income less any preferred dividends and then divided by weighted-average common shares outstanding. *(p. 548)*

Betterments Expenditures to make a plant asset more efficient or productive; also called *improvements*. *(p. 456)*

Blank endorsement Depositor signs the back of the check and the check is payable to the bearer of the check. *(p. 184)*

Bond Written promise to pay the bond's par (or face) value and interest at a stated contract rate; often issued in denominations of $1,000. *(p. 568)*

Bond indenture Contract between the bond issuer and the bondholders; identifies the parties' rights and obligations. *(p. 569)*

Bond sinking fund A fund designed to accumulate assets to pay a bond's maturity value. *(p. 576)*

Book value Asset's acquisition costs less its accumulated depreciation (or depletion, or amortization); also sometimes used synonymously as the *carrying value* of an account. *(pp. 109 & 450)*

Book value per common share Recorded amount of equity applicable to common shares divided by the number of common shares outstanding. *(p. 523)*

Book value per preferred share Equity applicable to preferred shares (equals its call price [or par value if it is not callable] plus any cumulative dividends in arrears) divided by the number of preferred shares outstanding. *(p. 523)*

Break-even point Output level at which sales equals fixed plus variable costs; where income equals zero. *(p. 808)*

Budget Formal statement of future plans, usually expressed in monetary terms. *(p. 678)*

Budget report Report comparing actual results to planned objectives; sometimes used as a progress report. *(p. 778)*

Budgetary control Management use of budgets to monitor and control company operations. *(p. 778)*

Business entity assumption Concept that assumes a business will be accounted for separately from its owner(s) and any other entity. *(pp. 11 & B-4)*

Call option The right of a bond issuer to retire bonds early. *(p. 575)*

Call price Amount that must be paid to call and retire a callable preferred stock or a callable bond. *(p. 523)*

Callable bonds Bonds that give the issuer the option to retire them at a stated amount prior to maturity. *(p. 578)*

Callable preferred stock Preferred stock that the issuing corporation, at its option, may retire by paying the call price plus any dividends in arrears. *(p. 523)*

Canceled checks Checks that the bank has paid and deducted from the depositor's account. *(p. 186)*

Capital expenditures Additional costs of plant assets that provide material benefits extending beyond the current period; also called *balance sheet expenditures*. *(p. 456)*

Capital stock General term referring to a corporation's stock used in obtaining capital (owner financing). *(p. 518)*

Carrying (book) value of bonds Net amount at which bonds are reported on the balance sheet; equals the par value of the bonds less any unamortized discount or plus any unamortized premium; also called *carrying amount* or *book value*. *(p. 572)*

Cash Includes currency, coins, and amounts on deposit in bank checking or savings accounts. *(p. 178)*

Cash basis accounting Accounting system that recognizes revenues when cash is received and recognizes expenses as cash is paid; not consistent with GAAP. *(p. 104)*

Cash disbursements journal Special journal normally used to record all payments of cash; also called *cash payments journal*. *(p. 294)*

Cash discount Reduction in the price of merchandise granted by a seller to a buyer when payment is made within the discount period. *(p. 263)*

Cash equivalents Short-term, investment assets that are readily convertible to a known cash amount or sufficiently close to their maturity date (usually within 90 days) so that market value is not sensitive to interest rate changes. *(p. 339)*

Cash flow on total assets Ratio of operating cash flows to average total assets; not sensitive to income recognition and measurement; partly reflects earnings quality. *(p. 614)*

Cash Over and Short Income statement account used to record cash overages and cash shortages arising from errors in cash receipts or payments. *(p. 179)*

Cash receipts journal Special journal normally used to record all receipts of cash. *(p. 270)*

Change in an accounting estimate Change in an accounting estimate that results from new information, subsequent developments, or improved judgment that impacts current and future periods. *(pp. 454 & 548)*

Chart of accounts List of accounts used by a company; includes an identification number for each account. *(p. 76)*

Check Document signed by a depositor instructing the bank to pay a specified amount to a designated recipient. *(p. 184)*

Check register Another name for a cash disbursements journal when the journal has a column for check numbers. *(pp. 169 & 294)*

Circular E IRS federal income tax withholding tables. *(p. 210)*

Classified balance sheet Balance sheet that presents assets and liabilities in relevant subgroups, including current and noncurrent classifications. *(p. 349)*

Clock card Source document used to record the number of hours an employee works and to determine the total labor cost for each pay period. *(p. 719)*

Closing entries Entries recorded at the end of each accounting period to transfer end-of-period balances in revenue, gain, expense, loss, and withdrawal (dividend for a corporation) accounts to the capital account (to retained earnings for a corporation). *(p. 134)*

Closing process Necessary end-of-period steps to prepare the accounts for recording the transactions of the next period. *(p. 133)*

Columnar journal Journal with more than one column. *(p. 266)*

Common stock Corporation's basic ownership share; also called *capital stock* or *contributed capital*. *(p. 518)*

Common-size financial statement Statement that expresses each amount as a percent of a base amount. In the balance sheet, total assets is usually the base and is expressed as 100%. In the income statement, net sales revenue is usually the base. *(p. 647)*

Comparability A qualitative characteristic of accounting information suggesting that information is more useful if it can be related to an industry or competitor benchmark. *(p. B-4)*

Comparative financial statement Statement with data for two or more successive periods placed in side-by-side columns, often with changes shown in dollar amounts and percents. *(p. 645)*

Complex capital structure Capital structure that includes outstanding rights or options to purchase common stock, or securities that are convertible into common stock. *(p. 549)*

Conservatism concept Concept that prescribes the less optimistic estimate when two estimates are about equally likely. *(pp. 423 & B-4)*

Consistency concept Concept that prescribes use of the same accounting method(s) over time so that financial statements are comparable across periods. *(pp. 421 & B-4)*

Continuous improvement Concept requiring every manager and employee to continually look to improve operations. *(p. 679)*

Contra account Account linked with another account and having an opposite normal balance; reported as a subtraction from the other account's balance. *(pp. 51 & 108)*

Contract rate Interest rate specified in a bond indenture (or note); multiplied by the par value to determine the interest paid each period; also called *coupon rate, stated rate,* or *nominal rate.* *(p. 570)*

Contribution margin per unit Amount that the sale of one unit contributes toward recovering fixed costs and earning profit; defined as sales price per unit minus variable expense per unit. *(p. 807)*

Contribution margin ratio Product's contribution margin divided by its sale price. *(p. 807)*

Control Process of monitoring planning decisions and evaluating the organization's activities and employees. *(p. 678)*

Controllable costs Costs that a manager has the power to control or at least strongly influence. *(pp. 681 & 758)*

Controlling account General ledger account, the balance of which (after posting) equals the sum of the balances in its related subsidiary ledger. *(p. 267)*

Conversion costs Expenditures incurred in converting raw materials to finished goods; includes direct labor costs and overhead costs. *(p. 685)*

Convertible bonds Bonds that bondholders can exchange for a set number of the issuer's shares. *(p. 578)*

Convertible preferred stock Preferred stock with an option to exchange it for common stock at a specified rate. *(p. 522)*

Copyright Right giving the owner the exclusive privilege to publish and sell musical, literary, or artistic work during the creator's life plus 70 years. *(p. 462)*

Corporation Business that is a separate legal entity under state or federal laws with owners called *shareholders* or *stockholders.* *(p. 11)*

Cost All normal and reasonable expenditures necessary to get an asset in place and ready for its intended use. *(p. 449)*

Cost accounting system Accounting system for manufacturing activities based on the perpetual inventory system. *(p. 714)*

Cost-benefit A constraint of useful accounting information prescribing that information will only be provided if the benefits to users outweigh the costs of preparation. *(p. B-7)*

Cost center Department that incurs costs but generates no revenues; common example is the accounting or legal department. *(p. 751)*

Cost object Product, process, department, or customer to which costs are assigned. *(p. 681)*

Cost of goods sold Cost of inventory sold to customers during a period; also called *cost of sales.* *(p. 322)*

Cost principle Accounting principle that prescribes financial statement information to be based on actual costs incurred in business transactions. *(p. B-5)*

Cost variance Difference between the actual incurred cost and the standard cost. *(p. 784)*

Cost-volume-profit (CVP) analysis Planning method that includes predicting the volume of activity, the costs incurred, sales earned, and profits received. *(p. 806)*

Credit Recorded on the right side; an entry that decreases asset and expense accounts, and increases liability, revenue, and most equity accounts; abbreviated Cr. *(p. 46)*

Credit memorandum Notification that the sender has credited the recipient's account in the sender's records. *(p. 265)*

Credit period Time period that can pass before a customer's payment is due. *(pp. 263 & 289)*

Credit terms Description of the amounts and timing of payments that a buyer (debtor) agrees to make in the future. *(p. 263 & 288)*

Creditors Individuals or organizations entitled to receive payments. *(p. 22)*

Cumulative preferred stock Preferred stock on which undeclared dividends accumulate until paid; common stockholders cannot receive dividends until cumulative dividends are paid. *(p. 543)*

Current assets Cash and other assets expected to be sold, collected, or used within one year or the company's operating cycle, whichever is longer. *(p. 351)*

Current liabilities Obligations due to be paid or settled within one year or the company's operating cycle, whichever is longer. *(p. 351)*

Customer orientation Company position that its managers and employees be in tune with the changing wants and needs of consumers. *(p. 679)*

Cycle efficiency (CE) A measure of production efficiency, which is defined as value-added (process) time divided by total cycle time. *(p. 690)*

Cycle time (CT) A measure of the time to produce a product or service, which is the sum of process time, inspection time, move time, and wait time; also called *throughput time.* *(p. 689)*

Date of declaration Date the directors vote to pay a dividend. *(p. 540)*

Date of payment Date the corporation makes the dividend payment. *(p. 540)*

Date of record Date directors specify for identifying stockholders to receive dividends. *(p. 540)*

Days' sales in inventory Estimate of number of days needed to convert inventory into receivables or cash; equals ending inventory divided by cost of goods sold and then multiplied by 365; also called *days' stock on hand.* *(p. 423)*

Days' sales uncollected Measure of the liquidity of receivables computed by dividing the current balance of receivables by the annual credit (or net) sales and then multiplying by 365; also called *days' sales in receivables.* *(p. 652)*

Debit Recorded on the left side; an entry that increases asset and expense accounts, and decreases liability, revenue, and most equity accounts; abbreviated Dr. *(p. 46)*

Debit memorandum Notification that the sender has debited the recipient's account in the sender's records. *(p. 289)*

Debt ratio Ratio of total liabilities to total assets; used to reflect risk associated with a company's debts. *(p. 695)*

Debt-to-equity ratio Defined as total liabilities divided by total equity; shows the proportion of a company financed by non-owners (creditors) in comparison with that financed by owners. *(p. 578)*

Declining-balance method Method that determines depreciation charge for the period by multiplying a depreciation rate (often twice the straight-line rate) by the asset's beginning-period book value. *(p. 452)*

Departmental accounting system Accounting system that provides information useful in evaluating the profitability or cost effectiveness of a department. *(p. 750)*

Departmental contribution to overhead Amount by which a department's revenues exceed its direct expenses. *(p. 757)*

Depletion Process of allocating the cost of natural resources to periods when they are consumed and sold. *(p. 459)*

Deposits in transit Deposits recorded by the company but not yet recorded by its bank. *(p. 187)*

Deposit ticket Lists items such as currency, coins, and checks deposited and their corresponding dollar amounts. *(p. 183)*

Depreciation Expense created by allocating the cost of plant and equipment to periods in which they are used; represents the expense of using the asset. *(pp. 108 & 449)*

Diluted earnings per share Earnings per share calculation that requires dilutive securities be added to the denominator of the basic EPS calculation. *(p. 549)*

Dilutive securities Securities having the potential to increase common shares outstanding; examples are options, rights, convertible bonds, and convertible preferred stock. *(p. 549)*

Direct costs Costs incurred for the benefit of one specific cost object. *(p. 681)*

Direct expenses Expenses traced to a specific department (object) that are incurred for the sole benefit of that department. *(p. 751)*

Direct labor Efforts of employees who physically convert materials to finished product. *(p. 685)*

Direct labor costs Wages and salaries for direct labor that are separately and readily traced through the production process to finished goods. *(p. 685)*

Direct material Raw material that physically becomes part of the product and is clearly identified with specific products or batches of product. *(p. 685)*

Direct material costs Expenditures for direct material that are separately and readily traced through the production process to finished goods. *(p. 685)*

Direct method Presentation of net cash from operating activities for the statement of cash flows that lists major operating cash receipts less major operating cash payments. *(p. 603)*

Direct write-off method Method that records the loss from an uncollectible account receivable at the time it is determined to be uncollectible; no attempt is made to estimate bad debts. *(p. 374)*

Discount on bonds payable Difference between a bond's par value and its lower issue price or carrying value; occurs when the contract rate is less than the market rate. *(p. 571)*

Discount period Time period in which a cash discount is available and the buyer can make a reduced payment. *(pp. 263 & 289)*

Dividend in arrears Unpaid dividend on cumulative preferred stock; must be paid before any regular dividends on preferred stock and before any dividends on common stock. *(p. 544)*

Dividend yield Ratio of the annual amount of cash dividends distributed to common shareholders relative to the common stock's market value (price). *(p. 549)*

Double-entry accounting Accounting system in which each transaction affects at least two accounts and has at least one debit and one credit. *(p. 47)*

Earnings per share (EPS) Amount of income earned by each share of a company's outstanding common stock; also called *net income per share.* *(p. 548)*

Effective interest method Allocates interest expense over the bond life to yield a constant rate of interest; interest expense for a period is found by multiplying the balance of the liability at the beginning of the period by the bond market rate at issuance; also called *interest method.* *(p. 581)*

Efficiency Company's productivity in using its assets; usually measured relative to how much revenue a certain level of assets generates. *(p. 691)*

Efficiency variance Difference between the actual quantity of an input and the standard quantity of that input. *(p. 785)*

Electronic funds transfer (EFT) Use of electronic communication to transfer cash from one party to another. *(p. 185)*

Employee Someone whose work is under the direction of an employer. *(p. 206)*

Employee earnings records Record of an employee's net pay, gross pay, deductions, and year-to-date payroll information. *(p. 216)*

Employee's Withholding Allowance Certificate (Form W-4) A form which shows an employee's withholding allowances. *(p. 206)*

Employer identification number (EIN) A number issued by the federal government that uniquely identifies a business. *(p. 232)*

Employer's Quarterly Unemployment Tax Report A report filed with the state that shows an employer's unemployment taxes owed. *(p. 241)*

Endorsement A written authorization transferring ownership of a check. *(p. 184)*

EOM Abbreviation for *end of month;* used to describe credit terms for credit transactions. *(p. 263)*

Equity Owner's claim on the assets of a business; equals the residual interest in an entity's assets after deducting liabilities; also called *net assets. (p. 23)*

Equity ratio Portion of total assets provided by equity, computed as total equity divided by total assets. *(p. 653)*

Estimated tax liability The amount a corporation expects to pay in income taxes for a specific year. *(p. 538)*

Ethics Codes of conduct by which actions are judged as right or wrong, fair or unfair, honest or dishonest. *(p. 9)*

Events Those happenings that affect an entity's accounting equation *and* can be reliably measured. *(p. 23)*

Expanded accounting equation Assets = Liabilities + Equity; Equity equals [Owner capital − Owner withdrawals + Revenues − Expenses] for a noncorporation; Equity equals [Contributed capital + Retained earnings + Revenues − Expenses] for a corporation where dividends are subtracted from retained earnings. *(p. 23)*

Expenses Outflows or using up of assets as part of operations of a business to generate sales. *(p. 23)*

External transactions Exchanges of economic value between one entity and another entity. *(p. 23)*

External users Persons using accounting information who are not directly involved in running the organization. *(p. 6)*

Extraordinary repairs Major repairs that extend the useful life of a plant asset beyond prior expectations; treated as a capital expenditure. *(p. 457)*

Factory overhead Factory activities supporting the production process that are not direct material or direct labor; also called *overhead* and *manufacturing overhead. (p. 685)*

Factory overhead costs Expenditures for factory overhead that cannot be separately or readily traced to finished goods; also called *overhead costs. (p. 685)*

Favorable variance Difference in actual revenues or expenses from the budgeted amount that contributes to a higher income. *(p. 779)*

Federal depository bank Bank authorized to accept deposits of amounts payable to the federal government. *(p. 234)*

Federal Insurance Contributions Act (FICA) Taxes Taxes assessed on both employers and employees; for Social Security and Medicare programs. *(pp. 207 & 232)*

Federal Reserve Bank A bank that can accept payroll deposits from any business. *(p. 234)*

Federal unemployment taxes (FUTA) Payroll taxes on employers assessed by the federal government to support its unemployment insurance program. *(p. 232)*

Financial accounting Area of accounting mainly aimed at serving external users. *(p. 6)*

Financial Accounting Standards Board (FASB) Independent group of full-time members responsible for setting accounting rules. *(pp. 10 & B-2)*

Financial reporting Process of communicating information relevant to investors, creditors, and others in making investment, credit, and business decisions. *(p. 643)*

Financial statement analysis Application of analytical tools to general-purpose financial statements and related data for making business decisions. *(p. 642)*

Financing activities Transactions with owners and creditors that include obtaining cash from issuing debt, repaying amounts borrowed, and obtaining cash from or distributing cash to owners. *(p. 600)*

Finished goods inventory Account that controls the finished goods files, which acts as a subsidiary ledger (of the Inventory account) in which the costs of finished goods that are ready for sale are recorded. *(pp. 684 & 717)*

First-in, first-out (FIFO) Method to assign cost to inventory that assumes items are sold in the order acquired; earliest items purchased are the first sold. *(p. 418)*

Fiscal year Consecutive 12-month (or 52-week) period chosen as the organization's annual accounting period. *(p. 105)*

Fixed budget Planning budget based on a single predicted amount of volume; unsuitable for evaluations if the actual volume differs from predicted volume. *(p. 778)*

Fixed budget performance report Report that compares actual revenues and costs with fixed budgeted amounts and identifies the differences as favorable or unfavorable variances. *(p. 779)*

Fixed cost Cost that does not change with changes in the volume of activity. *(p. 680)*

Flexible budget Budget prepared (using actual volume) once a period is complete that helps managers evaluate past performance; uses fixed and variable costs in determining total costs. *(p. 780)*

Flexible budget performance report Report that compares actual revenues and costs with their variable budgeted amounts based on actual sales volume (or other level of activity) and identifies the differences as variances. *(p. 782)*

FOB Abbreviation for *free on board;* the point when ownership of goods passes to the buyer; *FOB shipping point* (or *factory*) means the buyer pays shipping costs and accepts ownership of goods when the seller transfers goods to carrier; *FOB destination* means the seller pays shipping costs and buyer accepts ownership of goods at the buyer's place of business. *(p. 290)*

Form 940 IRS form used to report an employer's federal unemployment taxes (FUTA) on an annual filing basis. *(p. 241)*

Form 940-EZ The Employer's Annual Federal Unemployment Tax Return. This shows the amount of FUTA tax the employer owes for the year. *(p. 241)*

Form 941 IRS form filed to report FICA taxes owed and remitted. *(p. 236)*

Form 8109 A preprinted Federal Tax Deposit Coupon. It is used when an employer deposits money into a federal depository bank. *(p. 235)*

Form 8109-B A Federal Tax Deposit Coupon used by new businesses or when the business does not have a supply of preprinted Forms 8109. *(p. 235)*

Form SS-4 An Internal Revenue Service form filed by a business in order to receive an employer identification number. *(p. 238)*

Form W-2 Annual report by an employer to each employee showing the employee's wages subject to FICA and federal income taxes along with amounts withheld. *(p. 239)*

Form W-3 The Transmittal of Wage and Tax Statements form. This form reports the total wages and tax withholding information for all the employer's employees for the year. *(p. 239)*

Form W-4 Withholding allowance certificate, filed with the employer, identifying the number of withholding allowances claimed. *(p. 206)*

Franchises Privileges granted by a company or government to sell a product or service under specified conditions. *(p. 462)*

Full disclosure principle Principle that prescribes financial statements (including notes) to report all relevant information about an entity's operations and financial condition. *(pp. 399 & B-6)*

General accounting system Accounting system for manufacturing activities based on the *periodic* inventory system. *(p. 714)*

General and administrative expenses Expenses that support the operating activities of a business. *(p. 348)*

General journal All-purpose journal for recording the debits and credits of transactions and events. *(pp. 77 & 266)*

General partner Partner who assumes unlimited liability for the debts of the partnership; responsible for partnership management. *(p. 487)*

General partnership Partnership in which all partners have mutual agency and unlimited liability for partnership debts. *(p. 487)*

Generally Accepted Accounting Principles (GAAP) Rules that specify acceptable accounting practices. *(pp. 10 & B-7)*

General-purpose financial statements Statements published periodically for use by a variety of interested parties; includes the income statement, balance sheet, statement of owner's equity (or statement of retained earnings for a corporation), statement of cash flows, and notes to these statements. *(p. 643)*

Going-concern assumption Concept that prescribes financial statements to reflect the assumption that the business will continue operating indefinitely. *(p. B-5)*

Goods in process inventory Account in which costs are accumulated for products that are in the process of being produced but are not yet complete; also called *work in process inventory*. *(pp. 684 & 717)*

Goodwill Amount by which a company's (or a segment's) value exceeds the value of its individual assets less its liabilities. *(p. 462)*

Gross margin (See *gross profit*.) *(p. 322)*

Gross margin ratio Gross margin (net sales minus cost of goods sold) divided by net sales; also called *gross profit ratio*. *(p. 657)*

Gross pay Total compensation earned by an employee. *(p. 206)*

Gross profit Net sales minus cost of goods sold; also called *gross margin*. *(p. 322)*

Gross profit method Procedure to estimate inventory when the past gross profit rate is used to estimate cost of goods sold, which is then subtracted from the cost of goods available for sale. *(p. 430)*

Horizontal analysis Comparison of a company's financial condition and performance across time. *(p. 644)*

Impairment Diminishment of an asset value. *(p. 454)*

Income (See *net income*.)

Income statement Financial statement that subtracts expenses from revenues to yield a net income or loss over a specified period of time; also includes any gains or losses. *(p. 29)*

Income Summary Temporary account used only in the closing process to which the balances of revenue and expense accounts (including any gains or losses) are transferred; its balance is transferred to the capital account (or retained earnings for a corporation). *(p. 133)*

Incremental cost Additional cost incurred only if a company pursues a specific course of action. *(p. 812)*

Indefinite useful life Asset life that is not limited by legal, regulatory, contractual, competitive, economic, or other factors. *(p. 460)*

Independent contractor Someone who does a job for an employer, but decides how to do the work. *(p. 206)*

Indirect costs Costs incurred for the benefit of more than one cost object. *(p. 681)*

Indirect expenses Expenses incurred for the joint benefit of more than one department (or cost object). *(p. 752)*

Indirect labor Efforts of production employees who do not work specifically on converting direct materials into finished products and who are not clearly identified with specific units or batches of product. *(p. 685)*

Indirect labor costs Labor costs that cannot be physically traced to production of a product or service; included as part of overhead. *(p. 685)*

Indirect material Material used to support the production process but not clearly identified with products or batches of product. *(p. 683)*

Indirect method Presentation that reports net income and then adjusts it by adding and subtracting items to yield net cash from operating activities on the statement of cash flows. *(p. 603)*

Individual employee earnings records Records that summarize each employee's earnings, deductions, and net pay during each calendar year. *(p. 216)*

Installment note Liability requiring a series of periodic payments to the lender. *(pp. 401 & 577)*

Intangible assets Long-term assets (resources) used to produce or sell products or services; usually lack physical form and have uncertain benefits. *(pp. 351 & 460)*

Interest Charge for using money (or other assets) loaned from one entity to another. *(p. 396)*

Interim financial statements Financial statements covering periods of less than one year; usually based on one-, three-, or six-month periods. *(pp. 105 & 430)*

Internal controls or **Internal control system** All policies and procedures used to protect assets, ensure reliable accounting, promote efficient operations, and urge adherence to company policies. *(p. 160)*

Internal transactions Activities within an organization that can affect the accounting equation. *(p. 23)*

Internal users Persons using accounting information who are directly involved in managing the organization. *(p. 5)*

International Accounting Standards Board (IASB) Group that identifies preferred accounting practices and encourages global acceptance; issues International Financial Reporting Standards (IFRS). *(pp. 10 & B-4)*

Inventory Goods a company owns and expects to sell in its normal operations. *(p. 286)*

Inventory turnover Number of times a company's average inventory is sold during a period; computed by dividing cost of goods sold by average inventory; also called *merchandise turnover*. *(p. 423)*

Investing activities Transactions that involve purchasing and selling of long-term assets; includes making and collecting notes receivable and investments in other than cash equivalents. *(p. 599)*

Investment center Center of which a manager is responsible for revenues, costs, and asset investments. *(p. 760)*

Investment center return on total assets Center net income divided by average total assets for the center. *(p. 760)*

Invoice Itemized record of goods prepared by the vendor that lists the customer's name, items sold, sales prices, and terms of sale. *(pp. 167 & 287)*

Invoice approval Document containing a checklist of steps necessary for approving the recording and payment of an invoice; also called *check authorization*. *(p. 168)*

Job Production of a customized product or service. *(p. 714)*

Job cost sheet Separate record maintained for each job. *(p. 716)*

Job lot Production of more than one unit of a customized product or service. *(p. 715)*

Job order cost accounting system Cost accounting system to determine the cost of producing each job or job lot. *(p. 716)*

Job order production Production of special-order products; also called *customized production*. *(p. 714)*

Journal Record in which transactions are entered before they are posted to ledger accounts; also called *book of original entry*. *(p. 74)*

Journalizing Process of recording transactions in a journal. *(p. 74)*

Just-in-time (JIT) manufacturing Process of acquiring or producing inventory only when needed. *(p. 679)*

Land improvements Assets that increase the benefits of land, have a limited useful life, and are depreciated. *(p. 448)*

Large stock dividend Stock dividend that is more than 25% of the previously outstanding shares. *(p. 541)*

Last-in, first-out (LIFO) Method to assign cost to inventory that assumes costs for the most recent items purchased are sold first and charged to cost of goods sold. *(p. 419)*

Lean business model Practice of eliminating waste while meeting customer needs and yielding positive company returns. *(p. 679)*

Lease Contract specifying the rental of property. *(pp. 462 & 577)*

Leasehold Rights the lessor grants to the lessee under the terms of a lease. *(p. 462)*

Leasehold improvements Alterations or improvements to leased property such as partitions and storefronts. *(p. 462)*

Ledger Record containing all accounts (with amounts) for a business; also called *general ledger*. *(p. 74)*

Lessee Party to a lease who secures the right to possess and use the property from another party (the lessor). *(p. 462)*

Lessor Party to a lease who grants another party (the lessee) the right to possess and use its property. *(p. 462)*

Liabilities Creditors' claims on an organization's assets; involves a probable future payment of assets, products, or services that a company is obligated to make due to past transactions or events. *(p. 22)*

Licenses (See *franchises*.) *(p. 462)*

LIFO conformity rule If LIFO is used for tax reporting it must also be used for financial reporting. *(p. 421)*

Limited liability company (LLC) Organization form that combines select features of a corporation and a limited partnership; provides limited liability to its members (owners), is free of business tax, and allows members to actively participate in management. *(p. 488)*

Limited liability partnership Partnership in which a partner is not personally liable for malpractice or negligence unless that partner is responsible for providing the service that resulted in the claim. *(p. 487)*

Limited partners Partners who have no personal liability for partnership debts beyond the amounts they invested in the partnership. *(p. 487)*

Limited partnership Partnership that has two classes of partners: limited partners and general partners. *(p. 487)*

Liquid assets Resources such as cash that are easily converted into other assets or used to pay for goods, services, or liabilities. *(p. 178)*

Liquidating cash dividend Distribution of assets that returns part of the original investment to stockholders; deducted from contributed capital accounts. *(p. 533)*

Liquidity Availability of resources to meet short-term cash requirements. *(pp. 178 & 643)*

List price Catalog (full) price of an item before any trade discount is deducted. *(p. 287)*

Long-term investments Long-term assets not used in operating activities such as notes receivable and investments in stocks and bonds. *(p. 351)*

Long-term liabilities Obligations not due to be paid within one year or the operating cycle, whichever is longer. *(p. 351)*

Look-back rule A rule used to classify business as monthly or semiweekly depositors. *(p. 234)*

Lower of cost or market (LCM) Required method to report inventory at market replacement cost when that market cost is lower than recorded cost. *(p. 422)*

Maker of the note Entity who signs a note and promises to pay it at maturity. *(p. 396)*

Managerial accounting Area of accounting mainly aimed at serving the decision-making needs of internal users; also called *management accounting*. *(pp. 5 & 678)*

Manufacturing statement Report that summarizes the types and amounts of costs incurred in a company's production process for a period; also called *cost of goods manufacturing statement*. *(p. 687)*

Margin of safety Excess of expected sales over the level of break-even sales. *(p. 810)*

Market prospects Expectations (both good and bad) about a company's future performance as assessed by users and other interested parties. *(p. 643)*

Market rate Interest rate that borrowers are willing to pay and lenders are willing to accept for a specific lending agreement given the borrowers' risk level. *(p. 570)*

Market value per share Price at which stock is bought or sold. *(p. 518)*

Matching principle Prescribes expenses to be reported in the same period as the revenues that were earned as a result of the expenses. *(pp. 105, 374, & B-6)*

Materiality Prescribes that accounting for items that markedly impact financial statements, and any inferences drawn from them, adhere to GAAP. *(p. B-7)*

Materiality constraint Prescribes that accounting for items that significantly impact financial statements and any inferences from them strictly adhere to GAAP. *(p. 374)*

Materials ledger card Perpetual record updated each time units are purchased or issued for production use. *(p. 717)*

Materials requisition Source document production managers use to request materials for production; used to assign materials costs to specific jobs or overhead. *(p. 718)*

Maturity date of a note Date when a note's principal and interest are due. *(p. 397)*

Merchandise (See *merchandise inventory*.) *(p. 262)*

Merchandise inventory Goods that a company owns and expects to sell to customers; also called *merchandise* or *inventory*. *(pp. 286 & 317)*

Merchandiser Entity that earns net income by buying and selling merchandise. *(pp. 262 & 286)*

Merit rating Rating assigned to an employer by a state based on the employer's record of employment. *(p. 232)*

Minimum legal capital Amount of assets defined by law that stockholders must (potentially) invest in a corporation; usually defined as par value of the stock; intended to protect creditors. *(p. 519)*

Mixed cost Cost that behaves like a combination of fixed and variable costs. *(pp. 680 & 807)*

Modified Accelerated Cost Recovery System (MACRS) Depreciation system required by federal income tax law. *(p. 454)*

Monetary unit assumption Concept that assumes transactions and events can be expressed in money units. *(p. B-5)*

Mortgage Legal loan agreement that protects a lender by giving the lender the right to be paid from the cash proceeds from the sale of a borrower's assets identified in the mortgage. *(pp. 403 & 577)*

Multiple-step income statement Income statement format that shows subtotals between sales and net income, categorizes expenses, and often reports the details of net sales and expenses. *(p. 347)*

Mutual agency Legal relationship among partners whereby each partner is an agent of the partnership and is able to bind the partnership to contracts within the scope of the partnership's business. *(p. 487)*

Natural resources Assets physically consumed when used; examples are timber, mineral deposits, and oil and gas fields; also called *wasting assets*. *(p. 459)*

Net income Amount earned after subtracting all expenses necessary for and matched with sales for a period; also called *income, profit,* or *earnings*. *(p. 23)*

Net loss Excess of expenses over revenues for a period. *(p. 23)*

Net pay Gross pay less all deductions; also called *take-home pay*. *(p. 213)*

Net purchases Net cost of merchandise purchased; computed as purchases minus purchase discounts, minus purchase returns and allowances, plus transportation-in. *(pp. 290 & 322)*

Net realizable value Expected selling price (value) of an item minus the cost of making the sale. *(p. 414)*

Net sales Net amount of merchandise sold; computed as sales minus sales returns and allowances minus sales discounts. *(p. 322)*

Noncumulative preferred stock Preferred stock on which the right to receive dividends is lost for any period when dividends are not declared. *(p. 544)*

Nonparticipating preferred stock Preferred stock on which dividends are limited to a maximum amount each year. *(p. 544)*

No-par value stock Stock class that has not been assigned a par (or stated) value by the corporate charter. *(p. 519)*

Non-value-added time The portion of cycle time that is not directed at producing a product or service; equals the sum of inspection time, move time, and wait time. *(p. 690)*

Note payable Liability expressed by a written promise to pay a definite sum of money on demand or on a specific future date(s). *(p. 400)*

Operating activities Activities that involve the production or purchase of merchandise and the sale of goods or services to customers, including expenditures related to administering the business. *(p. 599)*

Operating cycle Normal time between paying cash for merchandise or employee services and receiving cash from customers. *(p. 350)*

Opportunity cost Potential benefit lost by choosing a specific action from two or more alternatives. *(p. 681)*

Ordinary repairs Repairs to keep a plant asset in normal, good operating condition; treated as a revenue expenditure and immediately expensed. *(p. 456)*

Organization expenses (costs) Costs such as legal fees and promoter fees to bring an entity into existence. *(p. 517)*

Out-of-pocket cost Cost incurred or avoided as a result of management's decisions. *(p. 681)*

Outstanding checks Checks written and recorded by the depositor but not yet paid by the bank at the bank statement date. *(p. 187)*

Overapplied overhead Amount by which the overhead applied to production in a period using the predetermined overhead rate exceeds the actual overhead incurred in a period. *(p. 725)*

Overhead cost variance Difference between the total overhead cost applied to products and the total overhead cost actually incurred. *(p. 786)*

Owner, capital Account showing the owner's claim on company assets; equals owner investments plus net income (or less net losses) minus owner withdrawals since the company's inception; also referred to as *equity*. *(p. 23)*

Owner investment Assets put into the business by the owner. *(p. 23)*

Owner withdrawals (See *withdrawals*.) *(p. 23)*

Paid-in capital Total amount of cash and other assets a corporation receives from its stockholders in exchange for its stock. *(p. 519)*

Paid-in capital in excess of par value Amount received from issuance of stock that is in excess of the stock's par value. *(p. 520)*

Par value Value assigned a share of stock by the corporate charter when the stock is authorized. *(p. 519)*

Par value of a bond Amount the bond issuer agrees to pay at maturity and the amount on which cash interest payments are based; also called *face amount* or *face value* of a bond. *(p. 569)*

Par value stock Class of stock assigned a par value by the corporate charter. *(p. 519)*

Participating preferred stock Preferred stock that shares with common stockholders any dividends paid in excess of the percent stated on preferred stock. *(p. 544)*

Partner return on equity Partner net income divided by average partner equity for the period. *(p. 499)*

Partnership contract Agreement among partners that sets terms under which the affairs of the partnership are conducted; also called *articles of partnership* if in writing. *(p. 486)*

Partnership liquidation Dissolution of a partnership by (1) selling noncash assets and allocating any gain or loss according to partners' income-and-loss ratio, (2) paying liabilities, and (3) distributing any remaining cash according to partners' capital balances. *(p. 497)*

Patent Exclusive right granted to its owner to produce and sell an item or to use a process for 17 years. *(p. 461)*

Payout ratio Cash dividends declared on common stock dividend by net income. *(p. 549)*

Payee of the note Entity to whom a note is made payable. *(p. 396)*

Payroll bank account Bank account used solely for paying employees; each pay period an amount equal to the total employees' net pay is deposited in it and the payroll checks are drawn on it. *(p. 214)*

Payroll deductions Amounts withheld from an employee's gross pay; also called *withholdings*. *(p. 209)*

Payroll register Record for a pay period that shows the pay period dates, regular and overtime hours worked, gross pay, net pay, and deductions. *(p. 213)*

Period costs Expenditures identified more with a time period than with finished products costs; includes selling and general administrative expenses. *(p. 681)*

Periodic inventory system Method that records the cost of inventory purchased but does not continuously track the quantity available or sold to customers; records are updated at the end of each period to reflect the physical count and costs of goods available. *(pp. 371 & 415)*

Periodicity assumption (or principle) Assumption that an organization's activities can be divided into specific time periods such as months, quarters, or years. *(p. B-5)*

Permanent accounts Accounts that reflect activities related to one or more future periods; balance sheet accounts whose balances are not closed; also called *real accounts*. *(p. 133)*

Perpetual inventory system Method that maintains continuous records of the cost of inventory available and the cost of goods sold. *(p. 415)*

Petty cash Small amount of cash in a fund to pay minor expenses; accounted for using an imprest system. *(p. 180)*

Planning Process of setting goals and preparing to achieve them. *(p. 678)*

Plant assets Tangible long-lived assets used to produce or sell products and services; also called *property, plant and equipment (PP&E)* or *fixed assets*. *(pp. 107 & 446)*

Plant asset age Estimated by dividing accumulated depreciation expense. *(p. 464)*

Plant asset useful life Equals the plant asset cost divided by depreciation expense. It is the length of time an asset will be productively used in the operations of a business. *(p. 463)*

Post-closing trial balance List of permanent accounts and their balances from the ledger after all closing entries are journalized and posted. *(p. 137)*

Posting Process of transferring journal entry information to the ledger; computerized systems automate this process. *(p. 74)*

Posting reference (PR) column A column in journals in which individual ledger account numbers are entered when entries are posted to those ledger accounts. *(p. 78)*

Predetermined overhead rate Rate established prior to the beginning of a period that relates estimated overhead to another variable, such as estimated direct labor, and is used to assign overhead cost to production. *(p. 722)*

Preemptive right Stockholders' right to maintain their proportionate interest in a corporation with any additional shares issued. *(p. 518)*

Preferred stock Stock with a priority status over common stockholders in one or more ways, such as paying dividends or distributing assets. *(p. 522)*

Premium on bonds Difference between a bond's par value and its higher carrying value; occurs when the contract rate is higher than the market rate; also called *bond premium*. *(p. 573)*

Premium on stock (See *paid-in capital in excess of par value*.) *(p. 520)*

Prepaid expenses Items paid for in advance of receiving their benefits; classified as assets. *(p. 106)*

Price-earnings (PE) ratio Ratio of a company's current market value per share to its earnings per share; also called *price-to-earnings*. *(p. 549)*

Price variance Difference between actual and budgeted revenue or cost caused by the difference between the actual price per unit and the budgeted price per unit. *(p. 783)*

Prime costs Expenditures directly identified with the production of finished goods; include direct materials costs and direct labor costs. *(p. 685)*

Principal of a note Amount that the signer of a note agrees to pay back when it matures, not including interest. *(p. 396)*

Principles of internal control Principles prescribing management to establish responsibility, maintain records, insure assets, separate recordkeeping from custody of assets, divide responsibility for related transactions, apply technological controls, and perform reviews. *(p. 160)*

Prior period adjustment Correction of an error in a prior year that is reported in the statement of retained earnings (or statement of stockholders' equity) net of any income tax effects. *(p. 547)*

Process operations Mass production of products in a continuous flow of steps. *(p. 715)*

Product costs Costs that are capitalized as inventory because they produce benefits expected to have future value; include direct materials, direct labor, and overhead. *(p. 681)*

Pro forma financial statements Statements that show the effects of proposed transactions and events as if they had occurred. *(p. 133)*

Profit center Business unit that incurs costs and generates revenues. *(p. 751)*

Profit margin Ratio of a company's net income to its net sales; the percent of income in each dollar of revenue; also called *net profit margin*. *(p. 655)*

Profitability Company's ability to generate an adequate return on invested capital. *(p. 643)*

Promissory note (or **note**) Written promise to pay a specified amount either on demand or at a definite future date; is a *note receivable* for the lender but a *note payable* for the lendee. *(p. 396)*

Proxy Legal document giving a stockholder's agent the power to exercise the stockholder's voting rights. *(p. 517)*

Purchase discount Term used by a purchaser to describe a cash discount granted to the purchaser for paying within the discount period. *(p. 288)*

Purchase order Document used by the purchasing department to place an order with a seller (vendor). *(pp. 168 & 287)*

Purchase requisition Document listing merchandise needed by a department and requesting it be purchased. *(pp. 166 & 286)*

Purchases journal Journal normally used to record all purchases on credit. *(p. 292)*

Quantity variance Difference between actual and budgeted revenue or cost caused by the difference between the actual number of units and the budgeted number of units. *(p. 783)*

Ratio analysis Determination of key relations between financial statement items as reflected in numerical measures. *(p. 644)*

Raw materials inventory Goods a company acquires to use in making products. *(p. 683)*

Realizable value Expected proceeds from converting an asset into cash. *(p. 375)*

Receiving report Form used to report that ordered goods are received and to describe their quantity and condition. *(pp. 167, 287 & 717)*

Recordkeeping Part of accounting that involves recording transactions and events, either manually or electronically; also called *bookkeeping*. *(p. 4)*

Relevance A qualitative characteristic of accounting information that prescribes that information be useful, understandable, timely and pertinent for decision making. *(p. B-3)*

Relevant benefits Additional or incremental revenue generated by selecting a particular course of action over another. *(p. 811)*

Reliability The principle that information is verifiable and faithfully represents the substance of the underlying economic transaction. *(p. B-3)*

Responsibility accounting budget Report of expected costs and expenses under a manager's control. *(p. 759)*

Responsibility accounting performance report Responsibility report that compares actual costs and expenses for a department with budgeted amounts. *(p. 759)*

Responsibility accounting system System that provides information that management can use to evaluate the performance of a department's manager. *(p. 750)*

Restricted retained earnings Retained earnings not available for dividends because of legal or contractual limitations. *(p. 547)*

Restrictive endorsement The depositor transfers the check to a specific person, business, or bank for a specific purpose. *(p. 184)*

Retailer Intermediary that buys products from manufacturers or wholesalers and sells them to consumers. *(p. 262)*

Retained earnings Cumulative income less cumulative losses and dividends. *(p. 519)*

Retained earnings deficit Debit (abnormal) balance in Retained Earnings; occurs when cumulative losses and dividends exceed cumulative income; also called *accumulated deficit*. *(p. 548)*

Return on total assets *(p. 655)*

Revenue expenditures Expenditures reported on the current income statement as an expense because they do not provide benefits in future periods. *(p. 456)*

Revenue recognition principle The principle prescribing that revenue is recognized when earned. *(pp. 105 & B-6)*

Revenues Gross increase in equity from a company's business activities that earn income; also called *sales*. *(p. 23)*

Reversing entries Optional entries recorded at the beginning of a period that prepare the accounts for the usual journal entries as if adjusting entries had not occurred in the prior period. *(p. 356)*

S corporation Corporation that meets special tax qualifications so as to be treated like a partnership for income tax purposes. *(p. 488)*

Salary A fixed amount of compensation paid or received on a regular basis, such as every two weeks, monthly, or annually. *(p. 208)*

Sales discount Term used by a seller to describe a cash discount granted to buyers who pay within the discount period. *(p. 262)*

Sales journal Journal normally used to record sales of goods on credit. *(p. 266)*

Sales mix Ratio of sales volumes for the various products sold by a company. *(p. 815)*

Salvage value Estimate of amount to be recovered at the end of an asset's useful life; also called *residual value* or *scrap value*. *(p. 449)*

Sarbanes-Oxley Act Created the *Public Company Accounting Oversight Board,* regulates analyst conflicts, imposes corporate governance requirements, enhances accounting and control disclosures, impacts insider transactions and executive loans, establishes new types of criminal conduct, and expands penalties for violations of federal securities laws. *(pp. 9 & B-2)*

Schedule of accounts payable List of the balances of all accounts in the accounts payable ledger and their total. *(p. 294)*

Schedule of accounts receivable List of the balances for all accounts in the accounts receivable ledger and their total. *(p. 268)*

Secured bonds Bonds that have specific assets of the issuer pledged as collateral. *(p. 578)*

Securities and Exchange Commission (SEC) Federal agency Congress has charged to set reporting rules for organizations that sell ownership shares to the public. *(pp. 9 & B-2)*

Self-employment tax Social Security and Medicare taxes for persons who operate their own businesses. *(p. 208)*

Selling expenses Expenses of promoting sales, such as displaying and advertising merchandise, making sales, and delivering goods to customers. *(p. 347)*

Serial bonds Bonds consisting of separate amounts that mature at different dates. *(p. 578)*

Shareholders Owners of a corporation; also called *stockholders. (p. 11)*

Signature card Includes the signatures of each person authorized to sign checks on the bank account. *(p. 183)*

Simple capital structure Capital structure that consists of only common stock and nonconvertible preferred stock; consists of no dilutive securities. *(p. 549)*

Single-step income statement Income statement format that includes cost of goods sold as an expense and shows only one subtotal for total expenses. *(p. 349)*

Small stock dividend Stock dividend that is 25% or less of a corporation's previously outstanding shares. *(p. 541)*

Solvency Company's long-run financial viability and its ability to cover long-term obligations. *(p. 643)*

Source documents Source of information for accounting entries that can be in either paper or electronic form; also called *business papers. (p. 75)*

Special journal Any journal used for recording and posting transactions of a similar type. *(p. 266)*

Specific identification Method to assign cost to inventory when the purchase cost of each item in inventory is identified and used to compute cost of inventory. *(p. 417)*

Standard costs Costs that should be incurred under normal conditions to produce a product or component or to perform a service. *(p. 783)*

State unemployment taxes (SUTA) State payroll taxes on employers to support its unemployment programs. *(p. 232)*

Stated value stock No-par stock assigned a stated value per share; this amount is recorded in the stock account when the stock is issued. *(p. 519)*

Statement of cash flows A financial statement that lists cash inflows (receipts) and cash outflows (payments) during a period; arranged by operating, investing, and financing. *(p. 598)*

Statement of owner's equity Report of changes in equity over a period; adjusted for increases (owner investment and net income) and for decreases (withdrawals and net loss). *(p. 29)*

Statement of partners' equity Financial statement that shows total capital balances at the beginning of the period, any additional investment by partners, the income or loss of the period, the partners' withdrawals, and the partners' ending capital balances; also called *statement of partners' capital. (p. 493)*

Statement of retained earnings Report of changes in retained earnings over a period; adjusted for increases (net income), for decreases (dividends and net loss), and for any prior period adjustment. *(p. 547)*

Statement of stockholders' equity Financial statement that lists the beginning and ending balances of each major equity account and describes all changes in those accounts. *(p. 548)*

Stock dividend Corporation's distribution of its own stock to its stockholders without the receipt of any payment. *(p. 541)*

Stock split Occurs when a corporation calls in its stock and replaces each share with more than one new share; decreases both the market value per share and any par or stated value per share. *(p. 543)*

Stockholders' equity A corporation's equity; also called *shareholders' equity* or *corporate capital. (p. 519)*

Straight-line depreciation Method that allocates an equal portion of the depreciable cost of plant asset (cost minus salvage) to each accounting period in its useful life. *(pp. 108 & 450)*

Straight-line bond amortization Method allocating an equal amount of bond interest expense to each period of the bond life. *(p. 572)*

Subsidiary ledger List of individual sub-accounts and amounts with a common characteristic; linked to a controlling account in the general ledger. *(p. 267)*

Sunk cost Cost already incurred and cannot be avoided or changed. *(p. 681)*

T-account Tool used to show the effects of transactions and events on individual accounts. *(p. 46)*

Target cost Maximum allowable cost for a product or service; defined as expected selling price less the desired profit. *(p. 715)*

Taxable income A corporation's total revenues under tax laws minus its total expenses under tax laws. *(p. 538)*

Temporary accounts Accounts used to record revenues, expenses, and withdrawals (dividends for a corporation); they are closed at the end of each period; also called *nominal accounts. (p. 133)*

Term bonds Bonds scheduled for payment (maturity) at a single specified date. *(p. 578)*

Time ticket Source document used to report the time an employee spent working on a job or on overhead activities and then to determine the amount of direct labor to charge to the job or the amount of indirect labor to charge to overhead. *(p. 719)*

Times interest earned ratio Ratio of income before interest expense (and any income taxes) divided by interest expense; reflects risk of covering interest commitments when income varies. *(p. 403)*

Total asset turnover Measure of a company's ability to use its assets to generate sales; computed by dividing net sales by average total assets. *(p. 463)*

Total quality management (TQM) Concept calling for all managers and employees at all stages of operations to strive toward higher standards and reduce number of defects. *(p. 679)*

Trade discount Reduction from a list or catalog price that can vary for wholesalers, retailers, and consumers. *(p. 288)*

Trademark or **trade (brand) name** Symbol, name, phrase, or jingle identified with a company, product, or service. *(p. 462)*

Transportation-In Freight costs paid by the buyer. *(p. 287)*

Treasury stock Corporation's own stock that it reacquired and still holds. *(p. 545)*

Trial balance List of accounts and their balances at a point in time; total debit balances equal total credit balances. *(p. 55)*

Unadjusted trial balance List of accounts and balances prepared before accounting adjustments are recorded and posted. *(p. 110)*

Unavoidable expense Expense (or cost) that is not relevant for business decisions; an expense that would continue even if a department, product, or service is eliminated. *(p. 817)*

Unclassified balance sheet Balance sheet that broadly groups assets, liabilities, and equity accounts. *(p. 349)*

Uncontrollable costs Costs that a manager does not have the power to determine or strongly influence. *(p. 758)*

Underapplied overhead Amount by which overhead incurred in a period exceeds the overhead applied to that period's production using the predetermined overhead rate. *(p. 725)*

Unearned revenue Liability created when customers pay in advance for products or services; earned when the products or services are later delivered. *(pp. 52 & 324)*

Unfavorable variance Difference in revenues or costs, when the actual amount is compared to the budgeted amount, that contributes to a lower income. *(p. 779)*

Units-of-production depreciation Method that charges a varying amount to depreciation expense for each period of an asset's useful life depending on its usage. *(p. 451)*

Unlimited liability Legal relationship among general partners that makes each of them responsible for partnership debts if the other partners are unable to pay their shares. *(p. 487)*

Unsecured bonds Bonds backed only by the issuer's credit standing; almost always riskier than secured bonds; also called *debentures*. *(p. 578)*

Useful life Length of time an asset will be productively used in the operations of a business; also called *service life*. *(p. 449)*

Value-added time The portion of cycle time that is directed at producing a product or service; equals process time. *(p. 690)*

Value chain Sequential activities that add value to an entity's products or services; includes design, production, marketing, distribution, and service. *(p. 686)*

Variable cost Cost that changes in proportion to changes in the activity output volume. *(p. 680)*

Variance analysis Process of examining differences between actual and budgeted revenues or costs and describing them in terms of price and quantity differences. *(p. 783)*

Vendee Buyer of goods or services. *(p. 167)*

Vendor Seller of goods or services. *(pp. 161 & 287)*

Vertical analysis Evaluation of each financial statement item or group of items in terms of a specific base amount. *(p. 644)*

Voucher Internal file used to store documents and information to control cash disbursements and to ensure that a transaction is properly authorized and recorded. *(p. 164)*

Voucher register Journal (referred to as *book of original entry*) in which all vouchers are recorded after they have been approved. *(p. 169)*

Voucher system Procedures and approvals designed to control cash disbursements and acceptance of obligations. *(p. 164)*

Wage bracket withholding table Table of the amounts of income tax withheld from employees' wages. *(p. 210)*

Wages Money paid or received for work or services by the hour, day, or week or by the number of units produced. *(p. 208)*

Weighted average Method to assign inventory cost to sales; the cost of available-for-sale units is divided by the number of units available to determine per unit cost prior to each sale that is then multiplied by the units sold to yield the cost of that sale. *(p. 428)*

Wholesaler Intermediary that buys products from manufacturers or other wholesalers and sells them to retailers or other wholesalers. *(p. 262)*

Withdrawals Payment of cash or other assets from a proprietorship or partnership to its owner or owners. *(p. 23)*

Withholding allowance This determines the amount of federal income taxes to withhold from an employee's pay. *(p. 206)*

Workers' compensation insurance An insurance program that provides benefits to workers who are injured on the job. *(p. 233)*

Work sheet Spreadsheet used to draft an unadjusted trial balance, adjusting entries, adjusted trial balance, and financial statements. *(p. 128)*

Working capital Current assets minus current liabilities at a point in time. *(p. 650)*

Working papers Analyses and other internal documents prepared by accountants when organizing information for formal reports and financial statements. *(p. 128)*

Workplace fraud The deliberate misuse of an employer's assets for an employee's personal gain. *(p. 158)*

Credits

Chapter 1
Page 3 ©Ian Barkley/Getty Images
Page 6 SETH WENIG/Reuters/Landov
Page 10 ©Mel Curtis/Getty Images

Chapter 2
Page 21 Courtesy of Spanx
Page 23 ©Sam Sharpe/Corbis
Page 29 Courtesy of Spanx

Chapter 3
Page 45 ©REUTERS/HO/Landov
Page 52 ©Joe Robbins/Getty Images

Chapter 4
Page 73 Courtesy of Vosges Haut Chocolat
Page 76 Copyright 2009 NBAE (Photo by Allen Einstein/NBAE via Getty Images)

Chapter 5
Page 103 Courtesy of PopCap Games, Inc.
Page 105 ©Walt Disney Co./Courtesy Everett Collection

Chapter 6
Page 127 Courtesy of Kathryn Kerrigan.

Chapter 7
Page 157 Courtesy of Dylan's Candy Bar

Chapter 8
Page 177 Courtesy of YoungSong Martin
Page 179 ©Joe Raedle/Getty Images

Chapter 9
Page 205 Courtesy of Feed Granola Company

Chapter 10
Page 231 AP Images/CP, Jeremy Hainsworth

Chapter 11
Page 261 Courtesy of Life is Good®
Page 264 ©Spencer Platt/ Getty Images

Chapter 12
Page 285 Courtesy of Cocalo
Page 290 ©Christof Koepsel/Bongarts/Getty Images

Chapter 13
Page 315 Courtesy www.bigbadtoystore.com
Page 325 ©2009 NBAE (Photo by Steve Babineau/NBAE via Getty Images)

Chapter 14
Page 345 Courtesy of RockBottomGolf.com
Page 351 ©Brian Bahr/Getty Images

Appendix B
Page B-5 ©Mel Curtis/Getty Images
Page B-6 ©Getty Images

Appendix C
Page C-3 AP Images/Katsumi Kasahara
Page C-10 ©ATABOY/Getty Images/The Image Bank

Index

Note: Page numbers followed by *n* indicate material in footnotes.

Abnormal (credit) balance, 47, 80, 357
Account(s), 23
  adjusting
    in accrual basis accounting
      (*See* **Adjusting entries**)
    in preparing financial statements
      (*See* Adjusting accounts)
  asset accounts
    adjusting entries posted to, 111
    after closing process, 136
    balances of, 112
  balance column accounts, 80
  balance sheet accounts, 318
  cash accounts
    adjustments not made to, 318
    recording transactions in
      (illustrated), 48–53
  chart of accounts, 76, 89
  contra accounts (*See* **Contra accounts**)
  controlling accounts, 267–268, 271
  equity accounts, 111, 136
  expense accounts
    adjusting entries posted to, 111
    after closing process, 136
    closing to Income Summary, 134,
      135, 352
  income statement accounts, 318
  liability accounts
    adjusting entries posted to, 111
    after closing process, 136
    balances of, 112
  permanent, 133, 136, 137, 141, 353, 357
  revenue accounts
    adjusting entries posted to, 111
    after closing process, 136
    closing to Income Summary, 134,
      135, 352
    contra revenue accounts, 263–264, 274
  T-accounts, 46–47, 60
    adjusting entries, 106, 328, 329
    balance column accounts compared, 80
    recording transactions in
      (illustrated), 48–53, 54, 59
  temporary (*See* **Temporary accounts**)
  withdrawals account, closing, 135, 137, 352
  See also specific accounts
Account balance, 47
Accounting, 2–13
  accrual v. cash basis, 104–105, 115, 318
  adjustments (*See* **Adjusting entries**)
  defined, **4**

demonstration problem, 12
double-entry accounting, 44–60
financial accounting, 6, 7
fundamentals of, 9–12
  ethics, 9, 10
  GAAP, 10
  ownership structures, 11–12
importance of, 4–6, 13
managerial accounting, 5, 7
opportunities in, 7–8, 13
payroll accounting, 213–216
  demonstration problem, 219
  employee earnings records, 216, 219
  recording and settling payroll, 214–215
  using payroll register, 213–214
principles-based, 10, B-2–B-3, B-7
rules-based, 10, B-2–B-3, B-7
Accounting abuses, 9
Accounting assumptions, B-3, B-4–B-5, B-7
  business entity assumption, 11, B-3, B-4
  going-concern assumption, B-3, B-5
  monetary unit assumption, B-3, B-5
  periodicity assumption, B-3, B-5
  time period assumption, 105
Accounting books, 75
Accounting clerks, 7
Accounting constraints, B-3, B-6–B-7
  conservatism, B-3, B-7
  cost-benefit trade-off, B-3, B-7
  materiality, B-3, B-7
Accounting cycle, 137–138
  completing
    closing entries, 352–353, 355
    post-closing trial balance, 353, 357
    reversing entries, 353, 356–357
  steps in, 138, 141
Accounting distribution, 169
Accounting equation, 22–23,
  33, 46, 54, 78
  equity, 23
  expanded, 23, 33
  liabilities, 22–23
  summary of transactions using, 28, 32
  trial balance order and, 55
Accounting errors
  in balance sheet columns, 131
  bank errors, 187, 188
  computerized error-checking, 77
  correction of, 89
    after posting, 86
    in bank statement, 186

    before posting, 85–86
    searching for errors and, 55, 55n
  reducing by using work sheet, 128
  transposition errors, 55n
  See also Human error
Accounting information, 4–6
  confidentiality of, 216
  cross-country comparisons of, B-4
  feedback value of, B-3
  manipulation of, 6
  predictive value of, B-3
  qualitative characteristics of, B-3, B-7
    comparability, 10, B-3, B-4
    consistency, B-3, B-4
    relevance, 10, B-3, B-4
    reliability, 10, B-3–B-4
  timeliness of, B-3, B-5
  users of, 5–6, 12, 13
  uses of, 4–5
Accounting information systems, 5
Accounting principles, B-1–B-7
  accounting assumptions,
    B-3, B-4–B-5, B-7
    business entity assumption,
      11, B-3, B-4
    going-concern assumption, B-3, B-5
    monetary unit assumption, B-3, B-5
    periodicity assumption, B-3, B-5
    time period assumption, 105
  constraints, B-3, B-6–B-7
    conservatism, B-3, B-7
    cost-benefit constraint, B-3, B-7
    materiality, B-3, B-7
  key principles, B-3, B-5–B-6, B-7
    cost principle, B-3, B-5
    full disclosure principle, B-3, B-6
    matching principle, 105, B-3, B-6
    revenue recognition principle,
      105, 324, B-3, B-6
  qualitative characteristics of accounting
    information, B-3, B-7
    comparability, 10, B-3, B-4
    consistency, B-3, B-4
    relevance, 10, B-3, B-4
    reliability, 10, B-3–B-4
  rules-based v. principles-based
    accounting, B-7
  objectives of financial reporting,
    B-2–B-3, B-7
  Sarbanes-Oxley Act of 2002, B-2
Accounting-related professions, 7, 8

Account numbers in chart of accounts, 76
Accounts payable, 27, 294, 301
Accounts payable ledger, 294, 302
    demonstration problems, 298, 299, 300
    posting from cash disbursements journal,
        293, 294, 295–296, 298
    proving ledger, 294, 299, 301
Accounts receivable
    schedule of, 268, 270, 301
    special journals and subsidiary ledgers,
        266–272, 274
        cash receipts journal, 270–272,
            274, 299
        demonstration problem, 273
        sales journal, 266–267, 273, 274, 299
        See also **Accounts receivable ledger**
    transaction analysis, 26, 27
    See also Merchandise sales
Accounts receivable ledger, 267–270
    controlling account and, 267–268
    demonstration problem, 273, 299, 300
    posting
        to general journal, 268, 269, 273
        to subsidiary ledger, 268, 269
    proving ledgers, 268, 269, 270, 274
    schedule of accounts receivable
        drawn from, 270
Accrual(s)
    expenses (*See* **Accrued expenses**)
    revenues (*See* **Accrued revenues**)
Accrual basis accounting, 104, 115
    adjusting accounts in
        (*See* **Adjusting entries**)
    cash basis accounting compared,
        104–105, 115, 318
    required adjustments in, 318
    revenue and expense recognition, 105
Accrued expenses, 106, **109,** 318
    adjusting entries for, 109–110,
        115, 320, 331
    reversing entries for, 356–357
    salaries expense, 109–110, 320, 331
Accrued revenues, 106, 318, **324**
    adjusting entries for, 324, 331–332
    financial statement effects, 326, 328, 329
    revenue recognition, 105
    services revenue, 324
Accumulated Depreciation account,
    108–109
ACFE. *See* Association of Certified Fraud
    Examiners
acfe.com, 158, 217
Acquisitions, A-13–A-14
Adelphia Communications, 9
Adjusted bank balance, 188
Adjusted book balance, 188
Adjusted trial balance, 110, 115
    computations
        cost of goods sold, 322–323
        net purchases, 322
        net sales, 322
    financial statement prepared from,
        112–113, 115
    in partial work sheet, 320–321

preparation of
    from unadjusted trial balance, 110, 112
    with work sheet, 129, 130
    sorting to financial statements, 129, 130
Adjusting accounts, 105–112
    accrued expenses, 106, 109–110, 115
    framework for, 105–106
    journalizing and posting, 110, 111
    prepaid (deferred) expenses, 106–109, 115
        depreciation, 107–109, 110, 114
        other prepaids, 107
        prepaid insurance, 106–107, 110, 114
        supplies, 107, 110, 114
    three-step adjusting process, 106
Adjusting entries, 105–112, 115
    accrued expenses, 109–110, 115,
        318, 320, 331
    adjusted trial balance, preparing, 110, 112
    alternative accounting for prepayments,
        329–331, 332
        prepaid expenses, 329–330, 332
        unearned revenues, 330–331, 332
    defined, **106**
    demonstration problems, 114, 326–329
    explanation of transactions, 110, 114
    financial statement effects of, 328, 329
        balance sheet effects, 324, 325, 326
        income statement effects, 326
    framework for, 105–106
    for inventory, 316, 317–318, 331
    journalizing and posting, 110, 111, 133
    links to financial statements, 326
    prepaid (deferred) expenses, 106–109, 115
        depreciation, 107–109, 110,
            114, 319, 320
        equipment, 319–320
        financial statement effects, 326, 328, 329
        other expenses, 107
        prepaid insurance, 106–107,
            110, 114, 319
        supplies, 107, 110, 114, 319
    preparing from bank reconciliation
        check printing, 189
        collection of note, 188–189
        demonstration of, 190, 191
        interest earned, 189
        NSF check, 189
    prior period adjustments, 326
    revenue adjustments, 323–325
        accrued revenues, 324, 331–332
        financial statement effects, 326, 328, 329
        unearned (deferred) revenues, 324–325,
            330–331, 332
    reversing entries compared, 357
    shown in partial work sheet, 320–323
        adjusted trial balance, 320–321
        cost of goods sold computation,
            322–323
        gross profit computation, 323
        net purchases computation, 322
        net sales computation, 322
    from source documents, 108
    three-step process, 106, 318
    types of, 318

Adjustments
    to accumulated depreciation, 108–109
    entering in work sheet, 129, 130
    keying, 129, 130
    prior period adjustments, 326
    required in accrual basis accounting, 318
Advance ticket sales, 52, 325, B-6
Advertising costs, A-12
AICPA (American Institute of Certified
    Public Accountants), 9
Altered checks, 187
Amazon.com, 162
American Institute of Certified Public
    Accountants (AICPA), 9
Annual financial statements, 105
    adjusting accounts, 105–112, 115
    preparation of (*See* Financial
        statement(s))
    timing and reporting, 104–105
Annual reports
    examples of
        Best Buy, A-1, A-2–A-20
        RadioShack, A-1, A-21–A-26
    financial section of, A-1
    tax reports, 216
    of withholding taxes, 216, 238–239
Anonymous tips, 159, 165
AOL Time Warner, 9
Apple Computer, 4
Asset(s), 22
    book value of, 109
    current assets, 351
    fixed (*See* **Plant assets**)
    intangible, 351, A-9–A-10
    internal control of, 161
    liquid assets, 178
    misappropriation of, 158
    net assets, 23
    noncurrent, 350
    normal balance for, 47
    prepaid accounts as, 52
    prepaid expenses as, 107
    reporting on balance sheet, 31, 351
    restricted, A-9
    salvage value of, 108
    separation of duties regarding, 161
Asset accounts, 111, 112, 136
Association of Certified Fraud
    Examiners (ACFE)
    frauds reported by, 162, 165
    on payroll fraud, 217
    Report to the Nation (2008), 158, 165
    Web site: acfe.com, 158, 217
ATM cards, 161
ATMs. *See* Automated teller machines
Audit of financial statements
    internal, in fraud detection, 159, 165
    using work sheet in, 128
Auditors
    external, 6, 159, 165
    internal, 5, 8, 162
    for voucher systems, 169
Authorization forms, 217
Authorized depositories, 234

Automated teller machines (ATMs)
face-recognition software in
ATM cards, 161
"payroll cards" used in, 213
withdrawals shown on bank statement, 186
Automatic payments, 186

Balance column accounts, 80
Balance per bank, 188
Balance per book, 188
Balance sheet, 29, 31, 33
cash basis statement, 105
classified (*See* **Classified balance sheet**)
consolidated, examples of, A-4, A-22
effects of understatements, 324, 325, 326
preparation of
from adjusted trial balance, 112, 113
demonstration of, 32, 60, 141
from trial balance, 56–57, 60, 85
from work sheet, 132, 133
required adjustments to accounts, 318
unclassified, format of, 349
Bank, 184
Bank account(s), 183–185
payroll account, 214, 215, 219
regular account, payroll paid from, 215, 219
Bank errors, 187, 188
Banking activities, 183–189, 192
bank reconciliation (*See* **Bank reconciliation**)
bank statement, 185–186, 187, 192
basic services, 183–185
bank account, 183–185
checks (*See* **Check(s)**)
deposits, 183, 184
electronic funds transfer (EFT), 185, 214
demonstration problem, 190–191
online banking, 185
Bankrate.com, 188
Bank reconciliation, 186–189, 192
adjusting entries prepared from, 188–189
check printing, 189
collection of note, 188–189
demonstration of, 190, 191
interest earned, 189
NSF check, 189
illustration of, 187–188
purpose of, 187
Bank service charges (fees), 186
check printing fees, 187, 189
overdraft program fees, 188
Bank statement, 185–186, 187, 192
Barnes & Noble, 264
Behavioral cues to fraud, 159
Best Buy, 4, 12, 23, 52, 57, 262
financial statements of, A-1, A-2–A-20
consolidated balance sheets, A-4
consolidated statements of
cash flows, A-6
consolidated statements of changes in
shareholders' equity, A-7
consolidated statements of earnings, A-5
selected financial data, A-3
selected notes to, A-8–A-20

BestBuy.com, 23
BigBadToyStore, 315
BigBadToyStore.com, 315
Bill, as source document, 75
Billing fraud, 158
Blakely, Sara, 21
Blank endorsement of check, 184
Boards of directors, 6, A-1
Boblit, Joel, 315
Bonding of employees, 161, 164
Bonds payable, 351
Book(s) (accounting books), 75
Bookkeeping, 4
Bookkeeping careers, 7
Book of final entry, 74
Book of original entry, 74
Book value of asset, **109**
Borders Books, 264
Boston Celtics, 325
Bot-networking, 163
Bretton-woods.com, 188
Bribery, 159
Bristol-Myers Squibb, 9
Brown, Warren, 45
Business associates, 6
Business description, A-8
Business entity assumption, 11, B-3, **B-4**
Business segments, A-19–A-20
Business structures
corporations (*See* **Corporation(s)**)
partnerships, 11, 13, 351, B-4
proprietorships, 11, 13, 351, B-4
types of businesses, 11–12
Buyer, transfer of ownership to, 290

Cake Love, 45
CakeLove.com, 45
Canceled checks, 186
Cannondale, 290
Capital providers, 6, 29
Careers in accounting, 7–8, 13
career paths, 7–8
certifications for, 8
entry-level, 7
Cash, 178, 192
access to, 178–179, 192
note regarding, A-8
Cash accounts, 48–53, 318
Cash and cash equivalents, note
regarding, A-8
Cash basis accounting, 104–105, 115, 318
Cash controls, 176–192
banking activities as, 183–189, 192
bank reconciliation (*See* **Bank reconciliation**)
bank statement, 185–186
basic bank services, 183–185
demonstration problem, 190–191
cash disbursements
payment by check, 294
petty cash system (*See* **Petty cash** fund)
cash receipts
over-the-counter receipts, 178–180, 192
receipts by mail, 180, 192

cash registers as, 160
for entrepreneurs, 157, 177
establishing responsibilities, 160
Cash disbursements
control of, 294
petty cash system (*See* **Petty cash** fund)
Cash disbursements journal, 294–296, 302
cash purchases recorded in, 292
demonstration problem, 299, 300
journalizing, 294, 295
posting from, 293, 294, 295–296, 298
Cash discount(s), 262, 263
Cash equivalents, A-8
Cash over and short, 179–180, 182
Cash payments
recording in T-accounts, 50, 51, 52, 53
transaction analysis, 26, 27
Cash purchases
journalizing and posting, 79, 80, 82, 83
recorded in cash disbursements journal, 292
recording in T-accounts, 49, 53
transaction analysis, 24–25
Cash receipts
in advance, 325
cash sales, 270, 271
from credit customers, 270, 271
journalizing and posting, 79, 83, 179
from other sources, 270, 271
over-the-counter receipts, 178–180, 192
cash over and short, 179–180
proper handling of, 178–179
receipts by mail, 180, 192
recording in T-accounts, 51, 52
transaction analysis, 27, 51, 52
Cash receipts journal, 270–272, 274
crossfooting, 271–272
demonstration problem, 299
footing, 271, 272
journalizing, 270, 271
posting, 270, 271, 272
Cash registers, 75, 160, 178, 179
Cash register tape, 178
Cash sales, 262, 270, 271
Catalina Marketing, 10
Catalog price, 287
Cause and effect, B-6
CB (certified bookkeeper), 8
Center for Women's Business Research, 29
CEO (chief executive officer), 165
Certificate in management
accounting (CMA), 8
Certified bookkeeper (CB), 8
Certified forensic accountant (CrFA), 8
Certified fraud examiner (CFE), 8
Certified Internal auditor (CIA), 8
Certified payroll professional (CPP), 8
Certified public accountant (CPA), 8
CFE (certified fraud examiner), 8
CFO (chief financial officer), 165
Chart of accounts, 76, 89
Check(s), 164, 184–185
adjusting entries for, 189
canceled checks, 186
as cash control, 294

Check(s)—*Cont.*
  endorsement of, 184
  NSF checks, 187, 188, 189
  outstanding, 187, 188
  payroll check, 214, 215
  for petty cash fund, 181
  processed image as source document, 75
  uncollectible, 186
Check authorization, 168
Check fraud, 187
Check printing fees, 187, 189
Check protectors, 161
Check register, 169, 294
Chicago Bears, 52
Chief executive officer (CEO), 165
Chief financial officer (CFO), 165
CIA (certified Internal auditor), 8
Circular E (IRS), **210**
Classified balance sheet, 349
  format of, 349–351, 357
    categories, 350–351
    classification structure for, 350
    example of, 350
Closing entries, 134
  in completing accounting cycle, 352–353, 355
  demonstration of, 139, 355
  recording, 134–137, 141
    expense accounts, 134, 135
    income summary, 134, 135, 137
    revenue accounts, 134, 135, 352
    withdrawals, 135, 137
Closing process, 126–141
  accounting cycle and, 137–138
  closing entries, 352–353, 355
  defined, **133**
  demonstration problem, 138–141
  post-closing trial balance, 136, 137, 141,
    353, 357
  recording closing entries
    (*See* **Closing entries**)
  reversing entries, 353, 356–357
  steps in, 134, 135
  temporary and permanent accounts
    Income Summary account, 133–134, 317
    Owner, Capital account, 134,
      135, 137, 352
  work sheet as tool in, 128–133
    applications and analysis, 132–133
    benefits of, 128
    use of, 128–131
CMA (certificate in management accounting), 8
CoCaLo, 285
CoCaLo.com, 285
Code(s) of ethics, 9
Code of Professional Ethics (AICPA), 9
Collections, 187, 188–189
Collusion, 161, 180
Columnar journal, 266
Commitments, A-20
Communicating business activities, 4, 5
Comparability of accounting information,
  10, B-3, **B-4**
Compound journal entry, 79, 83
Comprehensive income, A-18

Computerized accounting systems, 77, 83
Computerized journals, 77
Computer viruses, 163
Confidentiality of information, 216
Consistency of accounting
    information, B-3, **B-4**
Consolidated financial statements,
    examples of
  balance sheets, A-4, A-22
  income statements, A-5, A-23–A-24
  statements of cash flows, A-6, A-26
  statements of shareholders'
      equity, A-7, A-25
Consumer, buyer as, 288
Contingencies, A-20
Contra accounts, 51, 108
  Accumulated Depreciation account, 108–109
  contra-assets account, 351
  contra-purchases account, 289
  revenue accounts
    Sales Discounts, 263–264
    Sales Returns and Allowances, 264, 274
Controlling accounts, 267, 267–268, 271
Convertible debentures, A-16
Corporation(s), 11, 13, 351, B-4
Corrected bank balance, 188
Corrected book balance, 188
Correcting entry, 86, 89
Corruption, 158–159
Cost-benefit principle, 163
Cost control, 127
Cost flows, 323
Cost of goods sold, 322
  computing, 331
    from adjusted trial balance, 322–323
      demonstration of, 327
  cost flows, 322–323
  note regarding, A-12
Cost principle, B-3, **B-5**
Counterfeit checks, 187
CPA (certified public accountant), 8
CPP (certified payroll professional), 8
Credit(s), 46, 60, **77,** 78, 82
Credit (abnormal) balance, 47
  in balance column account, 80
  reversing entries to correct, 357
Credit card number theft, 163
Credit facilities, A-15–A-16
Credit memoranda, 186, 187, 188, **265**
Creditors (lenders), 6, **22**
Credit period, 263, 288, **289**
Credit purchases, 25
  journalizing and posting, 79, 82
  recorded in purchases journal, 292
  recording in T-accounts, 49
Credit sales
  of merchandise, 262
  provision of services, 26
  recording cash receipts, 270, 271
  recording in sales journal, 263, 266–267
  revenue recognition principle and, B-6
  sales discounts, 263–264, 288
Credit terms, 263, 288
CrFA (certified forensic accountant), 8

Cross-country comparisons, B-4
Crossfooting, 271–272
  cash disbursements journal, 295, 296
  subsidiary journals, 299, 300–301
Current assets, 351
Current liabilities, 351
Custody of assets, 161
Customers, 6
Cyberfraud
  scc.gov/investor/pubs/cyberfraud.htm, 162
  types of, 163
Cybersleuthing, 164

Debit(s), 46, 60, **77,** 78, 81–82
Debit balance, 47
Debit memoranda, 186, 188, **289**
Debt, A-15–A-16
Debt securities, A-10, A-14
Decision making, B-2–B-3
Defective merchandise, 264, 289
Deferrals, 106
  expenses (*See* **Prepaid expenses**)
  revenues (*See* **Unearned revenues**)
Delphi, B-5
Demonstration problems
  accounting, 12
  adjusting entries, 114, 326–329
  banking activities, 190–191
  closing process, 138–141
  double-entry accounting, 58–60
  financial statement formats, 355
  financial statement preparation, 32, 60
  internal controls, 166
  merchandise sales, 272–273, 299
  payroll, 217–219
  payroll tax reporting, 245–246
  petty cash fund, 191–192
  special journals and ledgers, 296–301
  transaction analysis, 31–33
  transaction processing, 86–89
  trial balance, 59, 301
Deposits in transit, 187
Deposit ticket, 75, 183, 184
Depreciation, 108
  adjusting entries for, 107–109, 110,
    114, 319, 320
  as selling expense, 347–348
  straight-line, 108
Discount period, 263, 288, **289**
Distribution managers, 5
Documentation, 161
  electronic documents, 75
  internal controls and, 162
Domini Social Index (DSI), 10
Double-entry accounting, 44–60
  analyzing and recording transactions
    (*See* Transaction analysis)
  defined, **47**
  demonstration problem, 58–60
  unadjusted trial balance, 55–58
Double taxation, 11
DSI (Domini Social Index), 10
Dylan's Candy Bar, 157
DylansCandyBar.com, 157

Earnings per share (EPS), A-16–A-17
eBay, 162
Ebbers, Bernard, 6
ECG (electrocardiogram), 162
Echostar, 10, B-5
E-commerce
   increased, internal controls and, 162–163
   online banking services, 185
   risks of, 163
EDGAR (electronic data gathering, analysis, and retrieval) database (SEC), 23, A-1
EFT (electronic funds transfer), 185, 214
EIN (employer identification number), 232
Electrocardiogram (ECG), 162
Electronic data gathering, analysis, and retrieval (EDGAR) database (SEC), 23, A-1
Electronic Data Systems, 10, B-5
Electronic documents, 75
Electronic funds transfer (EFT), 185, 214
Employee(s), 206
   bonding of, 161, 164
   security of payroll data, 217
Employee benefit plans
   for accounting professionals, 8
   entrepreneurs and, 231
   note regarding, A-19
Employee earnings, 208–213
   computing gross pay, 208–209
   computing net pay, 213
   computing withholdings, 209–212
   demonstration problem, 217–219
Employee earnings records, 216, 219
Employee fraud. *See* **Workplace fraud**
Employee's Withholding Allowance Certificate (Form W-4), 206, 207, 211, 213
Employer
   benefits provided by, 231
   payroll taxes (*See* Payroll tax reporting)
Employer identification number (EIN), 232
Employer's Annual Federal Unemployment Tax Return (Form 940, Form 940-EZ), 241
Employer's Quarterly Federal Tax Return (Form 941), 236, 237–238, 246
Employer's Quarterly Unemployment Tax Report, 241
Encryption, 163
End of month (EOM), 263
Endorsement of checks, **184**
Enron Corporation, 6, 9, 10, B-2, B-4
Entrepreneurship
   accounting for merchandisers, 285, 315
   accounting information use, 6
   cash controls, 157, 177
   cost control, 127
   employer-provided benefits, 231
   financial statements, 73, 103, 345
   merchandise sales, 261
   monitoring accounts, 45
   monitoring receivables and payables, 205
   transaction analysis, 21

transaction-based accounting, 3
   women entrepreneurs, 21, 29, 73, 127, 157, 177, 285
EOM (end of month), 263
EPS (earnings per share), A-16–A-17
Equipment, 24–25, 319–320, A-9
Equity, 22, 23
   changes in, 56, 131, 132
   normal balance for, 47
   reporting on balance sheet, 31, 351
Equity accounts, 111, 136
Equity securities, A-10, A-14–A-15
Ernst and Young, 10
Error correction. *See* Accounting errors
Estimates, 105, A-8
Ethics, 9, 10, 13
Events, 23
Executive compensation, A-12–A-13, A-16
Expanded accounting equation, 23, 33
Expenditures, 164–165
Expense accounts
   adjusting entries posted to, 111
   after closing process, 136
   closing to Income Summary, 134, 135, 352
Expenses, 23
   accrued (*See* **Accrued expenses**)
   depreciation, 347–348
   general and administrative expenses, 348, A-12
   payment in cash, 26
   prepaid (*See* **Prepaid expenses**)
   recognition of, 105
   reported on income statement, 30
   selling expenses, 347–348, A-12
   utilities expense, 80, 83
   wages and salaries
      accrued, 109–110, 114, 320, 331
      payment of, 79, 80, 83
      reversing entries for, 356–357
Explanation of transactions
   adjusting entries, 110, 114
   for journal entries, 77, 78, 83
External transactions, 23
External users of accounting information, **6,** 12, 13

Face-recognition software, 161
Fair Labor Standards Act, 206
Fannie Mae, 9
FASB. *See* **Financial Accounting Standards Board**
Fastow, Andrew, 6
Federal depository bank, 234
Federal Insurance Contributions Act (FICA), 207, 232
   FICA taxes (*See* **FICA** taxes)
   self-employment tax, 208
Federal Reserve Banks, 234
Federal Tax Deposit Coupon (**Form 8109**), **235**–236, 246
Federal Trade Commission (FTC), 164
Federal unemployment (FUTA) taxes, 232
   computing, 234–235, 240–241, 246
   demonstration problem, 246

recording in general journal, 241, 242–243, 246
   reporting, 241–242, 243, 246
Feedback value of accounting information, B-3
FeedGranola.com, 205
Feed Granola Company, 205
Feite, Brian, 103
FICA (Federal Insurance Contributions Act), 207, 232
FICA taxes, 207–208, 232
   computing, 233, 234–235, 246
   computing withholdings, 209–212
   demonstration problem, 246
   employer's annual withholding report, 238–239
   income maximums for, 232
   legal issues in, 207–208, 232
   Medicare taxes, 207, 208
      computing, demonstration of, 246
      no income maximums on, 232
      quarterly reporting, 236, 237–238
   recording in general journal, 233
   Social Security taxes, 207, 208, 212, 214
      computing, demonstration of, 246
      income maximums, 232
      quarterly reporting, 236, 237–238
Finance.Google.com, 23
Finance.Yahoo.com, 23
Financial accounting, 6, 7
Financial Accounting Standards Board (FASB), 10, 13, B-2
Financial history and highlights, A-1, A-3
Financial reporting, objectives of, B-2–B-3, B-7
Financial section of annual reports, A-1
Financial statement(s), 29–31
   annual, 104–112, 115
   in annual reports, A-1
   audit of, 128, 159, 165
   balance sheet (*See* **Balance sheet**)
   certification requirement, 165
   entrepreneurship, 73, 103, 345
   examples of, 4, A-1–A-26
      Best Buy, A-1, A-2–A-20
      RadioShack, A-1, A-21–A-26
   fraudulent, 159
   general-purpose, 6
   income statement (*See* **Income statement**)
   interim statements, 105, 128
   notes to, A-8–A-13
   preparation of
      from adjusted trial balance, 112–113, 115
      demonstration, 32, 60, 140–141
      from trial balance, 56–58, 60, 85, 89
      work sheet as aid in (*See* **Work sheet**)
   presentation issues, 57–58
   pro forma statements, 133
   reporting owner investments in, 131
   sorting adjusted trial balance to, 129, 130
   statement of owner's equity
      (*See* **Statement of owner's equity**)

Financial statement effects of adjusting
  entries, 328, 329
  balance sheet effects, 324, 325, 326
  income statement effects, 326
Financial statement formats, 347–351
  classified balance sheet, 349–351, 357
    categories, 350–351
    classification structure for, 350
  demonstration problem, 355
  income statement, 357
    demonstration of, 355
    multiple-step, 347–348, 355
    single-step, 349
  statement of owner's equity, 349, 357
  unclassified balance sheet, 349
Firewalls, 163
Fiscal year, 105, A-8
Fixed assets. *See* **Plant assets**
Fleming, 262
FOB (free on board) **point, 290**
Footing(s), 47, 271, 272, 299, 300–301
Forged endorsements, 187
Forged signature on check, 187
**Form 940 (Employer's Annual Federal
  Unemployment Tax Return), 241**
**Form 940-EZ (Employer's Annual Federal
  Unemployment Tax Return), 241**
**Form 941 (Employer's Quarterly Federal
  Tax Return), 236,** 237–238, 246
Form 8109 (Federal Tax Deposit Coupon),
  235–236, 246
Form 8109-B, 235
Form 10-K (SEC), **A-1**
Form 10-K405 (SEC), A-1
Form 10-KSB (SEC), **A-1**
Form 10-KSB405 (SEC), A-1
Form 10-KT (SEC), A-1
Form 10-KT405 (SEC), A-1
Form SS-4, 232
**Form W-2 (Wage and Tax Statement),
  238–**239, 246
**Form W-3 (Transmittal of Wage and
  Tax Statements), 239,** 246
**Form W-4 (Employee's Withholding
  Allowance Certificate), 206,** 207,
  211, 213
Fraud. *See* **Workplace fraud**
fraud.org, 162
"Fraudsters," 159
Fraudulent financial statements, 159
Free on board (**FOB**) point, **290**
Freight charges, 287
Freight-in, 287, 290
Freight-out, 290
Fremont General, 10
FTC (Federal Trade Commission), 164
ftc.gov/bcp/consumer/shtm, 162
Full disclosure principle, B-3, **B-6**
FUTA taxes. *See* **Federal unemployment
  (FUTA) taxes**

**GAAP (Generally accepted accounting
  principles), 10,** 13, **B-7**
The Gap, 262

General and administrative expenses, 348,
  A-12
General and subsidiary ledgers kept in
  tandem, 267
General journal, 77–80, **266**
  adjusting entries in, 114
  demonstration of entries, 87–88
  journalizing, 77–80, 82–83
  merchandise purchases shown in,
    291–292, 299, 300
  payroll entries, 215, 219
  posting to, 82–83, 265, 268, 269, 273
  recording payroll taxes in
    demonstration problem, 246
    FICA tax, 233
    FUTA and SUTA taxes, 241, 242–243
    payroll tax deposits in, 236
    workers' compensation insurance, 244, 246
  recording transactions, 89, 265
General ledger, 74, 80–82
  after closing process, 136
  after posting adjusting entries, 111
  balance column account, 80
  merchandise purchases
    cash disbursements journal posted to,
      295–296
    demonstration problems, 297, 298–301
    posted to general ledger, 291, 292
    purchases journal posted to, 292–293
  posting transactions (*See* **Posting
    transactions**)
  recording merchandise sales, 266
  trial balance prepared from, 83–85, 89
**Generally accepted accounting principles
  (GAAP), 10,** 13, **B-7**
General-purpose financial statements, 6
Ghost employees, 217
Gift cards, 325, A-11
Gift certificates, 52
Global Crossing, 9
Going-concern assumption, B-3, **B-5**
Goodwill, A-9
Government agencies, 8
Government penalties, 234
Grant Thornton, 10
Gross pay, 206
  computing, 208–209, 219
  computing withholdings from, 209–212
  demonstration problem, 218
  reporting, 213
Gross profit, 322
  computing, 331
    from adjusted trial balance, 323
    demonstration of, 327
  shown in income statement, 347, 348

Halliburton, 9
Historical cost principle, B-6
Human error
  cash receipts by mail, 180
  internal control and, 163
  shortchanging customers, 179–180
Human fraud, 163
Human resource managers, 5

IASB. *See* **International Accounting
  Standards Board**
Identifying business activities, 4, 5
Illegal acts
  collusion, 161, 180
  credit card number theft, 163
  fraud (*See* **Workplace fraud**)
  identity theft, 216
  manipulation of accounting
    information, 6
  misappropriation of assets, 158
IMA (Institute of Management
  Accountants), 9
Immediate recognition of costs, B-6
Impersonation online, 163
Income
  comprehensive, A-18
  maximums, 232
  from operations, 347, 348
Income statement, 29, 30, 33
  accrual basis statement, 104
  consolidated, examples of
    Best Buy, A-5
    RadioShack, A-23–A-24
  demonstration problems
    format of statement, 355
    preparation of statement, 32, 60, 140
  effects of understatements, 326
  format of, 357
    combination format, 349
    demonstration problem, 355
    multiple-step, 347–348, 355
    single-step, 349
  items reported on
    gains/losses from nonoperating
      activities, 348
    gross profit, 347, 348
    income and expenses, 30
  for period of time, 56
  preparation of
    from adjusted trial balance,
      112, 113
    demonstration problems, 32,
      60, 140
    from trial balance, 56, 57, 85
    using work sheet, 132–133
  required adjustments to accounts, 318
Income Summary account, **133–**134
  closing temporary accounts to,
    133–134, 317
  closing to Owner, Capital account, 134,
    135, 137, 352
  demonstration of, 140
  shown in partial work sheet, 320–321
Income taxes
  double taxation, 11
  note regarding, A-10–A-11, A-19
  self-employment tax, 208
Independent auditors, 6, 159, 165
Independent contractor, 206
Inflation, B-3, B-5
Information systems, 162
Institute of Management Accountants
  (IMA), 9

Insurance
 against loss, 161
 prepaid (*See* Prepaid insurance)
 workers' compensation insurance, 233,
  244, 246
Intangible assets, 351, A-9–A-10
Interest
 on checking accounts, 186, 187, 188
 earned, adjusting entries for, 189
Interim financial statements, 105, 128
Internal control(s), 5, 160–165, 169
 demonstration problem, 166
 limitations of, 163, 169
 over payroll, 216–217, 219
  control procedures, 217
  payroll fraud, 217
 petty cash fund, 191–192
 principles of, 160–162, 192
  custody of assets, 161
  demonstration problem, 166
  establishing responsibilities, 160
  insurance and bonding, 161
  recordkeeping, 161
  regular reviews, 162
  separation of duties, 161
  technological controls, 161
 purpose of, 160
 Sarbanes-Oxley Act requirements,
  165, 169
 technology and, 169
  e-commerce, increased, 162–163
  limited evidence and, 162
  processing errors, 162
  record testing and, 162
  separation of duties crucial to, 162
  software and devices, 161–163
 voucher systems (*See* **Voucher system** of
  control)
 workplace fraud and (*See* **Workplace
  Fraud**)
Internal control systems, 160
Internal Revenue Service (IRS), 207
 as accounting information user, 6
 Circular E, 210
 payroll tax reporting
  Employer's Annual Federal
   Unemployment Tax Return (Form
   940), 241
  Employer's Quarterly Federal Tax
   Return (Form 941), 236,
   237–238, 246
  Federal Tax Deposit Coupon (Form
   8109), 235–236, 246
  Form SS-4, 232
  required payroll tax deposits, 234
  Transmittal of Wage and Tax Statements
   (Form W-3), 239, 246
  Wage and Tax Statement (Form W-2),
   238–239, 246
 Web site of (www.IRS.gov), 207, 210,
  232, 243
Internal transactions, 23
Internal users of accounting information, **5,**
 12, 13

**International Accounting Standards Board
 (IASB), 10,** B-4
*International Financial Reporting Standards
 (IFRS),* 10
Internet Crime Complaint Center (FTC), 164
Inventory. *See* **Merchandise inventory**
Investment(s)
 in debt securities, A-10, A-14
 in equity securities, A-10, A-14–A-15
 by owner (*See* **Owner investments**)
Investors (shareholders), 6, 11, 29
Invoice(s), 167, 287
 purchase invoice, 167, 287
 sales invoice, 167, 287
  credit sales, 266, 267
  as source document, 75
 verification of, 168
Invoice approval, 168
Invoice date, 288
IRS. *See* Internal Revenue Service

Jacobs, Bert, 261
Jacobs, John, 261
Jiangsu Five Star Appliance Co., Ltd.,
 A-13–A-14
Journal, 74
Journal entries
 for cash receipts, 79, 83, 179
 closing entries, 352–353, 355
 compound, 79, 83
 correcting entries, 86
 explanation of transactions for, 77,
  78, 83
 for payroll tax deposits, 236
 for petty cash fund, 192
 posting to general ledger, 81–82, 88
 to record credit sales, 263, 266–267
 reversing entries, 353, 356–357
Journalizing transactions, **74**
 adjusting entries, 110, 111
 cash disbursements journal, 294, 295
 general journal, 77–80
 transaction processing
  general ledger, 80–82
  illustration of, 82–83
  payroll entries, 215, 219
  using special journals
   (*See* **Special journals**)

K-2, Inc., 351
Kapalka, Jason, 103
Kathryn Kerrigan, 127
KathrynKerrigan.com, 127
"Keep Ghosts Off the Payroll" (ACFE), 217
Kerrigan, Kathryn, 127
Keying adjustments, 129, 130
KLD Research & Analytics, Inc., 10n
Kozlowski, L. Dennis, 6

Labor unions, 6
Lauren, Dylan, 157
Lease(s), A-18–A-19
Lease obligations, 351
Ledger, 74

Legal issues
 crime (*See* Illegal acts; **Workplace fraud**)
 in payroll, 206–207, 219
  Fair Labor Standards Act, 206
  federal and state withholding,
   206, 207
  FICA taxes, 207–208, 232
  fines and penalties, 216
 in payroll tax reporting, 246
  employer FICA tax, 232
  employer identification number, 232
  federal and state unemployment tax acts,
   232–233
  workers' compensation insurance, 233
Lenders (creditors), 6
Letter to shareholders, A-1
Liabilities, 22–23
 current, 351
 long-term, 351, A-11
 normal balance for, 47
 reporting on balance sheet, 31
 unearned revenue as, 52, 325
Liability accounts, 111, 112, 136
Life is good, 261
Lifeisgood.com, 261
Limited liability company (LLC), 11
Limited Too, 3
Liquid assets, 178
Liquidity, 178
List of directors and officers, A-1
List price, 287
LLC (limited liability company), 11
Long-lived assets. *See* **Plant assets**
Long-term assets. *See* Noncurrent assets
Long-term investments, 351
Long-term liabilities, 351, A-11
Look-back rule, 234
Love Café, 45
LoveSac, 3, 5, 12
LoveSac.com, 3
Lowe, Renee Pepys, 285

Management discussion and analysis
 (MD&A), A-1
Manager(s), 5
Managerial accounting, 5, 7
Mandatory vacation policy, 160
Manual accounting system, 83, 85–86
Manufacturing businesses, 12
Marketing managers, 5
Markoff, Katrina, 73
Martin, Youngsong, 177
Matching principle, 105, B-3, **B-6**
Materiality constraint, B-3, B-7
MD&A (management discussion and
 analysis), A-1
Medicare benefits, 207
Medicare taxes, 207, 208
 computing, demonstration of, 246
 no income maximums on, 232
 quarterly reporting, 236, 237–238
Memo line on check, 185
Merchandise, 262, 264, 289
Merchandise available for sale, 323

Merchandise inventory, 286, 317
  adjusting entries for, 316, 317–318, 331
  beginning balances, 353
  ending balances, 353
    added to work sheet, 346, 347
    cost flows, 323
    recording, 317–318
  note regarding, A-8–A-9
  physical count of, 317
  valuation of, B-7
Merchandise purchases, 286–291, 302
  entrepreneurship, 285
  freight charges, 287
  ownership transfer, 290, 291
  periodic inventory system, 289, 299, 300–301
  purchase discounts, 288–289
  purchase returns and allowances, 289
  purchasing procedures, 286–287
  special journals and ledgers, 291–296, 302
    accounts payable subsidiary ledger, 294
    cash disbursements journal, 294–296
    demonstration problems, 296–301
    purchases journal, 292–293
  trade discounts, 287–288
  transportation costs, 290, 291
Merchandisers, 262, 286
  adjusting entries used by (*See* Adjusting
    entries)
  closing process for (*See* Closing process)
  entrepreneurship, 285, 315
  financial statements for (*See* Financial
    statement(s))
  length of operating cycle for, 350
  trial balance for (*See* Trial balance)
  work sheet for (*See* **Work sheet**)
Merchandise sales, 262–266, 274
  demonstration problems, 272–273, 299
  entrepreneurship, 261
  kinds of, 262
  recording and posting, 265, 266
  sales discounts, 262–264, 274
    credit sales entries, 263–264
    credit terms, 263, 288
  sales returns and allowances, 274
    sales allowances, 264–265
    sales returns, 264
  special journals and subsidiary ledgers,
    266–272
    accounts receivable subsidiary ledger,
      267–270
    cash receipts journal, 270–272, 274, 299
    sales journal, 266–267, 273, 274, 299
  See also Accounts receivable
Merchandising businesses, 12
Merit rating, for SUTA taxes, **232–233,** 240
Miami Heat, 76
Monetary unit assumption, B-3, **B-5**
Mortgages payable, 351
**Multiple-step income statement,
  347–348,** 355, 357

National Basketball Association, 325
National Retail Federation, 325
Natural disasters, 23

Navistar, 10
Nelson, Shawn, 3, 5
Net amount. *See* **Book value** of asset
Net assets, 23
Net cost of purchases, 289
Net income, 23
  computing in work sheet, 129, 130, 131
  reported on income statement, 30, 347, 348
Net loss, 23
  computing in work sheet, 129, 130, 131
  reported on income statement, 30
Net pay, 213, 218
Net purchases, 290, 291, **322,** 327, 331
Net sales, 263–264, **322,** 327, 331
New England Patriots, B-6
Nominal accounts. *See* **Temporary accounts**
Noncurrent assets, 350
Noncurrent (long-term) investments, 351
Nonoperating activities, 348
Non-sufficient funds (NSF) checks, 187, 188
Normal balance, 47, 60, 80
Nortel Networks, 9, 10
Notes payable, 351
Notes to financial statements, A-1
  acquisitions, A-13–A-14
  advertising costs, A-12
  business description, A-8
  business segments, A-19–A-20
  cash, A-8
  commitments, A-20
  contingencies, A-20
  convertible debentures, A-16
  cost of goods sold, A-12
  credit facilities, A-15–A-16
  employee benefit plans, A-19
  estimates, A-8
  fiscal year, A-8
  gift cards, A-11
  income taxes, A-10–A-11, A-19
  intangible assets, A-9–A-10
  investments(s), A-10, A-15
    in debt securities, A-10, A-14
    in equity securities, A-10, A-14–A-15
  leases, A-18–A-19
  long-term liabilities, A-11
  merchandise inventories, A-8–A-9
  property and equipment, A-9
  restricted assets, A-9
  revenue recognition, A-11
  SG&A expenses, A-12
  shareholders' equity, A-16–A-18
    comprehensive income, A-18
    earnings per share, A-16–A-17
    stock compensation plans, A-12–A-13,
      A-16
    stock repurchase, A-17–A-18
Not-for-profit agencies, 8
NSF (non-sufficient funds) checks, 187, 188

Occupational Fraud and Abuse (ACFE), 217
1-800-GOT-JUNK, 231
1800gotjunk.com, 231
Operating cycle, 350
Osborn, Jason, 205

Other expenses and losses, 348
Other revenues and gains, 348
Outstanding checks, 187, 188
Outstanding deposits, 187
Over-the-counter cash receipts, 178–180, 192
  cash over and short, 179–180
  proper handling of, 178–179
Owner(s), 5
Owner, Capital account, **23,** 134
  closing Income Summary account to, 134,
    135, 137, 352
  demonstration of, 140
Owner investments, 23
  equity increased by, 47
  journalizing transaction, 77–78, 79, 82
  recording in T-accounts, 48
  reporting in financial statements, 131
  transaction analysis, 24
Owner's equity
  increases and decreases in, 47
  reporting (*See* **Statement of owner's
    equity**)
  updating, 131, 132
Ownership structures, 11–12
Ownership transfer, 290, 291
Owner withdrawals, 23
  in cash, 27, 51
  equity decreased by, 47
  journalizing transaction, 79, 83
  recording in T-accounts, 51
  transaction analysis, 27

Partnership(s), 11, 13, 351, B-4
Passwords, 160, 163
Payables, 23
Payee of check, 184
Payer of check, 184
Payless Shoe Source, B-2
Pay rates, 217
Payroll, 204–219
  demonstration problem, 217–219
  earnings and withholdings,
    208–213, 219
    computing gross pay, 208–209, 219
    computing net pay, 213
    computing withholdings from
      gross pay, 209–212
    demonstration problem, 217–219
  internal controls, 216–217
    control procedures, 217
    payroll fraud, 217
  legal aspects of, 206–207, 219
    Fair Labor Standards Act, 206
    federal and state withholding, 206, 207
    FICA taxes, 207–208, 232
    fines and penalties, 216
  "paperless," 213
  payroll accounting, 213–216
    demonstration problem, 219
    employee earnings records, 216, 219
    recording and settling payroll, 214–215
    using payroll register, 213–214
Payroll bank account, 214, 215, 219
Payroll check, 214, 215

Payroll clerks, 217
Payroll deductions, 209, 219
  computing from gross pay, 209–212
  demonstration problem, 218
  federal income tax, 210–212
  federal tax withholdings
    computing and recording, 234–235
    employer's annual withholding
      report, 238–239
    employer's quarterly tax return,
      236, 237–238
  FICA withholding, 212
  state income tax, 212
  voluntary deductions, 209, 212
Payroll register, 213–214, 219, 233, 234–235
  information from
    in computing FUTA and SUTA taxes,
      234–235, 240
    in making tax deposits, 234–235
  updating, 236
Payroll tax deposits, 234–236
  computing and recording, 234–236
    federal tax withholdings, 234–235
    Form 8109, 235–236
    general journal entries, 236
  timing of, 234
Payroll tax reporting, 230–246
  computing deductions (*See* **Payroll
    deductions**)
  demonstration problem, 245–246
  employer's payroll taxes, 233–236
    FICA tax computation, 233,
      234–235, 246
    payroll tax deposits, 234–236
    recording in general journal, 233
  employer's reporting, 236–239
    annual withholding report, 238–239
    quarterly tax return, 236, 237–238
  laws impacting, 246
    employer FICA tax, 232
    employer identification number, 232
    federal and state unemployment tax acts,
      232–233
    workers' compensation insurance, 233
  unemployment taxes, 240–243
    computing employer's taxes, 234–235,
      240–241
    reporting employer's taxes, 241–243
  workers' compensation insurance
    actual premium, 244
    estimated premium, 233, 244
PCAOB. *See* Public Company Accounting
  Oversight Board
Periodic inventory system, 287
  recording merchandise purchases in,
    289, 299, 300–301
  unadjusted trial balance under, 316, 317
Periodicity assumption, B-3, B-5
Period of time, 29, 56, 105
Permanent (real) **accounts, 133,** 136,
    137, 141, 353, 357
Personal financial specialist (PFS), 8
Personal scanners, 161
Petty cashbox, 180

Petty cash fund, **180–**182, 192
  cash over and short, 182
  demonstration problem, 191–192
  illustration of, 181–182
  increasing or decreasing fund, 182
  operation of, 180–181
Petty cashier, 180
Petty cash receipts, 180–181
PFS (personal financial specialist), 8
Pharming, 163
Phishing, 163
Pirates of the Caribbean (film), 105
Plant assets, 107
  depreciation of (*See* **Depreciation**)
  property and equipment, A-9
  shown in classified balance sheet, 351
P&L statement. *See* **Income statement**
Point in time, 29, 56–57
Point-of-sale cash registers, 179
PopCap.com, 103
PopCap Games, 103
Post-closing trial balance, 136, 137,
    141, 353, 357
Posting reference (PR) column, 78, 268
Posting transactions, **48, 74,** 89
  adjusting entries, 110
  cash transactions
    from credit customers, 270, 271
    from other sources, 270, 271
    sales, 270, 271
  credits, 82
  debits, 81–82
  demonstration problem, 88
  error correction, 89
    after posting, 86
    before posting, 85–86
  to general ledger, 81–82, 268, 269,
    272, 291, 292
    from cash disbursements journal,
      295–296
    closing entries, 352, 353
    demonstration problems, 297, 299–301
    journal entries, 81–82, 88
    merchandise sales, 266
    from purchases journal, 292–293
    from subsidiary ledger, 268, 269, 273
  in recording transactions, 48–53, 59, 60
  to subsidiary ledger, 268, 269, 273
  See also **Special journals**
PR (posting reference) column, 78, 268
Predictive value of accounting information, B-3
Prepaid assets, 52
Prepaid expenses (deferrals), **106–**109,
    115, 318
  adjusting accounts, 106
    depreciation, 107–109, 110, 114
    other prepaids, 107
    prepaid insurance, 106–107, 110, 114
    supplies, 107, 110, 114
  adjusting entries for, 331
    depreciation expense, 107–109, 110,
      114, 319, 320
    equipment, 319–320
    financial statement effects, 326, 328, 329

  prepaid insurance, 106–107, 110,
    114, 319
  supplies, 107, 110, 114, 319
  alternative accounting for, 329–330, 332
  rent, 52, 79
Prepaid insurance
  accrual basis accounting for, 104
  adjusting entries for, 106–107, 110, 114, 319
  cash basis accounting for, 105
  journalizing transaction, 79, 83
  recording, 52
Prepayments
  in cash, 51–52
    prepaid assets, 52
    unearned revenues, 52
  journalizing transaction, 79, 83
  recording in T-accounts, 51–52
Preprinted forms, 161
Presentation issues in financial statements,
    57–58
Principles-based accounting, 10, B-2
  rules-based accounting compared, B-7
  objectives of financial reporting,
    B-2–B-3, B-7
  Sarbanes-Oxley Act of 2002, B-2
Principles of internal control, 160–162
  custody of assets, 161
  demonstration problem, 166
  establishing responsibilities, 160
  insurance and bonding, 161
  recordkeeping, 161
  regular reviews, 162
  separation of duties, 161
  technological controls, 161
Prior period adjustments, 326
Private accounting, 7, 8
Processed check image, 75
Processing errors, 162
Production managers, 5
Profit and loss statement. *See* **Income
  statement**
Pro forma financial statements, 133
Property, plant, and equipment. *See* **Plant
  assets**
Proprietorships, 11, 13, 351, B-4
Proving balances, 55
Proving ledgers
  accounts payable ledger, 294, 299, 301
  accounts receivable ledger, 268, 269,
    270, 274
Public accounting, 7–8
Public Company Accounting Oversight
  Board (PCAOB), 6
Purchase(s)
  in cash (*See* Cash purchases)
  credit purchases, 25, 49, 79, 82, 292
  of merchandise (*See* Merchandise
    purchases)
  net (*See* **Net purchases**)
  net cost of, 289
  total purchases, 316, 317
  transaction analysis, 24–25
Purchase allowances, 289, 316, 317

Purchase discounts, 288–289
   journalizing, 294
   in unadjusted trial balance, 316, 317
Purchase invoice, 167, 287
Purchase orders, 167, 287
   verification of, 168
   in voucher systems, 167, 169
Purchase requisitions, 166, 286
   verification of, 168
   in voucher systems, 164, 166, 167, 169
Purchase returns, 289, 316, 317
Purchases journal, 292–293, 296–298,
      299, 300, 302
Purchasing managers, 5

Quarterly tax reports, 216
QuickBooks accounting software, 5
Qwest Communications, 9

RadioShack, 4, 12, 262
   financial statements of, A-1, A-21–A-26
      consolidated balance sheets, A-22
      consolidated statements of cash flows, A-26
      consolidated statements of income,
         A-23–A-24
      consolidated statements of stockholders'
         equity and comprehensive
         income, A-25
Rath, Todd, 345
Rath, Tom, 345
Real accounts. *See* **Permanent accounts**
Receivables, 22
   accounts receivable (*See* Accounts
      receivable)
   monitoring, 205
Receiving departments, 287
Receiving reports, 167, 287
   verification of, 168
   in voucher systems, 167–168
Reconciled bank balance, 188
Reconciled book balance, 188
Recording business activities, 4
Recording transactions
   illustration of (*See* Transaction analysis)
   in transaction processing, 74–76, 89
Recordkeeping, 4
   access to cash separate from, 178–179, 192
   employee time sheets, 208
   as internal control, 161, 164
   salaries for, 8
Record testing, 162
Regular reviews, 162
Regulatory agencies, 6
Relevance of accounting information,
      10, **B-3**, B-4
Reliability of accounting information,
      10, **B-3**–B-4
Remittance advice, 185
Rent, 26, 52, 79
Report to the Nation (ACFE; 2008), 158, 165
Research and Development managers, 5
Residual equity, 23, 33
Responsibility, 160, 164
Restricted assets, A-9

Restrictive endorsement of check, 184
Retailers, 262, 288
Revenue(s), 23
   accruals (*See* **Accrued revenues**)
   adjusting entries for, 323–325
      accrued revenues, 324, 326, 328,
         329, 331–332
      unearned (deferred) revenues, 324–325,
         330–331, 332
   deferrals (*See* **Unearned revenues**)
   equity increased by, 47
   other revenues and gains, 348
   reported on income statement, 30
Revenue accounts
   adjusting entries posted to, 111
   after closing process, 136
   closing to Income Summary, 134, 135, 352
   contra revenue accounts, 263–264, 274
Revenue recognition, A-11
Revenue recognition principle, 105,
      324, B-3, **B-6**
Reversing entries, 353, 356–357
Risk of loss, 290
RockBottomGolf.com, 345
Rounding, 57–58
Rubin, Jeff, 157
Rules-based accounting, 10, B-2
   principles-based accounting compared, B-7
      objectives of financial reporting,
         B-2–B-3, B-7
      Sarbanes-Oxley Act of 2002, B-2

Salaries, 208
   for accounting professionals, 8
   salaries expense
      accrued, 109–110, 114, 320, 331
      payment of, 79, 80, 83
      reversing entries for, 356–357
Sales
   in cash, 262, 270, 271
   on credit (*See* Credit sales)
   fraudulent commissions, 217
   net sales, 263–264, 322, 327, 331
   records of, 178
   selling expenses, 347–348, A-12
   selling price, 287–288
   total sales, 316, 317
   See also Merchandise sales
Sales allowances, 264–265, 316, 317
Sales commissions, overstated, 217
Sales discounts, 262–264, 274
   credit sales entries, 263–264
   credit terms, 263
   in unadjusted trial balance, 316, 317
Sales invoice, 167, 287
   credit sales, 266, 267
   as source document, 75
Sales journal, 266–267
   demonstration of, 273, 299
   journalizing, 266, 267, 274
Sales returns, 264, 316, 317
Sales slips, prenumbered, 161
Sales ticket, 266
Salvage value of asset, 108

Sarbanes-Oxley Act of 2002, 9, B-2
   internal control requirements, 165, 169
   principles-based accounting and, B-2
Schedule of accounts payable, 294, 301
Schedule of accounts receivable, 268, 270, 301
Scudamore, Brian, 231
SEC. *See* **Securities and Exchange
   Commission**
sec.gov/investor/pubs/cyberfraud.htm, 162
**Securities and Exchange
   Commission (SEC), 10,** 13, **B-2**
   as accounting information user, 6
   EDGAR database, 23, A-1
   reporting requirements, 9
Segment information, A-19–A-20
Self-employment tax, 208
Sellers, 290
Selling, general and administrative expenses
      (SG&A), 348, A-12
Selling expenses, 347–348, A-12
Selling price, 287–288
Separation of duties
   access to cash, 178–179, 192
   crucial to internal control, 162
   as internal control, 161, 164
   payroll duties, 217
Service businesses, 11–12, 350
Service managers, 5
Services
   accrued revenues for, 324
   banking services (*See* Banking activities)
   prior period adjustments, 326
   provision of
      for cash, 25
      credit sales, 26
      journalizing transaction, 79, 82, 83
      recording in T-accounts, 49, 50
      transaction analysis, 25, 26, 49, 50
Shareholder(s), 6, 11, 29
Shareholders' equity, notes regarding,
      A-16–A-18
   comprehensive income, A-18
   earnings per share, A-16–A-17
   stock compensation plans, A-12–A-13, A-16
   stock repurchase, A-17–A-18
Short-term assets, 351
Signature card, 183
Simply Accounting software, 5
Single-step income statement, 349, 357
Small Business Administration, 45
Social Security Administration, 207
Social Security benefits, 207
Social Security numbers, 216
Social Security taxes, 207, 208, 212
   computing, demonstration of, 246
   employer reporting, 236, 237–238
   income maximums, 214, 232
Software
   accounting software, 5
   computerized error-checking, 77
   computer viruses, 163
   errors in, 162
   face-recognition software in ATM cards, 161
Sole proprietorships, 11, 13, 351, B-4

Source documents, 75, 89, 108
SPANX, 21, 29
Speakeasy, Inc., A-13
Special journals, 266, 274
   cash receipts journal, 270–272, 274
     demonstration problem, 299
     footing, crossfooting, and posting,
       271–272
     journalizing, 270, 271
   footing and crossfooting, 299, 300–301
   sales journal, 266–267, 273, 274, 299
     demonstration of, 273, 299
     journalizing, 266, 267, 273, 274
Standard & Poor's (S&P) 500, 10
State income tax, 212
Statement of cash flows, A-6, A-26
Statement of changes in owner's equity.
     See **Statement of owner's equity**
Statement of earnings, 214, 215
Statement of Ethical Professional
     Practice (IMA), 9
Statement of owner's equity, 29, 30–31, 33
   demonstration problems, 32, 60, 140
   format of, 349, 357
   preparation of, 140
     from adjusted trial balance, 112, 113
     from trial balance, 56, 57, 60, 85
     using work sheet, 128, 132, 133
Statements of shareholders' equity,
     A-7, A-25
State unemployment (SUTA)
     taxes, 232–233
   computing, 234–235, 240–241, 246
   demonstration problem, 246
   recording in general journal, 241,
     242–243, 246
   reporting, 241, 242, 246
Stock-based compensation, A-12–A-13, A-16
Stockholder(s), 6, 11, 29
Stock repurchase, A-17–A-18
Straight-line depreciation, 108
Subscriptions, 52
Subsidiary ledgers, 267
   accounts receivable subsidiary ledger,
     267–270
     controlling account and, 267–268, 271
     demonstration of, 273
     posting to, 268, 269, 273
     proving ledgers, 268, 269, 270, 274
     schedule of accounts receivable
       drawn from, 270
   in balance with controlling accounts, 271
   posting to, 268, 269
SuperValue, 262
Suppliers, 6
Supplies
   cash purchase, 24
   credit purchase, 25
   prepaid, adjusting entries for, 107, 110,
     114, 319
SUTA taxes. *See* **State unemployment**
     (SUTA) taxes
SYSCO, 262
Systematic and rational allocation, B-6

T-accounts, 46–47, 60
   adjusting entries, 106, 328, 329
   balance column accounts compared, 80
   recording transactions in (illustrated),
     48–53, 54, 59
   in transaction analysis, 46–47, 54, 59
Take-home pay, 213
Target, 12
Tax accounting, 7
Tax reporting
   FICA taxes (*See* **FICA taxes**)
   forms used in (*See specific forms*)
   payroll taxes, 216
Technology
   accounting software, 5
   internal controls and, 169
     e-commerce, increased, 162–163
     electrocardiograms, 162
     embedded tags, 161
     face-recognition software, 161
     limited evidence and, 162
     processing errors, 162
     record testing and, 162
     separation of duties crucial to, 162
   "payroll cards," 213
Temporary (nominal) **accounts, 133**
   closing, 141
     to Income Summary, 133–134, 317
     for merchandisers, 352, 357
     using work sheet, 128
     zero balances, 133, 134, 136, 353
   Owner, Capital account, 23, 134, 135,
     137, 140, 352
   Withdrawals account, 135, 137
TicketMaster, 4
Time clocks, 161
Timeliness of accounting information, B-3, B-5
Time period assumption, 105
Time sheets, 208, 209, 217
Trade discounts, 287–**288**
Trade names, A-10
Transaction(s), 23, 33
   explanation of
     adjusting entries, 110, 114
     for journal entries, 77, 78, 83
   external and internal, 23
   journalizing (*See* **Journalizing**
     transactions)
   posting (*See* **Posting** transactions)
   recording
     illustration of (*See* Transaction analysis)
     in transaction processing, 74–76, 89
Transaction analysis, 20–33, 46–54
   accounting equation and, 22–23, 78
   cash purchases, 24–25, 49, 53
   cash receipts, 27, 51, 52
   cash withdrawal by owner, 27, 51
   credit purchases, 25, 49
   demonstration problem, 31–33
   double-entry accounting and, 47
   financial statements and
     (*See* Financial statement(s))
   illustration of, 23–27
   investment by owner, 24

payment of accounts, 27
payment of expenses, 26
provision of services, 49, 50
   for cash, 25
   for credit, 26
recording transactions illustrated, 48–53
   cash payments, 50, 51, 52, 53
   cash purchases, 49, 53
   cash receipts, 51, 52
   credit purchases, 49
   investment by owner, 48
   prepayments, 51–52
   provision of services, 49, 50
   withdrawal of cash by owner, 51
   summary of, 28, 32
   using T-accounts, 46–47, 54, 59
   See also Transaction processing
Transaction processing, 74–76, 89
   chart of accounts in, 76
   demonstration problem, 86–89
   identification and analysis in
     (*See* Transaction analysis)
   journalizing and posting, 77–86
     error correction, 85–86, 89
     general journal, 77–80, 82–83
     general ledger, 80–82
     illustration of, 82–83
     payroll entries, 215, 219
     trial balance, 83–85
   from source documents, 75
   steps in, 89
Transmittal of Wage and Tax Statements
     (Form W-3), 239, 246
Transportation-in, 287, 290, 316, 317
Transportation-out, 290
Transposition errors, 55*n*
Trial balance, 55–58, 60
   adjusted (*See* **Adjusted trial balance**)
   demonstration problems, 59, 301
   for merchandisers, 316–318
     adjusting entries for inventory,
      316, 317–318, 331
     use of, 316, 317, 331
   post-closing, 136, 137, 141, 353, 357
   preparation of, 55, 56, 83–85, 89
   unadjusted (*See* **Unadjusted trial balance**)
   using to prepare financial statements, 56–58,
     60, 85, 89
Tyco International, 6, 9
Typo-squatting, 163

Unadjusted statements, 56–58
Unadjusted trial balance, 55–58, **110,** 112
   adjusted trial balance prepared from, 110, 112
   entering in work sheet, 129, 130, 321
   for merchandiser, 316–318
Unclassified balance sheet, 349
Uncollectible items, 186, 187, 189
Unearned revenues, 52, 318, **324**–**325**
   adjusting entries for, 324–325, 330–331, 332
   from advance sales, 52, 325
   alternative accounting for, 330–331, 332
   financial statement effects, 326, 328, 329
   journalizing transaction, 79, 83

Unemployment taxes, 240–243
  computing, 234–235, 240–241
  income maximums, 213
  laws impacting, 246
    federal unemployment taxes (FUTA), 232
    state unemployment taxes (SUTA),
      232–233
  recording in general journal, 241,
    242–243
  reporting, 241–243
    federal unemployment taxes,
      241–242, 243
    state unemployment taxes, 241,
      242, 246
United States Army, 216
Unlimited liability, 11
Unsold merchandise, 264
Useful life of asset, 108
Users of accounting information, 5–6, 13
  demonstration problem, 12
  external, 6, 12, 13
  internal, 5, 12, 13
Utilities expense, 80, 83
Utility bills, 326

Vechey, John, 103
Vendee, 167
Vendor, 167, 287
Venture capitalists, 29
VosgesChocolate.com, 73
Vosges Haut Chocolat, 73
Voucher(s), 164, 168–169
Voucher register, 169
Voucher system of control, **164–**165
  items in, 166–169, 170
    invoice approval, 168
    invoices, 167
    purchase orders, 167, 169
    purchase requisitions, 164, 166, 167, 169

  receiving reports, 167–168
  voucher, 168–169

Wage and Tax Statement (Form W-2),
  238–239, 246
Wages, 114, **208**
Wal-Mart, 179, 262, B-2
Walt Disney Company, 105
Web sites
  accounting data on, 23
  See also specific Web sites
WeMarket4U.net/netops, 164
"What-if" transactions, 128, 133
Wholesaler(s), 262, 288
Wildflower Linen, 177
WildflowerLinens.com, 177
Wi-phishing, 163
Withdrawals account, closing, 135, 137, 352
Withholding allowances, 206
Withholdings. *See* **Payroll deductions**
Withholding tables, 210–212
Workers' compensation insurance, 233,
  244, 246
Working papers. *See* **Work sheet**
Workplace fraud, 158
  average loss per fraud, 165
  cash receipts by mail, 180
  certified fraud examiners, 8
  collusion in, 161, 180
  cyberfraud, 162, 163
  detection of, 159, 165
  elements of, 158, 169
  examples of, 162, 165
  internal control and, 163
  major types of, 169
    asset misappropriation, 158
    corruption, 158–159
    fraudulent financial statements, 159
  payroll fraud, 217

Work sheet, 128, 141, 346–347, 357
  accounting errors, 128, 131
  demonstration of, 139
  electronic (Excel), 131
  example of, 347
  in financial statement preparation
    adjusted trial balance, 129, 130
    balance sheet, 132, 133
    income statement, 132–133
    interim statements, 128
    statement of owner's equity, 128, 132, 133
  partial, adjusting entries shown in, 320–323
    adjusted trial balance, 320–321
    cost of goods sold computation, 322–323
    gross profit computation, 323
    net purchases computation, 322
    net sales computation, 322
  steps in preparing, 346, 347
  as tool in closing process, 128–133
    applications and analysis, 132–133
    benefits of, 128
    use of, 128–131
WorldCom, 6, 9
Wright, Jason, 205
www.acfe.com, 158, 217
www.aicpa.org, 9
www.imanet.org, 9
www.IRS.gov, 207, 210, 232, 243
www.SEC.gov, A-1
www.SEC.gov/edgar.shtml, 23
www.SSA.gov, 207
www.xe.com, B-5

Xerox, 9

Zero balance(s)
  in balance column account, 80
  preparing trial balance and, 55
  of temporary accounts, 133, 134, 136, 353

Chart of Accounts

Following is a typical chart of accounts. Each company has its own unique accounts and numbering system.

Assets

Current Assets

101 Cash
102 Petty cash
103 Cash equivalents
104 Short-term investments
105 Market adjustment, _____ securities (S-T)
106 Accounts receivable
107 Allowance for doubtful accounts
108 Legal fees receivable
109 Interest receivable
110 Rent receivable
111 Notes receivable
119 Merchandise inventory
120 _____ inventory
121 _____ inventory
124 Office supplies
125 Store supplies
126 _____ supplies
128 Prepaid insurance
129 Prepaid interest
131 Prepaid rent
132 Raw materials inventory
133 Goods in process inventory, _____
134 Goods in process inventory, _____
135 Finished goods inventory

Long-Term Investments

141 Long-term investments
142 Market adjustment, _____ securities (L-T)
144 Investment in _____
145 Bond sinking fund

Plant Assets

151 Automobiles
152 Accumulated depreciation—Automobiles
153 Trucks
154 Accumulated depreciation—Trucks
155 Boats
156 Accumulated depreciation—Boats
157 Professional library
158 Accumulated depreciation—Professional library
159 Law library
160 Accumulated depreciation—Law library
161 Furniture
162 Accumulated depreciation—Furniture
163 Office equipment
164 Accumulated depreciation—Office equipment
165 Store equipment
166 Accumulated depreciation—Store equipment
167 _____ equipment
168 Accumulated depreciation—_____ equipment
169 Machinery
170 Accumulated depreciation—Machinery
173 Building _____
174 Accumulated depreciation—Building _____
175 Building _____
176 Accumulated depreciation—Building _____
179 Land improvements _____
180 Accumulated depreciation—Land improvements _____
181 Land improvements _____
182 Accumulated depreciation—Land improvements _____
183 Land

Natural Resources

185 Mineral deposit
186 Accumulated depletion—Mineral deposit

Intangible Assets

191 Patents
192 Leasehold
193 Franchise
194 Copyrights
195 Leasehold improvements
196 Licenses
197 Accumulated amortization—_____

Liabilities

Current Liabilities

201 Accounts payable
202 Insurance payable
203 Interest payable
204 Legal fees payable
207 Office salaries payable
208 Rent payable
209 Salaries payable
210 Wages payable
211 Accrued payroll payable
214 Estimated warranty liability
215 Income taxes payable
216 Common dividend payable
217 Preferred dividend payable
218 State unemployment taxes payable
219 Employee federal income taxes payable
221 Employee medical insurance payable
222 Employee retirement program payable
223 Employee union dues payable
224 Federal unemployment taxes payable
225 FICA taxes payable
226 Estimated vacation pay liability

Unearned Revenues

230 Unearned consulting fees
231 Unearned legal fees
232 Unearned property management fees
233 Unearned _____ fees
234 Unearned _____ fees
235 Unearned janitorial revenue
236 Unearned _____ revenue
238 Unearned rent

Notes Payable

240 Short-term notes payable
241 Discount on short-term notes payable
245 Notes payable
251 Long-term notes payable
252 Discount on long-term notes payable

Long-Term Liabilities

253 Long-term lease liability
255 Bonds payable
256 Discount on bonds payable
257 Premium on bonds payable
258 Deferred income tax liability

Equity

Owner's Equity

301 _____, Capital
302 _____, Withdrawals
303 _____, Capital
304 _____, Withdrawals
305 _____, Capital
306 _____, Withdrawals

Paid-In Capital

307 Common stock, $ _____ par value
308 Common stock, no-par value
309 Common stock, $ _____ stated value
310 Common stock dividend distributable
311 Paid-in capital in excess of par value, Common stock
312 Paid-in capital in excess of stated value, No-par common stock
313 Paid-in capital from retirement of common stock
314 Paid-in capital, Treasury stock
315 Preferred stock
316 Paid-in capital in excess of par value, Preferred stock

etained Earnings

318 Retained earnings
319 Cash dividends (or Dividends)
320 Stock dividends

Other Equity Accounts

321 Treasury stock, Common
322 Unrealized gain—Equity
323 Unrealized loss—Equity

Revenues

401 _____ fees earned
402 _____ fees earned
403 _____ services revenue
404 _____ services revenue
405 Commissions earned
406 Rent revenue (or Rent earned)
407 Dividends revenue (or Dividend earned)
408 Earnings from investment in _____
409 Interest revenue (or Interest earned)
410 Sinking fund earnings
413 Sales
414 Sales returns and allowances
415 Sales discounts

Cost of Sales

Cost of Goods Sold

502 Cost of goods sold
505 Purchases
506 Purchases returns and allowances
507 Purchases discounts
508 Transportation-in

Manufacturing

520 Raw materials purchases
521 Transportation-in on raw materials
530 Factory payroll
531 Direct labor
540 Factory overhead
541 Indirect materials
542 Indirect labor
543 Factory insurance expired
544 Factory supervision
545 Factory supplies used
546 Factory utilities
547 Miscellaneous production costs
548 Property taxes on factory building
549 Property taxes on factory equipment
550 Rent on factory building
551 Repairs, factory equipment
552 Small tools written off
560 Depreciation of factory equipment
561 Depreciation of factory building

Standard Cost Variance

580 Direct material quantity variance
581 Direct material price variance
582 Direct labor quantity variance
583 Direct labor price variance
584 Factory overhead cost variance

Expenses

Amortization, Depletion, and Depreciation

601 Amortization expense—_____
602 Amortization expense—_____
603 Depletion expense—_____
604 Depreciation expense—Boats
605 Depreciation expense—Automobiles
606 Depreciation expense—Building _____
607 Depreciation expense—Building _____
608 Depreciation expense—Land
    improvements _____
609 Depreciation expense—Land
    improvements _____
610 Depreciation expense—Law library
611 Depreciation expense—Trucks
612 Depreciation expense—_____ equipment
613 Depreciation expense—_____ equipment
614 Depreciation expense—_____
615 Depreciation expense—_____

Employee-Related Expenses

620 Office salaries expense
621 Sales salaries expense
622 Salaries expense
623 _____ wages expense
624 Employees' benefits expense
625 Payroll taxes expense

Financial Expenses

630 Cash over and short
631 Discounts lost
632 Factoring fee expense
633 Interest expense

Insurance Expenses

635 Insurance expense—Delivery equipment
636 Insurance expense—Office equipment
637 Insurance expense—_____

Rental Expenses

640 Rent expense
641 Rent expense—Office space
642 Rent expense—Selling space
643 Press rental expense
644 Truck rental expense
645 _____ rental expense

Supplies Expenses

650 Office supplies expense
651 Store supplies expense
652 _____ supplies expense
653 _____ supplies expense

Miscellaneous Expenses

655 Advertising expense
656 Bad debts expense
657 Blueprinting expense
658 Boat expense
659 Collection expense
661 Concessions expense
662 Credit card expense
663 Delivery expense
664 Dumping expense
667 Equipment expense
668 Food and drinks expense
671 Gas and oil expense
672 General and administrative expense
673 Janitorial expense
674 Legal fees expense
676 Mileage expense
677 Miscellaneous expenses
678 Mower and tools expense
679 Operating expense
680 Organization expense
681 Permits expense
682 Postage expense
683 Property taxes expense
684 Repairs expense—_____
685 Repairs expense—_____
687 Selling expense
688 Telephone expense
689 Travel and entertainment expense
690 Utilities expense
691 Warranty expense
695 Income taxes expense

Gains and Losses

701 Gain on retirement of bonds
702 Gain on sale of machinery
703 Gain on sale of investments
704 Gain on sale of trucks
705 Gain on _____
706 Foreign exchange gain or loss
801 Loss on disposal of machinery
802 Loss on exchange of equipment
803 Loss on exchange of _____
804 Loss on sale of notes
805 Loss on retirement of bonds
806 Loss on sale of investments
807 Loss on sale of machinery
808 Loss on _____
809 Unrealized gain—Income
810 Unrealized loss—Income

Clearing Accounts

901 Income summary
902 Manufacturing summary

A. K. A.

The same financial statement sometimes receives different titles. Below are some of the more common aliases.*

Balance Sheet	Statement of Financial Position Statement of Financial Condition
Income Statement	Statement of Income Operating Statement Statement of Operations Statement of Operating Activity Earnings Statement Statement of Earnings Profit and Loss (P&L) Statement
Statement of Cash Flows	Statement of Cash Flow Cash Flows Statement Statement of Changes in Cash Position Statement of Changes in Financial Position
Statement of Owner's Equity	Statement of Changes in Owner's Equity Statement of Changes in Owner's Capital Statement of Shareholders' Equity[†] Statement of Changes in Shareholders' Equity[†] Statement of Stockholders' Equity and Comprehensive Income[†] Statement of Changes in Capital Accounts[†]

* The term **Consolidated** often precedes or follows these statement titles to reflect the combination of different entities, such as a parent company and its subsidiaries.
[†]Corporation only.

We thank Dr. Louella Moore from Arkansas State University for suggesting this listing.